DESKTOP GUIDE TO

CONTRACT MANAGEMENT TERMS

NATIONAL CONTRACT MANAGEMENT ASSOCIATION®

CONNECTING TO
CREATE WHAT'S NEXT

INTRODUCTION

The *Desktop Guide to Contract Management Terms* provides useful information on the fundamental meaning and everyday use of more than 4,000 contracting terms from over 100 sources. This book has greatly expanded upon our previous series, the *Desktop Guide to Basic Contracting Terms*, to include new and recent terms contract managers may encounter on the job.

All terms and their definitions have been compiled from official sources or from publications by recognized experts in the field. Entries have been adapted and edited for content, consistency, and clarity of meaning. Where appropriate, contextual relevance has been provided. NCMA encourages using the *Federal Acquisition Regulation* (*FAR*), its agency supplements, the United States Code (U.S.C.), the Uniform Commercial Code (UCC), and other official sources for more detailed information. Source codes accompany the definitions. These have been listed with their corresponding source information in the Source Code List beginning on page 301). If a definition is not accompanied by a source code, it is considered original to this edition.

The *Desktop Guide to Contract Management Terms* serves as a training tool and on-the-job reference for both new entrants into the field and more seasoned practitioners, as well as a study tool for certification examinations. Other study manuals and resources for professional certification examinations are also available from NCMA.

Aa

8(a)
Section 8(a) of the Small Business Act (15 U.S.C. 14A).

8(a) Program
See *Section 8(a) Business Development Program*.

8(a) contract
A contract with the Small Business Administration under the Section 8(a) Business Development Program—a program established by Section 8(a) of the Small Business Act (15 U.S.C. 14A). Under the program, the SBA is authorized to enter into all types of contracts with other agencies and let subcontracts for performing those contracts to firms eligible for program participation. *(GOAT)*
See *Section 8(a) Business Development Program*.

8(a) contractor
An SBA subcontractor under an 8(a) contract. *(GOAT)*
See Section 8(a)

1207 Program
See *Section 1207 Program*.

A

ABC analysis
Application of Pareto's Law, or the "80/20 rule." ABC analysis, as related to inventory, is a determination of the relative ratios between the number of items and the dollar value of items purchased repetitively. Typically, 5-10 percent of the items (A items) account for 75-80 percent of the investment, 20-25 percent of the items (B items) account for 15-20 percent of the investment, and 70-75 percent of the items (C items) account for 5-10 percent of the investment. Inventories should be managed accordingly, with more emphasis placed on the strategic management of the A items. *(GKPT)*

AbilityOne Program
The AbilityOne Program (formerly *Javits-Wagner-O'Day Act*) provides "employment opportunities for people who are blind or have significant disabilities." The program is administered by the Committee for Purchase From People Who Are Blind or Severely Disabled. The U.S. AbilityOne Commission® was founded to operate the program in accordance with the Committee for Purchase From People Who Are Blind or Severely Disabled statute. Two national nonprofit agencies—the National Industries for the Blind (NIB) and SourceAmerica®—are designated to implement the AbilityOne Program through employment opportunities for these individuals to produce goods and services under U.S. federal government contracts. (See https://www.abilityone.gov; see also *FAR* Subpart 8.7.)
See also *Committee for Purchase From People Who Are Blind or Severely Disabled statute*.

absolute standard
A type of standard used in competitive negotiations to evaluate a proposal. Includes both the maximum acceptable value and the minimum acceptable value for all selected evaluation criteria. *(STBP)*

absorption costing
A method of determining the actual cost of a unit of production (either at various stages of completion or when service is provided) which treats fixed indirect costs as product costs. Under absorption costing, a unit's total cost is equal to the sum of the allocated fixed indirect costs and the costs of direct material, direct labor, and applicable overhead. *(P&L II)*

abstract of bids
A list of the bidders for a particular sealed-bid procurement that shows the significant portions of each bid, such as price, responsiveness, etc. Also called *record of bids*. *(CMBOK; GCG)* (See also FAR 14.204 and FAR 14.403.)

abstract of offers
A list of the offerors for a particular procurement that shows the significant portions of each offer, such as price, responsiveness, etc. *(CMBOK)*

abstract of title
A condensed history of the title to property based on past records. *(GKPT)*

abuse of authority
An arbitrary and capricious exercise of authority that is inconsistent with the mission of the U.S. federal agency concerned or the successful performance of a contract of such agency. *(FAR 3.908-2)*

accelerated delivery
The advancing, in whole or in part, of the scheduled delivery of material in order to meet emergency requirements. *(AFIT)*

Aa

accelerated payment
A payment made prior to the due date. *(5 CFR 1315.2)*

accelerated procedure
Procedure under the Contract Disputes statute (41 U.S.C. Chapter 71) whereby an appellant before an agency board of contract appeals can elect, for claims at or under a stipulated dollar amount, to have a decision issued on a claim within six months after making the election. *(GCG)* (See also FAR 33.211.)
See also *expedited procedure*.

acceleration
Direction to complete performance in advance of a negotiated term, for example:
- Ahead of time, due to urgency; or
- On time, despite the existence of an excusable delay.

(CMBOK)
See also *constructive acceleration; excusable delay*.

acceptable accounting system
As it relates to the *Defense Federal Acquisition Regulation Supplement* (*DFARS*) Business Systems Rule, this term refers to an accounting system that provides reasonable assurance that—
- Applicable laws and regulations are complied with,
- The accounting system and cost data are reliable,
- Risk of misallocations and mischarges are minimized, and
- Contract allocations and charges are consistent with billing procedures.

(DFARS 252.242-7006)
See *acceptable contractor business systems; contractor business systems*.

acceptable contractor business systems
A term that only applies to covered contracts with the Department of Defense that are subject to the Cost Accounting Standards under 41 U.S.C. Chapter 15. Contractor business systems will be considered "acceptable" if they comply with the terms and conditions of the following *DFARS* business system clauses (if the covered contract includes them): 252.242-7006, 252.234-7002, 252.215-7002, 252.242-7004, 252.245-7003, and 252.244-7001. *(DFARS 252.242-7005)*
See also *contractor business systems; Cost Accounting Standards (CAS); Cost Accounting Standards Board (CASB)*.

acceptable material management and accounting system
As it relates to the *DFARS* Business Systems Rule, an "acceptable" material management and accounting system (MMAS), is one that generally complies with the system criteria specified in DFARS 252.242-7004. This criteria begins with stating the MMAS shall have adequate internal controls to ensure system and data integrity. *(DFARS 252.242-7004)*
See *material management and accounting system (MMAS)*.

acceptable past performance evaluation rating
Based on the offeror's performance record, an "acceptable" past performance evaluation rating means that the federal government has a reasonable expectation that the offeror will successfully perform the required effort, or the offeror's performance record is unknown. *(SSP)*
Contrast with *unacceptable past performance evaluation rating*.

acceptance
(1) In the case of an offer, a manifestation of assent to the terms thereof made by the offeree in a manner invited or required by the offer. Acceptance by performance requires that at least part of what the offer requests be performed or tendered and includes acceptance by a performance which operates as a return promise. Acceptance by promise requires that the offeree complete every act essential to the making of the promise. *(RSOC 50(1)-(3))*
(2) The act, either verbal or written, that conveys assent to contractual terms and conditions. This act creates contractual liabilities for both the offeror and the offeree. An acceptance must be communicated, and (in common law) it must be the mirror image of the offer. *(CMBOK; FBL; STBP)*
See also *implied acceptance*.
(3) The act of an authorized representative of the federal government by which the government, for itself or as agent of another, assumes ownership of existing identified supplies tendered or approves specific services rendered as partial or complete performance of a contract. *(FAR 46.101)*
See also *conditional acceptance; letter of offer and acceptance* (LOA).
(4) The drawee's signed agreement to pay a draft as presented. *(UCC 3-409(a)-(c))*

Aa

acceptance criteria

Those criteria, usually stated in a contract and/or statement of work (SOW), that include deliverables, performance requirements, and essential conditions that must be met to complete project deliverables and be accepted. *(CMBOK)*
See *acceptance*.

acceptance date

The date that appears on the acceptance portion of a letter of offer and acceptance and indicates the calendar date on which a buyer agrees to accept the items and conditions contained in the offer portion. *(DISCS)*
See *letter of offer and acceptance* (LOA).

acceptance of offer

See *acceptance*.

acceptance of work

See *acceptance*.

acceptance period

The number of calendar days available to the buyer to award a contract from the date specified in the solicitation. *(CMBOK; GOAT)*

acceptance procedures

The process followed by federal government personnel during acceptance of a supply or service. *(GOAT)*

acceptance sampling

A statistical method used in contrast to 100-percent lot inspection. This quality control practice involves evaluating the overall condition of a given lot by inspecting only a portion of the lot for the purpose of accepting or rejecting the entire lot as either "conforming" or "not conforming" to a quality specification. *(CMBOK; DGCQI; GKPT)*

acceptance time

A definite period of time that one party to a negotiation has to accept an offer by another party. Instead of forcing a quick decision, this tactic can be used to deliberately give the other negotiator more time to grasp a solution or ideas. *(GOAT)*

acceptor

In the context of negotiable instruments, a drawee who has accepted a draft. *(UCC 3-103(a)(1))*
See *drawee*.

access

In the case of an information system, the opportunity to make use of an information system resource. *(CNSSI 4009)*
See *information system* (IS); see also *access control*.

access control

(1) Limiting access to information system resources only to authorized users, programs, processes, or other systems. *(CNSSI 4009)*
See *access*; see also *information system* (IS).
(2) The process of granting or denying specific requests to—
- Obtain and use information and related information processing services; and
- Enter specific physical facilities (e.g., federal buildings, military establishments, border crossing entrances).
(FIPS 201-2)

access control officer (ACO)

A designated individual responsible for limiting access to information systems resources. *(CNSSI 4009)*
See *access; information system* (IS).

accessibility

(1) The availability of public conveyances, facilities, utilities, technologies, and other designated resources to all persons. *(36 CFR 1194)* (See FAR 39.203 for electronic and information technology accessibility requirements.)
(2) A measure of the relative ease of admission to the various areas of an item for the purpose of operation or maintenance. *(DAAT)*
(3) The ability of individuals with disabilities to have access to and use of information and data that is comparable to the access of those who are not individuals with disabilities, unless an undue burden would be imposed. *(29 U.S.C. 794d)*
See also *undue burden*.

accessorial cost

The cost of the packing, crating, handling, and transporting of goods, which is not typically included in the standard price or contract cost of the goods. *(DISCS)*

accessory item

An item that facilitates or enhances the operation of another item or assembly, but which is not essential for its operation. *(GOAT)*

Aa

accommodated party
A party to an instrument issued for value given for the benefit of said party. *(UCC 3-419(a))*
See also *accommodation party*.

accommodation party
A party that signs an instrument for the purpose of incurring liability on the instrument without being a direct beneficiary of the value given for the instrument. *(UCC 3-419(a))*
See also *accommodated party*.

accord and satisfaction
(1) An "accord" is a contract under which an obligee promises to accept a stated performance in satisfaction of the obligor's existing duty. Performance of the accord discharges the original duty. Until performance of the accord is completed, the original duty is suspended unless there is such a breach of the accord by the obligor as discharges the new duty of the obligee to accept the performance in "satisfaction." *(RSOC 281(1)–(3))*
(2) A phrase used to assert agreement and that consideration is agreed upon. An "accord" often occurs as a result of a contract modification or a claim. The "accord" is the agreement and the "satisfaction" is the execution or performance. *(CMBOK; BLD)*

account
(1) Any deposit or credit account with a bank, including a demand, time, savings, passbook, share draft, or like account, other than an account evidenced by a certificate of deposit. *(UCC 4-104(a)(1))*
(2) Except as used in "account for," this term means a right to payment of a monetary obligation, whether or not earned by performance. *(UCC 9-102(a)(2))*

accountability
The obligation imposed by law, lawful order, or regulation, accepted by an organization or person for keeping accurate records to ensure control of property, documents, or funds, with or without physical possession. *(DODI 5000.64)*

accounting
(1) The system of recording and summarizing business and financial transactions and analyzing, verifying, and reporting the results. *(MW)*
(2) Except as used in "accounting for," this term refers to a record:
- Authenticated by a secured party,
- Indicating the aggregate unpaid secured obligations as of a date not more than 35 days earlier or 35 days later than the date of the record, and
- Identifying the components of the obligations in reasonable detail.
(UCC 9-102(a)(4))

accounting and appropriation data
See *lines of accounting* (LOA).

accounting classification reference number (ACRN)
Any combination of a two-position alphanumeric code used (in accordance with DFARS 204.7107) as a method of relating the accounting classification citation to detailed line item information contained in the schedule. Use of ACRNs provides for accountability of funds. *(DFARS 204.7101)*

accounting period
Providing financial information over specified time periods. *(NCMA-CA)*

accounting system
(1) A system that identifies and categorizes business costs in a consistent manner, thus allowing for the proper reporting of costs and determining allocability and allowability of cost elements. *(CMBOK)*
(2) As it relates to the *DFARS* Business Systems Rule, this term refers to the contractor's system or systems for accounting methods, procedures, and controls established to gather, record, classify, analyze, summarize, interpret, and present accurate and timely financial data for reporting in compliance with applicable laws, regulations, and management decisions, and may include subsystems for specific areas such as indirect and other direct costs, compensation, billing, labor, and general information technology. *(DFARS 252.242-7006)*
See *"acceptable" accounting system; contractor business systems*.

accounts payable
Amounts owed by an accounting entity on open accounts (e.g., materials and services received, wages earned, and fringe benefits unpaid). (DAAT)

accounts receivable
(1) Amounts due from debtors on open accounts. *(DAAT)*
(2) Amounts due for goods that have been shipped or

Aa

for services rendered, but for which payment has not been made. *(NES-02)*

(3) Under appropriated funds, amounts due from debtors for reimbursements earned or for appropriation refunds due. *(DAAT)*

(4) *From the federal government*—Amounts due from U.S. government organizations or funds. *(DAAT)*

(5) *From the public*—All accounts receivable arising from the sale of goods and services and from operations involving other than federal government organizations (e.g., debts owed by military personnel and civilian employees, contractors, and foreign military sales). *(DAAT)*

accreditation
To provide with credentials, to recognize or vouch for as conforming with a standard, or to recognize an institution as maintaining standards that qualify its members or graduates for professional practice or for admission to higher or more specialized institutions. *(MW)*

accrual basis of accounting
Records the effects on a reporting entity of transactions and other events and circumstances in the periods in which those transactions, events, and circumstances occur rather than only in the periods in which cash is received or paid by the entity. Accrual accounting is concerned with an entity's acquiring of goods and services and using them to produce and distribute other goods. It recognizes that the buying, producing, selling, distributing, and other operations of an entity during a period, as well as other events that affect entity performance, often do not coincide with the cash receipts and payments of the period. *(FASAB Handbook)*
See also *matching principle*.

accrual of a claim
The date on which all events—that fix the alleged liability of either the federal government or the contractor, and permit assertion of the claim—were known or should have been known. For liability to be fixed, some injury must have occurred. However, monetary damages need not have been incurred. Also called *claim accrual. (FAR 33.201)* (See FAR 33.206 for *use of* accrual of a claim *to determine* the "limitation of a claim.")

accrual year
The 12-month period during which a contractor may limit an employee's accrual of paid sick leave. *(FAR 22.2101)* (See also 29 CFR 13.5(b)(1).)

See *paid sick leave*.

accrued benefit cost method
An actuarial cost method under which units of benefits are assigned to each cost accounting period and are valued as they accrue (e.g., the services performed by each employee in the period involved). The measure of normal cost under this method for each cost accounting period is the present value of the units of benefit deemed to be credited to employees for service in that period. The measure of the actuarial accrued liability at a plan's inception date is the present value of the units of benefit credited to employees for service prior to that date. Also called "unit cost method without salary projection." *(FAR 31.001)*
See also *projected benefit cost method*.

accrued costs
The financial value of delivered articles and services and incurred costs. Incurred costs represent disbursement for which no physical deliveries have yet occurred. Examples include progress payments to contractors and nonrecurring costs. *(DISCS)* (See also FAR 31.001.)

accumulating costs
Collecting cost data in an organized manner, such as through a system of accounts. *(FAR 31.001)*

acknowledgement
(1) A recognized practice used to assure buyers that sellers have received and understood the need to perform on predetermined actions. *(CMBOK)*

(2) A form used to inform the buyer that the supplier has accepted the purchase order. As a result of this acknowledgment, a bilateral agreement is consummated, as long as the terms of the acknowledgment are not substantively different from those of the purchase order. *(GKPT)* (See also FAR 13.302-3.)

(3) Use of the federal government's Standard Form 30 (SF30), requiring bidders/offerors to acknowledge amendments to solicitations. Failure to acknowledge amendments may cause the offer to be rejected. *(CMBOK)*

acquisition
(1) In general, a process that begins with the establishment of needs and includes a description of requirements, solicitations and source selection, contract award, contract financing, contract performance, contract administration, and all technical and management functions directly related to the process of fulfilling an

Aa

organization's needs by contract. *(CMBOK; AFIT)*
See also *procurement*.

(2) In a federal government context, the acquiring by contract with appropriated funds of supplies or services (including construction) by and for the use of the federal government through purchase or lease, whether the supplies or services are already in existence or must be created, developed, demonstrated, and evaluated. *(FAR 2.101)*

acquisition and cross-servicing agreement (ACSA)

In a U.S. military context, this is an agreement—negotiated on a bilateral basis with countries or international organizations—that allows U.S. forces to exchange the most common types of support, including food, fuel, transportation, ammunition, and equipment. *(DDMAT)*

Acquisition Category (ACAT)

Categories established by the Department of Defense (DOD) to facilitate decentralized decision-making and execution and compliance with statutorily imposed requirements concerning DOD acquisition. The categories determine the level of review, decision authority, and applicable procedures, and generally include:

- ACAT I—major defense acquisition programs (MDAPs);
- ACAT II—those acquisition programs that do not meet the criteria for an ACAT I program, but do meet the criteria for a "major system";
- ACAT III—those acquisition programs that do not meet the criteria for an ACAT II program;
- ACAT IV—specific to the U.S. Navy/U.S. Marine Corps, those programs not otherwise designated as ACAT III.

(DAAT)

acquisition cost

(1) The sum of the ordering, transporting, handling, and all inventory holding costs associated with the acquisition of a material, including the amount, net of both trade and cash discounts, paid for the material. *(CMBOK)*.

(2) In the context of economic order quantity analysis, includes all costs associated with generating and processing an order and its related paperwork. *(GKPT)*

acquisition decision memorandum (ADM)

A memorandum signed by the milestone decision authority that documents decisions and direction resulting from milestone and other major decision point reviews. *(DAAT)*
See also *milestone decision authority* (MDA).

acquisition environment

Internal and external factors that have an effect on and help shape acquisition programs. Often these factors often work at opposite extremes and contradict each other. They include political forces, policies, regulations, reactions to unanticipated requirements, and emergencies. *(DAAT)*

acquisition executive

In a federal government context, the individual within each department, agency, etc., who has the overall acquisition management responsibilities. *(DAAT)*

"acquisition function closely associated with inherently governmental functions"

An acquisition function supporting or providing advice or recommendations with regard to the following activities of a federal agency:

- Planning acquisitions;
- Determining what supplies or services are to be acquired by the government, including developing statements of work;
- Developing or approving any contractual documents, to include documents defining requirements, incentive plans, and evaluation criteria;
- Evaluating contract proposals;
- Awarding government contracts;
- Administering contracts (including ordering changes or giving technical direction in contract performance or contract quantities, evaluating contractor performance, and accepting or rejecting contractor products or services);
- Terminating contracts; and
- Determining whether contract costs are reasonable, allocable, and allowable.

(FAR 3.1101)

Acquisition Gateway

An online federal government portal, managed by the General Services Administration, that includes all acquisition categories, intended to drive down prices and price variation experienced by federal government agencies as well as to drive better buying decisions. (See https://hallways.cap.gsa.gov)

Acquisition.gov

The federal government website, managed by the General Services Administration, that provides informa-

tion about acquisition regulations, systems, resources, opportunities, and training. It is the GSA's Integrated Acquisition Environment, and it is here that one can access the *Federal Acquisition Regulation* (*FAR*) and the *Defense Federal Acquisition Regulation Supplement* (*DFARS*), as well as the procurement regulations for all federal agencies. (See https://www.acquisition.gov.)
See *Integrated Acquisition Environment* (IAE)

acquisition logistics
Technical and management activities conducted to ensure supportability implications are considered early and throughout the acquisition process to minimize support costs and to provide the user with the resources to sustain the system. *(DAAT)*
See also *life cycle logistics* (LCL); *product support*.

acquisition methodology
The process used to solicit, request, or invite bids, quotes, or offers with the intent to award a contract. *(CMBOK)*

acquisition phase
A period in which all the tasks and activities needed to bring a program to the next major milestone occur. Phases provide a logical means of progressively translating broadly stated capabilities into well-defined, system-specific requirements and ultimately into effective systems. *(DAAT)*

acquisition plan (AP)
A plan for an acquisition that serves as the basis for initiating the individual contracting actions necessary to acquire a system or support a program. The acquisition plan should identify the milestones at which decisions should be made and address all the technical, business, management, and other significant considerations that will control the acquisition. *(CMBOK; FAI; GOAT)* (See also FAR Part 7.)
See also *acquisition strategy*.

acquisition planning
The process by which efforts of all personnel responsible for an acquisition are coordinated and integrated through a comprehensive plan for fulfilling the customer need in a timely manner at a reasonable cost. It includes developing the overall strategy for managing the acquisition. *(FAR 2.101; CMBOK; CMS)*

acquisition program

A directed effort funded either through government procurement appropriation or a research, development, test, and evaluation appropriation with the goal of providing a new or improved capability for a validated need. An acquisition program may include either development or procurement, or modifications of systems, subsystems, equipment, or components, as well as supporting equipment, systems, projects, and studies. *(DSMC)*

acquisition program baseline (APB)
In a DOD context, an agreement between the program manager and the milestone decision authority (MDA) that reflects the approved program and contains schedule, performance, and cost parameters that are the basis for satisfying an identified mission need. *(DAAT)*
See also additional *performance attribute* (APA); *initial operational capability* (IOC); *milestone decision authority* (MDA); *program manager*.

acquisition risk
The probability that some element of an acquisition process produces an undesirable result with an adverse effect on system effectiveness, suitability, cost, or availability for deployment. *(CMBOK; DSMC)*

acquisition savings
In value engineering, savings resulting from the application of a value engineering change proposal to contracts awarded by the same contracting office or its successor for essentially the same unit. They include "instant contract savings," "concurrent contract savings," and "future contract savings." *(FAR 48.001)*
See also *value engineering* (VE); *value engineering change proposal* (VECP).

acquisition strategy
(1) A business and technical management approach designed to achieve program objectives within the resource constraints imposed. It is the conceptual framework for planning, directing, contracting for, and managing a program, and provides a master schedule for research, development, testing, production, fielding, modification, post-production management, and other activities essential for success. *(DAAT; DSMC)*
(2) In major systems acquisition, a strategy developed by the program manager tailored to the particular major system acquisition program. This strategy is the program manager's overall plan for satisfying the mission need in the most effective, economical, and timely

Aa

manner. *(FAR 34.000; FAR 34.004)*

acquisition streamlining
Any effort that results in more efficient and effective use of resources to design, develop, or produce quality systems. *(FAR 7.101)*

acquisition team
The acquisition team consists of all participants in the buyer's acquisition, including not only representatives of the technical, supply, and procurement communities, but also the customers they serve and the contractors who provide the products and services. *(FAR 1.102(c)-(d))* (See also FAR 1.102-3.)

acquisition value
(1) The users' perception of the relative worth of a product or service. Formally defined as the subjectively weighted difference between the most a buyer would be willing to pay for the product or service, less the actual price of the item. *(AMAD)*
(2) The total price or total estimated cost of the contract or task order, including the base period and all options. *(DODI 5000.74)*

acquisition workforce
In terms of the federal government acquisition workforce, means the persons serving in acquisition positions within the federal government, as designated pursuant to 10 U.S.C. 1721(a). *(10 U.S.C. 101)*

Act
(1) The term for legislation once it has passed both houses of Congress and has been signed (i.e., "enacted") by the president of the United States or passed over his or her veto, thus becoming law. *(DISCS)* Compare with *bill*; *Executive Order* (EO).
(2.) A law in place. *(DAAT)*

act of God
An unanticipated grave natural disaster or other natural phenomenon or event of an exceptional, inevitable, accidental, and/or irresistible character, the effects of which could not have been foreseen, prevented, avoided, or otherwise guarded against by the exercise of due care or foresight. Examples include lightning, tornadoes, and earthquakes. *(STBP; 42 U.S.C. 9601(1))* See also *emergency*.

act of terrorism
Any act determined to have met the following require-

ments or such other requirements as defined and specified by the secretary of homeland security:
* Is unlawful;
* Causes harm, including financial harm, to a person, property, or entity, in the United States, or in the case of a domestic air carrier or a U.S.-flag vessel (or a vessel based principally in the United States on which U.S. income tax is paid and whose insurance coverage is subject to regulation in the U.S.), in or outside the United States;
* Uses or attempts to use instrumentalities, weapons, or other methods designed or intended to cause mass destruction, injury, or other loss to citizens or institutions of the United States.
(FAR 50.201)

action
In the sense of a judicial proceeding, includes recoupment, counterclaim, set-off, suit in equity, and any other proceeding in which rights are determined. *(UCC 1-201(1))*

active contract
Any contract that has been awarded and on which any element of contractor performance, payment, or administrative closing action is outstanding. *(AFIT)*

active repair time
In the case of a system, that portion of down time during which one or more technicians are working on the system to effect a repair. This time includes preparation time, fault location time, fault correction time, and final checkout time for the system. *(MIL-HDBK 338B)*

activity
(1) In general, a function, mission, action, or collection of actions. *(DDMAT)*
(2) A task or measurable amount of work to complete a job or part of a project. *(DAAT)*
(3) A unit, organization, or installation performing a function or mission. *(DDMAT)*

activity accounting
A system of accounting that recognizes various responsibilities throughout the organization and that reflects the plans and actions of each of these centers by allocating particular revenues and costs to the one having the pertinent responsibility. Also known as *responsibility accounting* and *profitability accounting*. *(NCMA-CA)*

Aa

Activity Address Code (AAC)
A distinct six-position code consisting of a combination of alpha and/or numeric characters assigned to identify specific agency offices, units, activities, or organizations by the GSA for civilian agencies and by the DOD for defense agencies. *(FAR 2.101)*

actual authority
Authority that the principal intentionally confers on the agent or allows the agent to believe himself or herself to possess. *(BLD)*
See *agent; agency*; see also *apparent authority; express authority; implied authority*.

actual cash value
The cost of replacing damaged property with other property of like kind and quality in the physical condition of the property immediately before the damage. *(FAR 31.001)*

actual cost
A cost sustained in fact, on the basis of costs incurred, as distinguished from forecasted or estimated costs. Actual costs include standard costs properly adjusted for applicable variances. *(FAR 31.001; CMBOK)*
See also *actual cost of work performed* (ACWP).

actual cost basis
A means of pricing equitable adjustments that relies on direct costing, whereby the seller tracks all the actual direct costs that are incurred as a result of the change. This method requires that the pricing action occurs after the work has been completed (retrospectively), and that the seller segregates the actual costs. *(CMBOK; NCMA-WS)*
See also *jury verdict basis; modified total cost basis; total cost basis*.

actual cost of work performed (ACWP)
(1) The costs actually incurred and recorded in accomplishing the work performed within a given time period. *(DAAT)*
(2) The program's total incurred cost, based on summation from the accounting system. *(NES-93)*
See also *actual cost*.

actual damages
See *compensatory damages*.

actual duration (AD)
The number of workdays that have passed from the actual start of an activity up to present (i.e., in-process activities) or the actual finish (i.e., completed activities). *(NDIA II)*
See also *actual finish* (AF); *actual start* (AS).

actual finish (AF)
The historic date a specific scope of work (typically an activity) was completed. *(NDIA II)*
See also *actual duration* (AD); *actual start* (AS).

actual start (AS)
The historic date a specific scope of work (typically an activity) began. *(NDIA II)*
See also *actual duration* (AD); *actual finish* (AF).

actual time
The time taken by a worker to complete a task or an element of a task. *(DAAT)*

actuarial accrued liability
A pension cost attributable, under the actuarial cost method in use, to years prior to the current period considered by a particular actuarial valuation. As of such date, the actuarial accrued liability represents the excess of the present value of future benefits and administrative expenses over the present value of future normal costs for all plan participants and beneficiaries. *(FAR 31.001)*
See also *actuarial assumption; actuarial cost method; actuarial gain and loss; actuarial valuation*.

actuarial assumption
An estimate of future conditions affecting pension cost; e.g., mortality rate, employee turnover, compensation levels, earnings on pension plan assets, and changes in values of pension plan assets. *(FAR 31.001)*
See also *actuarial accrued liability; actuarial cost method; actuarial gain and loss; actuarial valuation*.

actuarial cost method
A technique that uses actuarial assumptions to measure the present value of future pension benefits and pension plan administrative expenses, and that assigns the cost of such benefits and expenses to cost accounting periods. The actuarial cost method includes the asset valuation method used to determine the actuarial value of the assets of a pension plan. *(FAR 31.001)*
See also *actuarial accrued liability; actuarial assumption; actuarial gain and loss; actuarial valuation*.

actuarial gain and loss

Aa

The effect on pension cost resulting from differences between actuarial assumptions and actual experience. *(FAR 31.001)*
See also *actuarial accrued liability; actuarial assumption; actuarial cost method; actuarial valuation*.

actuarial valuation
The determination, as of a specified date, of the normal cost, actuarial accrued liability, actuarial value of the assets of a pension plan, and other relevant values for the pension plan. *(FAR 31.001)*
See also *actuarial accrued liability; actuarial assumption; actuarial cost method; actuarial gain and loss*.

ad valorem
A Latin term literally meaning "according to value," which is usually applied to a customs duty charged on the value only of goods that are dutiable, irrespective of quality, weight, or any other considerations. *(GKPT)*

addressable spend
In the context of federal government category management strategies, the amount of spend within a category or sub-category that can be addressed by a federal strategic sourcing initiative. *(GWCM)*
See also *category; category management; sub-category*.

adequate evidence
Information sufficient to support the reasonable belief that a particular act or omission has occurred. *(FAR 2.101)*

adequate price competition
A price is based on adequate price competition if:
- Two or more responsible offerors, competing independently, submit priced offers that satisfy the federal government's expressed requirement and if—
  - Award will be made to the offeror whose proposal represents the best value where price is a substantial factor in source selection, and
  - There is no finding that the price of the otherwise successful offeror is unreasonable (as any finding that the price is unreasonable must be supported by a statement of the facts and approved at a level above the contracting officer);
- There was a reasonable expectation, based on market research or other assessment, that two or more responsible offerors, competing independently, would submit priced offers in response to the solicitation's expressed requirement, even

though only one offer is received from a responsible offeror, and if—
  - Based on the offer received, the contracting officer can reasonably conclude that the offer was submitted with the expectation of competition (e.g., circumstances indicate that the offeror believed that at least one other offeror was capable of submitting a meaningful offer, and the offeror had no reason to believe that other potential offerors did not intend to submit an offer); and
  - The determination that the proposed price is based on adequate price competition and is reasonable has been approved at a level above the contracting officer; or
- Price analysis clearly demonstrates that the proposed price is reasonable in comparison with current or recent prices for the same or similar items, adjusted to reflect changes in market conditions, economic conditions, quantities, or terms and conditions under contracts that resulted from adequate price competition.
(FAR 15.403-1(c)(1)(i)–(iii))

adjusted ceiling
A negotiated adjustment to the ceiling price for changes that reflect a change in the negotiated maximum liability of the federal government. *(AFIT)*
See also *negotiated ceiling*.

adjusted hourly rate (including uncompensated overtime)
The rate that results from multiplying the hourly rate for a 40-hour work week by 40, and then dividing by the proposed hours per week which includes uncompensated overtime hours over and above the standard 40-hour work week. For example, 45 hours proposed on a 40-hour work week basis at $20 per hour would be converted to an uncompensated overtime rate of $17.78 per hour ($20.00 × 40 ÷ 45 = $17.78). *(FAR 37.101)*

adjusted target
The accumulated price resulting from changes to the basic contract for in-program change, change in scope, and/or terminations reflecting the current negotiated target price for work authorized. *(AFIT)*

administer contract
In the context of the Contract Management Standard Publication™, "administer contract" is in the "post-

Aa

award" life cycle phase of contract management, within the "perform contract" domain. It is the process of:

- Establishing expectations,
- Maintaining communication channels,
- Processing contract documentation,
- Conducting post-award performance reviews, and
- Assessing contract performance.

The value added by this process is in managing risk and increasing the likelihood of satisfactory contract execution. *(CMS)*
See *post-award life cycle phase; perform contract; see also ensure quality; Contract Management Standard™ Publication (CMS™); manage changes; subcontract management.*

administered price

A price determined by the conscious price policy of a seller rather than by the competitive forces of the marketplace. *(GKPT)*

administrative and logistics delay time (ALDT)

See *mean logistics delay time* (MLDT).

administrative appeal authority

The administrative appeal authority—as identified in OMB Circular No. A-76—reviews appeals to ensure that all costs are properly accounted for. *(OMB A-76)*

administrative change

A unilateral contract change, in writing, that does not affect the substantive rights of the parties (e.g., a change in the paying office or the appropriation data). *(FAR 43.101)*

administrative closeout

The process of ensuring that all documentation—including releases, audits, reports, and final invoices—has been completed and that contract files have been properly stored or disposed of. *(FAR 4.804-5)*

administrative contracting officer (ACO)

The contracting officer who is assigned the responsibility for the administration of federal government contracts. The administrative contracting officer is authorized to:

- Perform post-award contract administration duties,
- Monitor the contractor's performance, and
- Perform post-award contractual functions delegated by the purchasing office.

(DISCS; DSMC; OPM)

See also *contracting officer; corporate administrative contracting officer* (CACO).

administrative control

Direction or exercise of authority over subordinate or other organizations in respect to administration and support. *(DDMAT)*

administrative costs

General overhead expenses incident to the issue, sale, and transfer of material. *(AFIT)*

Administrative Dispute Resolution Act of 1996 (ADRA)

A federal law (*Pub. L.* 104-320, amending *Pub. L.* 101-552 and *Pub. L.* 102-354) that provides federal agencies the authority and procedures for the use of dispute resolution proceedings for the resolution of an issue in controversy that relates to an administrative program, if the parties agree to such a proceeding. *(5 U.S.C. 571, et seq.)*

administrative lead time

The time interval between the initiation of a procurement action and the letting/award of a contract or the placing of an order. Also called "procurement administrative lead time" (PALT). *(DISCS)*

administrative merits determination

Certain notices or findings of labor law violations issued by an enforcement agency following investigation. An "administrative merits determination" may be final or be subject to appeal or further review. *(FAR 22.2002)*

administrative proceeding

A nonjudicial process that is adjudicatory in nature in order to make a determination of fault or liability (e.g., Securities and Exchange Commission Administrative Proceedings, Civilian Board of Contract Appeals Proceedings, and Armed Services Board of Contract Appeals Proceedings). This includes administrative proceedings at the federal and state level, but only in connection with performance of a federal contract or grant. It *does not* include agency actions such as contract audits, site visits, corrective plans, or inspection of deliverables. *(FAR 9.101)*

advance acquisition contract (AAC)

A preliminary contract committing the contractor to proceed with an effort, including planning and engineering,

Aa

placement of orders for material, and other production efforts necessary to protect the required delivery schedule for the contract end items cited in the contract. This type of contract is used when the lead time is too long to allow waiting for funds in the fiscal year for which the end items are to be procured. Long lead funds are specifically appropriated for this type of effort. The definitive contract is negotiated at a later date and supersedes the advance acquisition contract. *(HCS)*
See *advance procurement*.

advance agreement

An agreement between the seller and the buyer regarding the treatment of specified costs negotiated either before or during contract performance, but preferably before the cost covered by the agreement is incurred. *(PW)* (See also FAR 31.109.)

advance arrangement

A predefined shipping requirement for certain cargo types. *(GKPT)*

advance buy

(1) The commitment of purchases in anticipation of future requirements beyond current lead times. Organizations may buy ahead as a matter of strategy or because of anticipated shortages, strikes, or price increases. Also called *forward buying. (GKPT)*
(2.) Procurement to provide for components that require a longer lead time than the system of which they are a part. Also called *advance procurement. (AFIT)* (See also DFARS 217.103.)
See also *advance buy funding*.

advance buy funding

That part of the procurement funding for an end item that is separately identified in an earlier year as advance procurement. *(DAAT)*
See *advance buy; advance funding*.

advance funding

Budget authority provided in an appropriation act to be used, if necessary, to cover obligations incurred late in the fiscal year for benefit payments in excess of the amount specifically appropriated in the act for that year, where the budget authority is charged to the appropriation for the program for the fiscal year following the fiscal year for which the appropriations act is passed. When such budget authority is used, the budget records an increase in the budget authority for the fiscal year in which it is used and a reduction in the budget

authority for the following fiscal year. *(DAAT)*
See *budget authority*.

advance notice

A notice of projected requirements distributed to reach as many prospective offerors as practicable. *(GOAT)*

advance notification

Under cost-reimbursement contracts, even if the contractor has an approved purchasing system and consent to subcontract is not required, the seller is required by statute to notify the buyer before the award of:
- Any cost-plus-fixed-fee contract, or
- Any fixed-price subcontract that exceeds limits identified in the *Federal Acquisition Regulation* (*FAR*).

(GOAT)

advance payment

An advance of money made by the buyer to a seller prior to, in anticipation of, and for the purpose of performance under one or more contracts. *(FAR 32.102(a))* (See also *FAR* Subpart 32.4.)
See *contractor financing*.

advance payment bond

A type of bond that secures fulfillment of the contractor's obligations under an advance payment provision. *(FAR 28.001)* (See also FAR 32.409-3(d)(5).)
See *bond*; see also *advance payment*.

advance procurement (AP)

Authority provided in an appropriations act to obligate and disburse during a fiscal year before that in which the related end item is procured. The funds are added to the budget authority for the fiscal year and deducted from the budget authority of the succeeding fiscal year. Used in major acquisition programs to obtain components whose long lead time requires early purchase in order to reduce the overall procurement lead time of the major end item. *(DAAT)*

advanced charge

The amount of freight or other transportation service charge on a shipment advanced from one carrier to another, or to the shipper, that is collected from the consignee. *(GKPT)*

advanced development

Projects that have advanced to a point where the development of experimental hardware for technical or operational testing is required prior to the determi-

Aa

nation of whether these items should be designed or engineered for eventual use. *(AFIT)*

advanced encryption standard (AES)
A Federal Information Processing Standards (FIPS)-approved cryptographic standard used to encrypt and decrypt data. *(CNSSI 4009)*
See also *encryption; Federal Information Processing Standards (FIPS)*.

adverse claim
A claim that a claimant has a property interest in a financial asset and that it is a violation of the rights of the claimant for another person to hold, transfer, or deal with the financial asset. *(UCC 8-102(a)(1))*
See *claim; notice of an adverse claim;* see also *claimant; financial asset*.

adviser
In the case of a letter of credit, a person who—at the request of the issuer, a confirmer, or another advisor—notifies or requests another adviser to notify the beneficiary that a letter of credit has been issued, confirmed, or amended. *(UCC 5-102(a)(1))*
See also *beneficiary; issuer; letter of credit*.

advisory and assistance services (A&AS)
Those services provided under contract by nongovernmental sources to support or improve organizational policy development, decision-making, management and administration, program and/or project management and administration, or research and development activities. All advisory and assistance services are classified in one of the following definitional subdivisions:
- Management and professional support services;
- Studies, analyses, and evaluations; and
- Engineering and technical services.

(FAR 2.101) (See also *FAR* Subpart 37.2.)
See *engineering and technical services; management and professional support services; studies, analyses, and evaluations*.

Advisory Panel on Streamlining and Codifying Acquisition Laws
See *Section 809 Panel*.

affected CAS-covered contract/subcontract
A contract or subcontract subject to Cost Accounting Standards rules and regulations, for which a contractor or subcontractor—
- Used one cost accounting practice to estimate

costs and a changed cost accounting practice to accumulate and report costs under the contract or subcontract, or
- Used a noncompliant practice for purposes of estimating or accumulating and reporting costs under the contract or subcontract.

(FAR 30.001)
See *Cost Accounting Standards* (CAS); *Cost Accounting Standards Board* (CASB).

affidavit
A written statement sworn to and acknowledged by a notary. *(GKPT)*

affiliated concerns
With respect to a prospective contractor's responsibility determination as a requirement to enter into a contract with the federal government, this term refers to business entities that are normally considered separate entities in determining whether the concern that is to perform the contract meets the applicable standards for responsibility. However, the contracting officer shall consider the affiliate's past performance and integrity when they may adversely affect the prospective contractor's responsibility. *(FAR 9.104-3(c))*
See also *affiliates; responsible prospective contractor*.

affiliates
Business concerns, organizations, or individuals are "affiliates" of each other if, directly or indirectly:
- Either one controls or has the power to control the other, or
- A third party controls or has the power to control both.

(FAR 2.101; FAR 9.403)

affirmative action
A provision of the Equal Employment Opportunity Act of 1972 (*Pub. L.* 92-261) that requires all firms to take affirmative action to move toward achieving a workforce that accurately reflects the composition of the community. *(GKPT)*

affirmative action program
A contractor's program that complies with Department of Labor regulations to ensure equal opportunity in employment to minorities, women, persons with disabilities, and covered veterans. *(FAR 22.801)* (See also FAR 22.804.)
See *affirmative action*.

Aa

affordability
(1) A determination that the life cycle cost of an acquisition program is in consonance with the long-range investment plans of the organization. *(DAAT)*
(2) Conducting a program at a cost constrained by the maximum resources that the organization can allocate to that capability. *(DAAT)*

affordability analysis
Long-range planning and decision-making that determines the resources an organization can allocate for each of its desired objectives by ensuring that the total of all such allocations—together with all other fiscal demands that compete for resources in the organization—are not above the organization's future total budget projection for each year. *(DAAT)*

after-imposed federal tax
Any new or increased federal excise tax or duty, or tax that was exempted or excluded on the contract date but whose exemption was later revoked or reduced during the contract period, on the transactions or property covered by a contract that the contractor is required to pay or bear as the result of legislative, judicial, or administrative action taking effect after the contract date. This term *does not* include social security tax or other employment taxes. *(GOAT)*
See also *after-relieved federal tax*.

after-relieved federal tax
Any amount of federal excise tax or duty, except social security or other employment taxes, that would otherwise have been payable on the transactions or property covered by a contract, but which the contractor is not required to pay or bear, or for which the contractor obtains a refund or drawback, as the result of legislative, judicial, or administrative action taking effect after the contract date. *(GOAT)*
See also *after-imposed federal tax*.

agency
(1) A relationship whereby the principal authorizes another (i.e., the "agent") to act for and on behalf of the principal to perform all acts connected with, and in all matters relating to, the business of the principal, including the authority to bind the principal in contract. *(FBL; STBP)*
See *agent authority*.
(2) Any executive department, military department, government corporation, government-controlled corporation, or other establishment in the executive branch of the federal government (including the Executive Office of the

President), or any independent regulatory agency. *(FAR 24.101)*
See *executive agency*.

agency ethics official
The designated agency ethics official (as described in 5 CFR 2638.201) or other designated person, including:
- Deputy ethics officials (as described in 5 CFR 2638.204) to whom authority (under FAR 3.104-6) has been delegated by the designated agency ethics official; and
- Alternate designated agency ethics officials (as described in 5 CFR 2638.202(b)).

(FAR 3.104-1)

agency head
(1) In general, the head of a department, agency, or bureau of the U.S. federal government. *(40 U.S.C. 1102(1))*
(2) "Agency head" or "head of the agency" means the secretary, attorney general, administrator, governor, chairperson, or other chief official of an executive agency, unless otherwise indicated, including any deputy or assistant chief official of an executive agency. *(FAR 2.101)*

agency employee or officer
Includes the following individuals who are employed by a federal agency:
- An individual who is appointed to a position in the government under Title 5 of the United States Code (U.S.C.), including a position under a temporary appointment;
- A member of the uniformed services, as defined in 37 U.S.C. 101(3);
- A special government employee, as defined in 18 U.S.C. 202;
- An individual who is a member of a federal advisory committee, as defined by the Federal Advisory Committee Act (Title 5, U.S.C., appendix 2).

(FAR 3.801)

agency support
In a federal government context, includes items furnished to an agency or an organization, as contrasted to an individual. Examples are real estate (for office or warehousing space), police and fire protection, utilities, registration of agency vehicles, and communications services. *(DODM 1342.6-M)*
See also *individual support; logistic and administrative support*.

Aa

agent
(1) A person who acts under the direction of a principal for the principal's benefit in a legal relationship known as "agency." *(GOAT)*
See *agency;* see also *agent authority*.
(2) Any individual, including a director, an officer, an employee, or an independent contractor, authorized to act on behalf of the organization. *(FAR 22.1702)*
See also *employee; independent contractor*.
(3) An employee (usually a contract manager) empowered to bind his or her organization legally in contract negotiations. *(STBP)*
See *contract manager*.

agent authority
The power delegated by a principal to his or her agent; a right to exercise power. *(BLD)*
See *agent; agency;* see also *actual authority; apparent authority; express authority; implied authority*.

aggregate price index number
A quantity that measures relative price changes for a group of related products over time. *(GOAT)*

aggregate risk
The cumulative risk associated with a given performance measure, accounting for all significant risk contributors. *(NID 8000-108)*

aggregates
As it relates to an executive department of the federal government, this term refers to the total relating to the whole budget rather than a particular function, program, or line item. The seven budget aggregates are:
- Budget authority,
- Outlays,
- Revenues,
- Deficit/surplus,
- Level of public debt,
- New direct loan obligations, and
- New guaranteed loan commitments.
(DAAT)

agile
A group of project management methodologies that emphasize rapid adaptability. These methodologies have been designed to rapidly respond to change in order to develop and deliver high-quality solutions in an uncertain and/or turbulent environment. *(AAAG)*

agile software development
A method of software development that utilizes an iterative development process, designs services based on real user needs, and constantly improves software from user feedback. Agile software development principles apply to both pre-award and post-award contexts.

aging schedule
A report of the status of invoices that are outstanding. Used in collection activities. *(HECA)*

agreement
(1) As distinguished from a "contract," this term refers to the bargain of the parties in fact, as found in their language or inferred from other circumstances, including course of performance, course of dealing, or usage of trade. *(UCC 1-201(3))* (See also UCC 1-303.)
Contrast with *contract*.
(2) A written or oral understanding, arrangement, or association, and any modification or cancellation thereof. It is a negotiated and typically binding arrangement between parties. Examples include basic agreements, basic ordering agreements, or blanket purchase agreements. *(46 U.S.C. 40102(1)(A))*

agreement for electronic presentment
An agreement, clearing-house rule, or Federal Reserve regulation or operating circular providing that presentment of an item may be made by transmission of an image of an item or information describing the item (i.e., "presentment notice"), rather than delivery of the item itself. The agreement may provide for procedures governing retention, presentment, payment, dishonor, and other matters concerning items subject to the agreement. *(UCC 4-110(a))*

Alaska Native Corporation (ANC)
Any regional corporation, village corporation, urban corporation, or group corporation organized under the laws of the State of Alaska in accordance with the Alaska Native Claims Settlement Act, as amended (43 U.S.C. 1601, *et seq.*) and which is considered a minority and economically disadvantaged concern under the criteria at 43 U.S.C. 1626(e)(1). This definition also includes ANC direct and indirect subsidiary corporations, joint ventures, and partnerships that meet the requirements of 43 U.S.C. 1626(e)(2). *(FAR 19.701)*

alignment
(1) The degree of agreement, conformance, and consistency among organizational purpose, vision, and val-

ues; structures, systems, and processes; and individual skills and behaviors. *(AIMD)*

(2) Performing adjustments that are necessary to return an item to a specified condition. *(DAAT)*

allocability

A cost is allocable if it is assignable or chargeable to one or more cost objectives on the basis of relative benefits received or other equitable relationship. Subject to the foregoing, a cost is allocable to a Government contract if it:

- Is incurred specifically for the contract;
- Benefits both the contract and other work, and can be distributed to them in reasonable proportion to the benefits received; or
- Is necessary to the overall operation of the business, although a direct relationship to any particular cost objective cannot be shown.

(FAR 31.201-4)
See also *allocable cost*.

allocate

To assign an item of cost, or a group of items of cost, to one or more cost objectives. This term includes both direct assignment of cost and the reassignment of a share from an indirect cost pool. *(FAR 31.001)*

allocated budget

See *total allocated budget* (TAB).

allocation

(1) An authorization by a designated official of the federal government making funds available within a prescribed amount to an operating agency for the purpose of making funding allotments (i.e., the first subdivision of an apportionment of funds). *(DISCS)*
See also *allotment*.

(2) In the context of acquisition from nonprofit agencies employing people who are blind or severely disabled, an action taken by a central nonprofit agency to designate the AbilityOne participating nonprofit agencies that will furnish definite quantities of supplies or perform specific services upon receipt of orders from ordering offices. *(FAR 8.701)*
See also *AbilityOne Program; Committee for Purchase From People Who Are Blind or Severely Disabled statute*.

allotment

An authorization granted within and pursuant to an allocation for the purpose of incurring commitments,

obligations, and expenditures in the accomplishment of an approved budget. Therefore, an allotment is a subdivision of an appropriation that provides the funding authority for an official
to accomplish a specific function or mission. *(DISCS)*
See also *allocation; apportionment; appropriation*.

allowability

A cost is allowable only when the cost complies with all of the following requirements:

- Reasonableness;
- Allocability;
- Standards promulgated by the Cost Accounting Standards Board, if applicable, otherwise, generally accepted accounting principles and practices appropriate to the circumstances;
- Terms of the contract; and
- Any limitations set forth in this subpart.

(FAR 31.201-2)
See also *allocability; allocable cost; cost reasonableness; reasonable cost*.

alter

In the context of construction on or alteration of federal property in performance of a contract, this term includes–

- Preliminary planning, engineering, architectural, legal, fiscal, and economic investigations and studies, surveys, designs, plans, working drawings, specifications, procedures, and other similar actions necessary for the alteration of a public building; and
- Repairing, remodeling, improving, or extending, or other changes in, a public building.

(40 U.S.C. 3301(a)(1))
See also *public building*.

alteration

(1) With respect to a facility and similar real property, this term refers to remodeling, improving, extending, or making other changes to a facility, exclusive of maintenance repairs that are preventive in nature. This term includes planning, engineering, architectural work, and other similar actions. *(FMR 102-71.20)*

(2) With respect to negotiable instruments, this term means:

- An unauthorized change in an instrument that purports to modify in any respect the obligation of a party, or
- An unauthorized addition of words or numbers or other change to an incomplete instrument relating to the obligation of a party.

(UCC 3-407(a))

Aa

alternate

A substantive variation of a basic provision or clause prescribed for use in a defined circumstance. It adds wording to, deletes wording from, or substitutes specified wording for a portion of the basic provision or clause. The alternate version of a provision or clause is the basic provision or clause as changed by the addition, deletion, or substitution. *(FAR 2.101)* (See also FAR 52.105(a).)

alternate bid

One of two or more bids on the same item, submitted on different bases by the same bidder, as provided by the invitation for bids. *(AFIT)* (See also FAR 14.404-2(b).)

alternate item

An item selected by the responsible engineering activity in lieu of the forecast item. *(AFIT)*

alternate positions

In the context of negotiations, by offering two or more alternative positions at the same time, a negotiator can indicate a willingness to accept more than one way of settling a particular issue or group of issues. *(GOAT)*

alternate proposal

One of two or more proposals on the same item, submitted on different bases by the same offeror, as provided by the request for proposals. *(FAR 15.209(a) (2))*

alternative dispute resolution (ADR)

Any type of procedure or combination of procedures voluntarily used, in lieu of litigation, to resolve issues in controversy. These procedures may include, but are not limited to, conciliation, facilitation, mediation, fact-finding, mini-trials, arbitration, and use of ombudsmen. *(FAR 33.201)* (See also FAR 33.214.)
See also *arbitration; issue in controversy; nonbinding arbitration*.

ambiguous or erroneous evaluation criteria

In the case of a pre-award protest, a protestor may claim that the criteria stated to be used to evaluate proposals is flawed, inaccurate, or ambiguous in some material way that will negatively impact the protestor's ability to fairly compete. *(CMBOK)*

ambiguous or incomplete requirements

In the case of a pre-award protest, a protestor may claim that the statement of work is so incomplete or ambiguous that it precludes a clear understanding of the full nature and scope of the requirement to be performed. *(CMBOK)*

amendment

(1) See *congressional amendment*.
(2) A change (correction, deletion, or addition) to any information contained in an invitation for bids or request for proposals (or previous amendment thereto). The amendment becomes part of the solicitation and any resulting contract. *(FAI)* (See also FAR 15.206.)
See *contract modification*.

American-made end product

See *U.S.-made end product*.

American National Standards

Those standards that have been approved by the American National Standards Institute (ANSI), a private, not-for-profit membership organization that coordinates the U.S. voluntary, consensus-based standards system and represents the United States in the International Organization for Standardization (ISO). *(NES-97)*
See *American National Standards Institute* (ANSI); *International Organization for Standardization* (ISO); *standard*.

American National Standards Institute (ANSI)

A not-for-profit organization that oversees voluntary consensus standards. *(NES-97)*
See *standard*.

American Recovery and Reinvestment Act of 2009 (ARRA)

A federal law (*Pub. L.* 111-5) that fosters accountability and transparency in government spending. *(DGBCT)* (See also *FAR* Subpart 25.6.)

amortization

(1) The gradual reduction, redemption, or liquidation of the balance of an account according to a specified schedule of time and amounts. *(AFIT)*
(2) The process of spreading the cost of an intangible asset over the expected useful life of the asset. *(STBP)*

analogy cost estimate

An estimate of costs based on historical data of a similar (analogous) item. *(DAAT)*

Aa

analysis of alternatives (AOA)
An analytical comparison of the effectiveness, suitability, and life-cycle cost (or total ownership cost) of alternatives that satisfy established needs. *(DODI 5000.02)*

analysis of variance (ANOVA)
The terms used to analyze variation/variance in the regression model. These terms are commonly summarized in a format known as an "ANOVA table." *(GOAT)*

annual bid bond
A single bond furnished by a bidder, in lieu of separate bonds, which secure all bids (on other than construction contracts) requiring bonds submitted during a specific federal government fiscal year. *(FAR 28.001)* See *bond*; see also *bid bond*.

annual performance bond
A single bond furnished by a contractor, in lieu of separate performance bonds, to secure fulfillment of the contractor's obligations under contracts (other than construction contracts) requiring bonds entered into during a specific federal government fiscal year. *(FAR 28.001)* See *bond*; see also *performance bond*.

annual receipts
(1) A measure of the revenue received by a business concern each year. *(GOAT)*
(2) For a concern that has been in business for three or more complete fiscal years, the annual average gross revenue of the concern taken for the last thre fiscal years. *(GOAT)*
(3) For a concern that has been in business for less than three complete fiscal years, the total receipts for the period it has been in business, divided by the number of weeks, including fractions of a week, that it has been in business, and multiplied by 52. *(GOAT)*

anomalous indorsement
An indorsement made by a person who is not the holder of the negotiable instrument concerned. An anomalous indorsement does not affect the manner in which the instrument may be negotiated. *(UCC 3-205(d))* See *indorsement; negotiable instrument*; see also *negotiation*.

ANSI X12
A set of standards promulgated by the American National Standards Institute (ANSI) for use in formatting and handling purchasing-related documents transmitted by electronic data interchange. *(GKPT)*

anticipated inventory
Anticipated stocks are accumulated for a well-defined future need. They differ from buffer (safety) stocks in that they are committed in the face of certainty. *(GKPT)*

anticipated reimbursement
The amount of reimbursements expected to be earned and added to appropriation or other funding authority as a source of funds in order to cover obligations incurred in performance of work, services, procurement of material for others, or material delivered from stock. *(AFIT)*

anticipatory breach/anticipatory repudiation
(1) When either party repudiates the contract with respect to a performance not yet due, the loss of which will substantially impair the value of the contract to the other. *(UCC 2-610)*
(2) When the promisor, without justification and before he or she has committed a breach, makes a positive statement to the promisee indicating that he or she will not or cannot perform his or her contractual duties. *(BLD)*
Compare with *breach of contract*.
(3) A refusal by one party to a contract to perform his or her future obligations under the contract that is expressed either by a clear statement of refusal or by a statement or action that clearly implies refusal. *(MW)*
See also *repudiation*; compare with *breach of contract*.

anticipatory profit
Profits payable for work not performed. This payment is viewed as a reasonable sanction to be imposed upon defaulters in ordinary contractual relationships. Anticipatory profits are not allowed when the federal government terminates a contract for convenience. *(CMPA)*
(See also FAR 49.108-3.)
See *convenience termination*.

anticompetitive practices
Practices that eliminate competition or restrain trade, which usually lead to excessive prices and may warrant criminal, civil, or administrative action against the participants. *(FAR 3.301(a))*

anti-counterfeit
A risk-based approach to reduce the frequency and impact of counterfeit material within acquisition systems and life-cycle sustainment processes. *(DODI 4140.67)*

Aa

Antideficiency Act (ADA)

A federal law (31 U.S.C. 1341) prohibiting the obligation of government money in advance of an appropriation or in excess of the amount of an available appropriation. The salient features of this act include prohibitions against authorizing or incurring obligations or expenditures in excess of amounts apportioned by the Office of Management and Budget or in excess of amounts permitted by agency regulations and establishment of procedures for determining the responsibility for violations and for reporting violations to the president, through OMB, and to the Congress. *(AAPM)* (See also FAR 32.702.)
See also *Antideficiency Act violations*.

Antideficiency Act violations

The incurring of obligations or the making of expenditures (outlays) in violation of appropriation law as to purpose, time, and amounts as specified in the applicable appropriations act or appropriations of funds. *(DDMAT)*

Anti-Kickback Act

See *Kickbacks statute*.

Antitrust Act

Also known as the *Sherman Act*, this federal law (15 U.S.C. 1, *et seq.*), prohibits any unreasonable interference—by contract, combination, or conspiracy—with the ordinary, usual, and freely competitive pricing or distribution system of the open market in interstate trade. *(DGBCT)* (See also *FAR* Subpart 3.3.)
See *antitrust acts*; see also *Clayton Antitrust Act of 1914; Robinson-Patman Act*.

antitrust acts

Federal and state statutes to protect trade and commerce from unlawful restraints, price discriminations, price fixing, and monopolies. Most states have mini-antitrust acts patterned on the federal acts. The federal antitrust acts include:

- The Antitrust Act (also known as the Sherman Act; 15 U.S.C. 1, *et seq.*);
- Sections 73 and 74 of the Wilson Tariff Act (15 U.S.C. 8, 9);
- The Clayton Antitrust Act of 1914 (15 U.S.C. 12, *et seq.*);
- The Act of June 19, 1936 (15 U.S.C. 13, 13a, 13b, 21a);
- The Federal Trade Commission Act (15 U.S.C. 41, *et seq.*);

- The Antitrust Civil Process Act (15 U.S.C. 1311, *et seq.*); and
- Acts supplementary to those acts.
(BLD; 46 U.S.C. 40102(2))

antitrust violations

Anticompetitive practices such as collusive bidding, follow-the-leader pricing, rotated low bids, collusive price estimating systems, and sharing of the business. *(FAR 3.301)*

anything-as-a-service (XaaS)

Refers to the growing variety of services available over the internet via cloud computing, as opposed to being provided locally or on premises. The "X" in "XaaS" is a catch-all term for any type of service—software-as-a-service/storage-as-a-service (SaaS), network-as-a-service (NaaS), infrastructure-as-a-service (IaaS), platform-as-a-service (PaaS), etc. Also called "everything-as-a-service." *(WB)*
See also *cloud computing*.

apparent authority

Authority that a third party reasonably believes an agent has, based on the third party's dealings with the principal. *(BLD)*
See *agent; agent authority; principal*; see also *actual authority; express authority; implied authority*.

apparent withdrawal

A tactic used in negotiation where a negotiator gives the impression that his or her organization is withdrawing from the negotiation when that is not the actual intent. Instead, there is a plan to resume negotiations at some later time. *(GOAT)*

appeal

(1) To resort to a superior (i.e., appellate) court to review the decision of an inferior (i.e., trial) court or administrative agency. *(BLD)*
(2) A request for reconsideration of an action taken to adjust, reduce, or delete funding for an item during the congressional review of the defense budget (authorization and appropriation). *(DAAT)*

appeal notice

A notice to a board of contract appeals that a contracting officer's final decision will be appealed. *(GCG)* (See also FAR 33.211.)

Aa

applied research

The effort that—

- Normally follows basic research, but may not be severable from the related basic research;
- Attempts to determine and exploit the potential of scientific discoveries or improvements in technology, materials, processes, methods, devices, or techniques; and
- Attempts to advance the state of the art.

When being used by contractors in cost principle applications, this term does not include efforts whose principal aim is the design, development, or test of specific items or services to be considered for sale; these efforts are within the definition of "development." *(FAR 31.205-18(a); 35.001)* (See also *FAR* Part 35.) See *development*; see also *basic research*.

appointment letter/memorandum

A document used by the contracting officer to assign contractual responsibility to another federal government official. The letter or memorandum specifies the official's authority and is signed by the contracting officer. *(GOAT)*

apportioned effort

Effort that by itself is not readily measured or divisible into discrete work packages, but is related in direct proportion to the planning and performance of other measured effort involved with one or more discrete work packages. *(NDIA II)*

apportionment

A determination made by the Office of Management and Budget that limits the amount of obligations or expenditures that may be incurred during a specified time period. An apportionment may limit all obligations to be incurred during the specified period or it may limit obligations to be incurred for a specific activity, function, project, or a combination thereof. *(DISCS)* See *appropriation act; authorization act; obligation*; see also *reapportionment*.

apprentice

A person, who is—

- Employed and individually registered in a bona fide apprenticeship program registered with the Department of Labor, Employment and Training Administration, Office of Apprenticeship Training, Employer, and Labor Services (OATELS), or with a state apprenticeship agency recognized by OATELS; or

- Who is in the first 90 days of probationary employment as an apprentice in an apprenticeship program, and is not individually registered in the program, but who has been certified by the OATELS or a state apprenticeship agency (where appropriate) to be eligible for probationary employment as an apprentice.

(FAR 22.401)
Compare with *trainee*.

appropriate person

(1) With respect to an indorsement, the person specified by a security certificate or by an effective special indorsement to be entitled to the security. *(UCC 8-107(a) (1))*
See *indorsement; security; security certificate*.
(2) With respect to an instruction, the registered owner of an uncertificated security. *(UCC 8-107(a)(2))*
See *instruction; uncertificated security*.
(3) With respect to an entitlement holder, the entitlement holder. *(UCC 8-107(a)(3))* (See also UCC 8-107(a) (4)-(5).)
See *entitlement holder*.

appropriation (APPN)

A provision of U.S. law that makes funds available to the federal government for obligation and expenditure (other than borrowing authority), including the authority to obligate and expend the proceeds of offsetting receipts and collections. Appropriations generally follow authorizing legislation—i.e., an "appropriation act"—which provides a specified amount of funds to be used for designated purposes, and each appropriation has a finite period of time for incurring obligations. *(2 U.S.C. 622(2)(A)(i); DISCS)*
See *appropriation act; budget authority; reappropriation; supplemental appropriations*; see also *operation and maintenance (O&M) appropriations; procurement appropriations; research, development, test, and evaluation (RDT&E) appropriations*.

appropriation act/bill

Legislation initiated by both the House and Senate Appropriations Committees, passed through Congress, and signed into law by the president that provides authority for federal agencies to incur obligations and to make payments out of the U.S. Treasury for specified purposes. An appropriation act is the most common means of providing budget authority. There are 13 regular appropriation acts for each federal fiscal year. *(DISCS)*

Aa

See also *apportionment; appropriation; authorization act; budget authority; obligation; reappropriation; supplemental appropriations*.

appropriation limitations
Statutory and other special restrictions that impose a restriction on the availability of funds, or the authority to obligate or expend appropriations for certain objects or purposes, as determined by Congress within an appropriation. *(DAAT)*
See *appropriation* (APPN).

appropriation warrant
An official U.S. Treasury document that provides the dollar amounts established in the general and detailed appropriation accounts of the U.S. Treasury pursuant to appropriation acts authorized by law. It serves as a convenient source document for entries into accounts that establish the amount of money authorized to be withdrawn from the U.S. Treasury. *(DAAT)*

appropriations committees
See *appropriators*.

appropriators
The Senate and House Appropriations Committees. They recommend legislation granting funding for U.S. federal agencies and also have oversight authority to monitor how funds are spent. *(DAAT)*

approval
In the case of first article testing, the contracting officer's written notification to the contractor accepting the test results of the first article. *(FAR 9.301)*

approved program
In a Department of Defense context, the technical and operational, schedule, and quantity requirements reflected in the latest approved under secretary of defense for acquisition, technology, and logistics (USD(AT&L)) acquisition decision memorandum, or other document reflecting a more current decision of the USD(AT&L) or other appropriate approval authority (such as the President's Budget, the Future Years Defense Program, and supporting documentation). *(DAAT)*
See also *program of record* (POR).

approved project
In a Department of Defense context, a cooperative project under 22 U.S.C. 2767 that has DOD component approval for implementation, or a cooperative research and development project under 10 U.S.C. 2350(a) that has the Office of the Secretary of Defense approval for implementation, before any formal agreements have been negotiated or concluded and funds are released. *(DAAT)*

approved purchasing system
A contractor's purchasing system that has been reviewed and approved in accordance with the "Subcontracting Policies and Procedures," or *FAR* Part 44. *(FAR 44.101)*

arbitrage
A financial term meaning the simultaneous buying of a security, commodity, or currency in one market while selling the same item in another market. *(GKPT)*

arbitral award or decision
An arbitrator or arbitral panel determination that a labor law violation occurred, or that enjoined or restrained a violation of labor law. It includes an award or decision that is not final or is subject to being confirmed, modified, or vacated by a court, and includes an award or decision resulting from private or confidential proceedings. *(FAR 22.2002)*

arbitrary deadline
Every contract negotiation has real deadlines (e.g., funding availability or required delivery) that might be used to put pressure on one party or the other. However, an "arbitrary deadline" is a point in time set by one of the parties to the negotiation simply to put pressure on another party. *(GOAT)*

arbitration
A nonjudicial method or procedure for settling matters of dispute(s) between parties whereby the dispute is referred to an objective outside party (i.e., one or more impartial persons—called an "arbitrator"), selected by the disputing parties, acting as a fact-finder and a primary decision-maker, who will produce a final and binding determination. This final determination is made out of court, which saves the time and expense of litigation. *(FBL; GCG; HECA)* (See also FAR 32.214.)
See *binding arbitration; nonbinding arbitration*; see also *arbitrator*.

arbitrator
A third person chosen to decide a dispute between two other persons. *(FBL)*
See *arbitration*.

Aa

architectural and engineering selection authority

The person who makes the final selection decision concerning architectural and engineering (A-E) services for a federal agency. This person may be the agency head or a designated selection authority. *(GOAT)*
See *architectural and engineering (A-E) services*

architectural and engineering (A-E) services

This term—also called "architect-engineer services"—includes the following:

- Professional services of an architectural or engineering nature, as defined by state law, if applicable, that are required to be performed or approved by a person licensed, registered, or certified to provide such services;
- Professional services of an architectural or engineering nature performed by contract that are associated with research, planning, development, design, construction, alteration, or repair of real property; and
- Other professional services of an architectural or engineering nature, or incidental services, which members of the architectural and engineering professions (and individuals in their employ) may logically or justifiably perform, including studies, investigations, surveying and mapping, tests, evaluations, consultations, comprehensive planning, program management, conceptual designs, plans and specifications, value engineering, construction phase services, soils engineering, drawing reviews, preparation of operating and maintenance manuals, and other related services.

(FAR 36.6; 40 U.S.C. 1102(2))

architectural work

The design of a building as embodied in any tangible medium of expression, including a building, architectural plans, or drawings. The work includes the overall form as well as the arrangement and composition of spaces and elements in the design, but does not include individual standard features. *(17 U.S.C. 101)*

architecture design

A systems engineering technical process by which the program manager and systems engineer, often through system modeling, trade-offs, and decision analyses, capture the functional requirements and interdependencies in the system architecture. The architecture design process, combined with stakeholder requirements definition and requirements analysis, provides key insights into technical risks early in the acquisition life cycle, allowing for early development of mitigation strategies. *(DAAT)*

area of combat operations

An area of operations designated as such by the secretary of defense when enhanced coordination of contractors performing private security functions working for U.S. federal government agencies is required. *(FAR 25.302-2)*
See also *other significant military operations; private security functions*.

areawide contract

A contract entered into between the General Services Administration and a utility service supplier to cover utility service needs of federal agencies within the franchise territory of the supplier. Each areawide contract includes an "authorization" form for requesting service, connection, disconnection, or change in service. *(FAR 41.101)*

armed forces service medal veteran

Any veteran who, while serving on active duty in the U.S. military, ground, naval, or air service, participated in a U.S. military operation for which an armed forces service medal was awarded pursuant to Executive Order 12985. *(FAR 22.1301)*

Armed Services Board of Contract Appeals (ASBCA)

A neutral, independent board whose primary function is to hear and decide post-award contract disputes between government contractors and the DOD, NASA, the CIA, and other entities with who the ASBCA has entered into agreements to provide services.
See also *Civilian Board of Contract Appeals (CBCA)*.

Armed Services Committees

Standing committees of the Senate and House, respectively:

- The Senate Armed Services Committee (SASC), and
- The House Armed Services Committee (HASC).

They authorize Department of Defense programs and conduct oversight. *(DAAT)*

Armed Services Procurement Act (ASPA)

A general federal statute (10 U.S.C. 2301-2314) that governs contracting by the DOD and its military services. *(GCG)*

Aa

Armed Services Procurement Regulation (ASPR)

A set of procurement regulations issued in 1949 that once governed procurements by military agencies and that later (in 1978) became known as the *Defense Acquisition Regulation* (*DAR*). Today, procurement by the U.S. military departments is governed by the *Federal Acquisition Regulation*, as supplemented by the *Defense FAR Supplement*. *(GCG)*

Arms Export Control Act (AECA)

The basic U.S. law (22 U.S.C. 2751, *et seq.*) providing the authority and general rules for the conduct of foreign military sales and commercial sales of defense articles, defense services, and training. The AECA came into existence with the passage of the Foreign Military Sales Act (FMSA) of 1968. An amendment in the International Security Assistance and Arms Export Control Act of 1976 changed the name of FMSA to the AECA. *(DISCS)*

Arms Export Control Board (AECB)

An interagency board, chaired by the under secretary of state for security assistance (science and technology), that serves to advise the secretary of state on matters relating to security assistance program levels and arms transfer policies. *(DAAT)*

arms transfer

Defense articles and defense services (arms, ammunition, etc.–including components, training, manufacturing licenses, technical assistance, and related technical data) provided by the federal government under the Foreign Assistance Act of 1961 (22 U.S.C. 2151), as amended. *(DAAT)*
See *defense article; defense service*.

article

(1) A member of a particular and distinctive kind or class of things, such as an item of goods. *(MW)*
(2) A manufactured item which:
- Is formed to a specific shape or design during manufacture, and
- Has end-use functions dependent in whole or in part upon its shape or design during end use.

(40 CFR 372.3)

as is

(1) A contract phrase referring to the condition of property to be sold or leased. It generally pertains to a disclaimer of liability; property sold in "as-is" condition is generally not guaranteed. *(CMBOK; STBP)*
(2) In a federal government context, a phrase meaning that the U.S. government may, at its option, furnish government property in an "as-is" condition. In such cases, the government makes no warranty with respect to the serviceability and/or suitability of the government property for contract performance. Any repairs, replacement, and/or refurbishment shall be at the contractor's expense. *(PGI 245.201-70)*

as required

(1) Refers to an action that is absolutely necessary in order to complete a task. *(MW)*
(2) Constitutes an expressly stated term of a binding agreement. *(FAR 4.1005-1(c))*

assemblage

A collection of items that is designed to accomplish one general function and is identified and issued as a single item. *(AFIT)*
See also *assembly*.

assembly

(1) The fitting together of manufactured parts into a complete machine, structure, or unit of a machine. *(MW)*
(2) In the case of information technology equipment, a group of parts, elements, subassemblies, or circuits that are removable items of the equipment. *(CNSSI 4009)*

assertion of opinion

An assertion that expresses only a belief, without certainty, as to the existence of a fact or expresses only a judgment as to quality, value, authenticity, or similar matters. *(RSOC 168(1))*

assessment

(1) The action or an instance of making a judgment about something. *(MW)*
(2) An amount that a person is officially required to pay, especially as a tax (e.g., the tax assessment on property). *(MW)*
(3) In the case of business process improvement, an appraisal by a trained team of professionals to determine the state of an organization's current processes and to determine the high priority process-related issues facing an organization. An assessment may also result in organizational support for process improvement. *(AIMD)*
See *business process improvement* (BPI).

Aa

assessment criteria
Areas of consideration common to more than one evaluation factor. *(DGBCT)*

asset
(1) Property, funding, technical knowledge, or other valuable items owned by an organization. Investments also typically create assets. *(AIMD)*

(2) Property of all kinds (real and personal, tangible and intangible), including, among other things, for certain purposes, patents and causes of action that belong to any person, including a corporation. *(BLD)*
See *property*.

(3) The inventory that is the subject of a bulk sale and any tangible and intangible personal property used or held for use primarily in, or arising from, the seller's business and sold in connection with that inventory. In this context, this term *does not* include:
- Fixtures, other than readily removable factory and office machines;
- The lessee's interest in a lease of real property; or
- Property to the extent it is generally exempt from creditor process under nonbankruptcy law.

(UCC 6-102(1)(a))
See *bulk sale*.

assign
To convey or transfer to another, as to assign property, rights, or interests to another. *(STBP)*

assignment
(1) The alignment of duty to act or to receive an act. *(CMBOK)*

(2) A transfer of rights (usually contract rights) from an assignor to an assignee. *(FBL)*
See also *assignment of a right*

(3) A transference of a property right (such as a contract or purchase order) or title to another party. In shipping, it is commonly used with a bill of lading, which involves transfer of rights, title, and interest for the purpose of indorsement. Such indorsement gives, to the party named, the title to the property covered by the bill of lading. *(GKPT)*
See also *bill of lading*

assignment of a right
A manifestation of the assignor's intention to transfer a right by virtue of which the assignor's right to performance by the obligor is extinguished in whole or in part and the assignee acquires a right to such performance. A contractual right can be assigned unless—

- The substitution of a right of the assignee for the right of the assignor would materially change the duty of the obligor, materially increase the burden or risk imposed by the contract, materially impair the chances of obtaining return performance, or materially reduce its value;
- The assignment is forbidden by statute or is otherwise inoperative on grounds of public policy; or
- Assignment is validly precluded by contract.

(RSOC 317(1)-(2))

assignment of claims
The transfer or making over by the contractor to a bank, trust company, or other financing institution, as security for a loan to the contractor, of its right to be paid by the federal government for contract performance. *(FAR 2.101)* (See also FAR 32.8.)

assignment of contract administration
As provided in federal agency procedures, contracting officers may delegate contract administration or specialized support services, either through interagency agreements or by direct request to the cognizant contract administration office. Also called *delegation of contract administration*. *(FAR 42.202; GOAT)*
See *delegation*

assignment of contract audit services
As provided in federal agency procedures or interagency agreements, contracting officers may request audit services directly from the responsible audit agency. The audit request should include a suspense date and should identify any information needed by the contracting officer. The responsible audit agency may decline requests for services on a case-by-case basis if resources of the audit agency are inadequate to accomplish the tasks. *(GOAT)* (See also FAR 42.101.)

assist audit
An audit performed by one audit office at the request of another audit office; usually an adjunct to or an integral part of an audit being performed by the requestor. *(OPM)*

assisted acquisition
A type of interagency acquisition where a servicing agency performs acquisition activities on a requesting agency's behalf, such as awarding and administering a contract, task order, or delivery order. *(FAR 2.101)*
Compare with *direct acquisition*.

Aa

association standards

Result from agreements that have been reached between the key economic players in a sector (e.g., suppliers, users, and often governments). The players agree on specifications and standards that are to be applied consistently in their sector's classification of materials, manufacture of products, and provision of services. *(NES-97)*
See *standard*.

attach

(1) To join or make a part of (e.g., affidavits *attached* to the suit.). *(MW)*
(2) To obtain a court order against property of another person that directs an officer of the court to seize or take control of the property. *(MW)*
Compare with *garnishment; levy*.
(3) To create a security interest in property and so acquire the right to foreclose on or otherwise deal with property for payment of a debt and to exercise one's rights in the property against third parties. *(MW)*

attachment

(1) Any documentation, appended to a contract or incorporated by reference, which does not establish a requirement for deliverables. *(DFARS 204.7101)*
Compare with *exhibit*.
(2) A legal proceeding accompanying an act in court by which a plaintiff may acquire a lien on a defendant's property as a security for the payment of any judgment that the plaintiff may obtain. *(GKPT)*
See *attach*.

attorney-in-fact

An agent, independent agent, underwriter, or any other company or individual holding a power of attorney granted by a surety. *(FAR 28.001)*
See also *power of attorney*.

attribute screening

A methodology for assuring that technical/specification requirements and customer expectations are clearly defined, described, and reflected in the product. The process to be followed is to tabulate the functional and physical attributes, including inputs resulting from customer specification documents, government regulations, internal reviews, and industry standards. Next, these attributes are refined as to requirements and attendant priorities (the "must-have(s)," the "nice-to-have(s)," and the "can-do-without(s)"). This process is repeated until the impact of the requirement is clear to all parties. At the end of the procedure, there should be an accurate design definition and an understanding of the customer requirements and priorities. *(NC-MA-WS)*

attrition

The loss of a resource due to natural causes in the normal course of events, such as a turnover of employees or spoilage and obsolescence of material. *(DISCS)*

auction

Sale in which property, services, or merchandise are sold to the highest bidder. *(DGBCT)*
See also *bulk sale; reverse auction* (RA).

auctioneer

A person whom the seller engages to direct, conduct, control, or be responsible for a sale by auction. *(UCC 6-102(1)(b))*
See *auction; bulk sale*.

audit

(1) The systematic examination of records and documents and/or the securing of other evidence by confirmation, physical inspection, or otherwise, for one or more of the following purposes:
- Determining the propriety or legality of proposed or completed transactions,
- Ascertaining whether all transactions have been recorded and are reflected accurately in accounts,
- Determining the existence of recorded assets and inclusiveness of recorded liabilities,
- Determining the accuracy of financial or statistical statements or reports and the fairness of the facts they represent,
- Determining the degree of compliance with established policies and procedures in terms of financial transactions and business management, and
- Appraising an account system and making recommendations concerning it.

(OPM) (See also *FAR* Subpart 42.1.)
(2) *Synonymous with* "contract compliance audit."
See *contract compliance audit*.

audit liaison

A contractor employee who serves as the contractor point of contact to help satisfy auditors' document requests. *(DGBCT)*

auditor

(1) A person with general access to an offeror's or

Aa

contractor's books and financial records to perform an audit. *(GOAT)*

(2) In federal government contracting, a professional accountant acting as a principal advisor to contracting officers on contractor accounting and contract audit matters. *(OPM)*

(3) In a DOD context, the cognizant audit office designated by the Defense Contract Audit Agency or U.S. military service audit activities for conducting audit reviews of a government contractor's accounting system policies and procedures for compliance with the criteria. *(DISCS)*

authenticate

(1) In the case of a record or document, means:
- To sign the record or document; or
- With present intent to adopt or accept a record, to attach to or logically associate with the record an electronic sound, symbol, or process.

(UCC 9-102(a)(7))

(2) In the case of an information system, means:
- To verify the identity of a user, user device, or other entity in an information system;
- To verify the integrity of data stored, transmitted, or otherwise exposed to unauthorized modification in an information system;
- To establish the validity of an electronic transmission.

(CNSSI 4009)

See also *authentication; information system* (IS).

authentication

(1) In general, the process of establishing confidence of authenticity. *(FIPS 201-2)*

(2) Verifying the identity of a user, process, or device, often as a prerequisite to allowing access to resources in an information system. *(FIPS 200)*

See *authenticate; authentication system*; see also *challenge and reply authentication; multifactor authentication*.

(3) A security measure designed to protect a communications system against acceptance of a fraudulent transmission or simulation by establishing the validity of a transmission, message, or originator. *(CNSSI 4009)*

(4) A means of identifying individuals and verifying their eligibility to receive specific categories of information. *(DDMAT)*

(5) Evidence by proper signature or seal that a document is genuine and official. *(DDMAT)*

authority

See *agent authority*.

authorization

(1) To give permission or authorize. *(MW)*

(2) *Synonymous with* "authorization act."
See *authorization act*.

(3) The document executed by the ordering agency and the utility supplier to order service under an areawide contract. *(FAR 41.101)*
See *areawide contract*.

(4) In the case of an information system, refers to access privileges granted to a user, program, or process. *(CNSSI 4009)*
See *information system* (IS)

authorization act

Basic, substantive legislation that establishes or continues the legal operation of a federal program or agency, either indefinitely or for a specific period of time, or which sanctions a particular type of obligation or expenditure. It sets limits on funds that can be appropriated, but does not grant funding, which must be provided by a separate congressional appropriation. *(DAAT; DISCS)*

authorization bill

A bill authorizing the expenditures of public funds. *(BLD)*

authorization committees

See *authorizers*.

authorization form

See *authorization*.

Authorization or authority to proceed (ATP)

Official authority for the contractor to begin work. In the case of federal government contracting, it is usually issued by the procuring contracting officer. *(NDIA II)*

authorized account

In the case of a payment order, a deposit account of a customer in a bank designated by the customer as a source of payment of payment orders issued by the customer to the bank. If a customer does not so designate an account, any account of the customer is an "authorized account" if payment of a payment order from that account is not inconsistent with a restriction on the use of that account. *(UCC 4A-105(a)(1))*

authorized aftermarket manufacturer

An organization that fabricates an electronic part or other item under a contract with, or with the express written authority of, the original component manufactur-

Aa

er based on the original component manufacturer's designs, formulas, and/or specifications. *(DFARS 202.101)*
See *original component manufacturer* (OCM).

authorized official of a U.S. federal agency

An officer or employee responsible for contracting, program management, audit, inspection, investigation, or enforcement of any law or regulation relating to federal government procurement or the subject matter of the contract. *(FAR 3.901)*
See also *officer or employee of a U.S. federal agency*.

authorized official of the Department of Justice

Any person responsible for the investigation, enforcement, or prosecution of any law or regulation. *(FAR 3.901)*

authorized unpriced work (AUW)

A contract scope change which has been directed by an authorized buyer representative, but which has not yet been fully negotiated/definitized. It includes a value, excluding fee or profit, typically associated with the authorized, unpriced change order. *(NDIA II)*
See also *change order* (CO); *undefinitized contract action* (UCA); *contrast with authorized work*.

authorized vendor

A manufacturer of equipment authorized to produce quantities in excess of contractual requirements for direct sale to eligible buyers. Eligible buyers are typically U.S. government organizations or U.S. government contractors. *(CNSSI 4009)*
See also *Authorized Vendor Program* (AVP).

Authorized Vendor Program (AVP)

A program in which a vendor, producing a product under contract to the federal government, is authorized to produce that product in numbers exceeding the contracted requirements for direct marketing and sale to eligible buyers. In this context, "eligible buyers" are typically U.S. government organizations or U.S. government contractors. *(CNSSI 4009)*
See *authorized vendor*.

authorized work

Effort that has been definitized and is on contract, plus definitized contract costs that have not been agreed to, but for which written authorization has been received. This term can also include effort or work scope assigned by management. *(DAAT; NDIA)*

authorizers

The standing committees of Congress that have legislative authority, authorize programs, and conduct oversight over agency programs. For example, the primary authorizers for the DOD are the Senate Armed Services Committee and the House Armed Services Committee. *(DAAT)*

authorizing legislation

Legislation enacted by Congress to permit establishment or continuation of a federal program or agency. Authorizing legislation is normally required before enactment of budget authority. *(DAAT)*

automated clearing house (ACH)

A nationwide electronic funds transfer system used by financial institutions, corporations, and consumers. It serves as a centralized distribution and settlement point for wire transfers and other electronic exchanges. The Federal Reserve serves as the ACH for the Department of the Treasury. The National Automated Clearing House Association (NACHA) is the regulatory body for the entire ACH system. *(NES-98)*

automated data processing equipment (ADPE)

See *information technology* (IT).

automated information system (AIS)

A combination of computer hardware, computer software, data, or telecommunications that performs automated functions that require little to no human input, such as collecting, processing, storing, transmitting, and displaying information. *(DODI 5000.02)*
See also *automatic data processing* (ADP).

automatic data processing (ADP)

Data processing performed by an electronic system so interconnected and interacting as to reduce to a minimum the need for human assistance or intervention. *(AFIT)*
See also *automated information system* (AIS).

automatic data processing equipment (ADPE)

See *information technology* (IT).

auxiliary technique

A price analysis technique used to support results from primary or secondary comparisons. Example auxiliary techniques include value analysis (i.e., answering the question, "What is the item worth?") and visual analysis

Aa

(i.e., an estimating technique that uses visual inspection of an item to determine a worth). *(NCMA-WS)*
See *value analysis*; compare with *primary comparison; secondary comparison*.

availability
(1) Timely, reliable access to data and information services for authorized users. *(CNSSI 4009)*
(2) A measure of the degree to which an item is in an operable and committable state at any given time. *(MIL-HDBK-470A)*

average
The arithmetic mean—the measure of central tendency most commonly used in contract pricing. *(GOAT)*

average procurement lead time
The average time elapsing between the initiation of procurement actions and the receipt into the system of material purchased as a result of such actions. *(AFIT)*
See *administrative lead time*.

avoidable costs
Those costs that will not continue if an ongoing operation is changed or deleted, including department salaries and other costs that could be avoided by not operating the specific department. *(IMA)*

award
(1) The notification to a bidder or offeror of acceptance of a bid or proposal. *(AFIT)*
(2) The formal contractual agreement between buyer and seller. *(CMBOK)*
See *contract award*.
(3) The procurement decision to buy a supply or service from a specific concern on specified terms, including dollar amount. *(GOAT)*

award fee
A fee payable to the contractor consisting of a base amount fixed at inception of the contract (if applicable and at the discretion of the contracting officer) and an award amount that the contractor may earn in whole or in part during performance and that is sufficient to provide motivation for excellence in the areas of cost, schedule, and technical performance. Award fee contracts may be fixed-price or cost-reimbursement. *(FAR 16.404; FAR 16.405-2)*
See *award-fee contract*; see also *award-fee amount; award-fee plan*.

award-fee board
The team of individuals identified in the award-fee plan who have been designated to assist the fee-determining official in making award-fee determinations. *(FAR 16.001)*
See also *fee-determining official* (FDO).

award-fee contract
A type of incentive contract that is suitable for use when—
* The work to be performed is such that it is neither feasible nor effective to devise predetermined objective incentive targets applicable to cost, schedule, and technical performance;
* The likelihood of meeting acquisition objectives will be enhanced by using a contract that effectively motivates the contractor toward exceptional performance and provides the federal government with the flexibility to evaluate both actual performance and the conditions under which it was achieved; and
* Any additional administrative effort and cost required to monitor and evaluate performance are justified by the expected benefits as documented by a risk and cost benefit analysis to be included in the determination and findings.
(FAR 16.401(e)(1))
See *incentive contract; award fee*.

award-fee plan
A plan, required for all federal government contracts providing for award fees, that establishes the procedures for evaluating award fee and an "award-fee board" for conducting the award-fee evaluation. *(FAR 16.401(e)(3))* (See also FAR 16.401(e)(3)(iv), Table 16-1.)
See *award fee*; see also *award-fee board; fee-determining official* (FDO).

award life cycle phase
In the context of the *CMS™*, "award" is the second phase of the contract life cycle. The award process involves all the work by both the buyer and seller that produces an awarded contract. Some contracts are very simple and others are exceedingly complex, but the majority fall somewhere in between. There is only one domain in the award phase: "form contract." The job tasks and competencies of the "form contract" domain produce the contract. *(CMS)*
See *form contract*; see also *Contract Management Standard™ Publication (CMS™); pre-award life cycle phase; post-award life cycle phase*.

Bb

back order (BO)
(1) Items that have been ordered but which cannot be shipped due to a lack of stock or some other reason. This is widely used as a measure of supplier performance and customer service (e.g., percent back orders, number of occurrences, number of back-order days). *(GKPT)*
(2) The quantity of an item requisitioned by ordering activities that is not immediately available for issue but is recorded as a stock commitment for future issue. *(DISCS)*

backpay
A retroactive adjustment of prior years' salaries or wages. This term includes the following:
- Payments to employees resulting from underpaid work actually performed;
- Payments to union employees for the difference in their past and current wage rates for working without a contract or labor agreement during labor management negotiation; or
- Payments to nonunion employees based upon results of union agreement negation only if:
  - A formal agreement or understanding exists between management and the employees concerning these payments, or
  - An established policy or practice exists and is followed by the contractor so consistently as to imply, in effect, an agreement to make such payments.

(FAR 31.205-6(h))

bad debts
Include actual or estimated losses arising from uncollectable accounts receivable due from customers and other claims, and any directly associated costs such as collection costs, and legal costs. *(FAR 31.205-3)*

bail
To deliver personal property in trust to another for a special purpose and for a limited period. *(MW)*
See *bailment*; see also *bailee; delivery*.

bailee
(1) In the law of contracts, one to whom goods are bailed; the party to whom personal property is delivered under a contract of bailment. *(BLD)*
(2) A person that by a warehouse receipt, bill of lading, or other document of title acknowledges possession of goods and contracts to deliver them. *(UCC 7-102(a)(1))*
See *bailment; document of title*.

bailment
The transfer of possession, but not ownership, of personal property (e.g., goods) for a limited time or specified purpose (e.g., transportation) such that the individual or business entity taking possession is liable to some extent for loss or damage to the property. The typical elements of a bailment are:
- Delivery of the personal property,
- Acceptance of the delivery, and
- Possession or control of the property.

(MW)
See also *delivery*.

bank/banker's acceptance
An instrument used in financing foreign trade, making possible the payment of cash to an exporter covering all or part of the amount of a shipment made by him or her. *(GKPT)*

banker's credit
See *letter of credit*.

banking day
The part of a day on which a bank is open to the public for carrying on substantially all of its banking functions. *(UCC 4-104(a)(3))*

bargaining
Includes persuasion, alteration of assumptions and positions, give-and-take, and may apply to price, schedule, technical requirements, type of contract, or other terms of a proposed contract. *(FAR 15.306(d))*
See *negotiation*.

bargaining mix
The set of issues that are or could be considered during negotiations. *(GTY)*
See *negotiation*; see also *best alternative to a negotiated agreement* (BATNA)*; resistance point; settlement point; target point; zone of possible agreement* (ZOPA).

bargaining power
The perceived power of each party in the bargaining process. *(GOAT)*

Bb

bargaining range
See *zone of possible agreement* (ZOPA).

bartering
A type of trading involving the exchange of one product for another. Bartering is used when there is a shortage of cash, when financial conditions do not support a cash transaction, or when currency is protected through legislation in order to retain value. *(NES-94)*

base fee
As used in award-fee contracting, this term refers to a base amount fixed at inception of the contract. *(DG-BCT)*

base profit
Dollars remaining after costs, overhead, and general and administrative costs are subtracted from the price. *(CMBOK)*

base realignment and closure (BRAC)
A congressionally authorized process used to reorganize the Department of Defense base structure to more efficiently and effectively support its forces, increase operational readiness, and facilitate new ways of doing business. *(AFIT)*
See also *most efficient organization* (MEO).

base year (BY)
A reference period that determines a fixed price level for comparison in economic escalation calculations and cost estimates. The price level index for the base year is "1.000." *(DAAT; DISCS)*

based-on price
A price derived from established catalog or market prices of commercial items sold in substantial quantities to the general public. The item being purchased must be sufficiently similar to the commercial item to permit the difference between the prices of the items to be identified and justified without resort to cost analysis. *(OPM)*

baseline
A defined quantity or quality used as a starting point for subsequent efforts and progress measurement. It can be used for technical, cost, or schedule measurements. *(DAAT)*

baseline configuration
A documented set of specifications for an information system, or a configuration item within a system, that has been formally reviewed and agreed on at a given point in time, and which can be changed only through change control procedures. *(NIST SP 800-171)*
See *configuration audit; configuration control*.

baselining
A process whereby all managers concerned collectively agree on the specific description of the program, requirements, and funding, and make a commitment to manage the program along those guidelines. *(DCMC)*

base-stock system
In its simplest form, an inventory system in which a replenishment order is issued each time a withdrawal is made and the order quantity is equal to the amount of the withdrawal. This type of system is commonly referred to as a "par-stock system" (i.e., bringing stock back to "par" level). *(GKPT)*

basic agreement
A written instrument of understanding—negotiated between an agency or contracting activity and a contractor—which contains contract clauses applying to future contracts between the parties during its term and contemplates separate future contracts that will incorporate by reference or attachment the required and applicable clauses agreed upon in the basic agreement. A basic agreement is not a contract. It is commonly used in contingency contracting. *(CMBOK)*

basic ordering agreement (BOA)
An instrument of understanding (not a contract) executed between a buyer and a seller setting forth negotiated contract clauses applicable to future procurements entered into between the parties during the term of the agreement. As specifically as possible, it includes a description of the supplies or services and the method for determining pricing, issuing, and delivering of future orders. It must specify when an order actually becomes a binding contract. Depending on the circumstances, a contract could be established upon the issuance of an order, upon the contractor's failure to reject the order within a specified time, or upon actual acceptance of the order by the contractor through performance (e.g., shipping the goods) or formal acceptance. *(DAAT; DSMC; NCMA-WS)* (See also FAR 16.703.)
Compare with *blanket purchase agreement* (BPA).

basic research
Research directed toward increasing knowledge in

science. The primary aim of basic research is a fuller knowledge or understanding of the subject under study, rather than any practical application of that knowledge. *(FAR 2.101)*
See also *applied research*.

basic scientific and technical information
Information relating to fundamental theories, designs, and data for theoretical or experimental investigation into possible applications. It does not include manufacturing knowledge or information on operational systems or systems in development. *(DAAT)*

Bayh Amendment
A federal law (*Pub. L.* 92-570) requiring that no funds be spent for any contract or agreement with any foreign corporation, organization, person, or other entity for the performance of research and development in connection with any weapons system or other military equipment for the Department of Defense when there is a U.S. corporation, organization, person, or other entity equally competent to carry out such research and development at a lower cost. *(NCMA-WS)*

Bayh-Dole Trademark Amendments Act
A federal law (*Pub. L.* 96-517) that amended the Stevenson-Wydler Technology Act of 1980 (15 U.S.C. 3710a(d)(2)) to allow small businesses and nonprofit organizations to retain title to inventions under government contracts or grants in order to further assist the process of technology transfer. *(TIPS)*
See *Stevenson-Wydler Technology Act of 1980*.

bearer
A person in possession of a negotiable instrument, document of title, or certificated security that is payable to bearer or indorsed in blank. *(UCC 1-201(5))*
See also *certificated security; document of title; negotiable instrument*.

bearer form
In the case of a certificated security, a form in which the security is payable to the bearer of the security certificate according to its terms, but not by reason of an indorsement. *(UCC 8-102(a)(2))*
See *bearer*; see also *certificated security; indorsement; security certificate*.

benchmark
A standard or point of reference used in measuring or judging quality, value, performance, price, etc. Bench-

marks of purchasing performance, such as purchasing operating expense as a percent of company sales dollars, gives purchasing professionals a reference point that can be used to evaluate the firm's performance. *(GKPT)*

beneficial interest
The right to the use and benefit of property. *(MW)*

beneficiary
(1) Where a promise has been made, but performance will benefit a person other than the promisee, that person is a "beneficiary." *(RSOC 2(4))*
See *promise*; see also *promisee*.
(2) In the case of a payment order, the person to be paid by the beneficiary's bank. *(UCC 4A-103(a)(2))*
See also *payment order; successor of a beneficiary*.
(3) In the case of a letter of credit, a person who, under the terms of a letter of credit, is entitled to have its complying presentation honored. This term includes a person to whom drawing rights have been transferred under a transferrable letter of credit. *(UCC 5-102(a)(3))*
See also *letter of credit; successor of a beneficiary*.

benefit
A term used to indicate an advantage, profit, or gain attained by an individual or organization. *(AIMD)*
See also *intangible benefit; tangible benefit*.

benefit-cost analysis
See *cost-benefit analysis*.

benefits analysis and determination
In a federal government context, prior to the issuance of a solicitation, the "benefits analysis" (sometimes called "consolidation and bundling benefit analysis") makes the case for an acquisition strategy that consolidates and/or bundles requirements. It identifies, quantifies, and compares the benefits arising from the strategy's implementation to benefits that would result from alternative strategies on cost savings, quality improvements, reductions in acquisition cycle times, better terms and conditions, etc., and is part of the acquisition strategy. After reviewing the benefits analysis, a senior procurement executive makes a "determination" either in favor or against the issuance of the solicitation based on whether the benefits described substantially exceed the necessary thresholds (for consolidated requirements) or are measurably substantial (for bundled requirements). *(15 U.S.C. 644(e); 644(q))*

Bb

Berry Amendment
A federal law (10 U.S.C. 2533a) that requires appropriated or otherwise available funds of the Department of Defense to be given preference in procurement to domestically grown, reprocessed, reused, or produced items. *(10 U.S.C. 2533a)*
See *Buy American statute*.

best alternative to a negotiated agreement (BATNA)
The best alternative a negotiator has, other than completing the present negotiation with the other side if negotiations fail (e.g., reach a deal, reach no settlement at all and walk away, or other possible alternatives). It provides a measure of relative bargaining power and the long-term effect of negotiations. For example, sometimes accepting an unreasonable negotiation result may be better than the available alternatives (e.g., a contractor may accept an unreasonably low price in an effort to limit future competition). *(GOAT; GTY)*
See also *negotiation*.

best and final offer (BAFO)
A buyer requests a best and final offer to indicate that no further negotiation will take place. This is the seller's last opportunity to make changes to its cost and technical proposals. This term is used in commercial and state/local contracts, but not in federal government contracting since the FAR Part 15 rewrite of 1997 adopted the use of the term "final proposal revision (FPR)." *(CMBOK; DGBCT)*
See *proposal revision*.

best in class (BIC) contract vehicle
In the context of the federal government's category management strategies, a contract vehicle for best-in-class solutions, as identified by category teams based on their conformance to five key requirements:
- Rigorous requirements definitions and planning processes,
- Appropriate pricing strategies,
- Data-driven demand management strategies,
- Category and performance management practices, and
- Independently validated reviews.

(GWCM)
See *category management*.

best practice
(1) A superior method or innovative practice that contributes to the improved performance of an organization, usually recognized as "best" by other peer organizations. It implies accumulating and applying knowledge about what is working and not working in different situations and contexts, including lessons learned and the continuing process of learning, feedback, reflection, and analysis (what works, how, and why). *(GPMT)*
(2) A practical technique gained from experience that may be used to improve the procurement process and to help detect problems in acquisitions, as well as the management and administration of contracts. *(FAR 37.501)*

best value
(1) The expected outcome of an acquisition that, in the buyer's estimation, provides the greatest overall benefit in response to the requirement. The keys to successful best-value contracting include:
- Consideration of life cycle costs; and
- Marginal analysis (i.e., the use of quantitative as well as qualitative techniques to measure price and technical performance tradeoffs between various proposals).

The "best value" concept applies to acquisitions where price or price-related factors are not the primary determinant of who receives the contract award. *(FAR 2.101; TIPS)*
(2) In a federal government context, "best value" represents the most advantageous tradeoff between price and performance for the government. It is determined through a process that compares—in accordance with selection criteria—strengths, weaknesses, risk, price, and performance to select the value that is most advantageous to the government. An agency can obtain best value in negotiated acquisitions by using any one or a combination of source selection approaches. *(DAAT)*

best value continuum
Obtaining best value in negotiated acquisitions can be achieved by using any one or a combination of source selection approaches. In different types of acquisitions, the relative importance of cost or price may vary. For example, in acquisitions where the requirement is clearly definable and the risk of unsuccessful contract performance is minimal, cost or price may play a dominant role in source selection. The less definitive the requirement, the more development work required, or the greater the performance risk, the more technical or past performance considerations may play a dominant role in source selection. *(FAR 15.101; CMBOK)*
See also *lowest price technically acceptable* (LPTA); *tradeoff process (source selection)*.

Bb

beta model
See *preproduction model*.

Better Buying Power (BBP)
A continuing effort to increase the productivity, efficiency, and effectiveness of Department of Defense acquisition, technology, and logistics efforts.

bid
(1) In purchasing, a "bid" can be an offer to sell or an offer to buy. In public-sector purchasing, a "bid" is the offer in the sealed-bid process (as opposed to other than sealed-bid procurement, where the offer may be referred to as a "proposal" or a "quotation"). *(DGBCT)* See also *offer*.
(2) An offer in response to an invitation for bids. *(FAR 2.101)*
(3) Any response to a solicitation, including a proposal under a negotiated acquisition. *(FAR 28.001)*

bid and proposal (B&P) costs
Costs incurred in preparing, submitting, and supporting bids and proposals (whether or not solicited) on potential contracts. This term *does not* include the costs of efforts sponsored by a grant or cooperative agreement, or the costs required in the performance of a contract. *(FAR 31.205-18(a); CMBOK)*

bid bond
In federal government contracting, an insurance document in which a third party agrees to pay a specific amount of money if the bonded (insured) bidder fails to sign a contract as bid upon and accepted by the government. *(P&L II)* (See also FAR 28.101.)
See bid *guarantee*.

bid development
All of the work activities required to design and price the product and service solution and accurately articulate this in a proposal for a customer. *(STBP)*

bid guarantee
A form of security accompanying a bid or proposal as assurance that the bidder—
- Will not withdraw a bid within a period specified for acceptance; and
- Will execute a written contract and furnish required bonds, including any necessary coinsurance or reinsurance agreements, within the time specified in the bid, unless a longer time is allowed after receipt of the specified forms.

(FAR 28.001)

bid/no-bid decision
An internal determination made by the seller's management whether or not to submit an offer or bid in response to a solicitation. *(CMBOK)*

bid opening
The public announcement of all the bids submitted in response to an invitation for bids. *(GSFC)* (See also *FAR* Subpart 14.4.)
See also *invitation for bids* (IFB).

bid phase
The period of time a seller of goods and/or services uses to develop a bid/proposal, conduct internal bid reviews, and obtain stakeholder approval to submit a bid/proposal. *(STBP)*

bid protest
See *protest*.

bid sample
A product sample required to be furnished by an offeror to show characteristics of the offered products that cannot adequately be described by specifications, purchase descriptions, or the solicitation (e.g., balance, facility of use, or pattern). *(FAR 2.101)* (See also FAR 52.214-20.)

bidder
(1) One who makes a bid. *(BLD)*
(2) Any entity that is responding or has responded to a solicitation, including an offeror under a negotiated acquisition. *(FAR 28.001)*

bidders' conference
See *pre-bid conference*.

bidders list
A list—also known as a "bidders mailing list"—maintained by the procurement office, of contractors and suppliers that have expressed interest in furnishing a specific supply or service to the federal government. *(GSFC)*

bilateral change
See *bilateral modification*.

bilateral contract
A contract formed by the exchange of promises in which

Bb

the promise of one party is consideration supporting the promise of the other. It contrasts with a "unilateral contract," which is formed by the exchange of a promise for an act. Most contracts are "bilateral"; i.e., they consist of reciprocal promises between the parties. *(CMBOK; BLD)* Contrast with *unilateral contract*.

bilateral modification
A contract modification that is signed by the seller and the buyer. Bilateral modifications are used to make negotiated equitable adjustments resulting from the issuance of a change order, definitize letter contracts, and reflect other agreements of the parties modifying the terms of contracts. *(FAR 43.103(a))*
See *contract modification;* contrast with *unilateral modification*.

bilateral notice
Used when terminating a contract by mutual consent. Typically initiated when one party notifies the other that it is exercising a contractual right to terminate based on particular circumstances. Generally, both the circumstances permitting the termination and the process for termination are predetermined in the contract. *(DGBCT)*

bill
(1) An itemized account of the separate cost of goods sold, services performed, or work done. *(MW)*
(2) A legislative proposal originating in either the House or Senate, which, if passed in identical form by both houses and signed by the president of the United States, becomes an enacted law. Bills are designated by "HR" in the House of Representatives or "S" in the Senate, according to the house in which they originate, plus a number assigned in the order in which they are introduced during the two-year period of a congressional term. Appropriations bills always originate in the House. *(DISCS)*

bill of lading (B/L)
(1) A document evidencing receipt of goods for shipment issued by a person engaged in the business of transporting or forwarding goods. *(UCC 1-201(6))*
(2) A carrier's contractual agreement to transport goods from one place to another and to deliver them to a designated person or location for the compensation and under the terms stated in the agreement. *(SPP)*
(3) A transportation document, used as a receipt of goods, as documentary evidence of title, for clearing customs, and generally used as a contract of carriage. *(FAR 47.001)*

See *commercial bill of lading* (CBL); *government bill of lading* (GBL).

bill of material (BOM)
A descriptive and quantitative listing of materials, supplies, parts, and components required to complete the production of a designated, complete end item. When actual or expected prices are applied, it then becomes the "priced bill of material" (PBOM). *(NDIA; OPM)*
See also *priced bill of material* (PBOM).

bill of sale
A written document formally transferring ownership of personal property specified in the document from the supplier to the purchaser. *(GKPT)*

billing rate
An indirect cost rate established temporarily for interim reimbursement of incurred indirect costs and adjusted as necessary pending the establishment of final indirect cost rates. *(FAR 42.701)*

"binding"
(1) Imposing a legal obligation. *(MW)*
(2) Requiring submission to a specified authority. *(MW)*

binding arbitration
Parties that submit to "binding arbitration" submit their disputes to a neutral third person or panel for a decision that both parties must accept without further appeal. Binding arbitration is commonly used in private-sector contracting, but is rarely used in federal government contracting due to the absolute nature of the binding decision. *(DGBCT)*
See *arbitration; nonbinding arbitration*.

biobased product
A product determined by the Department of Agriculture to be a commercial or industrial product (other than food or feed) that is composed, in whole or in significant part, of biological products, including renewable domestic agricultural materials and forestry materials. *(FAR 2.101)* (See also FAR 23.403.)

biometric
A measurable, physical characteristic or personal behavioral trait used to recognize the identity, or verify the claimed identity, of an applicant. Facial images, fingerprints, and iris image samples are all examples of biometrics. *(FIPS 201-2)*
See also *biometric information*.

Bb

blank

(1) A space left unfilled in a written document, in which one or more words or marks are to be inserted to complete the sense. *(BLD)*

(2) This term is also used to refer to a "skeleton" or printed form for any legal document, in which the necessary and invariable words are printed in their proper order, with blank spaces left for the insertion of such names, dates, figures, additional clauses, etc., as may be necessary to adapt the instrument to the particular case and to the design of the party using it. *(BLD)*

blank acceptance

An acceptance of a draft written on the paper before the draft is made and delivered by the acceptor. *(BLD)*

blank check purchase order

An ordering technique that includes a bank draft as the bottom portion of the purchase order form. When the order is shipped, the supplier enters the amount due for payment on the draft and sends it to the firm's bank for deposit. Many firms that utilize this approach for numerous small purchases refer to it as a "purchase order draft system." *(GKPT)*

blanket order

A term commitment (usually one year or more) to a supplier for certain goods or services over a predetermined period of time at predetermined prices, most-favored customer prices, or prices to be revised due to market or other conditions. This practice is aimed at reducing the number of small orders and utilizing short-term releases to satisfy demand requirements. *(GKPT)*

blanket purchase agreement (BPA)

A method used to fill purchase requirements for related supplies, material, equipment, or services by establishing accounts with established sources of supply. It includes certain conditions and provisions that have been negotiated and agreed to in advance. It also allows a buyer to make frequent purchases or service calls and receive one monthly bill for all supplies or services purchased. A "blanket purchase agreement" is not a contract; it is viewed as a type of "charge account" with certain qualified vendors, and it serves as the baseline for future transactions between the parties. An individual blanket purchase agreement is considered complete when the amount purchased under it equals the total dollar limitation, if any, or when the stated time limitation (period of performance) expires. Regulations limit the federal government's use of blanket purchase agreements to small purchases of items or services needed to fill anticipated recurring needs. *(CMBOK; DSMC; NCMA-WS)* (See also FAR 13.303.) Compare with *basic ordering agreement* (BOA).

blanketing

A negotiation approach designed to get all the issues "on the table" at the beginning of the negotiation. Negotiators using the blanketing tactic open the negotiation by outlining all their demands at once. *(GOAT)*

block certification

Block certification means "SAFETY Act certification" of a technology class that the U.S. Department of Homeland Security has determined (pursuant to 6 U.S.C. 442(d), as further delineated in 6 CFR 25.8 and 25.9) to be an approved class of approved products for homeland security—i.e., it will perform as intended, conforms to the seller's specifications, and is safe for use as intended. *(FAR 50.201)*

See *qualified anti-terrorism technology* (QATT); see also *block designation*.

block designation

Block designation means "SAFETY Act designation" of a technology class that the U.S. Department of Homeland Security has determined (pursuant to 6 U.S.C. 441(b) and 6 U.S.C. 443(a), as further delineated in 6 CFR 25.4) to be a qualified anti-terrorism technology. *(FAR 50.201)*

See *qualified anti-terrorism technology* (QATT); see also *block certification; pre-qualification designation notice*.

blockchain

The technology that forms the basis of cryptocurrencies. It is an open, secure, distributed ledger that can record transactions between two parties efficiently and in a verifiable and permanent way. *(TTAB)*

board of contract appeals

A designated administrative tribunal within an executive agency that is authorized to hear, examine, and decide on written requests asking for a change (i.e., an "appeal") of a contracting officer's decision, and related to a contract made by that agency. *(P&L I)*

boilerplate

The term used for printed terms and conditions that are frequently found on the back of purchase order forms in contracts, usually attached as "general provisions." *(HECA)*

Bb

bona fide
(1) Latin for "in good faith"; means made or done honestly in good faith without fraud or deceit. *(GOAT; MW)*
(2) The lack of fraud or deceit. *(DDMAT)*
(3) Genuine. *(GOAT)*

bona fide agency
An established commercial or selling agency, maintained by a contractor for the purpose of securing business, that neither exerts nor proposes to exert improper influence to solicit or obtain federal government contracts, nor holds itself out as being able to obtain any government contract or contracts through improper influence. *(FAR 3.401)*
See also *improper influence*.

bona fide employee
A person, employed by a contractor and subject to the contractor's supervision and control as to time, place, and manner of performance, who neither exerts nor proposes to exert improper influence to solicit or obtain U.S. federal government contracts, nor holds himself or herself out as being able to obtain any government contract or contracts through improper influence. *(FAR 52.203-5)*
See also *improper influence*.

Bona Fide Needs Rule
A rule of appropriations law that mandates a fiscal year's appropriations only be obligated to meet a legitimate need arising in the fiscal year for which the appropriation was made. *(PFAL)*

bond
A written instrument executed by a bidder or contractor (i.e., the "principal") and a second party (i.e., the "surety" or "sureties") to assure fulfillment of the principal's obligations to a third party (i.e., the "obligee" or the "U.S. federal government") identified in the bond. If the principal's obligations are not met, the bond assures payment, to the extent stipulated, of any loss sustained by the obligee. The types of bonds are as follows:
• An "advance payment bond,"
• An "annual performance bond,"
• A "bid bond,"
• A "patent infringement bond,"
• A "payment bond," and
• A "performance bond."
(FAR 28.001)
See *advance payment bond; annual bid bond; annual performance bond; bid bond; patent infringement bond; payment bond; performance bond*.

bonding costs
Arise when the buyer requires assurance against financial loss to itself or others by reason of the act or default of the seller. They also arise in instances where the seller requires similar assurance. This term includes such bonds as "bid," "performance," "payment," "advance payment," "infringement," and "fidelity" bonds. *(FAR 31.205-4)*

Bonds statute
A federal law (40 U.S.C. Chapter 31, Subchapter III) that requires performance and payment bonds for any construction contract with the federal government exceeding a stipulated dollar amount. This requirement may be waived by the contracting officer for as much of the work as is to be performed in a foreign country upon finding that it is impracticable for the contractor to furnish such bond, or as otherwise authorized by the Bonds statute or other law. Formerly known as the Miller Act. *(FAR 28.102-1(a))*

bonuses and incentive compensation
Incentive compensation for management employees, cash bonuses, suggestion awards, safety awards, and incentive compensation based on production, cost reduction, or efficient performance. *(GOAT)*

book value
An accounting term for the value of assets as carried on the books; that is, cost less reserve for depreciation. *(BLD)*

borrower
A contractor, subcontractor (at any tier), or other supplier who receives a guaranteed loan. *(FAR 32.301)*
See also *guaranteed loan*.

borrowing authority
In a federal government context, the authority granted to a federal entity to borrow and obligate and expend the borrowed funds, including through the issuance of promissory notes or other monetary credits. *(2 U.S.C. 622(2)(A)(ii))*
See also *budget authority*.

bottom line
See *resistance point*.

Boyle Rule
See *government contractor defense*.

Bb

bracketing

In negotiation, a "bracket" is a group or class of issues or solutions that are linked together. Negotiators can use this technique to identify issues that are critical to a mutually satisfactory result. *(GOAT)*

brand

A name, term, design, symbol, or any other feature that identifies one seller's good or service as distinct from those of other sellers. The legal term for brand is "trademark." A brand may identify one item, a family of items, or all items of that seller. If used for the firm as a whole, the preferred term is "trade name." *(AMAD)*

brand name description

A purchase description that identifies a product by its brand name and model or part number or other appropriate nomenclature by which the product is offered for sale. Also known as "brand name or equal." *(GOAT)* (See also FAR 11.104.)

breach

(1) *Synonymous with* "breach of contract."
See *breach of contract*.
(2) In the context of the U.S. federal budget, this term means, for any fiscal year, the amount (if any) by which new budget authority or outlays for that year (within a category of discretionary appropriations) is above that category's discretionary spending limit for new budget authority or outlays for that year, as the case may be. *(2 U.S.C. 900(c)(3))*

breach of contract

The failure, without legal excuse, to perform any promise that forms the whole or part of a contract. *(BLD)* (See also FAR 52.233-4.)
Compare with *anticipatory breach*.

breach of warranty

Occurs when the material or product fails to meet the quality or other specification warranted by the supplier. *(GKPT)* (See also FAR 46.706.)
See *warranty*.

break bulk

The splitting up of one consolidated or large-volume shipment into smaller ones for ultimate delivery to consignees. This term is also used commonly to describe the process of splitting up case quantities and selling by the unit. *(GKPT)*

break even

A situation that exists when cost and revenue (e.g., contract prices) are equal. Profit is zero. *(GOAT)*

break-even analysis

An analysis of the relationships between revenue/sales, expenses/costs, and net income/profit which determines the point at which total revenues are exactly equal to total fixed and variable costs (i.e., the "break-even point"). *(IMA)*
See *break-even point*.

break-even point

(1) In business enterprises, the point at which revenues exactly equal total incurred costs (i.e., revenues = fixed costs + variable costs). *(DAAT)*
(2) In decision-making (such as make versus buy, lease versus buy, etc.), the point of indifference, meaning that level of activity in which either method results in exactly the same cost. These types of break-even decisions often involve making assumptions about levels of activity (such as number of units needed). *(DAAT)*

breakout

(1) In a federal government context, the execution of acquisition strategy to convert some parts or system components from contractor-furnished to government-furnished. Rather than having the prime contractor provide from its sources, the government procures items directly and provides them to the prime contractor. *(DAAT)*
(2) Specifically in a DOD context, the review of a major weapons system to determine if a particular component may be purchased as a separate item instead of buying it from the weapons system manufacturer. This subsystem would then be provided in the weapons system contract as government-furnished equipment, rather than contractor-furnished equipment. *(HCS)*

bridge contract

A noncompetitive contract or contracting action undertaken to "bridge" the time between the end of one contract action and the beginning of another. This term includes the noncompetitive increase of a contract ceiling, as well as the extension of a period of performance. *(DAAT)*

broad agency announcement (BAA)

A general announcement of a federal agency's research interest, including criteria for selecting proposals and soliciting the participation of all offerors capa-

Bb

ble of satisfying the government's needs. *(FAR 2.101)* (See also FAR 6.102(d)(2) and FAR 35.016.)

broker

(1) A third party, acting as an intermediary between a buyer and a seller—such as an agent who negotiates contracts of purchase and sale. Here, the broker is authorized to negotiate with a potential seller for the buyer, but not authorized to commit the buyer to the transaction via a contractual document. The broker has no ownership of the goods or services being sold or offered, with the payment and credit transactions remaining the responsibility of the buyer and seller. *(GKPT; HECA; MW)*
(2) A person defined as a broker or dealer under the federal securities laws, but without excluding a bank acting in that capacity. *(UCC 8-102(a)(3))*
(3) *(As a verb)*: To arrange or negotiate an agreement (e.g., "to *broker* a deal"). *(MW)*

Brooks Architect-Engineer Act

See *Selection of Architects and Engineers statute*

budget

(1) A plan of operations for a fiscal period expressed in terms of estimated costs, obligations, and expenditures. *(NCMA-CA)*
(2) A source of funds for financing, including anticipated reimbursements and other resources. *(DAAT)*
(3) The history and workload data for the projected program and activities. *(DAAT)*
(4) A comprehensive financial plan for the federal government, encompassing the totality of federal receipts and outlays (expenditures). *(DAAT)*
See also *federal budget*.

budget activity (BA)

In a federal government context, categories within each appropriated and fund account that identify the purposes, projects, or types of activities financed by the appropriation or fund. *(DAAT)*

budget at completion (BAC)

The budget, or planned value, at the end of a project. It consists of the sum of all authorized budgets for the contract scope of work. The project's scope of work forms the performance measurement baseline, which projects the cost to complete the entire program. The budget at completion equals the sum of all the allocated budgets plus any undistributed budget. (Management reserve and profit/fee are *not* included in the budget at completion.) *(DAAT; PMPM)*

budget authority (BA)

The authority Congress gives to federal government agencies, permitting them to enter into obligations that will result in immediate or future outlays (expenditures). Such financial obligations include:
- Provisions of law that make funds available for obligation and expenditure (i.e., "appropriations"), other than borrowing authority, including the authority to obligate and expend the proceeds of offsetting receipts and collections;
- Borrowing authority, which means authority granted to a federal entity to borrow and obligate and expend the borrowed funds, including through the issuance of promissory notes or other monetary credits;
- Contract authority, which means the making of funds available for obligation, but not for expenditure; and
- Offsetting receipts and collections as negative budget authority, and the reduction thereof as positive budget authority.

Budget authority *does not* include the authority to ensure the repayment of loans held by another person or government. Budget authority may be classified by its duration (one year, multiple year, or no year); by the timing of the legislation providing the authority (current or permanent); by the manner of determining the amount available (definite or indefinite); or by its availability for new obligations. *(DGBCT; DISCS; 2 U.S.C. 622(2)(A)(i)-(iv))*
See also *appropriation; borrowing authority; contract authority; limitations on budget authority; new budget authority*.

budget estimate

In the case of a federal department or agency, a cost estimate prepared for inclusion in the department's/agency's budget to support acquisition programs. *(DAAT)*

budget execution

See *execution*

budget outlays

In a federal government context, with respect to any fiscal year, means expenditures and net lending of funds under budget authority during such year. *(2 U.S.C. 622(1))*
See *budget authority*

Bb

budget resolution
Established through legislation developed by congressional budget committees, a "budget resolution" serves as an outline to determine ceilings for the federal government's budget authority and outlays for spending. The budget resolution is not legally binding. *(DLA)*

budget variance
The difference between the amount incurred and the budget figure. *(NCMA-CA)*

budget year (BY)
The fiscal year following the current fiscal year, and for which the new budget estimate is prepared. *(DISCS)*

budgeted cost
The sum of the budgets for completed work packages and portions of open work packages, plus the appropriate portion of the budgets for level of effort and apportioned effort. *(DAAT)*

budgeted cost of work performed (BCWP)
In earned value management terminology, a measurement of the work completed. It is the value of work performed, or "earned," when compared to the original budgeted cost of work scheduled/performance measurement baseline. Also called the *earned value*, it may be expressed as a value for a specific period or cumulative to date. *(AFIT; DAAT; NDIA; NES-93)*
See *budgeted cost*; compare with *actual cost of work performed* (ACWP); *budgeted cost of work remaining* (BCWR); *budgeted cost of work scheduled* (BCWS).

budgeted cost of work remaining (BCWR)
In earned value management terminology, the sum of the budgets for all work that has yet to be accomplished. *(NDIA II)*
Compare with *budgeted cost of work performed* (BCWP); *budgeted cost of work scheduled* (BCWS).

budgeted cost of work scheduled (BCWS)
In earned value management terminology, the sum of the budgets for all work (work packages, planning packages, etc.) scheduled to be accomplished (including in-process work packages), plus the budget for level of effort and apportioned effort scheduled to be accomplished within a given time period. It may be expressed as a value for a specific period or cumulative to date. Also called *planned value* or *performance measurement baseline*. *(AFIT; DGBCT; NDIA; NES-93)*

Compare with *actual cost of work performed* (ACWP); *budgeted cost of work remaining* (BCWR); *budgeted cost of work scheduled* (BCWS).

budgeting
The process of translating resource requirements into a funding profile. *(DAAT)*

building/work
Construction activity, as distinguished from manufacturing, furnishing of materials, or servicing and maintenance work. The terms "building" and "work" include, without limitation, buildings, structures, and improvements of all types, such as bridges, dams, plants, highways, parkways, streets, subways, tunnels, sewers, mains, power lines, pumping stations, heavy generators, railways, airports, terminals, docks, piers, wharves, ways, lighthouses, buoys, jetties, breakwaters, levees, canals, dredging, shoring, rehabilitation and reactivation of plants, scaffolding, drilling, blasting, excavating, clearing, and landscaping. The manufacture or furnishing of materials, articles, supplies, or equipment (whether or not a U.S. federal or state agency acquires title to such materials, articles, supplies, or equipment during the course of the manufacture or furnishing, or owns the materials from which they are manufactured or furnished) is not "building" or "work" within the meaning of this definition unless conducted in connection with and at the site of such building or work as is described in the foregoing sentence, or under the United States Housing Act of 1937 (*Pub. L.* 75-412) and the Housing Act of 1949 (Title V of *Pub. L.* 81-171) in the construction or development of the project. *(FAR 2.101)*
See also *architectural work*; compare to *public building/public work*.

building service contract
A contract for recurring services related to the maintenance of a public building. Recurring services are services that are required to be performed regularly or periodically throughout the course of a contract, and throughout the course of the succeeding or follow-on contract(s), at one or more of the same public buildings. Building services include, but are not limited to, contracts for the recurring provision of custodial or janitorial services; window washing; laundry; food services; guard or other protective services; landscaping and groundskeeping services; and inspection, maintenance, and repair of fixed equipment such as elevators, air conditioning, and heating systems. Building service contracts *do not* include contracts that provide mainte-

Bb

nance services only on a nonrecurring or irregular basis (e.g., a contract to provide servicing of fixed equipment once a year, or to mulch a garden on a one-time or annual basis, is a "nonrecurring maintenance contract"); contracts for daycare services in a federal office building; or concessions for sales of goods or services other than food services or laundry services. *(GOAT)*
See *nonrecurring maintenance contract; recurring services contract*.

bulk funding
A system whereby a contracting officer receives authorization from a fiscal and accounting officer to obligate funds on purchase documents against a specified lump sum of funds reserved for the purpose and for a specified period of time, rather than obtaining individual obligational authority on each purchase document. Bulk funding is particularly appropriate for use if numerous purchases using the same type of funds are to be made during a given period. *(FAR 13.101(b)(4))*

bulk sale
(1) In the case of a sale by auction or a sale or series of sales conducted by a liquidator on the seller's behalf, means a sale or series of sales not in the ordinary course of the seller's business of more than half of the seller's inventory, as measured by value on the date of the bulk-sale agreement, if on that date the auctioneer or liquidator has notice, or after reasonable inquiry would have had notice, that the seller will not continue to operate the same or a similar kind of business after the sale or series of sales. *(UCC 6-102(1)(c)(i))*
See also *auction; auctioneer; in the ordinary course of the seller's business; liquidator*.
(2) In all other cases aside from those listed in (1) of this definition, means a sale not in the ordinary course of the seller's business of more than half the seller's inventory, as measured by value on the date of the bulk-sale agreement, if on that date the buyer has notice, or after reasonable inquiry would have had notice, that the seller will not continue to operate the same or a similar kind of business after the sale. *(UCC 6-102(1)(c)(ii))*

bundling
Consolidating two or more requirements for supplies or services, previously provided or performed under separate smaller contracts, into a solicitation for a single contract, a multiple-award contract, or a task or delivery order that is likely to be unsuitable for award to a small business concern (even if it is suitable for award to a small business with a small business team-

ing arrangement) due to—
- The diversity, size, or specialized nature of the elements of the performance specified;
- The aggregate dollar value of the anticipated award;
- The geographical dispersion of the contract performance sites; or
- Any combination of these factors.
(FAR 2.101)
See *consolidation; contract bundling;* see also *separate smaller contract*.

burden
An aspect of indirect cost—i.e., costs that cannot be attributed or assigned as direct cost. Also called *overhead. (CMBOK; DAAT)*
See *indirect cost; overhead*.

burden center
See *cost center*.

burden rate
See *indirect cost rate*.

Bureau of Industry and Security (BIS)
A bureau of the Department of Commerce responsible for ensuring an effective export control and treaty compliance system and promoting continued U.S. strategic technology leadership.

burn rate
The monthly rate at which a contractor's funds are expended during the period of the contract. *(DAAT)*

business advisor
A person with proficient contract management experience and training to help guide the customer and other stakeholders through the contract management life cycle. Business advisors must have good analytical, problem-solving, and communication skills and be adaptable to change. They must also understand the regulatory environment in order to be legally creative, while managing risk in satisfying contract requirements and obligations. *(CMBOK)*

business capability
The core ability an organization needs in order to deliver requisite products and services and provide value. *(DAAT)*

business case
A structured method for organizing and presenting a

Bb

business improvement proposal. Organizational decision-makers typically compare business cases when deciding to expend resources. A business case typically includes an analysis of business process performance and associated needs or problems, proposed alternative solutions, assumptions, constraints, and a risk-adjusted cost/benefit analysis. *(AIMD)*

business cycle

The recurring expansions and contractions of the national economy (usually measured by real gross domestic product). A complete cycle typically lasts from three to five years, but could last 10 years or more. It is divided into four phases:
*   Expansion,
*   Peak,
*   Contraction, and
*   Trough.

(NOM)

business development

(1) A broad term applied to the process of strengthening ties with existing clients as well as cultivating customers in other market sectors. In order to accomplish this goal, business development normally crosses the traditional functions between sales, marketing, customer care, operations, and management. *(DGBCT)*

(2) In a contracting context, this process is in the "pre-award" life cycle phase of contract management, within the "develop offer" domain. It is the process of:
*   Organizing pre-sales activities to develop customer relations and market strategy, and
*   Assessing competition.

The value added in business development is to understand the customer's near- and long-term requirements and determine the organization's ability to successfully respond to a solicitation. *(CMS)*
See also *develop win strategy*.

business enterprise architecture (BEA)

A blueprint to guide the development of integrated business processes. It includes architectural viewpoints that display capabilities, activities, processes, data, information exchanges, business rules, system functions, services, system data exchanges, technical standards, terms, and linkages to laws, regulations, and policies. *(DODI 5000.75)*

business evaluation factors

Aspects used to assess performance of prospective contractors; e.g., relevant experience, past perfor-mance, management plan, company resources, and/or quality of products/services. *(DGBCT)*

business manager

Business managers use sound business principles and good judgment to develop innovative solutions that achieve the organization's needs. Business managers partner with their customers to better understand their requirements, which involves developing the best solution to help customers accomplish the organization's mission while optimizing resources. *(DGBCT)*

business operations

Engaging in commerce in any form, including by acquiring, developing, maintaining, owning, selling, possessing, leasing, or operating equipment, facilities, personnel, products, services, personal property, real property, or any other apparatus of business or commerce. *(FAR 25.702-1)*

business process

A collection of related, structured activities that produce a specific service or product for a particular customer or customers. *(AIMD)*

business process improvement (BPI)

A systematic, disciplined approach that critically examines, rethinks, and redesigns mission-delivery processes and sub-processes within a process management approach. Also called "business process reengineering" (BPR). *(AIMD)*
See *business process*.

business proposal

The instrument required of an offeror for the submission or identification of cost or pricing data, by which an offeror submits to the buyer a summary of estimated (or incurred) costs suitable for detailed review and analysis. It is also called *contract pricing proposal*. *(CMBOK)*

business system

In a Department of Defense context, information systems that are operated by, for, or on behalf of the DOD, including financial systems, financial data feeder systems, contracting systems, logistics systems, planning and budgeting systems, installations management systems, human resources management systems, and training and readiness systems. A "business system" *does not* include a national security system or an information system used exclusively by and within the

Bb

defense commissary system or the exchange system or other instrumentality of the DOD conducted for the morale, welfare, and recreation of members of the armed forces using non-appropriated funds. *(DODI 5000.75)*
See also *contractor business systems*.

Business Systems Rule
Also called the *DFARS Business Systems Rule*. See *contractor business systems*; see also *business system*.

business-to-business (B2B)
Business to business, also called B to B or B2B, is a type of transaction that exists between businesses, such as one involving a manufacturer and wholesaler, or a wholesaler and a retailer. Business to business refers to business that is conducted between companies, rather than between a company and individual consumers. Business to business stands in contrast to business to consumer (B2C) and business to government (B2G) transactions. *(INV)*
Contrast with *business-to-consumer* (B2C).

business-to-consumer (B2C)
Business to consumer, or B2C, refers to the transactions conducted directly between a company and consumers who are the end-users of its products or services. The business to consumer as a business model differs significantly from the business-to-business model, which refers to commerce between two or more businesses. Traditionally B2C has been about one-on-one retail sales, but increasingly the focus has shifted towards meeting the continuously evolving consumer needs of e-commerce. *(INV)*
Contrast with *business-to-business* (B2B).

business unit
Any segment of an organization, or an entire business organization that is not divided into segments. *(FAR 2.101)*

Buy American Act (BAA)
See *Buy American statute*.

Buy American statute
A federal law (41 U.S.C. Chapter 83) and policy stating that manufactured materials, supplies, or articles acquired for public use shall be substantially constituted from domestically mined or manufactured materials. Products are considered to be "not of domestic origin"

if the cost of foreign products used in them accounts for a specified percentage of the total cost. Formerly known as the *Buy American Act* (BAA). **(41 U.S.C. 8302)** (See also *FAR* Subparts 25.1 and 25.2.)

buy-in
See *buying-in*.

buy item
An item or work effort to be produced or performed by a subcontractor. *(GOAT)*

buyback
A type of countertrade that occurs when a firm builds a plant in a foreign country or supplies technology, equipment, training, or other services and agrees to take a certain portion of the plant's output as partial payment for the investment. *(GKPT)*

buyer
(1) A person who buys or contracts to buy goods or services. *(UCC 2-103(a))*
(2) A contracted party with a requirement for goods and/or services to be fulfilled by one or more sellers. *(CMS)* See also *seller*.
(3) A professional buying specialist. Buyers typically specialize in a given group of materials or commodities and are responsible for market analysis, purchase planning, coordination with users, and supplier qualification, as well as selection, order placement, and follow-up activities. *(GKPT)*
(4) In the case of a bulk sale by auction or liquidation, refers to the auctioneer or liquidator, as the case may be. *(UCC 6-108(1)(a))*

buyer's market
A competitive market condition where supply exceeds demand. It exits when goods and/or services can be secured easily and when the economic forces of business tend to cause prices to be close to the purchaser's estimate of value. *(GKPT)*

buying-in/buy-in
Submitting an offer below anticipated costs, expecting to:
- Increase the contract amount after award (e.g., through unnecessary or excessively priced change orders); or
- Receive follow-on contracts at artificially high prices to recover losses incurred on the buy-in contract.
(FAR 3.501-1)

Cc

Byrd Amendment

A common name for *Pub. L.* 101-121, Section 219, which instructed the Office of Management and Budget to issue governmentwide guidance restricting the use of public funds to pay for lobbying. *(TIPS)*
See also *lobbying activities; lobbying and political activity; lobbying contract; lobbying firm; lobbyist.*

C

CAGE code

See *Commercial and Government Entity (CAGE) code.*

cancellation

(1) Occurs when either party puts an end to the contract for breach by the other. Its effect is the same as that of "termination," except that the cancelling party also retains any remedy for breach of the whole contract or any unperformed balance. *(UCC 2-106(4))*
Compare with **termination**.
(2) In the case of a multiyear contract, refers to the cancellation (within a contractually specified time) of the total requirements of all remaining program years of the contract. Cancellation results when the contracting officer notifies the contractor of nonavailability of funds for contract performance for any subsequent program year, or if the officer fails to notify the contractor that funds are available for performance of the succeeding program year requirements. *(GOAT)*
See *multiyear contract.*
(3) Concerning a contract for sale, this term means the withdrawal of the requirement to purchase goods and/or services by the buyer. *(STBP)*
See *no-cost cancellation.*
(4) Concerning a lease contract, this term refers to when either party puts an end to the lease contract for default by the other party. *(UCC 2A-103(b))*

cancellation ceiling

The maximum cancellation charge that the contractor can receive in the event of a cancellation. *(FAR 17.103)*
See *cancellation.*

cannibalize

In the context of U.S. federal government property, to remove parts from government property for use or for installation on other government property. *(FAR 45.101)*

capability

The ability to complete a task or execute a course of action under specified conditions and level of performance. *(CJCSI 3170.011)*
See also *capability gap; capability gap assessment (CGA); capability requirement; capability requirement document; capability solution.*

capability gap

The inability to meet or exceed a capability requirement, resulting in an associated operational risk until closed or mitigated. *(CJCSI 3170.011)*
See *capability*; see also *capability gap assessment (CGA); capability requirement; capability solution.*

capability gap assessment (CGA)

In a Department of Defense context, a deliberate assessment of integrated priority lists and other issues and perspectives from the military services and other DOD components relative to fielded materiel and non-materiel capability solutions, and development efforts that may already be underway to address capability gaps. *(CJCSI 3170.011)*
See *capability*; see also *capability gap; capability solution.*

capability need

See *capability requirement.*

capability requirement

A capability required to meet an organization's roles, functions, and missions in current or future operations. *(CJCSI 3170.011)*
See *capability*; see also *capability gap; capability requirement document; capability solution.*

capability requirement document

Any document used to articulate either deliberate or urgent/emergent capability requirements and associated information pertinent to review and validation. *(CJCSI 3170.011)*
See *capability*; see also *capability requirement; validation.*

capability solution

In a Department of Defense context, a solution to satisfy one or more capability requirements and reduce or eliminate one or more capability gaps. *(CJCSI 3170.011)*
See *capability*; see also *capability gap; capability requirement.*

Cc

capital

(1) Accumulated assets invested or available for investment, including:

- Goods used to produce other goods, and/or
- Property used to create income.

(MW)

See *debt capital; equity capital; fixed capital; moneyed capital; paid-in capital; stated capital; venture capital; working capital.*

(2) A store of useful assets or advantages. *(MW)*

(3) The value of those accumulated assets specified in (1.) of this definition. *(MW)*

(4) Consists of machinery, tools, buildings, transportation and distribution facilities, and inventories of unfinished goods. *(ECON)*

See also *capital asset.*

capital asset

(1) Tangible property, including durable goods, equipment, buildings, installations, and land. *(GOAT)*

(2) In a federal government context, refers to land, structures, equipment, intellectual property (e.g., software), and IT (including IT service contracts) that are used by the federal government and that have an estimated useful life of two years or more. *(OMB A-11)*

capital budgeting

The process of evaluating and selecting long-term investment projects. *(NES-02)*

capital, cost of

See *cost of capital.*

capital equipment

For accounting purposes, most firms classify "capital equipment" as noncurrent assets, which are capitalized and depreciated over the course of their economic lives. *(DBL)*

capital programming

An integrated process within a federal agency for planning, budgeting, procurement, and management of the agency's portfolio of capital assets to achieve agency strategic goals and objectives with the lowest life cycle cost and least risk. *(OMB A-11)*

capital project (investment)

The acquisition of a capital asset and the management of that asset through its life cycle after the initial acquisition. *(OMB A-11)*

capital property

An organization's plant, equipment, and other facilities subject to depreciation. *(GOAT)*

captive insurer

An insurer owned by or under control of the organization for which it provides insurance coverage. *(FAR 31.205-19(b))*

capture manager

A person responsible for managing a pursuit from bid decision to contract award. *(APMP)*

See *pursuit manager.*

capture management

The art and science of winning more business. *(STBP)*

capture management life cycle

The art and science of winning more business throughout the entire business cycle. *(STBP)*

capture plan

Documented analysis, strategies, and actions initiated following the pursuit decision that details customer issues, considerations relating to competitor and internal positioning, approaches to be implemented, and management tasks to be implemented to guide the capture of a particular opportunity. *(APMP)*

See *pursuit plan.*

capture planning

The process of assessing the customer and competitive environment and implementing strategies oriented toward capturing a specific business opportunity. *(APMP)*

See *capture plan; pursuit plan.*

capture project plan

A document or game plan of who needs to do what, when, where, how often, and how much to win business. *(STBP)*

capture strategy

A strategy to win a specific, defined opportunity. *(APMP)*

capture team

A small group of individuals within an organization who are delegated responsibility to manage a pursuit from the pursuit decision to contract award, typically including a capture manager, a technical lead, and the prospective program manager at a minimum (depending on the specific requirements of the pursuit). *(APMP)*

cardinal change

A major change to a contract that is made outside the scope of the contract—i.e., having the effect of making the work as performed not essentially the same work as the parties bargained for when the contract was awarded. Therefore, such a change is unenforceable by the buyer, and may constitute a breach of contract by the buyer. *(CMBOK; GCG; GSFC)*

Caribbean Basin country

In the context of the federal government's "Buy American" policies, trade agreements, and other laws and regulations governing foreign acquisition, this term refers to any of the following countries: Antigua and Barbuda, Aruba, the Bahamas, Barbados, Belize, Bonaire, the British Virgin Islands, Curacao, Dominica, Grenada, Guyana, Haiti, Jamaica, Montserrat, Saba, St. Kitts and Nevis, St. Lucia, St. Vincent and the Grenadines, Sint Eustatius, Sint Maarten, or Trinidad and Tobago. *(FAR 25.003)*
See also *Caribbean Basin country end product; end product*.

Caribbean Basin country end product

An article that—
* Is wholly the growth, product, or manufacture of a Caribbean Basin country;
* In the case of an article that consists in whole or in part of materials from another country, has been substantially transformed in a Caribbean Basin country into a new and different article of commerce with a name, character, or use distinct from that of the article or articles from which it was transformed; and
* Is not excluded from duty-free treatment for Caribbean countries under 19 U.S.C. 2703(b).

This term also refers to a product offered for purchase under a supply contract, but for purposes of calculating the value of the acquisition, includes services (except transportation services) incidental to the article, provided that the value of those incidental services does not exceed that of the article itself. *(FAR 25.003)*
See *Caribbean Basin country*.

carrier

(1) "Carrier" or "commercial carrier" means a common carrier or a contract carrier. *(FAR 47.001)*
See *common carrier; contract carrier*.
(2) A military or commercial ship, aircraft, barge, train, or truck, or a commercial transport company that moves material from one location to another. *(DISCS)*
(3) In the case of a bill of lading, means a person that issues the bill of lading. *(UCC 7-102(a)(2))*
See *bill of lading* (B/L).

cash flow

(1) The liquidity of assets for other business purposes. *(CMBOK)*
(2) The net effect of cash receipts minus disbursements from a given asset, or group of assets, for a given period. *(BLD; NCMA-CA)*
(3) The cash generated from property. As opposed to net income, looks instead to the amount left after all payments are made, whether they are tax deductible or not. *(BLD)*

cash prior to delivery

A term of sale in which the seller collects payment from the buyer in advance of the delivery of goods and/or the performance of services to and/or for the buyer. *(DISCS)*
Compare with *cash with acceptance*.

cash proceeds

Proceeds that are money, checks, deposit accounts, or the like. *(UCC 9-102(a)(9))*
See *proceeds*.

cash with acceptance

A term of sale in which currency, check, or other negotiable instrument is submitted by the buyer concurrent with acceptance of a sales offer for the full amount shown as the estimated total cost. *(DISCS)*
Compare with *cash prior to delivery*.

cashier's check

A draft with respect to which the drawer and drawee are the same bank or branches of the same bank. *(UCC 3-104(g))*

category

(1) In the context of discretionary spending by the federal government, category refers to the subsets of discretionary appropriations in 2 U.S.C. 901(c). *(2 U.S.C. 900(c)(4)(F))*
(2) Governmentwide segmented areas of spending on a set of defined commodities (products and services) that function together, are procured together, and behave in a similar manner. *(GWCM)*
See *category management*; see also *subcategory*.
(3) In the context of information security, category refers to a restrictive label applied to classified or unclassified information to limit access. *(CNSSI 4009)*

Cc

category hallway
A set of sites under the Common Acquisition Platform (CAP) that guide a U.S. federal agency down virtual "corridors" to the most relevant available products and services based on the agency's need.
See also *Acquisition Gateway; Common Acquisition Platform (CAP)*.

category management
A "strategic business practice" the federal government is employing to "buy smarter and more like a single enterprise." The goals are:
- Boost "savings, value, and efficiency" for government acquisition programs,
- "Eliminate contract redundancies," and
- Deliver on the government's small business objectives.

Governmentwide category management involves "identifying core areas of spending," developing "levels of expertise," and "leveraging shared best practices" across federal agencies.

Category Management Leadership Council (CMLC)
A council of representatives from federal government agencies that comprise the majority of federal procurement spending. It is the governing body that sets the direction of the government's category management initiative. (Formerly known as the *Strategic Sourcing Leadership Council* (SSLC).) *(OMB M-13-02)*

caucus
A technique used to break away from formal negotiations for the team to consider a point. When a counter-offer is made, a "caucus" can be used to confer with the negotiation team to consider all aspects of the counter-offer. *(DGBCT)*

cause and effect diagram
A structured form of brainstorming—also called a *fishbone diagram* or *Ishikawa diagram*—that graphically shows the relationship of causes and subcauses to an identified effect (problem). *(DGCQI)*

caveat emptor
A Latin phrase that means "let the buyer beware" (i.e., the purchase is at the buyer's risk). *(GKPT)*

ceiling
See *adjusted ceiling; negotiated ceiling*.

central office of record (COR)
An office within a federal government department or agency that keeps records of accountable information or other material held by elements subject to its oversight. *(CNSSI 4009)*

central procurement activity
A level of federal government contracting activity in which assignments are performed by formal contracting and involve procurements up to major components of agency-critical programs and facilities and the equipment to support these programs. This term also includes coordinated interdepartmental and governmentwide commodity assignments, as well as area-wide support responsibilities. *(OPM)*

centralized purchasing
A purchasing system in which all the departments of a company with a wide geographical distribution can make purchases through a common purchasing organization. Centralized purchasing aids finding the best deals with local vendors for the corresponding location of the company department. Avoids duplicity of orders and promotes benefits arising from the high-volume bulk discounts, lower transportation and inventory management costs, organized transactions and improved vendor relationships. Usually located at company headquarters. Opposite of decentralized purchasing. *(BD)*
Compare with *decentralization of purchasing*.

certificate
(1) In a legal sense, a document containing a certified statement. *(MW)*
(2) A document certifying that a person has fulfilled the requirements of and may practice in a specified field. *(MW)*
(3) A document that is proof of ownership or indebtedness (e.g., a stock certificate). *(MW)*
(4) Used as a *transitive verb*—means to testify or authorize by a certificate (especially to recognize as having met special qualifications—as of a governmental agency or professional board—within a field). *(MW)*

certificate of appointment
The document that empowers a person to act on the behalf of the U.S. federal government as a contracting officer. *(GSFC)* (See also *FAR* 1.603-3.)
See *warrant*.

certificate of competency (COC)
The certificate issued by the Small Business Administration stating that the holder is responsible (with respect

Cc

to all elements of responsibility, including, but not limited to, capability, competency, capacity, credit, integrity, perseverance, tenacity, and limitations on subcontracting) for the purpose of receiving and performing a specific federal government contract. *(GOAT)* (See also *FAR* Subpart 19.6.)

certificate of conformance
A certificate signed by a contractor representative stating that the supplies or services required by the contract have been furnished in accordance with all applicable contract requirements. This certificate further states that the supplies or services are of the quality specified and conform in all respects with the contract requirements, including specifications, drawings, preservation, packaging, packing, marking requirements, and physical item identification (e.g., part number), and are in the quantity shown on it or on the attached acceptance document. *(GOAT)*

certificate of current cost or pricing data
A document required to be executed and submitted by the seller attesting that the cost or pricing data provided to the buyer were accurate, complete, and current as of the date negotiations were concluded and price agreement reached (or, if applicable, an earlier date agreed upon between the parties that is as close as practicable to the date of agreement on price), and that such data is "certified" under the Truthful Cost or Pricing Data statute (41 U.S.C. Chapter 35). *(GCG; GSFC; GOAT)* (See also FAR 15.406-2.)
See *certified cost or pricing data*.

certificate of deposit
An instrument containing an acknowledgment by a bank that a sum of money has been received by the bank and a promise by the bank to repay the sum of money. A certificate of deposit is a "note" of the bank. *(UCC 3-104(j))*

certificate of indirect costs
A certificate that the contractor's final indirect cost rate proposal does not include any costs that are expressly unallowable under applicable cost principles of the *FAR* or its supplements. (GOAT)

certificate of title
A certificate with respect to which a statute provides for the security interest in question to be indicated as a condition or result of the security interest's obtaining priority over the rights of a lien creditor with respect to the collateral. *(UCC 9-102(a)(10))*

certificated security
A security that is represented by a certificate. *(UCC 8-102(a)(4))*
See *security*; see also *security certificate*; contrast with *uncertificated security*.

certification
(1) The act of certifying (i.e., making something official), or the state of being certified. *(MW)*
(2) A certified statement. *(MW)*
(3) The process of verifying the correctness of a statement or claim and issuing a certificate as to its correctness. *(FIPS 201-2)*
(4) A document required to be submitted—as per FAR 33.207(c)—to the federal government by a contractor submitting any claim exceeding a designated dollar amount. *(FAR 33.207)*
See *certification of a claim*; see also *defective certification*.

certification of a claim
The requirement, under the Contract Disputes statute (41 U.S.C. Chapter 71), that contract claims over the dollar amount designated in the statute be accompanied by a statement that simultaneously asserts that the claim is made in good faith, supporting data is accurate and complete, and the amount requested reflects the contract adjustment believed due. *(GCG)* (See also FAR 33.207.)

certified check
A check accepted by the bank on which it is drawn. Acceptance may be made:
- When the check is signed, acknowledging acceptance (which may consist of a signature alone); or
- By a writing on the check which indicates that the check is certified.

The drawee of a check has no obligation to certify the check, and refusal to certify is not dishonor of the check. *(UCC 3-409(a)-(d))*
See also *acceptance*.

Certified Commercial Contract Manager (CCCM)
A professional certification, issued by the National Contract Management Association, that validates an individual's education, training, experience, and knowledge of the Uniform Commercial Code.
See also *Certified Federal Contract Manager* (CFCM); *Certified Professional Contract Manager* (CPCM).

certified cost or pricing data

Cost or pricing data that were required to be submitted in accordance with FAR 15.403-4 and FAR 15.403-5 and have been certified, or are required to be certified, in accordance with FAR 15.406-2. This certification states that, to the best of the person's knowledge and belief, the cost or pricing data are accurate, complete, and current as of a date certain before contract award. Cost or pricing data are required to be certified in certain procurements (per 10 U.S.C. 2306a and 41 U.S.C. Chapter 35). *(FAR 2.101)*
See *cost or pricing data*.

certified document

A document certified as a true original. Authenticity of the document is validated through the appropriate seal or markings of the issuer or by a validated reference or source number; or if the document is a notarized legal document or other document approved by the appropriate legal authority. *(DODM 1000.13-M-VI)*

Certified Federal Contract Manager (CFCM)

A professional certification, issued by the NCMA, that validates an individual's education, training, experience, and knowledge of the *FAR*.
See also *Certified Commercial Contract Manager (CCCM); Certified Professional Contract Manager (CPCM)*.

certified invoice

An invoice certified for payment under the terms of the contract in lieu of a separate receiving report. *(GOAT)*

Certified Professional Contract Manager (CPCM)

A professional certification, issued by the NCMA, that demonstrates an individual has met NCMA's highest standards for education, training, and experience, and has demonstrated knowledge of the contract management competencies in the *Contract Management Body of Knowledge* (*CMBOK*). The CPCM is NCMA's senior and most prestigious certification.
See also *Certified Commercial Contract Manager (CCCM); Certified Federal Contract Manager (CFCM); Contract Management Body of Knowledge (CMBOK)*.

change in scope

A change to approved program requirements or specifications after negotiation of a basic contract. It may result in an increase or decrease in cost or time for performance. *(AFIT)* (See also FAR 43.201.)

change management

The process of proactively preparing the affected community for changes that will occur to an organization. *(AIMD)*

change-of-name agreement

A legal instrument executed by the seller and the buyer that recognizes the legal change of name of the seller without disturbing the original contractual rights and obligations of the parties. *(FAR 2.101; CMBOK)* (See also *FAR* Subpart 42.12.)
See *novation agreement*.

change order (CO)

(1) Specific to government contracts, a written order by the buyer directing a change, as authorized by contract clause, to modify contractual requirements within the scope of the contract. *(CMBOK)*
(2) A written order, signed by the contracting officer, directing the contractor to make a change that the "Changes" clause authorizes the contracting officer to order without the contractor's consent. *(FAR 2.101)* (See also *FAR* Subpart 43.2.)
See *"Changes" clause*; compare with *administrative change; constructive change*.

change proposal

See *contract modification; engineering change proposal; equitable adjustment*.

"Changes" clause

Specific to government contracts, a contract clause in which the seller provides a contractual grant of authority to the buyer to alter particular matters pertaining to contract performance. *(CMBOK)* (See also FAR 43.205.)

channel of distribution

An organized network of agencies and institutions that, in combination, perform all the functions required to link producers with end customers. *(AMAD)*

chattel paper

A record or records that evidence both a monetary obligation and a security interest in specific goods, a security interest in specific goods and software used in the goods, a security interest in specific goods and license of software used in the goods, a lease of specific goods, or a lease of specific goods and license of software used in the goods. *(UCC 9-102(a)(11))*

check
Means:
- A draft, other than a documentary draft, payable on demand and drawn on a bank; or
- A cashier's check or teller's check.

An instrument may be a "check" even though it is described on its face by another term, such as a "money order." *(UCC 3-104(f))*

See *negotiable instrument*; see also *cashier's check; certified check*.

chief acquisition officer (CAO)
An executive-level acquisition official responsible for federal agency performance of acquisition activities and acquisition programs created pursuant to 41 U.S.C. 1702. *(FAR 2.101)*

Chief Acquisition Officers Council (CAOC)
Established pursuant to Section 16 of the Office of Federal Procurement Policy statute, as amended (41 U.S.C. Div. B of Subtitle I, except Sections 1704 and 2303), the council consists of a diverse group of federal government acquisition professionals in the executive branch established to provide a senior-level forum for monitoring and improving the federal acquisition system. *(DGBCT)*

Chief Financial Officers (CFO) Act
A federal law (31 U.S.C. 901-903) that calls for:
- Integration of accounting and budgeting information so that principles used in accounting for program costs are consistent with those used in developing budgets;
- The systematic measurement of performance at the agency level to identify cost trends and other types of performance indicators; and
- The preparation and audit of financial statements on a uniform, consistent basis and subsequent communication of results to financial decision-makers.

(DGBCT)

Chief Information Officers Council (CIOC)
A government council established by Executive Order 13011, "Federal Information Technology," on July 16, 1996 and later codified by the E-Government Act of 2002 (*Pub. L.* 107-347). The council serves as the principal interagency forum for improving practices in the design, modernization, use, sharing, and performance of U.S. federal agency information resources. *(DGBCT)*

chief of mission
The principal officer in charge of a diplomatic mission of the United States or of a U.S. office abroad which is designated by the secretary of state as diplomatic in nature, including any individual assigned under Section 502(c) of the Foreign Service Act of 1980 (*Pub. L.* 96-465) to be temporarily in charge of such a mission or office. *(FAR 2.101)*

child care services
In a services contracting context, means child protective services (including the investigation of child abuse and neglect reports), social services, health and mental health care, child (day) care, education (whether or not directly involved in teaching), foster care, residential care, recreational or rehabilitative programs, and detention, correctional, or treatment services. *(FAR 37.101)*

Christian Doctrine
A legal principle derived from *G.L. Christian & Assoc. v. United States* (312 F.2d at 424, 427). It states that if a contract clause is required either by a statute, regulation, or Executive Order to be included in a federal government contract, the contract will be read to include the clause by operation of law, even if the clause is not physically incorporated into the document. *(CMBOK; FGC)*

civil aircraft and related articles
Refers to–
- All aircraft other than aircraft to be purchased for use by the DOD or the U.S. Coast Guard;
- The engines (and parts and components for incorporation into the engines) of these aircraft;
- Any other parts, components, and subassemblies for incorporation into the aircraft; and
- Any ground flight simulators, and parts and components of these simulators, for use with respect to the aircraft, whether to be used as original or replacement equipment in the manufacture, repair, maintenance, rebuilding, modification, or conversion of the aircraft and without regard to whether the aircraft or articles receive duty-free treatment under Section 601(a)(2) of the Trade Agreements Act of 1979 (*Pub. L.* 96-39).

(FAR 25.003)

civil judgment
(1) A judgment or finding of a civil offense by any court of competent jurisdiction. *(FAR 9.403)*

Cc

(2) In the context of labor law, any judgment or order entered by any federal or state court in which the court determined that a labor law violation occurred, or the same enjoined or restrained a violation of labor law. It includes a judgment or order that is not final or is subject to appeal. *(FAR 22.2002)*

civil law

(1) The body of law developed from Roman law and used in the State of Louisiana, in continental Europe, and in many other countries outside of the English-speaking world, including especially those that were colonized by countries of continental Europe. *(MW)*
Compare with *common law; statutory law*.
(2) The law established by a nation or state that applies to its own jurisdiction. *(MW)*

civilian agency

A U.S. federal government agency other than the Department of Defense. *(DODM 4120.24)*

Civilian Agency Acquisition Council (CAAC)

A group composed of members from federal civilian agencies that have joint responsibility with the Defense Acquisition Regulatory Council for revision of the *FAR*. *(GCG)* (See also FAR 1.201-1.)
See *Defense Acquisition Regulatory Council* (DARC).

Civilian Board of Contract Appeals, The (CBCA)

Established by Section 847 of the National Defense Authorization Act for Fiscal Year 2006 to hear and decide contract disputes between federal government contractors and executive agencies under the provisions of the Contract Disputes statute (41 U.S.C. Chapter 71), as well as regulations and rules issued under that statute. *(48 CFR 733.270(a))*
See *Armed Services Board of Contract Appeals* (ASBCA).

claim

(1) In general, a demand in writing for a sum certain. *(42 U.S.C. 9601(4))*
See also *claimant; contract claim; termination claim*.
(2) An assertion by one of the parties in a contract that the other party (or parties) owes consideration. *(CMBOK)*
See *contract claim*; see also *consideration*.
(3) Usually based on an argument that the party making the demand is entitled to an adjustment by virtue of the contract terms or some violation of those terms by the other party. *(STBP)*
(4) Concerning claims for damages due to breach of contract, a claim for damages for total breach is one for damages based on all of the injured party's remaining rights to performance; a claim for damages for partial breach is one for damages based on only part of the injured party's remaining rights to performance. *(RSOC 236(1)-(2))*
(5) In a federal government context, a written demand or written assertion by one of the contracting parties seeking, as a matter of right, the payment of money in a sum certain, the adjustment or interpretation of contract terms, or other relief arising under or relating to the contract. *(FAR 2.101)*
(6) In the case of a bulk sale, means a right to payment from the seller, whether or not the right is reduced to judgment, liquidated, fixed, matured, disputed, secured, legal, or equitable. *(UCC 6-102(1)(d))*
See also *bulk sale*.

claim accrual

See *accrual of claim*.

claim certification

See *certification of a claim*.

claimant

(1) Any person who presents a claim for compensation. *(42 U.S.C. 9601(5))*
(2) In the case of a bulk sale, a person holding a claim incurred in the seller's business. *(UCC 6-102(1)(e))*
See also *bulk sale*.

claims court

See *U.S. Court of Federal Claims* (COFC).

clarification

(1) A type of communication that seeks to understand an ambiguous or unclear statement or response of a seller to a buyer. *(CMBOK)*
(2) Communication between a buyer and an offeror for the sole purpose of eliminating minor irregularities, informalities, or apparent clerical mistakes in the proposal. *(FAR 15.601)*
Contrast with *discussion*.
(3) Limited exchanges between the government and offerors that may occur when award without discussions is contemplated. If award will be made without conducting discussions, offerors may be given the opportunity to clarify certain aspects of proposals (e.g., the relevance of

Cc

an offeror's past performance information and adverse past performance information to which the offeror has not previously had an opportunity to respond) or to resolve minor or clerical errors. *(FAR 15.306(a)(1)-(2))* See also *clarification request* (CR).

clarification request (CR)
A written communication issued by the source selection evaluation board through the contracting officer for the purpose of eliminating minor irregularities, informalities, or apparent clerical mistakes. It does not give the offeror an opportunity to revise or modify its proposal. *(NCMA-WS)*
See also *deficiency report*.

class determination and finding
A class determination and finding provides authority for a class of contract actions. A class may consist of contract actions for the same or related supplies or services or other contract actions that require essentially identical justification. *(FAR 1.703)*

class deviation
A deviation from *FAR*-dictated procedures or guidance that affects more than one contract action. *(GOAT)*

classification
The determination that official information requires, in the interests of national security, a specific degree of protection against unauthorized disclosure, coupled with a designation signifying that such a determination has been made. *(DDMAT)*
See also *classified information*.

classified acquisition
An acquisition in which offerors must have access to classified information to properly submit an offer or quotation, to understand the performance requirements, or to perform the contract. *(FAR 2.101)*
See *classified information*; see also *classified contract; classified bid*.

classified bid
Any bid that contains classified information (i.e., "confidential," "secret," or "top secret"). *(GOAT)*
See *classified information*; see also *classified acquisition*.

classified contract
Any contract in which the contractor or its employees must have access to classified information during

contract performance. A contract may be a "classified contract" even though the contract document itself is unclassified. *(FAR 2.101)*
See *classified information*; see also *classified acquisition*.

classified information
Any knowledge that can be communicated or any documentary material, regardless of its physical form or characteristics, that–
* Is owned by, is produced by or for, or is under the control of the U.S. federal government, or has been classified by the Department of Energy as privately generated restricted data following the procedures in 10 CFR 1045.21; and
* Must be protected against unauthorized disclosure according to Executive Order 12958, "Classified National Security Information" (April 17, 1995), or classified in accordance with the Atomic Energy Act of 1954 (42 U.S.C. 2011).

Such information is required to be marked to indicate its classified status (i.e., "top secret," "secret," or "confidential"). *(FAR 2.101; CNSSI 4009)*

clause
See *contract clause*.

Clayton Antitrust Act of 1914
A federal law (15 U.S.C. 12, *et seq.*) enacted in 1914 as an amendment to the Antitrust Act (15 U.S.C. 1, *et seq.*) dealing with antitrust regulations and unfair trade practices. The act prohibits price discrimination, exclusive dealing contracts, mergers, and interlocking directorates where the effect may be substantially to lessen competition or tend to create a monopoly in any line of commerce. *(BLD)*
See also *Robinson-Patman Act; Antitrust Act*.

Clean Air Act (CAA)
A federal law (42 U.S.C. 7401) designed to accelerate, expand, and intensify efforts against air pollution in the United States. The act requires the U.S. Environmental Protection Agency (EPA) to identify each substance that it believes causes or contributes to air pollution. Further, the EPA must identify each substance, whether from numerous or diverse sources, that it reasonably believes endangers public health or welfare. *(NES-94)*
See also *Clean Water Act* (CWA).

Clean Water Act (CWA)
A federal law (33 U.S.C. 1251, et seq.) that regulates,

Cc

among other things, the discharge of pollutants into navigable waters. The CWA redirected the regulatory focus of water pollution control from water quality standards to limits (called "effluent limits") on the concentrations of chemicals in the water quality. *(NES-94)* See also *Clean Air Act* (CAA).

clearance
A formal security determination by an authorized adjudicative office of the federal government that an individual is authorized access, on a need-to-know basis, to a specific level of collateral classified information (i.e., "top secret," "secret," and "confidential"). *(CNSSI 4009)* See *classified information*.

clearing
(1) The settlement of accounts or exchange of financial instruments, especially between banks. *(MW)*
(2) In the case of an information system, means the removal of data from the information system, its storage devices, and other peripheral devices with storage capacity, in such a way that the data may not be reconstructed using common system capabilities (e.g., keyboard strokes); however, the data may be reconstructed using laboratory methods. *(CNSSI 4009)*

clearing corporation
Means:
- A person that is registered as a "clearing agency" under the federal securities laws;
- A federal reserve bank; or
- Any other person that provides clearance or settlement services with respect to financial assets that would require it to register as a clearing agency under the federal securities laws but for an exclusion or exemption from the registration requirement, if its activities as a clearing corporation, including promulgation of rules, are subject to regulation by a federal or state governmental authority.

(UCC 8-102(a)(5))
See *clearing*.

Clinger-Cohen Act (CCA)
See *Federal Acquisition Reform Act* (FARA).

cloud computing
A type of computing that relies on shared computing resources rather than having local servers or personal devices to handle applications. It involves taking services and moving them outside an organization's firewall. The organization's applications, storage, and

other services are then accessed via the internet. *(WB)* See also *anything-as-a-service* (XaaS).

close contract
In the context of the *CMS™*, "close contract" is one of two domains within the "post-award" phase of the contract life cycle (the other being "perform contract"). it is the domain of both the buyer and seller, and it is the process of:
- Verifying all the requirements of the contract are satisfied,
- Settling unresolved matters, and
- Reconciling the contract to make final payment.

(CMS)
Contrast with *perform contract*; see also *closeout; contract closeout; Contract Management Standard™ Publication (CMS™)*.

closed contract
A contract on which:
- All seller and buyer obligations and administrative actions have been completed,
- All performance has been accomplished and accepted and/or all deliverables have been supplied and accepted,
- Final payment has been made and accepted, and
- The contract has been reconciled.

(CMBOK; AFIT)
See *contract closeout*.

closeout
The process of declaring that the obligations under a contract have been satisfied and that a procurement file is both physically and administratively complete. A closeout can occur when the contractor's supplies or services have been accepted and paid for and all documentation on the procurement is finalized and properly assembled. *(SPP)* (See also FAR 4.804-5.)
See *administrative closeout; quick closeout; record retention;* see also *close contract; contract closeout*.

closing date
The last day on which offers will be accepted. *(CMBOK)* (See also FAR 15.208.)

code
(1) A systematic statement of a body of law, especially one given statutory force (e.g., the "United States Code"); or a system of principles or rules (e.g., a "moral code"). *(MW)*
(2) Electronic instructions for a computer or other electronic system (as within a piece of software). *(MW)*

Cc

code of ethical conduct

A code of conduct for federal government officers and employees set forth in Executive Order 11222 (May 8, 1965), which reads: "Where government is based on consent of the governed, every citizen is entitled to have complete confidence in the integrity of his government. Each individual officer, employee, or advisor of government must help to earn and must honor that trust by his own integrity and conduct in all official actions." *(GOAT)*

Code of Federal Regulations (CFR)

Official codification of U.S. administrative regulations. The *Federal Acquisition Regulation* is Title 48 of the *CFR*, and is thus part of the *CFR*. *(DGBCT; GCG)*

co-development

A joint development project between the U.S. government and a foreign government to satisfy a common requirement. *(DISCS)*

coercion

Means:
- Threats of serious harm to or physical restraint against any person;
- Any scheme, plan, or pattern intended to cause a person to believe that failure to perform an act would result in serious harm to or physical restraint against any person; or
- The abuse or threatened abuse of the legal process.

(FAR 22.1702)

cognizant

Knowledgeable or aware of something, especially through personal experience. For example, cognizant administrative contracting officer or cognizant auditor. *(MW)*

cognizant federal agency

An agency of the federal government that, on behalf of all federal agencies, is responsible for establishing final indirect cost rates and forward pricing rates, if applicable, and administering Cost Accounting Standards for all contracts in a business unit. *(FAR 2.101)*
See also *business unit; cognizant federal agency official* (CFAO); *Cost Accounting Standards* (CAS); *Cost Accounting Standards Board* (CASB).

cognizant federal agency official (CFAO)

The contracting officer assigned by the cognizant federal agency to administer the Cost Accounting Standards (CAS). *(FAR 30.001)*
See *cognizant federal agency; Cost Accounting Standards* (CAS); *Cost Accounting Standards Board* (CASB).

collateral

The property subject to a security interest. This term includes:
- Proceeds to which a security interest attaches;
- Accounts, chattel paper, payment intangibles, and promissory notes that have been sold; and
- Goods that are the subject of a consignment.

(UCC 9-102(a)(12))
See also *account; chattel paper; consignment; goods; payment intangibles; proceeds; promissory note*.

collateral benefit

The degree to which pursuit of an opportunity will improve the existing skill level or develop new skills that will positively affect other or future business opportunities. *(STBP)*

collateral costs

Costs of operation, maintenance, logistic support, or property. *(FAR 48.001)*

collateral savings

Those measurable net reductions resulting from a value engineering change proposal in a federal agency's overall projected collateral costs, exclusive of acquisition savings, whether or not the acquisition cost changes. *(FAR 48.001)*
ineering change proposal (VECP).

collective bargaining agreement (CBA)

(1) An agreement that regulates terms and conditions of employment between an employer and a labor union. *(BLD)*
(2) Section 4(c) of the Service Contract Labor Standards statute (41 U.S.C. Chapter 67) generally requires a contractor to pay the wages negotiated by its predecessor contractor under a collective bargaining agreement. *(NCMA-WS)* (See also FAR 22.1010.)

collusion

Any affirmative action between two or more sellers that creates an unfair competitive practice. *(CMBOK)* (See also FAR 3.303.)

color of money

A term used to describe the type of funds to be used for a particular item. For example, different kinds of

Cc

appropriated funds must be used for various procurements—such as research, development, test, and evaluation; operations and maintenance; and foreign military sales. Each appropriation may have a limitation on the funds used, some for one year, while others may be two or multiple years, while still others may be no-year funds. *(CMBOK; HCS)*
See also *appropriation; no-year funding*.

color team reviews

Many organizations conduct "color team reviews" as part of their business development and proposal processes. These reviews are designed to help select the right opportunities on which to bid, confirm win strategies, address proposal and performance risk, and support development of high-quality proposals. While different organizations define color team review labels differently, the most common teams and their definitions are:

- *Gold Team*: Approves final proposal and price.
- *Pink Team*: Ensures the proposal is complete and accurate.
- *Red Team*: Ensures the proposal makes sense and solves the customer's business problem.

(APMP)

combatant commander (CCDR)

The commander of a unified or specified combatant command established in accordance with 10 U.S.C. 161. *(FAR 2.101)*

Commerce Control List (CCL)

Governs private and government (non-munitions) sales and transactions of commodities subject to Department of Commerce export controls and identifies those products subject to licensing control. The Commerce Control List is Supplement No. 1 to Part 774 of the *Export Administration Regulation (EAR)*.
See also *Export Administration Regulation (EAR)*.

commercial activities

(1) In general, any particular transaction or act, or any regular course of conduct that is of a commercial character. *(28 U.S.C. 1603(d))*
(2) Activities undertaken for the primary purpose of producing a profit for the benefit of an individual or organization organized for profit. (Activities where commercial aspects are incidental to the primary purpose of expression of ideas or advocacy of causes are not typically considered "commercial activities.") *(FMR 102-71.20)*
(3) In the context of alteration or construction of federal government buildings, this term includes the opera-

tions of restaurants, food stores, craft stores, dry goods stores, financial institutions, and display facilities. *(40 U.S.C. 3306(a)(1))*

commercial activity

Related to OMB Circular A76, an activity which is operated by a federal executive agency and which provides a product or service that could be obtained from a commercial source. *(OMB A-76)*
See also *commercial source*.

commercial advance payment

A payment made before any performance of work under the contract *(FAR 32.202-2)*.
See also *commercial interim payment; delivery payment; Prompt Payment Act* (PPA).

Commercial and Government Entity (CAGE) code

(1) An identifier assigned to entities located in the United States or its outlying areas by the Defense Logistics Agency (DLA) Commercial and Government Entity (CAGE) Branch to identify a commercial or government entity. *(FAR 4.1801)*
(2) An identifier assigned by a member of NATO or by NATO's Support and Procurement Agency (NSPA) to entities located outside the United States and its outlying areas that the DLS's CAGE Branch records and maintains in the CAGE master file. Also called a *NATO Commercial and Government Entity code, or NCAGE code. (FAR 4.1801)*

commercial bill of lading (CBL)

(1) Represents the receipt of goods, the contract of carriage, and is documentary evidence of title to goods. It must contain a description of the articles comprising the shipment. A commercial bill of lading is subject to the terms and conditions set forth for a government bill of lading and any other applicable contract or agreement of the transportation service provider for the transportation of shipments for the United States on U.S. government bills of lading. *(FTH)*
See *"bill of lading (B/L); documents of title; government bill of lading (GBL)*.
(2) Unlike a government bill of lading, a commercial bill of lading is not an accountable transportation document. *(FAR 47.001)*
See *government bill of lading (GBL)*.

commercial carrier

See *carrier*.

Cc

commercial component

Any component that is a commercial item. *(41 U.S.C. 102)*
See *commercial item*.

commercial computer software

Any computer software that is a commercial item. *(FAR 2.101)*

commercial derivative military article (CDMA)

An item acquired by the DOD that is or will be produced using the same production facilities, a common supply chain, and the same or similar production processes that are used for the production of articles predominantly used by the general public or by non-governmental entities for purposes other than governmental purposes. *(DFARS 252.225-7009(a))*

commercial interim payment

Any payment that is not a commercial advance payment or a delivery payment. A "commercial interim payment" is given to the contractor after *some* work has been done, whereas a "commercial advance payment" is given to the contractor when *no* work has been done. *(FAR 32.001)*
See also *commercial advance payment; delivery payment; Prompt Payment Act* (PPA).

commercial item

(1) Any item, other than real property, that is of a type customarily used by the general public or by nongovernmental entities for purposes other than governmental purposes, and—
- Has been sold, leased, or licensed to the general public; and
- Has been offered for sale, lease, or license to the general public.

(FAR 2.101; 41 U.S.C. 103(1))
See also *of-a-type*.
(2) Any item that—
- Evolved from an item described in (1.) of this definition through advances in technology or performance; and
- Is not yet available in the commercial marketplace, but it *will* be available in the commercial marketplace in time to satisfy the delivery requirements under a U.S. federal government solicitation.

(FAR 2.101; 41 U.S.C. 103(2))
(3) Any item that would satisfy a criterion expressed in (1) or (2) of this definition, were it not for—
- Modifications of a type customarily available in the

commercial marketplace; or
- Minor modifications of a type not customarily available in the commercial marketplace made to meet U.S. federal government requirements.

(FAR 2.101; 41 U.S.C. 103(3))
See also *minor modification; of-a-type*.
(4) Any combination of items meeting the requirements of (1), (2), (3), or (5) of this definition that are of a type customarily combined and sold in combination to the general public. *(FAR 2.101; 41 U.S.C. 103(4))*
See also *of-a-type*.
(5) Installation services, maintenance services, repair services, training services, and other services if—
- Such services are procured for support of an item referred to in (1), (2), (3), or (4) of this definition, regardless of whether such services are provided by the same source or at the same time as the item; and
- The source of the services provides similar services contemporaneously to the general public under terms and conditions similar to those offered to the federal government.

(FAR 2.101; 41 U.S.C. 103(5))
(6) Services of a type offered and sold competitively in substantial quantities in the commercial marketplace based on established catalog or market prices for specific tasks performed or specific outcomes to be achieved and under standard commercial terms and conditions. *(FAR 2.101; 41 U.S.C. 103(6))*
See *catalog price; market price*; see also *of-a-type*.
(7) Any item, combination of items, or service referred to in (1), (2), (3), (4), (5), and (6) of this definition, notwithstanding the fact that the item, combination of items, or service is transferred between or among separate divisions, subsidiaries, or affiliates of a contractor. *(FAR 2.101; 41 U.S.C. 103(7))*
(8) A nondevelopmental item, if the procuring agency determines, in accordance with conditions in the *FAR*, that the item was developed exclusively at private expense and has been sold in substantial quantities, on a competitive basis, to multiple state and local governments. *(FAR 2.101; 41 U.S.C. 103(8))* (See also *FAR* Part 12.)
See *commercial off-the-shelf* (COTS); *nondevelopmental item*.

commercial item description (CID)

An indexed, simplified product description—indexed and controlled by the GSA—that describes, by function or performance characteristic, the available, acceptable commercial items that will satisfy the U.S. federal government's needs. These documents are listed in

Cc

the GSA Index of Federal Specifications, Standards, and Commercial Item Descriptions. *(CMBOK; DODM 4120.24)*
See also *General Services Administration (GSA) Index of Federal Specifications, Standards, and Commercial Item Descriptions*

commercial item determination (CID)
(1) In accordance with *FAR* Part 10, agencies shall use the results of market research to make a determination whether commercial items are available to meet the agency's needs at either the item or component level. (FAR 10.001(a)(3))
See *commercial item*.
(2) In a DOD context, a determination in writing by the contracting officer when using *FAR* Part 12 procedures for acquisitions exceeding $1 million in value, except for acquisitions made pursuant to FAR 12.102(f)(1), that the acquisition meets the definition of commercial item in FAR 2.101 and DFARS 212,102(a)(1).
See also *Contractor Determination of Commerciality for Subcontracts*.

commercial item offer
An offer of a commercial item that the vendor wishes to see introduced in the U.S. federal government's supply system as an alternate or a replacement for an existing supply item. This term does not include innovative or unique configurations or uses of commercial items that are being offered for further development and that may be submitted as an unsolicited proposal. *(FAR 15.601)*

commercial off-the-shelf (COTS)
Any item of supply (including construction material) that is—
* A "commercial item" (as defined in FAR 2.101 and 41 U.S.C. 103(1));
* Sold in substantial quantities in the commercial marketplace; and
* Offered to the federal government, under a contract or subcontract at any tier, without modification, in the same form in which it is sold in the commercial marketplace.

Commercial off-the-shelf items *do not* include "bulk cargo" (as defined in 46 U.S.C. 40102(4)), such as agricultural products and petroleum products. Also called *commercially available off-the-shelf*. *(41 U.S.C. 104; FAR 2.101; FAR 22.1801)*
See also *off-the-shelf*.

commercial plan
A subcontracting plan (including goals) that covers the offeror's fiscal year and that applies to the entire production of commercial items sold by either the entire company or a portion thereof (e.g., division, plant, or product line). *(FAR 19.701)*

commercial sale
See *direct commercial sale* (DCS).

commercial sex act
In the context of federal policies prohibiting the trafficking of persons in relation to government solicitations and contracts, this term refers to any sex act on account of which anything of value is given to or received by any person. As per the Trafficking Victims Protection Act of 2000 (22 U.S.C. Chapter 78) and Executive Order 13627, U.S. government solicitations and contracts prohibit contractors, contractor employees, subcontractors, subcontractor employees, and their agents from procuring commercial sex acts during the period of performance of the contract. *(FAR 22.1702; FAR 22.1703)*
See also *sex trafficking; severe forms of trafficking in persons*.

commercial source
Related to OMB Circular A-76, a business or other non-federal activity located in the United States, its territories and possessions, the District of Columbia or the Commonwealth of Puerto Rico, which provides a commercial product or service. *(OMB A-76)*
See also *commercial activity*.

commercial tort claim
A claim arising in tort with respect to which:
* The claimant is an organization, or
* The claimant is an individual and the claim:
  * Arose in the course of the claimant's business or profession, and
  * Does not include damages arising out of personal injury to or the death of an individual.
(UCC 9-102(a)(13))
See also *claim; tort*.

commercial-type items
Any items, including those expended or consumed in use, which, in addition to military use, are used and traded in normal civilian enterprise, and may be imported/exported through normal international trade channels. *(DISCS)*
See *commercial item; of-a-type*.

commercially available off-the-shelf
See *commercial off-the-shelf*.

commingled goods
Goods that are physically united with other goods in such a manner that their identity is lost in a product or mass. (UCC 9-336(a))

Commission on Government Procurement (COGP)
In 1969, *Pub. L.* 91-129 established this commission, which consisted of 12 members representing Congress, the executive branch, and the public. The COGP report released in December 1972 contained 149 recommendations for improvements of the federal procurement process. Among the recommendations were establishment of an independent, centralized office for governmentwide procurement policy matters, a federal procurement institute for the uniform training and development of government procurement personnel, and a single uniform procurement system for all government agencies. *(FGP)*

Commission on Wartime Contracting (CWC)
An independent, bipartisan legislative commission established to study wartime contracting in Iraq and Afghanistan. Created by Section 841 of the National Defense Authorization Act for Fiscal Year 2008, this eight-member Commission was mandated by Congress to study federal agency contracting for the reconstruction, logistical support of coalition forces, and the performance of security functions in Iraq and Afghanistan. The Commission issued two reports to Congress in June 2009 and February 2011, as well as five special reports on specific issues. The Commission was sunset on September 30, 2011.

Committee for Purchase from People Who Are Blind or Severely Disabled statute
A federal law (41 U.S.C. Chapter 85) that requires the government to buy some of its supplies and services from nonprofit agencies that employ Americans who are blind or have other severe limitations. Formerly known as the *Javits-Wagner-O'Day Act* and recodified as the "Committee for Purchase from People Who are Blind or Severely Disabled statute." *(41 U.S.C. 8502)*
See *mandatory sources*.

commodity
An economic good, such as:
- A product of agriculture or mining;
- An article of commerce, especially when delivered for shipment; or
- A mass-produced, unspecialized product.

(MW)

commodity account
An account maintained by a commodity intermediary in which a commodity contract is carried for a commodity customer. *(UCC 9-102(a)(14))*
See also *account; commodity contract; commodity customer; commodity intermediary*.

commodity contract
A commodity futures contract, an option on a commodity futures contract, a commodity option, or another contract if the contract or option is:
- Traded on or subject to the rules of a board of trade that has been designated as a contract market for such a contract pursuant to federal commodities laws, or
- Traded on a foreign commodity board of trade, exchange, or market, and is carried on the books of a commodity intermediary for a commodity customer.

(UCC 9-102(a)(15))
See also *commodity; commodity customer; commodity intermediary*.

commodity customer
A person for which a commodity intermediary carries a commodity contract on its books. *(UCC 9-102(a)(16))*
See *commodity contract; commodity intermediary*.

commodity intermediary
A person that:
- Is registered as a futures commission merchant under federal commodities law, or
- In the ordinary course of its business provides clearance or settlement services for a board of trade that has been designated as a contract market pursuant to federal commodities law.

(UCC 9-102(a)(17))

Common Acquisition Platform (CAP)
A framework of digital services developed to redefine the end-to-end acquisition workflow within the U.S. federal government and to support the government's category management initiatives. *(GWCM)*
See *category management*.

common carrier

In general, a person holding itself out to the general public to provide transportation (of persons, goods, or other cargo) for compensation. *(FAR 47.001)*
See also *contract carrier*.

common cost

See *joint cost*.

common criteria (CC)

Criteria that provide comprehensive, rigorous methods for specifying security functions and assurance requirements for products and systems. *(ISO/IEC)*

common item

(1) Material that is common to the applicable federal government contract and the contractor's other work. *(FAR 2.101)*
(2) A term loosely used to denote any consumable item except repair parts or other technical items. *(DDMAT)*
(3) Readily available commercial items. *(DDMAT)*
(4) Any item of materiel that is required for use by more than one Department of Defense activity. *(DDMAT)*
(5) Any item of materiel that is procured for, owned by (i.e., "service stock"), or used by any military department of the DOD and is also required to be furnished to a recipient country under the grand-aid military assistance program. *(DDMAT)*
(6) Items used by two or more military services of similar manufacture or fabrication that may vary between the services as to color or shape (as vehicles or clothing). *(DDMAT)*
(7) Any part or component that is required in the assembly of two or more complete end-items. *(DDMAT)*

common law

A body of law that is based on custom and general principles and embodied in case law that serves as precedent or is applied to situations not covered by statute. In the United States, it is the body of law, originally developed in England, that is the basis of U.S. federal law and of state law in all U.S. states except Louisiana. *(MW)*
Compare with *civil law; statutory law*.

common parent

That corporate entity that owns or controls an affiliated group of corporations that files its federal income tax returns on a consolidated basis, and of which the offeror is a member. *(FAR 4.901)*

commonality

In a military context, a quality that applies to materiel or systems:
• Possessing like and interchangeable characteristics enabling each to be utilized, or operated and maintained, by personnel trained on the others without additional specialized training;
• Having interchangeable repair parts and/or components; and
• Applying to consumable items interchangeably equivalent without adjustment.
(DDMAT)

communications

(1) In a general sense, conveying information from one person or organization to another effectively. *(DGBCT)*
(2) In a government negotiated acquisition, "communications" are exchanges between the buyer and offerors, after receipt of proposals, which lead to establishment of the competitive range. Communications are limited to offerors whose past performance information is the determining factor preventing them from being placed within the competitive range and offerors whose exclusion from, or inclusion in, the competitive range is uncertain. *(FAR 15.306(b))*

company/consortium standards

Developed by a company or group of companies and maintained for internal use. These standards are usually developed without outside comment, applied across products, and may be licensed to outside parties. *(NES-97)*
See *standard*.

comparative analysis

A type of secondary comparison used in performing price analysis. Comparative analysis may be accomplished by a comparison of previous contract prices with a current quotation for the same or similar items. *(NCMA-WS)*
See *secondary comparison*.

compartmentalization

The process of separating into isolated compartments or categories. *(MW)*

compartmented mode

A mode of operation wherein each user with direct or indirect access to an information system, its peripherals, remote terminals, or remote hosts has *all* of the following:

- Valid security clearance for the most restricted information processed in the system,
- Formal access approval and signed nondisclosure agreements for that information which a user is to have access, and
- Valid need-to-know for information which a user is to have access.

(CNSSI 4009)

compensable delay

(1) Any delay for which the buyer has a duty to reimburse. *(CMBOK)*

(2) In federal government contracting, a delay for which the government is contractually responsible that excuses the contractor's failure to perform and is compensable, including:

- Suspension of work,
- Work stoppage due to a stop-work order, and
- Government-caused delay of work.

(FAR 52.242-14-17)

See *government-caused delay; stop-work order; suspension of work;* contrast with *excusable delay*.

compensation

(1) Wages, salaries, honoraria, commissions, professional fees, and any other form of compensation, provided directly or indirectly for services rendered. Compensation is indirectly provided if it is paid to an entity other than the individual, specifically in exchange for services provided by the individual. *(FAR 3.104-1)*

(2) Any payments made to, or on behalf of, an employee or offered to an applicant as remuneration for employment, including but not limited to salary, wages, overtime pay, shift differentials, bonuses, commissions, vacation and holiday pay, allowances, insurance and other benefits, stock options and awards, profit sharing, and retirement. *(48 CFR 52.222-26)*

(3) The total amount of wages, salary, bonuses, deferred compensation, and employer contributions to defined contribution pension plans for the fiscal year, whether paid, earned, or otherwise accruing, as recorded in the contractor's cost accounting records for the fiscal year. *(FAR 31.205-6(p)(1)(i))*

compensation clause

Also sometimes called the "payment" clause, this clause sets out the amount payable under the contract, supporting data required to be furnished with invoices, and other payment terms, such as time for payment and retention. *(HECA)*

See also *compensation*.

compensation for personal services

All remuneration paid currently or accrued, in whatever form and whether paid immediately or deferred, for services rendered by employees to the contractor. *(FAR 31.001)*

compensation information

The amount and type of compensation provided to employees or offered to applicants. *(48 CFR 52.222-26)*

compensated personal absence

Any absence from work for reasons such as illness, vacation, holidays, jury duty, military training, or personal activities for which an employer pays compensation directly to an employee in accordance with a plan or custom of the employer. *(FAR 31.001)*

compensatory damages

Damages that will compensate the injured party for the loss sustained and nothing more. They are awarded by a court as the measure of actual loss and not as punishment for outrageous conduct or to deter future transgressions. Also called *actual damages*. *(STBP)*

competency

(1) An ability or skill. *(MW)*

(2) In a legal sense, the quality or state of being legally qualified or adequate. *(MW)*

(3) In the context of the CMS™, processes and skills utilized to produce the expected contract management outcome of a specific domain. The processes and skills that make up a "competency" involve the ability to perform multiple job tasks, both simultaneously and sequentially, while achieving meaningful results. *(CMS)*

See *Contract Management Standard™ Publication (CMS™); domains; job tasks;* see also *Contract Management Body of Knowledge (CMBOK)*.

competent authority approval (CAA)

An approval from the national agency responsible under a country's national law for the regulation of certain activities (e.g., the competent authority that regulates hazardous materials transportation within the United States is the Department of Transportation.) *(DISCS)*

competition

(1) The desired outcome where two or more sellers, independently and without collusion, respond to the same solicitation. *(CMBOK)*

(2) Part of an acquisition strategy whereby more than one organization is asked to submit an offer (quote, bid,

Cc

or proposal) to deliver supplies or perform services. The winner is selected on the basis of criteria established in the solicitation (i.e., request for quotations, invitation for bids, or request for proposals). *(DSMC)* See also *full and open competition*.

competition advocate
A position established by the Competition in Contracting Act of 1984 (41 U.S.C. 253). Each federal agency is required to have a competition advocate who, in turn, designates a competition advocate for each procuring activity of the agency. The competition advocate is responsible for promoting full and open competition and for challenging any barriers to such competition. *(HCS)* See *Competition in Contract Act of 1984* (CICA); see also *full and open competition*.

Competition in Contracting Act of 1984 (CICA)
A federal law (41 U.S.C. 253) designed to foster competition and promote cost savings. It requires the use of advance procurement planning and market research, as well as the use of commercial products whenever practicable. *(DGBCT)* (See also *FAR* Part 6.)

competitive bidding
A common method of source selection; it is the offer of prices and specified elements of performance by firms competing for a contract *(GKPT)*
See also *sealed-bidding*.

competitive intelligence
Information on competitors or competitive teams that is specific to an opportunity. *(STBP)*

competitive negotiation
In federal government contracting, a procurement involving:
*   A request for proposals that states the government's requirements and criteria for evaluation;
*   The submission of timely proposals by a maximum number of offerors;
*   Discussions with those offerors found to be within the competitive range; and
*   Award of a contract to the offeror whose offer, price, and other evaluation factors are most advantageous to the government.

(OPM)
See also *competition competitive proposal*.

competitive procedures
Procedures available for use in fulfilling the requirement for full and open competition such as sealed bids, competitive proposals, a combination of competitive procedures, and other competitive procedures. *(FAR 6.102)*
See also *competition; competitive negotiation; competitive proposal; sealed-bidding*.

competitive proposal
A competitive procurement practice in buyer purchasing that:
*   Is initiated by a request for proposals,
*   Contemplates the submission of timely proposals by the maximum number of possible suppliers,
*   Permits discussions with those suppliers found to be within the competitive range, and
*   Concludes with the award of a contract to the one supplier whose proposal is most advantageous to the buyer (considering price and the other factors included in the solicitation).

(CMBOK; DISCS; GKPT)
See also *competition; competitive negotiation*.

competitive range
In federal government contracting, a range of acceptable standards determined by the contracting officer on the basis of price, cost, or technical factors and comprised of all of the most highly rated proposals, determined based on the ratings of each proposal against all evaluation criteria, unless the range is further reduced for purposes of efficiency. The contracting officer must conduct written or verbal discussions with all responsible offerors that submit proposals within this range. *(GOAT; OPM)* (See also FAR 15.306(c).)

completion form
A form of cost-plus-fixed-fee contract that describes the scope of work by stating a definite goal or target and specifying an end product. This form of contract normally requires the contractor to complete and deliver the specified end product (e.g., a final report of research accomplishing the goal or target) within the estimated cost, if possible, as a condition for payment of the entire fixed fee. However, in the event the work cannot be completed within the estimated cost, the Government may require more effort without increase in fee, provided the Government increases the estimated cost. *(FAR 16.306(d)(1))*
Compare with *term form*.

Cc

compliance
The act or process of conformity in fulfilling official requirements—such as those imposed by law, regulation, or contractual obligation. *(MW)*

compliance audit
See *contract compliance audit*.

compliance evaluation
(1) In general, any one or combination of actions used to examine compliance with applicable laws, regulations, contractual obligations, etc. Also sometimes referred to as a "compliance audit" or "contract compliance audit."
See also *contract compliance audit*.
(2) In the context of equal employment opportunity requirements, any one or combination of actions that the Office of Federal Contract Compliance Programs may take to examine a federal contractor's compliance with one or more of the requirements of Executive Order 11246, which established the government's equal employment opportunity requirements. *(FAR 22.801)*

compliance management
A means of obtaining what the purchase order required, within the terms and conditions of the purchase, as agreed upon by the buyer and the seller. *(NCMA-WS)*

compliance matrix
A common technique used to identify gaps in the seller's ability to meet the buyer's needs as defined in the request for proposals. It lists all the solicitation references and functional requirements, along with indicators of the level of compliance (i.e., "full," "partial," or "none"). *(CMBOK)*

compliance program
A program that establishes and maintains a system to ensure that the seller complies with the buyer's contract requirements and applicable procurement laws and regulations. (In U.S. federal government contracting, the Federal Sentencing Guidelines contain seven criteria that such a program must satisfy.) *(TIPS)*
See *Federal Sentencing Guidelines*.

compliance system
An IT system that translates contract requirements (such as pricing, warranty, service requirements, and product changes) into executable instructions to internal systems. It includes connectivity to enterprise resource planning tools and other customer resource management tools that the organization uses to communicate internally and externally. *(DGBCT)*

component
(1) An article, material, or supply incorporated directly into an end product or construction material. *(FAR 25.003)*
See also *end product; construction material*.
(2) Any item supplied to the U.S. federal government as part of an end item or of another component. *(FAR 2.101; 41 U.S.C. 105)* (See *FAR* Part 25 and FAR 52.225-1 for exceptions.)

component breakout
An acquisition strategy to convert some items, usually parts or self-contained elements of a complete operating equipment end item, from contractor-furnished to government-procured items. *(P&L II)*

component costs
(1) For components purchased by the contractor, the acquisition cost, including transportation costs to the place of incorporation into the end product or construction material (whether or not such costs are paid to a domestic firm), and any applicable duty (whether or not a duty-free entry certificate is issued). *(FAR 25.003)*
See *component*; see also *construction material; duty; end product*.
(2) For components manufactured by the contractor, all costs associated with the manufacture of the component, including transportation costs (as described in (1.) of this definition), plus allocable overhead costs, but excluding profit. Cost of components does not include any costs associated with the manufacture of the end product. *(FAR 25.003)*
See also *component; end product*.

compound interest
Interest computed on the sum of the original principal and accrued interest. *(MW)*

Comprehensive Environmental Response, Compensation, and Liability Act (CERCLA)
Also known as the "Superfund," this federal law (42 U.S.C. 9601, et seq.) regulates environmental cleanup when wastes have been dumped or spilled in the environment. *(NES-94)*

compromise
In the context of information security, a type of incident

Cc

where information is disclosed to unauthorized individuals or a violation of the security policy of a system in which unauthorized intentional or unintentional disclosure, modification, destruction, or loss of an object, or the copying of information to unauthorized media, may have occurred. *(CNSSI 4009; DFARS 202.101)*
See also *object*.

comptroller general
The head of the Government Accountability Office (GAO). *(TIPS)*

computer
A device that performs logical operations and processes data. Computers are composed of, at a minimum:
- A central processing unit (CPU) to perform operations;
- User input devices such as a keyboard, mouse, digitizer, or game controller; and
- A computer display screen to output information.

Computers include both stationary and portable units, including desktop computers, integrated desktop computers, notebook computers, thin clients, and workstations. Although computers must be capable of using input devices and computer displays, computer systems do not need to include these devices on shipment to meet this definition. This definition *does not* include server computers, gaming consoles, mobile telephones, portable hand-held calculators, portable digital assistants (PDAs), MP3 players, or any other mobile computing device with displays less than four inches, measured diagonally. *(FAR 23.701)*

computer abuse
Intentional or reckless misuse, alteration, disruption, or destruction of information processing resources. *(CNSSI 4009)*

Computer-Aided Acquisition and Logistics Support (CALS)
See *Continuous Acquisition and Life-cycle Support (CALS)*.

computer-aided design/computer-aided manufacturing (CAD/CAM)
An electronic data interchange methodology to help improve the speed and quality of manufacturing processes. CAD/CAM applications provide standardization in the pre-design stage in order to facilitate data transfer between CAD systems of different manufacturers and for transfers between CAD and CAM systems *(DBL; EDIW)*

computer cryptography
Use of a crypto-algorithm program by a computer to authenticate or encrypt/decrypt information. *(CNSSI 4009)*

computer database
See *database*.

computer program
A set of statements or instructions to be used directly or indirectly in a computer in order to bring about a certain result. *(17 U.S.C. 101)*

computer software
See *software*.

computer software documentation
Owner's manuals, user's manuals, installation instructions, operating instructions, and other similar items, regardless of storage medium, that explain the capabilities of the computer software or provide instructions for using the software. *(FAR 2.101)*
See *software*.

computer security
Measures and controls that ensure confidentiality, integrity, and availability of information system assets, including hardware, software, firmware, and information being processed, stored, and communicated. *(CNSSI 4009)*
See also *incident; information system (IS); information systems security (INFOSEC)*.

concept exploration contract
A type of contract used to refine the proposed concept and to reduce the concept's technical uncertainties. *(FAR 34.005-3)*
See also *demonstration contract; full production contract; full-scale development contract*.

concern
Any business entity organized for profit (even if its ownership is in the hands of a nonprofit entity) with a place of business located in the United States or its outlying areas and that makes a significant contribution to the U.S. economy through payment of taxes and/or use of American products, material, and/or labor, etc. This term includes, but is not limited to, an individual, partnership, corporation, joint venture, association, or cooperative. For the purpose of making affiliation findings, this term includes any business entity, whether organized for profit or not, and any foreign business

entity—i.e., any entity located outside the United States and its outlying areas. *(FAR 19.001)*

concerted refusals to deal

Agreements or understandings by which two or more organizations jointly refuse to do business with a specific third party. *(BOE)*

concession strategy

A plan of the goals and positions, and sometimes the underlying interests, one party trades with the other party in a negotiation. *(NED)*

concessions contract

A contract under which the federal government grants a right to use federal property, including land or facilities, for furnishing services. This term includes, but is not limited to, a contract the principal purpose of which is to furnish food, lodging, automobile fuel, souvenirs, newspaper stands, and/or recreational equipment, regardless of whether the services are of direct benefit to the government, its personnel, or the general public. *(29 CFR 13.2)*

concurrent contract savings

In value engineering, the net reductions in the prices of other contracts that are definitized and ongoing at the time the value engineering change proposal is accepted. *(GOAT)*
See also *value engineering* (VE); *value engineering change proposal* (VECP).

concurrent inspection

A judgment of a product or procedural acceptability conducted concurrently by the seller's inspection personnel and the buyer's quality assurance personnel. *(AFIT)*

concurrent resolution

A "concurrent resolution" must be adopted by both houses of Congress, but it is not sent to the president for signature and therefore does not have the force of law. A concurrent resolution, for example, is used as the vehicle for expressing the sense of Congress on various foreign policy and domestic issues. *(DISCS)*
See also *concurrent resolution on the budget*.

concurrent resolution on the budget

A resolution passed by both houses of Congress, but not requiring the signature of the president, which sets forth, reaffirms, or revises specified congressional budget totals for the federal government for a fiscal year.

(DISCS; 2 U.S.C. 622(4))
See *concurrent resolution*.

condition

An event, not certain to occur, which must occur, unless its non-occurrence is excused, before performance under a contract becomes due. *(RSOC 224)*

condition concurrent

A dependent condition of a contract that must be performed by all parties. *(BLD)*
See also *condition precedent; condition subsequent*.

condition precedent

(1) That which occurs before an event. *(CMBOK)*
(2) A condition that activates a term in a contract. *(STBP)*
Contrast with *condition subsequent*; see also *"condition concurrent"*.

condition subsequent

(1) That which occurs should some other defined actions precede it. *(CMBOK)*
(2) A condition that suspends a term in a contract. *(STBP)*
Contrast with *condition precedent*; see also *condition concurrent*.

conditional acceptance

Acceptance of supplies or services that do not conform to contract quality requirements, or are otherwise incomplete, that the contractor is required to correct or otherwise complete by a specified date. *(FAR 46.101)*
See *acceptance; contract quality requirements*.

conduct negotiations

In the context of the *CMS™*, "conduct negotiations" is in the "award" life cycle phase of contract management, within the "form contract" domain. It is the process of communicating between the buyer and seller regarding all aspects of the offer and its terms, and often involves clarifying requirements and parties requesting changes or consideration of an alternate approach that may be consistent with the solicitation requirements. The value added by this process is where both parties work to find common ground or offer compromises among their differences in quantity, price, delivery, quality, or other factors. *(CMS)*
See *Contract Management Standard™ Publication (CMS™)*; see also *award life cycle phase*.

conference committee

A meeting between representatives of the House and the Senate to reconcile differences when each chamber passes a dissimilar version of the same bill. *(DISCS)*
See also *bill*.

confidence interval

A probability statement about an interval that is likely to contain the true population mean. *(GOAT)*
See also *confidence level*.

confidence level

A measure of the confidence that a particular interval includes the population mean. *(GOAT)*
See also *confidence interval*.

confidentiality

(1) Preserving authorized restrictions on information access and disclosure, including means for protecting personal privacy and proprietary information. *(44 U.S.C. 3542)*
(2) Assurance that information is not disclosed to unauthorized individuals, processes, or devices. *(CNSSI 4009)*

confidentiality agreement

See *nondisclosure agreement* (NDA).

configuration

A collection of an item's descriptive and governing characteristics that can be expressed in functional terms (i.e., what performance the item is expected to achieve) and in physical terms (i.e., what the item should look like and consist of when it is built). *(DSMC)*

configuration control

The process of controlling modifications to hardware, firmware, software, and documentation to ensure an information system is protected against improper modifications prior to, during, and after system implementation. *(CNSSI 4009)*

configuration management

(1) Procedures for applying technical and administrative direction and surveillance to identify and document the functional and physical characteristics of an item or system, control any changes to such characteristics, and record and report the change, process, and implementation status. *(DAAT; DSMC)*
(2) A collection of activities focused on establishing and maintaining the integrity of IT products and information systems through control of processes for initializing, changing, and monitoring the configurations of those products and systems throughout the system development life cycle. *(NIST SP 800-171)*
See also *information system* (IS); *information technology* (IT).
(3) The management of security features and assurances through control of changes made to hardware, software, firmware, documentation, test, test fixtures, and test documentation throughout the life cycle of an information system. *(CNSSI 4009)*
See also *configuration control*.

configuration settings

The set of parameters that can be changed in hardware, software, or firmware that affect the security posture and/or functionality of the information system. *(NIST SP 800-171)*
See *information system* (IS); see also *configuration management*.

conflict of interest (COI)

This term is used in connection with public officials and fiduciaries and their relationship to matters of private interest or gain to them. A "conflict of interest" arises when an employee's personal or financial interest conflicts or appears to conflict with his or her official responsibility. *(BLD)* (See also FAR 3.101 and *FAR* Subpart 3.11.)
See also *organizational conflict of interest* (OCI).

congressional committee

A division of the House or Senate that prepares legislation for action by the parent chamber or makes investigations as directed by the parent chamber. Most standing committees are divided into subcommittees, which study specific types of legislation, hold hearings, and report bills, with or without amendments, to a full committee. Only a full committee can report legislation to the House or Senate. *(DISCS)*
See also *congressional defense committees; congressional intelligence committees*.

congressional defense committees

A term that refers to the following committees:
• The Senate Committee on Armed Services,
• The Senate Committee on Appropriations,
• The House Committee on Armed Services, and
• The House Committee on Appropriations.
(10 U.S.C. 101)

congressionally directed spending

A statutory provision or report language included primarily at the request of a senator or a member, delegate, or resident commissioner of the House of Representatives providing, authorizing, or recommending a specific amount of discretionary budget authority, credit authority, or other spending authority for a contract, loan, loan guarantee, grant, loan authority, or other expenditure with or to an entity, or targeted to a specific U.S. state, locality, or congressional district, other than through a statutory or administrative formula-driven or competitive award process. *(42 U.S.C. 5133(n)(1))*

connection charge

All nonrecurring costs, whether refundable or nonrefundable, to be paid by the U.S. federal government to a utility supplier for the required connecting facilities, which are installed, owned, operated, and maintained by the utility supplier. *(FAR 41.101)*
See also *termination liability*.

consensus decision

A decision made after all aspects of an issue, both positive and negative, have been brought out to the extent that everyone openly understands and supports the decision and the reasons for making it. *(DGCQI)*

consensus standards

See *voluntary consensus standards*.

consent of surety

An acknowledgment by a surety that its bond given in connection with a contract continues to apply to the contract as modified. *(FAR 28.001)*
See *surety*.

consent to subcontract

The contracting officer's written consent for the prime contractor to enter into a particular subcontract. *(FAR 2.101)* (See also FAR 44.201-1 and *FAR* Part 51.)

consequential damages

(1) Those costs that result from a particular cause. For example, a product failure may mean that the purchaser has incurred not only the added cost necessary to replace the product, but has also lost income that would have resulted had the product not failed. The lost income would be a "consequential damage." The extent to which consequential damages may be recovered depends on the language contained in the contract and the law in a particular jurisdiction. *(CMBOK; HECA)*
See *damages; incidental damages*.
(2) In the case of the seller's breach of warranty, consequential damages to the buyer include:

- Any loss resulting from general or particular requirements and needs of which the seller at the time of contracting had reason to know and which could not reasonably be prevented by cover or otherwise, and
- Injury to person or property proximately resulting from any breach of warranty. *(UCC 2-715(2))*

See also *cover; damages*.

conservatism

An accounting convention that provides guidance for accountants where solutions to uncertain elements should be chosen on the basis that would least likely overstate assets and income. Historically, this has been the most pervasive approach that accountants have used in preparing financial statements. *(NCMA-CA)*

consideration

(1) Anything of value that is exchanged between the parties to a contract. *(CMBOK)*
(2) The inducement to a contract—i.e., the cause, motive, price, or impelling influence that induces a contracting party to enter a contract. *(STBP)*

consignee

(1) A merchant to which goods are delivered in a consignment. *(UCC 9-102(a)(19))*
See *consignment; consignor*.
(2) The person, group of persons, or organization named in a bill of lading to whom a shipment of supplies or services is to be delivered—whether by land, sea, or air—and to whose order the bill promises delivery. *(DISCS; SPP; UCC 7-102(a)(3))*
See *bill of lading*.

consignment

A transaction, regardless of its form, in which a person delivers goods to a merchant for the purpose of sale and:

- The merchant:
  - Deals in goods of that kind under a name other than the name of the person making delivery;
  - Is not an auctioneer; and
  - Is not generally known by its creditors to be substantially engaged in selling the goods of others;

- With respect to each delivery, the aggregate value of the goods is above a specified dollar amount at the time of delivery;
- The goods are not consumer goods immediately before delivery; and
- The transaction does not create a security interest that secures an obligation.

(UCC 9-102(a)(20))
See also *consignee; consignor; goods*.

consignor

(1) A person that delivers goods to a consignee in a consignment. *(UCC 9-102(a)(21))*
See *consignee; consignment*.
(2) A person named in a bill of lading as the person from whom goods have been received for shipment. *(UCC 7-102(a)(4))*

consistency

An accounting principle that is vital in order to provide comparable financial information to interested users from period to period. *(NCMA-CA)*

consolidated facilities contract

A combination of a facilities acquisition and a facilities use contract. *(GOAT)*
See *facilities contract*; see also *facilities acquisition contract; facilities use contract*.

Consolidated List of Debarred, Suspended, and Ineligible Contractors

A single, comprehensive listing–prepared by the General Services Administration–of business firms and individuals debarred, suspended, or otherwise excluded by U.S. government agencies from receiving government contracts. *(AAPM)*
See *debarment; suspension*.

consolidated requirement

See *consolidation*.

consolidation

A federal government solicitation for a single contract, a multiple-award contract, a task order, or a delivery order to satisfy–

- Two or more requirements of the federal agency for supplies or services that have been provided to or performed for the federal agency under two or more separate contracts, each of which was lower in cost than the total cost of the contract for which offers are solicited; or

- Requirements of the federal agency for construction projects to be performed at two or more discrete sites.

Also called consolidated requirement. *(FAR 2.101)*
See also *separate contract*.

constant dollar values

Economic units measured in terms of constant purchasing power. Constant dollar values are not affected by general price inflation. *(GOAT)*
See *constant year dollars; current year dollars*.

constant year dollars

A method of relating dollar values for various years by removing the annual effects of inflation and showing all dollars at the value they would have had in a selected base year. *(DISCS)*
See *constant dollar values*; see also *current year dollars*.

constraints

Restrictions or boundary conditions that impact overall capability, priority, and resources in system acquisition. *(DSMC)*

construct

In the context of alteration or construction of federal government property, this term includes preliminary planning, engineering, architectural, legal, fiscal, and economic investigations and studies, surveys, designs, plans, working drawings, specifications, procedures, and other similar actions necessary for the construction of a public building. *(40 U.S.C. 3301(a)(2))*
See also *public building*.

construction

Construction, rehabilitation, alteration, conversion, extension, repair, or improvement (including dredging, excavating, and painting) of buildings, highways, or other real property. For purposes of this definition, the terms "buildings, structures, or other real property" include, but are not limited to, improvements of all types, such as bridges, dams, plants, highways, parkways, streets, subways, tunnels, sewers, mains, power lines, cemeteries, pumping stations, railways, airport facilities, terminals, docks, piers, wharves, ways, lighthouses, buoys, jetties, breakwaters, levees, canals, and channels. Construction does not include the manufacture, production, furnishing, construction, alteration, repair, processing, or assembling of vessels, aircraft, or other kinds of personal property (except as described in *FAR* Subpart 22.5). *(FAR 2.101; FAR 22.502)*

Cc

construction material
An article, material, or supply brought to the construction site by a contractor or subcontractor for incorporation into the building or work. This term also includes an item brought to the site preassembled from articles, materials, or supplies. However, emergency life safety systems, such as emergency lighting, fire alarm, and audio evacuation systems, that are discrete systems incorporated into a public building or work and that are produced as complete systems, are evaluated as a single and distinct construction material regardless of when or how the individual parts or components of those systems are delivered to the construction site. Materials purchased directly by the federal government are "supplies," *not* "construction material." *(FAR 25.003)*

constructive
That which is established by the interpretation of the law in construing facts, conduct, circumstances, or instruments. That which has not the character assigned to it in its own essential nature, but acquires such character in consequence of the way in which it is regarded by a rule or policy of law; hence, inferred, implied, or made out by legal interpretation. Notably, the word "legal" is sometimes used in lieu of "constructive." *(BLD)*

constructive acceleration
A requirement (based on the reasonable interpretation of the words, acts, or inaction of authorized buyer employees) that a seller complete its work by a date earlier than one that would reflect the time extensions to which it is entitled because of excusable delays. *(CMBOK; GCG)*
See also *acceleration; constructive*.

constructive acceptance
A concept borne out of the Prompt Payment Act (31 U.S.C. Chapter 39), which requires federal government officials to fulfill their administrative responsibilities under a contract with regards to payment deadlines to contractors, otherwise interest penalties accrue to the government. The government's acceptance of a proper invoice is deemed to occur constructively on the seventh day after the contractor delivers supplies or performs services in accordance with the terms and conditions of the contract, unless there is a disagreement over quantity, quality, or contractor compliance with a contract requirement. *(CMBOK)* (See also FAR 32.904.)
See *prompt payment; Prompt Payment Act* (PPA); see also *acceptance; "constructive."*

constructive change
A change resulting from the buyer's actions or directives that impacts the cost or schedule for performance that is of such a nature that it is construed by the seller to have the same effect as a formal change order. A "constructive change" generally occurs when a buyer employee (other than the contracting officer in the case of the U.S. federal government) implies or expressly orders the seller to perform work that is not in the contract. In government contracting, equitable adjustment is granted for constructive changes only if the change causes the seller injury or liability. *(CMBOK; OPM)*
Compare with *change order*; see also *"constructive"; equitable adjustment*.

consumable supplies and material
See *expendable supplies and material*.

consumer
(1) The ultimate user of goods, ideas, and services. *(AMAD)*
(2) An individual who enters into a transaction primarily for personal, family, or household purposes. *(UCC 1-201(11))*

consumer account
An account established by an individual primarily for personal, family, or household purposes. *(UCC 3-103(a)(2))*

consumer behavior
The behavior of the consumer or decision-maker in the marketplace of products and services. This term is often used to describe the interdisciplinary field of scientific study that attempts to understand and describe such behavior. *(AMAD)*
See *consumer*.

consumer transaction
A transaction in which:
- An individual incurs an obligation primarily for personal, family, or household purposes;
- A security interest secures the obligation; and
- The collateral is held or acquired primarily for personal, family, or household purposes.

This term includes consumer-goods transactions. *(UCC 3-103(a)(3); UCC 9-102(a)(26))*

contamination
In the context of information security, a type of incident involving the introduction of data of one security classification or security category into data of a lower

Cc

security classification or different security category. **(CNSSI 4009)**
See *incident*; see also *information security; information systems security* **(INFOSEC)**.

contiguous United States (CONUS)
The 48 contiguous (i.e., sharing a common boarder) U.S. states and the District of Columbia, including the adjacent territorial waters. (Also called "continental United States (CONUS).") This term *does not* include Alaska, Hawaii, or other U.S. territories outside of the contiguous United States. *(FAR 2.101; DISCS)*
See also *outlying areas; outside of the contiguous United States* **(OCONUS)**.

contiguous Western States
In certain contexts, this term is used to refer to the 11 contiguous Western States of the United States, which include: Arizona, California, Colorado, Idaho, Montana, Nevada, New Mexico, Oregon, Utah, Washington, and Wyoming. Also called the "11 contiguous Western States." *(43 U.S.C. 1702(o))*

continental United States (CONUS)
See *contiguous United States* **(CONUS)**.

contingency
(1) A possible future event or condition arising from presently known or unknown causes, the outcome of which is indeterminable at the present time. *(FAR 31.205-7)*
(2) In a Department of Defense context, a situation requiring military operations in response to natural disasters, acts of terrorism, subversive activity, or as otherwise directed by appropriate authority to protect U.S. interests. *(DDMAT)*
See also *contingency contract; contingency contracting; contingency operation*.

contingency contract
A legally binding agreement for supplies, services, and construction let by U.S. government contracting officers in an operational area, as well as other contracts that have a prescribed area of performance within a designated operational area. *(DDMAT)*
See also *contingency; contingency contracting*.

contingency contracting
The process of obtaining goods, services, and construction via contracting means in support of contingency operations. Usually, contingency contracting occurs in an emergency involving military forces, caused by declared national emergencies or U.S. Secretary of Defense–designated military operations. *(CMBOK; DDMAT)*
See also *contingency; contingency contracting; contingency operation*.

contingency operation
A military operation that—
- Is designated by the U.S. secretary of defense as an operation in which members of the U.S. armed forces are or may become involved in military actions, operations, or hostilities against an enemy of the United States or against an opposing military force; or
- Results in the call or order to, or retention to, active duty of members of the uniformed services under Section 688, 12301(a), 12302, 12304, 12304a, 12305, or 12406 of Title 10, U.S. Code; Chapter 15 of Title 10; Section 712 of Title 14; or any other provision of law during a war or during a national emergency declared by the president or Congress. *(FAR 2.101; 10 U.S.C. 101(a)(13))*

contingency plan
In the case of an information system, a plan maintained for emergency response, backup operations, and post-disaster recovery to ensure the availability of critical resources and to facilitate the continuity of operations in an emergency situation. *(CNSSI 4009)*
See also *continuity of operations plan* **(COOP)**; *information system* **(IS)**.

contingent contract
A contract that provides for the possibility of its termination when a specified occurrence takes place or does not take place. *(STBP)*

contingent fee
Any commission, percentage, brokerage, or other fee that is contingent upon the success that a person or concern has in securing a federal government contract. *(FAR 3.401)*

contingent interest
A future interest whose vesting is dependent upon the occurrence or non-occurrence of a future event. *(MW)*
Compare with *vested interest*; see also *future interest*.

continuation statement
An amendment of a financing statement which:
- Identifies, by its file number, the initial financing statement to which it relates; and

- Indicates that it is a continuation statement for, or that it is filed to continue the effectiveness of, the identified financing statement. *(UCC 9-102(a)(27))*
See also *financing statement*.

continued portion of the contract
The portion of a contract that the contractor must continue to perform following a partial termination. *(FAR 2.101)*

continuing resolution (CR)
Appropriations legislation enacted by Congress to provide temporary budget authority and make funds available for U.S. federal agencies to keep them in operation and to continue performance of work when their regular appropriations bill has not been enacted by the beginning of the fiscal year and where failure to obtain a continuing resolution will shut down the government. A continuing resolution usually specifies a designated period and maximum rate at which the agency may incur obligations, based on the rate of the prior year, the president's budget request, or an appropriation bill passed by either or both houses of the Congress. Normally, new programs cannot be started under a continuing resolution. *(DAAT; DISCS)*
See also *appropriation act/bill; continuing resolution authority (CRA); sequester/sequestration*.

continuing resolution authority (CRA)
The authority to obligate funds for use by federal agencies for the new fiscal year under a continuing resolution granted by Congress in a joint resolution making temporary appropriations prior to passage of the regular appropriations act, or in lieu of such an act. Normally, however, the continuing resolution authority is for a designated period less than a fiscal year, and such authority does not usually allow funding for the start of any new programs. *(DISCS)*
See *continuing resolution (CR)*.

Continuous Acquisition and Life Cycle Support (CALS)
A DOD initiative that mandates the sharing between contractors and government agencies of technical information, documents, support information, and other integrated digital product data—including cost and schedule details—through a set of standards to achieve efficiencies in business and operational mission areas. Formerly known as *Computer-aided Acquisition and Logistics Support* (CALS). *(DAAT; EDIW)*

continuous inventory
See *cycle count*.

continuous quality improvement
Based on the precept—"nothing is perfect"—continuous quality improvement assumes that all work processes are grounds for constant evaluation and potential improvement. *(DGCQI)*

continuous review system
A popular inventory control system in which the remaining quantity of an item is reviewed either manually or electronically each time a withdrawal is made from inventory to determine whether it is time to reorder. *(GKPT)*

continuous risk management (CRM)
A systematic and iterative process that efficiently identifies, analyzes, tracks, controls, and communicates and documents risks associated with implementation of designs, plans, and processes. *(NID 8000-108)*

contra proferentem
Latin for "against the one bringing forth." In contract interpretation, when choosing the reasonable meanings of a promise or agreement, or terms thereof, that meaning is generally preferred which operates against the party who supplies the words, or from whom a writing otherwise proceeds. In other words, an ambiguous contract provision is construed most strongly against the party who selected the language. Also called the *Doctrine of Contra Proferentem* and the "nondrafter's rule." *(CMBOK; BLD; RSOC 206)*
See also *contract interpretation*.

contract (CNT; Kt; K)
(1) A type of binding agreement formed between two or more persons who are legally capable of making a binding agreement, for the breach of which the law gives a remedy, or the performance of which the law in some way recognizes as a duty. A "contract" typically includes the following elements:
- A promise (or set of promises);
- A consideration (i.e., something of value promised or given);
- A reasonable amount of understanding between the persons as to what the agreement means; and
- A legal means for resolving any breach of the agreement.

(DISCS; RSOC 1)
See *contract elements*; see also *promise; promisee; promisor*.

Cc

(2) In the sense of a contract for the sale of supplies or services, it is a mutually binding legal relationship obligating the seller to furnish supplies or services and the buyer to provide consideration for them. *(CMS)*

(3) In federal government contracting, means a mutually binding legal relationship obligating the seller to furnish the supplies or services (including construction) and the buyer to pay for them. It includes all types of commitments that obligate the government to an expenditure of appropriated funds and that, except as otherwise authorized, are in writing. In addition to bilateral instruments, contracts include (but are not limited to) awards and notices of awards; job orders or task letters issued under basic ordering agreements; letter contracts; orders, such as purchase orders, under which the contract becomes effective by written acceptance or performance; and bilateral contract modifications. Contracts do not include grants and cooperative agreements covered by 31 U.S.C.6301, *et seq. (FAR 2.101)* (See *FAR* Part 16 for discussion of various types of contracts.)
See also **contract action**.

(4) In a commercial contracting context, as distinguished from "agreement," this term means the total obligation that results from the parties' agreement as determined by the UCC as supplemented by any other applicable laws. *(UCC 1-201(12))*
See also **Uniform Commercial Code** (UCC); contrast with **agreement**.

contract action

(1) An action resulting in a contract, including actions for additional supplies or services outside the existing contract scope, but not including actions that are within the scope and under the terms of the existing contract, such as contract modifications issued pursuant to the "changes" clause, or funding and other administrative changes. Also called **contracting action**. *(FAR 5.001; 32.001)*

(2) In federal government contracting, any oral or written action that results in the purchase, rent, or lease of supplies or equipment, services, or construction using appropriated dollars, or modifications to these actions regardless of dollar value. In this context, this term *does not* include grants, cooperative agreements, other transactions, real property leases, requisitions from federal government stock, training authorizations, or other transactions not subject to the *FAR. (FAR 4.601; FAR 23.101)*

contract action report (CAR)

Contract action data required to be entered into the Federal Procurement Data System. *(FAR 4.601)*
See also **contract action; Federal Procurement Data System** (FPDS).

contract adjustment board

A federal agency head may establish a "contract adjustment board" with authority to approve, authorize, and direct appropriate extraordinary contractual actions and to make all appropriate determinations and findings. *(GOAT)*

contract administration

(1) All the activities associated with the performance of a contract, from pre-award to closeout or termination—including ensuring compliance with contractual terms and conditions. *(DISCS; STBP)*
See also **administer contract; contract management; post-award life cycle phase**.

(2.) The oversight of a contractor's (or a supplier's) performance pursuant to the fulfillment of the terms, conditions, and specifications of a contract. *(OPM)*

contract administration file

A contract administration file contains the documents supporting all actions reflecting the basis for and the performance of contract administration responsibilities. Included are the copy of the contract and all modifications, together with official record copies of supporting documents executed by the contract administration office. *(GOAT)*
See **contract administration**; see also **contract administration office** (CAO).

contract administration office (CAO)

An office that performs assigned post-award functions related to the administration of contracts, as well as assigned pre-award functions. *(FAR 2.101)*
See also **contract administration**.

contract administration plan

The buyer's plan for performing the functions required for contract administration. *(GOAT)*
See **contract administration**.

contract audit

The evaluation of the accuracy and propriety of contractors' cost representations and claims by the review and analysis of contractors' and subcontractors' policies, systems, and controls. This term includes the

examination of books, accounts, basic records, and operations. *(AFIT)*
See also *contract compliance audit*.

Contract Audit Manual (CAM)
See *Defense Contract Audit Agency Contract Audit Manual* (CAM).

contract authority
Budget authority contained in an authorization bill that permits an agency of the federal government to enter into contracts or other obligations for future payments from funds not yet appropriated by Congress. Funds are made available for obligation, but not for expenditures. The assumption is that the necessary funds will be made available for payment in a subsequent appropriations act. *(DISCS; 2 U.S.C. 622(2)(A)(iii))*
See also *budget authority*.

contract award
Occurs when a buyer has signed and distributed a contract to a seller. *(DSMC; CMBOK)*
See *award*.

contract bond
A guarantee—backed by cash or other security—of the faithful performance and fulfillment of the undertakings, covenants, terms, and conditions contained in a contract. *(FAR 28.1; AFIT)*

contract budget base (CBB)
The sum of the negotiated contract cost plus the estimated cost of authorized unpriced work. This represents the total amount of performance measurement budget that may be allocated to contract work. *(NDIA II)*
See also *authorized unpriced work* (AUW); *total allocated budget* (TAB).

contract bundling
The act of combining two or more requirements. *(CMBOK)*
See *bundling*.

contract carrier
(1) A person providing transportation for compensation under continuing agreements with one person or a limited number of persons. *(FAR 47.001)*
(2) A person providing telecommunications services for compensation under continuing agreements with one person or a limited number of persons. *(GOAT)*

contract change proposal (CCP)
Document provided by a main (client) for effecting adjustments to the ambit of work (not of specifications or requirements) of a deal.

contract claim
Any request for relief, adjustment, or consideration by a party to the contract for an act which, in the opinion of the claimant, is not within the scope or intent of the original contract. *(FAR 33.206)*
See *claim*.

contract clause
A term or condition used in contracts or in both solicitations and contracts, and applying after contract award or both before and after award. Clauses state the rights and obligations of the parties to a contract. *(FAR 2.101; CMBOK)*
Contrast with *provision*.

contract closeout
In the context of the *CMS™*, "contract closeout" is in the "post-award" life cycle phase of contract management, within the "close contract" domain. It is the process of ensuring:
* All performance has been accomplished,
* Final payment has been made, and
* The contract has been reconciled.
The value added by this process is in the completion, delivery, and acceptance of the contract requirement(s) in accordance with the terms and conditions of the contract. *(CMS)*
See *close contract; Contract Management Standard™ Publication (CMS™); post-award life cycle phase*; see also *closeout*.

contract compliance audit
A process to assess a contractor's adherence to the terms of the contract. *(SFFF)*

contract cost
The aggregate dollar amount paid to the contractor/seller. *(AFIT)*

contract data requirements list (CDRL)
(1) Document used to order/buy and require delivery of data. It tells the seller what data to deliver, when and how such data will be accepted, and where to look for instructions. *(DSMC)*
(2) A list of authorized data requirements for a specific procurement that forms part of a contract. It provides a

Cc

contractual method to direct the contractor to prepare and deliver data that meets specific approval and acceptance criteria. The CDRL is the standard format for identifying potential data requirements in a solicitation, and deliverable data requirements in a contract. DFARS Subpart 215.470 requires the use of the CDRL in solicitations when the contract will require delivery of data. *(DAAT-A)*
See also *technical data package*; see also *contract requirements; exhibit*.

contract date
The date set for bid opening or, in the case of a negotiated contract or a modification, the effective date of a contract or modification. *(FAR 52.229-3(a); GOAT)*

contract debt
An amount that—
* Has been paid to a seller to which the seller is not currently entitled under the terms and conditions of the contract, or
* Is otherwise due from the seller under the terms and conditions of the contract.

(FAR 32.601(a)) (See also FAR 32.601(b) for specific examples under federal government contracts.)
See also *demand for payment of contract debt*.

contract dispute
A post-award disagreement between the buyer and a seller. *(CMBOK)*
See also *Contract Disputes statute; government contract disputes process*.

Contract Disputes Act of 1978 (CDA)
See *Contract Disputes statute*.

Contract Disputes statute
A federal law (41 U.S.C. Chapter 71) that establishes procedures and requirements for asserting and resolving claims by or against contractors arising under or relating to a contract subject to the statute. The statute provides for payment of interest on contactor claims in excess of a dollar amount specified in the statute, contractor certification of claims in excess of that dollar amount, and for a civil penalty for contractor claims that are fraudulent or based on a misrepresentation of fact. Formerly known as the "Contract Disputes Act of 1978" (CDA). *(41 U.S.C. 7104)* (See also FAR 33.2.)
See *contract dispute*; see also *government contract disputes process*.

contract elements
A legally enforceable contract must include the following elements:
* An offer,
* An acceptance,
* Consideration,
* Execution by competent parties,
* Legality of purpose, and
* Clear terms and conditions.

(GOAT)

contract execution
The process of working toward the accomplishment of contractual obligations. A contract is considered "executed" when all the parties have fully performed their contractual obligations. *(CMBOK)*

contract field services (CFS)
Services performed for the federal government by commercial or industrial companies. These services provide instruction and training on the installation, operation, and maintenance of government items, equipment, and systems. *(DISCS)*

contract financing
(1) In a commercial contracting context, contract financing may include obtaining loans and lines of credit from financial institutions, obtaining advance funding of accounts receivable or funding of purchase orders from private firms, or obtaining funds from venture capitalists. It may also include negotiating favorable payment clauses such as a sizable down payment or milestone payments as the work progresses. Commercial contract financing could also include such methods as commercial advance payments made before performance has begun, commercial interim payments made after some work has been done, and delivery payments made after receiving and accepting a portion of the total work to be performed. *(DGBCT)*
(2) In some cases within a federal government contracting context, successfully completing a government contract may require the government's assistance with some form of contract financing. For example, contract financing might be appropriate in a multimillion-dollar contract for goods that require the contractor to make substantial initial investments in labor, materials, and production costs. In cases where the government determines that some type of contract financing is appropriate, it usually takes one of two forms, private or government. When a contractor requests financing, the government contracting officer considers the following

Cc

order of preference for methods of contract financing:
- Private financing,
- Customary contract financing other than loan guarantees,
- Loan guarantees,
- Unusual contract financing, and
- Advance payments.

(DGBCT)
See also *advance payment; customary contractor financing; contractor financing; contract financing payment; guaranteed loan; private financing; unusual contract financing.*

contract financing payment
An authorized federal government disbursement of monies to a contractor prior to acceptance of supplies or services by the government. Contract financing payments include:
- Advance payments;
- Performance-based payments;
- Commercial advance and interim payments;
- Progress payments based on cost under the clause at FAR 52.232-16, "Progress Payments";
- Progress payments based on a percentage or stage of completion (see FAR 32.102(e)), except those made under the clause at FAR 52.232-5, "Payments Under Fixed-Price Construction Contracts," or the clause at FAR 52.232-10, "Payments Under Fixed-Price Architect-Engineer Contracts"; and
- Interim payments under a cost-reimbursement contract, except for a cost-reimbursement contract for services when Alternate I of the clause at FAR 52.232-25, "Prompt Payment," is used.

Contract financing payments do not include invoice payments, payments for partial deliveries, or lease and rental payments. *(FAR 32.001)*
See also *customary contract financing.*

contract for sale
Includes both a present sale of goods and a contract to sell goods at a future time.

contract formation
See *contract elements.*

contract fulfillment
The joint buyer and seller actions taken to successfully perform and administer a contractual agreement and meet or exceed all contractual obligations, including effective change management and timely contract closeout. *(STBP)*
See also *close-out, contract closeout.*

contract interpretation
The entire process of determining what the parties to a contract agreed to in the contract. *(AGC)*
See also *contra proferentem; Four Corners Doctrine; Plain Meaning Rule; Rule of Blue and Gold.*

contract life cycle phases
Contracts have a distinct beginning, middle, and end. This "contract life cycle" generally consists of three contract phases:
- "Pre-award,"
- "Award," and
- "Post-award."

(CMBOK; CMS)
See *award life cycle phase; pre-award life cycle phase; post-award life cycle phase.*

contract line item number (CLIN)
In federal government contracting, the supplies or services to be delivered under a contract, as set forth in the solicitation, are categorized into line items and subline items (in accordance with FAR 4.10 and DFARS 204.71), with a CLIN established for each line/subline item in accordance with agency procedures. *(FAR 4.1005-1(a)(1); NES-90)*
See also *line item; subline item.*

contract management (CM)
The actions of a contract manager to develop solicitations, develop offers, form contracts, perform contracts, and close contracts. *(CMS)*
See also *contract manager (CM); contract management profession.*

Contract Management Body of Knowledge® (CMBOK)
A body of knowledge published by the National Contract Management Association (NCMA) that outlines the key terms, skills, and knowledge necessary to work in the contract management profession. *(CMBOK)*
See *contract management; contract management profession.*

contract management profession
A specialized profession with broad responsibilities that include managing contract features such as deliverables, deadlines, and contract terms and conditions. *(CMBOK)*

contract management domains
In the context of the *CMS™*, this term refers to contract management processes performed by contract

Cc

managers, which generally fall into five categories of significant outcomes (i.e., "domains") within the three contract life cycle phases:
- "Solicitation,"
- "Offer,"
- "Contract,"
- "Contract performance," and
- "Close contract."

(CMBOK)
See *Contract Management Standard™ Publication (CMS™)*

contract management life cycle phases
See *contract life cycle phases*.

contract management review
Related to U.S. government agencies, an appraisal of the effectiveness of local offices' interpretation and application of policies, directives, and procedures, and of the capability of field activities to comply with them. *(OPM)*

Contract Management Standard™ Publication (CMS™)
Developed by NCMA, the purpose of the *Contract Management Standard™* is to describe the nature of contract management in terms of the contract management processes created through the integration and interaction of job tasks and competencies, and the purposes they serve. The common and repeated use of the *CMS™* will improve productivity, increase efficiency, and reduce costs. *(CMS)*
See *competencies; contract life cycle phases; contract management domains; job tasks*; see also *Contract Management Body of Knowledge (CMBOK)*.

contract manager (CM)
The authorized representative or agent for a contracting party. *(CMS)*
See also *agent; contract management*.

contract manufacturer
A company that produces goods under contract for another company under the label or brand name of that company. *(DFARS 202.101)*

contract modification
Any written change in the terms of a contract may be unilateral or bilateral. *(FAR 2.101)* (See also *FAR* Subpart 43.103.)
See *bilateral modification; unilateral modification; see also change order; supplemental agreement*.

contract negotiation
See *negotiation*; see also *contract negotiation process*.

contract negotiation process
A three-phased approach composed of planning, negotiating, and documenting a contractual agreement between two or more parties to buy or sell products and/or services. *(STBP)*
See *negotiation*.

contract price
The total amount of a contract for the term of the contract (excluding options, if any). *(GOAT)*

contract pricing proposal
See *cost proposal*; see also *business proposal; proposal*.

contract quality requirements
The technical requirements in the contract relating to the quality of a product or service and those contract clauses prescribing inspection, and other quality controls incumbent on the contractor, to assure that the product or service conforms to the contractual requirements. *(FAR 46.101)*
See also *contract requirements; government contract quality assurance*.

contract requirements
In addition to specified performance requirements, contract requirements include those defined in:
- The statement of work (SOW);
- Specifications, standards, and related documents;
- The contract data requirements list;
- Management systems; and
- Contract terms and conditions.

(OPM)
See also *contract data requirements list (CDRL); statement of work (SOW)*.

contract schedule
The complete statement of the requirement in the solicitation, including not only the statement of work and specifications, but also the terms and conditions with respect to packaging and marking, inspection and acceptance, deliveries or performance, contract administration data, and other special contract requirements. The schedule includes Sections A through H of the uniform contract format. *(FAI)*
See *uniform contract format*.

Cc

contract target cost (CTC)

See *negotiated contract cost* (NCC).

contract termination

(1) Cessation or cancellation, in whole or in part, of work under a prime contract, or a subcontract thereunder, due to failure of the contractor to perform in accordance with the terms of the contract. *(DISCS)*
See also *termination; termination for cause; termination for default* (T4D).
(2) Cessation or cancellation, in whole or in part, of work under a prime contract, or a subcontract thereunder, for the convenience of, or at the option of, the U.S. federal government. *(DISCS)*
See also *termination; termination for convenience*.

contract type

(1) Categories of contracts that are differentiated according to the degree and timing of the responsibility assumed by the contractor for the costs of performance, and the amount and nature of the profit incentive offered to the contractor for achieving or exceeding specified standards or goals. *(FAR 16.101)*
See *cost-plus-award-fee* (CPAF) *contract; cost-plus-fixed-fee* (CPFF) *contract; cost-plus-incentive-fee* (CPIF) *contract; firm-fixed-price* (FFP) *contract; fixed-price-incentive* (FPI) *contract; fixed-price level of effort term contract; fixed-price redeterminable* (FPR) *contract; fixed-price with economic price adjustment* (FPEPA) *contract; indefinite delivery/indefinite quantity contract; labor hour contract; time and materials contract*.
(2.) A specific pricing arrangement, or combination of pricing arrangements, employed for the performance of work under the contract. *(CMBOK)*

contract under seal

A formalized writing with a special seal attached. *(DGBCT)*
See *formal contract*.

contract work breakdown structure (CWBS)

The complete work breakdown structure for a contract. It includes the customer-approved work breakdown structure for reporting purposes and its discretionary extension to lower levels by the contractor, in accordance with customer direction and the contract work statement. It provides for the product-oriented decomposition of contract work into major elements that include all the hardware, software, data, and services that are the responsibility of the contractor. *(NDIA II)*
See *work breakdown structure* (WBS).

Contract Work Hours and Safety Standards Act (CWHSSA)

See *"Contract Work Hours and Safety Standards* (CWHSS) *statute*.

Contract Work Hours and Safety Standards (CWHSS) statute

A federal law (40 U.S.C. Chapter 37) requiring certain contracts to contain a clause (See FAR 52.222-4) specifying that no laborer or mechanic doing any part of the work contemplated by the contract shall be required or permitted to work more than 40 hours in any workweek unless paid for all additional hours at not less than one times the basic rate of pay. Formerly known as the *Contract Work Hours and Safety Standards Act* (CWHSSA). *(40 U.S.C. 3701, et seq.)* (See also *FAR* Subpart 22.3.)

contracted savings

Net life cycle cost savings realized by contracting for the performance of a value engineering study or by a value engineering change proposal submitted by a contractor. *(OMB A-131)*
See *value engineering* (VE); *value engineering change proposal* (VECP).

Contracts for Materials, Supplies, Articles, and Equipment Exceeding $15,000 statute

A federal law (41 U.S.C. Chapter 65) that requires a contractor that furnishes materials, supplies, articles, and/or equipment exceeding $15,000 to the government under a single contract to be either a manufacturer or regular dealer of said items. The statute includes stipulations on minimum wages, maximum hours, labor practices, and working conditions. (Formerly known as the *Walsh-Healey Public Contracts Act. (41 U.S.C. 6502)*

contracting

(1) The entire spectrum of action associated with obtaining supplies or services, from initial description through solicitation and contract award and all phases of contract administration. *(NCMA-SS)*
See also *contract management*.
(2) In a federal government context, includes purchasing, renting, leasing, or otherwise obtaining supplies or services from nonfederal sources. It includes a description (but not a determination) of supplies and services required, selection and solicitation of sources, preparation and award of contracts, and all phases of contract administration. It *does not* include making grants or cooperative agreements. *(FAR 2.101)*

contracting action
See *contract action*.

contracting activity
An element of an agency of the federal government that is designated by the agency head and delegated broad authority regarding acquisition functions. *(FAR 2.101)*

contracting agency
Any department, agency, establishment, or instrumentality in the executive branch of the federal government, including any wholly-owned government corporation, that enters into contracts. *(GOAT)*

contracting office
(1) An office that awards or executes a contract for supplies or services and performs post-award functions not assigned to a contract administration office. This term includes any contracting office that the acquisition is transferred to, such as another branch of the U.S. federal agency or another agency's office that is performing a joint acquisition action. *(FAR 2.101; FAR 48.001)*
Contrast with *contract administration office* (CAO).
(2) An office that performs contract management. *(CMBOK)*

contracting officer (CO; KO)
(1) An individual who, by appointment in accordance with applicable regulations, has the authority to enter into a federal agency procurement contract on behalf of the government and to make determinations and findings with respect to the contract. *(41 U.S.C. 2101(1))*
(2) A person with the authority to enter into, administer, and/or terminate contracts and make related determinations and findings. The term includes certain authorized representatives of the contracting officer acting within the limits of their authority as delegated by the contracting officer. "Administrative contracting officer (ACO)" refers to a contracting officer who is administering contracts. "Termination contracting officer (TCO)" refers to a contracting officer who is settling terminated contracts. *(FAR 2.101)*
See also *administrative contracting officer* (ACO); *contracting officer's representative* (COR); *termination contracting officer* (TCO).

contracting officer's representative (COR)
(1) An individual, including a contracting officer's technical representative (COTR), designated and authorized in writing by the contracting officer to perform specific technical or administrative functions. *(FAR 2.101)*
(2) A qualified individual appointed by the contracting officer to assist in the technical monitoring or administration (i.e., inspection, acceptance) of a contract. *(CMBOK)*
See *contracting officer* (CO; KO).

Contracting Officer's Representative Tracking (CORT) Tool
A tool used by the DOD to electronically track contracting officer's representative nominations, appointments, terminations, and training certifications for service contracts. *(DPAP)*
See *contracting officer's representative* (COR).

contracting officer's technical representative (COTR)
See *contracting officer's representative* (COR).

contracting out
The process by which a government activity contracts with private enterprise (as opposed to performing work in-house) for commercial or industrial products or services. *(OPM)*
See also *cost comparison; service contract.*

contractor (KR; Kr; KTR; Ktr)
(1) A seller having a contract (commitment) to provide specific supplies or services. *(CMBOK; SPP)*
(2) Any individual or other legal entity that—
- Directly or indirectly (e.g., through an affiliate) submits offers for or is awarded, or reasonably may be expected to submit offers for or be awarded, a U.S. federal government contract, including a contract for carriage under government or commercial bills of lading, or a subcontract under a government contract; or
- Conducts business, or reasonably may be expected to conduct business, with the federal government as an agent or representative of another contractor.

(FAR 9.403)
(3) For subcontracting requirements, the total contractor organization or a separate entity of it, such as an affiliate, division, or plant, that performs its own purchasing. *(FAR 44.101)*
(4) Includes a subcontractor at any tier whose subcontract is subject to the provisions of the Service Contract Labor Standards statute (41 U.S.C. Chapter 67). *(FAR 22.1001)*
See *Service Contract Labor Standards statute.*

(5.) Includes the terms "prime contractor" and "subcontractor." *(GOAT)*
See *prime contractor; subcontractor*.

contractor-acquired property (CAP)

Property acquired, fabricated, or otherwise provided by the contractor for performing a contract and to which the federal government has title. Contractor-acquired property that is subsequently delivered and accepted by the government for use on the same or another contract is considered "government-furnished property." *(FAR 45.101)* (See also FAR 45.402.)
See also *government-furnished property* (GFP).

contractor acquisition team

Contractor members of the acquisition team. *(GOAT)*
See *acquisition team; contrast with government acquisition team*.

contractor-approved supplier

A supplier that does not have a contractual agreement with the original component manufacturer for a transaction, but has been identified as trustworthy by a contractor or subcontractor. *(DFARS 202.101)*

contractor attributional/proprietary information

Information that identifies the contractor(s), whether directly or indirectly, by the grouping of information that can be traced back to the contractor(s) (e.g., program description, facility locations), personally identifiable information, as well as trade secrets, commercial or financial information, or other commercially sensitive information that is not customarily shared outside of the company. *(DFARS 204.7301)*
See *controlled unclassified information* (CUI)*; proprietary information*.

contractor bid or proposal information

In a federal government context, any of the following information submitted to a federal agency as part of or in connection with a bid or proposal to enter into a federal agency procurement contract, if that information has not been previously made available to the public or disclosed publicly:
- Cost or pricing data (as defined by 10 U.S.C. 2306a(h) with respect to procurements subject to that section and Section 304A(h) of the Procurement statute (41 U.S.C. Div. C of Subtitle I) with respect to procurements subject to that section);
- Indirect costs and direct labor rates;

- Proprietary information about the Committee for Purchase from People Who Are Blind or Severely Disabled statute (41 U.S.C. Chapter 85), manufacturing processes, operations, or techniques marked by the contractor in accordance with applicable law or regulation;
- Information marked by the contractor as "contractor bid or proposal information" in accordance with applicable law or regulation; and
- Information marked by the contractor as "contractor bid or proposal information" in accordance with FAR 52.215-1(e).

(FAR 3.104-1; CMBOK) (See also FAR 52.215-1(e).)

contractor business systems

For the purposes of covered contracts with the DOD that are subject to the Cost Accounting Standards under 41 U.S.C. Chapter 15, this term includes the following systems:
- Accounting system (if the contract includes the clause at DFARS 252.242-7006),
- Earned value management system (if the contract includes the clause at DFARS 252.234-7002),
- Estimating system (if the contract includes the clause at DFARS 252.215-7002),
- Material management and accounting system (if the contract includes the clause at DFARS 252.242-7004),
- Property management system (if the contract includes the clause at DFARS 252.245-7003), and
- Purchasing system (if the contract includes the clause at DFARS 252.244-7001).

(DFARS 252.242-7005)
See *"acceptable" contractor business systems; significant deficiency*; see also **business system**.

contractor cost data report

A contractual report that provides a consistent, disciplined, historical database for use in cost estimate/cost analysis studies. *(AFIT)*

contractor disclosure program

A program for Department of Defense contractors to submit disclosures in response to FAR 52.203-13, "Contractor Business Ethics Compliance Program and Disclosure Requirements." The program—
- Furnishes contractors with a "means of reporting certain violations of criminal law and violations of the civil False Claims Act discovered during self-policing activities";
- Offers a "framework for government verification of

the matters disclosed";
- Affords "an additional means for a coordinated evaluation of administrative, civil, and criminal actions" suitable to the situation; and
- Gives contractors the ability to "report suspected counterfeit parts or non-conforming parts through the submission of a contractor disclosure."
(See https://www.dodig.mil/Programs/Contractor-Disclosure-Program; see also DFARS 203.1003.)

contractor determination of commerciality for subcontracts
In a DOD context, contractors are responsible to make decisions about whether subcontracts meet the definition of commercial items. In doing so, they are expected to exercise reasonable business judgement. *(GACI)*

contractor employee
An employee of a firm or individual under contract or subcontract to the federal government, designated as providing services or support to the government. *(DODM 1000.13-M-VI)*
See also *employee of an agency*.

contractor financing
The provision of capital to a contractor through equity capital, private financing, customary progress payments, guaranteed loans, unusual progress payments, or advance payments. *(OPM)*
See *contract financing*; see also *advance payment; guaranteed loan; liquidation; progress payment*.

contractor-furnished equipment (CFE)
Standard items of hardware, electrical equipment, and other standard production or commercial items furnished by a prime contractor as part of a larger assembly. *(DAAT)*

contractor inventory
(1) Any raw materials, works in progress, or completed goods that are in the possession of the seller. *(CMBOK)*
(2) Any property acquired by and in the possession of a contractor or subcontractor under a contract for which title is vested in the buyer and which exceeds the amounts needed to complete full performance under the entire contract;
any property that the buyer is obligated or has the option to take over under any type of contract—e.g., as a result either of any changes in the specifications or plans thereunder or of the termination of the contract (or subcontract thereunder)—before completion of the work,

for the convenience or at the option of the buyer; and buyer-furnished property that exceeds the amounts needed to complete full performance under the entire contract.
(FAR 45.101)

contractor management
In a federal government context, the oversight and integration of contractor personnel and associated equipment providing support to government operations. *(DDMAT)*

contractor managerial personnel
A contractor's directors, officers, managers, superintendents, or equivalent representatives who have supervision or direction of:
- All or substantially all of the contractor's business,
- All or substantially all of the contractor's operation at any one plant or separate location, or
- A separate and complete major industrial operation.
(FAR 45.101)

contractor-owned, contractor-operated (COCO) facility
A facility owned and operated by a private contractor performing a service, under contract, for the buyer. *(AFIT)*

contractor performance assessment report (CPAR)
A detailed document that presents the performance and tasks a seller has performed for an organization. The report provides a record, both positive and negative, of a seller's performance on a given contract during a specific period of time, and it assesses how well the seller addressed the organization's needs, how well the budget was utilized, and the general outcome from the seller's work in comparison to the expectations set forth in the contract. Each assessment is based on objective facts and supported by program and contract management data, such as cost performance reports, customer comments, quality reviews, technical interchange meetings, financial solvency assessments, construction/production management reviews, contractor operation reviews, functional performance evaluations, and earned contract incentives. *(DGBCT)*
See also *Contractor Performance Assessment Reporting System* (CPARS)

Contractor Performance Assessment Reporting System (CPARS)
The federal government's evaluation reporting tool for all

Cc

past performance reports on contracts and orders. It is the government's policy for past performance evaluations to be prepared at least annually and at the time the work under a contract or order is completed (as specified in FAR 42.1502(b)–(f)), including for contracts and orders performed outside the United States, and all past performance information is required to be entered into the CPARS. Also referred to as "contractor performance assessment reports," these evaluations are generally for the entity, division, or unit that performed the contract or order. Data from the Past Performance Information Retrieval System (PPIRS) has been merged into the CPARS, making the CPARS—effective January 15, 2019—the official system for past performance information. *(FAR 42.1502(a))* See also *Past Performance Information Retrieval System* (PPIRS).

contractor purchasing system review (CPSR)
(1) The complete evaluation of a contractor's purchasing of material and services, subcontracting, and subcontract management from development of the requirement through completion of subcontract performance. *(FAR 44.101)* (See also FAR 44.301 and FAR 44.302.)
(2) An evaluation of the efficiency and effectiveness with which the prime contractor spends government funds and complies with government policy when subcontracting. *(CMBOK)*

contractor team arrangement (CTA)
A relationship between two or more sellers for the express purpose of conducting business together. *(CMBOK)*

contractor teaming agreement (CTA)
(1) An arrangement in which two or more companies form a partnership or joint venture to act as a potential prime contractor. (Also referred to as a "contractor team arrangement" (CTA).) *(FAR 9.601)*
(2) An arrangement where a potential prime contractor agrees with one or more other companies to have them act as its subcontractors under a specified U.S. federal government contract or acquisition program. *(FAR 9.601)*
See *joint venture*.

contractor's development and implementation costs
In value engineering, those costs the contractor incurs on a value engineering change proposal (VECP) specifically in developing, testing, preparing, and submitting the VECP, as well as those costs the contractor incurs to

make the contractual changes required by the federal government's acceptance of a VECP. *(FAR 48.001)* See *value engineering change proposal* (VECP).

contractor's headquarters
The highest organizational level from which executive compensation costs are allocated to federal government contracts. *(FAR 31.205-6(p)(1)(iv))*

contractor's managerial personnel
See *contractor managerial personnel*.

contractor's plant
Includes, but is not limited to, government-owned contractor-operated plants, federal installations, and federal and non-federal industrial operations, as may be required under the scope of the contract. *(FAR 2.101)*

Contracts for the International Sale of Goods (CISB)
See *Convention on Contracts for the International Sale of Goods* (CISB).

contracts with commercial organizations
All contracts and contract modifications for supplies, services, or experimental, developmental, or research work negotiated with organizations other than educational institutions, construction and architectural/engineering contracts, state and local governments, and nonprofit organizations on the basis of cost. *(GOAT)*

contribution
A concept, suggestion, or idea presented to the federal government for its use with no indication that the source intends to devote any further effort to it on the government's behalf. *(FAR 15.601)*

control account (CA)
The assignment of lower-level work segments to responsible lower-level managers, which provides a key management point for planning and control. It represents the portion of work scope (i.e., a single work breakdown structure element) assigned to one responsible organizational element. The control account identifies the plan for work task accomplishment; defines the effort required; identifies elements of cost (labor, material, etc.); and estimates the resources required to do the work. The control account is the minimum level where technical, schedule, and budget responsibility exists. It is also the minimum level where the budgeted cost for work scheduled (BCWS), actual cost of work

Cc

performed (ACWP), and budgeted cost for work performed (BCWP) values are compared for performance analysis. *(EVMIG; NDIA)*
See *earned value management* (EVM); see also *actual cost of work performed* (ACWP)*; budgeted cost for work performed* (BCWP)*; budgeted cost for work scheduled* (BCWS).

control account manager (CAM)
A single manager within the project organizational structure that has the authority and responsibility to manage one or more control accounts. *(NDIA II)*
See *control account* (CA).

control account plan (CAP)
Represents the work assigned to one responsible organizational element on one program work breakdown structure element. This is the lowest level in the structure at which the comparison of actual costs to planned budgets and earned value is required. It is also the cost collection point that identifies the cost elements with the factors contributing to cost and/or schedule variances. *(NDIA)*

control chart
A chart showing sequential or time-related performance of a process that is used to determine when the process is operating in or out of statistical control using control limits defined on the chart. *(DGCQI)*

control limit
A statistically derived limit for a process that indicates the spread of variations attributable to chance variation in the process. Control limits are based on averages. *(DGCQI)*

controlled space
In the case of an information system, the three-dimensional space surrounding information system equipment, within which unauthorized individuals are denied unrestricted access and are either escorted by authorized individuals or are under continuous physical or electronic surveillance. *(CNSSI 4009)*

controlled substance
A drug or other substance, or immediate precursor, included in schedules I through V of Section 202 of the Controlled Substances Act (21 U.S.C. 812), and as further defined in regulation at 21 CFR 1308.11-1308.15. *(FAR 23.503)*

controlled technical information
Technical information with military or space application that is subject to controls on the access, use, reproduction, modification, performance, display, release, disclosure, or dissemination. This term does not include information that is lawfully publicly available without restrictions. *(DFARS 204.7301)*
See also *technical information*.

controlled unclassified information (CUI)
Information the federal government creates or possesses, or that an entity creates or possesses for or on behalf of the government, that a law, regulation, or governmentwide policy requires or permits an agency to handle using safeguarding or dissemination controls. However, CUI does not include classified information or information a non-executive branch entity possesses and maintains in its own systems that did not come from, or was not created or possessed by or for, an executive branch agency or an entity acting for an agency. *(32 CFR 2002.4(h))* (See also FAR 4.1903; FAR 52.204-21; *DFARS* Subpart 204.73; DFARS 252.204-7008; DFARS 252.204-7012; and EO 13556.)
See also *covered defense information; covered contractor information system; federal contract information; contrast with classified information*.

Controlled Unclassified Information (CUI) Program
The executive branch-wide program to standardize CUI handling by all federal agencies. The program includes the rules, organization, and procedures for CUI, established by Executive Order 13556; 32 CFR 2002; and the CUI Registry. *(32 CFR 2002.4(n))* (See also FAR 4.1903; FAR 52.204-21; *DFARS* Subpart 204.73; DFARS 252.204-7008; and DFARS 252.204-7012.)
See *controlled unclassified information* (CUI).

convenience termination
See *termination for convenience*.

Convention on Contracts for the International Sale of Goods (CISG)
The United Nations Convention on Contracts for the International Sale of Goods (CISG) is a uniform international sales law governing the formation of international sales contracts and the rights and obligations of the buyer and seller. The CISG applies automatically to all contracts for the sale of goods between traders from two different countries that have both ratified the CISG. Also referred to as the "Vienna Convention." *(NES-94)*

Cc

See *United Nations Convention on Contacts for the International Sale of Goods* (CISG).

conversion from contract (to in-house performance)
In a federal government context, the change of a commercial activity from performance by contract with a commercial source to performance by federal employees with government resources. It also includes the conversion of expansions and/or new requirements (work) from contract performance to in-house performance. *(OMB A-76)*
See also *"conversion to contract" (from in-house performance)*.

conversion to contract (from in-house performance)
In a federal government context, the change of performance of an activity from in-house performance by federal employees to performance by a commercial source. *(OMB A-76)*
See *cost comparison*; see also *"conversion from contract" (to in-house performance)*.

conviction
A judgment or conviction of a criminal offense by any court of competent jurisdiction, whether entered upon a verdict or a plea, and includes a conviction entered upon a plea of *nolo contendere*. *(FAR 2.101)* (See also FAR 25.503.)
See also *final conviction; nolo contendere*.

cooperative agreement
Cooperative agreements and grants are a means of providing federal government assistance. The cooperative agreement differs from the grant because the sponsoring federal agency is involved, collaboratively, in management of the undertaking, and because cooperative agreements are often established with private enterprise organizations. Such agreements may provide for sharing the cost as well as management of the undertaking. *(GPM)* (See also FAR 35.003(a))
See *federal assistance; grant*.

cooperative arrangement
An arrangement in which one or more organizations work jointly with one or more separate entities pursuant to an enforceable arrangement (e.g., joint ventures, limited partnerships, teaming agreements/arrangements, and collaboration and consortium arrangements). *(FAR 31.205-18(e)(1))*

cooperative development
Any method by which governments cooperate to make better use of their collective research and development resources to include technical information exchange, harmonizing of requirements, co-development, interdependent research and development, and agreement on standards. *(DOD-MMH)*

cooperative purchasing
A means of combining buying power through consolidated purchasing *(CMBOK)*

cooperative research and development
A method by which two or more organizations or governments cooperate to make better use of their collective research and development resources, to include technical data exchanges and co-development of new systems. *(DISCS)*
See also *cooperative research and development agreement*.

cooperative research and development agreement
Any agreement between one or more U.S. federal laboratories and one or more nonfederal parties under which the government, through its laboratories, provides personnel, services, facilities, equipment, intellectual property, or other resources with or without reimbursement (but not funds to nonfederal parties) and the nonfederal parties provide funds, personnel, services, facilities, equipment, intellectual property, or other resources toward the conduct of specified research or development efforts that are consistent with the missions of the laboratory. This term does not include a procurement contract or cooperative agreement. *(15 U.S.C. 3710a(d)(1))*
See also *cooperative research and development*.

Copeland Anti-Kickback Act
See *Kickbacks statute*.

coproduction
A program implemented by a government-to-government or commercial licensing arrangement which enables a foreign government or firm to acquire the know-how to manufacture or assemble, repair, maintain, and operate, in whole or in part, an item. *(DISCS)*

copyright
Notwithstanding fair use and other limitations on exclusive rights, this term refers to the exclusive legal rights of the creator of an intellectual production for its

Cc

use and distribution. Copyright protection is granted to original works of authorship fixed in any tangible medium of expression, now known or later developed, from which they can be perceived, reproduced, or otherwise communicated, either directly or with the aid of a machine or device. For works copyrighted after 1978, the copyright is valid for the life of the author plus an additional 70 years. *(BLD; 17 U.S.C. 102(a))*

core capability
A commercial activity operated by a cadre of highly skilled employees in a specialized technical or scientific development area to ensure that a minimum capability is maintained. The "core capability" does not include the skills, functions, or full-time equivalent employees that may be retained in-house for reasons of national defense, including military mobilization, security, or rotational necessity; patient care; or research and development activities. *(OMB A-76)*

corporate administrative contracting officer (CACO)
Contractors with more than one operational location (e.g., division, plant, or subsidiary) often have corporate-wide policies, procedures, and activities requiring U.S. federal government review and approval and affecting the work of more than one administrative contracting officer (ACO). In these circumstances, effective and consistent contract administration may require the assignment of a "corporate administrative contracting officer" (CACO) to deal with corporate management and to perform selected contract administration functions on a corporate-wide basis. *(FAR 42.601)*
See *administrative contracting officer* (ACO).

corporate responsibility and personal conduct
Laws and standards governing both corporate and individual behavior, including standards of ethics and conduct, social responsibility, law, regulation, and public policy. *(DGBCT)*

corporate surety
A surety licensed under various insurance laws and, under its charter, has legal power to act as surety for others. *(FAR 2.101)*
See *surety*.

cost(s)
(1) The amount or equivalent paid or charged for something. *(MW)*

(2) The amount of funds expended in acquiring a product or obtaining a service. *(CMBOK; ASPM)*
(3) Notwithstanding the meaning in (2) of this definition, "costs" may include direct and indirect initial costs plus any periodic or continuing costs for operation and maintenance. *(AIMD)*
(4) That which is not price or profit. *(CMBOK)*
(5) In a federal government context, refers to "allowable costs" (in accordance with *FAR*, Part 31) in effect on the date of a contract. *(GOAT)*
See *allowable cost*.
(6) (*As a verb*)—To require expenditure or payment (*intransitive*), or to have a price of (*transitive*). *(MW)*

cost account
See *control account*.

cost accounting
A system of accounting analysis and reporting on production costs of goods or services, or operation costs of programs, activities, functions, or organizational units. This term includes cost estimating, determination of cost standards based on engineering data, and/or comparison of actual and standard costs for the purpose of aiding cost control. Also known as "management accounting" and *managerial accounting*. *(OPM)*

cost accounting practice
Any disclosed or established accounting method or technique that is used for allocation of costs to cost objectives, assignment of costs to cost accounting periods, or measurement of cost. *(GOAT)*

Cost Accounting Standards (CAS)
The CAS consist of nineteen standards promulgated by the Cost Accounting Standards Board (CASB) designed to ensure uniformity and consistency in the measurement, assignment and allocation of costs to contracts with the United States Government. CAS covers a variety of costs such as depreciation, pension plans, personal compensation, indirect costs and other areas of cost accounting. *(DAU)* (See also *FAR* Part 30.)
See *Cost Accounting Standards Board* (CASB); see also *cost accounting standards-covered contract*.

Cost Accounting Standards Board (CASB)
An independently established statutory board within the federal government. The CASB has the exclusive authority to make, promulgate, and amend cost accounting standards and interpretations designed to achieve uniformity and consistency in the cost accounting practices

Cc

governing the measurement, assignment, and allocation of costs to contracts with the United States. *(41 U.S.C. 1501, et seq. (*formerly 41 U.S.C. 422))*
See *Cost Accounting Standards* (CAS).

Cost Accounting Standards Board (CASB) disclosure statement
A written description of a contractor's cost accounting practices and procedures. *(48 CFR 9903.202-1(a)))*
See *Cost Accounting Standards* (CAS); *Cost Accounting Standards Board* (CASB).

cost allocability
A cost is "allocable" if it is assignable or chargeable to one or more cost objectives on the basis of relative benefits received or other equitable relationship, and if it:
* Is incurred specifically for the contract;
* Benefits both the contract and other work, and can be distributed to them in reasonable proportion to the benefits received; or
* Is necessary to the overall operation of the business, although a direct relationship to any particular cost objective cannot be shown.

(FAR 31.201-4)

cost analysis
(1) As opposed to "price analysis," refers to the process of reviewing and evaluating any separate cost elements and profit or fee in an offeror's proposal—and of the judgmental factors applied in projecting from the data to the estimated costs—to determine the degree to which the offeror's proposed costs represent what the cost of contract performance should cost, assuming reasonable economy and efficiency. The value added by this process is the buyer's ability to ascertain a fair and reasonable price and/or determine the realism of the price in preparation for contract negotiations, discussions, and for reducing risk in contract performance. In the context of the CMS™, this is in the "award" life cycle phase of contract management, within the "form contract" domain. *(CMS)*
Compare with *price analysis*; see also *award life cycle phase*; *Contract Management Standard™ Publication (CMS™)*; *form contract*.
(2) Cost analysis is the review and evaluation of any of the separate cost elements and profit or fee in an offeror's or contractor's proposal as needed to determine a fair and reasonable price or to determine cost realism, and the application of judgment to determine how well the proposed costs represent what the cost of the contract should be, assuming reasonable economy and efficiency. *(FAR 15.404-1(c))*

cost as an independent variable (CAIV)
A methodology used to acquire and operate affordable systems by setting aggressive, achievable life cycle cost objectives and managing achievement of these objectives by trading off performance and schedule as necessary. *(DAAT)*

cost avoidance
An action taken in the immediate time frame that will decrease costs in the future. For example, an engineering improvement that increases the mean time between failures and thereby decreases operation and maintenance costs is a cost avoidance action. *(OMB A-131)*

cost-benefit analysis
A technique used to compare the various costs associated with an investment with the benefits that it proposes to return. Both tangible and intangible factors should be accounted for and addressed in a cost-benefit analysis. *(AIMD)*

cost center
(1) The smallest unit of activity or area of responsibility for which costs are accumulated. *(NCMA-CA)*
(2) Any subdivision of an organization comprised of workers, equipment areas, activities, or combination of these that is established for the purpose of assigning or allocating costs. Cost centers are also used as a base for performance standards. Also known as "burden center" and *cost pool*. *(DOD-MMH)*

cost comparison
The process whereby the estimated cost of government performance of a commercial activity is formally compared, in accordance with the principles and procedures of OMB Circular A-76 and Supplement, to the cost of performance by commercial or inter-service support agreement sources. *(OMB A-76)*

cost contract
(1) A contract that provides for payment to the contractor of allowable costs, to the extent prescribed in the contract, incurred in performance of the contract. *(DISCS)*
(2) A cost-reimbursement contract in which the contractor receives no fee. A cost contract may be appropriate for research and development work, particularly with nonprofit educational institutions or other nonprofit organizations. *(FAR 16.302(a)-(b))*
See *cost-reimbursement contract*; see also *cost-sharing contract*.

Cc

cost-effectiveness

A systematic, quantitative method for comparing the costs of alternative means of achieving the same stream of benefits or a given objective. *(GOAT)*

cost element

See *element of cost* (EOC).

cost estimate

A judgment or opinion regarding the cost of an object, commodity, or service that results from an estimating procedure that specifies the expected dollar cost required to perform a stipulated task or to acquire an item. A cost estimate may constitute a single value or a range of values. *(DAAT)*

cost estimating

A set of techniques used to aid in the process of forecasting expected costs, as related to goods or services, for budgetary purposes. *(CMBOK; 48 CFR 9904.401-30(3))*

cost estimating relationship (CER)

A type of secondary comparison used in performing price analysis. CERs are used to adjust comparisons by establishing a common denominator between different items. For example, dollars per pound, per foot, or per loaded labor hour are yardsticks to measure a relationship between offers. *(NCMA-WS)*
See *secondary comparison*.

cost growth

A term related to the net change of an estimated or actual amount over a base figure previously established. The base must be relatable to a program, project, or contract and be clearly identified—including source, approval authority, specific items included, specific assumptions made, date, and the amount. *(DAAT)*

cost incentives

A type of incentive that often takes the form of a profit or fee adjustment formula within an incentive-type contract. Cost incentives are intended to motivate the seller to effectively manage costs over the course of a contract. Most incentive contracts include only cost incentives. *(FAR 16.402-1)*
See *incentive contract*; see also *cost-plus-incentive-fee* (CPIF) *contract*.

cost input

The cost, except general and administrative expenses, which for contract costing purposes is allocable to the production of goods and services during a cost accounting period. *(FAR 31.001)*

cost objective

A function, organizational subdivision, contract, or other work unit for which cost data are desired and for which provisions are made to accumulate and measure the cost of processes, products, jobs, capitalized projects, etc. *(FAR 31.001)* (See also *FAR* Subpart 31.6.)

cost of capital

Under the net-present-value method, a manager determines some minimum desired rate of return. This minimum rate is often called "cost of capital." All expected future cash flows are discounted to the present using this minimum desired rate. If the result is zero or positive, the project is desirable, and if negative, it is undesirable. *(IMA)*

cost of capital committed to facilities

An imputed cost determined by applying a cost of money rate to facilities capital. *(GOAT)*
See also *cost of money; facilities capital; facilities capital cost of money* (FCCM).

cost of components

See *component costs*.

cost of goods sold

(1) Inventoriable costs released to the current period (i.e., an expense) as a result of the sale of goods. *(NCMA-CA)*
(2) Direct costs of producing finished goods for sale. *(STBP)*

cost of money

An imputed cost that is not a form of interest on borrowings. It is also an "incurred cost" for cost-reimbursement purposes under applicable cost-reimbursement contracts and for progress payment purposes under fixed-price contracts. Specifically, this term refers to facilities capital cost of money (48 CFR 9904.414) and the cost of money as an element of the cost of capital assets under construction (48 CFR 9904.417). *(FAR 31.205-10(a))*

cost or price evaluation

Information used to evaluate what the proposed offer will most likely cost the buyer. Cost/price should not be scored or rated. Examples include cost/price reason-

ableness, cost/price realism, life cycle cost, and cost risk. When contracting on a cost-reimbursement basis, evaluations include a cost realism analysis to determine what the buyer should realistically expect to pay for the proposed effort, the offeror's understanding of the work, and the offeror's ability to perform the contract. *(DGBCT)*
See also *cost analysis; price analysis*.

cost or price negotiation objectives
Goals for contract action cost or price. Without an overall price objective, negotiations will often flounder and result in settlements that can be neither explained nor defended. *(GOAT)*

cost or pricing data
All facts that, as of the date of price agreement or, if applicable, an earlier date agreed upon between the parties that is as close as practicable to the date of agreement on price, prudent buyers and sellers would reasonably expect to affect price negotiations significantly. Cost or pricing data are factual, not judgmental, and are verifiable. While they do not indicate the accuracy of the prospective contractor's judgment about estimated future costs or projections, they do include the data forming the basis for that judgment. Cost or pricing data are more than historical accounting data; they are all the facts that can be reasonably expected to contribute to the soundness of estimates of future costs and to the validity of determinations of costs already incurred. They also include, but are not limited to, such factors as:
- Seller quotations,
- Nonrecurring costs,
- Information on changes in production methods and in production or purchasing volume,
- Data supporting projections of business prospects and objectives and related operations costs,
- Unit-cost trends such as those associated with labor efficiency,
- Make-or-buy decisions,
- Estimated resources to attain business goals, and
- Information on management decisions that could have a significant bearing on costs.

(FAR 2.101)
See *certified cost or pricing data*; see also *cost or pricing data threshold*.

cost or pricing data index
An offeror listing of all cost or pricing data and information accompanying or identified in a proposal. It

includes any supplemental additions and/or revisions up to the date of agreement on price, or an earlier date agreed upon by the parties. *(GOAT)*
See *cost or pricing data*.

cost or pricing data submission
In federal government contracting, the requirement for submission of cost or pricing data is met when all accurate cost or pricing data reasonably available to the offeror have been submitted, either actually or by specific identification, to the contracting officer or an authorized representative. *(FAR 15.408 Table 15-2)*
See *cost or pricing data*.

cost or pricing data threshold
In federal government contracting, the threshold for obtaining cost or pricing data—as listed at *FAR* Part 15—for new contracts. The threshold for each existing contract is specified in the contract. *(FAR 15.403-4(a)(1))*

cost overrun
(1) The amount by which a seller exceeds the estimated cost and/or the final limitation (ceiling) of the contract. *(DAAT)*
(2) A net change in contractual amount beyond that contemplated by a contract target price (fixed-price-incentive contract), estimated cost plus fee (any cost-reimbursable contract), or redeterminable price (fixed-price-redeterminable contract) due to the contractor's actual costs being over target or anticipated contract costs. *(OPM)*

cost performance index (CPI)
A measure of the cost efficiency relative to the performance of tasks and completion of those tasks. It is calculated by dividing the budgeted cost for work performed (BCWP) by the actual cost of work performed (ACWP) (i.e., BCWP ÷ ACWP = CPI). A value greater than "1" is favorable; a value less than "1" is unfavorable (i.e., CPI > 1.0 = under budget; CPI < 1.0 = over budget). It may be expressed as a value for a specific time period or cumulative to date. *(NDIA II; PMPM)*

cost performance report
A monthly, contractually required report procured by the government program manager from the contractor to obtain data from the contractor's management system. It provides the status of progress made on the contract, is usually in a standard format, and is used in the program manager's decision-making process. *(DSMC)*

cost-plus-a-percentage-of-cost (CPPC) contract

A contract type that bases the seller's fee on the amount of funds it expends. Thus, the fee paid to the seller rises as the seller's costs rise. Because this type of contract provides no incentive for the seller to control costs, it is rarely used. Per FAR 16.102(c), a cost-plus-a-percentage-of-cost "system" of contracting is prohibited in federal government contracting. *(CMBOK)*

cost-plus-award-fee (CPAF) contract

(1) A cost-reimbursement type contract with special incentive fee provisions used to provide motivation for excellence in contract performance in such areas as quality, timeliness, ingenuity, and cost-effectiveness. *(CMBOK)*
See also *cost incentives; incentive contract*.
(2) In federal government contracting, a cost-reimbursement contract that provides for a fee consisting of:
- A base amount (which may be zero) fixed at inception of the contract, if applicable and at the discretion of the contracting officer; and
- An award amount that the contractor may earn in whole or in part during performance (based upon a judgmental evaluation by the federal government) and that is sufficient to provide motivation for excellence in the areas of cost, schedule, and technical performance.

(FAR 16.305; 16.405-2)
See *cost-reimbursement contract*.

cost-plus-fixed-fee (CPFF) contract

A cost-reimbursement contract that provides for payment to the seller of a negotiated fee that is fixed at the inception of the contract. The fixed fee does not vary with actual cost, but it may be adjusted as a result of changes in the work to be performed under the contract. This contract type permits contracting for efforts that might otherwise present too great a risk to contractors, but it provides the contractor only a minimum incentive to control costs. *(FAR 16.306(a))*
See *cost-reimbursement contract*; see also *cost incentives; incentive contract*.

cost-plus-incentive-fee (CPIF) contract

A cost-reimbursement contract that provides for the initially negotiated fee to be adjusted later by a formula based on the relationship of total allowable costs to total target costs. This contract type specifies:
- A target cost,
- A target fee,

- Minimum and maximum fees, and
- A fee adjustment formula.

After contract performance, the fee payable to the seller is determined in accordance with the formula. The formula provides, within limits, for increases in fee above target fee when total allowable costs are less than target costs, and for decreases in fee below target fee when total allowable costs exceed target costs. This increase or decrease is intended to provide an incentive for the seller to manage the contract effectively. When total allowable cost is greater than or less than the range of costs within which the fee-adjustment formula operates, the seller is paid total allowable costs, plus the minimum or maximum fee. *(FAR 16.405-1)*
See *cost-reimbursement contract*; see also *cost incentives; incentive contract*.

cost pool

See *cost center*.

cost principles

The regulations that establish rules and policies relating to the general treatment of costs in federal government contracts, particularly the allowability of costs. *(GCG)*
See *allocable costs; allowable costs*; see also *cost principles for contracts with commercial organizations; cost principles for contracts with educational institutions; cost principles for contracts with nonprofit organizations; cost principles for contracts with state, local, and federal recognized Indian tribal governments*.

cost principles for contracts with commercial organizations

Found at FAR 31.2, principles for determining the allowable costs of contracts and contract modifications for supplies, services, or experimental, developmental, or research work negotiated with organizations other than educational institutions, construction and architect-engineer contracts, state and local governments, and nonprofit organizations on the basis of cost. *(FAR 31.103)* (See also *FAR* Subpart 31.2.)
See *cost principles*; see also *cost principles for contracts with educational institutions; cost principles for contracts with nonprofit organizations; cost principles for contracts with state, local, and federally recognized Indian tribal governments*.

cost principles for contracts with educational institutions

Found at FAR 31.3, principles for determining the allowable costs of contracts and contract modifications

Cc

for research and development, training, and other work performed by educational institutions (defined as institutions of higher education in the OMB's "Uniform Administrative Requirements, Cost Principles, and Audit Requirements for Federal Awards" at 2 CFR Part 200, Subpart A, and 20 U.S.C. 1001). *(FAR 31.104)* (See also *FAR* Subpart 31.3.)

See *cost principles*; see also *cost principles for contracts with commercial organizations; cost principles for contracts with nonprofit organizations; cost principles for contracts with state, local, and federally recognized Indian tribal governments; OMB Uniform Guidance*.

cost principles for contracts with nonprofit organizations

Found at FAR 31.7, principles and standards for determining the costs applicable to contracts with nonprofit organizations other than educational institutions, state and local governments, and those nonprofit organizations exempted under the OMB's "Uniform Administrative Requirements, Cost Principles, and Audit Requirements for Federal Awards" (at 2 CFR Part 200, Appendix VIII). *(FAR 31.108)* (See also *FAR* Subpart 31.7.)

See *cost principles*; see also *cost principles for contracts with commercial organizations; cost principles for contracts with educational institutions; cost principles for contracts with state, local, and federally recognized Indian tribal governments; OMB Uniform Guidance*.

cost principles for contracts with state, local, and federally recognized Indian tribal governments

Found at FAR 31.6, principles and standards for determining costs applicable to contracts with state, local, and federally recognized Indian tribal governments. *(FAR 31.107)* (See also *FAR* Subpart 31.6.)

See *cost principles*; see also *cost principles for contracts with commercial organizations; cost principles for contracts with educational institutions; cost principles for contracts with nonprofit organizations*.

cost proposal

The instrument required of an offeror for the submission or identification of cost or pricing data by which an offeror submits to the buyer a summary of estimated (or incurred) costs, which are suitable for detailed review and analysis. *(CMBOK, STBP)*

cost realism

This term means that the costs in an offeror's proposal—
- Are realistic for the work to be performed,
- Reflect a clear understanding of the requirements, and
- Are consistent with the various elements of the offeror's technical proposal.

(FAR 2.101)

See also *cost realism analysis*.

cost realism analysis

The process of independently reviewing and evaluating specific elements of each offeror's proposed cost estimate to determine whether the estimated proposed cost elements are:
- Realistic for the work to be performed,
- Reflect a clear understanding of the requirements, and
- Are consistent with the unique methods of performance and materials described in the offeror's technical proposal.

In federal government contracting, cost realism analyses are required to be performed on cost-reimbursement contracts to determine the probable cost of performance for each offeror. Cost realism analyses may also be used on competitive fixed-price contracts or, in exceptional cases, on other competitive fixed-price-type contracts when new requirements may not be fully understood by competing offerors, there are quality concerns, or past experience indicates that sellers' proposed costs have resulted in quality or service shortfalls. Results of the analysis may be used in performance risk assessments and responsibility determinations; however, proposals are required to be evaluated using the criteria in the solicitation, and the offered prices are prohibited from being adjusted as a result of the analysis. *(FAR 15.404-1(d)(1)–(3))* See *cost realism*.

cost reasonableness

A cost is "reasonable" if, in its nature and amount, it does not exceed that which would be incurred by a prudent person in the conduct of competitive business. Reasonableness of specific costs must be examined with particular care in connection with firms or their separate divisions that may not be subject to effective competitive restraints. No presumption of reasonableness shall be attached to the incurrence of costs by a contractor. If an initial review of the facts results in a challenge of a specific cost by the contracting officer or the contracting officer's representative, the burden of proof shall be upon the contractor to establish that such cost is reasonable. *(FAR 31.201-3(a))*

Cc

cost reimbursement (CR)
Payment of allowable incurred costs, to the extent prescribed in the contract. *(FAR 16.301-1)*

cost-reimbursement contract
A contract type that provides for payment of allowable incurred costs, to the extent prescribed in the contract. These contracts establish an estimate of total cost for the purpose of obligating funds and establishing a ceiling that the seller may not exceed (except at its own risk) without the approval of the buyer. Types of cost-reimbursement contracts include:
- Cost contracts,
- Cost-sharing contracts,
- Cost-plus-incentive-fee (CPIF) contracts,
- Cost-plus-award-fee (CPAF) contracts, and
- Cost-plus-fixed-fee (CPFF) contracts.

(FAR 16.301-1)

cost-reimbursement incentive contract
A cost-reimbursement type contract that incorporates an incentive arrangement based on contractor performance. The two types of cost-reimbursement incentive contracts are:
- Cost-plus-incentive-fee (CPIF) contracts, and
- Cost-plus-award-fee (CPAF) contracts.

(FAR 16.405)
See *cost-reimbursement contract; incentive contract*; see also *cost-plus-award-fee* (CPAF) *contract; cost-plus-incentive-fee* (CPIF) *contract*.

cost risk
(1) An assumption of possible monetary loss or gain in light of the job or work to be done. Cost risk is an element to be considered in the negotiation of a fair and reasonable price, as well as in the determination of contract type. *(OPM)*
(2) In program management, the risk that a program will not meet its acquisition strategy cost objectives that were developed using cost as an independent variable or cost objectives established by the acquisition authority. *(DAAT)*
See also *cost as an independent variable* (CAIV).

cost savings
A reduction in actual expenditures below the projected level of costs to achieve a specific objective. *(DAAT; OMB A-131)*

cost/schedule control systems criteria (C/SCSC)
A method of project management previously used by the federal government that has since been replaced by the ANSI Standard 748 earned value management system in many agencies.
See *earned value management system* (EVMS).

cost sharing
An explicit arrangement under which the seller bears some of the burden of reasonable, allocable, and allowable contract cost. *(FAR 2.101; CMBOK)*

cost-sharing contract
A cost-reimbursement contract in which the contractor receives no fee and is reimbursed only for an agreed-upon portion of its allowable costs. A cost-sharing contract may be used when the contractor agrees to absorb a portion of the costs, in the expectation of substantial compensating benefits. *(FAR 16.303(a)-(b))*
See *cost-reimbursement contract; cost contract*.

cost-type contract
See *cost-reimbursement contract*.

cost variance (CV)
(1) The difference between planned and actual costs for completed work. It is a true measure of cost performance as it compares the actual cost incurred to the value of work accomplished. It eliminates the distortions that are inherently present in a simple comparison of actual costs to a total budget when work is being performed ahead of or behind schedule. *(NDIA; PMPM)*
(2) An output of the earned value management system that measures cost overrun or cost underrun relative to the program performance measurement baseline. It is equal to the difference between budgeted cost of work performed (BCWP) and actual cost of work performed (ACWP); that is, CV = BCWP - ACWP. (A negative result indicates the contract is over budget.) *(DAAT; PMPM)*
See *earned value management system* (EVMS); *see also actual cost of work performed* (ACWP); *budgeted cost of work performed* (BCWP).

cost-volume-profit analysis
An examination of the relationship between revenue, fixed cost, variable cost, and profit. *(GOAT)*
See also *break-even analysis*.

cost-volume-profit equation
Used in cost-volume-profit analysis. In the equation,

revenue is equal to fixed cost plus variable cost plus profit. *(GOAT)*
See *cost-volume-profit analysis*.

costs of idle facilities or idle capacity

Costs such as maintenance, repair, housing, rent, and other related costs (e.g., property taxes, insurance, and depreciation). *(FAR 31.205-17(a))*
See also *facilities; idle capacity; idle facilities*.

cosurety

One of two or more sureties that are jointly liable for the penal sum of the bond. A limit of liability for each surety may be stated. *(FAR 2.101)*
See *surety*.

counterfeit

(1) In general, something made in imitation of a genuine article (e.g., an item or document) without authorization and especially with intent to deceive or defraud. *(MW)*
(2) An item that is an unauthorized copy or substitute that has been identified, marked, or altered by a source other than the item's legally authorized source and has been misrepresented to be an authorized item of the legally authorized source. *(DAAT)*

counteroffer

(1) An offer made in response to an original offer that proposes changes to the terms of the original offer. In making a counteroffer, the offeree rejects the original offer. *(CMBOK; FBL; RSOC 39(1))*
(2) In federal government contracting, the non-acceptance of the government's offer to buy as presented. In this context, a "counteroffer" introduces a new condition, item, quantity, or quality, or it varies from the original terms in the government's offer. Counteroffers by suppliers under sealed-bid procedures are rejected. However, under negotiated procedures (including small purchases), counteroffers are permissible and may be negotiated; e.g., a purchase order is only an offer to buy and the terms of acceptance may be negotiated. *(SPP)*

counter-purchase

A form of countertrade that occurs when a firm agrees to purchase a specified dollar volume of materials from a country in return for a sale made to that country. *(GKPT)*

countertrade

A requirement imposed by a country on a foreign exporter or supplier to purchase materials in the re-

ceiving country as part of the original sales transaction. Payment is made either partially or fully with goods instead of money. *(NES-94)*

course of dealing

A sequence of conduct concerning previous transactions between the parties to a particular transaction that is fairly to be regarded as establishing a common basis of understanding for interpreting their expressions and other conduct. *(UCC 1-303(b))*
See also *course of performance; usage of trade*.

course of performance

A sequence of conduct between the parties to a particular transaction that exists if:
- The agreement of the parties with respect to the transaction involves repeated occasions for performance by a party, and
- The other party, with knowledge of the nature of the performance and opportunity for objection to it, accepts the performance or acquiesces in it without objection.

(UCC 1-303(a))
See also *course of dealing; usage of trade*.

Court of Appeals for the Federal Circuit
See *U.S. Court of Appeals for the Federal Circuit*.

Court of Claims
See *United States Court of Federal Claims* (COFC).

cover

After a breach, the buyer may "cover" by making—in good faith and without unreasonable delay—any reasonable purchase of or contract to purchase goods in substitution for those due from the seller. *(UCC 2-712)*

covered agency

The federal government agency subject to the requirements (of the particular statute, regulation, etc.) at issue, or on behalf of which the requirements call for some action to take place.

covered area

(1) The geographical area described in a solicitation for a contract.
(2) Effective, January 1, 2020, a geographical area that the SBA has designated in approving a petition submitted by a state governor for HUBZONE designation of an area within their state. Also called a "Governor-Designated Covered Area."

Cc

covered contract

A contract that is subject to the requirements (of the particular statute, regulation, etc.) at issue. For example, in the context of the Cost Accounting Standards (CAS), a "covered contract" is one that is subject to the CAS. See also *Cost Accounting Standards* (CAS).

covered contractor information system

(1) In the context of safeguarding federal government information within contractor information systems, an information system that is owned or operated by a contractor and that processes, stores, or transmits federal contract information. *(FAR 4.1901)*
See also *controlled unclassified information* (CUI); *federal contract information; information system* (IS).
(2) In the context of safeguarding covered defense information, means an unclassified information system that is owned, or operated by or for, a contractor that processes, stores, or transmits covered defense information. *(DFARS 204.7301)*
See *covered defense information; controlled unclassified information* (CUI).

covered defense information

Unclassified controlled technical information or other information (as described in the Controlled Unclassified Information (CUI) Registry) that requires safeguarding or dissemination controls pursuant to and consistent with law, regulations, and governmentwide policies, and is–
- Marked or otherwise identified in the contract, task order, or delivery order and provided to the contractor by or on behalf of the DOD in support of the performance of the contract; or
- Collected, developed, received, transmitted, used, or stored by or on behalf of the contractor in support of the performance of the contract.

(DFARS 204.7301)
See *controlled unclassified information* (CUI).

covered employee

In the context of preventing personal conflicts of interest for contractor employees performing acquisition functions, an individual who performs an acquisition function closely associated with inherently governmental functions and is:
- An employee of the contractor, or
- A subcontractor that is a self-employed individual treated as a covered employee of the contractor because there is no employer to whom such an individual could submit the required disclosures.

(FAR 3.1101)
See also *personal conflict of interest* (PCI).

covered federal action

In the context of the inappropriate use of appropriated funds to influence certain federal contracting and financial transactions, refers to any of the following actions:
- Awarding any federal contract,
- Making any federal grant,
- Making any federal loan,
- Entering into any cooperative agreement, and/or
- Extending, continuing, renewing, amending, or modifying any federal contract, grant, loan, or cooperative agreement.

(FAR 3.801)

covered funds

In the context of whistleblower protections under the American Recovery and Reinvestment Act of 2009 (*Pub. L. 111-5*), any contract payment, grant payment, or other payment received by a contractor if:
- The federal government provides any portion of the money or property that is provided, requested, or demanded; and
- At least some of the funds are appropriated or otherwise made available by the Recovery Act.

(FAR 3.907-1)
See also *American Recovery and Reinvestment Act of 2009* (ARRA); *qui tam action*

covered information

In the context of whistleblower protections under the American Recovery and Reinvestment Act of 2009 (Pub. L. 111-5), information that the employee reasonably believes is evidence of gross mismanagement of the contract or subcontract related to covered funds, gross waste of covered funds, a substantial and specific danger to public health or safety related to the implementation or use of covered funds, an abuse of authority related to the implementation or use of covered funds, or a violation of law, rule, or regulation related to an agency contract (including the competition for or negotiation of a contract) awarded or issued relating to covered funds. *(FAR 3.907-1)*
See also *American Recovery and Reinvestment Act of 2009* (ARRA); *covered funds*.

covered personnel

In the context of contracts for advisory and assistance services, whether made with individuals or organizations, that involve either personal or nonpersonal

Cc

services, this term refers to:
- An officer or an individual who is appointed in the civil service by one of the following acting in an official capacity:
  - The president of the United States,
  - A member of Congress,
  - A member of the uniformed services,
  - An individual who is an employee (under 5 U.S.C. 2105),
  - The head of a U.S. federal government-controlled corporation, or
  - An adjutant general appointed by the secretary concerned (under 32 U.S.C. 709(c));
- A member of the armed services of the United States; or
- A person assigned to a U.S. federal agency who has been transferred to another position in the competitive service in another agency. *(FAR 37.201)*

cradle-to-grave
The total life cycle of a given system, from concept through development, acquisition, operations phases, and final disposition. Also called "womb-to-tomb." *(DAAT)*

credential
(1) Evidence attesting to one's right to credit or authority. *(FIPS 201-2)*
(2) In the context of information systems security, information, passed from one entity to another, used to establish the sending entity's access rights. *(CNSSI 4009)*

credit authority
In a federal government context, the authority to incur direct loan obligations or to incur primary loan guarantee commitments. *(2 U.S.C. 622(10))*

credit guaranty
In a foreign military sales context, a guaranty to any individual corporation, partnership, or other judicial entity doing business in the United States (excluding U.S. government agencies other than the Federal Financing Bank) against political and credit risks of nonpayment arising out of their financing of credit sales of defense articles and defense services to eligible countries and international organizations. *(DISCS)*

creditor
(1) Includes a general creditor, a secured creditor, a lien creditor, and any representative of creditors, in-cluding an assignee for the benefit of creditors, a trustee in bankruptcy, a receiver in equity, and an executor or administrator of an insolvent debtor's or assignor's estate. *(UCC 1-201(13))*
See also *creditor process; insolvent; representative*.
(2) In the case of a bulk sale, means a claimant or other person holding a claim. *(UCC 6-102(1)(f))*
See also *bulk sale; claimant*.

creditor process
Levy, attachment, garnishment, notice of lien, sequestration, or similar process issued by or on behalf of a creditor or other claimant with respect to an account. *(UCC 4A-502(a))*
See *creditor*.

critical dependencies
The interrelationships existing within or among processes that are primary drivers of defects or errors in a product or service. *(DGCQI)*

critical design review (CDR)
Determines that the detail design satisfies the performance and engineering specialty requirements of the development; that the specification establishes the detail design compatibility among the item and other items of equipment facilities, computer programs, and personnel; that the detail design assesses producibility and risk areas; and that it reviews the preliminary product specifications. *(DOD-MMH)*

critical infrastructures
Those physical and cyber-based systems essential to the minimum operations of the economy and government. *(CNSSI 4009)*

critical item
(1) A subsystem, component, material, or other item that could seriously jeopardize the successful completion of program requirements if not available when required during the procurement/production. *(DSMC)*
(2) An item that could have an adverse impact on cost, schedule, quality, and/or technical performance specifications. *(DSMC)*

critical nonconformance
A nonconformance with a contract's quality and/or quantity requirements that is likely to result in hazardous or unsafe conditions for individuals using, maintaining, or depending upon the supplies or services; or is likely to prevent performance of a vital U.S. federal

agency mission. *(FAR 46.101)*
See *contract quality requirements*; see also *major nonconformance; minor nonconformance; patent defect*.

critical path
The longest continuous sequence of tasks driving project completion, such that a delay on any task on the critical path will result in a corresponding delay to the end of the project. *(NDIA II)*
See *critical path method* (CPM).

critical path method (CPM)
A technique that aids understanding the interdependency of events in a project and the time required to complete them. It is used to predict project duration by analyzing which sequence of activities, or "path," has the least amount of scheduling flexibility, thus increasing the need for management attention. Activities that, when delayed, have an impact on the total project schedule are "critical" and said to be on the "critical path." *(DAAT; NDIA II)*
See *total float* (TF).

critical path scheduling
A tool that can be used to manage project buying activities, construction projects, research and development projects, etc. The critical path approach quantifies information about uncertainties faced by the activities responsible for meeting a predetermined time schedule. The process of analyzing these uncertainties focuses the manager's attention on the most critical series of activities in the total project—i.e., those that constitute the "critical path." *(DBL)*

critical process
A structured set of key practices that, when performed collectively, contributes to the attainment of a goal. *(AIMD)*

critical subcontract
A subcontract, the failure of which seriously jeopardizes the successful completion of a program within cost, schedule, quality, and/or technical performance specifications. *(DSMC)*

critical success factors
Indicators developed by a customer that indicate the defect-free character of a product or service. *(DGCQI)*

critical technology
In the context of national security, a technology that is either a "national critical technology" or a "defense critical technology." *(10 U.S.C. 2500(6))*
See *defense critical technology; national critical technology*.

critical-value analysis
A modification of the "ABC analysis" concept in which the subjective value of criticalness, as opposed to the actual dollar value, is assigned to each inventory item. *(GKPT)*
See also *ABC analysis*.

cross-cutting risk
A risk that is generally applicable to multiple mission execution efforts, with attributes and impacts found in multiple levels of the organization or in multiple organizations within the same level. *(NID 8000-108)*

cross-servicing
In a military context, that function performed by one military service in support of another military service for which reimbursement is required from the service receiving support. *(DISCS)*

crypto-algorithm
A well-defined procedure or sequence of rules or steps, or a series of mathematical equations used to describe cryptographic processes such as encryption/decryption, key generation, authentication, signatures, etc. *(CNSSI 4009)*

cryptocurrency
A digital asset constructed to function as a medium or exchange, premised on the technology of cryptography, to secure the transactional flow, as well as to control the creation of additional units of the currency. *(CBTR)*
See *blockchain*.

cryptographic
Pertaining to, or concerned with, cryptography. *(CNSSI 4009)*
See *cryptography*.

cryptographic key
See *key*.

cryptography
An art or science concerning the principles, means, and methods for rendering plain information unintelligible and for restoring encrypted information to intelligible form. *(CNSSI 4009)*
See *encryption*.

cryptosystem

Associated information security items interacting to provide a single means of encryption or decryption. *(CNSSI 4009)*
See *information systems security* (INFOSEC).

cumulative discount

A variation of quantity discount that is based on the quantity purchased over a specified period of time, rather than being computed on the size of a single order placed at one time. This type of discount is commonly offered by suppliers as an incentive to a purchasing firm for continued or increased patronage. *(GKPT)*

cure notice

(1) In the case of a termination for default on a government contract, the contracting officer is required to give the contractor written notice specifying the failure and providing a period of at least 10 days in which to cure the failure. Upon expiration of the period, the contracting officer may issue a notice of termination for default unless the failure to perform has been cured. *(FAR 49.402(d).*
(2) Notice issued to a contractor by a buyer to inform the contractor that the buyer considers the contractor's failure to make progress or perform any other contract provision a serious risk to successful performance/completion of the contract. *(CMBOK)*
See *default termination*; see also *show cause notice*.

current fiscal year (CFY)

The fiscal year in progress, but not yet completed. For the U.S. federal government, between and including October 1 and September 30. *(DISCS)*
See also *budget year* (BY); *current year*.

current year (CY)

The fiscal year in progress. *(DISCS)*
See also *budget year* (BY).

current year dollars

Dollar values of a given year that include the effects of inflation or escalation for that year, or which reflect the price levels expected to prevail during the year at issue. Also known as escalated dollars or "then-year dollars." *(DISCS)*
See also *constant dollar values; constant year dollars*.

customary contract financing

Financing deemed by a federal agency to be available for routine use by contracting officers. Most customary contract financing arrangements should be usable by contracting officers without specific reviews or approvals by higher management. *(FAR 32.001)*
Contrast with *unusual contract financing*.

customer

(1) Anyone for whom an organization provides goods or services. *(DGCQI)*
(2) In the private sector, those who pay or exchange value for products or services. *(DGBCT)*
(3) An individual, group of individuals, or organizational entity for whom the product or service is rendered. *(AIMD)*
(4) *Synonymous with* "end user." *(AIMD)*
See *end user*.
(5) In a federal government context, "customers" consist of, but are not limited to:
- The taxpayers,
- Taxpayer representatives in Congress,
- The sponsors of the agency,
- The managers of an agency program, and
- The recipients of the agency's products and services.

(DGBCT)
See also *stakeholder*.

customer service

Interaction with the designated end users of the contracted products and services. Includes actions to resolve customer complaints and facilitates use of products or access to services. *(DGBCT)*

customs territory of the United States

The 50 U.S. states, the District of Columbia, and Puerto Rico. *(FAR 2.101)*

cyber incident

See *incident*.

cybersecurity

A condition that results from the establishment and maintenance of protective measures that enable an enterprise to perform its mission or critical functions despite risks posed by threats to its use of information systems. Protective measures may involve a combination of deterrence, avoidance, prevention, detection, recovery, and correction that should form part of the enterprise's risk management approach. *(NIST SP 800-171)*

Dd

cybersecurity incident
See *incident*.

cyberspace
A global domain within the information environment consisting of the interdependent network of information technology infrastructures and resident data, including the internet, telecommunications networks, computer systems, and embedded processors and controllers. *(DDMAT)*

cycle count
A physical stock checking system in which the inventory is divided into 52 equal groups, one of which is physically counted each week. Thus, the physical inventory operation goes on continuously without interrupting operations or storeroom activities. Also called *continuous inventory*. *(GKPT)*

cycle stock
The active portion of an inventory; i.e., that part of inventory that is depleted through regular withdrawals or use and is replenished through repetitive orders. *(GKPT)*

cycle time
In a purchasing context, the period of time in replenishment cycle required to order and make available the required stock (e.g., the time between receipt of the requisition and delivery of the material to the requisitioner). *(GKPT)*

D

damage limitation clause
The limit of liability on a contract for the party that is caused by neglect or other cause. *(BLD)*

damages
(1) In general, refers to—
- A pecuniary compensation or indemnity, which may be recovered in the courts by any person who has suffered loss, detriment, or injury, whether to his person, property, or rights, through the unlawful act or omission or negligence of another; or
- A sum of money assessed by a jury, on finding for the plaintiff or successful party in an action, as a compensation for the injury done him by the opposite party.

(BLD)

See *consequential damages; incidental damages*.
(2) In a purchasing context, compensation of a specific value, determined by a court, to be paid for loss or injury suffered by one party to a contract as a result of the other contractual party's breach of the contract. *(GKPT)*
See also *liquidated damages*.

data
Recorded information, regardless of form or the media on which it may be recorded. This term includes technical data and computer software, but does not include information incidental to contract administration—such as financial, administrative, cost or pricing, or management information. *(FAR 27.401)*

data documentation costs
Costs of converting source data to the documents prescribed in the contract for delivery to the buyer. *(AFIT)*

data encryption standard (DES)
A cryptographic algorithm designed for the protection of unclassified data and published by the National Institute of Standards and Technology (NIST) in Federal Information Processing Standard (FIPS) "Publication 46." *(CNSSI 4009)*

data flow control
Synonymous with "information flow control."
See *information flow control*.

data integrity
A condition existing when data is unchanged from its source and has not been accidentally or maliciously modified, altered, or destroyed. *(CNSSI 4009)*
See also *data security*.

data item description (DID)
A completed form that defines the data required of a contractor. Data item descriptions specifically define the data content, preparation instructions, format, and intended use. *(DODM 4120.24)*

data management
Use of commercially available software tools to manage contract information, including repositories for contract documents, reporting systems, contracting process management, and portfolio management. *(DGBCT)*

data origin authentication
The process of corroborating that the source of the data is as claimed. *(CNSSI 4009)*

Dd

data other than certified cost or pricing data

Pricing data, cost data, and judgmental information necessary for the contracting officer to determine a fair and reasonable price or to determine cost realism. Such data may include the identical types of data as certified cost or pricing data, but without the certification. The data may also include, for example, sales data and any information reasonably required to explain the offeror's estimating process, including, but not limited to:

- The judgmental factors applied and the mathematical or other methods used in the estimate, including those used in projecting from known data; and
- The nature and amount of any contingencies included in the proposed price.

(FAR 2.101)
Compare with *certified cost or pricing data*; see also *cost realism; fair and reasonable price*.

data requirements review board

A board appointed by a responsible manager to assist and advise in the determination of data requirements. *(AFIT)*

data rights

(1) Rights of ownership of data under any contract. *(DGBCT)*
See *"Data Rights"/"Rights in Data" clause*; see also *copyright; patent; trade secret*.
(2) In federal government contracting, the government recognizes rights in data developed at private expense, and limits its demands for delivery of such data. When such data are delivered, the government will acquire only those rights essential to its needs. There are four types of rights the government can obtain for use of data developed under federal contracts:

- Unlimited rights,
- Limited rights,
- Restricted rights (which apply only to computer software), and
- Government purpose license rights.

(DGBCT)
See *"Data Rights"/"Rights in Data" clause; government purpose license rights (GPLR); limited rights; restricted rights; unlimited rights*.

"Data Rights"/"Rights in Data" clause

A contract provision, negotiated between the parties, identifying who owns the rights to data developed under the contract. *(DGBCT)*
See *data rights*.

Data Universal Numbering System (DUNS) number

The DUNS number is a unique nine-digit identifier for businesses, and it is the "first step" to register with the federal government's System for Award Management (SAM). Also known as a unique entity identifier, Dun & Bradstreet is the organization which assigns them for "business credit monitoring and tracking purposes." (See https://www.unitedstatesbusinessregistration.us/duns-number-unique-entity-identifier.)
See *System for Award Management* (SAM); *unique entity identifier*.

data security

Protection of data from unauthorized (i.e., accidental or intentional) modification, destruction, or disclosure. *(CNSSI 4009)*
See also *data integrity*.

database

A collection of recorded information in a form capable of, and for the purpose of, being stored in, processed, and operated on by a computer or other compatible information system. This term *does not* include computer software. Also called *computer database*. *(FAR 2.101)*
See *software*.

database management system (DBMS)

Software that organizes, catalogs, locates, retrieves, and maintains data in a database. *(F&F)*

Davis-Bacon Act (DBA)

See *Wage Rate Requirements (Construction) statute*.

DAWIA Certification

The procedure through which a military service or DOD component determines that an employee meets the education, training, and experience standards required for a career level in any acquisition, technology, and logistics career field. There are three levels of DAWIA Certification (i.e., "Level I," "Level II," and "Level III"), which are assigned based upon the workforce member's acquisition position. *(10 U.S.C. 1701(a); 10 U.S.C. 1748)*
See *Defense Acquisition Workforce Improvement Act (DAWIA)*

day

(1) Unless otherwise specified, a calendar day. *(FAR 2.101)*

(2) In the computation of any time period, "day" means:
- The day of the act, event, or default from which the designated period of time begins to run is not included; and
- The last day after the act, event, or default is included unless—
  - The last day is a Saturday, Sunday, or U.S. federal holiday; or
  - In the case of a filing of a paper at any appropriate administrative forum, the last day is a day on which weather or other conditions cause the closing of the forum for all or part of the day, in which event the next day on which the appropriate administrative forum is open is included.

(FAR 33.101)

de facto

A Latin term meaning "in fact," "in deed," or "actually." This phrase is used to characterize a position, entity, place, object, action, or state of affairs which currently exists and must be accepted for all practical purposes, but which, for all intents and purposes, is not "official"—its acceptance is typically due to a lack of an officially mandated position, entity, place, object, action, or state of affairs. *(BLD)*

de facto standards

Widely recognized standards that have gained widespread acceptance in the marketplace, but which have not been "officially" sanctioned by any international, national, or government organization. Because they are (usually) not formally documented by an accepted standards-developing organization, *de facto* standards should *not generally* be used in federal government contracting. *(NES-97)*
See *standard*.

de novo

A Latin term meaning "over again," or "as if for the first time." This phrase is typically used in legal proceedings where a previous action is conducted once again, usually to determine the adequacy/accuracy of when it was conducted the first time. For example, lower court decisions are generally "subject to *de novo* review at the next level" or higher.

debarment

Action taken by a debarring official to exclude a contractor from federal government contracting and government-approved subcontracting for a reasonable, specified period. The following are some causes for debarment:

- Conviction of or civil judgment for any offense indicating a lack of business integrity (e.g., fraud, antitrust violations, theft, bribery, etc.);
- Violation of the terms of a government contract so serious as to justify debarment;
- Violations of the Drug-Free Workplace statute (41 U.S.C. Chapter 81); or
- Any other cause of so serious or compelling a nature that it affects the present responsibility of a government contractor or subcontractor.

(FAR 2.101; 9.406-2)

Compare with *suspension*; see also *Consolidated List of Debarred, Suspended, and Ineligible Contractors; debarred; debarring official; Drug-Free Workplace statute*.

debarred

Means to be excluded from federal government contracting and government-approved subcontracting for a reasonable, specified period. *(FAR 2.101)*
See *debarment*.

debarring official

An agency head or a designee authorized by the agency head to impose debarment. *(FAR 9.403)*
See *debarment*.

debrief(ing)

In federal government contracting, offerors excluded from the competitive range or otherwise excluded from the competition may request a "pre-award debriefing" before award or, at the offeror's request, this debriefing may be delayed until after award (in which case, the debriefing will include all information normally provided in a post-award debriefing). Otherwise, should the offeror receive notification of contract award to another offeror, the unsuccessful offeror may, upon timely written request to the awarding agency, request a "post-award debriefing." *(FAR 15.505(a)(1)-(2); FAR 15.506(a)(1))*
See *pre-award debriefing; post-award debriefing*.

debt

(1) In a law or business context, means the common-law action for the recovery of money held to be due. "Debt" is a liability, meaning that the lender has a claim on a company's assets. Debt due within one year is generally classified as "short-term debt" on a company's balance sheet. Debt due in more than one year is considered "long-term debt." *(MW)*
(2) Liability on a claim. *(UCC 6-102(1)(i))*
See also *claim*.

Dd

debt bondage

The status or condition of a debtor arising from a pledge by the debtor of his or her personal services or of those of a person under his or her control as a security for debt, if the value of those services as reasonably assessed is not applied toward the liquidation of the debt or the length and nature of those services are not respectively limited and defined. *(FAR 22.1702)*

debt capital

Capital that is raised by borrowing (as by issuing bonds or securing loans). *(MW)*
See *capital*.

debtor

In the context of secured transactions, this term refers to any of the following:

- A person having an interest, other than a security interest or other lien, in the collateral, whether or not the person is an obligor;
- A seller of accounts, chattel paper, payment intangibles, or promissory notes; or
- A consignee.

(UCC 9-102(a)(28))
See also *new debtor; original debtor*.

decentralization of purchasing

Occurs when personnel from other functional areas outside of purchasing—production, engineering, marketing, finance, etc.—decide on sources of supply, negotiate with vendors directly, or perform any of the other major functions of purchasing. *(DBL)*
Compare with *centralization of purchasing*.

declared value

See *released value*.

decoupling inventory

Inventory retained to make possible the independent control of two operations. (Sometimes referred to as "line-balancing stock.") *(GKPT)*

decrement factor

(1) A percentage used to indicate the relative differences between a proposed price and a recommended, "should-pay" price. *(GOAT)*
(2) A percentage by which a subcontract reduces its subcontract price if, for example, the prime contractor purchases more than a specified amount of supplies. *(GOAT)*

deductive change

A change resulting in a reduction in contract price because of a net reduction in the contractor's work. *(GCG)*

default

(1) The actual or anticipated failure of a seller to fulfill the terms and conditions of the contract, thus giving the buyer the right to terminate the contract. *(CMBOK; NES-89)*
See *termination for default* (T4D).
(2) The failure to perform a legal obligation or duty. *(FBL)*
See *anticipatory default; anticipatory repudiation*.

default termination

See *termination for default* (T4D).

defect

(1) The absence of something necessary for completeness or perfection. *(BLD)*
(2) A deficiency in something essential to the proper use for the purpose for which a thing is to be used. *(BLD)*
(3) Some structural weakness in a part or component that is responsible for damage. *(BLD)*
(4) Any condition or characteristic in any supplies or services furnished by the seller under the contract that is not in compliance with the requirements of the contract. *(CMBOK; GOAT)*
See *latent defect; patent defect*.

defective certification

With respect to a claim, a certificate that alters or otherwise deviates from the language in the *FAR* or that is not executed by a person duly authorized to bind the seller with respect to the claim. Failure to certify shall not be deemed to be a defective certification. *(FAR 33.201; CMBOK)*

defective cost or pricing data

Certified cost or pricing data subsequently found to have been inaccurate, incomplete, or not current as of the date of final agreement on price or an earlier date agreed upon by the parties given on the contractor's or subcontractor's certificate of current cost or pricing data. *(OPM)*

defective pricing action

If after contract award, cost or pricing data relied upon by the procuring contracting officer are found to be inaccurate, incomplete, or not current as of the date of final agreement on price given on the contractor's or

Dd

subcontractor's certificate of current cost or pricing data, the federal government is entitled to a price adjustment, including profit or fee, of any amount by which the price was increased because of the defective data. *(HCS)*

defective specifications
Mistakes and omissions in the requirements set forth are generally identified in this way. This area is frequently the basis for claims and litigation between contracting parties. *(HECA)*

defendant
Includes a person in the position of defendant in a counterclaim, cross-claim, or third-party claim. *(UCC 1-201(14))*

Defense Acquisition Circular (DAC)
Circular that is issued to revise or supplement the *Defense Federal Acquisition Regulation Supplement*. *(GCG)*

defense acquisition executive (DAE)
The under secretary of defense for acquisition & sustainment (as of February 1, 2018) who has responsibility for supervising the defense acquisition system. The defense acquisition executive takes precedence on all acquisition matters after the secretary of defense and the deputy secretary of defense. *(DODD 5000.01)* See *defense acquisition system*.

Defense Acquisition Regulation (DAR)
The regulation that governed DOD procurements directly before the *FAR* became effective in 1984. Today, DOD procurements are governed by the *Federal Acquisition Regulation*, as supplemented by the *Defense FAR Supplement*. *(GSFC)*

Defense Acquisition Regulation System (DARS)
The DARS develops and maintains acquisition rules and guidance to facilitate the DOD acquisition workforce as they acquire goods and services. *(DAAT H)*

Defense Acquisition Regulatory Council (DARC)
Overseen by the DOD, the DARC is comprised of representatives from each U.S. military branch, the Defense Logistics Agency, and NASA. Among other responsibilities, this council, along with the Civilian Agency Acquisition Council, maintain the *FAR*. *(FAI)* (See also FAR 1.201.)
See *Civilian Agency Acquisition Council* (CAAC)

Defense Acquisition Workforce Improvement Act (DAWIA)
A federal law (10 U.S.C. Chapter 87, *et seq.*) requiring the DOD to establish policies and procedures for the effective management (including accession, education, training, and career development) of persons serving in acquisition positions in DOD. *(10 U.S.C. 1701(a); 10 U.S.C. 1748)*

defense agency
An organizational entity of the Department of Defense—
* That is established by the secretary of defense under Section 191 of Title 10, U.S.C. (or under the second sentence of Section 125(d) of Title 10 (as in effect before October 1, 1986)) to perform a supply or service activity common to more than one military department (other than such an entity that is designated by the secretary as a DOD field activity); or
* That is designated by the secretary of defense as a defense agency. *(10 U.S.C. 101)*

Defense Contract Audit Agency (DCAA)
A separate and independent entity within the DOD that provides contract audit functions and accounting/financial advisory services for all DOD components, as well as for other U.S. federal government agencies. For contractors other than educational institutions and nonprofit organizations, DCAA is normally the agency responsible for performing government contract audits. *(GCG; GOAT)*

Defense Contract Audit Agency Contract Audit Manual (CAM)
An official publication of the Defense Contract Audit Agency (DCAA). It prescribes auditing policies and procedures and furnishes guidance in auditing techniques for personnel engaged in the performance of the DCAA mission. *(DGBCT)*

Defense Contract Management Agency (DCMA)
A DOD component that provides unified contract administration services to DOD components and the U.S. National Aeronautics and Space Administration, working directly with suppliers to help ensure that DOD, federal, and allied government supplies and services are delivered on time, at projected cost, and meet all performance requirements. *(DISCS)*

Dd

defense critical technology

A technology that is identified under 10 U.S.C. 2505 as "critical" for attaining the national security objectives set forth in 10 U.S.C. 2501(a). *(10 U.S.C. 2500(8))*
See also *national critical technology*.

Defense Federal Acquisition Regulation Supplement (DFARS)

Establishes for the DOD uniform policies and procedures that implement the *Federal Acquisition Regulation*, as well as supplementary material that is unique to DOD. The *Defense FAR Supplement* is not a standalone document and must be read in conjunction with the *FAR*. *(HCS)*

defense industrial base

The capability of U.S. industry to respond to the needs of and to produce end items for the DOD. This term also includes that part of the total privately-owned and government-owned industrial production and maintenance capacity located in the United States expected to be available during emergencies to manufacture and repair items required by the U.S. military services. Also referred to as *domestic industrial base*. *(DISCS)*

defense industrial cooperation

U.S. activities performed in conjunction with selected foreign countries, which are intended to stimulate the development of foreign defense industrial capabilities, particularly in emerging technologies, for the mutual benefit of all participants. *(DISCS)*

Defense Logistics Agency (DLA)

A DOD component organization that provides consumable supply items and logistics services common to the military services. It is responsible for approximately 95 percent of consumable items and approximately 85 percent of all spare parts in the DOD supply system. *(DISCS; GCG)*
See also *Defense Logistics Agency Disposition Services; Defense Logistics Agency Logistics Information Service*.

Defense Logistics Agency Disposition Services

An organization with the Defense Logistics Agency that provides redistribution and disposal services for the DOD. The Foreign Military Sales program is one of the many programs qualified to receive DLS Disposition Services property. *(DISCS)*
See *Defense Logistics Agency* (DLA); see also *foreign military sales* (FMS).

Defense Logistics Agency Logistics Information Service

An organization within the Defense Logistics Agency that serves as the U.S. National Codification Bureau and also provides cataloging services in support of allied defense ministries. *(DISCS)*
See *Defense Logistics Agency* (DLA).

Defense Pricing and Contracting (DPC)

The DPC functions within the Office of the Secretary of Defense (OSD) and is "responsible for all pricing, contracting, and procurement policy matters, including e-Business," in the DOD. It is headed by the principal director of defense, pricing and contracting who serves as the "principal advisor to the under secretary of defense for acquisition and sustainment on procurement negotiation strategies for all major weapon systems programs, and major automated information systems." The DPC "executes policy" through timely updates to the *DFARS* and the Procedures, Guidance, and Information (PGI) resource."
See *Procedures, Guidance, and Information* (PGI)

Defense Priorities and Allocations System (DPAS)

The DPAS is "used to prioritize national defense-related contracts/orders throughout the U.S. supply chain." Its purpose is to provide "timely availability of industrial resources." The DPAS supports "military, energy, homeland security, emergency preparedness, and critical infrastructure requirements." It can also be used to deliver "military or critical infrastructure assistance to foreign nations." Rules for the DPAS are found at 15 CFR 700, under the part heading "Defense Priorities and Allocations System."
See *Defense Production Act of 1950, as amended* (DPA)

Defense Production Act of 1950, as amended (DPA)

A federal law (50 U.S.C. App. 2061–2171, *et seq.*) that establishes U.S. policy concerning the ability of the defense industrial base to supply materials and services for the national defense and to prepare for and respond to military conflicts, natural or man-caused disasters, or acts of terrorism within the United States. This law provides the president of the United States with an array of authorities to shape national defense preparedness programs, such as the Defense Priorities and Allocations System, and to take appropriate steps to maintain and enhance the defense industrial base. Under Title I of the DPA, the president is authorized to require preferential acceptance and performance of

Dd

contracts or orders (other than contracts of employment) supporting certain approved national defense and energy programs, and to allocate materials, services, and facilities in such a manner as to promote these approved programs. *(DGBCT; 50 U.S.C. App. 2062(a)(1)-(4))*
See also *defense industrial base; Defense Priorities and Allocations System (DPAS)*

defense service

As defined in Section 644(f) of the Foreign Assistance Act of 1961 (22 U.S.C. 2151, et seq.) and Section 47(4) of the Arms Export Control Act (22 U.S.C. 2751, et seq.), this term includes any service, test, inspection, repair, training, publication, technical or other assistance, or defense information used for the purpose of furnishing military assistance or foreign military sales, but does not include military education and training activities or design and construction services (under Section 29 of the Arms Export Control Act). *(DISCS)*
See *nonstandard service*; see also *Foreign Assistance Act of 1961 (FAA); Arms Export Control Act (AECA)*

defense specification

A document that describes the essential technical requirements for military-unique materiel or substantially modified commercial items. *(DODM 4120.24)*
Contrast with *federal specification*.

defense standard

A document that establishes uniform engineering and technical requirements for military-unique or substantially modified commercial processes, procedures, practices, and methods. *(DODM 4120.24)*
See *standard*.

deferred compensation

An award made by an employer to compensate an employee in a future cost accounting period or periods for services rendered in one or more cost accounting periods before the date of the receipt of compensation by the employee. This definition *does not* include the amount of year-end accruals for salaries, wages, or bonuses that are to be paid within a reasonable period of time after the end of a cost accounting period. *(FAR 31.001)*

deferred procurement

A decision that the initial procurement quantity of high-cost items is to be less than the originally estimated quantity during a specified support period. *(OPM)*

deficiency

A material failure of a proposal to meet a buyer requirement or a combination of significant weaknesses in a proposal that increases the risk of unsuccessful contract performance to an unacceptable level. *(FAR 15.001; CMBOK)*

deficiency report (DR)

In the context of U.S. federal government source selection, a written communication that is issued by the source selection evaluation board through the contracting officer for the purpose of identifying portions of a proposal that, when compared with the pertinent standard, fail to meet the government's minimum level of compliance. *(NCMA-WS)*
See *clarification request*; see also *deficiency; source selection; source selection evaluation board (SSEB)*.

deficit

In a federal government context, the amount by which outlays exceed receipts during a fiscal year. *(2 U.S.C. 622(6))*

definite-quantity contract

A contract that provides for delivery of a definite quantity of specific supplies or services for a fixed period, with deliveries or performance to be scheduled at designated locations upon order. *(FAR 16.502(a))*

definitive contract

Any contract that must be reported to the Federal Procurement Data System (FPDS) other than an indefinite delivery vehicle. (This definition applies only to contracts subject to the FPDS, and is not intended to apply to contracts governed by FAR Part 16.) *(FAR 4.601)*
See also *Federal Procurement Data System (FPDS); indefinite delivery vehicle (IDV)*.

definitization

(1) The agreement on, or determination of, contract terms, specifications, and price, which converts the undefinitized contract action to a definitive contract. *(DFARS 217.7401(b))*
(2) In the context of foreign military sales, the process of tailoring a standard DOD system to the international partner's operational requirements by making adjustments to the item configuration, the type and quantity of spare parts, and the logistics support package. *(DISCS)*

definitize

(1) To make definite. *(CMBOK)*

Dd

(2) A final determination of an agreement, arrangement, or contract, such as about its cost, duration, or scope. *(CMBOK)*
Contract with *undefinitized contractual action* (UCA).

definitized item
An item for which a firm price has been established in the basic contract or by modification. *(DFARS 204.7101)*
Contrast with *undefinitized item*.

deflated hourly rates
See *uncompensated overtime*.

deflation
Decreases in the price for identical or similar items that results in a decrease in purchasing power. *(GOAT)*

delay
See *excusable delay; government-caused delay*.

delegation
Conferring authority, from one government agency or representative to another, to accomplish contract administrative tasks. Such authority may be shared or recalled. *(P&L II)*
See also *delegation of performance of duty*.

delegation of contract administration
See *assignment of contract administration*.

delegation of performance of condition
Where a performance by a person is made a condition of a duty, performance by a person delegated by him or her satisfies that requirement unless the delegation is contrary to public policy or the terms of the agreement. Unless otherwise agreed, an agreement requires performance of a condition by a particular person only to the extent that the obligor has a substantial interest in having that person perform or control the acts required. *(RSOC 319(1)-(2))*
See *delegation*.

delegation of performance of duty
An obligor can properly delegate the performance of his or her duty to another unless the delegation is contrary to public policy or the terms of his or her promise. Unless otherwise agreed, a promise requires performance by a particular person only to the extent that the obligee has a substantial interest in having that person perform or control the acts promised. Unless the obligee agrees otherwise, neither delegation of performance nor a contract to assume the duty made with the obligor by

the person delegated discharges any duty or liability of the delegating obligor. *(RSOC 318(1)-(3))*
See *delegation*.

deliberation
The formal or informal process for communication and collective consideration, by stakeholders designated in the risk management plan, of all pertinent information, especially risk information, in order to support the decision maker. *(NID 8000-108)*

delinquency
The actual or potential failure by the seller to meet or maintain the contract delivery or performance schedule. *(CMBOK; AFIT)*
See *delivery schedule; performance schedule*.

deliverable
An item or service required to be delivered under a contract or other agreement.

deliverable subline item
May be used for several related items that require separate identification. For example, instead of establishing multiple separate line items, subline items may be established for—
- Items that are basically the same, except for minor variations such as size or color; accounting classification; or date of delivery, destination, or period or place of performance;
- Separately priced collateral functions that relate to the primary product, such as packaging and handling, or transportation; or
- Items to be separately identified at the time of shipment or performance.

(FAR 4.1004(a))
See *informational subline item*; see also *contract line item number* (CLIN); *line item; subline item* (SLIN).

delivery
(1) A transfer of possession. *(SPP)*
(2) Includes constructive or actual delivery of articles; also includes the performance of services for the customer or requisitioner, as well as accessorial services, when they are normally recorded in the billing and collection cycle immediately following performance. *(DISCS)*
(3) Applied to shipping, "delivery" occurs when a bill of lading is surrendered and title of goods passes to the receiver or consignee. *(SPP)*
(4) A voluntary transfer of possession of an instrument, document of title, or chattel paper. *(UCC 1-201(15))*

Dd

delivery forecast

A periodic estimate of contract production deliveries used as a measure of the effectiveness of production and supply availability scheduling and as a guide to corrective actions to resolve procurement or production bottlenecks. These forecasts provide estimates of deliveries under obligation against procurement from appropriated or other funds. *(DISCS)*
See also *delivery*.

delivery incentives

Contractually-specified incentives contingent upon some aspect of delivery under a contract or agreement. Delivery incentives should be considered when improvement from a required delivery schedule is a significant objective of the buyer. It is important to determine the buyer's primary objectives in a given contract (e.g., earliest possible delivery or earliest quantity production). *(FAR 16.402-3; CMBOK)*
See *incentive contract*.

delivery order (DO)

(1) An order for supplies placed against an established contract or with government sources. *(FAR 2.101)*
(2) An order for supplies placed against an established contract or with buyer sources. *(CMBOK)*
(3) A written order to a seller pursuant to an indefinite-delivery type contract, which then becomes the basic obligating document for the transaction. *(CMBOK)*
See *indefinite-delivery/indefinite-quantity* (IDIQ) *contract*.
(4) A record that contains an order to deliver goods directed to a warehouse, carrier, or other person that in the ordinary course of business issues warehouse receipts or bills of lading. *(UCC 7-102(a)(5))*

delivery order contract

A contract for supplies that does not procure or specify a firm quantity of supplies (others than a minimum or maximum quantity) and that provides for the issuance of orders for the delivery of supplies during the period of the contract. *(FAR 16.501-1)*

delivery payment

A payment for accepted supplies or services, including payments for accepted partial deliveries. Commercial financing payments are liquidated by deduction from these payments. Delivery payments are invoice payments for prompt payment purposes. *(FAR 32.001)*

delivery schedule

A realistic schedule to meet the delivery requirements of an acquisition. *(FAR 11.401(a))*
See also *performance schedule*.

demand for payment

See *demand for payment of contract debt*.

demand for payment of contract debt

A demand for a refund due the buyer under a contract. (Also called a *demand for payment* or *demand letter*.) *(FAR 32.604)*
See *contract debt*.

demand letter

See *demand for payment of contract debt*.

demilitarization (DEMIL)

In the context of federal government property, to render a product unusable for, and not restorable to, the purpose for which it was designed or is customarily used. *(FAR 45.101)*

demonstration contract

A type of contract for the demonstration phase of a major system acquisition that provides for contractors to submit, by the end of the phase, priced proposals, totally funded by the U.S. federal government, for full-scale development. *(FAR 34.005-4)*
See also *concept exploration contract; full production contract; full-scale development contract*.

demurrage

A fee charged by a carrier against a consignee, consignor, or other responsible party to compensate for the detention of the carrier's equipment (rail car, container, etc.) in excess of allowable free time for loading, unloading, reconsigning, or stopping in transit. This term is also used by suppliers of material delivered in a variety of returnable containers, such as gas cylinders, etc. *(GKPT)*

Department of Defense (DOD) acquisition official

Means:
- DOD contracting officer, or
- Any other DOD official authorized to approve a direct acquisition or an assisted acquisition on behalf of DOD.

(FAR 17.701)

dependent demand

Derived or contingent upon the demand for a component or a finished product; e.g., the demand for axles

Dd

used in the assembly of automobiles is dependent on the demand for the finished automobiles. *(GKPT)*

deposit account
A demand, time, savings, passbook, or similar account maintained with a bank. This term does not include investment property or accounts evidenced by an instrument. *(UCC 9-102(a)(29))*
See *account*; see also *investment property; instrument; negotiable instrument*.

deposition
Testimony that is taken under oath and subject to cross-examination in order to discover what the witness is going to say and to ensure the preservation of the witness' testimony should the witness otherwise be unable to testify at trial. *(FBL)*

depot
In terms of supply, an activity for the receipt, classification, storage, accounting, issue, maintenance, procurement, manufacture, assembly, research, salvage, or disposal of material. *(DDMAT)*

depot-level maintenance
Maintenance performed on material requiring a major overhaul or a complete rebuilding of parts, assemblies, subassemblies, and end items, including the manufacture of parts, modification, testing, and reclamation as required. *(DISCS)*

depot maintenance
Not to be confused with "depot-level maintenance." See *full maintenance*.

depreciation
(1) Amount of expense charged against earnings by an organization to write off the cost of a plant or machine over its useful life, giving consideration to wear and tear, obsolescence, and salvage value. *(STBP)*
(2) A charge to current operations that distributes the cost of a tangible capital asset, less estimated residual value, over the estimated useful life of the asset in a systematic and logical manner. It *does not* involve a process of valuation. *(FAR 2.101)*

descriptive literature
Information provided by an offeror, such as cuts, illustrations, drawings, and brochures, that shows a product's characteristics or construction of a product or explains its operation. This term includes only that information needed to evaluate the acceptability of the product and excludes other information for operating or maintaining the product. *(FAR 2.101)*

descriptive top-level specification
A top-level specification, an informal design notation, or a combination of the two. *(CNSSI 4009)*
See *formal top-level specification*.

design
(1) Turning a concept or idea into a configuration, drawing, model, mold, pattern, plan, or specification on which the actual or commercial production of an item is based, and which helps achieve the item's designated objective(s). *(DGBCT)*
(2) The process that defines a construction requirement (including the functional relationships and technical systems to be used, such as architectural, environmental, structural, electrical, mechanical, and fire protection), producing the technical specifications and drawings, and preparing the construction cost estimate. *(FAR 36.102)*

design-bid-build
The traditional construction delivery method where design and construction are sequential and contracted for separately with two contracts and two contractors. *(FAR 36.102)*
See also *construction; design; design-build*.

design-build
Combining design and construction in a single contract with one contractor. *(FAR 36.102)* (See also *FAR* Subpart 36.3.)
Contrast with *design-bid-build*; see also *two-phase design-build selection procedures*.

design criteria
Design constraints or preferred or accepted techniques to be used in achieving an acceptable approach to a design requirement. *(AFIT)*

design statement of work (design SOW)
Most often used when the buyer requires a specific manufactured good. Design SOWs are extremely detailed, and usually define all required materials, production processes, and specifications such as size, shape, color, tolerances, etc. *(CMBOK)*
See *functional statement of work (functional SOW); performance statement of work (performance SOW)*

Dd

design-to-cost (DTC)
A concept that establishes cost elements as management goals to achieve the best balance between life cycle cost, acceptable performance, and schedule. Under this concept, cost is a design constraint during the design and development phases and a management discipline throughout the acquisition and operation of the system or equipment. *(FAR 2.101)*

designated billing office
The office or person (governmental or nongovernmental) designated in the contract where the contractor first submits invoices and contract financing requests. The contract might designate different offices to receive invoices and contract financing requests. *(FAR 32.001)*
See also *designated payment office*.

designated country
In the context of the federal government's "Buy American" policies, trade agreements, and other laws and regulations governing foreign acquisition, this term refers to any of the following countries:
- A World Trade Organization Government Procurement Agreement country,
- A free trade agreement country,
- A least-developed country, or
- A Caribbean Basin country.

(FAR 25.003) (See FAR 25.003 for *precise list of countries* identified as "designated countries.")
See *Caribbean Basin country; free trade agreement country; least-developed country; World Trade Organization Government Procurement Agreement (WTO GPA) country*.

designated operational area
A geographic area designated by the combatant commander or subordinate joint force commander for the conduct or support of specified military operations. *(FAR 2.101)*
See also *combatant commander* (CCDR).

designated payment office
The office designated in the contract to make invoice payments or contract financing payments. In the context of federal government contracting, this will normally be the government disbursing office. *(FAR 32.001)*
See also *designated billing office*.

desirable change
A compliant change to a contractor's established or disclosed cost accounting practices that the cognizant federal agency official finds is desirable and not detrimental to the federal government and is, therefore, not subject to the increased cost prohibition provisions of Cost Accounting Standards–covered contracts and subcontracts affected by the change. *(FAR 30.001)*
See *Cost Accounting Standards* (CAS); see also *cognizant federal agency official* (CFAO)

desk audit
An examination of limited scope made at a point removed from the site of operations by means of reference to documents and other available information. *(AFIT)*
See *audit*.

detail planning
(1) In earned value management terminology, the action of breaking down the scope, schedule, and budget of a planning package into one or more detailed work packages with earned value techniques. *(NDIA II)*
(2) Notwithstanding the meaning in (1.) of this definition, the action of further breaking down the scope, schedule, and budget of a summary level planning package into one or more control accounts and related work packages/planning packages. *(NDIA II)*

detail specification
See *design specification*.

determination and findings (D&F)
A special form of written approval by an authorized official that is required by statute or regulation as a prerequisite to taking certain contract actions. The "determination" is a conclusion or decision supported by the "findings." The findings are statements of fact or rationale essential to support the determination and must cover each requirement of the statute or regulation. *(FAR 1.701)*

determination of responsibility
The process by which a seller is determined to be a responsible offeror. Also called a responsibility determination. *(CMBOK; OPM)*
See *responsible offeror*.

develop offer
In the context of the *CMS™*, the "develop offer" is one of two domains within the "pre-award" life cycle phase of contract management (the other being "develop solicitation"). It is primarily the domain of the seller. It is the process of—
- Developing foundational business practices and

Dd

strategies to compete in the marketplace, and

- Responding to solicitations with the intent of winning contracts and meeting performance requirements.

The value added by this process is to provide the buyer with a comprehensive solution to the buyer's requirements that enhances the seller's competitive position in the marketplace while delivering customer value. *(CMBOK; CMS)*
See *Contract Management Standard™ Publication (CMS™)*; contrast with *develop solicitation*.

develop solicitation

In the context of the *CMS™*, the "develop solicitation" is one of two domains within the "pre-award" life cycle phase of contract management (the other being "develop offer"). This domain applies to the buyer. It is the process of describing all the elements of the customer requirements (technical, business, regulatory, etc.) to the sellers. The value added by this process is the accurate presentation of the customer requirement through a solicitation in order to create a viable contract that can be performed. *(CMBOK; CMS)*
See *Contract Management Standard™ Publication (CMS™)*; contrast with *develop offer*.

develop win strategy

In the context of the *CMS™*, this is in the "pre-award" life cycle phase of contract management, within the "develop offer" domain. This term refers to the seller organization's ability to execute the business development plan as it assembles an offer to win business. The value added in developing a win strategy is in exploiting and increasing organizational strengths and efficiencies in order to enhance marketplace positioning. *(CMBOK; CMS)*
See *Contract Management Standard™ Publication (CMS™)*; see also *business development*.

development

The systematic use, under whatever name, of scientific and technical knowledge in the design, development, testing, or evaluation of a potential new product or service (or of an improvement in an existing product or service) for the purpose of meeting specific performance requirements or objectives. This term includes the functions of design engineering, prototyping, and engineering testing; it excludes subcontracted technical effort that is for the sole purpose of developing an additional source for an existing product, or development effort for manufacturing or production materials, systems,

processes, methods, equipment, tools, and techniques not intended for sale. *(FAR 31.205-18(a); FAR 35.001)*

deviation

(1) Departing from an established course or standard.
(2) Departing from *Federal Acquisition Regulation* requirements—also called a "*FAR* deviation" or a "deviation from the *FAR*." Deviations from the *FAR* include any one or combination of the following:

- The issuance or use of a policy, procedure, solicitation provision, contract clause, method, or practice of conducting acquisition actions of any kind at any stage of the acquisition process that is inconsistent with the *FAR*;
- The omission of any solicitation provision or contract clause when its prescription requires its use;
- The use of any solicitation provision or contract clause with modified or alternate language that is not authorized by the *FAR*;
- The use of a solicitation provision or contract clause prescribed by the *FAR* on a "substantially as follows" or "substantially the same as," if such use is inconsistent with the intent, principle, or substance of the prescription or related coverage on the subject matter in the *FAR*;
- The authorization of lesser or greater limitations on the use of any solicitation provision, contract clause, policy, or procedure prescribed by the *FAR*; and/or
- The issuance of policies or procedures that govern the contracting process or otherwise control contracting relationships that are not incorporated into agency acquisition regulations in accordance with FAR 1.301(a).

(FAR 1.401(a)-(f))

DFARS

See *Defense Federal Acquisition Regulation Supplement (DFARS)*.

DFARS Business Systems Rule

Also simply called the Business Systems Rule.
See *contractor business systems*.

differing site conditions

A provision in construction contracts that provides for adjustment of the contract price and/or schedule should the contractor discover physical conditions of an unusual nature that differ from those ordinarily encountered. *(GSFC)*
See also *differing site conditions–Category I; differing site conditions–Category II*.

Dd

differing site conditions–Category I

A subsurface or latent physical condition differing materially from conditions that are indicated in the contract documents or that may be implied from other language in the contract documents. *(AGC)*
See *differing site conditions*; see also *differing site conditions–Category II*.

differing site conditions–Category II

Conditions that are unknown and unusual, differing materially from those ordinarily encountered and not generally recognized as inherent in such work. *(AGC)*
See *differing site conditions*; see also *differing site conditions–Category I*.

digital services

The delivery of digital information (i.e., data or content) and transactional services (e.g., online forms, benefits applications) across a variety of platforms, devices, and delivery mechanisms (e.g., websites, mobile applications, and social media). *(OMB M-17-06)*

digital services playbook

An online playbook consisting of thirteen key "plays" drawn from successful practices from the private sector and the federal government that, if followed together, will help government build effective digital services. Also called the "U.S. Digital Services Playbook." *(OMB M-17-06)*
See *digital services*.

digital transmission

A transmission in whole or in part in a digital or other non-analog format. *(17 U.S.C. 101)*

diminishing manufacturing sources and material shortages (DMSMS)

The loss or impending loss of manufacturers of items, suppliers of items, or raw materials needed to support and maintain a system. *(DISCS)*

direct acquisition

A type of interagency acquisition where a requesting agency places an order directly against a servicing agency's indefinite-delivery contract. The servicing agency manages the indefinite-delivery contract but does not participate in the placement or administration of an order. *(FAR 2.101)*
See *interagency acquisition*; compare with *assisted acquisition*; see also *requesting agency; servicing agency*.

direct allocation of salary costs

See *uncompensated overtime*.

direct commercial sale (DCS)

A sale of defense articles or defense services made under a Department of State–issued license by U.S. industry directly to a foreign buyer, and which is not administered by the DOD through foreign military sales procedures. Also simply called a commercial sale. *(DISCS)* (See also DFARS 245.302.)
See also *foreign military sales* (FMS).

direct cost

(1) Any cost that is identified specifically with a particular final cost objective. Direct costs are not limited to items that are incorporated in the end product as material or labor. Costs identified specifically with a contract are direct costs of that contract All costs identified specifically with other final cost objectives of the contractor are direct costs of those cost objectives. *(FAR 2.101)*
(2) Those costs that are assignable to a specific product, primarily classified as "direct labor cost," "direct material cost," or "purchased cost." These costs are usually treated as variable and do not include general overhead or common cost allocations. *(GKPT)*

direct costing

A type of product costing that charges fixed manufacturing overhead immediately against the revenue of the period in which it was incurred, without assigning it to specific units produced. (Also known as *marginal costing* and *variable costing*.) *(NCMA-CA)*

direct labor

(1) In general, a direct cost related to labor. *(CMBOK)*
(2) All labor that is obviously related and specifically and conveniently traceable to specific products. *(NCMA-CA)*
(3) Includes all work required for preparation, processing, and packing of a product, or work directly relating to the performance of a service; but *does not* include supervision, administration, inspection, or shipping. *(41 U.S.C. 8501(3))*
(4) Labor specifically identified with a particular final cost objective. *(CMBOK)*

direct material

Those materials that enter directly into the end product, or that are used or consumed directly in connection with the furnishing of the end product or service. *(FAR 16.601(a))*

Dd

direct offset

A general type of industrial or commercial compensation practice required of a seller by a buyer as a condition for the purchase of goods or services. The form of compensation, which generally offsets a specific percentage of the cost of the purchase, is directly associated with the items purchased, such as the production of components for installation of the purchased end-item. *(DISCS)*

direct procurement

The procurement of defense supplies in the United States by a foreign government, contractor, or organization in which the supplies are purchased through commercial channels for use outside of the United States. *(AFIT)*

direct product profitability

Calculation of the net profit contribution attributable to a specific product or product line. *(GKPT)*

direct selling

Acts or actions to induce particular customers to purchase particular products or services of a seller. It is characterized by person-to-person contact and includes such efforts as familiarizing a potential customer with the seller's products or services, conditions of sale, service capabilities, etc. It also includes negotiation, liaison between customer and seller personnel, technical and consulting efforts, individual demonstrations, and any other efforts having as their purpose the application or adaptation of the seller's products or services for a particular customer's use. *(FAR 31.205-38(b)(5))*
See *selling*.

directed change

Most contracts contain a "Changes" clause that gives the buyer the right to direct changes during contract performance. The clause describes what type of changes the buyer can direct, the procedure for ordering the change, and a provision for equitable adjustment to the contract amount or period of performance if there is a resultant change in cost or schedule. A directed change usually must be within the original scope of the contract. *(FAR 43.205)*
See *"Changes" clause*.

directly affected employees

Employees whose work is being competed in a streamlined or standard competition using the OMB Circular A-76, "Performance of Commercial Activities." *(OMB A-76)*

directly associated cost

Any cost which is generated solely as a result of the incurrence of another cost, and which would not have been incurred had the other cost not been incurred. *(FAR 31.001)*

disabled veteran

(1) A veteran of the U.S. military, ground, naval, or air service, who is entitled to compensation (or who, but for the receipt of military retired pay, would be entitled to compensation) under laws administered by the secretary of Veterans Affairs. *(FAR 22.1301)*
(2) A person who was discharged or released from active duty because of a service-connected disability. *(FAR 22.1301)*

Disaster Response Registry

A voluntary registry of contractors who are willing to perform debris removal, distribution of supplies, reconstruction, and other disaster or emergency relief activities established in accordance with 6 U.S.C. 796, "Registry of Disaster Response Contractors." The registry contains information on contractors who are willing to perform disaster or emergency relief activities within the United States and its outlying areas. The registry is accessed via www.acquisition.gov and alternately through www.fema.gov. *(FAR 2.101)*
See *Robert T. Stafford Disaster Relief and Emergency Assistance Act*.

disbursement

See *gross disbursement; net disbursement*.

discharge of a contract

Results when the obligations incurred by the parties when they entered into the agreement are excused, and the parties are no longer bound to perform as promised. *(FAI)*

disclosure statement

An official statement in which persons or firms are required to describe their contract cost accounting practices by providing data responsive to the requirements of the U.S. federal government's Cost Accounting Standards. *(OPM)*
See *Cost Accounting Standards* (CAS).

discount

See *prompt payment discount; quantity discount; trade discount*.

Dd

discount for prompt payment
An invoice payment reduction offered by the seller for payment made by the buyer prior to the due date. Also called a *prompt payment discount*. *(FAR 32.902)*

discount rate
The interest rate used in calculating the present value of expected yearly benefits and costs. *(GOAT)*

discounted hourly rates
See *uncompensated overtime*.

discovery
A pretrial or prehearing procedure designed to promote full disclosure of all relevant facts related to a contract dispute. *(GCG)*

discrepancies incident to shipment
Any differences (e.g., count or condition) between the items documented to have been shipped and items actually received. *(FAR 45.101)*

discrete effort
Tasks that are related to the completion of specific end products or services, which can be separately planned and measured. *(NDIA II)*

discretionary appropriation
In a federal government context, those budgetary resources that are provided in appropriation acts other than those that fund mandatory programs. Also called "discretionary amount." *(GAO-05-734SP)*

discretionary spending
In a federal government context, outlays from budget authority provided in and controlled by appropriation acts. *(GAO-05-734SP)*

discretionary spending limit
In a federal government context, and as mandated by 2 U.S.C. 901, the mandatory restrictions placed on new budget authority levels. *(2 U.S.C. 901(c))*
See *nonsecurity category; security category*.

discriminatory price
A selling situation in which a supplier offers similar or identical items for sale, in identical quantities, at different prices to different buyers. *(GKPT)*

discussion
(1) Any oral or written communication between the buyer and a seller/offeror (other than communications conducted for the purpose of minor clarification), whether or not initiated by the buyer, that—
- Involves information essential for determining the acceptability of a proposal, or
- Provides the seller/offeror an opportunity to revise or modify its proposal.

(FAR 15.601)
(2) Negotiations conducted in a competitive acquisition that take place after establishment of the competitive range. *(FAR 15.306(d))*
See *negotiation*.

dishonor
(1) In the case of a negotiable instrument, means when a negotiable instrument is either not paid or not accepted, according to its tenor, on presentment for that purpose, or without presentment where that is excused. *(BLD)*
See also *negotiable instrument*.
(2) In the case of a letter of credit, means a failure to timely honor or to take an interim action, such as acceptance of a draft, that may be required by the letter of credit. *(UCC 5-102(a)(5))*
See *notice of dishonor*; see also *acceptance; honor; letter of credit*.

dismantling, demolition, or removal of improvements contract
A contract for dismantling or demolition of buildings, ground improvements, and other real property structures and for the removal of such structures or portions of them. *(FAR 37.300)*

dispute
See *contract dispute*.

dispute resolution communication
Any oral or written communication prepared for the purposes of a dispute resolution proceeding, including any memoranda, notes, or work product of the neutral parties or nonparty participant—except that a written agreement to enter into a dispute resolution proceeding, or final written agreement or arbitral award reached as a result of a dispute resolution proceeding, is not a "dispute resolution communication." *(5 U.S.C. 571(5))*
See also *dispute resolution proceeding*.

dispute resolution proceeding
Any process in which an alternative means of dispute

Dd

resolution is used to resolve an issue in controversy in which a neutral person is appointed, and in which specified parties participate. *(5 U.S.C. 571(6))*
See also *issue in controversy; neutral person*.

"Disputes" clause

A contract provision providing for administrative consideration and relief for disputes concerning questions of fact under a U.S. federal government contract that cannot be resolved by agreement between the parties to the contract. *(OPM)*
See also *government contract disputes process*.

dissemination

The government-initiated distribution of information to the public. It is not considered "dissemination" if the distribution is limited to government employees or agency contractors or grantees, intra-agency or inter-agency use, or sharing of government information and responses to requests for agency records under the Freedom of Information Act (5 U.S.C. 552) or the Privacy Act (5 U.S.C. 552a). *(OMB A-130)*

diversity programs

Programs designed to encourage a diverse workforce or education and training group such as programs that prohibit employment or workplace discrimination based on race, color, religion, sex, national origin, age, or disability. *(DGBCT)*

diverting

Redirecting materials that might otherwise be placed in the waste stream to recycling or recovery, excluding diversion to waste-to-energy facilities. *(FAR 36.001)*

Doctrine of *Contra Proferentem*

See *contra proferentem*.

document

(1) An original or official paper relied on as the basis, proof, or support of something. *(MW)*
(2) To furnish documentary evidence of something. *(MW)*
(3) In the case of a letter of credit, means a draft or other demand, document of title, investment security, certificate, invoice, or other record, statement, or representation of fact, law, right, or opinion—
- Which is presented in a written or other medium permitted by the letter of credit or, unless prohibited by the letter of credit, by the standard practice referred to in UCC 5-108(e); and
- Which is capable of being examined for compli-

ance with the terms and conditions of the letter of credit.
A "document" *may not* be oral. *(UCC 5-102(a)(6))*
See also *letter of credit*.

document of title

Includes a bill of lading, dock warrant, dock receipt, warehouse receipt or order for the delivery of goods, and also any other document which in the regular course of business or financing is treated as adequately evidencing that the person in possession of it is entitled to receive, hold, and dispose of the document and the goods it covers. To be a "document of title," a document must purport to be issued by or addressed to a bailee and purport to cover goods in the bailee's possession, which are either identified or are fungible portions of an identified mass. *(UCC 1-201(16))*
See also *negotiable document of title; nonnegotiable document of title*.

documentary draft

A draft to be presented for acceptance or payment if specified documents, certificated securities or instructions for uncertificated securities, or other certificates, statements, or the like are to be received by the drawee or other payor before acceptance or payment of the draft. *(UCC 4-104(a)(6))*

documentation

In the case of an agreement, documented information explaining the facts upon which the parties to the agreement based the agreement. The purpose of documentation is to establish that both parties accepted the final agreement. Negotiation documentation summarizes the agreements and concessions. It presents each step from solicitation to proposal to negotiation objectives to concessions to final agreement. *(FAR 15.406)*

domain

(1) In a cybersecurity context, the unique context (e.g., access control parameters) in which a program is operating. *(CNSSI 4009)*
See also *information system* (IS)*; object*.
(2) In the context of the *CMS™*, an area within the contract life cycle phases that produces significant contract management outcomes. *(CMS)*
See *contract management domains; Contract Management Standard™ Publication (CMS™)*; see also *competencies; contract life cycle phases; job tasks*.

Dd

domestic construction material

(1) An unmanufactured construction material mined or produced in the United States (in which case, the Buy American statute (41 U.S.C. Chapter 83) applies). *(FAR 25.003; 25.601)*
See *Buy American statute; construction material*.
(2) A construction material manufactured in the United States—if the cost of the components mined, produced, or manufactured in the United States exceeds 50 percent of the cost of all its components (components of foreign origin of the same class or kind for which nonavailability determinations have been made are treated as domestic) or the construction material is a commercial off-the-shelf item. *(FAR 25.003)*
See *construction material; commercial off-the-shelf* (COTS).
(3) A manufactured construction material that is manufactured in the United States and, if the construction material consists wholly or predominantly of iron or steel, the iron or steel was produced in the United States (in which case, Section 1605 of the American Recovery and Reinvestment Act (*Pub. L.* 111-5) applies). *(FAR 25.601)*
See *American Recovery and Reinvestment Act of 2009* (ARRA); *manufactured construction material*.

domestic end product

An unmanufactured end product mined or produced in the United States or an end product manufactured in the United States—if the cost of its components mined, produced, or manufactured in the United States exceeds 50 percent of the cost of all its components. Components of foreign origin of the same class or kind as those that the U.S. federal agency determines are not mined, produced, or manufactured in sufficient and reasonably available commercial quantities of a satisfactory quality are treated as domestic. Scrap generated, collected, and prepared for processing in the United States is considered domestic. This definition includes an end product that is a commercial off-the-shelf item. *(FAR 25.003)*
See also *Buy American statute; commercial off-the-shelf* (COTS); *end product*.

domestic industrial base

See *defense industrial base*.

domestic offer

An offer of a domestic end product. When the solicitation specifies that award will be made on a group of line items, a domestic offer means an offer where the proposed price of the domestic end products exceeds 50 percent of the total proposed price of the group. *(FAR 25.003)*
See also *end product*.

domestic preference

Any one of a number of policies adopted by a nation's government that maintain discriminatory government procurement rules designed to establish a preference in favor of domestic suppliers. *(TIPS)*
See *Buy American statute*.

domestic services

Services performed in the United States. *(GOAT)*

double counting

A Cost Accounting Standards violation that can result from allocating cost items directly to a cost objective without eliminating like cost items from indirect cost pools. *(NCMA-WS)*
See also *Cost Accounting Standards* (CAS).

down select

To reduce the number of contractors working on a program by eliminating one or more for the next phase. *(DAAT)*

draft

(1) A negotiable instrument that is an "order" (as defined in UCC 3-103). Also called a "bill of exchange." *(UCC 3-104(e))*
See *negotiable instrument; order; see also documentary draft*.
(2) An item, other than a negotiable instrument, that is an "order" (as defined in UCC 3-103). *(UCC 4-104(a)(7))*
See *item; negotiable instrument; order*.

draft request for proposals (DRFP)

(1) A tentative solicitation submitted to prospective offerors for review and comment. *(GOAT)*
(2) Usually sent out to prospective industry offerors authorized by the U.S. federal government to receive it in advance of a final request for proposals. A draft request for proposals solicits offerors' recommendations to add, delete, or modify requirements, and gives them advance notice of the government's requirements. *(DAAT)*

drawee

A person ordered in a draft to make payment. *(UCC 3-103(a)(4); UCC 4-104(a)(8))*
See also *drawer*.

Dd

drawer
A person who signs or is identified in a draft as a person ordering payment. *(UCC 3-103(a)(5))*
See also *drawee*.

driving path
The longest continuous sequence of tasks driving a selected interim contract or project event. A driving path may or may not be on the project's critical path. *(NDIA II)*
See also *critical path*.

drug-free workplace
The site(s) for the performance of work done by the contractor in connection with a specific contract where employees of the contractor are prohibited from engaging in the unlawful manufacture, distribution, dispensing, possession, or use of a controlled substance. *(FAR 2.101)*
See *controlled substance; Drug-Free Workplace statute*.

Drug-Free Workplace statute
A federal law (41 U.S.C. Chapter 81) establishing prohibitions on the unlawful manufacture, distribution, dispensation, possession, or use of controlled substances at sites where a contractor performs work in connection with a specific U.S. federal government contract. Formerly known as the "Drug-Free Workplace Act." *(41 U.S.C. 8102)*

dry bulk carrier
A vessel used primarily for the carriage of shipload lots of homogenous, unmarked, nonliquid cargoes such as grain, coal, cement, and lumber. *(FAR 47.501)*

dry cargo liner
A vessel used for the carriage of heterogeneous marked cargoes in parcel lots. However, any cargo may be carried in these vessels, including part cargoes of dry bulk items or, when carried in deep tanks, bulk liquids such as petroleum and vegetable oils. *(FAR 47.501)*

"dual-use"
Products, services, standards, processes, or acquisition practices, respectively, that are capable of meeting requirements for military and nonmilitary applications. *(10 U.S.C. 2500(2))*
See also *dual-use critical technology*.

dual-use critical technology
A critical technology that has military applications and nonmilitary applications. *(10 U.S.C. 2500(3))*
See *critical technology; dual-use*.

due bill
A bill levied by a government on the importation, exportation, or use and consumption of goods. *(GKPT)*

due date
The date on which payment should be made. *(FAR 32.001)*

due diligence
(1) In general, such diligence as a reasonable person under the same circumstances would use—i.e., reasonable but not exhaustive efforts. *(MW)*
(2) An organization exercises "due diligence" if it maintains reasonable routines for communicating significant information to a person conducting a transaction and there is reasonable compliance with the routines *(UCC 1-202(f))*

Dun & Bradstreet number
See *Data Universal Numbering System* (DUNS) *number*.

duty
(1) A task, service, or function that arises from one's position. *(MW)*
(2) An obligation assumed (as by contract) or imposed by law to conduct oneself in conformance with a certain standard or to act in a particular way. *(MW)*
(3) A tax imposed by the customs authority of the receiving country on imported goods and services:
- *Ad valorem*: "according to value,"
- Specific: determined by product weight or quantity, and
- Compound: a combination of the above two types.

(NES-94)

duty of good faith and fair dealing
Every contract imposes upon each party a duty of good faith and fair dealing in its performance and its enforcement. *(RSOC 205)*
See *fair dealing; good faith*.

Dynamic Small Business Search (DSBS)
Maintained by the Small Business Administration, this tool provides government contracting professionals the ability to identify potential small business contractors for upcoming contracting opportunities. Small

Ee

businesses can also use DSBS to identify other small businesses for teaming and joint ventures.

E

e-Verify
An internet-based system that allows businesses to determine the eligibility of their employees to work in the United States. *(DGBCT)*

early supplier involvement (ESI)
A practice that involves one or more selected suppliers with a buyer's product design team early in the specification development process. The objective is to utilize the supplier's expertise and experience in developing a product specification that is designed for effective and efficient manufacturability. *(GKPT)*

earned schedule (ES)
The amount of time originally planned, according to the spread of the budgeted cost for work scheduled, to reach the current total of budgeted cost for work performed. In a broad sense, earned schedule is also an analytical technique that uses the exact same data as earned value management, except the resulting schedule indicators are time-based, not cost-based. *(NDIA II)*
See *earned value management* (EVM); see also *"budgeted cost of work performed* (BCWP); *budgeted cost of work scheduled* (BCWS).

earned value (EV)
The value of completed work expressed in terms of the budget assigned to that work, also referred to as the "budgeted cost of work performed" (BCWP). It provides an objective measure of the value of completed work expressed in terms of the budget assigned to that work. *(NDIA II)*
See *budgeted cost of work performed* (BCWP); *earned value management* (EVM).

earned value management (EVM)
A project management methodology that integrates a project's technical scope, schedule, and resources with project risk in a baseline plan, against which progress is measured to provide metrics indicative of progress and performance trends useful for management decision-making. *(NDIA II)*
See also *earned value management system* (EVMS).

earned value management system (EVMS)
(1) A project management tool that effectively integrates the project scope of work with cost, schedule and performance elements for optimum project planning and control. The qualities and operating characteristics of an earned value management system are described in Electronic Industries Alliance Standard 748 (EIA-748), Earned Value Management Systems. *(FAR 2.101)*
(2) A system to manage costs through the measurement of performance, in dollars, over time.

earned value technique (EVT)
A specific technique such as milestone, percent complete, 50/50, 0/100, units complete, apportioned effort, or level of effort selected to represent the measurement of work scope progress and accomplishment in a work package. *(NDIA II)*

economic order quantity (EOQ)
A concept holding that the most economical quantity of material to order may be the one that tends to minimize all the costs associated with the order–i.e., carrying costs, acquisition costs, and the cost of the material itself. *(DBL)*

economic planning costs
The costs of general long-range management planning, which is concerned with the future overall development of the organization's business and which may take into account the eventual possibility of economic dislocations or fundamental alterations in those markets in which the organization currently does business. *(FAR 31.205-12)* (See also FAR 31.205-27 *and* 31.205-38.)

economic purchase quantity
A supply acquisition quantity that produces economic benefit to the buyer. Evaluation should consider the costs related to purchasing and holding the supply item. *(CMBOK)*

economically disadvantaged women-owned small business (EDWOSB) concern
A small business concern that is at least 51-percent directly and unconditionally owned by, and the management and daily business operations of which are controlled by, one or more women who are citizens of the United States and who are economically disadvantaged in accordance with 13 CFR Part 127. Such a concern automatically qualifies as a women-owned small business (WOSB) concern eligible under the WOSB

Ee

Program. *(FAR 2.101)*
See *Women-Owned Small Business* (WOSB) *Program.*

economies of scale
(1) The reduction in long-term average unit costs as the size (scale) of a firm or operation increases. *(GKPT)*
(2) Reductions in unit cost of output resulting from the producing additional units. *(DAAT)*

economies of scope
First cousins to economies of scale are economies of scope, factors that make it cheaper to produce a range of products together than to produce each one of them on its own. Such economies can come from businesses sharing centralized functions, such as finance or marketing. Or they can come from interrelationships elsewhere in the business process, such as cross-selling one product alongside another, or using the outputs of one business as the inputs of another. (See "Economies of Scale," the *Economist*, https://www.economist.com/node/12446567.)

economy
A particular system of organization for the production, distribution, and consumption of all things people use to achieve a certain standard of living. *(ECON)*

Economy Act
A federal law (31 U.S.C. 1535) that authorizes agencies to enter into agreements to obtain supplies or services from another agency. The *FAR* applies when one agency uses another agency's contract to obtain supplies or services. If the interagency business transaction does not result in a contract or an order, then the *FAR* does not apply. The Economy Act also provides authority for placement of orders between major organizational units within an agency; procedures for such intra-agency transactions are addressed in agency regulations. *(FAR 17.502-2(a))*

effective competition
A market condition that exists when two or more contractors, acting independently, actively contend for the U.S. federal government's business in a manner that ensures that the government will be offered the lowest cost or price alternative or best technical design meeting its minimum needs. *(FAR 34.001)*

effective date (ED)
(1) For a solicitation amendment, change order, or administrative change, the "effective date" is the issue date of the amendment, change order, or administrative change. *(FAR 43.101)*
(2) For a supplemental agreement, the "effective date" is the date agreed upon by the contracting parties. *(FAR 43.101)*
(3) For a modification issued as a confirming notice of termination for the convenience of the U.S. federal government, the "effective date" of the confirming notice shall be the same as the "effective date" of the initial notice. *(FAR 43.101)*
(4) For a modification converting a termination for default to a termination for the convenience of the U.S. federal government, the "effective date" is the same as the "effective date" of the termination for default. *(FAR 43.101)*
See *effective date of termination.*
(5) For a modification confirming the termination contracting officer's previous letter determination of the amount due in settlement of a contract termination for convenience, the "effective date" is the same as the "effective date" of the previous letter determination. *(FAR 43.101)*

effective date of termination
The date on which the notice of termination requires the contractor to stop performance under the contract. If the contractor receives the termination notice after the date fixed for termination, then the "effective date of termination" means the date the contractor receives the notice. *(FAR 2.101)*

effectiveness
Degree to which an activity or initiative is successful in achieving a specified goal. *(DGBCT)*

efficiency
Degree of capability or productivity of a process, such as the number of contracts awarded or contracts won per year. *(DGBCT)*

elasticity of demand
Degree of responsiveness of quantity demanded to a change in price. *(ECON)*

electronic and information technology (EIT)
Has the same meaning as "information technology" except EIT also includes any equipment or interconnected system or subsystem of equipment that is used in the creation, conversion, or duplication of data or information. This term includes, but is not limited to, telecommunication products (such as telephones),

Ee

information kiosks and transaction machines, websites, multimedia, and office equipment (such as copiers and fax machines). *(FAR 2.101)*

electronic commerce (EC)
Electronic techniques for accomplishing business transactions, including e-mail or electronic messaging, internet technology, electronic bulletin boards, purchase cards, electronic funds transfer, and electronic data interchange. *(41 U.S.C. 2301(a); FAR 2.101)*

electronic data interchange (EDI)
A technique for electronically transferring and storing formatted information between computers utilizing established and published formats and codes, as authorized by the applicable Federal Information Processing Standards (FIPS). *(FAR 2.101)*
See also *Federal Information Processing Standards* (FIPS).

electronic funds transfer (EFT)
Any transfer of funds, other than a transaction originated by cash, check, or similar paper instrument, that is initiated through an electronic terminal, telephone, computer, or magnetic tape for the purpose of ordering, instructing, or authorizing a financial institution to debit or credit an account. This term includes automated clearing house transfers, Fedwire transfers, and transfers made at automatic teller machines and point-of-sale terminals. (For purposes of compliance with 31 U.S.C. 3332 and implementing regulations at 31 CFR Part 208, the term "electronic funds transfer" includes a governmentwide commercial purchase card transaction.) *(FAR 2.101)*
See also *automated clearing house* (ACH); *Fedwire; funds-transfer system*.

electronic funds transfer indicator
A four-character suffix to the unique entity identifier. The suffix is assigned at the discretion of the commercial, nonprofit, or U.S. federal government entity to establish additional System for Award Management records for identifying alternative electronic funds transfer accounts for the same entity. *(FAR 2.101)* (See also *FAR* Subpart 32.11.)
See *electronic funds transfer* (EFT); *System for Award Management* (SAM).

electronic funds transfer information
Information necessary for making a payment by electronic funds transfer (EFT) through specified EFT mechanisms. *(FAR 32.1102)*
See *electronic funds transfer* (EFT).

electronic payment
Any method of making payments electronically. *(EDI)*

Electronic Product Environmental Assessment Tool (EPEAT) Registry
A resource for purchasers, manufacturers, resellers and others wanting to find or promote electronic products with positive environmental attributes. The definitive resource for finding technology products designed to minimize impact on the planet. The sustainability standards on which the EPEAT ecolabel is based are developed through a balanced voluntary consensus process involving multiple stakeholders, including sustainability advocates, manufacturer representatives, purchasing professionals, academics, recycling providers, and policy representatives. *(FAR 23.704(a)(1))*

electronic products
Products that are dependent on electronic currents or electromagnetic fields in order to work properly. *(FAR 23.701)*

Electronic Subcontracting Reporting System (eSRS)
The governmentwide, electronic, web-based system for small business subcontracting program reporting. *(FAR 19.701)*

elements of a contract
Elements that must be present in a contract if the contract is to be binding. These include the following:
- Offer,
- Acceptance,
- Consideration, and
- Intent to create a legal relationship.

(CMBOK)

element of cost (EOC)
(1) Those cost categories that directly or indirectly influence the cost of producing material or providing services and that can be apportioned to the contract. *(CMBOK)*
(2) The categories of cost—such as direct labor, direct material, direct subcontractor, and other direct costs as well as indirect costs—that directly influence the cost of producing material or providing services, and which can be apportioned to the contract. *(NDIA II; OPM)*

eligible end product
In the context of the U.S. federal government's "Buy American" policies, trade agreements, and other laws

and regulations governing foreign acquisition, this term refers to a foreign end product, construction material, or service that, due to applicability of a trade agreement to a particular acquisition, is not subject to discriminatory treatment. *(FAR 25.003)*
Contrast with *domestic end product*.

eligible offer

In the context of the federal government's "Buy American" policies, trade agreements, and other laws and regulations governing foreign acquisition, this term refers to an offer of an eligible product. When the solicitation specifies that award will be made on a group of line items, an "eligible offer" means a foreign offer where the combined proposed price of the eligible products and the domestic end products exceeds 50 percent of the total proposed price of the group. *(FAR 25.003)*
Contrast with *domestic offer*.

emergency

An occasion or instance for which, in the determination of the President, federal assistance is needed to supplement state or local efforts and capabilities to save lives and to protect property and public health and safety, or to lessen or avert the threat of a catastrophe in any part of the United States. *(FAR 2.101)*
See also *emergency response contract; major disaster*.

emergency acquisition flexibilities

Flexibilities provided with respect to any acquisition of supplies or services by or for an executive agency that, as determined by the head of an executive agency, may be used—
* In support of a contingency operation;
* To facilitate the defense against or recovery from nuclear, biological, chemical, or radiological attack against the United States; or
* When the president issues an emergency declaration or a major disaster declaration.

(FAR 18.001)

emergency response contract

A contract with private entities that supports assistance activities in a major disaster or emergency area, such as debris clearance, distribution of supplies, or reconstruction. *(FAR 26.201)*
See also *local firm; major disaster or emergency area*.

employee

(1) A person employed for wages or salary, usually below the executive level. *(MW)*
Contrast with *independent contractor*.
(2) An employee of the contractor directly engaged in the performance of work under the contract who has other than a minimal impact or involvement in contract performance. *(FAR 22.1702)*
See *contractor employee*; see also *employee assigned to the contract*.
(3) Any person engaged in performing work on or in connection with a contract covered by Executive Order 13706, and whose wages under such contract are governed by the Service Contract Labor Standards statute (41 U.S.C. Chapter 67); the Wage Rate Requirements (Construction) statute (40 U.S.C. Chapter 31, Subchapter IV); or the Fair Labor Standards Act (29 U.S.C. Chapter 8)—including employees who qualify for an exemption from the Fair Labor Standards Act's minimum wage and overtime provisions, regardless of the contractual relationship alleged to exist between the individual and the employer. *(FAR 22.2101)*
See also *paid sick leave; performance in connection with a contract; performance on a contract*.
(4) Notwithstanding the meaning provided in (3) of this definition, this term also includes any person performing work on or in connection with the contract and individually registered in a bona fide apprenticeship or training program registered with the Department of Labor's Employment and Training Administration, Office of Apprenticeship, or with a U.S. state apprenticeship agency recognized by the Office of Apprenticeship. *(FAR 22.2101)*

employee of an agency

Includes the following individuals who are employed by an agency of the federal government:
* An individual who is appointed to a position in the government, including a position under a temporary appointment;
* A member of the uniformed services;
* A special government employee; and
* An individual who is a member of a federal advisory committee.

(GOAT)

employer's identification number

An Employer Identification Number (EIN) is also known as a Federal Tax Identification Number. It is used to identify a business entity. Generally, businesses need an EIN.

Ee

encumbrance

(1) A right, other than an ownership interest, in real property. This term includes mortgages and other liens on real property. *(UCC 9-102(a)(32))*

(2) In the context of real estate, includes real estate mortgages and other liens on real estate and all other rights in real estate that are not ownership interests. *(UCC 2A-309(1)(e))*

end item (EI)

An assembled whole system or equipment, or a final combination of end products, component parts, and/or materials, which is ready for its intended use (e.g., an aircraft, a ship, or a smart phone). *(CMBOK; AFIT; DISCS)*

end product

(1) Supplies delivered under a line item of a contract. *(FAR 2.101; CMBOK)*

(2) Those articles, materials, and supplies to be acquired for public use. *(FAR 25.003)*

end-to-end security

In a cybersecurity context, safeguarding information in an information system from point of origin to point of destination. *(CNSSI 4009)*

See also *information system* (IS).

end user

The individual or groups who will operate the system for its intended purpose when it is deployed. *(AIMD)*

endorsement

(1) As opposed to "indorsement," the act or process of endorsing. *(MW)*

(2) In a cybersecurity context, U.S. National Security Agency approval of a commercially developed product for safeguarding national security information. *(CNSSI 4009)*

energy conservation

The use of energy resources in an efficient manner as to promote continued and sustainable use. Some contracts contain clauses that implement federal government policies to acquire goods and services that promote energy conservation, advance the use of renewable energy products, and help foster markets for emerging technology. *(DGBCT)*

energy-efficient product

A product that meets Department of Energy and Environmental Protection Agency criteria for use of the "Energy Star" trademark label, or is in the upper 25 percent of efficiency for all similar products as designated by the Department of Energy's Federal Energy Management Program. (As used in this definition, the term "product" *does not* include any energy-consuming product or system designed or procured for combat or combat-related missions (per 42 U.S.C. 8259b).) *(FAR 2.101)*

See *Energy Star*.

energy-efficient standby power devices

Products that use external standby power devices (or that contain an internal standby power function) and no more than one watt of electricity in their standby power–consuming mode, or which meet the recommended low standby levels as designated by the Department of Energy Federal Energy Management Program. *(FAR 2.101)*

energy facility

Any equipment or facility which is or will be used primarily in the exploration for, or the development, production, conversion, storage, transfer, processing, or transportation of, any energy resource. *(16 U.S.C. 1453(6))*

energy-savings performance contract

A contract that requires the contractor to:

- Perform services for the design, acquisition, financing, installation, testing, operation, and (where appropriate) maintenance and repair of an identified energy conservation measure or series of measures at one or more locations;
- Incur the costs of implementing the energy savings measures, including at least the cost (if any) incurred in making energy audits, acquiring and installing equipment, and training personnel in exchange for a predetermined share of the value of the energy savings directly resulting from implementation of such measures during the term of the contract; and
- Guarantee future energy and cost savings to the federal government.

(FAR 2.101)

Energy Star

A voluntary program designed to help businesses and individuals save money and protect the environment through superior energy efficiency. The Energy Star label signifies that a product has been independently

Ee

certified to save energy without sacrificing features or functionality.

engineering and technical services
A subdivision of advisory and assistance services. They are contractual services used to support a U.S. federal government program office during the acquisition cycle by providing such services as systems engineering and technical direction to ensure the effective operation and maintenance of a weapon system or major system (as defined in OMB Circular A-109) or to provide direct support of a weapon system that is essential to research, development, production, operation, or maintenance of the system. *(FAR 2.101)* (See also *FAR Subpart 37.2.*)
See *advisory and assistance services* (A&AS); see also *management and professional support services; studies, analyses, and evaluations*.

engineering change proposal (ECP)
(1) A document proposing any design change requiring revision to contract specifications or engineering drawings. It may be originated by either party to a contract. It requires detailed documentation and an evaluation of technical, cost, and schedule effects. *(CMBOK; OPM)*
(2) A proposal to a responsible authority recommending that a change to an original item of equipment be considered, and the design or engineering change be incorporated into the article to modify, add to, delete, or supersede original parts. *(DAAT)*

engineering data
Engineering documents such as specifications, drawings, standards, lists, or other information prepared by a design activity relating to the design, performance, manufacture, test, or inspection of items and services. *(CMBOK; AFIT)*

ensure quality
In the context of the *CMS™*, "ensure quality" is in the "post-award" life cycle phase of contract management, within the "perform contract" domain. It is the process of:
* Planning for contract performance delivery and monitoring, and
* Inspecting and accepting contract performance.
The value added by this process is to ensure the delivered product or service meets the terms and conditions of the contract. *(CMS)*
See *Contract Management Standard™ Publication (CMS™); perform contract; post-award life cycle*

phase; see also *administer contract; manage changes; subcontract management*.

enterprise resource planning (ERP)
An industry term for the broad set of activities that helps an organization manage the important parts of its business. The information made available through an ERP system provides visibility for key performance indicators required for meeting organizational objectives. ERP software applications can be used to manage product planning, parts purchasing, inventories, interacting with suppliers, providing customer service, and tracking orders. *(DGBCT)*
See *manufacturing/enterprise resource planning (M/ERP) system*.

enterprise software agreement
An agreement or a contract that is used to acquire designated commercial software or related services such as software maintenance. *(DFARS 208.7401)*

entitlement holder
A person identified in the records of a securities intermediary as the person who has a security entitlement against the securities intermediary. If a person acquires a security entitlement by virtue of UCC 8-501(b)(2) or UCC 8-501(b)(3), that person is the entitlement holder. *(UCC 8-102(a)(7))*
See also *entitlement order; securities entitlement; securities intermediary*.

entitlement order
A notification communicated to a securities intermediary directing transfer or redemption of a financial asset to which the entitlement holder has a security entitlement. *(UCC 8-102(a)(8))*
See also *entitlement holder; financial asset; securities intermediary; security entitlement*.

entitlement program
A federal government program that guarantees a certain level of benefits to persons or other entities who meet requirements set by law, such as Social Security, farm price supports, or unemployment benefits. *(FAR 4.601)*
See also *entitlements*.

entitlements
Benefits provided by the federal government to persons or other entities who meet requirements set by law (e.g., Social Security, farm price supports, or unemployment benefits). *(FAR 4.601)*

Ee

entity of the government
See *government*.

entrust/entrusting
Concerning goods, this term includes any delivery and any acquiescence in retention of possession regardless of any condition expressed between the parties to the delivery or acquiescence and regardless of whether the procurement of the entrusting or the possessor's disposition of the goods have been such as to be larcenous under the criminal law. *(UCC 2-403(3))*

environment
(1) For federal government purposes concerning the physical environment—
- The navigable waters, the waters of the contiguous zone, and the ocean waters of which the natural resources are under the management authority of the United States under the Magnuson-Stevens Fishery Conservation and Management Act (16 U.S.C. 1801, *et seq.*), and
- Any other surface water, ground water, drinking water supply, land surface or subsurface strata, or ambient air within the United States or under the jurisdiction of the United States.

(42 U.S.C. 9601(8))
(2) In an information technology context, a computer interface from which various tasks can be performed (e.g., a programming environment). *(MW)*
(3) In a cybersecurity context, the aggregate of external procedures, conditions, and objects affecting the development, operation, and maintenance of an information system. *(CNSSI 4009)*
See *information system* (IS).

environmental
In a federal government context, means environmental aspects of internal agency operations and activities, including those aspects related to energy and transportation functions. *(FAR 23.001)*

environmental assessment (EA)
A document used by federal agencies to determine whether an environmental impact statement (EIS) is required for a proposed system or action. The EA discusses the proposal, alternatives to the proposal, and a list of the people consulted. If the information contained in the EA convincingly evidences that the proposed action will not significantly affect the environment, no EIS is required. If a proposed system or action will adversely affect the environment or be environmentally

controversial, an EIS is required. *(DAAT; NES-94)* (See also FAR 7.105(b)(17).)
See *environmental impact statement* (EIS).

environmental contracting
A broad category that covers contracts for analysis, investigation, and studies in support of compliance, pollution prevention, conservation, recycling, and remediation to comply with all federal, state, and local environmental laws and regulations. *(DGBCT)*

environmental impact statement (EIS)
(1) A detailed written statement prepared to describe the effects for proposed activities on the environment. In federal government contracting, an EIS is required by Section 102(2)(C) of the National Environmental Policy Act (42 U.S.C. 4321, et seq.) for any proposed major federal action that will significantly affect the quality of the environment. *(42 U.S.C. 4332(C)(i))* (See also FAR 7.105(b)(17).)
(2) The primary purpose of an environmental impact statement is to serve as an action-forcing device to insure that the policies and goals defined in the act are infused into the ongoing programs and actions of the federal government. It shall provide full and fair discussion of significant environmental impacts and shall inform decisionmakers and the public of the reasonable alternatives which would avoid or minimize adverse impacts or enhance the quality of the human environment. *(40 CFR Part 1502)*
See also *environmental assessment* (EA).

Environmental Protection Agency (EPA)-designated item
A product that is or can be made with recovered material—
- That is listed by the EPA in a procurement guideline (40 CFR Part 247), and
- For which the EPA has provided purchasing recommendations in a related "Recovered Materials Advisory Notice."

(FAR 23.401)
See *recovered material*.

environmental laws
Policies and procedures supporting the government's program for protecting and improving the quality of the environment through pollution control, energy conservation, identification of hazardous material, and use of recovered materials. *(DGBCT)*

Ee

"environmentally preferable"

Products or services that have a lesser or reduced effect on human health and the environment when compared with competing products or services that serve the same purpose. This comparison may consider raw materials acquisition, production, manufacturing, packaging, distribution, reuse, operation, maintenance, or disposal of the product or service. *(FAR 2.101)*
See also *environmentally preferable purchasing* (EPP).

environmentally preferable purchasing (EPP)

Ensures that environmental considerations are included in purchasing decisions, along with traditional factors such as product price and performance. *(CMBOK; DGBCT)*
See *Environmentally Preferable Purchasing Program*.

Environmentally Preferable Purchasing Program

A U.S. Environmental Protection Agency program that helps the federal government harness private-sector innovation by utilizing marketplace standards and ecolabels to identify and procure environmentally preferable products and services. In turn, the program leverages the significant federal purchasing power to prevent pollution, realize life cycle cost savings, and increase U.S. industry competitiveness. (See https://www.epa.gov.)
See also *environmentally preferable; environmentally preferable purchasing* (EPP).

Equal Access to Justice Act (EAJA)

A federal law (5 U.S.C. 504; 28 U.S.C. 2412) designed to aid small businesses and individuals in recovering attorney fees if they prevail in certain actions against the government. *(GCG)*

equal employment opportunity (EEO)

The right of every individual under the law to be considered for employment without discrimination based on race, color, sex, national origin, age, religion, non-disqualifying mental or physical handicap, or any other nonmerit factor. *(HCS)*

"Equal Opportunity" clause

The clause at FAR 52.222-26, "Equal Opportunity," as prescribed in FAR 22.810(e). *(FAR 22.801)*

equipment

(1) A tangible item that is functionally complete for its intended purpose, durable, non-expendable, and needed for the performance of a contract. Equipment is not intended for sale and does not ordinarily lose its identity or become a component part of another article when put into use. Equipment does not include material, real property, special test equipment, or special tooling. *(FAR 45.101)*
Contrast with *article; item*.
(2) In the context of goods in a secured transaction, refers to goods other than inventory or consumer goods. *(UCC 9-102(a)(33))*

equitable adjustment

(1) A contractual remedy to make the seller whole. *(CMBOK)*
(2) The compensation or price adjustment to which a seller is entitled upon the occurrence of a contract change or special event. *(OPM)*
See *request for equitable adjustment*.

equitable interest

An interest that is held by virtue of equitable title, or which may be claimed on the ground of equitable relief. *(MW)*

equitable remedies

Legal remedies to address equitable adjustment, which include an order of specific performance, restitution, and recession. In the case of goods or real property, an order of specific performance can require the breaching party to perform in accordance with the contract. *(CMBOK)*

equity capital

Capital, as retained earnings, that is free of debt. *(MW)*
See *capital*; see also *paid-in capital*.

escalated dollars

See *current year dollars*.

escalation

(1) A term traditionally used to indicate an upward or downward movement of price. *(OPM)*
See *economic price adjustment*.
(2) Use of a price index to convert past to present prices or to convert present to future prices. *(DAAT)*
(3) An increase due to inflation and outlay rates for the appropriation and the branch or the service involved. *(DAAT)*

escalator clause

A contract clause generally permitting an increase in the price of goods or services in the event of certain outcomes, such as an increase in the supplier's raw materials or labor costs. Escalation clauses in a contract typically also provide for de-escalation. **(GKPT)** See **economic price adjustment**.

escrow
A legal document or other property delivered into the hands of a third person to be held until the happening of a contingency or performance of a condition. **(BLD)**

escrow agreement
See **ownership**.

essential job functions
The fundamental job duties of the employment position an individual holds. A job function may be considered "essential" if—
- The access to compensation information is necessary in order to perform that function or another routinely assigned business task; or
- The function or duties of the position include protecting and maintaining the privacy of employee personnel records, including compensation information.

(48 CFR 52.222-26)

established catalog price
A price that is regularly maintained by a seller, published or made available for inspection by customers, and states prices at which sales are currently, or were last, made to a significant number of buyers constituting the general public. **(CMBOK; OPM)**

established government source
Government and nongovernment sources of supplies, equipment, and services that are designated by law or regulation as mandatory sources, in a set order of priority, for particular items and services. **(CMBOK; SPP)**

established market price
A current price, established in the usual and ordinary course of trade between buyers and sellers free to bargain, which can be substantiated from sources independent of the manufacturer or vendor. **(CMBOK; OPM)**

estimate at completion (EAC)
(1) The current estimated total cost for authorized project work. It equals the cumulative-to-date actual cost of work performed (ACWP) plus the estimated costs to complete (i.e., the estimate to complete (ETC)) the authorized work remaining. The estimate at completion

does not include profit or fee. **(NDIA II)**

(2) A re-estimate of the total project budget. The original budget is multiplied by the actual cost and divided by the earned value. It is a way of saying that if the current cost performance trends continue, the final cost can be predicted. (EAC = budget at completion (BAC) × cost performance index (CPI).) **(PMPM)**

estimate to complete (ETC)
An estimate of costs to complete all work from a point in time to the estimated completion date. **(NDIA II)**

estimated actual charges
A systematic and documented estimate of actual costs. The procedure is used in the absence of an established cost accounting system. Sometimes referred to as a "cost finding technique." **(DISCS)**

estimated completion date (ECD)
The estimated date to complete all remaining work. **(NDIA II)**

estimating costs
The process of forecasting a future result in terms of cost, based upon information available at the time. Also called **cost estimating**. **(FAR 31.001)**

estimating system
The seller's policies, procedures, and practices for budgeting and planning controls, and generating estimates of costs and other data included in proposals submitted to customers in the expectation of receiving contract awards. Components include the seller's:
- Organizational structure;
- Established lines of authority, duties, and responsibilities;
- Internal controls and managerial reviews;
- Flow of work, coordination, and communication; and
- Budgeting, planning, estimating methods, techniques, accumulation of historical costs, and other analyses used to generate cost estimates.

(DFARS 252.215-7002(a))

estoppel
A rule of law that bars, prevents, and precludes a party from alleging or denying certain facts because of a previous allegation or denial or because of his or her previous conduct or admission. **(FBL)**

Ee

ethical leadership

The individual leaders in an organization define what is ethical through their own actions or inactions. *(DGBCT)*

ethics

(1) Of or relating to moral action, conduct, motive, or character. *(BLD)*

(2) Containing the precepts of morality, and approaching duties or conduct following such precepts. *(BLD)*

(3) Professionally right or befitting; conforming to professional standards of conduct. *(BLD)*

(4) In federal government contracting, refers to the requirement for contractors to have a satisfactory record of integrity and business ethics, especially for future source selection purposes (should the government possess past performance information regarding a contractor's actions under previously awarded contracts or orders). *(FAR 9.104-1(d); FAR 42.1501(a)(6))*

evaluation board

See *source selection evaluation board* (SSEB).

evaluation factors/significant subfactors

(1) The basis for the award decision, evaluation factors and significant subfactors must represent the key areas of importance and emphasis to be consider in the source selection decision; and support meaningful comparison and discrimination between and among competing proposals. *(FAR 15.304)*

(2) Evaluation factors and subfactors represent those specific characteristics that are tied to significant RFP requirements. They are the uniform baseline against which each offeror's proposal is evaluated allowing the government to make a determination of acceptability. The evaluation factors and subfactors shall be set forth in the solicitation in enough depth to communicate what will be evaluated. The evaluation factors and subfactors shall be the primary determinant of the detailed information requested in the solicitation's instructions to offerors. *(SSP)*

(3) Factors that will be considered in evaluating proposals tailored to each acquisition and which have an impact on the source selection decision. Price or cost to the buyer shall be included as an evaluation factor in every source selection. Quality shall also be addressed in every source selection. Quality may be expressed in terms of technical excellence, management capability, personnel qualifications, prior experience, past performance, and schedule compliance. Any other relevant factors, such as cost realism, may also be included. *(CMBOK)*

evaluation notice (EN)

In the context of source selection, this term refers to the procuring contracting officer's written notification to the offeror for purposes of clarifications, communications, or in support of discussions. *(SSP)*

evaluation standards

The uniform means by which proposals are measured. *(CMBOK)*

See *evaluation factors/significant subfactors*.

exception

An approved departure from the established design, content, specifications, terms, conditions, etc. *(GOAT)*

"Exceptional" performance rating

In the case of a past performance evaluation, an "Exceptional" performance rating signifies that performance meets contractual requirements and exceeds many to the U.S. federal government's benefit. The contractual performance of the element or sub-element being evaluated was accomplished with few minor problems for which corrective actions taken by the contractor were highly effective. (To justify an "Exceptional" rating, multiple significant events should be identified, and how they were of benefit to the government should be stated. A singular benefit, however, could be of such magnitude that it alone constitutes an "Exceptional" rating. Also, there should have been *no* significant weaknesses identified.) *(FAR Table 42-1)*

See *past performance evaluation*; contrast with *"Marginal" performance rating; "Satisfactory" performance rating; "Unsatisfactory" performance rating; "Very Good" performance rating*.

excess defense articles (EDA)

Defense articles owned by the U.S. federal government which are items (except construction equipment) that are in excess of the approved force acquisition objective and approved force retention stock of all DOD components at the time such articles are dropped from inventory by the supplying agency. *(DISCS)*

See also *defense article*.

excess funds

Funds relating to a specific line item or deliverable that was not performed on a contract. Under U.S. federal government contracts, funds identified as "excess" are deobligated by contract/order modification. *(CMBOK; DCMA-INST 135)*

See *remaining funds*.

Ee

excess personal property

Any personal property under the control of a federal agency that the agency head determines is not required for its needs or for the discharge of its responsibilities. Also called *excess property*. *(40 U.S.C. 102(3); FAR 2.101)*
See also *foreign excess property*.

excess property

See *excess personal property*.

excess reprocurement costs

(1) Under a contract terminated for default, any excess costs incurred by the buyer to repurchase supplies or services similar to those terminated for default—and for any other damages, whether or not repurchase was effected—to which the seller is liable to the buyer. *(FAR 49.402-2(e))* (See also FAR 49.402-6 and FAR 49.402-7.)
(2) Occurs when the seller is liable to the buyer for any excess costs incurred by the buyer to repurchase supplies or services similar to those terminated for default. *(CMBOK)*

Excluded Parties List System (EPLS)

See *exclusion records*.

exclusion records

Identifies those parties excluded from receiving federal government contracts, certain subcontracts, and from certain types of federal financial and nonfinancial assistance and benefits. The exclusion records were previously contained in the Excluded Parties List System (EPLS), and in 2012 were consolidated into the System for Award Management (SAM). These records are also known as "SAM exclusions," "suspensions," and "debarments."
See *System for Award Management (SAM)*.

exclusive/non-exclusive license

A license covering a patent(s), technical or proprietary data, technical assistance, know-how, or any combination of these granted by a U.S. firm to a foreign firm or government to produce, co-produce, or sell a defense article or service within a given sales territory without competition from any other licensees or from the licensor. A "non-exclusive license" is similar, except that competition may be permitted with other licensees and/or the licensor. *(MSA)*

exculpatory clause

Contract language designed to shift responsibility to the other party—e.g., a "No Damages for Delay" clause. *(HECA)*

excusable delay

(1) An unforeseen occurrence that causes a delay in contract performance and for which an equitable adjustment is due. *(CMBOK)*
See also *force majeure*.
(2) A contractual provision designed to protect the seller from sanctions for late performance. To the extent that contract performance has been excusably delayed, the seller is protected from default termination, liquidated damages, or excess costs of reprocurement or completion. Excusable delays may also lead to recovery of additional compensation if the buyer constructively accelerates performance. *(AGC)*
See also *government-caused delay*.
(3) When a failure to perform is excusable because it arose out of causes beyond the control and without the fault or negligence of the contractor. Examples these causes are:
• Acts of God or the public enemy,
• Acts of the buyer in either its sovereign or contractual capacity,
• Fires,
• Floods,
• Epidemics,
• Quarantine restrictions,
• Strikes,
• Freight embargoes, and
• Unusually severe weather.
(FAR 49.401(b); FAR 52.249-14.)

executed contract

A written document, signed by both parties and mailed or otherwise furnished to each party, which expresses the requirements, terms, and conditions to be met by both parties in the performance of the contract. *(CMBOK; OPM)*

execution

(1) The final consummation of a contract action, including all formalities (e.g., signature and any necessary approvals) needed to complete the action. *(GOAT)*
See also *contract action; contract execution*.
(2) The operation of carrying out a program as contained in the approved budget. Also called *budget execution*. *(DISCS)*

Ee

execution date

Concerning a payment order, the day on which the receiving bank may properly issue a payment order in execution of the sender's order. The execution date may be determined by instruction of the sender, but this date cannot be earlier than the day the order is received and, unless otherwise determined, is the day the order is received. If the sender's instruction states a payment date, the execution date is the payment date or an earlier date on which execution is reasonably necessary to allow payment to the beneficiary on the payment date. *(UCC 4A-301(b))*
See *executed*; see also *payment date*.

executive

Officers, managing partners, or any other employees in management positions. *(FAR 52.204-10(a))*

executive agency

A generic term that refers to any of the following components of the federal government:

- An executive department (5 U.S.C. 105),
- A military department (5 U.S.C. 102),
- An independent establishment (5 U.S.C. 101; 5 U.S.C. 102; 5 U.S.C. 104(1)), and
- A wholly owned government corporation (31 U.S.C. 9101).

(41 U.S.C. 133)
See *executive department; independent establishment; military department; wholly owned government corporation*.

executive agreement

A government-to-government agreement, including agreements with international organizations, to which the United States is a party. *(GOAT)*

executive and senior management

(1) Any employee:

- Compensated on a salary basis at a specified rate, exclusive of board, lodging, or other facilities;
- Whose primary duty consists of the management of the enterprise in which the individual is employed or of a customarily recognized department or subdivision thereof;
- Who customarily and regularly directs the work of two or more other employees; and
- Who has the authority to hire or fire other employees or whose suggestions and recommendations as to the hiring or firing and as to the advancement and promotion or any other change of status of

other employees will be given particular weight. *(FAR 22.1301)*

(2) Any employee who owns at least a *bona fide* 20-percent equity interest in the enterprise in which the employee is employed, regardless of whether the business is a corporate or other type of organization, and who is actively engaged in its management. *(FAR 22.1301)*

executive facility

A facility owned or leased by an office or entity within the executive branch of the federal government. The term includes a facility owned or leased by the GSA on behalf of an office or entity within the judicial branch of the government. *(40 U.S.C. 590(f)(1))*

Executive Order (EO)

A rule or regulation, issued by the president of the United States, a governor, or some other administrative authority, that has the effect of law. Executive Orders are used to implement and give administrative effect to provisions of the Constitution, to treaties, and to statutes. They may be used to create or modify the organization or procedures of administrative agencies or may have general applicability as law. Under the Administration Procedure Act of 1946, all federal Executive Orders must be published in the *Federal Register*. *(DISCS)*

executory contract

A contract that has not yet been fully performed by one or more parties. *(DGBCT)*

executory interest

A future interest other than a remainder or reversion that may take effect upon the divesting of a prior interest or one created simultaneously. *(MW)*
See *future interest*.

exempt commodities

(1) Goods that are not subject to import duties. *(GKPT)*
(2) Specific goods that can be transported exempt of regulation by the Interstate Commerce Commission. *(GKPT)*

exempt employee

An employee that is "exempt" from the provisions of the Service Contract Labor Standards statute (41 U.S.C. Chapter 67). Professional services and the like are deemed "exempt." *(NCMA-WS)*
See *uncompensated overtime; compare with service employee*.

Ee

exhibit

A document, referred to in a contract, which is attached and establishes requirements for deliverables. This term should not be confused with any other kind of "attachment" to a contract. (e.g., the DD Form 1423, "Contract Data Requirements List," is always an "exhibit," rather than an "attachment.") *(DFARS 204.7101)* Compare with *attachment*.

exhibit line item number (ELIN)

A separately identifiable contract line item that may be used instead of putting a long list of contract line items or subline items in the contract schedule. If an ELIN is established, the exhibit to which it refers should also be referred to. *(PGI 204.7105(a)-(b))* (See also DFARS 204.7105.)
See *exhibit*.

expectancy interest

See *expectation interest*.

expectation damages

See *"expectation interest"*

expectation interest

In the context of judicial remedies, the interest of a party to a breached contract in receiving the benefit of the bargain by being put in a position as good as that which would have resulted had the contract been performed. Also called "expectancy interest." *(RSOC 344(a); MW)*
See *"reliance interest"*; see also *restitution interest*.

expedited procedure

A procedure under the Contract Disputes statute (41 U.S.C. Chapter 71) whereby an appellant before an agency board of contract appeals can elect, for claims of a specified dollar amount or below, to have a decision issued on a claim within four months after making the election. *(GKPT)* (See also FAR 33.211.)
See *accelerated procedure*.

expendable supplies and material

Supplies that are consumed in use (e.g., ammunition, paint, fuel, cleaning and preserving materials, surgical dressings, drugs, medicines), or which lose their identity (e.g., spare parts). Sometimes called *consumable supplies and material*. *(DISCS)*
Contrast with *non-expendable supplies and material*.

expired appropriation/account

An appropriation or fund account in which the balanc-es are no longer available for incurring new obligations because the time available for incurring such obligations has ended. However, the account/appropriation remains available for five years to process disbursements, collections, and within-scope adjustment of original obligations. During this five-year period, obligations may be adjusted, and outlays may be made from these accounts. Unobligated balances may not be withdrawn from expired accounts. After the five-year period has elapsed, all obligated and unobligated balances are cancelled and the expired account is closed. *(DAAT)*

expired cost

A cost that should be released to the current period as an expense or loss. *(NCMA-CA)*

Export Administration Regulation (EAR)

Export of commodities not regulated by the U.S. Department of State through the *International Traffic in Arms Regulation* (*ITAR*) are administered by the U.S. Department of Commerce through the *EAR*. Under the *EAR*, most commodities can be exported under the authority of a general license. *(TIPS)*
See *International Traffic in Arms Regulation* (ITAR)

export controls

The comprehensive set of controls established to protect U.S. national security interests and to foster foreign policy initiatives. The U.S. Department of State monitors and controls the export and re-export of goods and services in accordance with the *ITAR*, and the U.S. Department of Commerce—through the *EAR*—enforces the export of commodities not regulated by the *ITAR*. *(DGBCT)*
See also *"Export Administration Regulation* (EAR); *International Traffic in Arms Regulation* (ITAR).

Export-Import Bank of the United States (Ex-Im Bank; EXIMBANK)

An independent U.S. federal government agency that provides loans, loan guarantees, and credit risk insurance coverage to U.S. exporters and foreign importers. *(NES-94)*

exporting

The act of sending or carrying merchandise abroad, especially for trade or sale. *(NES-94)*

express authority

Authority delegated to an agent intentionally, distinctly,

Ff

and plainly expressed verbally or in writing. *(BLD)*
See *agent; agent authority*; see also *actual authority; apparent authority; implied authority*.
A contract in which the terms of the contract are stated in either written or spoken words and are assented to by both parties. *(CMBOK)*

express warranty
A written statement arising out of a sale to the consumer of a consumer good, pursuant to which the manufacturer, distributor, or retailer undertakes to preserve or maintain the utility or performance of the consumer good or provide compensation if there is a failure in utility or performance. It is not necessary to the creation of an express warranty that formal words such as "warrant" or "guarantee" be used, or that a specific intention to make a warranty be present. For commercial contracts, an express warranty must be included in the contract by addendum. *(CMBOK; DGBCT)*

expressly unallowable cost
A particular item or type of cost which, under the express provisions of an applicable law, regulation, or contract, is specifically named and stated to be unallowable. *(FAR 31.001)*

ex-ship
Concerning delivery of goods, this term means "from the carrying vessel" (e.g., "delivery of goods ex ship"). *(UCC 2-322(1))*

extended overhead
A means of recovering management and other fixed costs during a period of delay where the overhead during the period will not be fully recovered by the formula of overhead as a "markup" on direct costs. Equity requires that the buyer pay for the additional management attention given to the project during delays. In such cases, sellers need to recover their fixed overhead costs using a different formula than overhead as a "markup" on direct costs. *(CMBOK; NES-87)*

external network
A network not controlled by the organization. *(NIST SP 800-171)*
See *network*; contrast with *internal network*.

extraordinary contractual action
A contractual action authorized by authority of *Pub. L.* 85-804 and Executive Order 10789. *Pub. L.* 85-804 empowers the president of the United States to authorize federal agencies exercising functions in connection with the national defense to enter into, amend, and modify contracts, without regard to other provisions of law related to making, performing, amending, or modifying contracts (as authorized by Executive Order 10789), whenever the president considers that such action would facilitate the national defense. *(GOAT)*

extraordinary contractual relief
A form of relief for contractors pursuant to the performance of extraordinary contractual actions necessitated to facilitate the national defense.

extrinsic evidence
An element of contract interpretation that consists of:
• Discussions and concurrent actions,
• Prior course of dealing between the parties, and
• Custom and trade usage.
Extrinsic evidence is used to determine the intent of the parties regarding disputed contract terms. *(CMBOK)*

F

fabrication
(1) The construction of a part from raw material. *(DAAT)*
(2) The development of software code. *(DAAT)*

facilities
(1) Property used in production, maintenance, research, development, or testing (including plant equipment and real property). *(NCMA-WS)*
(2) A plant or any portion thereof (including land integral to the operation), equipment, individually or collectively, or any other tangible capital asset, wherever located, and whether owned or leased by the contractor. *(FAR 31.205-17(a))*
See also *facility*.

facilities acquisition contract
A facilities contract providing for the acquisition, construction, and installation of facilities. *(GOAT)*
See *facilities contract*.

facilities capital
The net book value of tangible capital assets and of those intangible capital assets that are subject to amortization. *(DGBCT)*

Ff

facilities capital cost of money (FCCM)
An imputed cost of capital committed to facilities determined by applying a cost-of-money rate determined by the secretary of the treasury to facilities capital employed in contract performance. *(48 CFR 9904.414)*

facilities contract
A contract under which federal government facilities are provided to a contractor or subcontractor by the government for use in connection with performing one or more related contracts for supplies or services. It is used occasionally to provide special tooling or special test equipment. *(GOAT)*
See also *consolidated facilities contract; facilities acquisition contract; facilities use contract*.

facilities use contract
A facilities contract providing for the use, maintenance, accountability, and disposition of facilities. *(GOAT)*
See *facilities contract*.

facility
Any building, plant, installation, structure, vessel, location, or site of operations owned, leased, or supervised by a contractor or subcontractor and used in the performance of a contract or subcontract. *(GOAT)*

fact finding
The process of identifying and obtaining information necessary to complete the evaluation of proposals. This may include fact-finding sessions with offerors. *(CMBOK; FAI)*

factory burden
See *factory overhead*.

factory overhead
All factory costs other than direct labor and direct material. Also known as *factory burden, indirect manufacturing costs*, and *manufacturing overhead. (CMBOK; NCMA-CA)*

failure
The inability of a system or component to perform its required functions within specified performance requirements. *(AIMD)*

FAIR Act agencies
The agencies required under the Federal Activities Inventory Reform Act (FAIR Act; *Pub. L.* 105-270) to submit inventories annually of the activities performed by government personnel. *(FAR 4.1701)*

fair and reasonable
A subjective evaluation of what each party deems as equitable consideration in areas such as terms and conditions, cost or price, assured quality, and timeliness of contract performance, and/or any other areas subject to negotiation. *(CMBOK; P&L II)*

fair and reasonable price
A price that is fair to both parties, considering the agreed-upon conditions, promised quality, and timeliness of contract performance. Although generally a fair and reasonable price is a function of the law of supply and demand, there are statutory, regulatory, and judgmental limits on the concept. *(CMBOK; ASPM)* (See also FAR 15.402.)

fair and reasonable price determination
An assessment by the U.S. federal government that an offeror's proposed price for a supply or service can be considered "fair and reasonable" on the basis of applying one or more price analysis techniques. *(DODM 1338.10)*
See *fair and reasonable price*.

fair dealing
The transacting of business in a manner characterized by candor and full disclosure and free of self-dealing. *(MW)*
See *duty of good faith and fair dealing*.

Fair Labor Standards Act of 1938 (FLSA)
A federal law (29 U.S.C. 201, *et seq.*) that set a minimum standard wage (periodically increased by later statutes) and a maximum work week of 40 hours in industries engaged in interstate commerce. The act also prohibited the labor of children under 16 years of age in most employments, and under 18 years of age in dangerous occupations. The act also created the Wage and Hour Division in the U.S. Department of Labor. *(BLD)*
See *professional services*.

fair market price
A price based on reasonable costs under normal competitive conditions and not on lowest possible cost. *(FAR 19.001)*
See *market price*.

fair market value
(1) A price at which buyers and sellers with a reasonable knowledge of pertinent facts, and not acting under any compulsion, are willing to do business. *(MW)*

(2) The value of an item as determined by negotiation between purchasers and suppliers, which would be acceptable as a basis for a purchase and sale. *(GKPT)*

fair value

Examines product or service features that enhance profits for the final product and the ability of a commercial firm to maintain a competitive advantage in the marketplace. *(DGBCT)*

family of products

Includes all products of the same classification, design, construction, material, type, and other design characteristics. These products are manufactured within the same production facilities and have the same processes, quality of materials, quality controls, and are produced under the same management, yet have the acceptable variety of physical and functional characteristics defined and specified in an applicable specification. *(DODM 4120.24)*
See also *product*.

fast payment procedure

A procedure utilized with simplified acquisitions that provides payment to the seller immediately upon receipt of its invoice (and before inspection and acceptance has taken place), provided the seller certifies that the supplies have been delivered to a "point of first receipt" (such as a common carrier) and are as ordered. *(CMBOK; GSFC)*
See *point of first receipt*.

FedBizOpps (FBO)

See *governmentwide point of entry*.

federal

Of or relating to the central government of the United States, as distinguished from the governments of its constituent units (i.e., state and local governments). *(MW)*

Federal Acquisition Certification in Contracting (FAC-C)

A certification for federal government personnel performing acquisition activities and functions. The purpose of this program is to establish general education, training, and experience requirements for those acquisition professionals. The FAC-C applies to all executive agencies, except the Department of Defense.

Federal Acquisition Circular (FAC)

Document issued by the DARC and the CAAC to announce proposed, interim, and final changes to the *Federal Acquisition Regulation*. *(GCG)*
See also **Defense Acquisition Regulatory Council, The (DARC)*; *Civilian Agency Acquisition Council, The (CAAC)**.

Federal Acquisition Institute (FAI)

Responsible for promoting the development of a professional acquisition workforce for U.S. federal agencies. In conjunction with its partners, it seeks to ensure the availability of training, provide research, promote professionalism, and improve acquisition workforce management. (See https://www.fai.gov.)

Federal Acquisition Reform Act (FARA)

A federal law (41 U.S.C. 263) that established rules to improve the efficiency of competition, clarify commercial item procedures from the Federal Acquisition Streamlining Act, and eliminate certain certification requirements. Also called the **Clinger-Cohen Act**. *(DGBCT)*

Federal Acquisition Regulation (FAR)

The *FAR* is the primary regulation for use by all federal executive agencies in their acquisition of supplies and services with appropriated funds. It became effective on April 1, 1984, and is issued within applicable laws under the joint authorities of the administrator of general services, the secretary of defense, and the administrator of for the National Aeronautics and Space Administration, under the broad policy guidelines of the administrator of the Office of Federal Procurement Policy, Office of Management and Budget. *(FAR, Forward)*

Federal Acquisition Regulation System (*FAR* System)

The *Federal Acquisition Regulations* System is established for the codification and publication of uniform policies and procedures for acquisition by all executive agencies. The *FAR* System consists of the *Federal Acquisition Regulation* (*FAR*), which is the primary document, and agency acquisition regulations that implement or supplement the *FAR*. *(FAR 1.101)*

Federal Acquisition Regulatory Council (FARC)

The council was established in 41 U.S.C. 1302 to assist in the direction and coordination of governmentwide procurement policy and governmentwide procurement regulatory activities in the federal government. It is comprised of the administrator for the Office of Federal

Ff

Procurement Policy, the secretary of defense, the administrator of the National Aeronautics and Space Administration, and the administrator of the General Services Administration. *(41 U.S.C. 1302)*

Federal Acquisition Streamlining Act (FASA)

A U.S. federal law (*Pub. L.* 103-355) that changed over 200 existing statutes and shifted the emphasis in federal procurement to using commercial practices, empowering contracting officers to exercise business judgment and emphasizing the importance of past performance. *(DGBCT)*

federal agency

Any executive agency of the U.S. federal government or any independent establishment in the legislative or judicial branch of the government (except the Senate, the House of Representatives, and the Architect of the Capitol and any activities under the architect's direction). *(42 U.S.C. 5122(9); FAR 2.101; FMR 102-71.20)* See *executive agency*.

federal agency procurement

The acquisition (by using competitive procedures and awarding a contract) of goods or services (including construction) from nonfederal sources by a federal agency using appropriated funds. For broad agency announcements and small business innovation research programs, each proposal received by an agency constitutes a separate procurement for the purposes of the Restrictions on Obtaining and Disclosing Certain Information statute (41 U.S.C. Chapter 21). *(FAR 3.104-1)*

federal assistance (grants and cooperative agreements)

The furnishing of assistance (i.e., anything of value, including financing) by the federal government through extra-contractual vehicles (i.e., by grant or cooperative agreement) to a recipient to accomplish a public purpose. This differs from "procurement" in that it is not an acquisition of products or services for the direct benefit or use of the federal government. *(CMBOK; GPM; OPM)* See *cooperative agreement; grant*.

Federal Awardee Performance & Integrity Information System (FAPIIS)

A web-enabled application that is used to collect contractor and grantee performance information including Terminations for Cause or Default, Defective Cost and Pricing Data, Determinations of Non-Responsibility, Terminations for Material Failure to Comply (grants), Recipient Not

Qualified Determinations (grants), DOD Determination of Contractor Fault, Administrative Agreements, Information on Trafficking in Persons, and Subcontractor Payment Issues. Once records are completed in FAPIIS, they become available in the Federal Past Performance Information Retrieval System (PPIRS) where they are used to support future acquisitions. See FAR 52.209-7 and FAR 52.209-9.)

federal budget

The U.S. federal government's budget for a particular fiscal year transmitted in January (the first Monday after January 3rd) to the Congress by the president, in accordance with the Budget and Accounting Act of 1921 (*Pub. L.* 67-13). Also called the "president's budget," it includes funding requests for all agencies and activities of the executive, legislative, and judicial branches. *(DISCS)*

Federal Business Opportunities (FedBizOpps; FBO)

See *governmentwide point of entry* (GPE).

Federal Catalog Program (FCP)

A governmentwide program to provide a uniform system of item identification, preclude or eliminate different identifications of like items, reveal interchangeability among items, aid in parts standardization, facilitate intra- and inter-departmental logistics support, and improve logistics management and effectiveness by promoting efficiency and economy in logistics operations. *(DODM 4100.39)*

Federal Cataloging System (FCS)

A federal government program administered by the DOD in conjunction with the General Services Administration (GSA). It names, describes, classifies, and numbers each item the government repetitively uses, buys, stocks, or distributes so that only one distinctive combination of letters and numerals identifies the same item throughout the U.S. government. *(DODM 4100.39)*

federal contract information

In the context of safeguarding federal government information within contractor information systems, this term refers to information, not intended for public release, that is provided by or generated for the government under a contract to develop or deliver a product or service to the government, but not including information provided by the government to the public (such as that on public websites) or simple transactional information, such as that necessary to process payments. *(FAR 4.1901)*
See also *covered contractor information system; infor-*

Ff

mation; information system.

Federal Courts Administration Act

A federal law (*Pub. L.* 102-572) that, in 1992, changed the name of the U.S. Claims Court to the U.S. Court of Federal Claims. *(DGBCT)*

federal excise taxes

Federal taxes levied on the sale or use of particular supplies or services. *(FAR 29.201(a))*

federal grant program

A federal program to provide assistance in carrying out economic and community development activities. *(40 U.S.C. 15101(3))*

Federal Information Processing Standard (FIPS)

A standard for adoption and use by federal departments and agencies that has been developed within the Information Technology Laboratory and published by the National Institute of Standards and Technology, a part of the U.S. Department of Commerce. A FIPS covers some topics in information technology to achieve a common level of quality or some level of interoperability. *(FIPS 201-2)*

federal information system

An information system used or operated by an executive agency of the federal government, by a contractor of an executive agency, or by another organization on behalf of an executive agency. *(40 U.S.C. 11331)* See also *executive agency; information system* (IS); contrast with *nonfederal information system*.

Federal Information Technology Acquisition Reform Act (FITARA)

A federal law (enacted December 19, 2014, as Title VIII, Subtitle D, of the National Defense Authorization Act (NDAA) for Fiscal Year 2015 (*Pub. L.* 113-291)) outlining specific requirements related to agency chief information officer authority enhancements, enhanced transparency and improved risk management in IT investments, portfolio review, federal data center consolidation, expansion of training and use of IT cadres, maximizing the benefit of strategic sourcing, and governmentwide software purchasing programs. While FITARA passed the House as a standalone act, it was ultimately incorporated as Subtitle D of the 2015 NDAA (titled "Federal Information Technology Acquisition Reform"), though it is still commonly referred to as "FITARA." *(OMB M-15-14)*

Federal Logistics Information System (FLIS)

The central repository for all logistics identification data. It is the primary computer system through which all users access, store, and retrieve necessary information related to an item of supply and that is generally considered a database of record. *(DISCS; DODM 4120.24)*

federal power and water marketing agency

A federal government entity that produces, manages, transports, controls, and sells electrical and water supply service to customers. *(FAR 41.101)*

Federal Prison Industries (FPI)/UNICOR

Federal Prison Industries, Inc. (FPI), also known as *UNICOR*, is a self-supporting, wholly owned government corporation of the District of Columbia. FPI provides training and employment for prisoners confined in federal penal and correctional institutions through the sale of its supplies and services to government agencies. *(FAR 8.601)* See *required sources of supplies and service*.

Federal Procurement Data System (FPDS)

A federal government reporting system that provides a comprehensive web-based tool for agencies to report contract actions. *(FAR 4.602(a))* (See also *FAR* Subpart 4.6.)

Federal Procurement Regulations (FPR)

The rules that governed the purchases made by civilian agencies before the *FAR* became effective. Issued in 1959, they provided detailed procurement guidance and requirements for the nonmilitary agencies. The lead agency for the *FPR* was the General Services Administration. The *FPR* was authorized by the Procurement statute (41 U.S.C. Div. C of Subtitle I). *(FGP; GSFC)*

Federal Property and Administrative Services Act of 1949

See *Procurement statute*.

Federal Register

A daily federal government publication that informs the public of proposed rules, final rules, and other legal notices issued by federal agencies. *(FAI)*

federal regulations

Applicable directives and instructions issued by the several departments and agencies that establish and implement acquisition policies. One example is the FAR. *(DGBCT)*

Ff

Federal Sentencing Guidelines

Guidelines published by the U.S. Sentencing Commission that establish the parameters and set policies for judges in sentencing convicted companies. Under the guidelines, there are three possible penalties:
- Restitution,
- Monetary fine, and
- Probation.

A company may experience more severe punishment if it does not have an effective compliance program to prevent and detect violations of law. *(TIPS)*
See *compliance program*.

federal specification (FEDSPEC)

A specification issued or controlled by the General Services Administration (and listed in the GSA Index of Federal Specifications, Standards, and Commercial Item Descriptions) for commercial or modified commercial products that contains requirements or tests too extensive to be suitable for a commercial item description. *(DODM 4120.24)*
See *commercial item description* (CID); *federal standard; General Services Administration* (GSA) *Index of Federal Specifications, Standards, and Commercial Item Descriptions; specification*.

federal standard

A standard issued or controlled by the General Services Administration (and listed in the GSA Index of Federal Specifications, Standards, and Commercial Item Descriptions) that covers processes, procedures, practices, and methods for use by all federal agencies. *(DODM 4120.24)*
See *General Services Administration* (GSA) *Index of Federal Specifications, Standards, and Commercial Item Descriptions; standard*.

federal statute

See *statute*.

federal supply class (FSC)

A four-digit coding structure used by the federal government to group products into logical families in the Federal Supply Classification system for supply management purposes. *(DODM 4120.24)*
See *Federal Supply Classification* (FSC); *federal supply group* (FSG).

Federal Supply Classification (FSC)

A federal government system by which all items of personal property that are used by all participating activities are classified. Federal Supply Classification contains groups and classes of commodities with emphasis on the items known to be in participating activities' supply systems. *(DODM 4100.39)*
See also *federal supply class* (FSC); *federal supply group* (FSG).

federal supply group (FSG)

A two-digit coding structure used by the federal government to group related federal supply classes under logical families in the Federal Supply Classification system for supply management purposes. The first two digits of each federal supply class represent the related federal supply group. *(DODM 4120.24)*
See *federal supply class* (FSC); *Federal Supply Classification* (FSC).

Federal Supply Schedule (FSS) Program

Directed and managed by the General Services Administration, it provides federal agencies with a simplified process for obtaining commonly used supplies and services at prices associated with volume buying. The Federal Supply Schedule Program is also known as the **GSA Schedules Program** or the **Multiple Award Schedule (MAS) Program**. *(FAR 8.402(a))* (See also *FAR* Subpart 8.4 and *FAR* Part 38.)
See **Multiple Award Schedule and Single Award Schedule**.

federally controlled facilities

A term that applies to any of the following:
- Federally-owned buildings or leased space, whether for single or multi-tenant occupancy, and its grounds and approaches, all or any portion of which is under the jurisdiction, custody, or control of a federal government department or agency;
- Federally-controlled commercial space shared with nongovernment tenants (e.g., if a department or agency leased the 10th floor of a commercial building, this term applies to the 10th floor only);
- Government-owned, contractor-operated facilities, including laboratories engaged in national defense research and production activities; and
- Facilities under a management and operating contract, such as for the operation, maintenance, or support of a government-owned or controlled research, development, special production, or testing establishment.

(FAR 2.101; OMB M-05-24)

Ff

federally-controlled information system

Information systems used or operated by a federal agency or by a contractor of an agency or other organization on behalf of an agency. Applicability for access to federal systems from a non-federally-controlled facility should be based on the risk determination required by existing National Institute of Standards and Technology (NIST) guidance. *(FAR 2.101; OMB M-05-24)*

Federally Funded Research and Development Center (FFRDC)

Activities that are sponsored under a broad charter by a U.S. federal government agency (or agencies) for the purpose of performing, analyzing, integrating, supporting, and/or managing basic or applied research and/or development, and that receive 70 percent or more of their financial support from the government; and—

- A long-term relationship is contemplated;
- Most or all of the facilities are owned or funded by the government; and
- The FFRDC has access to government and supplier data, employees, and facilities beyond that common in a normal contractual relationship.

(FAR 2.101) (See also *FAR* Subpart 35.017.)

Fedwire

An online credit transfer service operated by the U.S. Federal Reserve Banking System that is used primarily for large-value, time-critical payments. Also called the "Fedwire Funds Service." *(NES-98)*

fee

An agreed-to amount of reimbursement beyond the initial estimate of costs. (The term "fee" is used when discussing cost-reimbursement contracts, whereas "profit" is used in relation to fixed-price contracts.) *(CMBOK; DGBCT; OPM)*
See also *profit*.

fee-determining official (FDO)

The designated agency official(s) who reviews the recommendations of the award-fee board in determining the amount of award fee to be earned by the contractor for each evaluation period. *(FAR 16.001)* (See also 16.401(e)(3).)
See also *award fee board*.

felony

Any federal or state offense classified by applicable federal or state law as a felony. *(21 U.S.C. 802(13))*

fences

Explicit limitations (i.e., ceilings and floors) established by Congress on the use of funds provided in an appropriations act. *(DISCS)*
See also *earmarks*.

fiduciary

(1) A person who handles another person's money or property in a capacity that involves a confidence or trust. Examples of fiduciaries are executors or guardians of the estates of minors or deceased persons. *(CMBOK; FBL)*
See *"fiduciary duty"*
(2) With respect to a negotiable instrument, this term means an agent, trustee, partner, corporate officer or director, or other representative owing a fiduciary duty. *(UCC 3-307(a)(1))*
See also *negotiable instrument; represented person*.

fiduciary duty

A duty obligating a fiduciary (as an agent or trustee) to act with loyalty and honesty and in a manner consistent with the best interests of the beneficiary of the fiduciary relationship (as a principal or trust beneficiary). *(MW)*
See *fiduciary; represented person*.

field contracting activity

A level of federal government contracting activity that supports the operational requirements of a post, camp, station, national park, hospital, institute, or field installation, and involves a highly diversified range of assignments. *(OPM)*

field pricing support

The analysis of contractor pricing proposals by any or all field technical and other specialists. *(OPM)*

file protection

In a cybersecurity context, the aggregate of processes and procedures designed to inhibit unauthorized access, contamination, elimination, modification, or destruction of a file or any of its contents. *(CNSSI 4009)*

file security

In a cybersecurity context, a means by which access to computer files is limited to authorized users only. *(CNSSI 4009)*

"filed"

The complete receipt of any document by an entity before its close of business. Documents received after close of business are considered filed as of the next day. Unless otherwise stated, the close of business of a federal agency is presumed to be 4:30 p.m. local time. *(FAR 33.101)*

filing office
An office designated as the place to file an official document or statement. *(UCC 9-102(a)(37))*
See *filed*.

fill rate
The proportion of all stock requisitions that are filled from stock that is present on the shelf. The inverse of this is "stock-out rate." These measurements can be calculated for any time period (in some retail or distribution firms it might be computed daily or weekly). *(GKPT)*

final conviction
A conviction, whether entered on a verdict or plea, including a plea of *nolo contendere*, for which a sentence has been imposed. *(FAR 3.702)*
See *conviction*; see also *nolo contendere*.

final cost objective
A cost objective that has allocated to it both direct and indirect costs and, in the contractor's accumulation system, is one of the final accumulation points. *(FAR 31.001)*

final decision
For purposes of the Contract Disputes statute (41 U.S.C. Chapter 71), this is a contracting officer's unilateral adjudication of a contract claim that is a prerequisite to jurisdiction over the claim by a board of contract appeals or federal court. *(CMBOK; GCG)*
See also *"government contract disputes process"*

final indirect cost rate
The indirect cost rate established and agreed upon by the federal government and the contractor as not subject to change. It is usually established after the close of the contractor's fiscal year (unless the parties decide upon a different period) to which it applies. For cost-reimbursement research and development contracts with educational institutions, it may be predetermined; that is, established for a future period on the basis of cost experience with similar contracts, together with supporting data. *(FAR 2.101)*
See *indirect cost rate*.

final proposal revision (FPR)
A final proposal submission by all offerors in the competitive range submitted at a common cut-off date at the request of the buyer after conclusion of negotiations. *(NCMA-SS)* (See also FAR 15.307(b).)
See *proposal revision*.

final voucher
Under cost-reimbursement contracts, a type of invoice submitted when the contract is completed. *(NCMA-WS)*
See *invoice*.

finance lease
A lease with respect to which the lessor does not select, manufacture, or supply the goods; the lessor acquires the goods or the right to possession and use of the goods in connection with the lease. *(UCC 2A-103(g))*
See also *goods; lease; lease contract; lessee; lessor*.

financial accounting
Measuring and recording financial data of an enterprise for purposes of providing relevant financial information to interested users both internal and external to the entity. *(NCMA-CA)*

financial accounting data sheet
Commits the buyer to availability of funds for specific amounts as displayed on the data sheet. It is the final proof the buyer needs to show that funds are available for obligation. The financial accounting data sheet is attached to the procurement request and indicates funding availability. *(HCS)*

Financial Accounting Standards Board (FASB)
Established in 1973, the Financial Accounting Standards Board (FASB) is the independent, private-sector, not-for-profit organization based in Norwalk, Connecticut, that establishes financial accounting and reporting standards for public and private companies and not-for-profit organizations that follow generally accepted accounting principles *(GAAP)*. (See https://www.fasb.org.)

financial asset
Means:
- A security;
- An obligation of a person or a share, participation, or other interest in a person or in property or an enterprise of a person, which is, or is of a type, dealt in or traded in financial markets, or which is recognized in any area in which it is issued or dealt in as a medium for investment; or

Ff

- Any property that is held by a securities intermediary for another person in a securities account if the securities intermediary has expressly agreed with the other person that the property is to be treated as a financial asset.

As context requires, this term means either the interest itself or the means by which a person's claim to it is evidenced, including a certificated or uncertificated security, a security certificate, or a security entitlement. *(UCC 8-102(a)(9))*
See also *certificated security; security; securities account, security certificate; security entitlement; securities intermediary; uncertificated security.*

financial data addendum sheet
A document that indicates funds are available for a particular procurement. It indicates the appropriate funding citation and dollar limitation that is established for procuring the designated item. It is attached to the procurement request or forwarded by separate funding procurement request to initiate the funding action. The financial data addendum sheet is distinguished from the data sheet, which becomes part of the executed contract. *(HCS)*
See also *financial accounting data sheet.*

financing
See *contract financing; contractor financing.*

financing entity
A bank, finance company, or other person who, in the ordinary course of business, makes advances against goods or documents of title or who by arrangement with either the seller or the buyer intervenes in ordinary course to make or collect payment due or claimed under the contract for sale, as by purchasing or paying the seller's draft or making advances against it or by merely taking it for collection, whether or not documents of title accompany the draft. "Financing entity" also includes a bank or other person who similarly intervenes between persons who are in the position of seller and buyer in respect to the goods. *(UCC 2-104(2))*

financing statement
A record or records composed of an initial financing statement and any filed record relating to the initial financing statement. *(UCC 9-102(a)(39))*

finished goods inventory
The cost of a manufacturer's completed product that is being held for sale. *(NCMA-CA)*

firewall
A system designed to defend against unauthorized access to or from a private network. *(CNSSI 4009)*

firm bid rule
A rule that prohibits the bidder from withdrawing its bid for the period specified in the invitation for bids; usually 60 days after bid opening. *(GSFC)*
See also *invitation for bids* (IFB).

firm-fixed-price (FFP) contract
A contract that provides for a price that is not subject to any adjustment by reasons of costs experienced by the seller in performance of the contract. This contract type places upon the seller maximum risk and full responsibility for all costs and resulting profit or loss. It provides maximum incentive for the seller to control costs and perform effectively and imposes a minimum administrative burden upon the contracting parties. *(FAR 16.202-1)*

firm-fixed-price, level-of-effort (FFP-LOE) term contract
A fixed-price type contract that requires the seller to provide a specified level of effort over a stated period of time on work that can be stated only in general terms, and the same requires the buyer to pay the seller a fixed dollar amount. *(FAR 16.207-1)*
See also *fixed-price, level-of-effort* (FPLOE) *contract.*

firmware
Computer programs and data stored in hardware–i.e., recorded in permanent or semi-permanent computer memory–such that the programs and data cannot be dynamically written or modified during execution of the programs. *(CNSSI 4009; NIST SP 800-17;)*
See also *hardware; software.*

first article
A preproduction model, initial production sample, test sample, first lot, pilot lot, or pilot model submitted for testing and evaluation for conformance with specified contract requirements before or in the initial stages of production. *(FAR 2.101)*
See also *"first article testing* (FAT).

first article testing (FAT)
(1) Testing and evaluating the first article for conformance with specified contract requirements before or in the initial stage of production. *(FAR 2.101)*
See *first article.*
(2) Used by the buyer to ensure that the seller can fur-

Ff

nish a product that conforms to all contract requirements for acceptance. This procedure, although costly, can be a significant contributor to risk reduction. Assuming that more than one product is to be built, the risk to the remaining products is minimized based on the lessons learned during the first article inspection. *(CMBOK)*

first-in, first-out (FIFO)
An inventory accounting method where the stock of merchandise or material that is acquired earliest is assumed to be used first; the stock acquired latest is assumed to be still on hand. *(IMA)*
Compare with *last-in, first-out*.

first-tier subcontract
A subcontract awarded directly by the contractor for the purpose of acquiring supplies or services (including construction) for performance of a prime contract. It does not include the contractor's supplier agreements with vendors, such as long-term arrangements for materials or supplies that benefit multiple contracts and/or the costs of which are normally applies to a contractor's general and administrative expenses or indirect costs. *(FAR 4.1701)*
See also *first-tier subcontractor*.

first-tier subcontractor
A subcontractor holding a subcontract with a prime contractor. *(FAR 22.801)*
See *first-tier subcontract*.

fiscal year (FY)
(1) An accounting period of 12 months. *(MW)*
(2) The federal government's accounting period, which runs from October 1 to September 30 of the following year, for which annual financial statements are regularly prepared, generally a period of 12 months, 52 weeks, or 53 weeks. *(FAR 31.001; DISCS)*
(3) The fiscal year established by the contractor for accounting purposes. *(FAR 31.205-6(p)(1)(iii))*

fishbone diagram
See *cause and effect diagram*.

fixed capital
Capital that is invested on a long-term basis—especially capital invested in fixed assets. *(MW)*
See *capital*.

fixed-ceiling-price with retroactive price redetermination contract
A fixed-price type contract that provides for a fixed ceiling price and a retroactive price redetermination within the ceiling after completion of the contract. *(FAR 16.206-1)*
See *fixed-price contract*.

fixed cost
(1) A cost which, for a given period of time and range of activity, does not change. *(NCMA-CA)*
(2) Costs that do not vary with the volume of business, such as property taxes, insurance, depreciation, security, and water/utility fees. *(DISCS)*

fixed price
A form of pricing that includes a ceiling beyond which the buyer bears no responsibility for payment. *(OPM)*

fixed-price-award-fee (FPAF) contract
(1) A fixed-price type contract with award-fee provisions included. Often used when the buyer wishes to motivate a seller and other incentives cannot be used because the seller's performance cannot be measured objectively. Such contracts establish a fixed price (including normal profit) for the effort. This price will be paid for satisfactory contract performance. Award fee earned (if any) will be paid in addition to that fixed price. *(FAR 16.404)*
See *fixed-price contract*; see also *award fee*.
(2) Operating expenses that are incurred to provide facilities and organization that are kept in readiness to do business without regard to actual volumes of production and sales. Examples of fixed costs consist of rent, property tax, and interest expense. *(CMBOK)*

fixed-price contract
A contract that provides for a firm price or, in appropriate cases, an adjustable price, and are so designed as to facilitate proper pricing under varying circumstances. Fixed-price types of contracts providing for an adjustable price may include a ceiling price, a target price (including target cost), or both. Unless otherwise specified in the contract, the ceiling price or target price is subject to adjustment only by operation of contract clauses providing for equitable adjustment or other revision of the contract price under stated circumstances. *(FAR 16.201)* (See also FAR 30.001.)
See *"firm-fixed-price (FFP) contract; fixed-ceiling-price with retroactive price redetermination contract; fixed-price incentive (FPI) contract; fixed-price, level-of-effort (FLOE) contract; fixed-price with economic price*

Ff

adjustment (FPEPA) *contract; fixed-price with prospective price redetermination contract.*

fixed-price contract with retroactive price redetermination

See *fixed-ceiling-price contract with retroactive price redetermination*

fixed-price-incentive (FPI) contract

A fixed-price contract that provides for adjusting profit and establishing the final contract price by application of a formula based on the relationship of total final negotiated cost to total target cost. The final price is subject to a price ceiling, negotiated at the outset. There are two types of FPI contracts:
- "Fixed-price-incentive (firm target) contract," and
- "Fixed-price-incentive (successive target) contract."

(FAR 16.204; 16.403(a))

See *fixed-price-incentive (firm target) (FPIF) contract; fixed-price-incentive (successive targets) (FPIS) contract.*

fixed-price-incentive (firm target) (FPIF) contract

A fixed-price-incentive (FPI) contract that specifies a target cost, a target profit, a price ceiling (but not a profit ceiling or floor), and a profit adjustment formula. These elements are all negotiated at the outset. The price ceiling is the maximum that may be paid to the contractor, except for any adjustment under other contract clauses. When the contractor completes performance, the parties negotiate the final cost, and the final price is established by applying the formula. When the final cost is less than the target cost, application of the formula results in a final profit greater than the target profit; conversely, when final cost is more than target cost, application of the formula results in a final profit less than the target profit, or even a net loss. If the final negotiated cost exceeds the price ceiling, the contractor absorbs the difference as a loss. Because the profit varies inversely with the cost, this contract type provides a positive, calculable profit incentive for the contractor to control costs. *(FAR 16.403-1(a))*

See *fixed-price-incentive (FPI) contract; contrast with fixed-price-incentive (successive targets) (FPIS) contract.*

fixed-price-incentive (successive targets) (FPIS) contract

A fixed-price-incentive (FPI) contract that specifies the following elements, all of which are negotiated at the outset:

- An initial target cost;
- An initial target profit;
- An initial profit adjustment formula to be used for establishing the firm target profit, including a ceiling and floor for the firm target profit;
- The production point at which the firm target cost and firm target profit will be negotiated; and
- A ceiling price that is the maximum that may be paid to the contractor, except for any adjustment under other contract clauses providing for equitable adjustment or other revision of the contract price under stated circumstances.

When the production point specified in the contract is reached, the parties negotiate the firm target cost, giving consideration to cost experience under the contract and other pertinent factors. The firm target profit is established by the formula. At this point, the parties have two alternatives: They may negotiate a firm fixed price (using the firm target cost plus the firm target profit as a guide) or, if negotiation of a firm fixed price is inappropriate, they may negotiate a formula for establishing the final price using the firm target cost and firm target profit. The final cost is then negotiated at completion. *(FAR 16.403-2(a))*

See *fixed-price-incentive (FPI) contract;* contrast with *fixed-price-incentive (firm target) (FPIF) contract.*

fixed-price level of effort term contract

A fixed-price type of contract that requires the contractor to provide a specific level of effort, over a stated period of time, on work that can be stated only in general terms. *(FAR 16.207-1)*

fixed-price redeterminable (FPR) contract

A fixed-price type of contract that contains provisions for subsequently negotiated adjustment, in whole or in part, of the initially negotiated base price. *(OPM)* (See also FAR 16.205 and FAR 16.206.)

fixed-price type contract

See *fixed-price contract.*

fixed-price with economic price adjustment (FPEPA) contract

A fixed-price contract that provides for upward and downward revision of the stated contract price upon the occurrence of specified contingencies. *(FAR 16.203-1)*

See *fixed-price contract.*

Ff

fixed-price with prospective price redetermination contract

A fixed-price contract that provides for a firm-fixed-price for an initial period of contract deliveries or performance and prospective redetermination (at a stated time or times during performance) of the price for subsequent periods of performance. *(FAR 16.205-1)* See *fixed-price contract*.

flexible budget

A budget, usually referring to overhead costs only, which is prepared for a range, rather than a single level of activity; one which can be automatically geared to changes in the level of volume. Also known as a *variable budget*. *(NCMA-CA)*

flexibly priced contract/subcontract

Means—
- Fixed-price contracts and subcontracts described at FAR 16.203-1(a)(2), FAR 16.204, FAR 16.205, and FAR 16.206;
- "Cost-Reimbursement Contracts" and subcontracts (*FAR* Subpart 16.3);
- Incentive contracts and subcontracts where the price may be adjusted based on actual costs incurred (*FAR* Subpart 16.4);
- Orders issued under "Indefinite-Delivery Contracts" and subcontracts where final payment is based on actual costs incurred (*FAR* Subpart 16.5); and
- The materials portion of "Time-and-Materials" contracts and subcontracts (*FAR* Subpart 16.6).

(FAR 30.001)

flow down

(1) The transfer and translation of requirements from a prime contract to a subcontract in support of the prime contract. The "flow down" may be required or optional. *(NES-89)*
See *mandatory flow down clauses*.
(2) The further flow-down of the requirements described in (1.) of this definition from subcontracts to lower-tier subcontracts. *(CMBOK)*

forbearance

An intentional failure of a party to enforce a contract requirement, usually done for an act of immediate or future consideration from the other party. It is sometimes referred to as a "nonwaiver" or as a "one-time waiver," but not as a relinquishment of rights. *(DGBCT)*

force majeure

French for "superior force." It refers to an unexpected or uncontrollable event that upsets a plan or releases one from an obligation. In contracting, it is often used to refer to excusable conditions for nonperformance under a contract (e.g., strikes, acts of God, etc.). In this context, it is synonymous with the term "excusable delay." *(CMBOK; HECA; TIPS)*
See *excusable delay*.

forced labor

Knowingly providing or obtaining the labor or services of a person—
- By threats of serious harm to, or physical restraint against, that person or another person;
- By means of any scheme, plan, or pattern intended to cause the person to believe that, if the person did not perform such labor or services, that person or another person would suffer serious harm or physical restraint; or
- By mean s of the abuse or threatened abuse of law or the legal process.

(FAR 22.1702) (See also *FAR* Subpart 22.15.)

forecast

An estimation of the future demand for a product. It is usually stated as a quantity (or value) over a specific time period. There are a number of inputs into a forecast, such as historical data, market trends, marketing data, and sales force feedback. *(DGBCT)*

Foreign Assistance Act of 1961 (FAA)

The basic law (22 U.S.C. 2151, et seq.) providing the authority and the general rules for the conduct of foreign assistance grant activities/programs by the federal government. *(DISCS)*

foreign construction material

A construction material other than a domestic construction material. *(FAR 25.003; FAR 25.601)*
See *construction material*; contrast with *domestic construction material*.

foreign contractor

In the context of the federal government's "Buy American" policies, trade agreements, and other laws and regulations governing foreign acquisition, this term refers to a contractor or subcontractor organized or existing under the laws of a country other than the United States. *(FAR 25.003)*

Ff

Foreign Corrupt Practices Act (FCPA)

A federal law (15 U.S.C. 78dd-1, *et seq.*) making certain payments to foreign government officials illegal, even if such payments are legal or a common practice in the foreign country. *(TIPS)*

foreign end product

An end product other than a domestic end product. *(FAR 25.003)*

See *end product*; contrast with *domestic end product*.

foreign-flag vessel

Any vessel of foreign registry including vessels owned by U.S. citizens but registered in a nation other than the United States. *(FAR 47.501)*

foreign military sales (FMS)

(1) That portion of U.S. security assistance authorized by the Arms Export Control Act (22 U.S.C. 2751, *et seq.*) and conducted on the basis of formal contracts or agreements between the U.S. government and an authorized recipient government or international organization. Foreign military sales include government-to-government sales of defense articles or defense services, from DOD stocks or through new procurements under DOD-managed contracts, regardless of the source of financing. *(DISCS)*

See also *Arms Export Control Act* (AECA); *defense article; defense service.*

(2) Actions on the part of the DOD on behalf of another government to make procurements using that government's funds. *(OPM)*

Foreign Military Sales (FMS) Program

That portion of U.S. security assistance authorized by the Foreign Assistance Act (FAA) of 1961, and the Arms Export Control Act (AECA). The recipient provides reimbursement for defense articles and services transferred from the United States. This includes cash sales from stocks (inventories, services, or training) by the Department of Defense. (See https://www.dau.mil.)

See *conventional arms transfer* (CAT); *foreign military sales* (FMS); see also *Arms Export Control Act* (AECA); *Foreign Assistance Act of 1961* (FAA).

foreign offer

In the context of the federal government's "Buy American" policies, trade agreements, and other laws and regulations governing foreign acquisition, this term refers to any offer other than a domestic offer. *(FAR 25.003)*

See *domestic offer; eligible offer.*

foreign services

In the context of the federal government's "Buy American" policies, trade agreements, and other laws and regulations governing foreign acquisition, this term refers to any services other than domestic services. *(GOAT)*

foreign trade zone

A site sanctioned by U.S. Customs and Border Protection that provides special customs exemptions to U.S. plants engaged in international trade-related activities. Duty-free treatment is accorded items that are processed in foreign trade zones and then re-exported, and duty payment is deferred on items until they are brought out of the foreign trade zone for sale in the U.S. market. This helps to offset customs advantages available to overseas producers who compete with domestic industry. *(DGBCT; GKPT)*

form contract

In the context of the *CMS™*, "form contract" is the only domain within the "award" phase of the contract life cycle. It is the process of:

- Determining reasonable cost and pricing,
- Conducting negotiations,
- Selecting the source, and
- Managing challenges and disagreements.

The value added by this process is to mitigate or eliminate contract performance risk by selecting the best source and negotiating prices and terms and conditions. *(CMS)*

See *award life cycle phase; Contract Management Standard™ Publication (CMS™)*; see also *conduct negotiations; cost analysis; price analysis; manage legal conformity; source selection.*

form, fit, and function data

(1) Data relating to items, components, or processes that are sufficient to enable physical and functional interchangeability, and data identifying source, size, configuration, mating and attachment characteristics, functional characteristics, and performance requirements. *(FAR 27.401)*

(2) For computer software, this term means data identifying source, functional characteristics, and performance requirements, but specifically excludes the source code, algorithms, processes, formulas, and flow charts of the software. *(FAR 27.401)*

formal contract

A contract that requires a special form or method of formation (creation) in order to be enforceable. *(CMBOK)*

See *contract under seal; letter of credit; recognizance; negotiable instrument.*

Ff

formal reprogramming
In project management, the process of establishing an "over target baseline" or "over target schedule." (NDIA II)
See over target baseline (OTB); over target schedule (OTS).

forward buying
The practice of buying materials in a quantity exceeding specified current requirements, but not beyond the actual foreseeable requirements (DBL)

forward pricing
An action involving negotiations and a resultant agreement between a seller and the buyer to use certain rates and/or indices for a specified future period of time in pricing contracts or contract modifications. (CMBOK; P&L II)

forward pricing rate agreement (FPRA)
A written agreement negotiated between a seller and a buyer to make certain rates available during a specified period for use in pricing contracts or modifications. These rates represent reasonable projections of specific costs that are not easily estimated for, identified with, or generated by a specific contract, contract end item, or task. These projections may include rates for such things as labor, indirect costs, material obsolescence and usage, spare parts provisioning, and material handling. (FAR 2.101)
See forward pricing; see also forward pricing rate proposal (FPRP); forward pricing rate recommendation.

forward pricing rate proposal (FPRP)
A proposal submitted by a seller to a buyer for certification of the seller's cost and labor rates over a period of time. The buyer is responsible for performing the appropriate reviews of contractor cost proposals to establish well-supported negotiation positions and to negotiate effectively to ensure contract prices are fair and reasonable. This leads up to a "forward pricing rate agreement." (NDIA II)
See forward pricing rate agreement (FPRA).

forward pricing rate recommendation
A rate set unilaterally by the administrative contracting officer for use by the federal government in negotiations or other contract actions when forward pricing rate agreement negotiations have not been completed or when the contractor will not agree to a forward pricing rate agreement. (FAR 2.101)
See also forward pricing rate agreement (FPRA).

Four Corners Doctrine
A theory of contract interpretation that the contract itself should include all of the terms and conditions that the parties wish to be part of the agreement—i.e., the notion that the entire agreement should be contained within the "four corners" of the document. (CMBOK)
See contract interpretation.

framework pricing arrangement
A contract that is definitive in all respects except pricing. The agreement or contract specifies a predetermined index, formula, or algorithm (i.e., the "framework") for the calculation of price at the point of sale. (CMBOK)

franchise territory
A geographical area that a utility supplier has a right to serve based upon a franchise, a certificate of public convenience and necessity, or other legal means. (FAR 41.101)
See also utility service.

fraud
(1) An intentional perversion of truth for the purpose of inducing another in reliance upon it to part with something of value belonging to him or her or to surrender a legal right. (BLD)
(2) A false representation of a matter of fact, whether by words or conduct, by false or misleading allegations, or by concealment of that which should have been disclosed, which deceives and is intended to deceive another so that he or she shall act upon it to his or her legal injury. (BLD)
See fraudulent misrepresentation.
(3) Anything calculated to deceive. (BLD)
(4) Includes:
* Acts of fraud or corruption or attempts to defraud the U.S. federal government or to corrupt its agents,
* Acts which constitute a cause for debarment or suspension under FAR 9.406-2(a) and FAR 9.407-2(a), and
* Acts which violate the False Claims Act (31 U.S.C. 3729-3731) or the Kickbacks statute (41 U.S.C. Chapter 87).
(FAR 31.205-47(a))

fraudulent misrepresentation
A misrepresentation is fraudulent if the maker intends his or her assertion to induce a party to manifest his or her assent and the maker—

Ff

- Knows or believes that the assertion is not in accord with the facts,
- Does not have the confidence that he or she states or implies in the truth of the assertion, or
- Knows that he or she does not have the basis that he or she states or implies for the assertion.

(RSOC 162(1))
Contrast with *material misrepresentation*.

free on board (FOB)

This term is used in conjunction with a physical point to determine the responsibility and basis for payment of freight charges and, unless otherwise agreed, the point where title for goods passes to the buyer or consignee. *(FAR 2.101)*
See also *free on board at destination (FOB destination); free on board at origin (FOB origin)*.

free on board at destination (FOB destination)

The seller or consigner delivers the goods on the seller's or consigner's conveyance at destination. Unless the contract provides otherwise, the seller or consignor is responsible for the cost of shipping and risk of loss. *(FAR 2.101)* (See also FAR 52.247-34.)
See *free on board* (FOB); see also *free on board at origin* (FOB origin).

free on board at origin (FOB origin)

The seller or consignor places the goods on the conveyance by which they are to be transported. Unless the contract provides otherwise, the buyer or consignee is responsible for the cost of shipping and risk of loss. *(FAR 2.101)* (See also FAR 52.247-29.)
See *free on board* (FOB); see also *free on board at destination* (FOB destination).

Freedom of Information Act (FOIA)

A federal law (5 U.S.C. 552, *et seq.*) requiring disclosure of government records to any person, except as stated in specific exceptions. The information is to be made available either by:
- Publishing it in the *Federal Register*,
- Providing an opportunity to read and copy records at convenient locations, or
- Upon request, providing a copy of a reasonably described record.

(FAR 24.201; TIPS)

free trade agreement (FTA)

A treaty between two or more countries that do not impose tariffs for commerce conducted across their borders. This doesn't mean capital and labor moves freely between them, and tariffs are still imposed upon nonmember countries. The idea is to open markets and provide opportunities for businesses to compete globally. *(DGBCT)*

free trade agreement country

In the context of the federal government's "Buy American" policies, trade agreements, and other laws and regulations governing foreign acquisition, this term refers to: Australia, Bahrain, Canada, Chile, Colombia, Costa Rica, Dominican Republic, El Salvador, Guatemala, Honduras, Korea (Republic of), Mexico, Morocco, Nicaragua, Oman, Panama, Peru, or Singapore. *(FAR 25.003)*
See *foreign trade agreement (FTA)*; see also *designated country; free trade agreement country end product*.

free trade agreement country end product

In the context of the federal government's "Buy American" policies, trade agreements, and other laws and regulations governing foreign acquisition, this term refers to an article that is wholly the growth, product, or manufacture of a free trade agreement (FTA) country, or in the case of an article that consists in whole or in part of materials from another country, has been substantially transformed in an FTA country into a new and different article of commerce with a name, character, or use distinct from that of the article or articles from which it was transformed. *(FAR 25.003)*
See *foreign trade agreement (FTA); foreign trade agreement country*; see also *end product*.

freight

Supplies, goods, and transportable property. Also called "general freight." *(FAR 2.101; FAR 47.201)*

freight forwarder (FF)

A commercial import/export company who arranges transportation of freight from a specified point to a final destination. *(DISCS)*
See also *freight*.

fringe benefits

Allowances and services provided by an employer to its employees as compensation in addition to regular wages and salaries. Fringe benefits may include, but are not limited to, vacations, sick leave, holidays, military leave, employee insurance, and supplemental unemployment benefit plans. *(FAR 31.205-6(m)(1))*

Ff

Fulford Doctrine

A legal doctrine arising from *Fulford Manufacturing Co.* (ABSCA Nos. 2143, 2144; 6 CCF ~ 61,185) holding that the imposition of excess costs of reprocurement entitles the contractor to an additional opportunity to question the propriety of the original (default) termination.

full and open competition

With respect to a contract action, means that all responsible sources are permitted to compete. *(FAR 2.101)*
See also *responsible source*.

full cost

(1) *Synonymous with* "acquisition cost."
(2) When applied to the expenses incurred in the operation of an organization, they are comprised of all direct, indirect, general, and administrative costs incurred in the operation of the organization. These costs include, but are not limited to personnel, equipment, software, supplies, contracted services, space occupancy, etc. *(OMB A-130)*

full disclosure

An accounting principle that states the accountant should adequately disclose all relevant information to facilitate a clear understanding of the preparation of financial statements and to avoid erroneous implications. *(NCMA-CA)*

full maintenance

The complete diagnostic repair, modification, and overhaul of equipment, including repair of defective assemblies by piece part replacement. Also known as "depot maintenance." *(CNSSI 4009)*
Compare with *"limited maintenance*.

full production contract

A contract for full production of successfully tested major systems selected from the full-scale development phase. *(FAR 34.005-6)*
See *full-scale development* (FSD); see also *concept exploration contract; demonstration contract; full-scale development contract*.

full-scale development (FSD)

The phase of a major system acquisition when the system/equipment and the principal items necessary for its support are designed, fabricated, tested, and evaluated. The intended output is, at a minimum, a pre-production system that closely approximates the final product, the documentation necessary to enter the production phase, and the test results that demonstrate that the production product will meet stated requirements. *(DOD-MMH)* (See also FAR 34.005-5.)
See also *full-scale development contract*.

full-scale development (FSD) contract

A contract type for use in major systems acquisition that should provide for the contractors to submit priced proposals for production that are based on the latest quantity, schedule, and logistics requirements and other considerations that will be used in making the production decision. *(FAR 34.005-5)*
See *full-scale development* (FSD); see also *concept exploration contract; demonstration contract; full production contract*.

full-time work schedule

Full-time employment with a basic 40-hour work week. *(DODM 1000.12-M-VI)*
See *uncompensated overtime*.

functional requirement

A contract requirement stated in terms of the objectives that must be achieved under the contract. Each offeror is permitted to define how those objectives will be achieved in its proposal. *(GOAT)*

functional specification

A purchase description that describes the deliverable in terms of performance characteristics and intended use, including those characteristics that at a minimum are necessary to satisfy the intended use. *(FAI)*

functional statement of work (functional SOW)

Describe requirements in terms of the end purpose, expected result, or final objective rather than in terms of how the work effort is to be performed. The functional SOW is the least restrictive of the three basic SOW types. *(DGBCT)*
Compare with *design SOW; performance SOW*.

fund cite

See *lines of accounting* (LOA)

funded pension cost

The portion of pension cost for a current or prior cost accounting period that has been paid to a funding agency. *(FAR 31.001)*

Ff

funds transfer

The series of transactions, beginning with the originator's payment order, made for the purpose of making payment to the beneficiary of the order. A funds transfer is completed by acceptance by the beneficiary's bank of a payment order for the benefit of the beneficiary of the originator's payment order. *(UCC 4A-104(a))*
See also *beneficiary; funds-transfer system; electronic funds transfer (EFT); originator; payment order*.

funds-transfer system

A wire transfer network, automated clearing house, or other communication system of a clearing house or other association of banks through which a payment order by a bank may be transmitted to the bank to which the order is addressed. *(UCC 4A-105(a)(5))*
See also *electronic funds transfer (EFT); funds transfer; funds-transfer system rule*.

funds-transfer system rule

A rule of an association of banks:

- Governing transmission of payment orders by means of a funds-transfer system of the association or rights and obligations with respect to those orders, or
- To the extent the rule governs rights and obligations between banks that are parties to a funds transfer in which a Federal Reserve Bank, acting as an intermediary bank, sends a payment order to the beneficiary's bank.

A funds-transfer system rule governing rights and obligations between participating banks using the system may be effective even if the rule indirectly affects another party to the funds transfer who does not consent to the rule. A funds-transfer system rule may also govern rights and obligations of parties other than participating banks using the system. *(UCC 4A-501(b))*
See also *funds transfer; funds-transfer system; payment order*.

future goods

Goods which are not both existing and identified. A purported present sale of future goods or of any interest therein operates as a contract to sell. *(UCC 2-105(2))*
See *goods*.

future unit cost reduction

In value engineering, the instant unit cost reduction adjusted as the contracting officer considers necessary for projected learning or changes in quantity during the sharing period. It is calculated at the time the value engineering change proposal is accepted and applies either throughout the sharing period (unless the contracting officer decides that recalculation is necessary because conditions are significantly different from those previously anticipated) or to the calculation of a lump-sum payment (which cannot later be revised). *(FAR 48.001)*
See *value engineering; value engineering change proposal (VECP)*.

future years defense program (FYDP)

DOD database and internal accounting system that summarizes forces and resources associated with programs approved by the secretary of defense. Its three parts are the organizations affected, appropriations accounts (research, development, test, and evaluation (RDT&E); operation and maintenance (O&M); etc.), and the 11 major force programs (strategic forces, mobility forces, research and development (R&D), etc.). The FYDP allows a "crosswalk" between DOD's internal system of accounting via 11 major force programs and congressional appropriations. The primary data element in the FYDP is the "program element" (PE). The FYDP is updated twice during the planning, programming, budgeting and execution (PPBE) process cycle: submission of the concurrent Program Objectives Memorandum (POM)/Budget Estimate Submission (BES) (usually July/August), and submission of the president's budget (PB) to Congress (early February the year following). *(DAAT)*

futures contract

A contract for the purchase or sale and delivery of commodities at a future date, primarily used as a hedging device against market price fluctuations or unforeseen supply shortages. *(GKPT)*

Gg

gaining contract

A contract with firm requirements that necessitate the transfer of property used under another contract (i.e., the "losing contract"). *(FAR 45.106)*
See *losing contract*.

gap

See *capability gap*.

gap-filler

An interim agreement that defines the rights and obligations of the parties and establishes the basis for the conduct of business prior to the establishment of a long-term contractual relationship. Examples of "gap-fillers" include memorandums of understanding, letter contracts, teaming agreements, and other short-term agreements. *(CMBOK)*

garnishment

(1) A process under which money owed or paid to a borrower is given to a creditor instead. *(MW)*
(2) A legal summons or warning concerning the attachment of property to satisfy a debt. *(MW)*
See also *attachment; levy*.
(3) A stoppage of a specified sum from wages to satisfy a creditor or a legal obligation. *(MW)*

General Agreement on Tariffs and Trade (GATT)

A multilateral treaty first implemented in 1947 to reduce escalated tariffs and promote free trade. In 1995, it was succeeded by the World Trade Organization. *(NES-94)*

general and administrative (G&A) expense

(1) An expense related to the overall operation of the business—including indirect expenses for an organization's general and executive offices, executive compensation, staff services, and other miscellaneous support purposes. *(CMBOK; OPM)*
(2) In a federal government context, any management, financial, and other expense which is incurred by or allocated to a business unit and which is for the general management and administration of the business unit as a whole. A G&A expense *does not* include those management expenses whose beneficial or causal relationship to cost objectives can be more directly measured by a base other than a cost input base representing the total activity of a business unit during a cost accounting period. *(FAR 2.101)*
See also *business unit*.

general contracting concepts

Include such notions as principal and agency, types of authority, essential elements of a contract, market research, competition, fair and reasonable prices, and ethics. *(CMS)*

general intangible

Any personal property, including things in action (other than accounts, chattel paper, commercial tort claims, deposit accounts, documents, goods, instruments, investment property, letter-of-credit rights, letters of credit, money, and oil, gas, and other minerals before extraction). This term includes payment intangibles and software. *(UCC 9-102(a)(42))*
See also *payment intangible*.

general ledger

A complete record of financial transactions over the life of an organization. The ledger holds account information that is needed to prepare financial statements, and includes accounts for assets, liabilities, equity, revenues, and expenses. *(NDIA II)*

general provisions

A collection of contract clauses that are not specific to a given procurement, but also are part of a common contract language. *(OPM)*

General Services Administration (GSA) Index of Federal Specifications, Standards, and Commercial Item Descriptions

The index that publishes "alphabetic, numeric, and federal supply classifications listings" for federal specifications, standards, and qualified products lists and commercial item descriptions. (See https://www.gsa. gov; see also *FAR* Subpart 11.201.)

General Services Administration (GSA) specifications and standards

See *commercial item description* (CID); *federal specification* (FEDSPEC); see also *specification; standard*.

generally accepted accounting principles (GAAP)

The standard framework of guidelines for financial accounting used in any given jurisdiction. Also called "accounting standards" and "standard accounting practices." *(NDIA II)*

Gg

generic entity identifier

A number or other identifier assigned to a category of vendors and not specific to any individual or entity. *(FAR 4.601)*
See also *unique entity identifier*.

genuine

Free of forgery or counterfeiting. *(UCC 1-201(19))*

global sourcing

The procurement of goods or services outside the continental limits of the United States. In many firms, the term "global" infers the development of a longer term, planned continuing relationship with international suppliers. *(GKPT)*

go/no-go decision

(1) A determination to proceed with or abandon a plan or project. *(CMBOK)*
(2) In quality control, "go" denotes that a product conforms to the specifications; when it does not, it is "no go." *(CMBOK)*

goals of the acquisition process

Performance standards of the acquisition process. They include:

- Satisfying the customer in terms of cost, quality, and timeliness of the delivered product or service;
- Minimizing administrative operating costs;
- Conducting business with integrity, fairness, and openness; and
- Fulfilling public policy objectives.

(FAR 1.102)
See also *guiding principles for the federal acquisition system*.

going concern concept

An accounting concept that assumes the economic entity will last indefinitely (without evidence to the contrary). This concept is critical in order to support and justify important accounting concepts such as depreciation of property, amortization of assets, and other considerations. *(NCMA-CA)*

golden parachute payment

A term commonly used to refer to costs incurred in making any payment which is—

- In an amount in excess of the normal severance pay paid by an organization to an employee upon termination of employment, and
- Is paid to the employee contingent upon, and following, a change in management control over,

or ownership of, the organization or a substantial portion of the organization's assets.
In U.S. federal government contracting, such a payment is an "unallowable cost." *(FAR 31.603(b)(11))*
See *unallowable cost*.

good faith

Honesty in fact in the conduct or transaction concerned. Every contract or duty imposes an obligation of "good faith" in its performance and enforcement. *(UCC 1-201(20); UCC 1-304; UCC 5-102(a)(7); UCC 7-102(a)(6); UCC 9-102(a)(43))*
See *duty of good faith and fair dealing*; see also *fair dealing*.

goods

(1) Any articles, materials, supplies, or manufactured products, including inspection and test equipment. Goods must be both existing and identified before any interest in them can pass. Goods which are not both existing and identified are "future goods." *(UCC 2-105(1)–(4); UCC 2A-103(h); UCC 9-102(a)(44))*
(2) All things that are treated as "movable" for the purposes of a contract for storage or transportation. *(UCC 7-102(a)(7))*

goodwill

(1) One of the intangible values beyond its net worth that a business acquires from suppliers and customers. It is promoted by granting more business as a reward for good service, sharing plans and forecasts, working together to solve problems, mutual research and development, etc. *(GKPT)*
(2) An unidentifiable intangible asset, which originates under the purchase method of accounting for a business combination when the price paid by the acquiring company exceeds the sum of the identifiable individual assets acquired less liabilities assumed, based upon their fair values. The excess is commonly referred to as "goodwill." Goodwill may also arise from the acquisition of a company as a whole or a portion thereof. *(FAR 31.205-49)*

government

In the case of the federal government, refers to any entity of the legislative or judicial branches, any executive agency, military department, government corporation, or independent establishment, the U.S. Postal Service, or any nonappropriated-fund instrumentality of the armed forces of the federal government. *(FAR 8.701)*

Gg

Government Accountability Office (GAO)

An agency of the legislative branch, headed by the comptroller general of the United States and responsible solely to the Congress, that functions to audit all negotiated government contracts and investigate all matters relating to the receipt, disbursement, and application of public funds. It is also charged by law to settle and adjust claims by and against the government. *(DISCS; GCG)*

government acquisition team

The federal government members of the acquisition team, including representatives of the technical, supply, and procurement functions, and the customers they serve. *(GOAT)*
See *acquisition team*; contrast with *contractor acquisition team*.

government bill of lading (GBL)

An accountable transportation document that has been authorized and prepared by a federal government official. *(FAR 47.001)*
See *bill of lading* (B/L); *commercial bill of lading* (CBL).

government-caused delay

Acts of the federal government in either its sovereign or contractual capacity may be found to be excusable causes of delay. For a contractor to be excused by an act of the government in its contractual capacity, the contractor must prove that the government act causing the delay was wrongful. Sovereign acts that delay the contractor's performance are grounds for excusable delays. *(AGC)*
See *excusable delay*; see also *government delay of work*.

government contract disputes process

The disputes process in federal government contracts is governed by the Contract Disputes statute (41 U.S.C. Chapter 71) and is set forth in *FAR* Subpart 33.2, "Disputes and Appeals." In this context, a "dispute" is a post-award disagreement between the government and a contractor, typically concerning conflicting points of view regarding contract provisions or performance. *(CMBOK)*

government contractor defense

A legal defense, based upon the U.S. Supreme Court's findings in *Boyle v. United Technologies Corp.* (487 U.S. 500(1988)), that allows a federal government contractor to escape liability from state law claims brought by injured persons when those claims arise from a contractor's compliance with federal government specifications. Also known as the *Boyle Rule*. *(BP; TIPS)*

government contract quality assurance

The various functions, including inspection, performed by the U.S. federal government to determine whether a contractor has fulfilled the contract obligations pertaining to quality and quantity. *(FAR 46.101)*
See also *acceptance; conditional acceptance; contract quality requirements; testing*.

government corporation

An agency of the federal government, established by Congress to perform a public purpose, which provides a market-oriented product or service and is intended to produce revenue that meets or approximates its expenditures. *(FGCO; 5 U.S.C. 103(1); 31 U.S.C. 9101(1))*
See also *government-sponsored enterprise* (GSE); *mixed-ownership government corporation; wholly owned government corporation*.

government costs

In value engineering, means those U.S. federal agency costs that result directly from developing and implementing the value engineering change proposal (VECP), such as any net increases in the cost of testing, operations, maintenance, and logistics support. This term *does not* include the normal administrative costs of processing the VECP or any increase in instant contract cost or price resulting from negative instant contract savings. *(FAR 48.001)*
See *value engineering; value engineering change proposal* (VECP).

government delay of work

Delays and interruptions in the contract work caused by the acts, or failures to act, of the contracting officer. The "Government Delay of Work" clause (FAR 52.242-17) provides for the administrative settlement of contractor claims that arise from any delays and interruptions in the contract work caused by the federal government. (However, this clause is not applicable if the contract otherwise specifically provides for an equitable adjustment because of the delay or interruption—e.g., when the "Changes" clause is applicable.) *(FAR 42.1304(a); DGBCT)*
See *government-caused delay*.

government estimate (GE)

See *independent government cost estimate* (IGCE).

Gg

government financing

Payments made to a contractor before supplies have been delivered or services rendered, including advance payments, progress payments based on cost, loan guarantees, partial payments, progress payments based on a percentage or stage of completion, or performance-based payments. *(GOAT)*

government-furnished equipment (GFE)

Items in the possession of, or acquired by, the federal government and delivered to or otherwise made available to a contractor. *(DISCS)*

See also *government-furnished property* (GFP); *government-furnished material* (GFM).

government-furnished material (GFM)

U.S. government property which may be incorporated into, or attached to, an end item to be delivered under a contract or which may be consumed in the performance of a contract. It includes, but is not limited to, raw and processed material, parts, components, assemblies, small tools, and supplies. *(DISCS)*

See also *government-furnished equipment* (GFE); *government-furnished property* (GFP).

government-furnished property (GFP)

Property in the possession of, or directly acquired by, the U.S. federal government and subsequently furnished to a contractor for performance of a contract. Government-furnished property includes, but is not limited to, spares and property furnished for repair, maintenance, overhaul, or modification. Government-furnished property also includes contractor-acquired property if the contractor-acquired property is a deliverable under a cost contract when accepted by the government for continued use under the contract. *(FAR 45.101)*

See *government property*; see also *government-furnished equipment* (GFE); *government-furnished material* (GFM).

government information

Information created, collected, processed, disseminated, or disposed of by or for the federal government. *(OMB A-130)*

Government Management Reform Act of 1994 (GMRA)

A federal law (*Pub. L.* 103-356; 108 Stat. 3410) designed to provide a more effective, efficient, and responsive government primarily through reform in the areas of human resources and financial management. Notably, the act requires—

- The executive branch to make all federal wage, salary, and retirement payments to recipients by electronic funds transfer, unless another means of payment has been determined to be appropriate by the secretary of the treasury;
- All major federal departments and agencies to prepare and submit to the director of the OMB annual audited financial statements covering all accounts and associated activities of each office, bureau, and activity of the agency; and
- Annual governmentwide financial statements reflecting the consolidated financial position and results of operation of the entire federal government. *(DGBCT)*

government-owned, contractor-operated (GOCO) facility

A facility owned by the federal government but provided to a contractor for operation to produce goods for the government's use. *(OPM)*

government-owned, government-operated (GOGO) facility

A facility that is both owned and operated by the federal government. *(DAAT)*

Government Performance and Results Act (GPRA)

A federal law (*Pub. L.* 103-62, as amended) requiring agencies to prepare and publish:

- A strategic plan,
- An annual performance plan for the applicable fiscal year, and
- An annual performance report. *(DGBCT)*

See also *GPRA Modernization Act of 2010* (GPRAMA).

government production and research property

U.S. federal government–owned facilities, special test equipment, and special tooling to which the government has title or the right to acquire title. *(GOAT)*

government property

All property owned or leased by the federal government—including both government-furnished property and contractor-acquired property. Government property includes material, equipment, special tooling, special test equipment, and real property. Government proper-

Gg

ty does not include intellectual property and software. *(FAR 45.101)*
See also *contractor-acquired property* (CAP); *government-furnished property* (GFP); *loss of government property*.

government publication
Information that is published as an individual document at government expense, or as required by law. *(OMB A-130)*

government purchase card (GPC; P card)
A purchase card, similar in nature to a commercial credit card, issued to authorized federal government personnel for use in acquiring and paying for supplies, services, and construction (as authorized by law or regulation). The purchase card may be used to—
- Make micro-purchases;
- Place a task or delivery order (if authorized in the basic contract, basic ordering agreement, or blanket purchase agreement); or
- Make financing and delivery payments when the contractor agrees to accept payment by the card.

The purchase card is an electronic funds transfer (EFT) method and it may be used as a means to meet applicable requirements to pay by EFT, to the extent that purchase card limits do not preclude such payments. Also known as a governmentwide commercial purchase card" or simply as a purchase card or a P card. *(FAR 13.001; FAR 13.301(a); FAR 13.301(c); FAR 32.1102)*
See also *electronic funds transfer* (EFT).

government purpose license rights (GPLR)
Rights to use, duplicate, or disclose technical data for federal government purposes only, and to have or permit others to do so for government purposes only. Government purposes include competitive procurement, but do not include the right to permit others to use for commercial purposes. *(DAAT)*
See also *rights in technical data*.

government rate tender
An offer by a common carrier to the United States at a rate below the regulated rate offered to the general public. *(FAR 47.001)*
See *common carrier*.

government spend
The sum of dollars obligated against orders (including purchase orders, delivery orders, blanket purchase agreements, or definitive contract actions). These are action types where money is obligated to an actual order/contract with the intent to purchase supplies or services. *(GWCM)*

government-sponsored enterprise
A corporate entity created by a law of the United States that—
- Has a federal charter authorized by law;
- Is privately owned, as evidenced by capital stock owned by private entities or individuals;
- Is under the direction of a board of directors, a majority of which is elected by private owners;
- Is a financial institution with power to:
  - Make loans or loan guarantees for limited purposes such as to provide credit for specific borrowers or one sector, and
  - Raise funds by borrowing (which does not carry the full faith and credit of the federal government) or to guarantee the debt of others in unlimited amounts;
- Does *not* exercise powers that are reserved to the government as sovereign (such as the power to tax or to regulate interstate commerce);
- Does *not* have the power to commit the government financially (but it may be a recipient of a loan guarantee commitment made by the government); and
- Has employees whose salaries and expenses are paid by the enterprise and are not federal employees subject to Title 5 of the United States Code.

(2 U.S.C. 622(8)(A)-(B))

government vessel
A vessel owned by the U.S. federal government and operated directly by the government or for the government by an agent or contractor, including a privately-owned U.S.-flag vessel under bareboat charter to the government. *(FAR 47.501)*

governmental accounting
Similar to financial accounting, which involves the measuring and recording of financial data of governmental units to interested users; however, governmental accounting utilizes accounting conventions that are different from those applied to financial accounting. *(NCMA-CA)*

governmental unit
A subdivision, agency, department, county, parish, municipality, or other unit of the government of the United States, a U.S. state, or a foreign country. This term

Gg

includes an organization having a separate corporate existence if the organization is eligible to issue debt on which interest is exempt from income taxation under the laws of the United States. *(UCC 9-102(a)(45))*

governmentwide acquisition contract (GWAC)

A federal government task-order or delivery-order contract established by one agency for governmentwide use that is operated by an executive agent designated by the U.S. Office of Management and Budget (pursuant to 40 U.S.C. 11302(e)) or under a delegation of procurement authority issued by the GSA prior to August 7, 1996, under authority granted GSA by former section 40 U.S.C. 759 (repealed by *Pub. L.* 104-106). The Economy Act (31 U.S.C. 1535) *does not* apply to orders under a GWAC. *(FAR 2.101)*

governmentwide commercial purchase card (GPC; P card)

See *government purchase card* (GPC; P card)

governmentwide point of entry (GPE)

Commonly known as *FedBizOpps*, it is the single point where federal business opportunities valued at or greater than a specified dollar threshold—including synopses of proposed contract actions, solicitations, and associated information—can be accessed electronically by the public. The GPE is located at www.fedbizopps.gov. *(FAR 2.101)*

GPRA Modernization Act of 2010 (GPRAMA)

A federal law (*Pub. L.* 111-352) that amended the Government Performance and Results Act (GPRA) (*Pub. L.* 103-62) to require agencies to publish their strategic plans, performance plans, and performance reports (a requirement of the original GPRA) in machine-readable formats, and to identify possible factors beyond agencies' control that could prevent the achievement of the objectives detailed in these plans.
See also *Government Performance and Results Act (GPRA)*

grandfather clause

A contractual or legal provision that protects the existing interests of affected parties. *(GKPT)*

grant

An award of financial assistance, the principal purpose of which is to transfer a thing of value from a federal agency to a recipient to carry out a public purpose of support or stimulation authorized by a law of the United States (see 31 U.S.C. 6101(3)). A grant is distinguished from a contract, which is used to acquire property or services for the federal government's direct benefit or use; whereas grants are frequently made conditional upon an action specified by the grantee, such as the maintenance of certain standards or a proportional contribution of funds, and there is often little or no federal involvement in the management of the work being funded. *(31 U.S.C. 6304(1)–(2))*
See *cooperative agreement; federal assistance*.

gratuity

Something of monetary value freely given to another party with no explicit expectation of return or reward. *(SPP)*

green contracting

Contract actions, including task and delivery orders, for products and services meeting environmentally preferred requirements, such as being energy-efficient, water-efficient, bio-based, non-ozone-depleting, or containing recovered materials. Procured products should also be nontoxic or less toxic than alternatives. *(FAR 23.103(a))*
See also *environmentally preferable purchasing; sustainable acquisition*.

gross disbursement

In budgetary usage, gross disbursements represent the amount of checks issued, cash, or other payments made, less refunds received. *(DISCS)*
See also *outlays*; contrast with *net disbursement*.

gross domestic product (GDP)

A measure of a nation's domestic output, which is the total value of all finished goods and services produced within the country during a specified time period (typically one calendar year). *(GKPT)*

gross national product (GNP)

The total dollar value of all the final goods (as distinguished from goods still in the process of production) produced by all the firms in the economy. *(ECON)*

GSA eLibrary

This is the GSA's online resource for the "latest contract award information" for GSA Schedules, Department of Veterans Affairs (VA) Schedules, and Technology Contracts. Formerly the Schedules e-Library, it also provides information on Schedule Program changes, a listing of available contractors, as well as an "updated"

Hh

category guide. (See https://www.gsa.gov/tools/supply-procurement-etools/gsa-elibrary.)

GSA Schedules Program
See *Federal Supply Schedule* (FSS) *Program*.

guaranteed loan
(1) Loan guarantees made by Federal Reserve banks, on behalf of designated guaranteeing agencies, to enable contractors to obtain financing from private sources under contracts for the acquisition of supplies or services for the national defense. *(FAR 32.102.(c))*
(2) A loan, revolving credit fund, or other financial arrangement made pursuant to Regulation V of the Federal Reserve Board, under which the guaranteeing agency is obligated, on demand of the lender, to purchase a stated percentage of the loan and to share any losses in the amount of the guaranteed percentage. Also called a "V loan." *(FAR 32.301)*
See *guaranteeing agency*; see also *contractor financing*.

guaranteeing agency
Any U.S. federal agency that the president of the United States has authorized to guarantee loans, through Federal Reserve Banks, for expediting national defense production. *(FAR 32.301)*

guiding principles for the federal acquisition system
To deliver on a timely basis the best value product or service to the customer, while maintaining the public's trust and fulfilling public policy objectives. Participants in the acquisition process should work together as a team and should be empowered to make decisions within their area of responsibility.
The federal acquisition system will:
- Satisfy the customer in terms of cost, quality, and timeliness of the delivered product or service by, for example—
  - maximizing the use of commercial products and services,
  - using contractors who have a track record of successful past performance or who demonstrate a current superior ability to perform, and promoting competition;
- Minimize administrative operating costs;
- Conduct business with integrity, fairness, and openness; and
- Fulfill public policy objectives.
(FAR 1.102)
See also *goals of the acquisition process*.

hacker
An unauthorized user who attempts to or gains access to an information system. *(CNSSI 4009)*

hand-to-mouth buying
Purchasing over a short period of time to meet only immediate short-term requirements. *(GKPT)*

hard savings
Cost reductions that are reasonable, measurable, and that reduce the established level of approved expenditures. *(AFIT)*

hardware
In the case of an information system, the physical components of the system. *(NIST SP 800-171)*
See also *firmware; software*.

head of contracting activity (HCA)
The federal government official who has overall responsibility for managing the contracting activity. *(FAR 2.101)*

head of the agency
See *agency head*.

high-value item
Concerning federal government property, a contract end item that has a high unit cost, such as an aircraft, an aircraft engine, a communication system, a computer system, a missile, or a ship—and which is designated by the contracting officer as a "high-value item." *(FAR 46.101)*

high-value material
Major components, assemblies, or critical piece-part items that are identified based on an analysis of material categories a contractor needs to procure and consume in the integration and build of an end item. *(NDIA II)*

highest-level owner
The entity that owns or controls an immediate owner of the offeror, or that owns or controls one or more entities that control an immediate owner of the offeror. No entity owns or exercises control of the highest-level owner. *(FAR 4.1801)*
See also *immediate owner*.

Hh

historical costs

An accounting convention that is the foundation for the valuation of assets and the initial recording of economic transactions. There are various other costing methods that have evolved over time (e.g., present value of future cash flow, etc.), but the historical costs method has been generally accepted by accountants to be the most useful and reliable basis for accounting because historical costs are definite and determinable, as well as objective and verifiable. Also known as "sunk costs." *(NCMA-CA)*

historical prices

A type of secondary comparison used in performing price analysis. The current quotation can be compared with historical prices from past acquisitions to determine the reasonableness of a currently offered price. Some adjustment to a historical price is probably necessary, however, to account for changes such as increased costs, improved technology, different specifications, size or quantity of the purchase, delivery terms, government-furnished property, and packaging requirements. *(NCMA-WS)*
See also *secondary comparison*.

historically black college or university

An institution determined by the secretary of education to meet the requirements of 34 CFR 608.2. Also referred to as a *part B institution*. *(FAR 2.101)*
See also *minority institution*.

historically underutilized business zone (HUBZone)

An area located within one or more qualified census tracts, qualified nonmetropolitan counties, lands within the external boundaries of a Native American reservation, qualified base closure areas, or redesignated areas, as defined in 13 CFR 126.103. *(FAR 2.101)*
See also *historically underutilized business zone (HUBZone) contract*.

historically underutilized business zone (HUBZone) contract

A contract awarded to a SBA-certified "historically underutilized business zone (HUBZone) small business concern" through any of the following procurement methods:
- A sole-source award to a HUBZone small business concern,
- Set-aside awards based on competition restricted to HUBZone small business concerns, or
- Awards to HUBZone small business concerns

through full and open competition after a price evaluation preference in favor of HUBZone small business concerns. *(FAR 2.101)*
See *historically underutilized business zone (HUBZone)*; see also *historically underutilized business zone (HUBZone) small business concern*.

historically underutilized business zone (HUBZone) small business concern

A small business concern, certified by the Small Business Administration (SBA), that appears on the List of Qualified HUBZone Small Business Concerns maintained by SBA (13 CFR 126.103). *(FAR 2.101)*
See *historically underutilized business zone (HUBZone)*; see also *historically underutilized business zone (HUBZone) contract*.

holder

A term that refers to:
- The person in possession of a negotiable instrument that is payable either to bearer or to an identified person that is the person in possession, or
- The person in possession of a document of title if the goods are deliverable either to bearer or to the order of the person in possession.

(UCC 1-201(21))

honor

In the case of a letter of credit, means performance of the issuer's undertaking in the letter of credit to pay or deliver an item of value. Unless the letter of credit otherwise provides, "honor" occurs:
- Upon payment;
- If the letter of credit provides for acceptance, upon acceptance of a draft and, at maturity, its payment; or
- If the letter of credit provides for incurring a deferred obligation, upon incurring the obligation and, at maturity, its performance.

(UCC 5-102(a)(8))
See also *letter of credit*.

hourly rate

The rate(s) prescribed in the contract for payment for labor that meets the labor category qualification of a labor category specified in the contract that are performed by the contractor; performed by the subcontractors; or transferred between divisions, subsidiaries, or affiliates of the contractor under a common control. *(FAR 16.601(a))*

hub and spoke

A distribution model. Stock is held at the "hub" location and then sent out to the "spoke" locations (i.e., distribution centers) when needed. This model usually allows for reduced overall inventory because the safety stock is mostly held at the hub rather than at numerous spokes. *(DGBCT)*

humanitarian or peacekeeping operation

A military operation in support of the provision of humanitarian or foreign disaster assistance or in support of a peacekeeping operation under Chapter VI or VII of the Charter of the United Nations. This term *does not* include routine training, force rotation, or stationing. *(FAR 2.101)*

identical bids

Bids for the same line item that are determined to be identical as to unit price or total line item amount, with or without the application of evaluation factors (e.g., discount or transportation cost). *(FAR 3.302)*

idle capacity

The unused capacity of partially used facilities. It is the difference between that which a facility could achieve under 100-percent operating time on a one-shift basis, less operating interruptions resulting from time lost for repairs, setups, unsatisfactory materials, and other normal delays, and the extent to which the facility was actually used to meet demands during the accounting period. A multiple-shift basis may be used in the calculation instead of a one-shift basis if it can be shown that this amount of usage could normally be expected for the type of facility involved. *(FAR 31.205-17(a))*
See *costs of idle facilities or idle capacity; facilities*; see also *idle facilities*.

idle facilities

Completely unused facilities that are excess to the contractor's current needs. *(FAR 31.205-17(a))*
See *facilities*; see also *idle capacity*.

immateriality

See *materiality and immateriality*.

immediate gain actuarial cost method

Any of the several actuarial cost methods under which actuarial gains and losses are included as part of the unfunded actuarial liability of the pension plan, rather than as part of the normal cost of the plan. *(FAR 31.001)*
See also *actuarial cost method*.

immediate owner

An entity, other than the offeror, that has direct control of the offeror. Indicators of control include, but are not limited to, one or more of the following:
* Ownership or interlocking management,
* Identity of interests among family members,
* Shared facilities and equipment, and
* The common use of employees.

(FAR 4.1801)
See also *highest-level owner*.

implied acceptance

In the case of a bilateral contract, acceptance of an offer need not be expressed, but it may be shown by any words or acts indicating the offeree's assent to the proposed bargain. *(DGBCT)*

implied authority

Authority implied from the principal's conduct. It includes only such acts as are incident and necessary to the exercise of the authority expressly granted. *(BLD)*
See *agent; agent authority*; see also *actual authority; apparent authority; express authority*.

implied contract

A contract (sometimes called an "implied in fact contract") in which the terms of the contract are wholly or partly inferred from the conduct (as opposed to the words) of the parties or surrounding circumstance. In order to establish an implied contract:
* The seller must have furnished some service or property to the buyer,
* The seller must have reasonably expected to be paid and the buyer knew or should have known that a reasonable person in the seller's shoes would have expected to be paid for the service or property rendered by the seller, and
* The buyer must have had the opportunity to reject the services or property and failed to do so.

(CMBOK)

implied-in-law contract

See *quasi contract*.

implied warranty

A promise arising by operation of law that something that is sold shall be merchantable and fit for the purpose for which the seller has reason to know that it is required. Some types of implied warranties are as follows: implied warranty of fitness for a particular purpose, implied warranty of merchantability, implied warranty of title, and implied warranty of wholesomeness. *(DGBCT)*
See *Spearin Doctrine*.

implied warranty of merchantability

The implication by sale of the item that it is reasonably fit for the ordinary purposes for which items are used. Items must be of at least "average," "fair," or "medium"-grade quality and must be comparable in quality to those that will pass without objection in the trade or market for items of the same description. *(GOAT)*

implied warranty of specifications

See *Spearin Doctrine*.

imply

To indirectly convey meaning or intent; to leave the determination of meaning up to the receiver of the communication based upon circumstances, general language used, or conduct of those involved. *(P&L I)*

import

The purchase of commodities by one country from a source in a foreign country for trade or resale by the purchaser. *(NES-94)*

imprest fund

A cash fund of a fixed amount established through an advance of funds, without charge to an appropriation, to an authorized imprest fund cashier to effect immediate cash payments of relatively small amounts for authorized purchases of supplies and nonpersonal services. A non-government equivalent is a "petty cash" account. *(CMBOK; DDMAT)*

improper influence

Any influence that induces or tends to induce a U.S. federal government employee or officer to give consideration or to act regarding a government contract on any basis other than the merits of the matter. *(FAR 3.401)*

improper payment

Any payment that should not have been made or that was made in an incorrect amount under statutory, contractual, administrative, or other legally applicable requirements. Improper payments occur when—
- Funds go to the wrong recipient,
- The recipient receives the incorrect amount of funds (including overpayments and underpayments),
- Documentation is not available to support a payment, or
- The recipient uses funds in an improper manner.
(31 U.S.C. 3321 note)

Improper Payments Elimination and Recovery Act of 2010 (IPERA)

A federal law (*Pub. L.* 111-204) that amended Section 2 of the Improper Payments Information Act of 2002 (31 U.S.C. 3321 note) to expand requirements for identifying programs and activities susceptible to improper payments. *(31 U.S.C. 3321 note)*
See *improper payment*; see also *Improper Payments Elimination and Recovery Improvement Act of 2012* (IPERIA)*; Improper Payments Information Act of 2002* (IPIA).

Improper Payments Elimination and Recovery Improvement Act of 2012 (IPERIA)

A federal law (*Pub. L.* 112-248) that amended the Improper Payments Information Act of 2002 (31 U.S.C. 3321 note) to intensify efforts to identify, prevent, and recover payment error, waste, fraud, and abuse within federal spending, including the "Do Not Pay Initiative." *(31 U.S.C. 3321 note)*
See *improper payment*; see also *Improper Payments Elimination and Recovery Act of 2010* (IPERA)*; Improper Payments Information Act of 2002* (IPIA).

Improper Payments Information Act of 2002 (IPIA)

A federal law (31 U.S.C. 3321 note), as amended by the Improper Payments Elimination and Recovery Act of 2010 (IPERA; *Pub. L.* 111-204) and the Improper Payments Elimination and Recovery Improvement Act of 2012 (IPERIA; *Pub. L.* 112-248), that directs each executive agency to review all of its programs and activities annually, identify those that may be susceptible to significant improper payments, estimate the annual amount of improper payments, and submit those estimates to Congress. *(31 U.S.C. 3321 note)*
See *improper payment*; see also *Improper Payments Elimination and Recovery Act of 2010* (IPERA)*; Improper Payments Elimination and Recovery Improvement Act of 2012* (IPERIA).

improvement curve
See *learning curve*.

"in-scope"
Phrase used to denote that an action performed or requested to be performed by a seller for the buyer could reasonably be considered to be within the requirements of the contract. *(P&L II)*

"in writing"/"writing"/"written"
Any worded or numbered expression that can be read, reproduced, and later communicated, and includes electronically transmitted and stored information. *(FAR 2.101)*

inappropriate sole-source requirement
A requirement advertised as a sole-source procurement that is not, in fact, a valid use of sole-source authority—the possibility for competition exists. *(CMBOK)*

incentive
Motivating the seller in calculable monetary terms to turn out a product that meets significantly advanced performance goals, improve on the contract schedule up to and including final delivery, substantially reduce costs of the work, or complete the project under a weighted combination of some or all of these objectives. *(CMBOK; DAAT)*

incentive arrangement
A negotiated pricing arrangement that structures a series of relationships designed to motivate and reward the seller for performance in accordance with the contract specifications. It involves target costs, fees, and/or profits. In the case of award fee arrangements, it involves the payment of a fee tied to negotiated incentive criteria. *(OPM)*
See *incentive*.

incentive contract
A contract type appropriate for use when a firm-fixed-price contract is not appropriate and the required supplies or services can be acquired at lower costs and, in certain instances, with improved delivery or technical performance, by relating the amount of profit or fee payable under the contract to the seller's performance. Incentive contracts are designed to obtain specific acquisition objectives by establishing reasonable and attainable targets that are clearly communicated to the seller—including appropriate incentive arrangements designed to motivate seller efforts that might not other-

wise be emphasized and to discourage seller inefficiency and waste. The two basic categories of incentive contracts are:
- Fixed-price incentive contracts, and
- Cost-reimbursement incentive contracts.

(FAR 16.401(a)–(c))
See *cost incentives; delivery incentives; multiple-incentive contracts; performance incentives*; see also *award-fee contract; cost-reimbursement incentive contract; fixed-price-award-fee* (FPAF) *contract; fixed-price-incentive* (FPI) *contract*.

incident
In a cybersecurity context, an occurrence that—
- Actually, potentially, or imminently jeopardizes the confidentiality, integrity, or availability of an information system or the information the system processes, stores, or transmits; or
- Constitutes a violation or imminent threat of violation of law, security policies, security procedures, or acceptable use policies.

Also called a "cyber incident" or a "cybersecurity incident." *(44 U.S.C. 3552(b)(2); FIPS 200; DFARS 202.101)*
See *information; information system* (IS).

incidental damages
(1) Damages to the seller due to a breach by the buyer that include any commercially reasonable charges, expenses, or commissions incurred in stopping delivery; in the transportation, care, and custody of goods after the buyer's breach; or in connection with the return or resale of the goods or otherwise resulting from the breach. *(UCC 2-710)*
(2) Damages to the buyer due to a breach by the seller that include expenses reasonably incurred in inspection, receipt, transportation, and care and custody of goods rightfully rejected; any commercially reasonable charges, expenses, or commissions in connection with effecting cover; and any other reasonable expense incident to the delay or other breach. *(UCC 2-715(1))*
See *consequential damages; cover; damages*.

incidentals
Small items and expenses. In small purchases procurement, incidentals are usually taken care of from the imprest fund/petty cash account. *(SPP)*

incomplete instrument
A signed writing, whether or not issued by the signer, the contents of which show at the time of signing that

it is incomplete but that the signer intended it to be completed by the addition of words or numbers. *(UCC 3-115(a))*
See also **negotiable instrument**.

incoterms

Short for "international commercial terms." The terms clarify destination, risk and liability, point of title transfer, and cost inclusions. When referenced in contract documents, incoterms enable parties contracting for the purchase and sale of goods internationally to simply and concisely allocate their responsibilities for transportation costs, customs fees and documentation requirements, risks of loss or damage, insurance, and other responsibilities. *(NES-94)*

incremental budget

The budget is based on the previous period's budget and actual results. The budget amount is then changed in accordance with expectations for the next period. *(IMA)*

incremental cost

The additional cost associated with increases in a given set of costs. For example, the incremental costs of increasing production for 1,000 units to 1,200 per week would be the additional costs of the extra 200 units. An incremental cost may be a positive or negative amount. *(IMA)*

incremental funding

(1) The obligation of funds to a contract (which contains a total price or estimated cost) in periodic installments as the work progresses, rather than a lump sum. *(GKPT)*
(2) The provision (or recording) of budgetary resources for a program or project based on obligations estimated to be incurred within a fiscal year when such budgetary resources will cover only a portion of the obligations to be incurred in completing the program or project as programmed. This differs from full funding, where budgetary resources are provided or recorded for the total estimated obligations for a program or project in the initial year of funding. Most commonly used for research and development, as opposed to production, which must be fully funded. *(DAAT)*

indefinite delivery contract

A contract that may be used to acquire supplies and/or services when the exact times and/or exact quantities of future deliveries are not known at the time of contract award. *(GOAT)*

indefinite delivery/indefinite quantity (IDIQ) contract

A type of contract in which the exact date of delivery or the exact quantity, or a combination of both, is not specified at the time the contract is executed; provisions are placed in the contract to later stipulate these elements of the contract. *(OPM)*

indefinite delivery vehicle (IDV)

An indefinite delivery contract or agreement that has one or more of the following Federal Acquisition Regulation clauses:
- FAR 52.216-18, "Ordering";
- FAR 52.216-19, "Order Limitations";
- FAR 52.216-20, "Definite Quantity";
- FAR 52.216-21, "Requirements";
- FAR 52.216-22, "Indefinite Quantity"; and/or
- Any other clause allowing ordering.
(FAR 4.601)

indefinite quantity contract

Commonly referred to as a "term contract," provides for the furnishing of an indefinite quantity, within stated limits, of specific property or services during a specified contract period, with deliveries to be scheduled by the timely placement of orders with the contractor. *(FMR 102-71.20)*

indemnification

Protections provided by the parties to each other to restore a loss, either in whole or in part, by payment, repair, or replacement. It can also be a contract provision whereby one party engages to secure another against an anticipated loss resulting from an act or forbearance on the part of one of the parties or some third party. *(DGBCT; STBP)*

indemnification clause

This clause describes protections provided by the parties to each other. *(HECA)*

Indemnification under Public Law 85-804

The inclusion of a clause in government contracts where the approving official has determined that the contractor shall be indemnified against unusually hazardous or nuclear risks. *(FAR 50.104-4)* (See also FAR 52.250-1.)

indemnify

To make good; to compensate; to reimburse a person in case of an anticipated loss. *(STBP)*

independent contractor (IC)

One that contracts to do work or perform a service for another and that retains total and free control over the means or methods used in doing the work or performing the service–being responsible only under the contract with the client for the result obtained. *(GKPT; MW)*

Independent cost analysis (ICA)

An analysis of program office (PO) and/or component Life Cycle Cost Estimates (LCCEs) conducted by an impartial body disassociated from the management of the program. *(DAAT)*

independent cost estimate (ICE)

An independent estimate for a Major Defense Acquisition Program (MDAP) or Major Automated Information System (MAIS). The term "independent" refers to both organizational and analytic independence. Organizational independence means that the cost estimate is prepared by an entity not within any organization that would unduly influence the estimate. Analytic independence means that the cost estimate is free of any bias or preconceived notions about the program's most likely cost. The estimate covers the entire life cycle of the program and includes sunk costs; Research, Development, Test and Evaluation (RDT&E) costs; procurement; military construction; military pay; and operations and maintenance costs. The Director, Cost Assessment and Program Evaluation (DCAPE) conducts ICEs and cost analyses for MDAPs for which the Under Secretary of Defense (Acquisition, Technology and Logistics) is the Milestone Decision Authority (MDA) and as requested by the MDA for other MDAPs. The ICE is also known as the "Will Cost" Estimate. *(DAAT; DODI 5000.02)*
See also *independent government cost estimate* (IGCE); *Major Automated Information System* (MAIS); *Major Defense Acquisition Program* (MDAP).

independent establishment

A generic term for either of the following components of the U.S. federal government:
- An establishment in the executive branch (other than the U.S. Postal Service or the Postal Regulatory Commission) which is *not* an executive department, military department, government corporation, or part thereof, or part of an independent establishment; and
- The Government Accountability Office (GAO).
(5 U.S.C. 104)

independent government cost estimate (IGCE)

The federal government's detailed estimate of the resources and projected cost of the resources a contractor will incur in the performance of a contract. These costs include direct costs (such as labor, products, equipment, travel, and transportation) and indirect costs (such as labor overhead, material overhead, general and administrative expenses, and profit or fee). This estimate is developed by the government technical activity based on the requirements of the statement of work, performance work statement, etc. and without the influence of potential contractors' efforts. Also called *independent government estimate* (IGE) and *government estimate* (GE). *(CMBOK; PAN 16-06)*
See also *independent cost estimate* (ICE).

independent government estimate (IGE)

See *independent government cost estimate* (IGCE).

independent research and development (IR&D)

The cost of effort that is neither sponsored by a grant nor required in performing a contract, and which falls within any of the following four areas:
- Basic research,
- Applied research,
- Development, and
- Systems and other concept formulation studies.
(FAR 31.001; FAR 31.205-18(a))
See *applied research; basic research; development; systems and other concept formulation studies*.

independent review officer (IRO)

The agency official who certifies–prior to a bid opening–that the federal government's performance and cost comparison estimates have been prepared in accordance with OMB Circular A-76 and its supplement. *(OMB A-76)*

index numbers

Detailed data for use in cost estimating–such as price movements at the primary market level, price indexes for groups of products and commodities, retail price changes, the purchasing power of the consumer's dollar, and effects of inflation–developed and published by the U.S. Department of Labor's Bureau of Labor Statistics. *(CE)*

Index of Federal Specifications, Standards, and Commercial Item Descriptions

Ii

See *General Services Administration (GSA) Index of Federal Specifications, Standards, and Commercial Item Descriptions*.

Indian

For federal government purposes, this term refers to any person who is a member of any Native American tribe/tribal organization, band, group, pueblo, or community that is recognized by the federal government as eligible for services from the U.S. Bureau of Indian Affairs in accordance with 25 U.S.C. 1452(c) and any "Native" as defined in the Alaska Native Claims Settlement Act (43 U.S.C. 1601). *(FAR 26.101; 25 U.S.C. 5304(d))*

Indian Incentive Program (IIP)

A federal government policy that states that Indian (i.e., Native American) organizations and Indian-owned economic enterprises, including Alaska Natives, shall have the maximum practicable opportunity to participate in performing contracts awarded by federal agencies. The policy also provides for incentive payments to Indian organizations and Indian-owned economic enterprises that perform as subcontractors. *(FAR 26.102)*

Indian organization

The governing body of any Indian (i.e., Native American) tribe or entity established or recognized by the governing body of an Indian tribe for the purposes of 25 U.S.C. Chapter 17. *(FAR 26.101)*
See also *Indian*.

Indian-owned economic enterprise

Any Indian-owned (as determined by the U.S. secretary of the interior) commercial, industrial, or business activity established or organized for the purpose of profit, provided that "Indian" (as the term is defined for federal government purposes) ownership constitutes not less than 51 percent of the enterprise. *(FAR 26.101)*

Indian tribal government

For U.S. federal government purposes, this term refers to the governing body of any Indian (i.e., Native American) or Alaska Native tribe, band, nation, pueblo, village, or community that the Secretary of the Interior acknowledges to exist as an Indian tribe under the Federally Recognized Indian Tribe List Act of 1994 (25 U.S.C. 479a, *et seq.*). *(42 U.S.C. 5122(6))*
Compare with *tribal organization*; see also *Indian*.

indictment

(1) A formal accusation of a crime by a grand jury. (FBL)
(2) Indictment for a criminal offense. An information or other filing by competent authority charging a criminal offense is given the same effect as an indictment. *(FAR 9.403)*

indirect cost

(1) Any cost not directly identifiable with a single final cost objective but also identified with two or more final cost objectives or with at least one intermediate cost objective. Also called *overhead* or "burden costs." *(FAR 2.101; NDIA II)*
See also *indirect cost rate*.

indirect cost pools

Groupings of incurred costs identified with two or more cost objectives but not identified specifically with any final cost objective. *(FAR 31.001)* (See also *FAR* Subpart 31.3 and *FAR* Subpart 31.6.)

indirect cost rate

The percentage or dollar factor that expresses the ratio of indirect expense incurred in a given period to direct labor cost, manufacturing cost, or another appropriate base for the same period. *(FAR 2.101)*
See also *final indirect cost rate*.

indirect labor

All labor that is not specifically associated with or cannot be practically traced to specific units of output. *(NCMA-CA)*

indirect manufacturing costs

See *factory overhead*.

indirect observation

Usually obtained through the receipt of various types of reports from the seller, from reviews or audits performed by either the buyer's management staff or by internal or external auditors, from various forms of pre- and post-production testing and sampling, and a variety of other methods. *(DGBCT)*
See *direct observation; observation*.

indirect offset

A general type of industrial or commercial compensation practice required of a contractor by a purchasing government as a condition for the purchase of articles/services. The form of compensation, which generally offsets a specific percentage of the cost of the purchase, is unrelated to the items purchased, and may include contractor purchases of commodities and manufactured goods produced in the purchasing country. *(DISCS)*

individual
(1) A citizen of the United States or an alien lawfully admitted for permanent residence. *(FAR 24.101)*
(2) An offeror/contractor that has no more than one employee including the offeror/contractor. *(FAR 23.503)*

individual subcontracting plan
A subcontracting plan that covers the entire contract period (including option periods), applies to a specific contract, and has goals that are based on the offeror's planned subcontracting in support of the specific contract, except that indirect costs incurred for common or joint purposes may be allocated on a prorated basis to the contract. *(FAR 19.701)*
See *subcontracting plan*; see also *master subcontracting plan*.

individual surety
One person, as distinguished from a business entity, who is liable for the entire penal amount of the bond. *(FAR 2.101)*
See *surety*.

indorsee
The person to whom a draft, promissory note, bill of lading, etc. is assigned by indorsement. *(BLD)*

indorsement
A signature, other than that of a signer as maker, drawer, or acceptor, that alone or accompanied by other words is made on an instrument for the purpose of:
• Negotiating the instrument,
• Restricting payment of the instrument, or
• Incurring the indorser's liability on the instrument.
However, regardless of the intent of the signer, a signature and its accompanying words is an "indorsement" unless the accompanying words, terms of the instrument, place of the signature, or other circumstances unambiguously indicate that the signature was made for a purpose other than indorsement. *(UCC 3-204(a))*
See also *anomalous indorsement; blank indorsement; fraudulent indorsement; indorsee; indorser; special indorsement*.

indorser
A person who makes an indorsement. *(UCC 3-204(b))*
See *indorsement*.

industrial base
A nation's resources that represent the nation's capacity and capability to produce goods at an appropriate rate in terms of national defense and commercial competitiveness. The defense industrial base is only one portion of the whole industrial base; i.e., those industries that at any particular time support the nation's security through the provision of defense material and supporting goods and services. *(TIPS)*
See also *defense industrial base*.

industrial standardization
The process of establishing agreement on uniform identifications for definite characteristics of quality, design, performance, quantity, service, etc. A uniform identification is called a "standard." *(DGBCT)*

industry
All concerns primarily engaged in similar lines of activity, as listed and described in the North American Classification System (NAICS) manual. *(FAR 19.001)*

industry specification
A type of specification prepared by technical or industry associations that is approved for use by U.S. federal agencies. *(GCG)*

ineligible
Excluded from federal government contracting (and subcontracting, if appropriate) pursuant to statutory, Executive Order, or regulatory authority other than the *Federal Acquisition Regulation* and its implementing and supplementing regulations; for example, pursuant to—
• The Wage Rate Requirements (Construction) statute (40 U.S.C. Chapter 31, Subchapter IV) and its related statutes and implementing regulations;
• The Service Contract Labor Standards statute (41 U.S.C. Chapter 67);
• The Equal Employment Opportunity Acts and Executive Orders;
• The Contracts for Material, Supplies, Articles, and Equipment Exceeding $15,000 statute (41 U.S.C. Chapter 65);
• The Buy American statute (41 U.S.C. Chapter 83); or
• The Environmental Protection Acts and Executive Orders.
(FAR 2.101)

inflation
An ongoing general rise in prices. The steeper this rise,

the faster the decline of a dollar's purchasing power. *(ECON)*

influencing or attempting to influence
Making, with the intent to influence, any communication to or appearance before an officer or employee of any U.S. federal government agency, a member of Congress, an officer or employee of Congress, or an employee of a member of Congress in connection with any covered federal action. *(FAR 3.801)*
See also *covered federal action; officer or employee of a U.S. federal agency*.

informal contract
A contract that does not require a specified form or method of formation in order to be valid. *(DGBCT)*

information
Any communication or representation of knowledge such as facts, data, or opinions in any medium or form, including textual, numerical, graphic, cartographic, narrative, or audiovisual. *(OMB A-130)*

information assurance (IA)
Measures that protect and defend information and information systems by ensuring their availability, integrity, authentication, confidentiality, and nonrepudiation. These measures include providing for restoration of information systems by incorporating protection, detection, and reaction capabilities. *(CNSSI 4009)*
See also *information system* (IS).

information assurance product
A product or technology whose primary purpose is to:
- Provide security services (e.g., confidentiality, authentication, integrity, access control, and nonrepudiation of data);
- Correct known vulnerabilities; and/or
- Provide layered defense against various categories of non-authorized or malicious penetrations of information systems or networks.

Examples include such products as data/network encryptors, firewalls, and intrusion detection devices. *(CNSSI 4009)*
See *information assurance* (IA).

information management
The function of managing an organization's information resources for the handling of data and information acquired by one or many different systems, individuals, and organizations in a way that optimizes access by all

who have a share in that data or a right to that information. *(DDMAT)*

information other than cost or pricing data
Any type of information that is not required to be certified and is necessary to determine price reasonableness or cost realism. For example, such information may include pricing, sales, or cost information, and includes cost or pricing data for which certification is determined inapplicable after submission. *(GOAT)*

information resources
In a federal government cybersecurity context, information and related resources, such as personnel, equipment, funds, and information technology. *(OMB A-130; 44 U.S.C. 3502(6))*
See also *information resources management*.

information resources management
In the context of federal government information management, this term refers to the process of managing information resources to accomplish agency missions and to improve agency performance, including through the reduction of information collection burdens on the public. *(OMB A-130; 44 U.S.C. 3502(7))*
See *information resources*.

information security
Protecting information and information systems from unauthorized access, use, disclosure, disruption, modification, or destruction in order to provide confidentiality, integrity, and availability. *(44 U.S.C. 3552(b)(3))*
See also *availability; confidentiality; information systems security* (INFOSEC); *integrity*.

information system (IS)
A discrete set of information resources organized for the collection, storage, processing, maintenance, use, sharing, dissemination, disposition, display, or transmission of information in accordance with defined procedures, whether automated or manual. *(FAR 4.1901; AIMD; CNSSI 4009; 44 U.S.C. 3502(8))*

information system component
A discrete, identifiable IT asset (e.g., hardware, software, firmware) that represents a building block of an information system. Information system components include commercial IT products. *(NIST SP 800-128)*
See *information system* (IS).

information system life cycle

The phases through which an information system passes, typically characterized as initiation, development, operation, and termination. *(OMB A-130)*
See *information system* (IS).

information system service

A capability provided by an information system that facilitates information processing, storage, or transmission. *(NIST SP 800-171)*
See *information system* (IS).

information systems security (INFOSEC)

Protection of information systems against unauthorized access to or modification of information—whether in storage, processing, or transit—and against the denial of service to authorized users, including those measures necessary to detect, document, and counter such threats. *(CNSSI 4009)*
See also *information system* (IS).

information systems security product

An item (i.e., chip, module, assembly, or equipment), technique, or service that performs or relates to information systems security. *(CNSSI 4009)*
See also *information systems security* (INFOSEC).

information technology (IT)

Any equipment or interconnected system or subsystem of equipment that is used in the automatic acquisition, storage, analysis, evaluation, manipulation, management, movement, control, display, switching, interchange, transmission, or reception of data or information. For the purposes of this definition, equipment is used by a U.S. federal agency if the equipment is used by the agency directly or is used by a contractor under a contract with the agency that requires its use or, to a significant extent, requires its use in the performance of a service or the furnishing of a product. The term "information technology" includes computers, ancillary equipment (including imaging peripherals, input, output, and storage devices necessary for security and surveillance), peripheral equipment designed to be controlled by the central processing unit of a computer, software, firmware and similar procedures, services (including support services), and related resources. This term *does not* include any equipment acquired by a contractor incidental to a federal contract or which contains embedded information technology that is used as an integral part of the product, but the principal function of which is not the acquisition, storage, analysis, evaluation, manipulation, management, movement, control,

display, switching, interchange, transmission, or reception of data or information. For example, HVAC (heating, ventilation, and air conditioning) equipment, such as thermostats or temperature control devices, and medical equipment where information technology is integral to its operation, are not "information technology." *(FAR 2.101; OMB A-130; 40 U.S.C. 11101(6)(A)-(C); AIMD)*

informational subline item

This type of subline item identifies information that relates directly to the line item and is an integral part of it (e.g., parts of an assembly or parts of a kit). *(FAR 4.1004(b))*
See *deliverable subline item*; see also *contract line item number* (CLIN); *line item; subline item*.

inherently governmental function

As a matter of policy, a function that is so intimately related to the public interest as to mandate performance by U.S. federal government employees. This definition is a policy determination, not a legal determination. An "inherently governmental function" includes activities that require either the exercise of discretion in applying government authority, or the making of value judgments in making decisions for the government. Governmental functions normally fall into two categories: the act of governing (i.e., the discretionary exercise of government authority), and monetary transactions and entitlements. An inherently governmental function involves, among other things, the interpretation and execution of the laws of the United States so as to:

- Bind the United States to take or not to take some action by contract, policy, regulation, authorization, order, or otherwise;
- Determine, protect, and advance United States' economic, political, territorial, property, or other interests by military or diplomatic action, civil or criminal judicial proceedings, contract management, or otherwise;
- Significantly affect the life, liberty, or property of private persons;
- Commission, appoint, direct, or control officers or employees of the United States; or
- Exert ultimate control over the acquisition, use, or disposition of the property, real or personal, tangible or intangible, of the United States, including the collection, control, or disbursement of federal funds.

"Inherently governmental functions" do not normally include gathering information for or providing advice, opinions, recommendations, or ideas to government officials. They also do not include functions that are primarily ministerial and internal in nature, such as building security, mail operations, operation of cafeterias, housekeeping, facilities operations and maintenance, warehouse operations, motor vehicle fleet management operations, or other routine electrical or mechanical services. *(FAR 2.101)*

initial product inspection
The product verification inspection performed during the early stages of production on selected characteristics of an item to obtain confidence that the seller can produce the item in accordance with contract requirements. *(AFIT)*

initial provisioning
The process of determining the range and quantity of items (i.e., spares and repair parts, special tools, test equipment, and support equipment) required to support and maintain an item for an initial period of operation. Its phases include the identification of items of supply; the establishment of data for catalog, technical manual, and allowance list preparation; and the preparation of instructions to ensure delivery of necessary support items with related end articles. *(DISCS)*

initial spares
Spare parts procured for the logistics support of a system during its initial period of operation. *(DISCS)*

injunction
An order of a court of equity that tells a person to do or refrain from doing some act or acts. *(FBL)*

input
Resources (funds, labor, time, equipment, space, technology, etc.) used to produce outputs and outcomes. *(DGBCT)*

insider trading
Trading in securities, or buying or selling property or assets, on the basis of nonpublic information acquired during a consultancy contract. *(UNI)*

insolvency proceeding
Includes an assignment for the benefit of creditors or other proceeding intended to liquidate or rehabilitate the estate of the person involved. *(UCC 1-201(22))* See also *insolvent*.

insolvent
In a financial sense, this term means:

- Having generally ceased to pay debts in the ordinary course of business other than as a result of bona fide dispute,
- Being unable to pay debts as they become due, or
- Being insolvent within the meaning of federal bankruptcy law.
(UCC 1-201(23))

inspection
Examining and testing supplies and services (including, when appropriate, raw materials, components, and intermediate assemblies) to determine whether the supplies and services conform to the contract requirements. *(FAR 2.101)*

inspection requirements
Instructions issued by the purchasing officer or technical representative regarding the type and extent of government inspections required for specific contracts. *(AFIT)*

inspector general
(1) An inspector general appointed under the Inspector General Act of 1978, as amended (e.g., the DOD inspector general). In the case of an executive agency that does not have an inspector general, the duties shall be performed by an official designated by the head of the executive agency. *(FAR 3.901)*
(2.) An "inspector general," appointed under the Inspector General Act of 1978, as amended (*Pub. L.* 95-452), leads an organization charged with examining the actions of a federal government agency, military organization, or contractor as a general auditor of their operations to ensure they are operating in compliance with generally established policies of the government, to audit the effectiveness of security procedures, or to discover the possibility of misconduct, waste, fraud, theft, or certain types of criminal activity by individuals or groups related to the organization's operation, usually involving some misuse of the organization's funds or credit. There are numerous offices of inspector general at the federal, state, and local levels. In the case of an executive agency that does not have an Inspector General, these duties are performed by an official designated by the head of the executive agency. *(TAS)*

installment contract
A contract that requires or authorizes the delivery of goods in separate lots to be separately accepted, even if the contract contains a clause stating "each delivery is a separate contract" or its equivalent. *(UCC 2-612)*

installment lease contract

A lease contract that authorizes or requires the delivery of goods in separate lots to be separately accepted, even if the lease contract contains a clause stating "each delivery is a separate lease" or its equivalent. *(UCC 2A-103(i))*

instant contract

(1) In value engineering, the contract under which the value engineering change proposal (VECP) is submitted. It *does not* include increases in quantities after acceptance of the VECP that are due to contract modifications, exercise of options, or additional orders. If the contract is a multiyear contract, this term *does not* include quantities funder after VECP acceptance. *(FAR 48.001)*
See *value engineering; value engineering change proposal* (VECP).
(2) In a fixed-price contract with prospective price redetermination, this term refers to the period for which firm prices have been established. *(FAR 48.001)*

instant unit cost reduction

In value engineering, the amount of the decrease in unit cost of performance (without deducting any of the contractor's development and implementation costs) resulting from using the value engineering change proposal (VECP) on the instant contract. In service contracts, the instant unit cost reduction is normally equal to the number of hours per line-item task saved by using the VECP on the instant contract, multiplied by the appropriate contract labor rate. *(FAR 48.001)*
See *value engineering; value engineering change proposal* (VECP); see also *contractor's development and implementation costs; instant contract.*

institutional risk

Risks to infrastructure, IT, resources, personnel, assets, processes, occupational safety, environmental management, or security that affect capabilities and resources necessary for mission success, including institutional flexibility to respond to changing mission needs and compliance with external requirements (e.g., Environmental Protection Agency or Occupational Safety and Health Administration regulations). *(NID 8000-108)*

instrument

A negotiable instrument or any other writing that:
- Evidences a right to the payment of a monetary obligation,
- Is not itself a security agreement or lease, and
- Is of a type that in ordinary course of business is

transferred by delivery with any necessary indorsement or assignment.
This term *does not* include investment property, letters of credit, or writings that evidence a right to a payment arising out of the use of a credit or charge card or information contained on or for use with the card. *(UCC 9-102(a)(47))*
See *negotiable instrument.*

insurance

A contract that provides that for a stipulated consideration, one party undertakes to indemnify another against loss, damage, or liability arising from an unknown or contingent event. *(FAR 2.101)*

insurance administration expenses

The contractor's costs of administering an insurance program—e.g., the costs of operating an insurance or risk-management department, processing claims, actuarial fees, and service fees paid to insurance companies, trustees, or technical consultants. *(FAR 31.001)*

intangible benefit

A benefit that may be easy to identify, but difficult to quantify—e.g., more efficient decision-making, greater data accuracy, improved data security, reduced customer burden, or increased organizational knowledge. *(AIMD)*
See *benefit*; contrast with *tangible benefit.*

intangible capital asset

An asset that has no physical substance, has more than minimal value, and is expected to be held by an enterprise for continued use or possession beyond the current accounting period for the benefits it yields. *(FAR 31.001)*
Compare with *tangible capital asset.*

Integrated Acquisition Environment (IAE)

See *Acquisition.gov.*

integrated agreement

A writing or writings constituting a final expression of one or more terms of an agreement. *(RSOC 209(1))*

integrated baseline review (IBR)

A joint assessment by the offeror or contractor and the U.S. federal government of the—
- Ability of the project's technical plan to achieve the objectives of the scope of work;
- Adequacy of the time allocated for performing the defined tasks to successfully achieve the project schedule objectives;

- Ability of the performance measurement baseline to successfully execute the project and attain cost objectives, recognizing the relationship between budget resources, funding, schedule, and scope of work;
- Availability of personnel, facilities, and equipment when required to perform the defined tasks needed to execute the program successfully; and
- The degree to which the management process provides effective and integrated technical/schedule/cost planning and baseline control.

(FAR 34.202(c))
See also *performance measurement baseline* (PMB).

integrated logistics support (ILS)
The composite of actions necessary to ensure the effective and economical performance of the systems and equipment that, functioning together, comprise a total system and, in turn, an operating force. *(HCS)*

integrated materiel management (IMM)
The exercise of total Department of Defense management responsibility for a federal supply group and class, commodity, or item by a single agency, including requirements, funding, budgeting, storage, issuing, cataloging, standardizing, and procurement. *(DISCS)*

integrated priority list (IPL)
Annual submittal by Combatant Commands (CCMDs) which represent prioritized issues (capability gaps associated with validated or proposed capability requirements), that limit CCDM ability to successfully achieve assigned roles, functions and missions. The IPLs are the official submissions of these prioritized capability gaps to the Joint Staff for review under the CGA process. *(CJCSI 3170.011)*

integrated project/product team (IPT)
A multidisciplinary team of acquisition professionals led by a program/project manager, which is responsible and accountable for planning, budgeting, procurement, and life-cycle management of an investment to achieve its cost, schedule, and performance goals. *(NDIA II)*

integrated supply
A special type of partnering arrangement usually developed between a purchaser and a distributor on an intermediate to long-term basis. The objective of an integrated supply relationship is to minimize, for both buyer and supplier, the labor and expense involved in the

acquisition and possession of maintenance, repair, and operating products and items that are repetitive, generic, high transaction, and have a low unit cost. *(GKPT)*

integration
The process of providing systems engineering and technical direction for a system for the purpose of achieving capabilities that satisfy program requirements. *(10 U.S.C. 2500(15))*

integrity
In the context of information security, guarding against improper information modification or destruction, including ensuring information nonrepudiation and authenticity. *(44 U.S.C. 3542)*

intellectual property (IP)
Includes inventions, trademarks, patents, industrial designs, copyrights, and technical information including software, data designs, technical know-how, manufacturing information and know-how, techniques, technical data packages, manufacturing data packages, and trade secrets. *(DAAT)*

interagency acquisition
A procedure by which a federal agency needing supplies or services (i.e., the "requesting agency") obtains them from another agency (i.e., the "servicing agency") by an assisted acquisition or a direct acquisition. This term includes acquisitions under the Economy Act (31 U.S.C. 1535) and non-Economy Act acquisitions completed under other statutory authorities (e.g., the GSA's Federal Supply Schedules (FSS) and governmentwide acquisition contracts (GWACS)). *(FAR 2.101)*
See *requesting agency; servicing agency*; see also *assisted acquisition; direct acquisition*.

interchangeability
A condition that exists when two or more items possess such functional and physical characteristics as to be equivalent in performance and durability and are capable of being exchanged one for the other without alteration to the items themselves or to adjoining items, except for adjustment. *(DODM 4120.24)*
See also *interchangeability and substitutability* (I&S)

interchangeability and substitutability (I&S)
Conditions that permit the exchange of one item for another without affecting design or performance beyond acceptable limits. *(DODM 4100.39)*
See also *interchangeability*.

interdivision work authorization (IDWA)/ interdivision work order (IDWO; IWO)
See *inter-organizational transfer*.

interest
(1) A charge for the use of another's money that is usually a percentage of the money being used. *(MW)*
See *compound interest; legal interest; simple interest*.
(2) A right, title, claim, or share in property. *(MW)*
See *beneficial interest; contingent interest; controlling interest; equitable interest; executory interest; expectation interest; future interest; insurable interest; legal interest; life interest; possessory interest; purchase-money security interest; reliance interest; reversionary interest; security interest; terminable interest; vested interest*.
(3) A specific concern or level of involvement (e.g., financial involvement), especially that warrants recognition or causes bias. *(MW)*
See *conflict of interest* (COI).
(4) Something that causes or warrants particular attention, such as:
- A principle, purpose, or object of concern; or
- A right, such as from a constitution (e.g., the U.S. Constitution)—especially such a right considered as an issue or claim created in or involving a particular situation or thing.

(MW)
See *public interest*; see also *privacy interest; property interest*.
(5) In the context of judicial remedies, a sum that may be calculated and awarded in addition to any damages awarded. *(CMBOK)*

interested party
(1) With respect to a contract or a solicitation or other request for offers, an actual or prospective offeror whose direct economic interest would be affected by the award of the contract or by the failure to award the contract. A protest may only be filed by an "interested party." *(31 U.S.C. 3551(2)(A); FAR 33.101)*
See *protest*.
(2) A prime contractor or an actual or prospective offeror whose direct economic interest would be affected by the award of a subcontract or by the failure to award a subcontract. *(FAR 26.101)*
See also *prime contractor; subcontract*.
(3) With respect to a public-private competition conducted under OMB Circular A-76 with respect to the performance of an activity or function of a U.S. federal agency, or a decision to convert a function performed by

federal employees to private-sector performance without a competition under OMB Circular A-76, includes:
- Any official who is responsible for submitting the agency tender in such competition; and
- Any one individual who, for the purpose of representing the federal employees engaged in the performance of the activity or function for which the public-private competition is conducted in a protest that relates to such public-private competition, has been designated as the "agent" of the federal employees by a majority of such employees.

(31 U.S.C. 3551(2)(B))
See also *agent; OMB Circular A-76*.

intergovernmental relations
A range of cooperative activities among governments, including various forms of intergovernmental cooperative purchasing, joint or shared use of facilities and supplies, and procurements made by one government from another. *(DGBCT)*

interim voucher
Under cost-reimbursement contracts, a type of invoice submitted prior to completion of the contract. *(NCMA-WS)*
See *invoice*.

internal confidentiality agreement/ statement
A confidentiality agreement or any other written statement that the contractor requires any of its employees or subcontractors to sign regarding nondisclosure of contractor information. This term does not include confidentiality agreements arising out of civil litigation or confidentiality agreements that contractor employees or subcontractors sign at the behest of a U.S. federal agency. *(FAR 3.901)*

internal controls
The plan of an organization and all its methods and measures adopted within an organization to safeguard its assets, check the accuracy and reliability of its data, promote operational efficiency, and encourage adherence to prescribed managerial policies. *(NCMA-CA)*
See also *internal security controls*.

internal network
A network where:
- The establishment, maintenance, and provisioning of security controls are under the direct control of organizational employees or contractors; or

- Cryptographic encapsulation or similar security technology implemented between organization-controlled endpoints, provides the same effect (at least with regard to confidentiality and integrity).

An internal network is typically organization-owned, yet the same may be organization-controlled while not being organization-owned. *(NIST SP 800-171)*
See *network*; contrast with *external network*.

internal security controls
In a cybersecurity context, hardware, firmware, or software features within an information system that restrict access to resources only to authorized subjects. *(CNSSI 4009)*
See also *information system* (IS).

international commercial terms (incoterms)
See *incoterms*.

international coproduction
A program implemented by a government-to-government or commercial licensing arrangement that enables a foreign government or firm to acquire the knowledge to manufacture or assemble, repair, maintain, and operate, in whole or in part, a defense item. *(DGBCT)*

international logistics
The planning, negotiating, and implementation of supporting logistics arrangements between nations, their forces, and agencies. It includes furnishing logistics support (major end items, materiel, and/or services) to, or receiving logistics support from, one or more friendly foreign governments, international organizations, or military forces, with or without reimbursement. *(DISCS)*

International Organization for Standardization (ISO)
An independent, non-governmental international organization with a membership of 162 national standards bodies. (See https://www.iso.org.)
See *International Organization for Standardization (ISO) 9000; International Organization for Standardization (ISO) 9001; standard*.

International Organization for Standardization (ISO) 9000
The ISO 9000 family addresses various aspects of quality management and contains some of ISO's best-known standards. The standards provide guidance and tools for companies and organizations who want to ensure that their products and services consistently meet customer's requirements, and that quality is consistently improved.

International Organization for Standardization (ISO)9001
ISO 9001sets out the criteria for a quality management system and is the only standard in the 9000 family that can be certified to (although this is not a requirement). It can be used by any organization, large or small, regardless of its field of activity. The 9001 standard is based on a number of quality management principles including a strong customer focus, the motivation and implication of top management, the process approach and continual improvement.

international standardization agreement (ISA)
The record of an agreement among several or all of the member nations of a multinational treaty organization to adopt like or similar equipment, supplies, and stores. *(DODM 4120.24)*

International Trade Commission (ITC)
Responsible for monitoring trade and determining when goods that are imported from overseas at less than their normal value ("dumped" goods) cause, or threaten to cause, material injury to any U.S. industrial product. *(NES-94)*

International Traffic in Arms Regulation (ITAR)
A document prepared by the Directorate of Defense Trade Control, Bureau of Political-Military Affairs, U.S. Department of State, providing licensing and regulatory provisions for the import and export of defense articles, technical data, and services. The *ITAR* includes the U.S. Munitions List. Published in the *Federal Register* as 22 CFR 120-130. *(DISCS)*
See *Export Administration Regulation (EAR)*.

internet
Collectively, the myriad computer and telecommunications facilities, including equipment and operating software, which comprise the interconnected worldwide network of networks that employ the Transmission Control Protocol/Internet Protocol, or any predecessor or successor protocol to such protocol, to communicate information of all kinds. *(21 U.S.C. 802(50))*

interoperability
(1) The ability of systems or items to provide or accept data, information, material, and services from other

systems or items. *(DODM 4120.24)*
(2) The ability of people to operate in synergy in the execution of assigned tasks. *(CJCSI 2700.01E)*
(3) The ability of systems, units, or forces to provide services to and accept services from other systems, units or forces, and to use the services so exchanged to enable them to operate effectively together. *(DISCS)*

inter-organizational transfer (IOT)
The assignment of work under a contract to one or more separate divisions or subunits of the prime contractor. Also known as *interdivision work authorization* (IDWA)/ *interdivision work order* (IDWO; IWO). *(NES-89)*

inter-service support agreement (ISSA)
The provision of a commercial activity, in accordance with an ISSA, on a reimbursable basis. This includes franchise funds, revolving funds, and working capital funds. *(OMB A-76)*

interveners
Awardees of the protested procurement or all other offerors who had a "reasonable prospect" of receiving an award. *(DGBCT)*

intervention
In the context of utility services, this term refers to action by the GSA or a delegated agency to formally participate in a utility regulatory proceeding on behalf of all U.S. federal executive agencies. *(FAR 41.101)*
See also *delegated agency; utility service*.

intrusion
In a cybersecurity context, the unauthorized act of bypassing the security mechanisms of a system. *(CNSSI 4009)*

invention
Any invention or discovery that is or may be patentable or otherwise protectable under Title 35 of the United States Code, or any variety of plant that is or may be protectable under the Plant Variety Protection Act (7 U.S.C. 2321, *et seq.*). *(FAR 27.301)*
See also *subject invention*.

inventoriable cost
A cost associated with units produced; a cost that may be looked upon as "attaching" or "clinging" to units produced. *(NCMA-CA)*

inventory
The amount of property on hand at any given time. This includes raw materials, goods in process, and finished goods. *(NES-02; SPP)*

inventory control
The effective management of inventories, including decisions about which items to stock at each location, how much stock at each location, how much stock to keep on hand at various levels of operation, when to buy, how much to buy controlling pilferage and damage, and managing shortages and backorders. *(GKPT)*

inventory holding (carrying) cost
The cost of keeping inventory on hand, including the opportunity cost of invested funds, storage and handling costs, taxes, insurance, shrinkage, and obsolescence-risk costs. Firms usually state an item's holding cost per time period as a percentage of the item's value, typically between 20 and 40 percent per year. *(GKPT)*

inventory position
A measure of an inventory item's ability to satisfy future demand, considering scheduled receipts and on-hand inventory. *(GKPT)*

inventory recovery
A systematic, central organizational effort to manage the surplus equipment/material and scrap recovery/ marketing/disposition activities in a manner that recovers as much of the original capital investment as possible. *(GKPT)*

inventory turnover
A measure of the velocity of total inventory movement through the firm, found by dividing annual sales (at cost) by the average aggregate inventory value maintained during the year. Many firms calculate production inventory turnover rate as the annual inventory purchase value divided by the average production inventory value. *(GKPT)*

inverted domestic corporation
A corporation that used to be incorporated in the United States, or used to be a partnership in the United States, but now is incorporated in a foreign country, or is a subsidiary whose parent corporation is incorporated in a foreign country, that meets the criteria specified in 6 U.S.C. 395(b), applied in accordance with the rules and definitions of 6 U.S.C. 395(c). *(FAR 9.108-1)*

investment goods
See *capital*.

investment property
A security, whether certificated or uncertificated, security entitlement, securities account, commodity contract, or commodity account. *(UCC 9-102(a)(49))*

invitation for bids (IFB)
The method of solicitation for the sealed bid process. The IFB must describe the federal government's requirements clearly, accurately, and completely. Unnecessarily restrictive specifications or requirements that might unduly limit the number of bidders are prohibited. The IFB includes all documents (whether attached or incorporated by reference) to be furnished by prospective bidders for the purpose of bidding. *(DGBCT; NCMA-SB)* (See also FAR 14.201.)

invoice
A seller's bill or written request for payment under the contract for supplies delivered or services performed. *(FAR 2.101)*
See also *final voucher; interim voucher; proper invoice*.

invoice payment
A federal government disbursement of monies to a contractor under a contract or other authorization for supplies or services accepted by the government. Invoice payments include:
- Payments for partial deliveries that have been accepted by the government;
- Final cost or fee payments where amounts owed have been settled between the government and the contractor;
- For purposes of *FAR* Subpart 32.9 only, all payments made under the clause "Payments Under Fixed-Price Construction Contracts" (FAR 52.232-5) and the clause "Payments Under Fixed-Price Architect-Engineer Contracts" (FAR 52.232-10); and
- Interim payments under a cost-reimbursement contract for services when Alternate I of the clause "Prompt Payment"(FAR 52.232-25) is used.

Invoice payments *do not* include contract financing payments. *(FAR 32.001)*
See *invoice*; see also *contract financing payments*.

Invoicing, Receipt, Acceptance and Property Transfer (iRAPT)
A secure web-based system for electronic invoicing, receipt, and acceptance. The iRAPT system replaced wide-area workflow (WAWF) and is part of the e-Business Suite. It creates a virtual folder to combine the three documents required to pay a vendor:
- The contract,
- The invoice, and
- The receiving report.

The iRAPT application enables electronic form submission of invoices, government inspection, and acceptance documents in order to support the DOD's goal of moving to a paperless acquisition process.

irrevocable letter of credit
A written commitment by a federally insured financial institution to pay all or part of a stated amount of money, until the expiration date of the letter, upon the U.S. federal government's (the beneficiary) presentation of a written demand for payment. Neither the financial institution nor the offeror/contractor can revoke or condition the letter of credit. *(FAR 2.101)*

Ishikawa Diagram
See *Fishbone Diagram*.

Israeli end product
In the context of the federal government's "Buy American" policies, trade agreements, and other laws and regulations governing foreign acquisition, this term refers to an article that is wholly the growth, product, or manufacture of Israel, or in the case of an article that consists in whole or in part of materials from another country, has been substantially transformed in Israel into a new and different article of commerce with a name, character, or use distinct from that of the article or articles from which it was transformed. *(FAR 25.003)*

issue
As it pertains to a negotiable instrument, this term means the first delivery of the instrument by the maker or drawer, whether to a holder or nonholder, for the purpose of giving rights on the instrument to any person. *(UCC 3-105(a))*
See also *issuer*.

issue in controversy
A material disagreement between the buyer and the seller that may result in a claim or is all or part of an existing claim. *(FAR 33.201)*

issuer
(1) In the case of a negotiable instrument, applies to issued and unissued instruments and means a maker or

drawer of an instrument. *(UCC 3-105(c))*
See also *issue; negotiable instrument.*
(2) In the case of a letter of credit, means a bank or other person that issues a letter of credit, but does not include an individual who makes an engagement for personal, family, or household purposes. *(UCC 5-102(a)(9))*
See also *issue; letter of credit.*
(3) A bailee that issues a document of title or, in the case of an unaccepted delivery order, the person that orders the possessor of goods to deliver. This term includes a person for which an agent or employee purports to act in issuing a document if the agent or employee has real or apparent authority to issue documents, even if the issuer did not receive any goods, the goods were misdescribed, or in any other respect the agent or employee violated the issuer's instructions. *(UCC 7-102(a)(8))*
See also *bailee; delivery order; document of title; goods.*

item

(1) *Synonymous with "item of supply."*
See *item of supply.*
(2) An instrument or a promise or order to pay money handled by a bank for collection or payment. This term *does not* include a payment order governed by Article 4A of the Uniform Commercial Code or a credit or debit card slip. *(UCC 4-104(a)(9))*
See also *instrument; order; promise.*

item identification

A collection and compilation of data to describe an item. The minimum data to develop an item identification are a combination of the item name, CAGE code, manufacturers' identifying part or reference number, reference number category code, and reference number variation code. It may also include the item name, all of the physical and performance characteristics data that a specific item identification guide prescribes, the manufacturers' identifying part or reference number, and additional related reference numbers. *(DODM 4100.39)*
See also *Commercial and Government Entity (CAGE) code.*

item of production

A part, piece, object, equipment, or material that is produced by a manufacturer, is grouped within a manufacturer's identifying number, and conforms to the same engineering drawing, standard, specification, and inspection. *(DODM 4100.39)*

item of supply

Any individual part, component, subassembly, assembly, or subsystem integral to a major system, and other property which may be replaced during the service life of the system. This term includes spare parts and replenishment parts, but the same does not include packaging or labeling associated with shipment or identification of an "item." *(FAR 34.101;)*

item reduction activity (IRA)

An organization in a federal government department or agency responsible for reviewing federal supply classes or item name codes for reducing, to the highest degree practicable, the number of sizes and kinds of items that are generally similar. *(DODM 4120.24)*
See also *federal supply class.*

item reduction study

An analysis to identify unneeded items currently in the supply system that involves a technical review of supply items to identify duplicating or overlapping items. It leads to a reduction in the number of similar items. *(DODM 4120.24)*

item unique identification and valuation

A system of marking, valuing, and tracking items delivered to the federal government that enhances logistics, contracting, and financial business transactions supporting the United States. *(DFARS 211.274-1)*

J

Javits-Wagner-O'Day Act (JWOD)

See *Committee for Purchase from People Who Are Blind or Severely Disabled statute.*

job analysis

A detailed examination of a job to determine the duties, responsibilities, and specialized requirements necessary for its performance. *(DAAT)*

job class of employees

Employees performing in positions within the same job. *(FAR 31.001)*

job order cost system

One in which a contractor accounts for output and costs incurred by specifically identifiable physical units. A job order may cover the production of one unit

or represent a composite number of identical units. *(HECA)*

job tasks

In the context of the *CMS™*, refers to the tasks performed on a routine basis by contract managers. Contract managers systematically process the job tasks to achieve the expected results of the competencies. *(CMS)*
See also *Contract Management Standard™ Publication (CMS™); competencies; domains*.

joint contract

A contract in which the parties bind themselves both individually and as a unit. *(STBP)*

joint cost

A cost that is common to all the segments in question and that is not clearly or practically allocable except by some questionable allocation base. Also known as *common cost*. *(NCMA-CA)*

joint products cost

Costs of two or more manufactured goods, of significant sales values, that are produced by a single process and that are not identifiable as individual products up to a certain state of production known as the split-off point. *(NCMA-CA)*

joint resolution (J Res)

A legislative resolution, designated H J Res (House) or S J Res (Senate), which requires the approval of both houses and the signature of the president of the United States, just as a bill does, and which has the force of law if approved. There is no practical difference between a bill and a joint resolution. A joint resolution generally is used to deal with a limited matter, such as a single appropriation. *(DISCS)*

joint settlement

Joint negotiation of two or more termination settlement proposals from the same contractor under different contracts. *(GOAT)*

joint venture

(1) The parties jointly own and manage either a partnership or a corporation established for the express purpose of entering into a contract with the customer. Neither party alone enjoys direct privity of contract with the customer; only the joint venture itself has direct privity. *(AI)*
(2) For size determination purposes, an association

of persons or concerns with interests in any degree or proportion by way of contract, express or implied, consorting to engage in and carry out a single specific business venture for joint profit, for which purpose they combine their efforts, property, money, skill, or knowledge, but not on a continuing or permanent basis for conducting business generally. A joint venture is viewed as a business entity in determining power to control its management. *(FAR 19.101(7))*
See *teaming arrangement*.

joint work statement

A proposal prepared for a federal agency by the director of a government-owned, contractor-operated laboratory describing the purpose and scope of a proposed cooperative research and development agreement, and assigning rights and responsibilities among the agency, the laboratory, and any other party or parties to the proposed agreement. *(15 U.S.C. 3710a(d)(3))*

jurisdiction

(1) In a legal sense, the authority (i.e., of a board of contract appeals, federal court, or arbitrator) to hold a hearing, grant relief, and make determinations that are binding on the parties. *(GCG)*
(2) With respect to a registered organization, this term refers to the jurisdiction under whose law the organization is formed or organized (i.e., "jurisdiction of organization"). *(UCC 9-102(a)(50))*
See also *registered organization*.

jury verdict basis

A means of pricing equitable adjustments used when the two parties rely on different costing approaches. This technique is not limited to use in court; it can also be used during negotiations. It requires compromise. The evidence is presented by both parties, the information is evaluated, and the "jury verdict" method is used to determine a reasonable claim amount. *(NCMA-CA)*
See *actual cost basis; modified total cost basis; total cost basis*.

just-in-time (JIT) inventory

(1) A manufacturing and inventory philosophy that minimizes inventory at all levels—materials are purchased, transported, and processed just in time for their use in a subsequent stage of the manufacturing process. The dual objectives of the JIT concept are to reduce waste and to increase productivity. *(EDI; DGBCT)*
(2) The minimum inventory required to meet production schedules. *(DGCQI)*

justification and approval (J&A)
A document to justify procurement using other than full and open competition. This document is required prior to commencing negotiation for a contract resulting from an unsolicited proposal or any other contract award that does not provide for full and open competition. *(HCS)*

Kanban system
A system of production flow control that pulls in-process inventories through a manufacturing process where items are called for only as they are needed in the next step of the production process. *(GKPT)*

key
In a cybersecurity context, a parameter used in conjunction with a cryptographic algorithm that determines the specific operation of that algorithm. Also called cryptographic key. *(FIPS 201-2)*

key contract terms
In the context of contract interpretation, U.S. courts and boards of contract appeals generally use three sources to define "key contract terms":

- The definitions that the parties have incorporated into the contract document, or which are referenced by law (e.g., the *Federal Acquisition Regulation*);
- If the definitions are not incorporated into the contract, or are not referenced by law, then dictionaries or common usage are used; or
- If the key contract term is not defined in the contract and circumstances indicate that the intent of the parties was a technical term, not in common usage, then an appropriate technical definition will be selected.

(CMBOK)

key functional characteristics
Those functional qualities or characteristics that critically affect a configuration item's ability to fulfill operational requirements. *(AFIT)*

key personnel clause
A solicitation provision that requires offerors to identify which personnel will be working on the contract. The buyer states its personnel qualification requirements and the seller responds with documentation (e.g., résumés) detailing how its key personnel meet the buyer's requirements. Some key personnel clauses may require the seller to price its effort based on each key person's actual rate rather than the average bid rate used on the majority of proposals. The seller must bid the key personnel in good faith, but generally has a right of substitution, with the buyer's approval. The buyer has certain recourse, such as renegotiation and right of refusal, if the promised key personnel are not provided. *(TIPS)*

key practices
The infrastructures and activities that contribute most to the effective implementation and institutionalization of a critical process. *(AIMD)*

kickback
(1) Payment back of a portion of the purchase price to a buyer or public official by the seller to induce purchase or to improperly influence future purchases or leases. The federal Kickbacks statute (41 U.S.C. Chapter 87) makes kickbacks a criminal offense in connection with a government contract. *(BLD)*
See *Kickbacks statute*.
(2) Any money, fee, commission, credit, gift, gratuity, thing of value, or compensation of any kind that is provided to any prime contractor, prime contractor employee, subcontractor, or subcontractor employee for the purpose of improperly obtaining or rewarding favorable treatment in connection with a prime contract, or in connection with a subcontract relating to a prime contract. *(FAR 3.502-1)*

Kickbacks statute
A federal law (41 U.S.C. Chapter 87) passed to deter subcontractors from making payments and contractors from accepting payments for the purpose of improperly obtaining or rewarding favorable treatment in connection with a prime contract or a subcontract relating to a prime contract. Formerly known as the *Anti-Kickback Act* and the *Copeland Anti-Kickback Act*. *(FAR 3.502-2)*

L

label
A display of written, printed, or graphic matter upon the immediate container of any article; as well as a requirement made by or under authority of Title 21, Chapter 9 of the United States Code that any word, statement, or other information appear on the label shall not be considered to be complied with unless such word, statement, or other information also appears on the outside container or wrapper, if any there be, of the retail package of such article, or is easily legible through the outside container or wrapper. *(21 U.S.C. 321(k))*
See also *labeling*.

labeling
All labels and other written, printed, or graphic matter—
- Upon any article or any of its containers or wrappers, or
- Accompanying such article.

(21 U.S.C. 321(m))

labor compliance agreement
An agreement entered into between a contractor or subcontractor and an enforcement agency to address appropriate remedial measures, compliance assistance, steps to resolve issues to increase compliance with the labor laws, or other related matters. *(FAR 22.2002)*
See *labor laws*; see also *enforcement agency*.

labor cost at standard
A pre-established measure of the labor element of cost, computed by multiplying labor-rate standard by labor-time standard. *(FAR 31.001)*
See *labor-rate standard; labor-time standard*.

labor efficiency variance
A variance relative to labor that is equal to the earned labor hours less actual labor hours multiplied by the earned hourly rate (i.e., (earned hours - actual hours) × earned rate). It reflects the number of hours actually expended versus the number of hours earned to complete the planned work. *(NDIA II)*

labor hour contract
(1) A contract that provides for reimbursement of the contractor's labor costs at a fixed hourly rate. *(GSFC)*
(2) A variation of the time-and-materials contract, differing only in that materials are not supplied by the contractor. *(FAI)*

labor law decision
An administrative merits determination, arbitral award or decision, or civil judgment, which resulted from a violation of one or more labor laws. *(FAR 22.2002)*
See *labor laws*; see also *administrative merits determination; arbitral award or decision; civil judgment*.

labor laws
Laws that define and protect the rights of employees. They include the following laws and Executive Orders:
- The Fair Labor Standards Act (29 U.S.C. Chapter 8);
- The Occupational Safety and Health Act of 1970 (29 U.S.C. Chapter 15);
- The Migrant and Seasonal Agricultural Worker Protection Act (Pub. L. 97-470);
- The National Labor Relations Act (Pub. L. 74-198);
- The Wage Rate Requirements (Construction) statute (40 U.S.C. Chapter 31, Subchapter IV—formerly known as the "Davis-Bacon Act");
- The Service Contract Labor Standards statute (41 U.S.C. Chapter 67—formerly known as the "Service Contract Act");
- Executive Order 11246 of September 24, 1965 ("Equal Employment Opportunity");
- Section 503 of the Rehabilitation Act of 1973 (29 U.S.C. 794d);
- The Vietnam Era Veterans' Readjustment Assistance Act of 1972 and the Vietnam Era Veterans' Readjustment Assistance Act of 1974 (38 U.S.C. 4212);
- The Family and Medical Leave Act (Pub. L. 103-3);
- Title VII of the Civil Rights Act of 1964 (Pub. L. 88-352);
- The Americans with Disabilities Act of 1990 (Pub. L. 101-336);
- The Age Discrimination in Employment Act of 1967 (29 U.S.C. 621–634); and
- Equivalent U.S. state laws.

(Note: The only equivalent state laws implemented in the *FAR* are OSHA-approved state plans, which can be found at www.osha.gov/dcsp/osp/approved_state_plans.html.) (FAR 22.2002)

labor market
A place where individuals exchange their labor for compensation. Labor markets are identified and defined by a combination of geography, education and/or technical background required, experience required by the job, licensing or certification requirements, occupational membership, and industry. *(FAR 31.001)*

labor productivity

The rate of output of a worker or group of workers per unit of time, usually compared to an established standard or expected rate of output. *(DAAT)*

labor-rate standard

A preestablished measure, expressed in monetary terms, of the price of labor. *(FAR 31.001)*
Contrast with *labor-time standard*.

labor-rate variance

A variance relative to labor that is equal to the earned labor rate less actual labor rate multiplied by the actual labor hours used to execute the effort (i.e., (earned rate - actual rate) × actual hours). It reflects the difference between the earned labor rate and the actual labor rate. *(NDIA II)*

labor relations

Maintaining satisfactory relations between the employer and its employees, including such activities as establishing labor management committees, employee publications, and other related activities. *(FAR 31.205-21(a))*

labor surplus area

A geographic area identified by the U.S. Department of Labor in accordance with 20 CFR 654, Subpart A, as an area of concentrated unemployment or underemployment or an area of labor surplus. *(FAR 2.101)*
See also *labor surplus area concern*.

labor surplus area concern

A concern that together with its first-tier subcontractors will perform substantially in labor surplus areas. Performance is substantially in labor surplus areas if the costs incurred under the contract on account of manufacturing, production, or performance of appropriate services in labor surplus areas exceed 50 percent of the contract price. *(FAR 2.101)*
See *labor surplus area*.

labor-time standard

A preestablished measure, expressed in temporal terms, of the quantity of labor. *(FAR 31.001)*
Contrast with *labor-rate standard*.

laborers or mechanics

In the context of labor standards for contracts involving construction, means:

- Workers, utilized by a contractor or subcontractor at any tier, whose duties are manual or physical in nature (including those workers who use tools or who are performing the work of a trade), as distinguished from mental or managerial;
- Apprentices, trainees, helpers, and, in the case of contracts subject to the Contract Work Hours and Safety Standards statute, watchmen and guards;
- Working foremen who devote more than 20 percent of their time during a workweek performing duties of a laborer or mechanic, and who do not meet the criteria of 29 CFR Part 541 for the time so spent; and
- Every person performing the duties of a laborer or mechanic, regardless of any contractual relationship alleged to exist between the contractor and those individuals.

This term does not include workers whose duties are primarily executive, supervisory, administrative, or clerical, rather than manual. Persons employed in a bona fide executive, administrative, or professional capacity (as defined in 29 CFR Part 541) are not deemed to be "laborers or mechanics." *(FAR 22.401)*

Lanham Act

The common name for the federal law (15 U.S.C. 1051, *et seq.*)—titled "An Act to provide for the registration and protection of trademarks used in commerce, to carry out the provisions of certain international conventions, and for other purposes"—that establishes U.S. policy concerning the registration and enforcement of trademarks. *(15 U.S.C. 1051(a)-(e))*

large-scale construction project

In the case of a federal government construction project, a construction project where the total cost to the government is $25 million or more. *(FAR 22.502)*

last-in, first-out (LIFO)

A cost-flow assumption that the stock acquired earliest is still on hand; the stock of merchandise or material acquired latest is used first. *(IMA)*
Compare with *first-in, first-out*.

late bid

A bid received in the office designated in the invitation for bids after the exact time set for receipt of bids. *(FAR 14.304(b)(1))*

latent defect

A defect that exists at the time of acceptance but cannot be discovered by a reasonable inspection. *(FAR 2.101)*
Contrast with *patent defect*.

law of agency
See *agency*.

lead time
(1) The period of time from the initiation and the completion of a process. *(DAAT)*
(2) The period of time from the date of a purchase order to the date of delivery of the order. *(GKPT)*

leader-follower concept
A contractual relationship for the delivery of an end item through a prime or subcontract relationship or to provide assistance to another company. Variants include:

- A prime contract awarded to an established source (leader) who is obligated to subcontract to and assist another source (follower);
- A contract is awarded requiring the leader to assist the follower, who has the prime contract for production; or
- A prime contract awarded to the follower for production, and the follower is obligated to subcontract with a designated leader for assistance (the leader may be producing under another contract).

(DAAT)

Lean
A set of tools used for process improvement. It is a systematic method for the elimination of waste from a process with the goal of providing what is of value to the customer. Although Lean's roots are in the manufacturing and production environments, it is widely applied to transactional processes as well. (Note that *Lean* and the "Lean" within *Lean Six Sigma* are the same thing. When Lean is brought in as "Lean Six Sigma," it is reorganizing Lean tools through a Six Sigma view.) *(GLSS)*
See also *Lean Six Sigma* (LSS); *Six Sigma*.

Lean Six Sigma (LSS)
The name given to the combination of the "Lean" and "Six Sigma" process improvement methods. Lean traditionally focuses on removing waste from the system, with the objective of a streamlined process. Six Sigma focuses on reducing variation in the system, with an emphasis on increasing predictability. Both models focus on satisfying the needs of the customer by incrementally improving processes. *(GLSS)*
See also *Lean; Six Sigma*.

learning curve
A tool of calculation used primarily to project resource requirements, in terms of direct manufacturing labor hours or the quantity of material (for this purpose, usually referred to as an "improvement curve") required for a production run. The concept of a learning curve was adopted from the observation that individuals who perform repetitive tasks exhibit a rate of improvement due to increased manual dexterity. *(ASPM)*

lease
(1) A legally binding agreement between two parties—the lessor, who owns the asset, and the lessee, who uses the asset. *(NES-02)*
See *lease agreement; lease contract*.
(2) In reference to goods, refers to a transfer of the right to possession and use of goods for a term in return for consideration, but a sale, including a sale on approval or a sale on return, or retention or creation of a security interest is not a "lease." Unless the context clearly indicates otherwise, this term includes a "sublease." *(UCC 2A-103(j))*
See also *lease agreement; lease contract; purchase money lease; sublease*.
(3) In reference to tangible personal property, refers to a contract by which the owner of such property grants another the right to possess, use, and enjoy it for a specified period of time in exchange for periodic payment of a stipulated price. *(BLD)*

lease agreement
The bargain, with respect to the lease, of the lessor and the lessee in fact as found in their language or by implication from other circumstances, including course of dealing, usage of trade, or course of performance. Unless the context clearly indicates otherwise, this term includes "sublease agreement." *(UCC 2A-103(k))*
See also *lease; sublease agreement*; contrast with *lease contract*.

lease contract
The total legal obligation that results from the lease agreement and any other applicable rules of law. Unless the context clearly indicates otherwise, this term includes a "sublease contract." *(UCC 2A-103(l))*
See also *lease; sublease agreement*.

lease or buy decision
The decision concerning whether to contract for the possession and use of an asset owned by another party for a period of time in return for lease payments, as opposed to purchasing the asset. *(GKPT)*

leasehold interest

The interest of the lessor or the lessee under a lease contract. *(UCC 2A-103(m))*
See also *lease; lessee; lessor*.

lease-to-ownership program (LTOP)

A contract for the lease of property that provides for the automatic transfer of property title to the buyer upon the expiration of the lease. *(F&F)*
Compare with *lease with option to purchase* (LWOP).

lease with option to purchase (LWOP)

A contract for the lease of property that provides the buyer with the option of purchasing the property at one or more points during the lease, or upon its expiration. *(F&F)*
Compare with *lease-to-ownership program* (LTOP).

least-developed country

In the context of the federal government's "Buy American" policies, trade agreements, and other laws and regulations governing foreign acquisition, this term refers to any of the following countries: Afghanistan, Angola, Bangladesh, Benin, Bhutan, Burkina Faso, Burundi, Cambodia, Central African Republic, Chad, Comoros, Democratic Republic of Congo, Djibouti, Equatorial Guinea, Eritrea, Ethiopia, Gambia, Guinea, Guinea-Bissau, Haiti, Kiribati, Laos, Lesotho, Liberia, Madagascar, Malawi, Mali, Mauritania, Mozambique, Nepal, Niger, Rwanda, Samoa, Sao Tome and Principe, Senegal, Sierra Leone, Solomon Islands, Somalia, South Sudan, Tanzania, Timor-Leste, Togo, Tuvalu, Uganda, Vanuatu, Yemen, or Zambia. *(FAR 25.003)*
See also *least-developed country end product*.

least-developed country end product

In the context of the federal government's "Buy American" policies, trade agreements, and other laws and regulations governing foreign acquisition, this term refers to an article that is wholly the growth, product, or manufacture of a least developed country, or in the case of an article that consists in whole or in part of materials from another country, has been substantially transformed in a least-developed country into a new and different article of commerce with a name, character, or use distinct from that of the article or articles from which it was transformed. This term also refers to a product offered for purchase under a supply contract, but for purposes of calculating the value of the end product, includes services (except transportation services) incidental to the article, provided that the value of those incidental services does not exceed that of the article itself. *(FAR 25.003)*

See *least-developed country*; see also *end product*.

legal capital

See *stated capital*.

legal interest

(1) An interest that is recognized in law (e.g., by legal title). *(MW)*
(2) A lawful interest rate (i.e., at or below the highest rate allowed). *(MW)*
(3) Interest computed at a rate described in (2) of this definition. *(MW)*

legal proceedings

(1) Any criminal proceeding. *(FAR 9.403)*
(2) Any civil judicial proceeding to which the federal government is a party. *(FAR 9.403)*
(3) Any appeals from proceedings described in (1) or (2) of this definition. *(FAR 9.403)*

legally binding contract

In order for a contract to be "legally binding," it must—
- Involve two or more parties who possess the capacity to contract;
- Show agreement, including "offer," "acceptance," and "mutual assent";
- Show something of value exchanged between the contracted parties or other inducement that leads a person to make a promise;
- Be for a legal purpose; and
- Be in the correct form.
(CMBOK)

lessee

A person who acquires the right to possession and use of goods under a lease. Unless the context clearly indicates otherwise, this term includes a "sublessee." *(UCC 2A-103(n))*
See also *goods; lease; lessor; sublease*.

lessons learned

Capitalizing on past errors in judgment, material failures, wrong timing, or other mistakes to ultimately improve a situation or system. *(DAAT)*

lessor

A person who transfers the right to possession and use of goods under a lease. Unless the context clearly indicates otherwise, this term includes a "sublessor." *(UCC 2A-103(p))*
See also *lease; lessee; lessor's residual interest; sublease*.

LI

lessor's residual interest

The lessor's interest in the goods after expiration, termination, or cancellation of the lease contract. *(UCC 2A-103(q))*
See also *goods; lease; lease contract; lessor*.

letter contract

A written preliminary contractual instrument that authorizes the contractor to begin immediately manufacturing supplies or performing services. *(FAR 16.603)*

letter of assist (LOA)

A contractual document issued by the United Nations to a government authorizing it to provide goods or services to a peacekeeping operation. *(DDMAT)*

letter of credit

(1) A definite undertaking by an issuer to a beneficiary at the request or for the account of an applicant or, in the case of a financial institution, to itself or for its own account, to honor a documentary presentation by payment or delivery of an item of value. *(UCC 5-102(a)(10))*
See also *proceeds*.
(2) An international business document that assures the seller that payment will be made by the bank issuing the letter of credit upon fulfillment of the sales agreement. In this context, it is a legally binding contract between the banks representing the exporter and the importer and includes all the terms and conditions of the sale. *(GKPT; NES-02)*
(3) In a contract for sale, means an irrevocable credit issued by a financing entity of good repute and, where the shipment is overseas, of good international repute. *(UCC 2-325(3))*
See also *financing entity; letter-of-credit right*.

letter-of-credit right

A right to payment or performance under a letter of credit, whether or not the beneficiary has demanded or is at the time entitled to demand payment or performance. This term *does not* include the right of a beneficiary to demand payment or performance under a letter of credit. *(UCC 9-102(a)(51))*
See *letter of credit*.

letter of intent (LOI)

An obligation instrument that can be used to protect price and availability of long-lead-time items and for other purposes. *(AFIT)*

letter of offer and acceptance (LOA)

A DOD letter by which the U.S. government offers to sell to a foreign government or international organization U.S. defense articles and defense services pursuant to the Arms Export Control Act, as amended (22 U.S.C. 2751, *et seq.*). The LOA lists the items and/or services, estimated costs, and the terms and conditions of sale. It also provides for the signature of an appropriate foreign government official to indicate acceptance. *(DISCS)*
See *foreign military sales* (FMS); see also *Arms Export Control Act (AECA); defense article; defense service*.

level of effort (LOE)

The devotion of talent or capability to a predetermined level of activity, over a stated period of time, on the basis of a fixed-price or cost-reimbursement pricing arrangement; payment is usually based on effort expended rather than results achieved. *(OPM)*

level of protection

The extent to which protective measures, techniques, and procedures must be applied to information systems and networks based on risk, threat, vulnerability, system interconnectivity considerations, and information assurance needs. Levels of protection include:
- "Basic": requiring implementation of standard minimum security.
- "Medium": requiring layering of additional safeguards above the standard minimum security.
- "High": requiring the most stringent protection and rigorous security.

(CNSSI 4009)

levy

(1) The imposition or collection of an assessment by legal authority (e.g., "the government imposed a *levy* on gasoline"). *(MW)*
(2) In a legal sense, an act of levying, such as: the imposition or collection of a tax, or the seizure according to a writ of execution of real or personal property in a debtor's possession to satisfy a debt. *(MW)*
See also *attach; garnishment*.

liabilities

The various claims against a firm, including accounts payable, notes payable, obligations under capital leases, and long-term debts. *(NES-02)*

license

Permits the usage of software, patents, trademarks, or technology by another entity without transferring ownership rights. *(DGBCT)*
See also *exclusive/non-exclusive license; licensing*.

licensing

Involves the many procedures administrative agencies perform in conjunction with issuance of various types of licenses. *(DGBCT)*
See *license*.

lien

(1) A legal claim on property for the purpose of satisfying a debt. *(GKPT)*
(2) Concerning goods, this term means a charge against or interest in goods to secure payment of a debt or performance of an obligation, but this term *does not* include a security interest. *(UCC 2A-103(r))*
See also *lien creditor*.

lien creditor

Means:
- A creditor that has acquired a lien on the property involved by attachment, levy, or the like;
- An assignee for benefit of creditors from the time of assignment;
- A trustee in bankruptcy from the date of the filing of the petition; or
- A receiver in equity from the time of appointment.

(UCC 9-102(a)(52))
See *lien*.

life cycle

(1) Concerning an item, refers to the total phases through which an item passes from the time it is initially developed until the time it is either consumed in use or disposed of as being excess to all known requirements. *(DDMAT)*
(2) *Synonymous with* "contract life cycle phases." *(CMBOK)*
See *contract life cycle phases*.

life cycle cost (LCC)

The total cost to the U.S. federal government of acquiring, operating, supporting, and (if applicable) disposing of the items being acquired. *(FAR 7.101)*

life cycle cost estimate (LCCE)

The overall estimated cost for a particular program alternative over the time period corresponding to the life of the program, including direct and indirect initial costs plus any periodic or continuing costs of operation and maintenance. *(DGBCT)*

likelihood

A measure of the possibility that a scenario will occur that also accounts for the timeframe in which the events represented in the scenario can occur. *(NID 8000-108)*

limitation of cost

A limitation on the funds available under a cost-reimbursement contract. The parties estimate that the contract cost will not exceed the limitation of cost. The contractor agrees to use its best efforts to perform the work specified in the contract and all obligations under the contract within the estimated cost, which, if the contract is a cost-sharing contract, includes both the U.S. federal government's and contractor's share of cost. *(GOAT)* (See also FAR 52.232-20.)
See *"Limitation of Costs" clause*.

"Limitation of Costs" clause

Applicable only to fully funded cost-reimbursement contracts. Under this clause, the contracting officer should be given 60 days' notice in writing when the costs incurred will exceed 75 percent of the estimated cost. The federal government is not obligated to reimburse the contractor for costs incurred in excess of the estimated costs, and the contractors are not obligated to continue performance under a contract causing them to incur costs in excess of the estimated costs. *(TIPS)* (See also FAR 52.232-20.)
See *limitation of costs*.

limitation of funds

A limit on the funds currently available under a cost-reimbursement contract when the available funding is less than the estimated amount of the contract. The parties contemplate that the U.S. federal government will allot additional funds incrementally to the contract up to the full estimated cost to the government specified in the schedule, exclusive of any fee. The contractor agrees to perform, or have performed, work on the contract up to the point at which the total amount paid and payable by the government under the contract approximates but does not exceed the total amount actually allotted by the government to the contract. *(GOAT)* (See also FAR 52.232-22.)
See *"Limitation of Funds" clause*.

LI

"Limitation of Funds" clause

Used for incrementally funded cost-reimbursement contracts. Similar to the "Limitation of Costs" clause, this clause recommends the contractor to give the contracting officer 60 days' written notice when costs incurred will exceed 75 percent of the funds allotted to the contract. *(TIPS)* (See also FAR 52.232-22.)
See *limitation of funds*.

limitations on budget authority

In a federal government context, a term that means any amount that is precluded from obligation in a fiscal year by a provision of law (such as a limitation or a benefit formula), which shall not be included in the budget authority in that year. *(2 U.S.C. 622(2)(B))*
See *budget authority*.

limited liability company (LLC)

A business structure that combines the limited personal liability feature of a corporation with the single taxation feature of a partnership or sole-proprietorship firm. Its profits and tax benefits are split any way the stockholders/shareholders (whether individuals or other firms) choose. *(BD)*

limited production

See *low rate initial production*.

limited rights

The rights of the U.S. federal government in limited rights data, as set forth in a "limited rights notice." *(FAR 27.401)*
See *limited rights data; limited rights notice;* contrast with *restricted rights; unlimited rights*.

limited rights data

(1) Data, other than computer software, that embody trade secrets or are commercial or financial and confidential or privileged, to the extent that such data pertain to items, components, or processes developed at private expense, including minor modifications. *(FAR 27.401)*
(2) Data, other than computer software, developed at private expense that embody trade secrets or are commercial or financial and confidential or privileged. *(FAR 27.409(b)(2))* (See also FAR 52.227-14, Alternate I.)
See *limited rights;* see also *limited rights notice*.

limited rights notice

A written request by the contracting officer to a contractor for delivery of limited rights data. *(FAR 27.409(b)(3))* (See also FAR 52.227-14, Alternate II, (g)(3).)

limits on exchanges

Limits imposed on federal government personnel involved in a competitive acquisition. These limits place restrictions on conduct that:
- Favors one offeror over another;
- Reveals an offeror's technical solution, including unique technology, innovative and unique uses of commercial items, or any information that would compromise an offeror's intellectual property to another offeror;
- Reveals an offeror's price without that offeror's permission—nevertheless, the contracting officer may inform an offeror that its price is considered by the government to be "too high," or "too low," and reveal the results of the analysis supporting that conclusion. It is also permissible, at the government's discretion, to indicate to all offerors the cost or price that the government's price analysis, market research, and other reviews have identified as reasonable;
- Reveals the names of individuals providing reference information about an offeror's past performance; or
- Knowingly furnishes source selection information in violation of FAR 3.104, 41 U.S.C. 2102 and 41 U.S.C.2107.

(FAR 15.306(e)) (See also FAR 15.201.)

line item

The basic structural element in a procurement instrument that describes and organizes the required product or service for pricing, delivery, inspection, acceptance, invoicing, and payment. The use of the term "line item" includes "subline item," as applicable. *(FAR 2.101)* (See also FAR Subpart 4.10.)
See also *contract line item number (CLIN); subline item*.

lines of accounting (LOA)

An accounting classification citation structure that identifies a specific department/agency, color of money, fiscal year, and purpose. Lines of accounting are assigned by the U.S. Department of the Treasury and each line of accounting is specified in a requirements document (such as a purchase request). Also known as *accounting and appropriation data* or a *fund cite*. *(QRFAL)*

liquidate

To decrease a payment for an accepted supply item or service under a contract for the purpose of recouping financing payments previously paid to the seller. *(FAR 32.001)*

LI

liquidated damages

A contract provision providing for the assessment of damages (i.e., a monetary amount) on the seller for its failure to comply with certain performance or delivery requirements of the contract. Used when the time of delivery or performance is of such importance that the buyer may reasonably expect to suffer damages if the delivery or performance is delinquent. Payments of liquidated damages are in lieu of actual damages related to the failure. The rate (e.g., dollars per day of delay) is fixed in the contract and must be reasonable considering probable actual damages related to any failure in contract performance. *(DGBCT; OPM)*

liquidation

Term used when the seller pays back or reimburses the buyer for contractor financing or a loan given in the form of progress payments. (A "progress payment" is a financing method to support the future delivery of a product.) When the product is delivered and accepted by the buyer, the progress payments are liquidated or offset against the delivery price. At delivery, instead of paying the full line-item price, the buyer will subtract from the line-item price a percentage (i.e., the "liquidation rate") as payback for the financing. Generally, the liquidation rate is the same percentage as the progress payment rate. *(CMBOK)* See *contractor financing; progress payment*.

liquidator

A person who is regularly engaged in the business of disposing of assets for businesses contemplating liquidation or dissolution. *(UCC 6-102(1)(j))*

litigation information

Any information, including sensitive information, that is furnished to the contractor by or on behalf of the federal government, or that is generated or obtained by the contractor in the performance of litigation support under a contract. This term *does not* include information that is lawfully, publicly available without restriction, including information contained in a publicly available solicitation. *(DFARS 204.7401)*

litigation support

Administrative, technical, or professional services provided in support of the federal government during or in anticipation of litigation. *(DFARS 204.7401)*

loan guarantees

See *guaranteed loan*.

"lobbying"

Refers to any of the following activities:

- Attempts to influence the outcomes of any U.S. federal, state, or local election, referendum, initiative, or similar procedure, through in kind or cash contributions, endorsements, publicity, or similar activities;
- Establishing, administering, contributing to, or paying the expenses of a political party, campaign, political action committee, or other organization established for the purpose of influencing the outcomes of elections;
- Any attempt to influence the introduction of U.S. federal, state, or local legislation or the enactment or modification of any pending federal, state, or local legislation through communication with any member or employee of the Congress or state legislature (including efforts to influence state or local officials to engage in similar lobbying activity), or with any federal government official or employee in connection with a decision to sign or veto enrolled legislation;
- Any attempt to influence the introduction of U.S. federal, state, or local legislation or the enactment or modification of any pending federal, state, or local legislation by preparing, distributing, or using publicity or propaganda or by urging members of the general public or any segment thereof to contribute to or participate in any mass demonstration, march, rally, fundraising drive, lobbying campaign, or letter writing or telephone campaign;
- Legislative liaison activities, including attendance at legislative sessions or committee hearings, gathering information regarding legislation, and analyzing the effect of legislation, when such activities are carried on in support of or in knowing preparation for an effort to engage in lobbying or political activities; or
- Attempting to improperly influence, either directly or indirectly, an employee or officer of the executive branch of the federal government to give consideration to or act regarding a regulatory or contract matter.

(FAR 31.205-22(a)) (See FAR 31.205-22(b) for *exceptions* to these activities.)

local area preference

When awarding emergency response contracts during the term of a major disaster or emergency declaration by the president of the United States, under the authority of the Robert T. Stafford Disaster Relief and

Emergency Assistance Act (42 U.S.C. 5121, *et seq.*), preference shall be given, to the extent feasible and practicable, to local firms. *(42 U.S.C. 5150(a)(1))*

local firm
In the context of disaster or emergency assistance activities, a private organization, firm, or individual residing or doing business primarily in a major disaster or emergency area. *(FAR 26.201)*
See also *emergency response contract; local area preference; major disaster or emergency area.*

local government
A unit of government within a U.S. state, including:
- A county, municipality, city, town, township, local public authority, school district, special district, intrastate district, council of governments (regardless of whether the council of governments is incorporated as a nonprofit corporation under state law), regional or interstate government entity, or agency or instrumentality of a local government;
- An Indian (i.e., Native American) tribe or authorized tribal organization, or Alaska Native village or organization, that is not an Indian tribal government (as defined in 42 U.S.C. 5122(6)); and
- A rural community, unincorporated town or village, or other public entity recognized as a "local government" by a U.S. state or political subdivision of a state.

If chartered, established, or otherwise recognized by a U.S. state for the performance of a governmental duty, includes a local public authority, a special district, an intrastate district, a council of governments, a sponsor group representative organization, and any other instrumentality of a local government. *(FAR 3.801; 42 U.S.C. 5122(8))*

local supplier
A business located within the purchasing activity's recognized metropolitan area. *(SPP)*

logistics
The process of planning, implementing, and controlling the efficient, cost-effective flow and storage of raw materials, in-process inventory, finished goods, and related information from point of origin to point of consumption for the purpose of conforming to customer requirements. *(GKPT)*

logistics management
That part of supply chain management that plans, imple-ments, and controls the efficient, effective forward and reverse flow and storage of goods, services, and related information between the point of origin and the point of consumption in order to meet customers' requirements. Logistics management activities typically include inbound and outbound transportation management, fleet management, warehousing, materials handling, order fulfillment, logistics network design, inventory management, supply/demand planning, and management of third-party logistics services providers. To varying degrees, the logistics function also includes sourcing and procurement, production planning and scheduling, packaging and assembly, and customer service. It is involved in all levels of planning and execution—strategic, operational, and tactical. Logistics management is an integrating function, which coordinates and optimizes all logistics activities, as well as integrates logistics activities with other functions including marketing, sales manufacturing, finance, and information technology. *(DGBCT)*

long-lead items/long-lead time materials
Those components of a system or piece of equipment for which the times to design and fabricate are the longest, and, therefore, to which an early commitment of funds may be desirable in order to meet the earliest possible date of system completion. *(DISCS)*

losing contract
A contract under which property is transferred to another contract (i.e., the "gaining contract") with firm requirements that necessitate the transfer of the original contract's property. *(FAR 45.106)*
See *gaining contract.*

loss
A situation that exists when cost is greater than revenue (e.g., contract price). Profit is negative. *(GOAT)*

loss of government property
The unintended, unforeseen, or accidental loss, damage, or destruction of U.S. federal government property that reduces the government's expected economic benefits of the property. Loss of government property *does not* include occurrences such as purposeful destructive testing, obsolescence, normal wear and tear, or manufacturing defects. Loss of government property includes, but is not limited to:
- Items that cannot be found after a reasonable search,
- Theft,
- Damage resulting in unexpected harm to prop-

Mm

erty requiring repair to restore the item to usable condition, or

- Destruction resulting from incidents that render the item useless for its intended purpose or beyond economical repair.

(FAR 45.101)
See *government property*.

lot

A parcel or a single article which is the subject matter of a separate sale, lease, or delivery, whether or not it is sufficient to perform the contract. *(UCC 2-105(5); UCC 2A-103(s))*
See also *lot size*.

lot size

The quantity of goods purchased or produced in anticipation of demand. *(GKPT)*

lowest price technically acceptable (LPTA)

This source selection process is appropriate when best value is expected to result from selection of the technically acceptable proposal with the lowest evaluated price. When using the lowest price technically acceptable process, the following apply:

- The evaluation factors and significant subfactors that establish the requirements of acceptability shall be set forth in the solicitation. Solicitations shall specify that award will be made on the basis of the lowest evaluated price of proposals meeting or exceeding the acceptability standards for non-cost factors. If the contracting officer documents the file pursuant to FAR 15.304(c)(3)(iii), past performance need not be an evaluation factor in lowest price technically acceptable source selections. If the contracting officer elects to consider past performance as an evaluation factor, it shall be evaluated in accordance with FAR 15.305. However, the comparative assessment in FAR 15.305(a)(2)(i) does not apply. If the contracting officer determines that a small business' past performance is not acceptable, the matter shall be referred to the Small Business Administration for a Certificate of Competency determination, in accordance with the procedures contained in *FAR* Subpart 19.6.
- Tradeoffs are not permitted.
- Proposals are evaluated for acceptability but not ranked using the non-cost/price factors.
- Exchanges may occur.

(FAR 15.101-2)

low rate initial production

A low rate of output at the end of full-scale development or beginning of production. It reduces the buyer's exposure to large retrofit problems and costs while still providing adequate numbers of hard-tooled production items for final development and operational tests prior to a full production decision. As part of an acquisition strategy, it is a risk reduction method that is also known as *limited production* and *pilot production*. *(DSMC)*

lower-tier subcontractor

A concern participating in a contract action as a subcontractor to a higher-tier subcontractor. *(GOAT)*

lump sum

A lot price or a fixed-total price paid in one sum. *(GKPT)*

made

(1) When used in relation to any invention other than a plant variety, means the conception or first actual reduction to practice of the invention. *(FAR 27.301)*
(2) When used in relation to a plant variety, means that the contractor has at least tentatively determined that the variety has been reproduced with recognized characteristics. *(FAR 27.301)*

Mailbox Rule

Under contract law, the idea that an offer is considered "accepted" at the time the acceptance is communicated (whether by mail, e-mail, etc.). *(CMBOK)*

maintainability

The ability of an item to be retained in or restored to a specified condition when maintenance is performed by personnel having specified skill levels, using prescribed procedures and resources, at each prescribed level of maintenance and repair. *(DOD-MMH)*

maintenance

(1) The upkeep of property, necessitated by wear and tear, which neither adds to the permanent value of the property nor appreciably prolongs its intended life, but keeps it in efficient operating condition. The term "preventive maintenance" involves deterring something from going wrong; the term "corrective maintenance"

involves restoring something to its proper condition. *(DISCS)*

(2) The process of modifying a system or component after delivery to correct faults, improve performance or other attributes, or adapt to a changed environment. *(AIMD)*

maintenance concept/plan

A description of maintenance considerations and constraints for system/equipment under development. *(DISCS)*

maintenance, repair, and operating/operations (MRO) items

Supplies that are consumed in the operations process, but which do not become part of the product of the operation (e.g., soap, lubricating oil, machine repair parts, and office supplies). *(GKPT)*

Major Automated Information System (MAIS)

An information system that requires special management attention because of its importance to a U.S. federal agency mission; its high development, operating, or maintenance costs; or its significant role in the administration of agency programs, finances, property, or other resources. *(DAAT; OMB A-130)*
See also *independent cost estimate* (ICE).

Major Defense Acquisition Program (MDAP)

An acquisition program that is designated by the Under Secretary of Defense for Acquisition, Technology and Logistics (USD(AT&L)) as an MDAP; or is estimated to require an eventual total expenditure for research, development, test, and evaluation (RDT&E), including all planned increments, of more than $480 million in Fiscal Year (FY) 2014 constant dollars or, for procurement, including all planned increments, of more than $2.79 billion in FY 2014 constant dollars. *(DODI 5000.02))*
See also *independent cost estimate* (ICE).

major defense equipment (MDE)

Any item on the U.S. Munitions List having a nonrecurring research and development cost of more than $50 million or a total production cost of more than $200 million. *(DISCS)*
See *Munitions List; significant military equipment* (SME).

major disaster

Any natural catastrophe (including any hurricane, tor-

nado, storm, high water, wind-driven water, tidal wave, tsunami, earthquake, volcanic eruption, landslide, mudslide, snowstorm, or drought), or, regardless of cause, any fire, flood, or explosion, in any part of the United States, which in the determination of the president causes damage of sufficient severity and magnitude to warrant major disaster assistance to supplement the efforts and available resources of U.S. states, local governments, and disaster relief organizations in alleviating the damage, loss, hardship, or suffering caused thereby. *(42 U.S.C. 5122(2))*
See also *emergency; major disaster or emergency area*.

major disaster or emergency area

The area included in the official presidential declaration(s) and any additional areas identified by the U.S. Department of Homeland Security. Major disaster declarations and emergency declarations are published in the *Federal Register* and are available at the U.S. Federal Emergency Management Agency website (www.fema.gov). *(FAR 26.201)*
See *emergency; major disaster; see also emergency response contract*.

major nonconformance

A nonconformance with a contract's quality and/or quantity requirements, other than critical, that is likely to result in failure of the supplies or services, or to materially reduce the usability of the supplies or services for their intended purpose. *(FAR 46.101)*
See *contract quality requirements*; see also *critical nonconformance; minor nonconformance; patent defect*.

major system

A combination of elements that will function together to produce the capabilities required to fulfill a mission need. These elements may include hardware, equipment, software, or any combination thereof, but exclude construction or other improvements to real property. A system is a "major system" if—

• The DOD is responsible for the system and the total expenditures for research, development, test, and evaluation for the system are estimated to be more than $185 million (based on fiscal year 2014 constant dollars) or the eventual total expenditure for procurement exceeds $835 million (based on fiscal year 2014 constant dollars) (or any update of these thresholds based on a more recent fiscal year);

• A civilian agency is responsible for the system and total expenditures for the system are estimated to

Mm

exceed $2 million or the dollar threshold for a "major system" established by the agency pursuant to OMB Circular A-109, "Major System Acquisitions," whichever is greater; or

- The system is designated a "major system" by the head of the agency responsible for the system (as specified by 10 U.S.C. 2302 and 41 U.S.C. 109). *(FAR 2.101; 10 U.S.C. 2302; 41 U.S.C. 109(a)-(b))* See *civilian agency; OMB Circular A-109*.

make-or-buy decision
A determination of whether it is more advantageous to make a particular item in-house or to buy it from a supplier. The choice involves both qualitative (e.g., quality control) and quantitative (e.g., relative cost) factors. *(BD)*

make-or-buy program
That part of a contractor's written plan for a contract identifying those major items to be produced or work efforts to be performed in the prime contractor's facilities (i.e., "make") and those to be subcontracted (i.e., "buy"). *(FAR 2.101)*

manage changes
In the context of the *CMS™*, "manage changes" is in the "post-award" life cycle phase of contract management, within the "perform contract" domain. It is the process of:

- Initiating, considering, negotiating, and issuing contract modifications; and
- Maintaining configuration control of the contract and subsequent contract performance.

The value added by this process is to allow flexibility in making necessary contract changes while protecting the integrity of the contract. *(CMS)*
See *Contract Management Standard™ Publication (CMS™)*; see also *perform contract; post-award life cycle phase*.

manage legal conformity
In the context of the *CMS™*, "manage legal conformity" is in the "award" life cycle phase of contract management, within the "form contract" domain. It is the process of resolving conflict between potential and actual contracted parties. The value added by this process is the ability to resolve issues related to the solicitation or source selection process through informal and formal means. *(CMS)*
See *Contract Management Standard™ Publication (CMS™)*; see also *award life cycle phase; form contract*.

management and operating contract
An agreement under which the federal government contracts for the operation, maintenance, or support, on its behalf, of a government-owned or controlled research, development, special production, or testing establishment wholly or principally devoted to one or more major programs of the contracting federal agency. *(FAR 17.601)*

management and professional support services
A subdivision of advisory and assistance services. They are contractual services that provide assistance, advice, or training for the efficient and effective management and operation of organizations, activities (including management and support services for research and development activities), or systems. These services are normally closely related to the basic responsibilities and mission of the U.S. federal agency originating the requirement for the acquisition of services by contract. Included are efforts that support or contribute to improved organization of program management, logistics management, project monitoring and reporting, data collection, budgeting, accounting, performance auditing, and administrative technical support for conferences and training programs. *(FAR 2.101)* (See also *FAR* Subpart 37.2.)
See *advisory and assistance services* (A&AS); see also *engineering and technical services; studies, analyses, and evaluations*.

management control system
The process by which managers ensure that resources are obtained and used effectively and efficiently in the accomplishment of the organization's objectives. A management control system is an explicit set of activities, policies, procedures, and reports intended to institutionalize the formal aspects of the management control process. *(MCS)*

management plan
The document that outlines the changes that will result in the government's most efficient organization to perform a commercial activity in-house. It provides the staffing patterns and operating procedures that serve as a baseline for in-house cost estimates. *(OMB A-76)*

management reserve (MR)
Budget to cover unexpected work that is deemed in-scope to the contract but cannot be identified in advance. *(EVMIG; NDIA)*

Mm

manager

One who is responsible for planning, organizing, staffing, directing, and controlling. *(DGBCT)*

managerial accounting

See *cost accounting*.

mandatory flow down clauses

Federal Acquisition Regulation clauses that are cited in the prime contract and specifically require the inclusion of the text of the clause either verbatim or substantially verbatim in all subcontracts entered into in support of the prime contract. *(OPM)*
See *flow down*.

mandatory sources

Refers to the prioritization of sources of supplies and services for use by the federal government. The government buyer must first examine sources offered from or through the government before fulfilling the requirement with an outside source. *FAR* Part 8 details the mandatory sources of supplies and services and their order of priority. *(FAR 8.000; 8.002)*
See *Committee for Purchase from People Who Are Blind or Severely Disabled statute; established government sources; Federal Prison Industries* (FPI)/*UNICOR; wholesale supply source*.

mandatory use schedule

See *Federal Supply Schedule* (FSS) *Program*.

manufactured construction material

Any construction material that is not unmanufactured construction material. *(FAR 25.601)*
See *unmanufactured construction material*.

manufactured end product

Any end product in product and service codes (PSC) 1000–9999, except:
- PSC 5510, "Lumber and Related Basic Wood Materials";
- Product or service group (PSG) 87, "Agricultural Supplies";
- PSG 88, "Live Animals";
- PSG 89, "Subsistence";
- PSC 9410, "Crude Grades of Plant Materials";
- PSC 9430, "Miscellaneous Crude Animal Products, Inedible";
- PSC 9440, "Miscellaneous Crude Agricultural and Forestry Products";
- PSC 9610, "Ores";
- PSC 9620, "Minerals, Natural and Synthetic"; and
- PSC 9630, "Additive Metal Materials."
(FAR 2.101)
See *Product Service Code/Product and Service Code* (PSC).

manufacturer

(1) Any business that, or person who, manufactures a consumer product. *(GOAT)*
(2) In a government contracting context, the producer responsible for the fabrication or assembly of the final product as defined in the government's specification. *(DODM 4120.24)*
See *producer*.

manufacturing and production engineering

This term refers to the following efforts:
- Developing and deploying new or improved materials, systems, processes, methods, equipment, tools, and techniques that are or are expected to be used in producing products or services;
- Developing and deploying pilot production lines;
- Improving current production functions, such as plant layout, production scheduling and control, methods and job analysis, equipment capabilities and capacities, inspection techniques, and tooling analysis (including tooling design and application improvements); and
- Material and manufacturing producibility analysis for production suitability and to optimize manufacturing processes, methods, and techniques.
(FAR 31.205-25(a))

manufacturing/enterprise resource planning (M/ERP) system

A method for planning all resources of a manufacturing firm, integrating all business functions. It includes functions such as business planning, production planning and scheduling, capacity requirement planning, job costing, financial management and forecasting, order processing, shop floor control, time and attendance, performance measurement, and sales and operations planning. *(NDIA II)*

manufacturing overhead

See *factory overhead*.

manufacturing resource planning (MRP)

A production planning and control system used to schedule production jobs, purchase materials, check capacity requirements, forecast product demands,

Mm

and redirect material supplies in the face of changing schedules. *(GKPT)*
See also *manufacturing resource planning II* (MRP II).

manufacturing resource planning II (MRP II)
An expansion of a basic MRP system that includes the following additional capabilities:
- A capacity planning capability,
- A financial interface that permits planning to be done in financial terms as well as operations planning terms, and
- A simulation capability that can be used in doing alternatives planning work.

(GKPT)
See *manufacturing resource planning* (MRP).

manufacturing technology (MANTECH)
Techniques and processes designed to establish or improve the quality, productivity, and practices of the manufacturing process—including quality control, shop floor management, inventory management, and worker training, as well as manufacturing equipment and software—required to support current and projected programs and the assurance of the availability to produce, reduce lead time, ensure economic availability of end items, reduce costs, increase efficiency, improve reliability, or to enhance safety and antipollution measures. *(DSMC; 10 U.S.C. 2500(10))*

march-in rights
With respect to any invention of a contractor conceived or first actually reduced to practice in the performance of work under a U.S. federal government contract in which a contractor has acquired title, refers to the rights of the government to require the contractor to grant a non-exclusive, partially exclusive, or exclusive license in any field of use to a responsible applicant or applicants. If the contractor refuses such a request, the agency is granted a license if the agency determines that such action is necessary. *(FAR 27.302(f))*

margin pricing
A pricing method where price is based on the relationship between cost and profit. *(DGBCT)*

marginal costing
See *direct costing*.

"Marginal" performance rating
In the case of a past performance evaluation, a "Marginal" performance rating signifies that performance

does not meet some contractual requirements. The contractual performance of the element or sub-element being evaluated reflects a serious problem for which the contractor has not yet identified corrective actions. The contractor's proposed actions appear only marginally effective or were not fully implemented. *(FAR Table 42-1)*
See *past performance evaluation*; contrast with *"Exceptional" performance rating; "Satisfactory" performance rating; "Unsatisfactory" performance rating; "Very Good" performance rating*.

mark-up pricing
Establishing prices based on estimated direct cost or total cost-plus-a-percentage-of-cost mark-up. *(CMBOK)*

market
The organized exchange of commodities (goods, services, or resources) between buyers and sellers within a specific geographic area and during a given period of time. Markets are the exchange between buyers who want a good—the demand-side of the market—and the sellers who have it—the supply-side of the market. In essence, a buyer gives up money and gets a good, while a seller gives up a good and gets money. From a marketing context, in order to be a "market" the following conditions must exist:
- The target consumers must have the ability to purchase the goods or services,
- They must have a need or desire to purchase,
- The target group must be willing to exchange something of value for the product, and
- They must have the authority to make the purchase.
If all these variables are present, a market exists. *(DGBCT)*

market data
A type of secondary comparison used in performing price analysis. Market data are used to evaluate trends and technology in a particular market. Newspapers and trade journals can be used to validate assumptions. *(NCMA-WS)*
See *secondary comparison*.

market division
(1) Agreements or understandings by which competitors divide a market in which they compete. *(BOE)*
(2) Exclusive allocation of customers, territories, or products within a market. *(BOE)*

market grade
A product that is of fair, average quality. This means

Mm

that the item meets the standards of the trade and that its quality is appropriate for ordinary use. It is used in applying the implied warranty of merchantability. *(GKPT)*
See also *implied warranty of merchantability*.

market intelligence
Information on competitors or competitive teams operating in the marketplace or industry. *(STBP)*

market planning
Involves market research and analysis and general management planning concerned with the development of an organization's business. *(FAR 31.205-38(b)(4))*

market price
A current price established in the course of ordinary trade between buyers and sellers free to bargain and that can be substantiated through competition or from sources independent of the offerors. *(FAR 2.101)*

market research
Collecting and analyzing information about capabilities within the market to satisfy the buyer's needs. *(FAR 2.101)*

market strategy
The action plan of how an organization will sell its services or products. The strategy must consider the organization's business environment, its abilities and competencies, the desires of top management, and overall mission objectives. *(DGBCT)*

market surveillance
Includes all the activities performed to continuously keep abreast of technology and product developments. *(DAAT)*

market survey
Attempts to ascertain whether qualified sources are available to satisfy the buyer's requirement. *(DGBCT)*

marketing channel
A set of institutions necessary to transfer the title to goods and to move goods from the point of origin to the point of consumption. *(AMA)*

marketing consultant
Any independent contractor who furnishes advice, information, direction, or assistance to an offeror or any other contractor in support of the preparation or submission of an offer for a federal government contract by that offeror. However, an independent contractor *is not* considered a "marketing consultant" when rendering:
- Services excluded in *FAR* Subpart 37.2;
- Routine engineering and technical services (such as installation, operation, or maintenance of systems, equipment, software, components, or facilities);
- Routine legal, actuarial, auditing, and accounting services; and
- Training services.
(FAR 9.501)

master agreement
A business arrangement in which the parties determine the underlying commercial arrangement governing the relationship (e.g., terms and conditions) but defer specific negotiation of elements of the contract to specific events or transactions (e.g., price). *(DGBCT)*

master subcontracting plan
A subcontracting plan that contains all the required elements of an individual subcontracting plan, except goals, and may be incorporated into individual subcontracting plans, provided the master subcontracting plan has been approved. *(FAR 19.701)*
See *subcontracting plan*; see also *individual subcontracting plan*.

master solicitation
A document containing special clauses and provisions that have been identified as essential for the acquisition of a specific type of supply or service that is acquired repetitively. *(FAR 2.101)*

matching principle
An accounting principle that provides the basis for accrual accounting. It is concerned with matching expenses to the related revenue as a means of providing an accurate presentation of an entity's performance. *(NCMA-CA)*
See *accrual accounting*.

material
(1) Property that may be consumed or expended during the performance of a contract, component parts of a higher assembly, or items that lose their individual identity through incorporation into an end-item. Material *does not* include equipment, special tooling, special test equipment, or real property. *(FAR 45.101)*

Mm

(2) In the case of a time-and-materials contract, means:
- Direct materials, including supplies transferred between divisions, subsidiaries, or affiliates of the contractor under a common control;
- Subcontracts for supplies and incidental services for which there is not a labor category specified in the contract;
- Other direct costs (e.g., incidental services for which there is not a labor category specified in the contract, travel, computer usage charges); and
- Applicable indirect costs.

(FAR 16.601)

material cost at standard
A pre-established measure of the material elements of cost, computed by multiplying material-price standard by material-quantity standard. *(FAR 31.001)*
See *material-price standard; material-quantity standard*.

material costs
Include the costs of such items as raw materials, parts, subassemblies, components, and manufacturing supplies, whether purchased or manufactured by the contractor, and may include such collateral items as inbound transportation and in-transit insurance. In computing material costs, the contractor shall consider reasonable overruns, spoilage, or defective work (unless otherwise provided in any contract provision relating to inspecting and correcting defective work). *(FAR 31.205-26(a))*

material inspection and receiving report
A validated report of seller-furnished supplies or services inspected and/or accepted by the buyer. *(AFIT)*

material(s) management
(1) The process of procuring and moving materials, parts, or finished inventory from the point of purchase to assembly plants, warehouses, or the final customer. *(F&F)*
(2) An integrated systems approach to the coordination of materials activities and the control of total materials costs. It advocates assigning to a single operating department all major activities that contribute to the cost of materials. *(DBL)*

material management and accounting system (MMAS)
A system or systems used by a contractor for the planning, controlling, and accounting for the acquisition, use, issuing, and disposition of material. Material management and accounting systems may be manual or automated and may be standalone systems or may integrate with planning, engineering, estimating, purchasing, inventory, accounting, or other systems. *(NDIA II; DFARS 252.242-7004)*
See also *"acceptable" material management and accounting system; contractor business systems*.

material misrepresentation
A misrepresentation is material if it would be likely to induce a reasonable person to manifest his or her assent, or if the maker knows that it would be likely to induce the recipient to do so. *(RSOC 162(2))*
Contrast with *fraudulent misrepresentation*.

material-price standard
A pre-established measure, expressed in monetary terms, of the price of material. *(FAR 31.001)*
Contrast with *material-quantity standard*.

material price variance
A variance relative to material that is equal to the earned unit price less the actual unit price multiplied by the actual quantity of material used (i.e., (earned unit price - actual unit price) × actual quantity). *(NDIA II)*

material-quantity standard
A preestablished measure, expressed in physical terms, of the quantity of material. *(FAR 31.001)*
Contrast with *material-price standard*.

Material Safety Data Sheets (MSDS)
In U.S. federal government contracting, a required document that details all applicable hazardous material data (as specified in the latest version of Federal Standard No. 313—including revisions adopted during the term of the contract), or data for any other material designated by a government technical representative as potentially hazardous and requiring safety controls, for a contract in which performance may carry a risk of exposure to such hazardous materials. *(FAR 23.302(b)–(c))*

material usage variance
A variance relative to material that is equal to the earned quantity less the actual quantity multiplied by the earned unit price (i.e., (earned quantity - actual quantity) × earned unit price). *(NDIA II)*

materiality and immateriality
An accounting principle holding that financial reporting is not concerned with insignificant items or minor

amounts that would not affect the decisions of interested users. Decisions have to be made regarding the relative importance and size (i.e., materiality) of these expense items in order to determine the most cost-effective and meaningful expression of a company's operating costs. *(NCMA-CA)*

materiel

(1) The supplies, weapons, and equipment associated with a military force. Includes all items (e.g., ships, tanks, self-propelled weapons, and aircraft, as well as related spares, repair parts, and support equipment, but excluding real property, installations, and utilities) necessary to equip, operate, maintain, and support military activities without distinction as to their application for administrative or combat purposes. *(CJCSI 3170.011; DGBCT)*

(2) The equipment, apparatus, and supplies used by an organization or institution. *(MW)*
See also ***materiel management***; compare with ***non-materiel capability solution***.

materiel management

Direction and control of those aspects of logistics that deal with materiel, including the functions of identification, cataloging, standardization, requirements determination, procurement, inspection, quality control, packaging, storage, distribution, disposal, maintenance, mobilization planning, industrial readiness planning, and item management classification. This term encompasses materiel control, inventory control, inventory management, and supply management. *(DISCS)*
See ***materiel***.

may

Denotes the permissive. However, the words "no person may…" mean that no person is required, authorized, or permitted to do the act described. *(FAR 2.101)*

mean time between failure(s) (MTBF)

For a particular interval, the total functional life of a population of an item divided by the total number of failures (requiring corrective maintenance actions) within the population. The definition holds for time, rounds, miles, events, or other measures of life unit. It is a basic technical measure of reliability recommended for use in the research and development contractual specification environment, where "time" and "failure" must be carefully defined for contractual compliance purposes. *(DAAT)*

mean time between maintenance (MTBM)

A measure of reliability that represents the average time between all maintenance actions—both corrective and preventive. *(DAAT)*

measuring unit

In accounting, a standard unit of measure is necessary to provide a "yardstick" for measuring and comparing performance on financial statements. The U.S. dollar is the unit of measure used by virtually all companies in the United States for financial reporting purposes *(NCMA-CA)*

media

In the context of information systems security, physical devices or writing surfaces onto which information is recorded, stored, or printed. *(DFARS 204.7301; FIPS 200)*
See also ***information systems security*** (INFOSEC).

mediation

A private, informal process in which the parties are assisted by one or more neutral third parties in efforts to achieve settlement. Mediators do not judge or arbitrate; they advise and consult impartially with the parties in an attempt to bring about a mutually agreeable resolution. *(DGBCT)*

memorandum of agreement (MOA)/ memorandum of understanding (MOU)

Formal documentation of the mutual recognition and acceptance of certain important matters or conditions for which the failure to agree would cause a delay or no deal. They are not legally binding on the parties and may express mutual understanding of an issue without implying commitments by the parties to the understanding. *(CMBOK; AFIT; DSMC)*

Mentor-Protégé Program

The U.S. Small Business Administration (SBA) program to enhance the capability of 8(a) program participants to compete more successfully for federal government contracts. The program encourages private-sector relationships and expands SBA's efforts to identify and respond to the developmental needs of 8(a) clients. Mentors provide technical and management assistance, financial assistance in the form of equity investments and/or loans, subcontract support, and assistance in performing prime contracts through joint venture arrangements with 8(a) firms. (See https://www.sba.gov/federal-contracting/contracting-assistance-programs; see also FAR 19.702(d).)

Mm

See *8(a) contractor*; see also *Small Business Act* (SBA); *Small Business Administration* (SBA).

method of procurements

The process employed for soliciting offers, evaluating offers, and awarding a contract. In U.S. federal government contracting, contracting officers use one of the following methods for any given acquisition:
- Simplified acquisitions,
- Sealed bidding,
- Negotiation, or
- Two-step sealed bidding.

(FAI)

methods of price analysis

See *auxiliary techniques; primary comparison; secondary comparison*.

micropurchase

An acquisition of supplies or services using simplified acquisition procedures, the aggregate amount of which does not exceed the micropurchase threshold (as defined in FAR 2.101). *(FAR 2.101)*

micropurchase threshold

The aggregate monetary amount for the acquisition of supplies or services defined in FAR 2.101. Exceptions to this amount include—
- The micropurchase threshold for acquisitions of construction subject to the Wage Rate Requirements (Construction) statute (40 U.S.C. Chapter 31, Subchapter IV);
- The micropurchase threshold for acquisitions of services subject to the Service Contract Labor Standards statute (41 U.S.C. Chapter 67); and
- The micropurchase threshold for acquisitions of supplies or services that, as determined by the head of the agency, are to be used to support a contingency operation or to facilitate defense against or recovery from nuclear, biological, chemical, or radiological attack, except for construction subject to the Wage Rate Requirements (Construction) statute in the case of any contract to be awarded and performed, or purchase to be made, inside or outside the United States.

(FAR 2.101)

milestone

A significant event in the project; usually completion of a major deliverable. A milestone is typically used to measure progress. *(AIMD; DGBCT)*

milestone decision authority (MDA)

The designated individual with overall responsibility for an acquisition program. The MDA has the authority to approve entry of an acquisition program into the next phase of the acquisition process and is accountable for cost, schedule, and performance reporting to a higher authority, including congressional reporting. *(DODD 5000.01)*

military assistance program (MAP)

See *conventional arms transfer*.

Military Standard Requisitioning and Issue Procedures (MILSTRIP)

A uniform procedure established by the DOD to govern requisition and issue of materiel within standardized priorities. *(AFIT)* (See also www.dla.mil.)

military-unique requirement

A design, construction, manufacturing, or performance requirement that is peculiar to the military, and cannot be met by a commercial products, processes, or practices. *(DODM 4120.24)*

Miller Act

See *Bonds statute*.

minimum reorder point

A predetermined inventory level that triggers a need to place an order. This minimum level (considering safety stock) provides inventory to meet anticipated demand during the time it takes to receive the order. *(GKPT)* See also *reorder point* (ROP).

mini-trial

A structured process where the attorney for each party presents an abbreviated version of that side's case. This information exchange allows each party to hear the strength and weaknesses of the other party's case as well as their own. Following the presentation, the attorneys meet to see if they can negotiate a settlement. A neutral party can oversee the process if desired and may provide an opinion on what the potential court outcome might be. *(DGBCT)*

minor modification

A modification that does not significantly alter the non-governmental function, or essential physical characteristics of an item or component, or change the purpose of a process. Factors to be considered in determining

whether a modification is "minor" include:
- The value and size of the modification, and
- The comparative value and size of the final product.

Dollar values and percentages may be used as guideposts, but these are not conclusive evidence that a modification is "minor." *(FAR 2.101)*
See also *modification*.

minor nonconformance

A nonconformance with a contract's quality and/or quantity requirements that is not likely to materially reduce the usability of the supplies or services for their intended purpose, nor is a departure from established standards having little bearing on the effective use or operation of the supplies or services. *(FAR 46.101)*
See *contract quality requirements*; see also *critical nonconformance; major nonconformance; patent defect*.

minority institution

An institution of higher education meeting the requirements of Section 365(3) of the Higher Education Act of 1965 (20 U.S.C. 1067k), including a "Hispanic-serving institution of higher education," as defined in Section 502(a) of the act (20 U.S.C. 1101a). *(FAR 2.101)*

misrepresentation of fact

A false statement of substantive fact, or any conduct that leads to the belief of a substantive fact material to proper understanding of the matter in hand, made with intent to deceive or mislead. *(FAR 33.201)*

mission

The enduring, chartered, long-term goal(s) of an organization. *(AIMD)*

mistake

Concerning a mistake in a contractor's bid or proposal that is not disclosed or discovered until after award of a U.S. federal government contract, the mistake may be corrected by contract modification if correcting the mistake would be favorable to the government without changing the essential requirements of the specifications. *(FAR 14.407-4)*
See also *mistake in bid*.

mistake in bid

A procedure that enables a bidder to correct or withdraw its bid when a mistake has been made in preparing the bid. *(GSFC)*

mixed invoice

An invoice that contains items with different payment due dates. *(FAR 32.902)*

mode of transportation

Means of moving freight traffic using transportation methods such as bills of lading, parcel post, bus service, air cargo, rail freight, carload and less than carload, motor freight, freight forwarder, and pipeline. *(DGBCT)*

model

A very detailed description or scaled representation of one component of a larger system that can be created, operated, and analyzed to predict actual operational characteristics of the final produced component. *(FIPS 201-2)*

modification

(1) In the case of a provision or clause, means a minor change in the details of the provision or clause that is specifically authorized by applicable laws and regulations and does not alter the substance of the provision or clause. *(FAR 52.101)*
See *"contract modification"*
(2) In the case of a system or component, means the act of changing a system or component to improve performance or some other attribute, or to adapt the system or component to function in a changed environment. *(AIMD)*

modified total cost basis

A means of pricing equitable adjustments. Under this approach, information on specific costs incurred is included in addition to a total cost portion of the claim. *(NCMA-WS)*
See also *actual cost basis; jury verdict basis; total cost basis*.

modular contracting

(1) Use of one or more contracts to acquire information technology systems in successive, interoperable increments. *(FAR 39.002)*
(2) A contracting approach under which the need for a system is satisfied in successive acquisitions of interoperable increments. Each increment complies with common or commercially acceptable standards applicable to the system in question so that the increments are compatible with the other increments comprising the system. *(CMBOK)*

Mm

money damages

In the case of a breach of contract, include compensatory damages for the purpose of putting the nonbreaching party in the position he or she would have been in if the contract had not been breached. *(DGBCT)*

moneyed capital

Capital that consists of or represents money that is used or invested (as by a bank or investment company) for the purpose of making a profit. *(MW)*
See *capital*.

monopolization

Maintaining or expanding a large market share through illegal or threatening tactics intended to impair the commercial viability of competitors. *(BOE)*

monopoly

A market structure in which the entire market for a good or service is supplied by a single seller or firm. *(ECON)*
Compare with *monopsony*.

monopsony

A market structure in which a single buyer purchases a good or service. *(ECON)*
Compare with *monopoly*.

mortgage

A consensual interest in real property, including fixtures, which secures payment or performance of an obligation. *(UCC 9-102(a)(55))*

most efficient organization (MEO)

Refers to the federal government's in-house organization to perform a commercial activity. It may include a mix of federal employees and contract support. *(OMB A-76)*

most favored customer (MFC)

A General Services Administration (GSA) policy stating that GSA requires MFC pricing from vendors; that is, GSA will not award a contract to a firm that does not offer the government a discount equal to or better than that offered to any other similar customer. *(NCMA-WS)*

moving average cost

An inventory costing method under which an average unit cost is computed after each acquisition by adding the cost of the newly acquired units to the cost of the units of inventory on hand and dividing this figure by the new total number of units. *(FAR 31.001)*

multi-agency contract (MAC)

A task-order or delivery-order contract established by one U.S. federal agency for use by government agencies to obtain supplies and services, consistent with the Economy Act (31 U.S.C. 1535).Multi-agency contracts include contracts for information technology established pursuant to 40 U.S.C. 11314(a)(2). (Not to be confused with "multiple-award contract" (MAC).) *(FAR 2.101)*
See *multiple-award contract* (MAC).

multiple-award contract (MAC)

A contract that is—
- A "Multiple Award Schedule" contract issued by the GSA (e.g., GSA Schedule Contract) or agencies granted "Multiple Award Schedule" contract authority by the GSA (e.g., the Department of Veterans Affairs) as described in *FAR* Part 38, "Federal Supply Schedule Contracting";
- A multiple-award task-order or delivery-order contract issued in accordance with FAR Subpart 16.5, including governmentwide acquisition contracts; or
- Any other indefinite-delivery/indefinite-quantity contract entered into with two or more sources pursuant to the same solicitation.

(FAR 2.101)
See *Federal Supply Schedule* (FSS) *Program; governmentwide acquisition contract* (GWAC); *Multiple Award Schedule* (MAS).

Multiple Award Schedule (MAS)

Contracts awarded by the General Services Administration or the Department of Veterans Affairs (VA)for similar or comparable supplies, or services, established with more than one supplier, at varying prices. The primary statutory authorities for the MAS program are 41 U.S.C. 152(3), "Competitive Procedures," and 40 U.S.C. 501, "Services for Executive Agencies." *(FAR 8.401)*
See *Federal Supply Schedule* (FSS) *Program*.

Multiple Award Schedule (MAS) Program

See *Federal Supply Schedule* (FSS) *Program*.

multiple-incentive contract

A contract designed to motivate the contractor to strive for outstanding results in all incentive areas and compel trade-off decisions among the incentive areas, consistent with the buyer's overall objectives for the acquisition. Because of the interdependency of the buyer's cost, the technical performance, and the delivery goals, a contract that emphasizes only one of the

goals may jeopardize control over the others. Because outstanding results may not be attainable for each of the incentive areas, all U.S. federal government multiple-incentive contracts must include a cost incentive (or constraint) that operates to preclude rewarding a contractor for superior technical performance or delivery results when the cost of those results outweighs their value to the buyer. *(FAR 16.402-4)*
See *incentive contract*.

multiple service locations
The various locations or delivery points in a utility supplier's service area to which it provides service under a single contract. *(FAR 41.101)*
See also *utility service*.

multiple-year contract
A contract having a term of more than one year, regardless of fiscal year funding. This term includes "multiyear contracts." *(FAR 22.1001)*
See *multiyear contract*.

multiyear contract
A contract for the purchase of supplies or services for more than one, but not more than five, program years. A multiyear contract may provide that performance under the contract during the second and subsequent years of the contract is contingent upon the appropriation of funds, and (if it does so provide) may provide for a cancellation payment to be made to the contractor if appropriations are not made. The key distinguishing difference between multiyear contracts and multiple-year contracts is that multiyear contracts, defined in the statutes cited at FAR 17.101, buy more than one year's requirement (of a product or service) without establishing and having to exercise an option for each program year after the first. *(FAR 17.103)*
Contrast with *multiple-year contract*.

Munitions List
The U.S. Munitions List is an enumeration of defense articles and defense services and is published in the U.S. Department of State's *International Traffic in Arms Regulation (ITAR)*. *(DISCS)*
See also *defense article; defense service; International Traffic in Arms Regulation (ITAR)*.

must
See *shall*.

mutual assent
Consists of an offer made by one party and the unconditional acceptance of that offer by another party. *(GKPT)*

mutual mistake
A mistake is a belief that is not in accord with the facts. If the buyer participated in the mistake, relief is sought by sellers under the theory of mutual mistake. *(AGC)*

national defense
Any activity related to programs for military or atomic energy production or construction, military assistance to any foreign nation, stockpiling, or space. *(FAR 2.101)* (See also *FAR* Subpart 11.06.)
See also *national defense program*.

national defense activity
A commercial activity that is approved by the secretary of defense, or designee, as being subject to deployment in a direct military combat support role. *(OMB A-76)*
See also *national security activity*.

national defense program
Programs for military and energy production or construction, military assistance to any foreign nation, stockpiling, space, and any directly related activity. This term includes emergency preparedness activities conducted pursuant to Title VI of The Robert T. Stafford Disaster Relief and Emergency Assistance Act (42 U.S.C. 5195, *et seq.*) and critical infrastructure protection and restoration (50 U.S.C. App. 2152). *(FAR 11.601)*
See also *National Defense Strategy* (NDS).

National Industries for the Blind (NIB)
See *AbilityOne Program*.

National Industries for the Severely Handicapped (NISH)
Rebranded as "SourceAmerica" in 2013.
See *AbilityOne Program*.

national security system
Any telecommunications or information system operated by a federal government agency or by a contractor of an agency, or other organization on behalf of an agency—

- The function, operation, or use of which–
  - Involves intelligence activities,
  - Involves cryptologic activities related to national security,
  - Involves command and control of military forces,
  - Involves equipment that is an integral part of a weapon or weapons system, or
  - Is critical to the direct fulfillment of military or intelligence missions; or
- Is protected at all times by procedures established for information that have been specifically authorized under criteria established by an Executive Order or an Act of Congress to be kept classified in the interest of national defense or foreign policy.

This term *does not* include a system that is to be used for routine administrative and business applications, such as payroll, finance, logistics, and personnel management applications. *(FAR 39.002; 40 U.S.C. 11103(a) (1); 44 U.S.C. 3552(b)(6)(A)-(B))*

national stock number (NSN)

A 13-digit stock number consisting of a four-digit Federal Supply Classification and a nine-digit national item identification number. Each NSN is assigned to identify an item of supply and equipment within the U.S. federal government's inventory. Only one NSN is assigned to an item. *(GSFC; MSA)*
See also *Federal Supply Classification* (FSC).

nationally recognized standards

Encompasses any standard or modification thereof that–
- Has been adopted and promulgated by a nationally recognized standards-producing organization under procedures whereby those interested and affected by it have reached substantial agreement on its adoption, or
- Was formulated through consultation by appropriate U.S. federal agencies in a manner that afforded an opportunity for diverse views to be considered. *(FMR 102-71.20)*

need

A capability shortfall such as those documented in a mission needs statement, deficiency report, or engineering change proposal. *(AIMD)*
See *requirement*.

negative instant contract savings

In value engineering, means the increase in the instant contract cost or price when the acceptance of a value engineering change proposal results in an excess of the contractor's allowable development and implementation costs over the product of the instant unit cost reduction multiplied by the number of instant contract units affected. *(FAR 48.001)*
See *value engineering; value engineering change proposal* (VECP); see also *contractor's development and implementation costs; instant contract; instant unit cost reduction*.

negotiable document of title

A document of title is "negotiable" if, by its terms, the goods are to be delivered to bearer or to the order of a named person. *(UCC 7-104(a))*
See *document of title*; contrast with *nonnegotiable document of title*.

negotiable instrument

(1) An unconditional promise or order to pay a fixed amount of money, with or without interest or other charges described in the promise or order, if it:
- Is payable to bearer or to order at the time it is issued or first comes into possession of a holder;
- Is payable on demand or at a definite time; and
- Does not state any other undertaking or instruction by the person promising or ordering payment to do any act in addition to the payment of money, but the promise or order may contain:
  - An undertaking or power to give, maintain, or protect collateral to secure payment;
  - An authorization or power to the holder to confess judgment or realize on or dispose of collateral; or
  - A waiver of the benefit of any law intended for the advantage or protection of an obligor.

(UCC 3-104(a))
See also *check; incomplete instrument; instrument; order; promise*.

(2) An order that meets all the requirements of (1.) of this definition, and otherwise falls within the definition of "check," is considered *both* a negotiable instrument and a check. *(UCC 3-104(c))*

(3) A promise or order other than a check is not a "negotiable instrument" if, at the time it is issued or first comes into possession of a holder, it contains a conspicuous statement, however expressed, to the effect that the promise or order is not negotiable or is not an instrument. *(UCC 3-104(d))*

(4) A negotiable instrument is a "note" if it is a promise and is a "draft" if it is an order. If an instrument falls

within the definition of both "note" and "draft," a person entitled to enforce the instrument may treat it as either. *(UCC 3-104(e))*

negotiated ceiling

Maximum negotiated value for which the buyer is liable for payment to the seller. *(AFIT)*
See *adjusted ceiling*.

negotiated contract cost (NCC)

The cost negotiated in a cost-plus-fixed-fee contract, or the negotiated contract target cost in either a fixed-price-incentive or cost-plus-incentive-fee contract. It does not include profit or fee, nor does it include the estimated value of undefinitized change orders (i.e., authorized unpriced work). Sometimes referred to as the *contract target cost* (CTC). *(NDIA II)*

negotiation

(1) A basic means of getting what you want from others. It is back-and-forth communication designed to reach an agreement when you and the other side have some interests that are opposed. *(GTY)*
See also *bargaining mix; best alternative to a negotiated agreement* (BATNA); *resistance point; settlement point; target point; zone of possible agreement* (ZOPA).
(2) A process between buyers and sellers seeking to reach mutual agreement on a matter of common concern through fact-finding, bargaining, and persuasion. *(P&L I)*
See *contract negotiation*.
(3) Federal government acquisition of supplies or services, including construction, by other-than-sealed-bidding procedures. *(P&L I)*
See *contract negotiation*.
(4) Exchanges, in either a competitive or sole-source environment, between the U.S. federal government and offerors, that are undertaken with the intent of allowing the offeror to revise its proposal. These negotiations may include bargaining. "Bargaining" includes persuasion, alteration of assumptions and positions, give-and-take, and may apply to price, schedule, technical requirements, type of contract, or other terms of a proposed contract. When negotiations are conducted in a competitive acquisition, they take place after establishment of the competitive range and are called "discussions." *(FAR 15.306(d))*
See *negotiation objectives; negotiation techniques*; see also *bargaining; discussions*.
(5) As it pertains to a negotiable instrument, means a transfer of possession, whether voluntary or involuntary, of an instrument by a person other than the issuer to a person who thereby becomes its holder. *(UCC 3-201(a))*

negotiation objectives

Determining the issues to be negotiated and the minimum and maximum positions for each issue. They address strategies that provide the overall framework that will guide the conduct of the negotiation. They include both win-lose and win-win strategies and all tactics and counter-tactics necessary to achieve the desired result. *(CMBOK)*

negotiation techniques

Specific methods used during negotiations to reach agreement. Example techniques include:
- "Win-win": less confrontational and tend to have better outcomes for both parties,
- "Win-lose": more confrontational with mistrust on both sides, and
- "Lose-lose": happens when there is a deadlock and the parties cannot reach a final agreement.

(DGBCT)

net acquisition savings

In value engineering, means total acquisition savings, including instant, concurrent, and future contract savings, less costs. *(FAR 48.001)*
See *value engineering*.

net contract price

In the case of a bulk sale, means the new consideration the buyer is obligated to pay for the assets less—
- The amount of any proceeds of the sale of an asset, to the extent the proceeds are applied in partial or total satisfaction of a debt secured by the asset; and
- The amount of any debt to the extent it is secured by a security interest or lien that is enforceable against the asset before and after it has been sold to a buyer.

If a debt is secured by an asset and other property of the seller, the amount of the debt secured by a security interest or lien that is enforceable against the asset is determined by multiplying the debt by a fraction, the numerator of which is the value of the new consideration for the asset on the date of the bulk sale and the denominator of which is the value of all property securing the debt on the date of the bulk sale. *(UCC 6-102(1)(k))*
See *bulk sale*; see also *assets; debt*.

Nn

net disbursement

In budgetary usage, net disbursements represent gross disbursement less income collected and credited to the appropriate fund account, such as amounts received for goods and services provided. *(DISCS)*
See also *outlays*; contrast with *gross disbursements*.

net proceeds

In the case of a bulk sale, means the new consideration received for assets sold at a sale by auction or a sale conducted by a liquidator on the seller's behalf less—

- Commissions and reasonable expenses of the sale;
- The amount of any proceeds of the sale of an asset, to the extent the proceeds are applied in partial or total satisfaction of a debt secured by the asset; and
- The amount of any debt to the extent it is secured by a security interest or lien that is enforceable against the asset before and after it has been sold to a buyer.

If a debt is secured by an asset and other property of the seller, the amount of the debt secured by a security interest or lien that is enforceable against the asset is determined by multiplying the debt by a fraction, the numerator of which is the value of the new consideration for the asset on the date of the bulk sale and the denominator of which is the value of all property securing the debt on the date of the bulk sale. *(UCC 6-102(1)(l))*
See *bulk sale*; see also *assets; auction; liquidator; debt*.

neutral person

An impartial third party who serves as a mediator, fact finder, or arbitrator, or otherwise functions to assist the parties to resolve issues in controversy. A neutral person may be a permanent or temporary officer or employee of the federal government or any other individual who is acceptable to the parties. A neutral person must have no official, financial, or personal conflict of interest with respect to the issues in controversy, unless the interest is fully disclosed in writing to all parties and all parties agree that the neutral person may serve. *(FAR 2.101)*
See also *issue in controversy*.

new budget authority

In a U.S. federal government context, the term "new budget authority" means, with respect to a fiscal year—

- Budget authority that first becomes available for obligation in that year, including budget authority that becomes available in that year as a result of reappropriation; or
- A change in any account in the availability of

unobligated balances of budget authority carried over from a prior year, resulting from a provision of law first effective in that year (and includes a change in the estimated level of new budget authority provided in indefinite amounts by existing law). *(2 U.S.C. 622(2)(C))*
See also *budget authority*.

new debtor

A person that becomes bound as debtor by a security agreement previously entered into by another person. *(UCC 9-102(a)(56))*
See *debtor*; compare with *original debtor*.

new requirement

A newly established need for a product or service. *(OMB A-76)*

new value

Means:
- Money;
- Money's worth in property, services, or new credit; or
- Release by a transferee of an interest in property previously transferred to the transferee.

This term *does not* include an obligation substituted for another obligation. *(UCC 9-102(a)(57))*

no-cost cancellation

A type of quasi-termination that usually occurs shortly after contract execution, often because the seller realizes that it will be unable to perform. If both parties agree, no debts or obligations are due, and if the buyer can obtain performance from other sources, a no-cost cancellation can be a quick and efficient way to sever a contractual relationship. *(CMBOK)*
See *cancellation*.

nolo contendere

Latin for "I do not wish to contend." It is a plea by a defendant in a criminal prosecution that without admitting guilt subjects the defendant to conviction, as in the case of a guilty plea, but which does not preclude denying the truth of the charges in a collateral proceeding (as in a civil action based on the same acts). Also called a "plea of no contest" and "*non vult contendere*." *(MW)*

nominated person

In the case of a letter of credit, means a person whom the issuer—

Nn

- Designates or authorizes to pay, accept, negotiate, or otherwise give value under a letter of credit; and
- Undertakes by agreement or custom and practice to reimburse.

(UCC 5-102(a)(11))
See *letter of credit*; see also *issuer; value*.

nonappropriated fund(s) (NAF)

In a federal government context, cash and other assets from sources other than monies appropriated by Congress. Nonappropriated funds are government funds and are used for the collective benefit of the department or agency personnel who generated them. These funds are separate and apart from funds recorded in the books of the treasurer of the United States. *(DODI 1015.15)*

nonbinding arbitration

Involves an evidentiary hearing before a third party, composed of one or more arbitrators, that draws conclusions regarding the issues in dispute. These hearings typically include broad fact-finding activities, which assist in educating the third party about the matters in dispute. Upon completion of presentations by each party, the third party renders its decision. The parties are not bound by the arbitrator's decision, and either or both sides may reject it. The intent of nonbinding arbitration is to predict the likely adjudicated outcome of the case as an aid to settlement. *(CMBOK)*
See *alternative dispute resolution; arbitration; binding arbitration*.

noncash proceeds

Proceeds other than cash proceeds. *(UCC 9-102(a) (58))*
See *cash proceeds; proceeds*.

noncompliance

(1) A failure to comply with laws or regulations.
(2) In the context of the Cost Accounting Standards (CAS), a failure in estimating, accumulating, or reporting costs to comply with applicable CAS or to consistently follow disclosed or established cost accounting practices. *(FAR 30.001)*
See also *Cost Accounting Standards* (CAS).

nonconforming services/supplies

Services or supplies that do not conform in all respects to contract requirements. *(DGBCT)*

noncontiguous domestic trade

Transportation (except with regard to bulk cargo, forest products, recycled metal scrap, waste paper, and paper waste) subject to regulation by the Surface Transportation Board involving traffic originating in or destined to Alaska, Hawaii, or a territory or possession of the United States. *(FAR 47.001)*

nondefense agency

Any department or agency of the federal government other than the Department of Defense. *(FAR 17.701)*

nondevelopmental item (NDI)

(1) Any previously developed item of supply used exclusively for governmental purposes by a U.S. federal agency, a state or local government, or a foreign government with which the United States has a mutual defense cooperation agreement. *(FAR 2.101)*
(2) Any item described in (1) of this definition that requires only minor modification or modifications of a type customarily available in the commercial marketplace in order to meet the requirements of the procuring department or agency. *(FAR 2.101)*
See also *of-a-type*.
(3) Any item of supply being produced that does not meet the requirements of (1) or (2) of this definition solely because the item is not yet in use. *(FAR 2.101)*

nondisclosure agreement (NDA)

A legally binding document setting forth the conditions under which proprietary information is offered and received between the parties. Also called a *proprietary information agreement* or *confidentiality agreement*. *(CMBOK)*

non-eligible offer

In the context of the federal government's "Buy American" policies, trade agreements, and other laws and regulations governing foreign acquisition, this term refers to an offer of a non-eligible product. *(FAR 25.003)*
Contrast with *eligible offer*; see also *non-eligible product*.

non-eligible product

In the context of the U.S. federal government's "Buy American" policies, trade agreements, and other laws and regulations governing foreign acquisition, this term refers to a foreign end product that is not an eligible product. *(FAR 25.003)*
Contrast with *eligible product*; see also *end product; foreign end product*.

DESKTOP GUIDE TO
CONTRACT MANAGEMENT TERMS

Nn

non-exclusive license
See *exclusive/non-exclusive license*.

non-expendable supplies and material
Supplies that are not consumed in use and retain their original identity, such as weapons, machines, tools, and equipment. *(DISCS)*
Contrast with *expendable supplies and material*.

nonfederal employer
In the context of whistleblower protections under the American Recovery and Reinvestment Act of 2009 (*Pub. L.* 111-5), any employer that receives Recovery Act funds, including a contractor, subcontractor, or other recipient of funds pursuant to a contract or other agreement awarded and administered in accordance with the *FAR. (FAR 3.907-1)*
See also *American Recovery and Reinvestment Act of 2009* (ARRA); *qui tam action*.

nonmanufacturer rule
Means that a contractor under a small business set-aside or 8(a) contract shall be a small business under the applicable size standard and shall provide either its own product or that of another domestic small business manufacturing or processing concern. *(FAR 19.001)* (See 13 CFR 121.406.)
See *8(a) contract*.

non-materiel capability solution
Changes to doctrine, organization, training, previously fielded materiel, leadership and education, personnel, facilities, and/or policy implemented to satisfy one or more capability requirements or needs and reduce or eliminate one or more capability gaps, without the need to develop or purchase new materiel capability solutions. *(CJCSI 3170.011)*
See *materiel*; see also *capability gap; capability requirement; capability solution*.

nonnegotiable document of title
A document of title is "negotiable" if, by its terms, the goods are to be delivered to bearer or the order of a named person. Any other document of title is "nonnegotiable." A bill of lading that states that the goods are consigned to a named person is not made negotiable by a provision that the goods are to be delivered only against an order in a record signed by the sane or another named person. A document of title is also considered "nonnegotiable" if, at the time it is issued, the document has a conspicuous legend, however expressed, that it is nonnegotiable. *(UCC 7-104(a)-(c))*
See *document of title*; contrast with *negotiable document of title*.

nonpersonal services
Contractual services other than personal and professional services. *(40 U.S.C. 102(8))*
See also *nonpersonal services contract*.

nonpersonal services contract
A contract under which the personnel rendering the services are not subject, either by the contract's terms or by the manner of its administration, to the supervision and control usually prevailing in relationships between the U.S. federal government and its employees. *(FAR 37.101)*
See *service contract*; see also *personal services contract*.

nonprobability sampling
See *sampling*.

nonprocurement common rule
The procedures used by federal executive agencies to suspend, debar, or exclude individuals or entities from participation in nonprocurement transactions under Executive Order 12549. Examples of nonprocurement transactions are grants, cooperative agreements, scholarships, fellowships, contracts of assistance, loans, loan guarantees, subsidies, insurance, payments for specified use, and donation agreements. *(FAR 9.403)*

nonprofit organization
(1) Any organization that is–
- Described in Section 501(c) of the Internal Revenue Code (Title 26, U.S.C.), and
- Exempt from tax under Section 501(a) of that code. *(FAR 26.401)*
(2) A university or other institution of higher education or an organization of the type described in section 501(c)(3) of the Internal Revenue Code (Title 26, U.S.C.) and exempt from taxation under Section 501(a) of that code. *(FAR 27.301)*
(3) Any nonprofit scientific or educational organization qualified under a U.S. state nonprofit organization statute. *(FAR 27.301)*

nonrecurring costs (NRC; NC)
(1) Those costs that are generally incurred on a one-time basis and include such costs as plant or equipment relocation, plant rearrangement, special tooling and special test equipment, preproduction engineering, initial spoilage and rework, and specialized work-

force training. *(FAR 17.103)*

(2) Those costs funded by a research, development, test, and evaluation appropriation to develop or improve a product or technology either through contract or in-house effort. *(DISCS)*

(3) Those one-time costs incurred in support of previous production of a specified model and those costs incurred in support of a total projected production run. *(DISCS)*

nonrecurring demand

A one-time requisition from a customer that is not used to compute demand-based requirements. *(DISCS)*

nonrecurring maintenance contract

Contracts that provide maintenance services only on a nonrecurring or irregular basis (e.g., a contract to provide servicing of fixed equipment once a year, or to mulch a garden on a one-time or annual basis). *(GOAT)*
Contrast with *recurring services contract*.

nonseverable

Concerning property, this term refers to property that cannot be removed after construction or installation without substantial loss of value or damage to the installed property or to the premises where installed. *(FAR 45.101)*

nonseverable deliverable

A deliverable item that is a single end product or undertaking, entire in nature, that cannot be feasibly subdivided into discrete elements or phases without losing its identity. *(DFARS 204.7101)*

nonseverable property

Property that cannot be removed after construction or installation without substantial loss of value or damage to the installed property or to the premises where installed. *(FAR 45.101)*

nonsponsor

In the context of a Federally Funded Research and Development Center (FFRDC), any other organization, in or outside of the U.S. federal government, which funds specific work to be performed by the FFRDC and is not a party to the sponsoring agreement. *(FAR 35.017(b))*
See *Federally Funded Research and Development Center* (FFRDC); see also *primary sponsor; sponsor*.

nontraditional defense contractor

An entity that is not currently performing and had not

performed, for at least the one-year period preceding the solicitation of sources by the DOD for the procurement or transaction, any contract or subcontract for DOD. *(10 U.S.C. 2302(9))*
See also *other transaction/other transaction authority* (OTA).

non-value-added work

Work activities that add no value to the mission of the organization. Such activities may or may not be necessary. Necessary ones may include utilities, supplies, travel and maintenance. Unnecessary ones may include searching for information, duplicating work, rework, time not working, etc. *(DGBCT)*

normal cost

The annual cost attributable, under the actuarial cost method in use, to current and future years as of a particular valuation date excluding any payment in respect of an unfunded actuarial liability. *(FAR 31.001)*

normal costing

A type of product costing that applies to units produced (as costs of production), the actual direct materials consumed, the actual direct labor used, and an estimated, predetermined portion of overhead calculated on the basis of a normal or average schedule of production. *(CMBOK)*

North American Industry Classification System (NAICS)

The standard for use by federal statistical agencies in classifying business establishments for the collection, tabulation, presentation, and analysis of statistical data describing the U.S. economy. Use of the standard provides uniformity and comparability in the presentation of these data. NAICS is based on a production-oriented concept, meaning it groups establishments into industries according to similarity in the processes used to produce goods or services. NAICS replaced the Standard Industrial Classification (SIC) system in 1997. *(DGBCT)*

North Atlantic Treaty Organization (NATO) Commercial and Government Entity (CAGE) code (NCAGE code)

An identifier assigned by a member of the North Atlantic Treaty Organization (NATO) or by the NATO Support and Procurement Agency (NSPA) to entities located outside the United States and its outlying areas that the U.S. Defense Logistics Agency CAGE Branch records

Nn

and maintains in the CAGE master file. *(FAR 4.1801)* See **Commercial and Government Entity (CAGE) code.**

no-setoff commitment

A contractual undertaking that, to the extent permitted by the Assignment of Claims Act of 1940, as amended (31 U.S.C. 3727, 41 U.S.C. 6305), payments by any department or agency of the executive branch of the U.S. federal government to the assignee under an assignment of claims will not be reduced to liquidate the indebtedness of the contractor to the government. *(FAR 32.801)*

not otherwise specified

A classification indicating commodities not completely identified. *(GKPT)*

notice

(1) A person has "notice" of a fact if the person:
- Has actual knowledge of it,
- Has received a notice or notification of it, or
- From all the facts and circumstances known to the person at the time in question, has reason to know it exists.

(UCC 1-202(a))

(2) A person "notifies" or "gives" a notice or notification to another person by taking such steps as may be reasonably required to inform the other person in ordinary course, whether or not the other person actually come to know of it. *(UCC 1-202(d))*

(3) A person "receives" a notice or notification when:
- It comes to that person's attention, or
- It is duly delivered in a form reasonable under the circumstances at the place of business through which the contract was made or at another location held out by that person as the place for receipt of such communications.

(UCC 1-202(e))

(4) Notice, knowledge, or a notice or notification received by an organization is effective for a particular transaction from the time it is brought to the attention of the individual conducting that transaction and, in any event, from the time it would have been brought to the individual's attention if the organization had exercised due diligence. *(UCC 1-202(f))*
See also **due diligence**.

notice of an adverse claim

A person has "notice of an adverse claim" if:
- The person knows of the adverse claim;
- The person is aware of facts sufficient to indicate

that there is a significant probability that the adverse claim exists and deliberately avoids information that would establish the existence of the adverse claim; or
- The person has a duty, imposed by statute or regulation, to investigate whether an adverse claim exists, and the investigation so required would establish the existence of the adverse claim.

(UCC 8-105(a))

notice of availability (NOA)

A written notification that material requiring special handling is ready to be shipped. The notice of availability is sent by the shipper to the purchaser or freight forwarder for oversized, hazardous, explosive, classified, or perishable material, and requires a response from the recipient with delivery instructions. *(DISCS)*
See also **freight forwarder (FF); shipper.**

notice of award

(1) A notification to the lowest, responsive seller that it must obtain a performance bond and a payment bond before it can be awarded a contract. *(GSFC)*

(2) A notification to the lowest, responsive construction seller that it must obtain a performance bond and a payment bond before it can be awarded a contract. *(CMBOK)*

notice of dishonor

When a negotiable instrument, such as a bill or note, is dishonored by non-acceptance on presentment for acceptance, or by nonpayment at its maturity, it is the duty of the holder to give immediate notice of such dishonor to the drawer (if it is a bill) and to the indorser (whether it is a bill or note). *(BLD)*
See **dishonor**; see also **drawer; holder; indorser; negotiable instrument.**

notice of intent to disallow costs

At any time during the performance of a cost-reimbursement contract, a fixed-price incentive contract, or a contract providing for price redetermination, the cognizant contracting officer responsible for administering the contract may issue the contractor a written notice of intent to disallow specified costs incurred or planned for incurrence. This notice usually results from monitoring contractor costs. Its purpose is to notify the contractor as early as practicable during contract performance that the cost is considered "unallowable" under the contract terms and to provide for timely resolution of any resulting disagreement. In the event of a disagreement, the

contractor may submit to the contracting officer a written response. Any such response shall be answered by withdrawal of the notice or by making a written decision within 60 days. *(FAR 42.801(a)-(b))*
See *unallowable cost*.

notice of termination
A written notice to the contractor that the contract is being terminated for convenience or default. *(CMBOKT; GOA)*

notification
See *notice*.

"Notification" clause
For certain types of cost reimbursable contracts, buyers will include provisions that they be notified when invoiced costs reach a percentage of the total contract. This is to allow for proper planning, particularly when it appears that costs identified for the job will not be sufficient to complete the work. *(HECA)*
See *"Limitation of Costs" clause; "Limitation of Funds" clause*.

notification of contract changes
When a contractor considers that the federal government has effected or may effect a change in the contract that has not been identified as such in writing and signed by the contracting officer, it is necessary that the contractor notify the government in writing as soon as possible. This will permit the government to evaluate the alleged change and—
- Confirm that it is a change, direct the mode of further performance, and plan for its funding;
- Countermand the alleged change; or
Notify the contractor that no change is considered to have occurred.
(FAR 43.104(a))

not-to-exceed (NTE) price
(1) A maximum price that the seller may not exceed while negotiations are underway to establish the final price. Permits the seller to perform the contract while negotiations are being conducted and protects the buyer from excessive expenditures. *(NCMA-SB)*
(2) A ceiling for a particular cost element in a cost-reimbursable contract. *(NCMA-SB)*

novation agreement
A legal instrument executed by the contractor (transferor), the successor in interest (transferee), and the buyer; and by which, among other things, the transferor

guarantees performance of the contract, the transferee assumes all obligations under the contract, and the buyer recognizes the transfer of the contract and related assets. *(FAR 2.101)* (See also *FAR* Subpart 42.12.)
See *change-of-name agreement*.

no-year funding
Congressional funding that does not require obligation in any specific year or years. *(DGBCT)*

O

objective
A brief statement of the goal to be achieved, the end product desired, or the basic purpose of the requirement. *(DGBCT)*

objectivity
An accounting principle that holds that financial accounting information should be verifiable and substantially capable of reproduction for reviews made by independent and qualified preparers utilizing the same set of facts and assumptions. This principle is critical to the audit process. *(NCMA-CA)*

obligation
(1) A legal requirement for the disbursement of funds according to orders placed, contracts awarded, services received, or other contractual documents. *(AFIT)*
(2) A duty to make a future payment of money. The duty is incurred as soon as an order is placed or a contract is awarded for the delivery of goods and the performance of services. An obligation legally encumbers a specified sum of money, which will require an outlay or expenditure in the future. *(DAAT)*
See also *obligor*.

obligation authority (OA)
(1) Congressional or administrative authority to incur obligations; it is independent from the authority to make expenditures in payment thereof. *(AFIT)*
(2) A congressional authorization to procure goods and services within a specified amount by appropriation or other authorization. *(DAAT)*
(3) The administrative extension of the authority described in (2) of this definition, as by apportionment or funding. *(DAAT)*
(4) The amount of authority, as described in (2) and (3) of this definition, so granted. *(DAAT)*

obligation of funds

Legally binding commitments, such as contract awards, made by U.S. federal agencies during a given period that will require outlays during the same or some future period. *(FAI)*

obligor

A person that, with respect to an obligation secured by a security interest in or a lien on the collateral:

- Owes payment or other performance of the obligation,
- Has provided property other than the collateral to secure payment or other performance of the obligation, or
- Is otherwise accountable in whole or in part for payment or other performance of the obligation.

This term does not include issuers or nominated persons under a letter of credit. *(UCC 9-102(a)(59))*
See *obligation*; see also *principal obligor; secondary obligor.*

observation

In addition to the information provided by a contractor in various meetings and reports, observation is a tool often used by the buyer's contract professionals and management staff to validate information received from other sources. *(DGBCT)*
See *direct observation; indirect observation.*

obsolete inventory

Inventory for which there is no forecast demand expected. A condition of being out of date. A loss of value occasioned by new developments that place the older property at a competitive disadvantage. *(DGBCT)*

of-a-type

In the context of commercial items and services, refers to an item or service that is similar to, but not necessarily identical to, items and services sold in the commercial marketplace. *(GACI)*
See *commercial item; commercial item determination* (CID).

off-the-shelf

(1) Procurement of existing systems or equipment without a research, development, test, and evaluation program or with minor development to make the system suitable for federal government needs. May be a commercial system or equipment or a system or equipment already in the government's inventory. *(DSMC)*
(2) An item produced and placed in stock by a contrac-

tor, or stocked by a distributor, before receiving orders or contracts for its sale. The item may be commercial or produced to military or federal specifications or description. *(FAR 46.101)*
See *commercial off-the-shelf* (COTS); *nondevelopmental item.*

offer

(1) A response to a solicitation that, if accepted, would bind the offeror to perform the resultant contract. Responses to invitations for bids (sealed bidding) are offers called "bids" or "sealed bids"; responses to requests for proposals (negotiation) are offers called "proposals"; however, responses to requests for quotations (simplified acquisition) are "quotations," *not* offers. *(FAR 2.101)* (See also *FAR* Subpart 15.6.)
(2) The manifestation of willingness to enter into a bargain, so made as to justify another person in understanding that his or her assent to that bargain is invited and will conclude it. *(STBP)*
(3) An unequivocal and intentionally communicated statement of proposed terms made to another party. An offer is presumed revocable unless it specifically states that it is irrevocable. Once made, an offer will be open for a reasonable period of time and is binding on the offeror unless revoked by the offeror before the other party's acceptance. *(STBP)*
See *bid; proposal.*

offeror

Any person who has submitted an offer in response to a request for proposal or a bid in response to an invitation for bids. Also called a *bidder. (FAR 2.101)*

Office of Federal Contract Compliance Programs (OFCCP)

An office within the Department of Labor, responsible for enforcing affirmative action and equal employment opportunity required of those who do business with the federal government. (See https://www.dol.gov/ofccp.)

Office of Federal Procurement Policy (OFPP)

An organization within the Office of Management and Budget that provides leadership and direction to federal procurement programs. (See https://www.whitehouse.gov/omb/management/office-federal-procurement-policy/.)
See *Office of Management and Budget* (OMB).

Office of Federal Procurement Policy statute

A law (41 U.S.C. Div. B of Subtitle I) that established the

Office of Federal Procurement Policy (OFPP) within the Office of Management and Budget to:
- Provide overall direction of governmentwide procurement policies, regulations, procedures, and forms for executive agencies of the U.S. federal government; and
- Promote economy, efficiency, and effectiveness in the procurement of property and services by the executive branch of the federal government.

Formerly known as the "Office of Federal Procurement Policy Act" (OFPPA). *(41 U.S.C. 1101(a)-(b))*

Office of Management and Budget (OMB)
A federal government office that recommends and monitors federal programs and funding levels, develops and issues governmentwide policy guidance on management concerns, and reviews proposed regulations. *(FAI)*

Office of Small and Disadvantaged Business Utilization (SADBU)
The Small Business Act (15 U.S.C. 14A) requires each agency with contracting authority to establish an Office of Small and Disadvantaged Business Utilization (see section (k) of the Small Business Act). Notably, for the DOD, in accordance with Section 904 of the National Defense Authorization Act for Fiscal Year 2006 (*Pub. L. 109-163*) (10 U.S.C. 144 note), the Office of Small and Disadvantaged Business Utilization has been redesignated as the "Office of Small Business Programs." *(FAR 2.101)*
See also *Small Business Act* (SBA).

officer or employee of a U.S. federal agency
Includes the following individuals who are employed by a federal agency:
- An individual who is appointed to a position in the government (under Title 5 of the United States Code), including a position under a temporary appointment;
- A member of the uniformed services (as defined in 37 U.S.C. 101(3));
- A special government employee (as defined in 18 U.S.C. 202); and
- An individual who is a member of a federal advisory committee (as defined by the Federal Advisory Committee Act, 5 U.S.C. Appendix 2).

(FAR 3.801)

official information
All information in the custody and control of a U.S. government department or agency that was acquired by U.S. government employees as a part of their official duties or because of their official status and has not been cleared for public release. *(CNSSI 4009)*

offset
(1) A cost balancing action whereby a claim may be canceled or lessened by a counterclaim. *(P&L II)*
(2) In the context of foreign military sales, see *offset agreement*.

offset agreement
An agreement, arrangement, or understanding between a U.S. supplier of defense articles or services and a foreign country under which the supplier agrees to purchase or acquire, to promote the purchase or acquisition by other U.S. persons, of goods or services produced, manufactured, grown, or extracted, in whole or in part, in that foreign country in consideration for the purchase by the country of defense articles or services from the supplier. *(DISCS)*
See *direct offset; indirect offset*; see also defense *article; defense service*.

oligopoly
A market dominated by a few sellers. *(ECON)*
Compare with *monopoly; monopsony*.

OMB Circular A-11, "Preparation, Submission, and Execution of the Budget"
A directive of the U.S. Office of Management and Budget (OMB) establishing policy concerning the basic laws that regulate the federal government budget process. It also establishes the requirement for an "earned value management system" to be used for major acquisitions for development. *(OMB A-11; FAR 34.201)*
See also *earned value management system* (EVMS).

OMB Circular A-76, "Performance of Commercial Activities"
A directive of the OMB that requires commercial government-operated activities be contracted out whenever it is cost effective. *(OMB A-76)*

OMB Circular A-108, "Federal Agency Responsibilities for Review, Reporting, and Publication under the Privacy Act"
A reissued directive of the OMB, which supplements its Circular A-130, and sets forth a series of requirements governing federal agency practices with respect to certain information about individuals, as set forth by the Privacy Act of 1974 (5 U.S.C. 552a). *(OMB A-108)*

OMB Circular A-109, "Major Systems Acquisition"

A directive of the OMB created as a result of the Commission on Government Procurement's recommendations that establishes policies to be followed by executive branch agencies in the acquisition of major systems. A "major system" is defined as a combination of elements that will function together to produce the capabilities required to fulfill a mission need. The circular states management objectives, management structure, and key decision points. *(OMB A-109)* (See also *FAR* Part 34.)

See *progressive down-selection*.

OMB Circular A-119, "Federal Participation in the Development and Use of Voluntary Consensus Standards and in Conformity Assessment Activities"

A revised directive of the OMB that established policies on federal use and development of voluntary consensus standards and on conformity assessment activities. *(OMB A-119)*

OMB Circular A-123, "Management's Responsibility for Internal Control"

A directive of the OMB which implements the Federal Managers' Financial Integrity Act of 1982, as amended by the Sarbanes-Oxley Act of 2002, and is intended to strengthen the requirements for conducting management's assessment of internal control over financial reporting, while also emphasizing the need for agencies to integrate and coordinate internal control assessments with other internal control-related activities. *(OMB A-123)*

OMB Circular A-127, "Financial Management Systems"

A directive of the OMB that prescribes policies and standards for executive departments and agencies to follow in developing, operating, evaluating, and reporting on financial management systems. *(OMB A-127)*

OMB Circular A-130, "Management of Federal Information Resources"

This circular provides uniform governmentwide information resources management policies as required by the Paperwork Reduction Act of 1980, as amended by the Paperwork Reduction Act 1995 (44 U.S.C. Chapter 35). To assist agencies in an integrated approach to information resources management, the act requires that the director of the OMB develop and implement uniform and consistent information resources management policies; oversee the development and promote the use of information management principles, standards, and guidelines; and evaluate agency information resources management practices with the policies, principles, standards, and guidelines promulgated by the director. *(OMB A-130)*

OMB Circular A-131, "Value Engineering"

A directive of the OMB requiring federal departments and agencies to use value engineering as a management tool, where appropriate, to reduce program and acquisition costs. *(OMB A-131)*

OMB Uniform Guidance

The OMB's "Uniform Administrative Requirements, Cost Principles, and Audit Requirements for Federal Awards" (2 CFR Part 200) is a "governmentwide framework for grants management." Commonly referred to as the Uniform Guidance, it "supersedes OMB Circulars A-21, A-87, A-89, A-102, A-110, A-122, and A-133, and the guidance in Circular A-50 on audit follow-up." Since its official launch in December 2014, two supplements have been implemented—one in April 2017 and another in May 2018. These follow the Uniform Guidance's aims to "reduce the administrative burden on award recipients" while guarding against "the risk of waste and misuse of federal funds." (See FAR 2.101.)

one-year appropriations

Appropriations generally used for current administrative, maintenance, and operational programs, including the procurement of items classified as "expense." These appropriations are available for obligation for one fiscal year. *(DAAT)*

online inspection

Any inspection or test that can be performed on an item without impeding the flow of the item through the receiving (or manufacturing) process. *(AFIT)*

open end contract

An agreement for the supply of goods or services that contains varying limits, or no limit, on time and quantity, and which usually involves recurring orders and changes of various types. *(AFIT)*

open market

The collective name for private, commercial business sources of supplies and services. For example, in federal government simplified acquisitions, open market sources can be used under two conditions:

Oo

- If no mandatory sources can meet the need, or
- If the open market can provide the same supplies or services at substantial savings.

(SPP)

open system
A system that implements specifications maintained by an open, public consensus process for interfaces, services, and support formats to enable properly engineered components to be utilized across a wide range of systems, with minimal change; to interoperate with other components on local and remote systems; and to interact with users in a manner that facilitates portability. *(DAAT)*

operating profit
The amount of gross profit earned from the normal operations of the company. This is the amount of sales in excess of total operating expenses. *(NES-02)*

operation and maintenance (O&M) costs
Costs associated with equipment, supplies, and services required to train, operate, and maintain forces in a recipient country, including the cost of spare parts other than concurrent spares and initial stockages, ammunition and missiles used in training or replacements for such items expended in training or operations, rebuild and overhaul costs (excluding modernization) of equipment subsequent to initial issue, training and other services that do not constitute investment costs, and administrative costs associated with overall program management and administration. *(DISCS)*

operation and maintenance (O&M) appropriations
In a DOD context, appropriations that fund expenses such as civilian salaries, travel, minor construction projects, operating military forces, training and education, depot maintenance, stock funds, and base operations support. *(DAAT)*

operation of a system of records
Performance of any activities associated with maintaining a system of records, including the collection, use, and dissemination of records. *(FAR 24.101)*

operationally critical support (OCS)
Supplies or services designated by the federal government as "critical" for airlift, sealift, intermodal transportation services, or logistical support that is essential to the mobilization, deployment, or sustainment of the

U.S. Armed Forces in a contingency operation. *(DFARS 252.204-7012)*

operations management
A subset of management activity that is primarily concerned with actions related to the directing and controlling functions of management. *(DGBCT)*

opportunity cost
The maximum alternative earning that might have been obtained if the productive good, service, or capacity had been applied to some alternative use. *(NCMA-CA)*

opportunity profile
A stage of the capture management life cycle during which a seller evaluates and describes the opportunity in terms of what it means to their customer, what it means to their company, and what will be required to succeed. *(STBP)*

option
A unilateral right in a contract by which, for a specified time, the buyer may elect to purchase additional supplies or services called for in the contract, or may elect to extend the term of the contract. *(FAR 2.101)*

option contract
A promise which meets the requirements for the formation of a contract and limits the promisor's power to revoke an offer. *(RSOC 25)*

Optional Use Schedule
See *Federal Supply Schedule* (FSS) *Program*.

oral presentations
May substitute for, or augment, written information. Use of oral presentations as a substitute for portions of a proposal can be effective in streamlining the source selection process. For government acquisitions, oral presentations may occur at any time in the acquisition process, and the same are subject to the same restrictions as written information, regarding timing (See FAR 15.208) and content (See FAR 15.306). Oral presentations provide an opportunity for dialogue among the parties. Pre-recorded videotaped presentations that lack real-time interactive dialogue are not considered "oral" presentations. *(DGBCT)*

order
(1) To request something to be made, supplied, or served.

(2) An order placed under a Federal Supply Schedule contract; or a task-order contract or delivery-order contract awarded by another agency.

(3) In the context of negotiable instruments, a written instruction to pay money signed by the person giving the instruction. The instruction may be addressed to any person, including the person giving the instruction, or to one or more persons jointly or in the alternative, but not in succession. An authorization to pay is not an "order" unless the person authorized to pay is also instructed to pay. *(UCC 3-103(a)(8))*

order of precedence

(1) A solicitation provision that establishes priorities so that contradictions within the solicitation can be resolved. *(GSFC)*

(2) A contract clause that specifies the sequential hierarchy of documents for the interpretation and resolution of any conflicting terms. *(DGBCT)*

(3) For federal government contracts, the order of precedence is established in FAR 52.215-8, "Order of Precedence—Uniform Contract Format." *(DGBCT)*
See *order of precedence process*.

order of precedence process

In the context of contract interpretation, refers to the process of establishing an order of precedence for contract provisions when one section of a contract conflicts with another. In such a case, the parties should use an "Order of Precedence" clause to specify which section(s) takes priority. In federal government contracts, the *Federal Acquisition Regulation* specifies the order of precedence process to be used. According to the *FAR*, any inconsistency shall be resolved by giving precedence in the following order:
- The schedule (excluding the specification);
- Representations and other instructions;
- Contract clauses;
- Other documents, exhibits, and attachments; and
- The specifications.

(FAR 52.214-29; FAR 52.215-8; CMBOK)

ordering activity

(1) An activity that originates a requisition or order for procurement, production, or performance of work or service by another activity. *(DISCS)*

(2) An activity that is authorized to place orders, or establish blanket purchase agreements, against the GSA Multiple Award Schedule contracts. *(FAR 8.401)*
See *Multiple Award Schedule* (MAS).

ordinary care

(1) In the case of a person engaged in business, this term means observance of reasonable commercial standards, prevailing in the area in which the person is located, with respect to the business in which the person is engaged. *(UCC 3-103(a)(9))*

(2) In the case of a bank that takes an instrument for processing for collection or payment by automated means, this term means that reasonable commercial standards do not require the bank to examine the instrument if the failure to examine does not violate the bank's prescribed procedures and the bank's procedures do not vary unreasonably from general banking usage. *(UCC 3-103(a)(9))*

organization

(1) An entity of any size, complexity, or positioning within an organizational structure. *(FIPS 200)*

(2) A "person" other than an individual. *(UCC 1-201(25))*
See *person*.

organization costs

Expenditures in connection with:
- Planning or executing the organization or reorganization of the corporate structure of a business, including mergers and acquisitions;
- Resisting or planning to resist the reorganization of the corporate structure of a business or a change in the controlling interest in the ownership of a business; and
- Raising capital.

Such expenditures include but are not limited to incorporation fees and costs of attorneys, accountants, brokers, promoters and organizers, management consultants, and investment counselors, whether or not employees of the business. *(FAR 31.205-27(a))*

organizational breakdown structure (OBS)

The project structure that depicts the organization established to manage the resources tasked with performing the work on a specific contract. *(NDIA II)*
See *work breakdown structure*.

organizational conflict of interest (OCI)

Because of other activities or relationships with other persons, a person is unable or potentially unable to render impartial assistance or advice to the federal government, the person's objectivity in performing the contract work is or might be otherwise impaired, or a person has an unfair competitive advantage. *(FAR 2.101)*
See *conflict of interest*.

organizational unit

An organization—such as a program, project, center, mission directorate, or mission support office—that is responsible for carrying out a particular activity. *(NID 8000-108)*

original complement of low-cost equipment

A group of items acquired for the initial outfitting of a tangible capital asset or an operation unit, or a new addition to either. The items in the group individually cost less than the minimum amount established by the contractor for capitalization for the classes of assets acquired, but in the aggregate, they represent a material investment. The group, as a complement, is expected to be held for continued service beyond the current period. Initial outfitting of the unit is completed when the unit is ready and available for normal operations. *(FAR 31.001)*

original contract price

(1) The award price of a contract. This term does not include the price of any options, except those options exercised at the time of contract award. *(FAR 28.102-2(a))*
(2) For requirements contracts, the price payable for the estimated total quantity. *(FAR 28.102-2(a))*
(3) For indefinite-quantity contracts, the price payable for the specified minimum quantity. *(FAR 28.102-2(a))*

original debtor

A person that, as debtor, entered into a security agreement to which a new debtor has become bound. *(UCC 9-102(a)(60))*
See *debtor*; compare with *new debtor*.

original component manufacturer (OCM)

An organization that designs and/or engineers a part and is entitled to any intellectual property rights to that part. *(DFARS 202.101)*
See also *original manufacturer*.

original equipment manufacturer (OEM)

A company that manufactures products that it has designed from purchased components and sells those products under the company's brand name. *(DFARS 202.101)*
See also *original manufacturer*.

original manufacturer

The original component manufacturer, the original equipment manufacturer, or the contract manufacturer. *(DFARS 202.101)*

See *contract manufacturer; original component manufacturer* (OCM); *original equipment manufacturer* (OEM).

originating activity

Those activities that are the source of data content and logistical responsibilities. *(DODM 4100.39)*

originator

In the case of a payment order, the sender of the first payment order in a funds transfer. *(UCC 4A-104(c))*
See also *funds transfer; payment order*.

other direct cost (ODC)

A cost that can be identified specifically with a final cost objective that is not otherwise treated as a direct labor, material, purchased services, or purchased equipment cost. *(NDIA II)*

other transaction/other transaction authority (OT; OTA)

An acquisition instrument other than a grant, cooperative agreement, or contract. Under the authority granted by 10 USC 2371, the Department of Defense may enter into these transactions to carry out basic, applied, and advanced research projects. The use of OTs/OTAs are governed by statute, but they are not subject to the *Federal Acquisition Regulation. (10 USC 2371; 2371b)*
See also *nontraditional defense contractor*.

other work

Any current or scheduled work of the contractor, whether government or commercial, other than work related to the terminated contract. *(FAR 49.001)*

outlays

Actual expenditures (e.g., checks issued, cash disbursed, interest occurred on the public debt, or other payments) by a U.S. federal department or agency. Total budget outlays consist of the sum of the outlays from appropriations and other funds in the budget, less receipts (i.e., refunds and reimbursements). *(DISCS; FAI)*
See *budget outlays*.

outlying areas

In the context of U.S. territories, refers to commonwealths such as Puerto Rico and the Northern Mariana Islands; territories such as American Samoa, Guam, and the U.S. Virgin Islands; and minor outlying islands such as Baker Island, Howland Island, Jarvis Island, Johnston

Atoll, Kingman Reef, Midway Islands, Navassa Islands, Palmyra Atoll, and Wake Atoll. *(FAR 2.101)*

output

Products and services delivered. Outputs are the immediate products of internal activity—the amount of work done within the organization or by its contractors (such as miles of road repaired or number of calls answered). *(DGBCT)*

outside of the contiguous United States (OCONUS)

All geographic areas not included within the territorial boundaries of the contiguous/continental United States, including Alaska and Hawaii. (Also called "outside of the continental United States (OCONUS)" and "outside CONUS (OCONUS).") *(DISCS)*
See *contiguous United States* (CONUS).

outsourcing

(1) A version of the make-or-buy decision in which a firm elects to purchase an item or service that previously was made or performed in-house. *(GKPT)*
See also *make-or-buy decision*
(2) To take a requirement and seek an alternative source outside a functional area. *(CMBOK)*

outyear

A fiscal year one or more years after the budget year. *(2 U.S.C. 932(2)(a))*

over target baseline (OTB)

In project management terminology, a performance measurement baseline that exceeds the contract budget base. It is implemented to produce a realistic schedule and budget plan for the project's remaining work. The difference between the total allocated budget and contract budget base is the amount of the overrun. It typically requires customer approval to implement. *(NDIA II)*
See also *contract budget base* (CBB); *performance measurement baseline* (PMB); *total allocated budget* (TAB).

over target schedule (OTS)

In project management terminology, a replanned schedule baseline that extends beyond contract milestone dates, delivery dates, or completion date. An "over target schedule" is usually accompanied by an increase in budgets resulting in a corresponding "over target baseline." It typically requires customer approval

to implement. *(NDIA II)*
See also *over target baseline* (OTB).

overhead

An accounting cost pool that generally includes general indirect expenses that are necessary to operate a business but not directly accountable to a specific good or service produced. Some examples are building rent, utilities, salaries of corporate officers, janitorial services, office supplies and furniture, etc. *(HCS)*
See *extended overhead*.

Overseas Private Investment Corporation (OPIC)

An independent government agency that offers finance and insurance for overseas investments, along with investment and foreign country information. *(NES-94)*

over-target baseline (OTB)

When the total budget allocated to work exceeds the contract budget base. Sometimes, available budgets for the remaining work are insufficient to ensure valid performance measurement. The need for an OTB could result from a major event or program review.

overtime

Time worked by an employee in excess of the employee's normal workweek. *(FAR 2.101)*
See *normal workweek; overtime premium*.

overtime premium

The difference between the regular rate of pay to an employee for the shift involved and the higher rate paid for overtime. This term does not include shift premium—i.e., the difference between the regular rate of pay to an employee and the higher rate paid for extra-pay-shift work. *(FAR 2.101)*

ownership

Legal title or right to something. Mere possession is not ownership. *(DGBCT)*

Pp

P

P card
See *government purchase card* (GPC; P card).

Packard Commission
Established by President Ronald Reagan in 1985 as the "President's Blue Ribbon Commission on Defense Management," it is commonly called the "Packard Commission" in reference to its chairperson, David Packard. The commission was tasked to examine defense issues, cite problems, and recommend solutions. In June 1986, the commission's final report, titled "A Quest for Excellence," was issued citing 37 broadly worded recommendations. *(TIPS)*

packing, crating, handling, and transportation (PCH&T)
The resources, processes, procedures, design considerations, and methods to ensure that all system, equipment, and support items are preserved, packaged, handled, and transported properly, including:
- Environmental considerations,
- Equipment preservation requirements for short- and-long-term storage, and
- Transportability.

One of the principal elements of integrated logistics support. *(DISCS)*

paid-in capital
Equity capital that is received in exchange for an interest (e.g., shares of stock) in the ownership of a business. *(MW)*
See *capital; equity capital*.

paid sick leave
Compensated absence from employment that is required by Executive Order 13706, "Establishing Paid Sick Leave for Federal Contractors," and 29 CFR Part 13. *(FAR 22.2101)*

Paperwork Reduction Act (PRA)
A federal law (44 U.S.C. Chapter 35) that, among other objectives, requires that automatic data processing and telecommunications technologies are acquired and used by the federal government in a manner that improves service delivery and program management. *(NS; OMB A-130)*

parametric cost estimating
A cost estimating methodology using statistical relationships between historical costs and other program variables such as system physical or performance characteristics, contractor output measures, or manpower loading. *(DAAT)*

parol evidence
Oral/verbal evidence; in contract law, the evidence drawn from sources exterior to the written instrument. *(STBP)*

Parol Evidence Rule
A common law rule used in contract interpretation that seeks to preserve the integrity of written agreements by refusing to permit contracting parties to attempt to alter a written contract with evidence of any contradictory prior or contemporaneous oral agreement (parol to the contract). *(STBP)*
See *parol evidence*.

part
(1) A division of a larger work (e.g., *FAR* Part 12). *(MW)*
(2) A constituent member of a machine or other apparatus (e.g., the parts of an aircraft). *(MW)*
See also *spare part*.

part B institution
See *historically black college or university*.

partial payment
(1) A payment authorized under a contract, to be made upon completion of the delivery of one or more complete units called for, delivered, and accepted by the buyer under the contract. *(OPM)*
(2) A payment made against a termination claim upon prior approval before final settlement of the total termination claim. *(OPM)*

partial set-aside
When small business sources cannot satisfy the federal government's entire requirement at a reasonable price (i.e., a total set-aside is not appropriate), the contracting officer shall set aside a portion of the acquisition for small businesses under conditions at FAR 19.502-3. *(NCMA-WS)* (See also FAR 19.502.)
See *set-aside*.

partial termination
The termination of a part, but not all, of the work that has not been completed and accepted under a contract. *(FAR 2.101)*
See also *terminated portion of the contract*.

Pp

participating personally and substantially in a federal agency procurement

Means:

- Active and significant involvement of an official in any of the following activities directly related to that procurement:
  - Drafting, reviewing, or approving the specification or statement of work for the procurement;
  - Preparing or developing the solicitation;
  - Evaluating bids or proposals, or selecting a source;
  - Negotiating price or terms and conditions of the contract; and
  - Reviewing and approving the award of the contract.
- "Participating personally" means participating directly, and this includes the direct and active supervision of a subordinate's participation in the matter.
- "Participating substantially" means that the official's involvement is of significance to the matter. Substantial participation requires more than official responsibility, knowledge, perfunctory involvement, or involvement on an administrative or peripheral issue. Participation may be substantial even though it is not determinative of the outcome of a particular matter. A finding of substantiality should be based not only on the effort devoted to a matter, but on the importance of the effort. While a series of peripheral involvements may be insubstantial, the single act of approving or participating in a critical step may be substantial. However, the review of procurement documents solely to determine compliance with regulatory, administrative, or budgetary procedures does not constitute substantial participation in a procurement.

(FAR 3.104-1)

parts management

The practice of considering the application, standardization, technology (new and aging), system reliability, maintainability, supportability, and cost in selecting parts and addressing availability, logistics support, and legacy issues in supporting them throughout the life of the systems. *(DODM 4120.24)*
See *part*.

parts per million (PPM)

A common quality measurement technique used to determine the defect rate of production. It is calculated by dividing the number of failures for a specific group of production by the total production, then multiplying that value by 1,000,000. A value of 1 PPM means one defect in one million. As an example, if a production run of 500 units contains 5 defective units, the defect rate would be 10,000 PPM (5/500 = 0.01 (i.e., 1 percent of the units are defective); 0.01 × 1,000,000 = 10,000 PPM). Also called "defects per million" (DPM).

party

(1) A person that has engaged in a transaction or made an agreement. *(UCC 1-201(26))*
(2) A party to an instrument. *(UCC 3-103(a)(10))*
See *negotiable instrument*; see also *accommodated party; accommodation party*.

pass-through charges

Costs (i.e., indirect costs, profit) added by the prime contractor or higher-tier subcontractors on work performed by subcontractors. *(CMBOK)*

pass-through contracts

Subcontracts awarded by a prime contractor representing more than 70 percent of the total cost of work to be performed under the prime contract, task or delivery order. *(FAR 15.404-1(h))*

past performance

An offeror's or contractor's performance on active and physically completed contracts. *(FAR 2.101)* (See also FAR 4.804-4.)

past performance information

Relevant information, for future source selection purposes, regarding a contractor's actions under previously awarded contracts or orders, including ratings and supporting narratives. It includes, for example, the contractor's record of—

- Conforming to requirements and to standards of good workmanship;
- Forecasting and controlling costs;
- Adherence to schedules, including the administrative aspects of performance;
- Reasonable and cooperative behavior and commitment to customer satisfaction;
- Reporting into databases;
- Integrity and business ethics; and
- Business-like concern for the interest of the customer.

(FAR 42.1501) (See also *FAR* Subpart 4.14, and the *reporting requirements* for solicitations in FAR 9.104-7.)
See also *Contractor Performance Assessment Reporting System* (CPARS); *Past Performance Information Retrieval System* (PPIRS).

Pp

Past Performance Information Retrieval System (PPIRS)

The governmentwide single repository of past performance data. The PPIRS consists for two components:

- The Report Card (RC), and
- The Federal Awardee Performance and Integrity Information System (FAPIIS).

The *Federal Acquisition Regulation* requires federal agencies to post all contactor performance evaluations in the PPIRS. (FAR 42.1503(f))

See also **Federal Awardee Performance and Integrity Information System (FAPIIS); Contractor Performance Assessment Reporting System (CPARS).**

past performance evaluation

One indicator of an offeror's ability to perform the contract successfully. The currency and relevance of the information, source of the information, context of the data, and general trends in contractor's performance shall be considered. *(FAR 15.305(a)(2))*

patent

(1) Readily visible or intelligible. *(MW)*

(2) A government grant of exclusive rights to an inventor that prohibits others from making, using, or selling an invention. The current term for patents is generally 20 years. This term was increased from 17 years in 1995 to coincide with the World Trade Organization guidance. *(DGBCT)*

patent ambiguity

A "patent ambiguity" in a contract is one that is, on its face, so glaring and obvious (e.g., a noticeably apparent omission, inconsistency, discrepancy, error, or gap) that it imposes an affirmative duty on a contractor to seek clarification on the matter from the drafter. *(PAS)*

patent costs

To the extent that such costs are incurred as requirements of a federal government contract, include the following costs:

- Costs of preparing invention disclosures, reports, and other documents;
- Costs for searching the art to the extent necessary to make the invention disclosures; and
- Other costs in connection with the filing and prosecution of a U.S. patent application where title or royalty-free license is to be conveyed to the government.

This term includes general counseling services relating to patent matters, such as advice on patent laws, regu-

lations, clauses, and employee agreements; but does not include patent costs not required by the contract. *(FAR 31.205-30)*

patent defect

(1) Any defect which exists at the time of acceptance and not a latent defect. *(FAR 46.101)*

See also **acceptance; latent defect.**

(2) Defects that can be discovered without undue effort. If the defects were actually known to the buyer at the time of acceptance, they are "patent defects," even if they might otherwise not have been discoverable by a reasonable inspection. *(AGC)*

See also **latent defect.**

patent infringement

The violation or encroachment upon a patent. *(BLD)*

See **patent.**

patent infringement bond

A type of bond that secures fulfillment of the contractor's obligations under a patent provision. *(FAR 28.001)*

See **bond.**

payee

(1) The person in whose favor a draft, promissory note, or check is made or drawn. *(BLD)*

See also **check; promissory note.**

(2) The person to whom or to whose order a note or check is made payable. *(BLD)*

See also **check.**

payment

The amount payable under the contract supporting data required to be submitted with invoices, and other payment terms such as "time for payment" and "retention." *(STBP)*

See *"Compensation" clause.*

payment bond

A type of bond that assures payment as required by law to all persons supplying labor or material in the prosecution of the work provided for in the contract. (FAR 28.001)

See **bond.**

payment date

(1) The date on which a check for payment is dated or, for an electronic funds transfer, the settlement date. *(FAR 32.902)*

See also **electronic funds transfer (EFT); settlement date.**

(2) In the case of a payment order, means the day on

which the amount of the order is payable to the beneficiary by the beneficiary's bank. The payment date may be determined by instruction of the sender, but this date cannot be earlier than the day the order is received by the beneficiary's bank and, unless otherwise determined, is the day the order is received by the beneficiary's bank. *(UCC 4A-401)*
See also *beneficiary; payment order*.

payment in due course

Where a payment is made to a holder in due course (i.e., a person holding a debt instrument not knowing it may have been fraudulently transferred). The true owner of the note cannot demand that the payor pay twice, but must seek redress from the party that committed the fraud. *(BLD)*
See also *holder*.

payment information

The payment advice provided by the buyer to the seller that identifies what the payment is for, any computations or adjustments made by the buyer, and any information required by the Prompt Payment Act (31 U.S.C. Chapter 39). *(FAR 32.1102)*
See also *Prompt Payment Act* (PPA).

payment intangible

A general intangible under which the account debtor's principal obligation is a monetary obligation. *(UCC 9-102(a)(61))*
See *general intangible*.

payment order

An instruction of a sender to a receiving bank, transmitted orally, electronically, or in writing, to pay, or to cause another bank to pay, a fixed or determinable amount of money to a beneficiary if:

- The instruction does not state a condition to payment to the beneficiary other than time of payment,
- The receiving bank is to be reimbursed by debiting an account of, or otherwise receiving payment from, the sender; and
- The instruction is transmitted by the sender directly to the receiving bank or to an agent, funds-transfer system, or communication system for transmittal to the receiving bank.

(UCC 4A-103(a)(1))
See also *beneficiary; funds-transfer system*.

payment recapture audit (PRA)

A review and analysis of a federal agency's books, sup-porting documents, and other information supporting its payments. The goal of the review is to identify over-payments to contractors that are due to payment errors. Also called a *recovery audit*. *(OMB M-03-07)*

pecuniary liability

The statutory obligation of an individual to reimburse the federal government for loss or improper application of funds or property. *(AFIT)*

penal sum

The amount of money specified in a bond (or a percentage of the bid price in a bid bond) as the maximum payment for which the surety is obligated or the amount of security required to be pledged to the U.S. federal government in lieu of a corporate or individual surety for the bond. Also called "penal amount." *(FAR 28.001)*

penalty

Includes the imposition by an agency or court of a fine or other punishment, a judgment for monetary damages or equitable relief, or the revocation, suspension, reduction, or denial of a license, privilege, right, grant, or benefit. This term *does not* include the costs of restitution, reimbursement, or compensatory damages resulting from a legal or other proceeding. *(FAR 31.205-47(a); 44 U.S.C. 3502(14))*

per diem

Latin for "per day"; however, it is used in various ways to take on more specific meanings. For example, from a transportation perspective, a *per diem* charge is the daily rate for use of rail cars of one railroad by another railroad. However, when dealing with federal government employee travel, *per diem* is a daily allowance for travel expenses. The U.S. *per diem* rate for government employee travel includes two components: for lodging and for meals and incidentals. The General Services Administration sets the *per diem* rate for each U.S. city and state and for foreign travel. *(GKPT)*

perform contract

In the context of the *Contract Management Standard*™, "perform contract" is one of two domains within the "post-award" phase of the contract life cycle (the other being "close contract"). The job tasks and competencies for this domain produce the contract performance. It is the process of establishing and maintaining communications, as well as tracking and documenting contract performance. The value added by this process is:

Pp

- Monitoring risk and assessing its impact on contract performance, and
- Ensuring compliance with contractual terms and conditions during contract performance up to contract closeout or termination.
(CMS)
Contrast with *close contract*; see also *administer contract; ensure quality; manage changes; subcontract management*.

performance
(1) The execution of the terms of a contract. If a buyer offers to purchase from a supplier, the supplier performs by furnishing the buyer's requirements. *(FAI)*
(2) An informal means of accepting an offer. *(DGBCT)*

performance-based acquisition (PBA)
An acquisition structured around the results to be achieved as opposed to the manner by which the work is to be performed. *(FAR 2.101)*

performance-based contract
A contract that is structured around the purpose of the work to be performed as opposed to either the manner in which the work is to be performed or a broad statement of work. Typically, a performance work statement is used to describe the requirement. *(STBP)*
See also *performance-based services acquisition*.

performance-based logistics (PBL)
The Department of Defense strategy of purchasing support in terms of systems readiness and performance outcome, rather than simply acquiring and stocking material on demand. *(DISCS)*
See *performance-based logistics contract*.

performance-based logistics contract
A Department of Defense contract with a manufacturer who is responsible for ensuring optimum system performance by providing complete logistics support to the customer. *(DISCS)*
See *performance-based logistics* (PBL).

performance-based payments
Contract financing payments made on the basis of:
- Performance measured by objective, quantifiable methods;
- Accomplishment of defined events; or
- Other quantifiable measures of results.
(FAR 32.102(f))

performance-based services acquisition (PBSA)
Acquisition strategies, methods, and techniques that describe and communicate measurable outcomes rather than direct performance processes. It is structured around defining a service requirement in terms of performance objectives and providing sellers the latitude to determine how to meet those objectives. *(GPBSA)*

performance bond
A type of bond that secures performance and fulfillment of the contractor's obligations under the contract. *(FAR 28.001)*
See *bond*; see also *annual performance bond*.

performance confidence assessment
In a source selection context, this term refers to an evaluation of the likelihood (or the buyer's confidence) that the offeror will successfully perform the solicitation's requirements. The evaluation is based upon past performance information. *(SSP)*

"performance in connection with a contract"
An employee "performs in connection with a contract" if the employee's work activities are necessary to the performance of a contract but are not the specific services called for by the contract. *(FAR 22.2101)*
Contrast with *performance on a contract*.

performance incentives
May be considered in connection with specific product characteristics (e.g., a missile range, an aircraft speed, an engine thrust, or a vehicle maneuverability) or other specific elements of the contractor's performance. These incentives should be designed to relate profit or fee to results achieved by the contractor, compared with specified targets. *(FAR 16.402-2)*
See *incentive contract*.

performance measure
A metric used to measure the extent to which a system, process, or activity fulfills its intended objectives. *(NID 8000-108)*

performance measurement
The process of developing measurable indicators of performance that can be systematically tracked to assess progress made in achieving predetermined goals and using such indicators to assess progress in achieving these goals. *(AIMD)*

Pp

performance measurement baseline (PMB)
See *budgeted cost for work scheduled* (BCWS).

performance on a contract
An employee "performs on a contract" if the employee directly performs the specific services called for by the contract. *(FAR 22.2101)*
Contrast with *performance in connection with a contract*.

performance risk assessment group (PRAG)
A group of experienced government personnel that are appointed by the source selection advisory council chairperson to permit performance risk to be used, if appropriate. Performance risk may be separately assessed for each evaluation factor or as a whole with the assessment provided directly to the source selection advisory council/authority for final decision or indirectly through the source selection evaluation board. *(DGBCT)*

performance schedule
A realistic schedule to meet the performance requirements of an acquisition. *(FAR 11.401(a))*
See also *delivery schedule*.

performance specification
A purchase description that describes the deliverable in terms of desired operational characteristics. It states requirements in terms of the required results with criteria for verifying compliance but without stating the methods for achieving the required results. A performance specification defines the functional requirements for the item, the environment in which it must operate, and interface and interchangeability characteristics. Performance specifications tend to be more restrictive than functional specifications in terms of limiting alternatives that the buyer will consider and in terms of defining separate performance standards for each such alternative. *(DODM 4120.24; FAI)*

performance standards
Establish the performance level required by the federal government to meet the contract requirements. These standards are measurable and structured to permit an assessment of the contractor's performance. *(FAR 37.603)*

performance work statement (PWS)
A statement of work for performance-based acquisitions that describes the required results in clear, specific, and objective terms with measurable outcomes. *(FAR 2.101)*

performing activity
An activity that is responsible for performing work or service, including the production of material and/or the procurement of goods and services from other contractors and activities. *(DISCS)*

period of performance (POP)
The number of working days or calendar days, from a specified start date to a specified completion date, as provided for in a contract or to complete a specific scope of work. *(NDIA II)*

periodic inventory method
An inventory accounting system that requires a physical count of inventory to determine the ending amounts of raw material, work in process, and finished goods, and, hence, also the costs of goods sold. *(NCMA-CA)*

periodic review system
A fixed-order interval inventory control system in which an item's inventory position is reviewed on a scheduled periodic basis, rather than continuously. An order is placed at the end of each review, and the order quantity usually varies. This system is different from a fixed-order quantity system in which the order quantity is typically fixed and the time between orders varies. *(GKPT)*

perpetual inventory method
An inventory accounting system whereby a continuous record is kept that tracks raw materials, work in process, finished goods, and cost of goods sold on a day-to-day basis. *(NCMA-CA)*

person
(1) In federal government contracting, this term includes corporations, companies, associations, firms, partnerships, societies, joint-stock companies, trusts, business associations of any kind, as well as individuals. *(FAR 52.203-7(a); 1 U.S.C. 1)*
(2) In commercial contracting, this term refers to an individual, corporation, business trust, estate, trust, partnership, limited liability company, association, joint venture, government, governmental subdivision, agency, or instrumentality, public corporation, or any other legal or commercial entity. *(UCC 1-201(27))*

person in the position of a seller
Includes, as against a principal, an agent who has paid or become responsible for the price of goods on behalf of his or her principal, or anyone who otherwise

Pp

holds a security interest or other right in goods similar to that of a seller. A person in the position of a seller may withhold or stop delivery and resell and recover incidental damages. *(UCC 2-707)*

personal computer product
A computer, computer display, desktop computer, integrated desktop computer, or notebook computer. *(FAR 23.701)*
See *computer*.

personal conflict of interest (PCI)
A situation in which a person has a financial interest, personal activity, or relationship that could impair the person's ability to act impartially and in the best interest of the buyer when performing under the contract. Among the sources of personal conflicts of interest are:

- Financial interests of the person, of close family members, or of other members of the person's household, including:
    - Compensation, including wages, salaries, commissions, professional fees, or fees for business referrals;
    - Consulting relationships (including commercial and professional consulting and service arrangements, scientific and technical advisory board memberships, or serving as an expert witness in litigation);
    - Services provided in exchange for honorariums or travel expense reimbursements;
    - Research funding or other forms of research support;
    - Investment in the form of stock or bond ownership or partnership interest (excluding diversified mutual fund investments);
    - Real estate investments;
    - Patents, copyrights, and other intellectual property interests; or
    - Business ownership and investment interests;
- Other employment or financial relationships (including seeking or negotiating for prospective employment or business); and
- Gifts, including travel.

(FAR 3.1101)
See also *organizational conflict of interest* (OCI).

personal property
Property of any kind or interest in it—*except* real property, records of the U.S. federal government, and naval vessels of the following categories: battleships, cruisers, aircraft carriers, destroyers, and submarines. *(FAR 2.101)*

personal services contract
A contract that, by its express terms or as administered, makes the contractor personnel appear to be, in effect, federal government employees. (Federal agencies are not permitted to award personal services contracts unless authorized by statute to do so.) It is characterized by the employer-employee relationship it creates between the government and the contractor's personnel. The government is normally required to obtain its employees by direct hire under competitive appointment or other procedures required by the civil service laws. Obtaining personal services by contract, rather than by direct hire, circumvents those laws unless Congress has specifically authorized acquisition of the services by contract. *(FAR 2.101; FAR 37.101)*
See also *nonpersonal services contract*.

personally identifiable information (PII)
Information that can be used to distinguish or trace an individual's identity, either alone or when combined with other information that is linked or linkable to a specific individual. (See OMB Circular A-130, "Managing Federal Information as a Strategic Resource.") *(FAR 24.101)*

physical configuration audit (PCA)
A technical examination of a designated configuration item to verify that the item "as built" conforms to the technical documentation that defines the item. *(DOD-MMH)*

pilot production
A limited production run of a new system used to demonstrate the capability to mass produce an item. Also known as *low rate initial production*. *(AFIT)*

place of manufacture
The place where an end product is assembled out of components, or otherwise made or processed from raw materials into the finished product that is to be provided to the buyer. If a product is disassembled and reassembled, the place of reassembly is not the place of manufacture. *(FAR 52.212-3(a))*

Plain Meaning Rule
When a contract is clear and unequivocal, a court will enforce it according to its plain terms, set forth on the face of the instrument, and there is no need for the court either to consider extrinsic evidence or to interpret the language of the contract. *(DGBCT)*

Pp

planned order release (POR)
A planned authorization for a supplier to release (ship) material against an existing contract. As used in material requirements planning system operation, the POR indicates when a release for a specified quantity of an item is to be issued. The release date is the planned receipt date minus the lead time. *(GKPT)*

planned value
See *budget at completion; budgeted cost for work scheduled*.

planner
The designated person or office responsible for developing and maintaining a written plan, or for the planning function in those acquisitions not requiring a written plan. *(FAR 7.101)*

planning estimate
The estimates of operational/technical characteristics, schedule, and program acquisition cost developed at the time of approval for program initiation. *(AFIT)*

planning factor
An estimating relationship used to compute the amount and type of effort or resources that will be necessary to develop, produce, acquire, and/or operate a given system. *(AFIT)*

planning package
The logical aggregation of future work (i.e., scope, schedule, and budget) within a control account that cannot yet be broken down into work package activities. Performance cannot be taken against a planning package. *(NDIA II)*

planning, programming, and budgeting system (PPBS)
An integrated system for the establishment, maintenance, and revision of the "future years defense program" and the Department of Defense budget. *(DISCS)*
See also *future years defense program* (FYDP).

plans and specifications
Drawings, specifications, and other data for and preliminary to the construction. *(FAR 36.102)*

plant clearance officer
In a federal government context, an authorized representative of the contracting officer, appointed in accordance with agency procedures, responsible for screening, redistributing, and disposing of contractor inventory from a contractor's plant or work site. The term "contractor's plant" includes, but is not limited to, government-owned contractor-operated plants, federal installations, and federal and nonfederal industrial operations, as may be required under the scope of the contract. *(FAR 2.101)*
See *contractor's plant*; see also *plant clearance period*.

plant clearance period
The period beginning on the effective date of the completion or termination of a federal government contract and ending 90 days (or such longer period as may be agreed to) after receipt by the contracting officer of acceptable inventory schedules for each property classification. The final phase of the plant clearance period means that period after receipt of acceptable inventory schedules. *(FAR 49.001)*
See also *plant clearance officer*.

plant protection costs
Costs of items such as:
- Wages, uniforms, and equipment of personnel engaged in plant protection;
- Depreciation on plant protection capital assets; and
- Necessary expenses to comply with any applicable federal government requirements (e.g., U.S. military plant protection requirements).
(FAR 31.205-29)

plant reconversion costs
Those costs incurred in restoring or rehabilitating an organization's plant facilities to approximately the same condition existing immediately before the start of a contract, fair wear and tear excepted. *(FAR 31.205-31)*

point of first receipt
Often referred to in discussions of "fast payment procedure," the point of first receipt is designated by the government. It is the point where goods or services leave the supplier's hands, and from which they are forwarded to the eventual user. Post offices or common carriers are examples of such points. *(SPP)*

point of origin
The location where a transportation company receives a shipment from the shipper. *(GKPT)*

point of sale (POS) data
Data that shows the actual units sold. Usually tracked by barcode scanning. *(DGBCT)*

Pp

point of sale (POS) transactions
Business arrangements in which the entire business arrangement between the parties is executed in a single event. *(DGBCT)*

pollution prevention
Any practice that:
- Reduces the amount of any hazardous substance, pollutant, or contaminant entering any waste stream or otherwise released into the environment (including fugitive emissions) prior to recycling, treatment, or disposal and reduces the hazards to public health and the environment associated with the release of such substances, pollutants, and contaminants;
- Reduces or eliminates the creation of pollutants through increased efficiency in the use of raw materials, energy, water, or other resources; or
- Protects natural resources by conservation.

(FAR 2.101)

pool
In the context of defense production pools and research and development pools, a group of concerns that have:
- Associated together in order to obtain and perform, jointly or in conjunction with each other, defense production or research and development contracts;
- Entered into an agreement governing their organization, relationship, and procedures; and
- Obtained approval of the agreement by either:
  - The Small Business Administration under Section 9 or 11 of the Small Business Act (15 U.S.C. 638 or 640); or
  - A designated official under Part V of Executive Order 10480 and Section 708 of the Defense Production Act of 1950, as amended (50 U.S.C. App. 2158).

(FAR 9.701)

port of debarkation (POD)
A military or commercial air or ocean port at which material is offloaded. Also called *port of discharge*. *(DISCS)*
See also *port of embarkation* (POE).

port of discharge (POD)
See *port of debarkation* (POD).

port of embarkation (POE)
A military or commercial air or ocean port at which a carrier begins the journey to deliver material to the consignee. Also called a *port of exit*. *(DISCS)*

port of exit (POE)
See *port of embarkation* (POE).

positive law codification
Pub. L. 107-217 and *Pub. L.* 111-350, codified and enacted as Title 40 and Title 41 of the United States Code, respectively, revised the historical titles of certain general and permanent laws related to public contracts and public buildings, property, and works. *(FAR 1.110(a)-(c))* (See FAR 1.110 for cross references between the historical titles of the acts and the current reference in Title 40 or Title 41.)

possessory interest
An interest involving or arising out of the possession of property. (Note that a "possessory interest" is based on *control* rather than *use*; thus, a lessee who occupies and controls the use of property has a possessory interest, while a party who has an easement does not.) *(MW)*

post-award conference/orientation
A conference, letter, or other form of written communication held or delivered after contract award to aid both government and contractor personnel in achieving a clear and mutual understanding of all contract requirements and significant elements of contract administration, and to identify and resolve potential problems. *(DGBCT)*

post-award debriefing
In federal government contracting, an offeror, upon its timely written request received by the awarding agency after the date on which that offeror received notification of contract award to another offeror, may request a post-award debriefing, which will furnish the basis for the selection decision and contract award. At a minimum, the post-award debriefing information shall include:
- The government's evaluation of the significant weaknesses or deficiencies in the offeror's proposal, if applicable;
- The overall evaluated cost or price (including unit prices) and technical rating, if applicable, of the successful offeror and the debriefed offeror, and past performance information on the debriefed offeror;
- The overall ranking of all offerors, when any ranking was developed by the agency during the source selection;

Pp

- A summary of the rationale for award;
- For acquisitions of commercial items, the make and model of the item to be delivered by the successful offeror; and
- Reasonable responses to relevant questions about whether source selection procedures contained in the solicitation, applicable regulations, and other applicable authorities were followed.

The post-award debriefing *shall not* include point-by-point comparisons of the debriefed offeror's proposal with those of other offerors. Moreover, the debriefing *shall not* reveal any information prohibited from disclosure by FAR 24.202 or exempt from release under the Freedom of Information Act (5 U.S.C. 552). *(FAR 15.505(d)–(e); FAR 15.506(a)(1))* (See *FAR* Subpart 15.5.)
See *debrief(ing)*; compare with *pre-award debriefing*.

post-award life cycle phase

In the context of the *Contract Management Standard*™, "post-award" is the third and final phase of the contract life cycle. It and begins once the "award" phase is completed. This involves all of the contract management functions known as "contract administration." The contract administration functions will vary greatly depending on the complexity of the contract. Both the buyer and seller are actively involved in contract administration to ensure satisfactory performance and to bring the contract to a successful conclusion. *(CMS)*
See *close contract; perform contract*; see also *award life cycle phase; pre-award life cycle phase*.

post-award protest issues

See *unequal treatment; unreasonable best value analysis*; see also *pre-award protest issues*.

postconsumer fiber

As defined by the Environmental Protection Agency, this term means:
- Paper, paperboard, and fibrous materials from retail stores, office buildings, homes, and so forth, after they have passed through their end-usage as a consumer item, including: used corrugated boxes; old newspapers; old magazines; mixed waste paper; tabulating cards; and used cordage; or
- All paper, paperboard, and fibrous materials that enter and are collected from municipal solid waste; but not
- Fiber derived from printers' over-runs, converters' scrap, and over-issue publications.

(FAR 52.204-4(a))
See *postconsumer material*.

postconsumer material

A material or finished product that has served its intended use and has been discarded for disposal or recovery, having completed its life as a consumer item. Postconsumer material is a part of the broader category of "recovered material." For paper and paper products, postconsumer material means "postconsumer fiber," as defined by the Environmental Protection Agency. *(FAR 11.301)*
See *postconsumer fiber*; see also *recovered material*.

post-MEO performance review

When services are performed in-house, as a result of a cost comparison, including those involving an inter-service support agreement, a formal review and inspection of the most efficient organization (MEO) should be conducted. Typically, this review should be conducted following the end of the first full year of performance. Post-MEO performance reviews confirm that the MEO has been implemented in accordance with the transition plan, established the MEO's ability to perform the services of the performance work statement and confirm that actual costs are within the estimates contained in the in-house cost estimate. Adjustments may be for formal mission or scope of work changes. *(OMB A-76)*
See *most efficient organization* (MEO).

potential impact

The potential consequences to organizational operations, organizational assets, or individuals that a loss of confidentiality, integrity, or availability caused by a cybersecurity incident could be expected to have. Such consequences include:
- A *limited* adverse effect ("low");
- A *serious* adverse effect ("moderate"); or
- A *severe* or *catastrophic* adverse effect ("high").

(FIPS 199)
See *impact; incident*.

power of attorney

The authority given one person or corporation to act for and obligate another, as specified in the instrument creating the power. In corporate suretyship, this term refers to an instrument under seal that appoints an attorney-in-fact to act in behalf of a surety company in signing bonds. *(FAR 2.101)*
See also *attorney-in-fact*.

practical application

(1) To manufacture a composition or product under such conditions as to establish that the invention is being

Pp

utilized and that its benefits are, to the extent permitted by law or federal government regulations, available to the public on reasonable terms. *(FAR 27.301)*
See *invention*.

(2) To practice a process or method under such conditions as to establish that the invention is being utilized and that its benefits are, to the extent permitted by law or federal government regulations, available to the public on reasonable terms. *(FAR 27.301)*
See *invention*.

(3) To operate a machine or system under such conditions as to establish that the invention is being utilized and that its benefits are, to the extent permitted by law or federal government regulations, available to the public on reasonable terms. *(FAR 27.301)*
See *invention*.

practical utility
In the context of federal government information management, this term refers to the ability of an agency to use information, particularly the capability to process such information in a timely and useful fashion. *(44 U.S.C. 3502(11))*

pre-award debriefing
In federal government contracting, offerors excluded from the competitive range or otherwise excluded before award may request a debriefing before award (as per 10 U.S.C. 2305(b)(6)(A) and 41 U.S.C. 3705).
At a minimum, pre-award debriefings shall include:
- The agency's evaluation of significant elements in the offeror's proposal;
- A summary of the rationale for eliminating the offeror from the competition, and
- Reasonable responses to relevant questions about whether source selection procedures contained in the solicitation, applicable regulations, and other applicable authorities were followed in the process of eliminating the offeror from the competition.

Pre-award debriefings *shall not* include:
- The number of offerors,
- The identity of other offerors,
- The content of other offerors' proposals,
- The ranking of other offerors,
- The evaluation of other offerors, or
- Any of the information prohibited in FAR 15.506(e).

(FAR 15.505(a)(1); FAR 15.505(e)–(f)) (See *FAR* Subpart 15.5.)
See *debrief(ing)*; compare with *post-award debriefing*.

pre-award inquiry
Questions and comments from prospective offerors about specifications, terms, and conditions in a solicitation received prior to the opening date of the invitation for bids or closing date of the request for proposals. *(FAI)*

pre-award life cycle phase
In the context of the *Contract Management Standard*™, "pre-award" is the first of three phases of the contract life cycle and includes:
- *For the buyer*–Assisting in defining the customer requirements for products or services, and then developing a comprehensive acquisition plan to fulfill those requirements in a timely manner at a reasonable price. This includes developing and executing an overall strategy for the purchase, which is accomplished through researching the marketplace, developing contracting strategies, preparing solicitations, and requesting offers.
- *For the seller*–Developing and executing a strategy for obtaining the award for a contract, including pre-sales activities, market strategies, and responding to the procurement.

(CMS)
See *develop offer; develop solicitation*; see also *award life cycle phase; post-award life cycle phase*.

pre-award process
(1) A process by which buyers develop a comprehensive plan for fulfilling requirements for products or services in a timely manner at a reasonable price. This term includes developing an overall strategy for the purchase, which is accomplished through researching the marketplace, developing strategies, initiating the procurement, and selecting a supplier. *(CMBOK)*
(2) A process by which sellers develop and execute a strategy for obtaining the award of a contract, including market strategies, pricing strategies, and responding to the procurement. *(CMBOK)*

pre-award protest issues
See *ambiguous or erroneous evaluation criteria; ambiguous or incomplete requirements; exclusion from the competitive range; inappropriate sole-source requirement; restrictive requirements; unfair evaluation criteria*; see also *post-award protest issues*.

pre-award survey
An evaluation of a prospective contractor's capability to perform a proposed contract. *(FAR 2.101)*

Pp

pre-bid conference
A conference held with prospective bidders in sealed-bid procurements prior to the submission of a bid to clarify any ambiguous situations, answer bidder questions, and ensure that all bidders have a common basis of understanding regarding the supplies or services required. Also known as a "*pre-proposal conference* in a negotiated procurement. *(OPM)*

pre-contract costs
Costs incurred before the effective date of the contract directly pursuant to the negotiation and in anticipation of the contract award when such incurrence is necessary to comply with the proposed contract delivery schedule. *(FAR 31.205-32)*

precious metal
Silver, gold, platinum, palladium, iridium, osmium, rhodium, and ruthenium. *(FAR 45.101)*
See also *refined precious metal*.

predecessor
An entity that is replaced by a successor and includes any predecessors of the predecessor. *(FAR 52.204-20(a))*
See also *successor*.

preferential procurement programs
These are special federal government "commercial" source programs, such as Federal Prison Industries/UNICOR and the Committee for Purchase from the Blind or Severely Disabled. *(OMB A-76)*

preliminary negotiations
A manifestation of willingness to enter into a bargain is not an offer if the person to whom it is addressed knows or has reason to know that the person making it does not intend to conclude a bargain until he or she has made a further manifestation of assent. *(RSOC 26)*
See *offer*.

pre-negotiation objectives
Establish the buyer's initial negotiation position. They assist in the contracting officer's determination of fair and reasonable price. They should be based on the results of the contracting officer's analysis of the offeror's proposal, taking into consideration all pertinent information including field pricing assistance, audit reports and technical analysis, fact-finding results, independent government cost estimates, and price histories. *(FAR 15.406-1)*

pre-performance meeting
This meeting can help avoid problems during contract performance and can set the foundation for good communication between the buyer and seller. When conducted, this meeting should be chaired by contracting professionals from the buyer and seller and include appropriate managers and staff personnel from the buyer's organization (i.e., the customer who will interface with and receive the benefits from the contractor's work) and appropriate managers and staff personnel from the seller's organization (i.e., the contactor's resources that will interface with and perform work for the customer). *(DGBCT)*
See *status review meeting*.

preponderance of the evidence
Proof by information that, compared with that opposing it, leads to the conclusion that the fact at issue is more probably true than not. *(FAR 2.101)*

pre-production inspection
Examination and testing performed, witnessed, or participated in by the government on one or more items submitted by a contractor to prove, prior to the initiation of production, that its production methods are capable of yielding items that comply with the technical requirements of the contract. *(AFIT)*
See also *preproduction model*.

pre-production model
A version of an item or equipment, prior to the initiation of its full-scale production, suitable for complete evaluation of form, design, and performance. Preproduction models are often called *beta models*. *(CNSSI 4009)*

pre-proposal conference
A meeting held with contractors after the request for proposals in negotiated procurements have been sent out. The goal is to promote uniform interpretation of work statements and specifications by all prospective contractors. *(NCMA-SS)*
See *pre-bid conference*.

pre-qualification
A buyer's announcement of interest, including criteria for selecting proposals, and selecting offerors capable of meeting the requirements. *(DGBCT)*

pre-qualification designation notice
A notice in a procurement solicitation or other publication by the federal government stating that the

Pp

technology to be procured either affirmatively or presumptively satisfies the technical criteria necessary to be deemed a "qualified anti-terrorism technology." A pre-qualification designation notice authorizes offeror(s) to submit streamlined SAFETY Act applications for SAFETY Act designation and receive expedited processing of those applications. *(FAR 50.201)* See *qualified anti-terrorism technology* (QATT); see also *block certification; block designation*.

present sale
A sale which is accomplished by the making of the contract. *(UCC 2-106(1))*

present value
The amount as of a date certain of one or more sums payable in the future, discounted to the date certain by use of either an interest rate specified by the parties if that rate is not manifestly unreasonable at the time the transaction is entered into; otherwise, the discount is determined by a commercially reasonable rate that takes into account the facts and circumstances of each case at the time the transaction was entered into. *(UCC 1-201(28); UCC 2A-103(u))*

present value of future cash flows
A dollar today is worth more because of the interest cost. Thus, dollar benefits that accrue in the future cannot be compared directly with investments made in the present. Discounting is a technique for converting various cash flows occurring over time to equivalent amounts at a common point in time considering the time value of money to facilitate a valid comparison. Also known as *time value of future cash flows*. *(AFIT)*

President's Blue Ribbon Commission on Defense Management
See *Packard Commission*.

pre-solicitation conference
A meeting held with potential contractors or subcontractors prior to a formal solicitation to discuss technical and other problems connected with a proposed procurement. The conference is also used to elicit the interest of prospective contractors in pursuing the task, such as a research and development effort. *(DSMC)*

pre-solicitation notice
Notices issued sufficiently in advance of the invitation for bids to stimulate the interest of the greatest number of prospective bidders. *(FAR 36.231-2(a))*

preventive maintenance
See *maintenance*.

price
(1) Cost plus any fee or profit applicable to the contract type. *(FAR 15.401)*
(2) The amount that one pays for goods or services. *(CMBOK)*

price analysis
(1) The process of examining and evaluating an offeror's proposed price without evaluation of the separate detailed cost elements and proposed profit of the offeror's price proposal. The value added by this process is the buyer's ability to evaluate an offer by comparing it with indicators of reasonableness, such as:
- Historical prices paid,
- Published prices,
- Competitive analysis,
- Comparative analysis, and
- Market data.

This process is part of the "award" life cycle phase. *(CMS)* Compare with *cost analysis*; see also *auxiliary techniques; secondary comparison; primary comparison*.
(2) Price analysis is the process of examining and evaluating a proposed price without evaluating its separate cost elements and proposed profit. Unless an exception from the requirement to obtain certified cost or pricing data applies under FAR 15.403-1(b)(1) or FAR 15.403-(b)(2), at a minimum, the contracting officer shall obtain appropriate data, without certification, on the prices at which the same or similar items have previously been sold and determine if the data is adequate for evaluating the reasonableness of the price. *(FAR 15.404-1(b))*

price fixing
Any agreement, understanding, or arrangement among competitors to raise, lower, fix, or stabilize prices, as well as any agreement between a supplier and customer as to the price at which the customer may resell goods purchased. *(BOE)*

price index
A number, usually a percentage, expressing the relation of the actual price of a commodity at a given point in time to its price during a specified base period. This information can be used to chart price level changes. *(GKPT)*

Pp

price negotiation memorandum (PNM)
(1) The contracting officer's documentation in the contract file of the principal elements of the negotiated agreement. *(FAR 15.406-3)*
(2) The document that relates the story of the negotiation. A sales document establishing the reasonableness of the agreement reached with the successful offeror, as well as a permanent record of the decisions made by the negotiator in establishing that the price was fair and reasonable. *(CMBOK)*

price or cost analysis
See *cost analysis; price analysis*.

price reduction
(1) A contract clause that entitles the buyer to obtain a price reduction of any significant amount, including profit or fee, by which the contract price was increased due to defective cost or pricing data. An audit investigation by an outside party (e.g., the U.S. Defense Contract Audit Agency) must precede this administrative action. Based on the audit results, a unilateral modification to the contract, reducing the price, is issued by the buyer. *(TIPS)*
(2) Ordering activities may request a price reduction at any time before placing an order, establishing a blanket purchase agreement (BPA), or in conjunction with the annual BPA review. However, the ordering activity shall seek a price reduction when the order or BPA exceeds the simplified acquisition threshold. Schedule contractors are not required to pass on to all schedule users a price reduction extended only to an individual ordering activity for a specific order or BPA. *(FAR 8.405-4)*

price-related factors
Factors that may be applicable in evaluation of bids for award and shall be included in the solicitation when applicable:
* Foreseeable costs or delays to the government resulting from such factors as differences in inspection, locations of supplies, and transportation. If bids are on an f.o.b. origin basis, transportation costs to the designated points shall be considered in determining the lowest cost to the government. (See FAR 47.303 and FAR 47.305.)
* Changes made, or requested by the bidder, in any of the provisions of the invitation for bids, if the change does not constitute a ground for rejection under FAR 14.404.
* Advantages or disadvantages to the government

that might result from making more than one award. The contracting officer shall assume, for the purpose of making multiple awards, that $500 would be the administrative cost to the government for issuing and administering each contract awarded under a solicitation. Individual awards shall be for the items or combinations of items that result in the lowest aggregate cost to the government, including the assumed administrative costs. (See FAR 14.201-6(q).)
* Federal, state, and local taxes.(See *FAR* Part 29.)
* Origin of supplies, and, if foreign, the application of the Buy American statute or any other prohibition on foreign purchases.(See *FAR* Part 25.)
(FAR 14.201-8)

price variance
The difference between the actual price and the standard price, multiplied by the total number of items acquired. *(NCMA-CA)*
Contrast with *rate variance*.

priced bill of material (PBOM)
A descriptive and quantitative listing of materials, supplies, parts, and components—complete with actual or expected prices applied—required to complete the production of a designated, complete end item. *(NDIA; OPM)*
See also *bill of material* (BOM).

pricing
The process of establishing a reasonable amount or amounts to be paid for supplies or services. *(FAR 2.101)*

pricing arrangement
An agreed-to basis between contractual parties for the payment of amounts for specified performance; usually expressed in terms of a specific cost-reimbursement or fixed-price type arrangement. *(OPM)*

pricing proposal
See *contract pricing proposal*.

primary comparison
A means of accomplishing price analysis. An example of a primary comparison is competitive evaluation, whereby independent, current, responsible, responsive offers are compared against each other. Another example of a primary comparison is published catalog prices. *(NCMA-WS)*
Compare with *auxiliary techniques; secondary comparison*.

Pp

primary sponsor

In the context of a Federally Funded Research and Development Center (FFRDC), the lead federal agency responsible for managing, administering, or monitoring overall use of the FFRDC under a multiple sponsorship agreement. *(FAR 35.017(b))*

See *Federally Funded Research and Development Center* (FFRDC); see also *nonsponsor; sponsor*.

prime

(1) *Synonymous with* "prime contractor."

(2) As an adjective—the first in rank, authority, or significance. *(MW)*

prime contract

(1) The contract between the buyer and the seller having complete responsibility for the work. *(CMBOK)*

(2) A contract or contractual action entered into by the U.S. federal government for the purpose of obtaining supplies, materials, equipment, or services of any kind. *(FAR 3.502-1)*

prime contractor

(1) Also simply called the *prime*, it is the entity with whom an agent of the United States enters into a prime contract for the purpose of obtaining supplies, materials, equipment, or services of any kind. *(DAAT)*

See also *prime contract; prime contractor employee*.

(2) The contractor who is under contract with the buyer and has complete responsibility for completion of a project or delivery of products or services under the contract. *(CMBOK)*

(3) A person who has entered into a prime contract with the U.S. federal government. *(FAR 3.502-1)*

(4) In an equal employment opportunity context, means any person who holds, or has held, a U.S. federal government contract subject to Executive Order 11246. *(FAR 22.801)*

See also *equal employment opportunity* (EEO).

prime contractor employee

Any officer, partner, employee, or agent of a prime contractor. *(FAR 3.502-1)*

See *prime contractor*.

prime cost

The sum of direct material and direct labor. *(NCMA-CA)*

prime-sub dispute

A dispute between the prime contractor and subcontractor to be settled at the local state court level. However, if the subcontractor has a protestable event against the U.S. federal government, the prime may protest on behalf of the subcontractor because the subcontractor does not have privity of contract with the government. *(DGBCT)*

See *Severin Doctrine*.

principal

An officer, director, owner, partner, or a person having primary management or supervisory responsibilities within a business entity (e.g., general manager, plant manager, head of a division or business segment, and similar positions). *(FAR 2.101)*

principal obligor

With respect to an instrument, this term means the accommodated party or any other party to the instrument against whom a secondary obligor has recourse under Article 3 of the Uniform Commercial Code. *(UCC 3-103(a)(11))*

See also *obligor*.

prior course of dealing

An important type of extrinsic evidence used in contract interpretation to establish the meaning of ambiguous language. Also used to demonstrate that an explicit requirement of the contract is not binding because that requirement was not enforced in the past. *(AGC)*

priority rating

(1) An identifying code assigned by a delegate agency or authorized person placed on all rated orders and consisting of the rating symbol and the program identification symbol. *(15 CFR 700)*

(2) "DO" and "DX" are the two types of priority ratings contained in the Defense Priorities and Allocations System (DPAS) Regulation that specify rules relating to the status, placement, acceptance, and treatment of priority-rated contracts and orders. "DO" ratings have equal preferential status and take priority over all unrated orders. "DX" ratings have equal preferential status and take priority over DO-rated and unrated orders. *(CMPA)*

See *Defense Priorities and Allocations System* (DPAS); *rated order*.

privacy interest

An interest in freedom from governmental intrusion into matters in which one has a reasonable expectation of privacy. *(MW)*

private financing

Financing without a federal government guarantee.

Pp

Such financing includes loans from financial institutions, sale of bonds or stocks, and loans from family members or other private sources. However, a contractor should not be required to obtain private financing at unreasonable terms or from other agencies. In addition, under assignment of claims provisions, a financing institution can receive payments directly from the government in consideration for making a private loan to a contractor. *(DGBCT)*

private sector

The part of an economy which is not controlled or owned by the government. *(MW)*
Contrast with *public sector*.

private-sector standards

Documents that are developed by companies, consortia, industry and trade associations, and technical societies. The groups are collectively referred to as "standard-developing organizations." *(NES-97)*
See *standard*.

private security functions

Activities engaged in by a federal government contractor consisting of:
- Guarding of personnel, facilities, designated sites, or property of a U.S. federal agency, the contractor or subcontractor, or a third party; or
- Any other activity for which personnel are required to carry weapons in the performance of their duties in accordance with the terms of the contract. *(FAR 25.302-2)*

privately-owned U.S.-flag commercial vessel

A vessel registered and operated under the laws of the United States, used in commercial trade of the United States, owned and operated by U.S. citizens (including a vessel under voyage or time charter to the government), and a U.S. federal government-owned vessel under bareboat charter to, and operated by, U.S. citizens. *(FAR 47.501)*

privatization

The process of changing a public entity or enterprise to private control and ownership. It does not include determinations as to whether a support service should be obtained through public or private resources, when the government retains full responsibility and control over the delivery of those services. *(OMB A-76)*

privity of contract

(1) The direct legal (contractual) relationship that exists between parties that allows either party to enforce contractual rights against the other party and seek remedy directly from the other party with whom this relationship exists. *(P&L II)*
(2) The legal relationship between two parties to the same contract. The federal government has privity of contract with the prime contractor. Therefore, the government's relationship with subcontractors is indirect in nature. Government involvement with subcontractors is channeled through prime contractor–directed activities; only the prime contractor is authorized to direct the subcontractor. *(DSMC)*

pro forma

(1) A Latin term meaning "as a matter of form." In most contexts, it is used to describe a document or practice made or carried out in a perfunctory manner or as a formality, provided as a courtesy or to satisfy minimum requirements, or to conform to a norm or doctrine. *(MW)*
(2) Provided or made in advance to describe items or projections (e.g., a *pro forma* invoice). *(MW)*
See also *pro forma invoice*.

pro forma invoice

A document prepared in advance of a sale to provide evidence of the final form and amount of invoice. *(GKPT)*

probability sampling

See *sampling*.

probable cost

In a cost realism context, a value determined by adjusting each offeror's proposed cost (and fee, when appropriate) to reflect any additions or reductions in cost elements to realistic levels based on the results of the cost realism analysis. The probable cost may differ from the proposed cost and should reflect the buyer's best estimate of the cost of any contract that is most likely to result from the offeror's proposal. In federal government contracts, the probable cost shall be used for purposes of evaluation to determine the best value. *(FAR 15.404-1(d)(2)(i)–(ii))*
See also *cost realism; cost realism analysis*.

procedure

(1) Established or official actions.
(2) The processes used by the administrative and judicial forums to resolve protests. *(DGBCT)*

(3) A written description of a sequence of actions to be taken to perform a given task. *(AIMD)*

(4) A traditional or established way of doing things. *(MW)*

(5) One or more methods or steps for the enforcement or administration of rights, duties, justice, or laws. *(MW)*

Procedures, Guidance, and Information (PGI)

Procedures, Guidance, and Information (PGI) is a companion resource to the *DFARS*. The PGI is a web-based tool for simply and rapidly accessing guidance and information relevant to *FAR* and *DFARS* topics. The *DFARS* remains the source for regulations, which include the implementation of statutes and DOD-wide contracting policies, authorities, and delegations. The PGI contains both mandatory and non-mandatory internal DOD procedures, guidance, and supplemental information. *(DAAT-A)*

See also *Defense Pricing and Contracting* (DPC);

proceeds

(1) In the case of a letter of credit, means the cash, check, accepted draft, or other item of value paid or delivered upon honor or giving of value by the issuer or any nominated person under the letter of credit. This term *does not* include a beneficiary's drawing rights or documents presented by the beneficiary. *(UCC 5-114(a))*

See *letter of credit*.

(2) Concerning collateral, refers to the following property:
- Whatever is acquired upon the sale, lease, license, exchange, or other disposition of collateral;
- Whatever is collected on, or distributed on account of, collateral;
- Rights arising out of collateral;
- To the extent of the value of collateral, claims arising out of the loss, nonconformity, or interference with the use of, defects or infringement of rights in, or damage to, the collateral; or
- To the extent of the value of collateral and to the extent payable to the debtor or the secured party, insurance payable by reason of the loss or nonconformity of, defects or infringement of rights in, or damage to, the collateral.

(UCC 9-102(a)(64))

See *collateral*.

process capability analysis

A statistical technique used during development and production cycles to analyze the variability of a process relative to product specifications. *(DGCQI)*

process costing

A method of costing products with average costs computed on the basis of total costs divided by equivalent units of work performed. Usually used in high-volume, similar-product situations. *(NCMA-CA)*

procurement

A process that includes all stages of the process of acquiring property or services, beginning with the process for determining a need for property or services and ending with contract completion and closeout. *(41 U.S.C. 111)*

See also *acquisition; procurement process; procurement system*.

procurement appropriations

In a federal government context, appropriations that fund those acquisition programs that have been approved for production (to include low rate initial production of acquisition objective quantities), and all costs integral and necessary to deliver a useful end item intended for operational use or inventory upon delivery. *(DAAT)*

See also *appropriation* (APPN); *procurement*.

procurement authorization

A document that establishes the approved material procurement program and authorizes and directs the action to be taken to place the approved material program under procurement. *(AFIT)*

procurement center representative

A representative of the Small Business Administration assigned to any contracting activity or contract administration office to carry out SBA policies and programs.

procurement contract for construction

A procurement contract for the construction, alteration, or repair (including painting and decoration) of public buildings or public works and which requires or involves the employment of mechanics or laborers, and any subcontract of any tier thereunder. This term includes any contract subject to the Wage Rate Requirements (Construction) statute (40 U.S.C. Chapter 31, Subchapter IV). *(29 CFR 13.2)*

See also *procurement contract for services*.

procurement contract for services

A contract the principal purpose of which is to furnish services in the United States through the use of service employees, and any subcontract thereunder. This term in-

Pp

cludes any contract subject to the Service Contract Labor Standards statute (41 U.S.C. Chapter 67). *(29 CFR 13.2)* See also *procurement contract for construction*.

procurement instrument identifier (PIID)

The government-unique identifier for each solicitation, contract, agreement, or order. For example, an agency may use as its PIID for procurement actions, such as delivery and task orders or basic ordering agreements, the order or agreement number in conjunction with the contract number. *(FAR 4.001)*

See also *supplementary procurement instrument identifier*.

procurement integrity

(1) A set of rules of conduct, contained in the 1989 amendments to the Office of Federal Procurement Policy statute (41 U.S.C. Div. B of Subtitle I), that were formalized for the purpose of upholding the integrity of the federal government procurement process. *(NS)* (See also FAR 3.104.)

(2) Procurement integrity encompasses a range of legislation, regulations, directives, actions, and attitudes for preserving the integrity of the federal procurement and assuring the fair treatment of bidders, offerors and contractors. The term "integrity" itself is defined as firm adherence to a code or standard of values. *(DAAT-A)*

Procurement Integrity Act (PIA)

See *Restrictions on Obtaining and Disclosing Certain Information statute*.

procurement lead time

The time interval (in months) between the initiation of procurement action and receipt into the supply system of the production model (excluding prototypes) or material purchased as the result of such actions. Procurement lead time is composed of two elements:
- Production lead time, and
- Administrative lead time.

(AFIT; DISCS)

See *administrative lead time; production lead time*.

procurement list

In the context of acquisition from nonprofit agencies employing people who are blind or severely disabled, a list of supplies (including military resale commodities) and services that the Committee for Purchase from People Who Are Blind or Severely Disabled has determined are suitable for purchase by the federal government under 41 U.S.C. Chapter 85. *(FAR 8.701)*

procurement package

All information required to obtain bids or proposals; the technical information necessary to accurately describe the item to be procured. *(AFIT)*

procurement process

Includes preparation and processing of a demand as well as the end receipt and approval of payment. It often involves:
- Purchase planning,
- Standards determination,
- Specifications development,
- Supplier research and selection,
- Value analysis,
- Financing,
- Price negotiation,
- Making the purchase,
- Supply contract administration,
- Inventory control and stores, and
- Disposals and other related functions.

The process of procurement is often a part of an organization's strategy because the ability to purchase certain materials will determine if operations will continue. *(BD)*

procurement request (PR)

Document that describes the required supplies or services so that a procurement can be initiated. Some procuring activities actually refer to the document by this title; others use different titles such as "procurement directive." Combined with specifications, the statement of work, and the contract data requirements list, it is called the "PR package," a basis for a solicitation. *(DGBCT)*

Procurement statute

A general federal statute (41 U.S.C. Div. C of Subtitle I) that governs contracting by the civilian agencies of the government. Formerly known as the *Federal Property and Administrative Services Act of 1949*, Title III. *(40 U.S.C. 101, et seq.)*

procurement system

The integration of the procurement process, the professional development of procurement personnel, and the management structure for carrying out the procurement function. *(41 U.S.C. 112)*

Procurement Technical Assistance Center (PTAC)

Centers designed to provide technical assistance, training, and counseling to businesses that want to sell

products and services to federal, state, and/or local governments. PTAC services are available either free of charge, or at a nominal cost. PTACs are part of the Procurement Technical Assistance Program," which is administered by the Defense Logistics Agency. (See https://www.dla.mil/SmallBusiness/PTAP/.)
See *Procurement Technical Assistance Program* (PTAP).

procurement technical assistance program (PTAP)

A program "established to expand the number of business capable of participating" in federal government contracts. The program is administered by the Defense Logistics Agency's Office of Small Business in coordination with states, local governments, and nonprofit organizations. (See https://www.dla.mil/SmallBusiness/PTAP/.)
See also *Procurement Technical Assistance Center* (PTAC).

procuring activity

In a federal government context, a component of an executive agency having a significant acquisition function and designated as such by the head of the agency. Unless agency regulations specify otherwise, the term "procuring activity" is synonymous with "contracting activity." *(FAR 2.101)*

procuring contracting officer (PCO)

The individual authorized to enter into contracts for supplies and services on behalf of the federal government by detailed bids or negotiations and who is responsible for overall procurement under such contracts. *(DISCS)*

producer

The actual manufacturer of parts or materials that are not used as end items, but are processed or incorporated into designed equipment. (This term distinguishes a producer from an equipment manufacturer, who uses the parts and materials in his or her equipment.) *(DODM 4120.24)*
Contrast with *manufacturer*.

product

Includes materials, parts, components, subassemblies, assemblies, and equipment. The term "product" also encompasses the term "family of products," which includes all products of the same classification, design, construction, material, type, and other design characteristics. These products are manufactured within the same production facilities and have the same processes, quality of materials, quality controls, and are produced under the same management, yet have the acceptable variety of physical and functional characteristics defined and specified in the applicable specification. *Synonymous with* "supplies." *(DODM 4120.24)*
See also *family of products*.

product description

A generic term for documents used for acquisition and management purposes, such as specifications, standards, commercial item descriptions, non-government standards, or purchase descriptions. *(DODM 4120.24)*
See *commercial item description* (CID); *non-government standard* (NGS); *purchase description; specification; standard*.

product support integrator (PSI)

An entity charged with integrating all sources of product support within the scope of a contract or agreement. *(DGBCT)*

product verification inspection

Physical inspection or test of a product by the government after inspection and acceptance by the contractor's quality organization. *(AFIT)*

production lead time

The time interval between the placement of a contract and receipt into the supply system of material purchased. *(DISCS)*
See also *administrative lead time*.

production lot testing

Performed to verify that the manufacturer can and has maintained the manufacturing capability, process, and facilities to produce a product in accordance with the requirements throughout the entire life of the contract. *(DGBCT)*

production readiness review (PRR)

A formal examination of a program to determine whether:
• The design is ready for production,
• Production engineering problems have been resolved, and
• The producer has accomplished adequate planning for the production phase.
(DOD-MMH)

Pp

production surveillance

A function of contract administration used to determine contractor progress and to identify any factors that may delay performance. Production surveillance involves federal government review and analysis of contractor performance plans, schedules, controls, and industrial processes—as well as the contractor's actual performance under them. *(FAR 42.1101)*

professional and consultant services

Services rendered by persons who are members of a particular profession or possess a special skill and who are not officers or employees of the contractor. Examples include those services acquired by contractors or subcontractors in order to enhance their legal, economic, financial, or technical positions. "Professional and consultant services" are generally acquired to obtain information, advice, opinions, alternatives, conclusions, recommendations, training, or direct assistance, such as studies, analyses, evaluations, liaison with U.S. federal government officials, or other forms of representation. *(FAR 31.205-33(a))*

professional employee

(1) Any person employed in a bona fide professional capacity. *(29 CFR 541)*
(2) Any employees who are members of those professions having a recognized status based upon acquiring professional knowledge through prolonged study. Examples of these professions include accountancy, actuarial computation, architecture, dentistry, engineering, law, medicine, nursing, pharmacy, and the sciences (such as biology, chemistry, and physics, and teaching). To be a "professional employee," a person must not only be a professional, but must be involved essentially in discharging professional duties. *(FAR 22.1102)*

professional services

The Fair Labor Standards Act (29 U.S.C. 201, et seq.) defines a "professional" employee as one who exercises discretion and independent judgment and who performs work that is predominantly intellectual and varied in character, as opposed to skilled or technical. The categories of executive, administrative, and professional employees are exempt from the Service Contract Labor Standards statute (41 U.S.C. Chapter 67) and provisions for minimum wage rates, fringe benefits requirements, and rules governing overtime compensation. *(NCMA-WS)*
See *Fair Labor Standards Act* (FLSA); *Service Contract Labor Standards statute; uncompensated overtime*.

profit

(1) The difference between total cost and revenue. *(DGBCT)*
(2) The amount realized by a contractor after the cost of performance (both direct and indirect) are deducted from the amount to be paid under the terms of the contract. *(DGBCT)*
See *anticipatory profit; fee*.
(3) The net proceeds from selling a product or service when costs are subtracted from revenues. May be positive (profit) or negative (loss). *(P&L I)*
(4) The surplus remaining after total costs are deducted from total revenue, and the basis on which tax is computed and dividend is paid. As an indicator of comparative performance, however, it is less valuable than return on investment (ROI). *(BD)*
Compare with *return on investment* (ROI).

profit center

The smallest organizationally independent segment of a company charged by the management with profit and loss responsibilities. *(FAR 31.001)* (See also *FAR* Subpart 31.3 and *FAR* Subpart 31.6.)

profit objective

The part of the estimated contract price objective that the contracting officer concludes is appropriate for the procurement at hand. Developed after a thorough review of proposed contract work and all available knowledge regarding an offeror, as well as an analysis of the offeror's cost estimate and a comparison of it with the U.S. federal government's estimate or projection of cost. *(OPM)*

program

A major, independent part of a capital asset or system that involves a planned effort to achieve an outcome, the progress toward which is discretely measurable. A program may be comprised of multiple projects, delivery orders, task orders, or other recognized terms indicating a bilateral agreement between contracting parties. *(NDIA II)*
See also *project*.

Program Evaluation and Review Technique (PERT)

A technique for management of a program through to completion by constructing a network model of integrated activities and events and periodically evaluating the time/cost implications of progress. It uses network diagrams to show time and dependency relationships

Pp

between the activities that make up the total project. The purpose of the technique is to keep all the "parts" arriving on schedule so that the total project can be completed as planned. *(DBL; DGBCT)*

program management
The process whereby a single leader exercises centralized authority and responsibility for planning, organizing, staffing, controlling, and leading the combined efforts of participating personnel and organizations for the management of a specific acquisition program or programs throughout the system life cycle. *(DAAT)*

program management review (PMR)
A management-level review held by a systems program office or systems program manager for the purpose of determining the status of an assigned system. Program management reviews are designed as tools to identify problems, if any, and to develop appropriate follow-up actions as required. *(DISCS)*

program manager (PM)
The individual designated with responsibility for and authority to accomplish program/project objectives for planning, budgeting, acquisition, and management to meet the user's operational needs. Also known as the *project manager* or *product manager*. *(NDIA II)* See also *milestone decision authority (MDA)*.

program office estimate (POE)
A detailed estimate of acquisition and ownership costs normally required for high-level decisions. The estimate is performed early in the program and serves as the base point for all subsequent tracking and auditing purposes. *(DGBCT)*

program risk-adjusted budget (PRB)
The total program budget that includes an additional amount of funding and schedule above the program budget that customer management determines may be necessary to ensure project/program success. The PRB for a U.S. federal government program should be established at a level of probability sufficient to provide acceptable confidence that a program can achieve 90 percent of its performance, cost, and schedule objectives within the approved budget as required by statute. The amount above the program budget covers risk not identifiable through the integrated baseline review and other risk management approaches, but that history on similar programs or the amount of total risk on the particular program indicates will likely be needed to en-

sure sufficient resources will be budgeted for project/program success. The difference between the program budget and PRB is held at a level above the program level to be released to the program when justified to fund cost and schedule overruns from the performance measurement baseline that happen through no fault of the program management process. *(NDIA II)*

program-unique specification
A specification that describes a product, process, or material developed and produced for use under a specific program or as part of a single system that has no application outside of that system. *(DODM 4120.24)*

program work breakdown structure (PWBS)
The work breakdown structure that encompasses an entire program. It consists of at least three levels of the program with associated definitions and is used by the U.S. federal government program manager and contractor to develop and extend a contract work breakdown structure. *(DAAT)*

progress payment
(1) A payment made as work progresses under a contract on the basis of percentage of completion accomplished, or for work performed at a particular stage of completion. *(OPM)*
(2) A payment made on the basis of costs incurred by the contractor as work progresses under the contract. This form of contract financing does not include payments based on the percentage or stage of completion accomplished, payments for partial deliveries accepted by the U.S. federal government, partial payments for a contract termination proposal, or performance-based payments. *(FAR 32.102(b))*
(3) In a Department of Defense context, those payments made to contractors or DOD industrial fund activities as work progresses under a contract. Payments are made on the basis of cost incurred or percentage of work completed, or of a particular stage of completion accomplished prior to actual delivery and acceptance of contract items. *(DISCS)*

progressive down-selection
A type of down-selection strategy for a phased acquisition. In this method, a single solicitation is issued for all phases of the program. The initial phase contracts are awarded and the contractors for subsequent phases are expected to be chosen through a down-selection from among the preceding phase contractors. In each phase, progressively fewer contracts are awarded until

Pp

a single contractor is chosen for the final phase. Normally, all down-selections are accomplished without issuing a new, formal solicitation. Also called "phased acquisition." *(DGBCT)*

project
An endeavor with a defined technical scope, schedule, and budget to achieve a specific result. Generally, a "project" comprises all effort authorized by a contract or other authorization document received from a customer, (e.g., a subcontract or inter-organizational transfer), but it may also be an internally defined and authorized effort. There may be multiple projects within a program. The terms "project" and "program" are often used interchangeably. *(NDIA II)*
See also *program*.

project labor agreement (PLA)
A pre-hire collective bargaining agreement with one or more labor organizations that establishes the terms and conditions of employment for a specific construction project and is an agreement described in 29 U.S.C. 158(f). *(FAR 22.502)*

project management
(1) The application of processes, methods, skills, and knowledge to achieve project objectives.
(2) A temporary endeavor to achieve planned objectives.

project manager
The individual with business responsibility for an entire project. This individual typically directs, controls, administers, and regulates a project developing or acquiring an information system. Also sometimes known as the *program manager* or "product manager." *(AIMD)*
See *program manager* (PM).

project plan
A document that describes the technical and management approach to be followed for a project. The plan typically describes the work to be done, the resources required, the methods to be used, the procedures to be followed, the schedules to be met, and the way that the project will be organized. *(AIMD)*

project team
A group of people, each with assigned responsibilities, who work closely together to achieve the shared objective of delivering, operating, or maintaining a deliverable under a given project. The project team may work together on tasks that are highly interdependent and may exercise a level of autonomy in managing their activities in pursuit of those objectives. The project team may vary in size from a single individual assigned part-time to a large organization assigned full-time. *(AIMD)*

projected average loss
The estimated long-term average loss per period for periods of comparable exposure to risk of loss. *(FAR 2.101)*

projected benefit cost method
(1) Any of the several actuarial cost methods that distribute the estimated total cost of all the employees' prospective benefits over a period of years, usually their working careers. *(FAR 31.001)*
(2) A modification of the accrued benefit cost method that considers projected compensation levels. *(FAR 31.001)*

promise
In the context of negotiable instruments, refers to a written undertaking to pay money signed by the person undertaking to pay. An acknowledgment of an obligation by the obligor is *not* a "promise" unless the obligor also undertakes to pay the obligation. *(UCC 3-103(a)(12))*
See also *obligation; obligor*; contrast with *order*.

promisee
The person to whom the manifestation of an intention to act or refrain from acting in a specified way is addressed. *(RSOC 2(3))*
See *promise*; see also *promisor*.

promisor
The person manifesting an intention to act or refrain from acting in a specified way, so made as to justify a promisee in understanding that a commitment has been made. *(RSOC 2(2))*
See *promise*; see also *promisee*.

promissory
Containing or consisting of a promise stipulating or engaging for a future act or course of conduct. *(BLD)*

promissory note
(1) A written promise from one party to another to pay a specific sum of money at a specific time to the bearer or other designated party. *(GKPT)*
(2) An instrument that evidences a promise to pay a monetary obligation—however, it *does not* evidence an

Pp

order to pay and does not contain an acknowledge-ment by a bank that the bank has received for deposit a sum of money or funds. *(UCC 9-102(a)(65))*

prompt payment
Pursuant to the requirements of the Prompt Payment Act (31 U.S.C. Chapter 39), the federal government has strict policies on making invoice payments to contrac-tors. Most payments are due the 30th day after the designated billing office has received a proper invoice from the contractor or the 30th day after government acceptance of supplies delivered or services per-formed by the contract, whichever is later. Agencies must pay an interest penalty, without request from the contractor, for late invoice payments or improperly taken discounts. *(GOAT)* (See also *FAR* Subpart 32.9.)
See *Prompt Payment Act* (PPA); see also *proper invoice*.

Prompt Payment Act (PPA)
A federal law (31 U.S.C. Chapter 39) requiring federal agencies to make timely payments, pay interest pen-alties when payments are late, and take discounts only when payments are made on or before the discount date. *(DGBCT)* (See also *FAR* Subpart 32.9.)
See also *prompt payment*.

prompt payment discount
See *discount for prompt payment*.

proper invoice
A bill or written request for payment that meets the mini-mum standards specified in the applicable "prompt pay-ment" clause and other terms and conditions contained in the contract for invoice submission. *(GOAT)*

property
All tangible property, both real and personal. *(FAR 45.101)*
See *personal property; real property*; see also *govern-ment property; government-furnished property (GFP)*

property administration
Upon receipt of U.S. federal government property, the contractor is responsible and accountable for the prop-erty as prescribed by the terms of the contract. This includes any government property in the possession or control of a subcontractor. Accordingly, the contrac-tor is required to establish and maintain a system to control, protect, and maintain all government property. *(NCMA-WS)*
See *property administrator; property control system*.

property administrator
In the context of U.S. federal government property, refers to an authorized representative of the con-tracting officer appointed in accordance with agency procedures, responsible for administering the contract requirements and obligations relating to govern-ment property in the possession of a contractor. *(FAR 45.101)*
See *government property*; see also *government-fur-nished property; property administration*.

property control system
Contractors' processes that adequately meet the prop-erty control requirements of the U.S. federal govern-ment's property clauses. *(NCMA-WS)*
See *property administration; property records*.

property interest
An interest in freedom from governmental deprivation of property and sources of financial gain without due process. In broad terms, this term refers to something (as in a job or benefit) to which one has a legitimate claim of entitlement and that cannot be taken away without due process, as distinguished from the unpro-tected object of a need, desire, or expectation. *(MW)*

property records
Concerning U.S. federal government property, refers to the records created and maintained by a contractor in support of its stewardship responsibilities for the man-agement of government property. *(FAR 45.101)*
See *government property; property administration; property control system*.

proposal
(1) An offer in response to a request for proposals. *(FAR 2.101)* (See also *FAR* Subpart 15.6.)
(2) Normally, a written offer by a seller describing its offering terms. Proposals may be issued in response to a specific request or may be made unilaterally when a seller feels there may be an interest in its offer (which is also known as an "unsolicited proposal"). *(HECA)*
See also *unsolicited proposal*.
(3) Any offer or other submission used as a basis for pricing a contract, contract modification, or termination settlement or for securing payments thereunder. *(FAR 31.001)*
See also *contract pricing proposal; offer*.
(4) A record authenticated by a secured party which includes the terms on which the secured party is willing to accept collateral in full or partial satisfaction of the

Pp

obligation it secures (pursuant to UCC 9-620, UCC 9-621, and UCC 9-622). *(UCC 9-102(a)(66))*

proposal center
A support organization dedicated to generating proposals and other responses to customer requests during the business acquisition cycle. *(DGBCT)*

proposal evaluation
(1) An assessment of both the proposal and the offeror's ability (as conveyed by the proposal) to successfully accomplish the prospective contract. An agency shall evaluate competitive proposals solely on the factors specified in the solicitation. Evaluations may be conducted using any rating method or combination of methods, including color or adjectival ratings, numerical weights, and ordinal rankings. The relative strengths, deficiencies, significant weaknesses, and risks supporting proposal evaluation shall be documented in the contract file. *(FAR 15.305(a))*
(2) It is the assessment of a proposal to determine the offeror's ability to successfully perform the prospective contract. It is also used to determine a fair and reasonable price for the contract requirement. *(DAAT-A)*

proposal management plan
The document that describes the roles, responsibilities, tasks, and deadlines before writers start developing proposal sections, volumes, and ultimately the complete proposal. *(DGBCT)*

proposal manager
The person responsible for proposal development, including maintaining schedules; coordinating input, reviews, and strategy implementation; resolving internal problems; and providing leadership. *(DGBCT)*

proposal modification
A change made to a proposal before the solicitation closing date and time, or made in response to an amendment, or made to correct a mistake at any time before award. *(FAR 15.001)*

proposal planning
The process for defining a proposal effort while sales efforts continue. *(DGBCT)*

proposal preparation
Activities and events required to submit an offer or quotation, usually in response to a customer request. *(DGBCT)*

proposal response
The process through which an organization analyzes customer requirements, defines a solution, and delivers a proposal to a given customer. *(DGBCT)*

proposal revision
A change to a proposal made after the solicitation closing date, at the request of or as allowed by a contracting officer, as the result of negotiations. *(FAR 15.001)*

proposal specialist
A member of the proposal team who understands and often prepares compliance checklists, outlines, cross-reference matrices, work breakdown structures (WBS), WBS dictionaries, and schedules. *(DGBCT)*

proposal strategy
A plan to write a persuasive, winning proposal; a subset of the capture strategy. *(DGBCT)*

proprietary data
A broad term used to describe data belonging to the contractor. These data could be intellectual property, financial data, etc. This is generally a term used in the submission of a proposal to protect the contractor's sensitive information from disclosure and is not a category of rights applicable to technical data under all contracts. *(DAAT)*
See also *proprietary information*.

proprietary information
(1) Material and information relating to or associated with a company's products, business, or activities, including but not limited to financial information, data or statements, trade secrets, product research and development, existing and future product designs and performance specifications, marketing plans or techniques, schematics, client lists, computer programs, processes, and know-how that has been clearly identified and properly marked by the company as proprietary information, trade secrets, or company confidential information. The information must have been developed by the company and not be available to the federal government or to the public without restriction from another source. *(CNSSI 4009)*
(2) Data owned by a contractor that is not publicly available, and which may be used only with the permission of the owner. *(CMBOK)*
See also *nondisclosure agreement (NDA)*.

proprietary information agreement
See *nondisclosure agreement (NDA)*.

Pp

prospective pricing

A pricing decision made in advance of performance, based on analysis of comparative prices, cost estimates, past costs, or combinations of such considerations. *(OPM)*

protected purchaser

In the case of a security, means a purchaser of a certificated or uncertificated security, or of an interest therein, who:

- Gives value,
- Does not have notice of any adverse claim to the security, and
- Obtains control of the certificated or uncertificated security.

(UCC 8-303(a))

See *security*; see also *adverse claim; certificated security; notice of an adverse claim; uncertificated security*.

protected veteran

A veteran who is protected under the nondiscrimination and affirmative action provisions of 38 U.S.C. 4212. This term specifically includes the following terms: "disabled veteran," "recently separated veteran," "active duty wartime or campaign badge veteran," and "armed forces service medal veteran." *(FAR 22.1301)*

protest

A written objection by an interested party to any of the following:

- A solicitation or other request by a federal agency for offers for a contract for the procurement of property or services;
- The cancellation of such a solicitation or other request;
- An award or proposed award of a federal agency procurement contract (pursuant to 31 U.S.C. Chapter 35, Subchapter V);
- A termination or cancellation of such an award of a contract, if the written objection contains an allegation that the termination or cancellation is based in whole or in part on improprieties concerning the award of the contract; or
- The conversion of a function that is being performed by U.S. federal employees to private-sector performance.

(41 U.S.C. 2101(6); 31 U.S.C. 3551(1); FAR 33.101)

See *interested party; protest venue*; see also *post-award protest issues; pre-award protest issues*.

protest venue

Protests may be filed with:

- The U.S. federal agency (see Executive Order 12979, "Agency Procurement Protests");
- The U.S. Government Accountability Office (see 4 CFR Part 21, "GAO Bid Protest Regulations"); or
- The U.S. Court of Federal Claims (see www.U.S.C.fc.U.S.C.ourts.gov/rules-and-forms).

U.S. District Courts do not have any bid protest jurisdiction. *(FAR 33.101; FAR 33.103; FAR 33.105)*

protester

An interested party to a federal government solicitation for, award of, or proposed award of (or cancellation or termination of a solicitation, award, or proposed award) a contract who files a protest with the appropriate protest venue.

See *interested party; protest; protest venue*; see also *post-award protest issues; pre-award protest issues*.

prove

With respect to a fact, to meet the burden of establishing the fact. *(UCC 3-103(a)(13))*

See also *burden of establishing*.

provide

Concerning property management, this term means to furnish, as in government-furnished property, or to acquire, as in contractor-acquired property. *(FAR 45.101)*

provision

See *solicitation provision*.

provisioned item

A line item in the contract for which firm requirements (quantity or type) are not known at the time of contract preparation. A line item is therefore established for generic types of supplies or services (e.g., spare and repair parts, support equipment, engineering support, government property repair, and data). Requirements for these line items are initiated by a requisition. *(HCS)*

provisioning

The process of determining or meeting the range and quantity of items required to support and maintain or function for a set period of time. *(OPM)*

See also *initial provisioning*.

prudent businessperson concept

A phrase used as a measure of reasonableness in assessing an offer, counter-offer, or other action taken

Pp

under a contract. It relates to making a procurement decision based on sound fiduciary or business principles. *(P&L II)*

public building/public work
(1) A building or work, the construction, prosecution, completion, or repair of which is carried on directly or indirectly by authority of, or with funds of, a federal agency to serve the interest of the general public, regardless of whether title thereof is in a federal agency. *(FAR 22.401)*
(2) Includes, without limitation, bridges, dams, plants, highways, parkways, streets, subways, tunnels, sewers, mains, power lines, pumping stations, heavy generators, railways, airports, terminals, docks, piers, wharves, ways, lighthouses, buoys, jetties, breakwaters, levees, and canals, and the construction, alteration, maintenance, or repair of such buildings and works. *(FAR 25.601)*

public-finance transaction
A secured transaction in connection with which:
* Debt securities are issued;
* All or a portion of the securities issued have an initial stated maturity of at least 20 years; and
* The debtor, obligor, secured party, account debtor or other person obligated on collateral, assignor or assignee of a secured obligation, or assignor or assignee of a security interest is a U.S. state or a governmental unit of a U.S. state.
(UCC 9-102(a)(67))

public information
In the context of federal government information management, this term refers to any information, regardless of form or format, that an agency discloses, disseminates, or makes available to the public. *(44 U.S.C. 3502(12))*

public interest
(1) The general welfare and rights of the public that are to be recognized, protected, and advanced. *(MW)*
(2) A specific public benefit or stake in something (e.g., the public interest in controlling crime). *(MW)*

Public Law (Pub. L)
A law that applies to the public at large, as opposed to a private law, which concerns private individual rights, duties, and liabilities. *(BLD)*

Public Law 85-804
A federal law granting the president of the United States the authority to authorize any department or

agency of the government which exercises functions in connection with the national defense to enter into contracts or into amendments or modifications of existing contracts, and to make advance payments thereon, without regard to other provisions of law relating to the making, performance, amendment, or modification of contracts, whenever he or she deems that such action would facilitate the national defense. This authority is granted only during a national emergency, as declared by Congress or the president, and with certain limitations, as specified in the statute. *(50 U.S.C. 1431)*
See *extraordinary contractual action*.

public organic record
A record that is available to the public for inspection and is:
* A record consisting of the record initially filed with or issued by a U.S. state or the United States to form or organize an organization and any record filed with or issued by the U.S. state or the United States which amends or restates the initial record;
* An organic record of a business trust consisting of the record initially filed with a U.S. state and any record filed with the state which amends or restates the initial record, if a statute of the state governing business trusts requires that the record be filed with the state; or
* A record consisting of legislation enacted by Congress or the legislature of a U.S. state which forms or organizes an organization, any record amending the legislation, and any record filed with or issued by the U.S. state or the United States which amends or restates the name of the organization.
(UCC 9-102(a)(68))

public-private partnership (PPP)
(1) An agreement or contractual relationship between a public agency and a private sector entity. Through this agreement, the skills and assets of each sector are shared in delivering a service or facility for the use of the general public. *(DGBCT)*
(2) In the context of government property management, this term refers to any partnership or working relationship between a federal agency and a corporation, individual, or nonprofit organization for the purpose of financing, constructing, operating, managing, or maintaining one or more federal real property assets. *(40 U.S.C. 621(7))*
(3) In the context of PPPs with the Department of Defense, DODI 4151.21 qualifies a public private partnership as a "cooperative arrangement between

Pp

an organic product support provider and one or more private sector entities to perform defense-related work, use DOD facilities and equipment, or both. Other government organizations, such as program offices, inventory control points, and sustainment commands, may be parties to such agreements." *(DAAT-A)*

public relations
All functions and activities dedicated to maintaining, protecting, and enhancing the image of a concern or its products, or maintaining or promoting reciprocal understanding and favorable relations with the public at large or any segment of the public. This term includes activities associated with areas such as advertising, customer relations, etc. *(FAR 31.205-1)*
See also *public relations and advertising costs.*

public relations and advertising costs
Include the costs of media time and space, purchased services performed by outside organizations, as well as the applicable portion of salaries, travel, and fringe benefits of employees engaged in the functions and activities of public relations and advertising. *(FAR 31.205-1(c))*
See *public relations*.

public sector
The part of an economy which is controlled or owned by the government. *(MW)*
Contrast with *private sector*.

public-work contract
Any contract for a fixed improvement or for any other project, fixed or not, for the public use of the United States or its allies, involving construction, alteration, removal, or repair, including projects or operations under service contracts and projects in connection with the national defense or with war activities, dredging, harbor improvements, dams, roadways, and housing, as well as preparatory and ancillary work in connection therewith at the site or on the project. *(FAR 28.305(a))*

pull system
A system for replenishing distribution center inventories where the inventory decisions are made at the distribution center and "pulled" from the manufacturing plant. This is decentralized decision-making. *(DGBCT)*
See *push system*.

punitive damages
In the context of judicial remedies, these are designed to punish the guilty party and are applicable only if the defendant is guilty of fraud, malice, or oppression. Punitive damages may not be applicable in breach of contract cases. *(CMBOK)*

purchase
Taking by sale, lease, discount, negotiation, mortgage, pledge, lien, security interest, issue or reissue, gift, or any other voluntary transaction creating an interest in property or goods. *(UCC 1-201(29); UCC 2A-103(v))*

purchase card (P card)
See *"government purchase card* (GPC; P card).

purchase description
(1) A description of the essential physical characteristics and functions required to meet the buyer's minimum needs. *(DGBCT)*
(2) A simplified specification that is used when an item is purchased infrequently. *(GSFC)*

purchase-money collateral
Goods or software that secures a purchase-money obligation incurred with respect to that collateral. *(UCC 9-103(a)(1))*
See *purchase-money obligation*; see also *purchase-money security interest in goods; purchase-money security interest in software*.

purchase-money lease
A lease is a "purchase-money lease" unless the lessee has possession or use of the goods or the right to possession or use of the goods before the lease agreement is enforceable. *(UCC 2A-309(1)(c))*

purchase-money obligation
An obligation of an obligor incurred as all or part of the price of the collateral or for value given to enable the debtor to acquire rights in or the use of the collateral if the value is in fact so used. *(UCC 9-103(a)(2))*

purchase-money security interest
(1) The security interest held by the seller of collateral to secure payment of all or part of the price. (MW)
See *security interest*.
(2) The security interest of a person that gives value to a debtor so that the debtor may acquire rights in or the use of collateral. *(MW)*

purchase-money security interest in goods
A security interest in goods is a "purchase-money secu-

Pp

rity interest":
- To the extent that the goods are purchase-money collateral with respect to that security interest;
- If the security interest is in inventory that is or was purchase-money collateral, also to the extent that the security interest secures a purchase-money obligation incurred with respect to other inventory in which the secured party holds or held a purchase-money security interest; and
- Also to the extent that the security interest secures a purchase-money obligation incurred with respect to software in which the secured party holds or held a purchase-money security interest.

(UCC 9-103(b))
See *purchase-money security interest*; see also *purchase-money collateral; purchase-money security interest in software*.

purchase-money security interest in software
A security interest in software is a "purchase-money security interest" to the extent that the security interest also secures a purchase-money obligation incurred with respect to goods in which the secured party holds or held a purchase-money security interest if:
- The debtor acquired its interest in the software in an integrated transaction in which it acquired an interest in the goods, and
- The debtor acquired its interest in the software for the principal purpose of using the software in the goods.

(UCC 9-103(c))
See *purchase-money security interest*; see also *purchase-money obligation; purchase-money security interest in goods*.

purchase order (PO)
(1) A document, signed by a contracting officer and addressed to a contractor, requesting the future delivery of supplies, equipment, or material, or the future performance of nonpersonal services in accordance with certain terms in exchange for a promise by the government to pay the stated price. Considered an offer to contract rather than an acceptance of contract. *(OPM)* (See also *FAR* 13.302.)
See also *simplified acquisition procedures*.
(2) The first official offer issued by a commercial buyer to a seller, indicating quantities and agreed prices for products and services.
(3) When issued by the federal government, means an offer by the government to buy supplies or services, including construction and research and development,

upon specified terms and conditions, using simplified acquisition procedures. *(FAR 2.101)*

purchase request
An exact description of a product or service used in invitations for bids, requests for proposals, and contracts to tell prospective suppliers precisely what is required. Also known as a *purchase description*. **(OPM)**

purchase requisition
A written or computerized request to the purchasing department for a procurement of goods or services from suppliers. *(GKPT)*

purchaser
A person that takes by purchase. *(UCC 1-201(30))*
See *purchase.*

purchasing
(1) The process of buying supplies and services utilizing a variety of contractual arrangements. *(P&L I)*
(2) In a U.S. federal government context, the process of buying readily available supplies and services utilizing procedures such as purchase orders, blanket purchase agreements, and pre-negotiated schedules. *(P&L I)*

pursuit
Acquisition project selected by the organization to be won; typically selected based on assessing newly identified leads to determine the organization's interest and whether they are winnable. *(DGBCT)*

pursuit criteria
Basis for determining whether a given opportunity aligns with the organization's goals for new business capture. *(DGBCT)*

pursuit decision
Making an informed decision about the opportunity to pursue effectively and to allocate appropriate resources for capture planning. *(DGBCT)*

pursuit manager
Person responsible for managing a pursuit from bid decision to contract award. *(DGBCT)*
See *capture manager*.

pursuit plan
Documented analysis, strategies, and actions initiated following the pursuit decision that details customer issues, considerations relating to competitor and internal

positioning, approaches to be implemented, and management tasks to be implemented to guide the capture of a particular opportunity. *(DGBCT)*
See *capture plan*.

push system

A system for replenishing distribution center inventories where the inventory decisions are made at the manufacturing location. The stock is then "pushed" out to the distribution centers. This is centralized decision-making. *(DGBCT)*
See *pull system*.

quadrennial defense review (QDR)

The secretary of defense is required to conduct a quadrennial defense review (QDR) and to submit a report on the QDR to Congress every four years. The QDR articulates a national defense strategy consistent with the most recent national security strategy by defining force structure, modernization plans, and a budget plan allowing the military to successfully execute the full range of missions within that strategy. *(DISCS)*

qualification

In federal government acquisition, refers to a process in advance of, and independent from, an acquisition by which a manufacturer's capabilities or a manufacturer's or distributor's products are examined, tested, and approved to be in conformance with specification requirements, and subsequent approval for inclusion of products in an electronic qualified products list or manufacturers in an electronic qualified manufacturers list. *(DODM 4120.24)*
See also *product; qualified manufacturer; qualified manufacturers list* (QML); *qualified product; qualified products list* (QPL).

qualification requirement

A buyer requirement for testing or other quality assurance demonstration that must be completed before award of a contract. *(FAR 2.101)*

qualifications-based selection (QBS)

Establishes the procurement process by which architects and engineers are selected for design contracts with U.S. federal government design and construction agencies. *(DGBCT)*

qualified anti-terrorism technology (QATT)

Any technology designed, developed, modified, procured, or sold for the purpose of preventing, detecting, identifying, or deterring acts of terrorism or limiting the harm such acts might otherwise cause, for which a SAFETY Act designation has been issued. Notably, for purposes of defining a QATT, "technology" means any product, equipment, service (including support services), device, or technology (including information technology) or any combination of the foregoing. Design services, consulting services, engineering services, software development services, software integration services, threat assessments, vulnerability studies, and other analyses relevant to homeland security may also be deemed a "technology." *(FAR 50.201)*
See *act of terrorism*; see also *block certification; block designation*.

qualified bidders list (QBL)

A list of bidders who have had their products examined and tested and who have satisfied all applicable qualification requirements for that product or have otherwise satisfied all applicable qualification requirements. *(FAR 9.201)*

qualified disabled veteran

A disabled veteran who has the ability to perform the essential functions of the employment positions with or without reasonable accommodation. *(FAR 22.1301)*
See *disabled veteran*.

qualified manufacturer

A manufacturer who has had its products examined and tested and who has satisfied all applicable qualification requirements for said products. *(FAR 9.201)*

qualified manufacturers list (QML)

In general, a list of manufacturers who have had their products examined and tested and who have satisfied all applicable qualification requirements for that product. *(FAR 9.201)*

qualified product

A product that has been examined and tested for compliance with specification requirements and approved for inclusion in a qualified products list. *(FAR 2.101)*
See also *product; qualified products list* (QPL).

Qq

qualified products list (QPL)

In general, a list of products that have been examined, tested, and have satisfied all applicable qualification requirements. *(FAR 2.101)*

quality

The composite of all attributes or characteristics, including performance, that satisfies a user's needs. *(QAC)*

quality assurance (QA)

A planned and systematic pattern of all actions necessary to provide confidence that adequate technical requirements are established; products and services conform to established laws, regulations, policy, and technical requirements; and satisfactory performance is achieved. *(AFIT)*

quality assurance surveillance plan (QASP)

(1) The key government-developed surveillance process document that is applied to Performance-Based Service Contracting (PBSC). The QASP is used for managing contractor performance assessment by ensuring that systematic quality assurance methods validate that contractor quality control efforts are timely, effective, and are delivering the results specified in the contract or task order. The QASP directly corresponds to the performance objectives and standards (i.e., quality, quantity, timeliness) specified in the Performance Work Statement (PWS). It provides specific details on how the government will survey, observe, test, sample, evaluate, and document contractor performance results to determine if the contractor has met the required standards for each objective in the PWS. *(DAAT-A)*
See also *performance-based acquisition* (PBA); *performance-based contract*.
(2) The method by which federal government employees will supervise in-house or contract performance to ensure that the standards of the performance work statement are met within the costs bid. *(OMB A-76)*

quality control (QC)

The process of measuring quality performance, comparing it with the standard, and acting on the difference. *(DGCQI)*

quantity discount

Voluntary price reduction offered by a firm to customers acquiring quantities of a product. Unit prices normally decline as volume increases, primarily because fixed costs are being divided by an increasing number of units. *(DGBCT)*
See *"trade discount."*

quantity variance

The standard price for a given resource, multiplied by the difference between the actual quantity used and the total standard quantity allowed for the number of good units produced. *(NCMA-CA)*

quasi contract

Obligations imposed by law to prevent the unjust enrichment of one person at another's expense. Sometimes called "implied in law contract." *(DGBCT)*

qui tam action

An action brought by an informer (also called a "whistleblower"). Part of the penalty goes to any person who brings such action and the remainder to the state or some other suit (e.g., the U.S. federal government). It is called a *"qui tam* action" because the plaintiff states that he or she sues for the state as well as for him- or herself. *(BLD)*

quick closeout

A faster method of completing the closeout process for a cost-reimbursement contract. Final indirect rates are negotiated on a contract basis, rather than by fiscal year as in regular closeout methods. Quick closeout can only be done in limited circumstances, such as if the contract is physically complete, the amount of unsettled indirect costs to be allocated to the contract is relatively insignificant, and an agreement can be reached on a reasonable estimate for allocable dollars. *(NCMA-WS)*
See *closeout*.

quotation

A statement of price, either written or verbal, which may include, among other things, a description of the product or service; the terms of sale, delivery, or period of performance; and payment. Such statements are usually issued by sellers at the request of potential buyers. In federal government procurement, quotations do not constitute an offer that can be accepted to form the basis of a binding contract. Rather, quotations are solicited to obtain market information for planning purposes. *(P&L II)*

Rr

R

Rainbow Series

This collection of computer security standards and guidelines is now considered "obsolete." First published by the DOD's Computer Security Center then by the National Computer Security Center during the 1980s and 1990s, the name "rainbow" comes from the varied colors in which the series was bound. Specific to the Department of Defense were CSC-STD-001-83 (i.e., Orange Book), CSC-STD-002-85 (i.e., Green Book), CSC-STD-003-85 (i.e., Light Yellow Book), and CSC-STD-004-85 (i.e., Yellow Book II). The National Institute of Standards and Technology, a part of the Department of Commerce, through its Computer Security Resource Center (CSRC) provides links to this collection "for historical purposes only." (See https://csrc.gov/publications.)
See *Federal Information Processing Standard* (FIPS).

rapid acquisition

A streamlined and tightly integrated iterative acquisition approach, acting upon validated urgent or emergent capability requirements, to:

- Conduct analysis and evaluate alternatives and identify preferred solutions;
- Develop and approve acquisition documents;
- Contract using all available statutory and regulatory authorities and waivers and deviations of such, as appropriate to the situation;
- Identify and minimize technical development, integration, and manufacturing risks; and
- Rapidly produce and deliver required capabilities. *(CJCSI 3170.011)*

See also *capability; capability requirement*.

rapidly report

In the context of safeguarding covered defense information and cyber incident reporting in relation to U.S. federal government contracts, refers to the requirement to report any cyber incident within 72 hours of discovery. *(DFARS 204.7301)*

rate

May include rate schedules, riders, rules, terms and conditions of service, and other tariff and service charges (e.g., facilities use charges). *(FAR 41.101)*

rate variance

The difference between actual wages paid and the standard wage rate, multiplied by the total actual hours of direct labor used. *(NCMA-CA)*
See *price variance*.

rated order

A prime contract, a subcontract, or a purchase order in support of an approved program issued in accordance with the provisions of the Defense Priorities and Allocations System (DPAS) Regulation (15 CFR part 700). *(FAR 11.601)*

ratification

(1) In general, the confirmation of a previous act done either by the party itself or by another, as confirmation of a voidable act; the affirmance by a person of a prior act that did not bind the person, but which was done or professedly done on his or her account, whereby the act, as to some or all persons, is given the effect as if originally authorized by the person. *(BLD)*
(2) The act of approving an unauthorized commitment by an official who has the authority to do so. *(FAR 1.602-3(a))*
(3) The formal action of the president of the United States in giving effect to a treaty that has been approved by the Senate. The treaty is then officially proclaimed and becomes legally enforceable. *(DISCS)*

rating/scoring system

A method of rating/scoring an evaluation factor in relationship to its corresponding standard such as numerical, adjective, color, etc. The source selection plan establishes the factors against which all proposals will be evaluated, the weights to be assigned to each factor, and the applicable rating system. A rating system may be based on colors, points, or adjectives. An example of a color-based rating system is as follows: blue = exceptional, green = acceptable, yellow = marginal, and red = unacceptable. An example of an adjective-based rating system is "excellent," "very good," "good," "fair," and "poor." (Also called a "scoring system.") *(CMBOK)*

real growth

The growth (decline) of a budget after considering inflation. For example, a $10,000 budget that goes to $11,000 is only five percent real growth if inflation for the covered period is five percent; with no inflation, it would be 10 percent growth. (Also known as "decline.") *(DLA)*

Rr

real property

(1) Any interest in land, together with the improvements, structures, and fixtures located thereon (including prefabricated movable structures, such as Butler-type storage warehouses and Quonset huts, and house trailers with or without undercarriages), and appurtenances thereto, under the control of any federal agency. For exceptions, see the *Federal Property Management Regulation*. *(CMBOK)*
(2) In English Common Law, real property, real estate, realty, or immovable property is any subset of land that has been legally defined and the improvements to it made by human efforts: any buildings, machinery, wells, dams, ponds, mines, canals, roads, various property rights, etc. *(DGBCT)*

reapportionment

A revision of an annual apportionment of funds either upwards or downwards, accomplished within the fiscal year for which the original apportionment applied. *(DISCS)*
See **apportionment**.

reappropriation

The congressional carrying over of funds unused in one year to the following year. For example, in the case of appropriated U.S. federal government funds, any funds which at the end of the fiscal year are not reserved or obligated are customarily made available by the Congress for use in the subsequent fiscal year. *(DISCS)*
See **appropriation**.

reasonable compensation

With respect to professional and other technical services, a payment in an amount that is consistent with the amount normally paid for such services in the private sector. *(FAR 3.801)*

reasonable cost

(1) A cost is "reasonable" if, in its nature and amount, it does not exceed that which would be incurred by a prudent person in the conduct of competitive business. *(FAR 31.201-3(a))*
(2) A business decision reached jointly by a buyer and seller; a product of judgment influenced by bargaining strength and economic realities dictated by the marketplace. *(DAAT)*

reasonable or competitive prices

The expected range of prices resulting from experience obtained through the competitive free enterprise system for like or similar activities. Determinations are to be made by the contracting officer. *(OMB A-76)*

rebate

A legitimate refund to a purchasing organization in consideration for the purchase of a stipulated quantity or dollar volume within a specified time frame. *(GKPT)*

receiving report

Written evidence that indicates buyer acceptance of supplies delivered or services performed. Receiving reports for U.S. federal government contracts must meet the requirements of FAR 32.905(c). *(FAR 2.101)*
(See also *FAR* Subpart 46.6.)

recency

As it pertains to past performance information, refers to a measure of the time that has elapsed since the past performance reference occurred. Recency is generally expressed as a time period during which past performance references are considered relevant. *(SSP)*
See also *"relevancy"*

recently separated veteran

Any veteran during the three-year period beginning on the date of such veteran's discharge or release from active duty in the U.S. military, ground, naval, or air service. *(FAR 22.1301)*

reciprocal defense procurement

Procurement actions which are implemented under memoranda of understanding/memoranda of agreement between the United States and various participating nations whereby the participants agree to effect complementary acquisitions of defense articles from each other's country. *(DISCS)*
See also *defense article; memorandum of agreement* (MOA)/*memorandum of understanding* (MOU).

reciprocity

An agreement or understanding that one company will buy goods or services from a supplier in exchange for the supplier's purchase of equipment, programs, or services from that company. *(BOE)*

recognizance

An acknowledgment in court by a person that he or she will perform some specified obligation or pay a certain sum if he or she fails to perform (e.g., personal recognizance bond). *(DGBCT)*

reconditioned

Restored to the original normal operating condition by readjustments and material replacement. *(FAR 11.001)*

Rr

record

Information that is inscribed on a tangible medium or that is stored in an electronic or other medium and is retrievable in perceivable form. *(UCC 1-201(31); UCC 5-102(a)(14); UCC 7-102(a)(10))*

record drawings

Drawings submitted by a contractor or subcontractor at any tier to show the construction of a particular structure or work as actually completed under the contract. *(FAR 36.102)*

record-keeping requirement

In the context of federal government information management, this term refers to a requirement imposed by or for an agency on persons to maintain specified records, including a requirement to—

- Retain such records;
- Notify third parties, the federal government, or the public of the existence of such records;
- Disclose such records to third parties, the federal government, or the public; or
- Report to third parties, the federal government, or the public regarding such records.

(44 U.S.C. 3502(13))

record retention

The storage of records no longer active. Government contract records are to be retained in accordance with *Federal Acquisition Regulation* 4.805, Table 4-1. *(FAR 4.805(a))*
See *closeout*.

record of bids

See *abstract of bids*.

records

(1) All books, papers, maps, photographs, machine-readable materials, or other documentary materials, regardless of physical form or characteristics, made or received by an agency of the government under federal law or in connection with the transaction of public business and preserved or appropriate for preservation by that agency or its legitimate successor as evidence of the organization, functions, policies, decisions, procedures, operations, or other activities of the government or because of the informational value of the data in them. Library and museum material made or acquired and preserved solely for reference or exhibition purposes, extra copies of documents preserved for only convenience of reference, and stocks of publications and of processed documents are not included. *(OMB A-130)*

(2) In the case of an information system, the recordings (automated and/or manual) of evidence of activities performed or results achieved (e.g., forms, reports, test results), which serve as a basis for verifying that the organization and the information system are performing as intended. *(NIST SP 800-171)*

(3) Units of related data fields—i.e., groups of data fields that can be accessed by a program and that contain the complete set of information on particular items. *(NIST SP 800-171)*

(4) Pertaining to an individual, means any item, collection, or grouping of information about an individual that is maintained by a federal agency, including, but not limited to, education, financial transactions, medical history, and criminal or employment history, and that contains the individual's name, or the identifying number, symbol, or other identifying particular assigned to the individual, such as a fingerprint, voiceprint, or photograph. *(FAR 24.101)*
See also *system of records on individuals*.

records management

The planning, controlling, directing, organizing, training, promoting, and other managerial activities involved with respect to records creation, records maintenance and use, and records disposition in order to achieve adequate and proper documentation of the policies and transactions of the federal government and effective and economical management of agency operations. *(OMB A-130)*

recoupment

The recovery by the federal government of government-funded nonrecurring costs from contractors that sell, lease, or license the resulting products or technology to buyers other than the federal government. *(FAR 35.001)*

recoverable item

An item that is normally not consumed in use and is subject to return for repair or disposal. *(DISCS)*
See also *reparable item*.

recovered material

(1) Waste materials and byproducts recovered or diverted from solid waste. This term does not include those materials and byproducts generated from, and commonly reused within, an original manufacturing process. *(FAR 2.101)*

Rr

See also *Environmental Protection Agency* (EPA)-*designated item*.

(2) For paper and paper products, defined by the U.S. Environmental Protection Agency as "recovered fiber," means the following materials:

- Postconsumer fiber; or
- Manufacturing wastes such as:
  - Dry paper and paperboard waste generated after completion of the papermaking process (that is, those manufacturing operations up to and including the cutting and trimming of the paper machine reel into smaller rolls or rough sheets) including; envelope cuttings, bindery trimmings, and other paper and paperboard waste resulting from printing, cutting, forming, and other converting operations; bag, box, and carton manufacturing wastes; and butt rolls, mill wrappers, and rejected unused stock; and
  - Repulped finished paper and paperboard from obsolete inventories of paper and paperboard manufacturers, merchants, wholesalers, dealers, printers, converters, or others.

(FAR 11.301)

Recovery Act
See *American Recovery and Reinvestment Act of 2009 (ARRA)*

Recovery Act–designated country
As mandated by Section 1605 in Division A of the American Recovery and Reinvestment Act of 2009 (*Pub. L. 111-5*) with regard to manufactured construction material and certain exceptions to the Buy American statute (41 U.S.C. Chapter 83) with regard to unmanufactured construction materials, this term refers to a World Trade Organization Government Procurement Agreement country, a free trade agreement country, or a least-developed country. *(FAR 25.601)*
See *manufactured construction material; unmanufactured construction material*; see also *free trade agreement country; least-developed country; World Trade Organization Government Procurement Agreement (WTO GPA) country*.

recovery audit
See *payment recapture audit* (PRA).

recruiting and training agency
Any person who refers workers to any contractor or provides or supervises apprenticeship or training for employment by any contractor. *(FAR 22.801)*

recruitment costs
This term refers to any of the following:

- Costs of help-wanted advertising (except if such advertising does not describe specific positions or classes of positions or includes material that not relevant for recruitment purposes, such as extensive illustrations or descriptions of the company's products or capabilities);
- Costs of operating an employment office needed to secure and maintain an adequate labor force;
- Costs of operating an aptitude and educational testing program;
- Travel costs of employees engaged in recruiting personnel;
- Travel costs of applicants for interviews; and
- Costs for employment agencies, not in excess of standard commercial rates.

(FAR 31.205-34)

recurring commercial activity
An activity that is required by the government on a consistent and long-term basis. This definition does not imply an hourly, daily, monthly, or annual requirement, but must, in a general sense, be repetitive in nature, wherein the expected workload can be reasonably estimated. *(OMB A-76)*

recurring costs
Costs that vary with the quantity being produced, such as labor and materials. *(FAR 17.103)*

recurring services contract
A contract for recurring services–i.e., those services that are required to be performed regularly or periodically throughout the course of a contract, and throughout the course of the succeeding or follow-on contract(s). Examples of recurring services include, but are not limited to, custodial or janitorial services; window washing; laundry; food services; guard or other protective services; landscaping and groundskeeping services; and inspection, maintenance, and repair of fixed equipment such as elevators, air conditioning, and heating systems. *(GOAT)*
Contrast with *nonrecurring maintenance contract*.

reduced payment
In the case of a subcontract, payment that is for less than the amount agreed upon in a subcontract in accordance with its terms and conditions, for supplies and services for which the U.S. federal government has paid the prime contractor. *(FAR 19.701)*

Rr

refined precious metal

Recovered silver, gold, platinum, palladium, iridium, rhodium, or ruthenium, in bullion, granulation, or sponge form, which has been purified to at least .999 percentage of fineness. *(DFARS 208.7301)*
See *precious metal*.

registered form

As applied to a certificated security, a form in which:

- The security certificate specifies a person entitled to the security, and
- A transfer of the security may be registered upon books maintained for that purpose by or on behalf of the issuer, or the security certificate so states.

(UCC 8-102(a)(13))
See *security*; see also *certificated security; issuer; security certificate*.

registered in the System for Award Management (SAM) database

A phrase that means:

- The contractor has entered all mandatory information, including the unique entity identifier and the electronic funds transfer indicator (if applicable), the Commercial and Government Entity (CAGE) code, as well as data required by the Federal Funding Accountability and Transparency Act of 2006, into the SAM database;
- The contractor has completed the Core, Assertions, Representations and Certifications, and Points of Contact sections of the registration in the SAM database;
- The U.S. federal government has validated all mandatory data fields, to include validation of the Taxpayer Identification Number (TIN) with the U.S. Internal Revenue Service (IRS) (with consent from the contractor to provide the TIN validation to the government as a part of the SAM registration process); and
- The government has marked the record "active."

(FAR 2.101)

registered organization

An organization organized solely under the law of a single U.S. state or the United States by the filing of a public organic record with, the issuance of a public organic record by, or the enactment of legislation by the state or the United States. This term includes a business trust that is formed or organized under the law of a single U.S. state if a statute of the state governing business trusts requires that the business trust's organic record be filed with the state. *(UCC 9-102(a)(71))*
See also *public organic record*.

regular dealer

A person that owns, operates, or maintains a store, warehouse, or other establishment in which the materials, supplies, articles, or equipment of the general character described by the specifications and required under the contract are bought, kept in stock, and sold to the public in the usual course of business. *(DGBCT)*

reimbursable expenditure

An expenditure made for another agency, fund, appropriation, or for a private individual, firm, or corporation, which subsequently will be recovered. *(DISCS)*

reimbursements

Amounts received by an activity for the cost of material, work, or services furnished to others, for credit to an appropriation or their fund account. *(DISCS)*

reinsurance

A transaction which provides that a surety, for a consideration, agrees to indemnify another surety against loss which the latter may sustain under a bond which it has issued. *(FAR 28.001)*

rejection

(1) An offeree's power of acceptance is terminated by his or her "rejection" of the offer, unless the offeror has manifested a contrary intention. *(RSOC 38(1))*
(2) A manifestation of intention not to accept an offer is "rejection" unless the offeree manifests an intention to take it under further advisement. *(RSOC 38(2))*

released value

The assigned value of the cargo for reimbursement purposes, not necessarily the actual value of the cargo. Released value may be more or less than the actual value of the cargo. The released value is the maximum amount that can be recovered by a party in the event of loss or damage for the shipments of freight and household goods. Also known as *declared value*. *(FAR 47.001)*

relevancy

As it pertains to past performance information, refers to a measure of the extent of similarity between the service/support effort, complexity, dollar value, contract type, and subcontract/teaming or other comparable attributes of past performance examples and the source solicitation requirements; and a measure of the

Rr

likelihood that the past performance is an indicator of future performance. *(SSP)*

reliability
(1) The duration or probability of failure-free performance under stated conditions. *(DOD-MMH)*
(2) The ability of a system and its parts to perform its mission without failure, degradation, or demand on the support system. *(DAAT)*
See *mean time between failure* and *"mean time between maintenance.*
(3) A fundamental characteristic of an item of material expressed as the probability that it will perform its intended function for a specified period of time under stated conditions. *(DISCS)*

reliance damages
Monetary damages, such as compensation for expenses or losses, that place the aggrieved party in the same position it was in before signing the contract. *(CMBOK)*
See also *reliance interest*.

reliance interest
In the context of judicial remedies, the interest of a party to a breached contract in being reimbursed for loss (i.e., detriments suffered or expenses incurred) caused by reliance on the contract by being put in as good a position as he or she would have been in had the contract not been made. *(RSOC 344(b); MW)*
See *reliance damages*; see also *expectation interest; restitution interest*.

relocation costs
Costs incident to the permanent change of assigned work location (for a period of 12 months or more) of an existing employee or upon recruitment of a new employee. *(FAR 31.205-35(a))*
See also *rental costs*.

remaining duration (RD)
The number of workdays forecasted to complete an in-process or "unstarted" activity (or other scope of work). The remaining duration of a completed activity is zero. *(NDIA II)*

remaining funds
Funds left on a contract due to quantity variances or price rounding and where all contract performance as required by the contract has been completed and paid in full. These funds are annotated accordingly and are automatically removed. *(DGBCT)*
See *excess funds*.

remanufactured
Factory rebuilt to original specifications. *(FAR 11.001)*

remedy
Any remedial right to which an aggrieved party is entitled with or without resort to a tribunal. *(UCC 1-201(32))*
See also *aggrieved party*.

remedy coordination official
The person or entity in a federal agency who coordinates within that agency the administration of criminal, civil, administrative, and contractual remedies resulting from investigations of fraud or corruption related to procurement activities. *(FAR 32.006-2)*

remitter
A person who purchases an instrument from its issuer if the instrument is payable to an identified person other than the purchaser. *(UCC 3-103(a)(15))*
See also *negotiable instrument*.

rental costs
The costs of renting or leasing real or personal property acquired under operating leases (as defined in the Financial Accounting Standards Board's Accounting Standards Codification 840, "Leases"), rental costs under a sale and leaseback arrangement, and charges in the nature of rent for property between any divisions, subsidiaries, or organizations under common control. *(FAR 31.205-36(a)-(b))*

reorder point (ROP)
The point at which time a stock replenishment requisition is submitted to maintain the predetermined stockage objective. *(DISCS)*

repair
Those additions or changes that are necessary for the protection and maintenance of items, equipment, or property to deter or prevent excessive or rapid deterioration or obsolescence, and to restore damaged items or equipment, or property damaged by storm, flood, fire, accident, or earthquake. *(FMR 102-71.20)*

reparable item
An item that can be reconditioned or economically repaired for reuse when it becomes unserviceable. *(DISCS)*
See also *recoverable item*.

Rr

replenishment spare parts

Items and equipment, both repairable and consumable, purchased as spares by inventory control points and which are required to replenish stocks for use in the maintenance, overhaul, and repair of equipment, such as ships, tanks, guns, aircraft, engines, etc. *(DISCS)*

replevin

A legal action whereby the owner of goods can legally recover them from someone who is holding them unlawfully. *(FBL)*

reporting

Contracts sometimes require contractors to provide reports to the buyer about performance and financial status to ensure contract completion on time and within budget. When required by the contract, the contractor should provide written status reports to keep the buyer's contacting professionals and customers aware of progress and issues. These reports can be narrative, statistical, or a combination of the two, consistent with the need for the information. *(DGBCT)*

reporting costs

The provision of cost information to others. *(48 CFR 9904.401-30(7))*

representative

A person empowered to act for another, including an agent, an officer of a corporation or association, and a trustee, executor, or administrator of an estate. *(UCC 1-201(33))*

represented person

The principal, beneficiary, partnership, corporation, or other person to whom a fiduciary duty is owed. *(UCC 3-307(a)(2))*
See *fiduciary; fiduciary duty*.

reprogramming

The transfer of funds between program elements or line items within an appropriation. *(DISCS)*

repudiation

Under a contract, the rejection or renunciation of a duty or obligation. A party aggrieved by a repudiation may consider a repudiated contract to have been breached and bring an action for relief. *(MW)*
See also *anticipatory repudiation*.

request for deviation

A specific written authorization to depart from a particular requirement of an item's current approved configuration documentation for a specific number of units or a specified period of time. It differs from an engineering change since a deviation does not affect a change to a configuration document. *(DGBCT)*
See *deviation*.

request for equitable adjustment (REA)

(1) A letter or proposal requesting a change to the contract price or schedule. *(CMBOK)*
(2) This term is commonly mentioned within the *FAR* and its supplement *DFARS*, but without a formal definition. However, the U.S. Court of Appeals cites a REA as anything but a "routine request for payment" and determined it "a remedy payable only when unforeseen or unintended circumstances, such as government modification of the contract, differing site conditions, defective or late-delivered government property or issuance of a stop work order, cause an increase in contract performance costs" (Reflectone, Inc. v. Dalton, 60 F.3d 1572 (Fed. Cir. 1995). *(DAAT-A)*
See *equitable adjustment*.

request for information (RFI)

(1) A document used to obtain price, delivery, other market information, or capabilities for planning purposes when the government does not presently intend to issue a solicitation. *(GOAT)*
(2) A formal invitation to submit general and/or specific information concerning the potential future purchase of goods and/or services. *(STBP)*

request for proposals (RFP)

(1) Used in negotiated acquisitions to communicate U.S. federal government requirements to prospective contractors and to solicit proposals. RFPs for competitive acquisitions shall, at a minimum, describe the following:
- The government's requirement;
- The anticipated terms and conditions that will apply to the contract:
  - The solicitation may authorize offerors to propose alternative terms and conditions, including the contract line item number (CLIN) structure; and
  - When alternative CLIN structures are permitted, the evaluation approach should consider the potential impact on other terms and conditions or the requirement;

Rr

- Information required to be in the offeror's proposal; and
- Factors and significant subfactors that will be used to evaluate the proposal and their relative importance.

(FAR 15.203(a))

(2) A solicitation document used in negotiated procurement when the buyer reserves the right to award without further verbal or written negotiation. Only the acceptance of the buyer is required to create a binding contract. Of course, the buyer can choose to negotiate further at its option. *(DSMC)*

(3) A formal invitation that contains a scope of work and seeks a formal response (proposal), describing both methodology and compensation, to form the basis of a contract. *(STBP)*

request for quotations (RFQ)

(1) A solicitation document used when a specification or statement of work already exists and the buyer needs to get information from potential sellers about price and delivery. The RFQ differs from the RFP in that an RFQ is not an offer and, consequently, the buyer cannot accept a quote to form a binding contract. *(CMBOK)*

(2)The solicitation form normally used in simplified acquisitions or negotiated procurement when award will be made after negotiation with the offeror. Since the prospective subcontractor's quotation is not a formal offer, the prime contractor and subcontractor must reach a bilateral negotiated agreement before a binding contract exists. *(DSMC)*

(3) A formal invitation to submit a price for goods and/or services as specified. *(STBP)*

request for technical proposals

A solicitation document used in two-step sealed bidding. Normally in letter form, it asks only for technical information; price and cost breakdowns are forbidden. *(DSMC)*

request for waiver

Used by a contractor to ask that a particular requirement for a product or service be overlooked or waived. The waiver request would ask for permission to ignore a specific requirement. *(NES-96)*

requesting agency

The U.S. federal agency that has the requirement for an interagency acquisition. *(FAR 2.101)*
See *interagency acquisition*; see also *servicing agency*.

requesting offers

The process of implementing the acquisition plan by soliciting responses from contractors in order to fulfill a customer need. The value added of requesting offers is producing a clear and concise solicitation that effectively communicates all the buyer's requirements and enables the sellers to provide comprehensive, responsive proposals. *(CMS)*

required change

In the context of the Cost Accounting Standards (CAS), means—

- A change in cost accounting practice that a contractor is required to make in order to comply with applicable CAS, modifications or interpretations thereto, that subsequently becomes applicable to an existing CAS-covered contract or subcontract due to the receipt of another CAS-covered contract or subcontract; or
- A prospective change to a disclosed or established cost accounting practice when the cognizant federal agency official determines that the former practice was in compliance with applicable CAS and the change is necessary for the contractor to remain in compliance.

(FAR 30.001)

See *Cost Accounting Standards* (CAS); see also *cognizant federal agency official* (CFAO); *Cost Accounting Standards Board* (CASB).

required receipt date

The date goods are due to be received at the place designated by the buyer is sometimes a determinant of transportation costs. The buyer and seller should be aware of the potential for increased transportation costs that may be a result of a specific receipt date, particularly when the delivery schedule is aggressive or when the delivery schedule is accelerated by modification due to a change in plans or to overcome some issue or problem in production. *(DGBCT)*

required sources of supplies and services

See *mandatory sources*.

requirement

A description of what is expected to be performed by one or both parties to an agreement:

- *Technical* requirements specify what the product should do and how the seller will support it.
- *Administrative* requirements specify how the customer/buyer relationship will work.

Rr

(CMBOK; NES-97)
See also **capability requirement**.

requirements contract
(1) A contract provides for filling all actual purchase requirements of designated government activities for supplies or services during a specified contract period (from one contractor), with deliveries or performance to be scheduled by placing orders with the contractor. *(FAR 16.503(a).)*
(2) A contract that provides for filling all actual purchase requirements of designated government activities for supplies or services during a specified contract period (from one contractor) with deliveries or performance to be scheduled by placing orders with the contractor. Appropriate for acquiring supplies or services when recurring requirements are anticipated but cannot be predetermined in precise quantities. *(OPM)*

requirements creep
The tendency of the user (or developer) to add capabilities or performance to the original mission responsibilities and/or performance requirements for a system while it is still in development. *(DGBCT)*

requirements documents
All aspects of the request for proposals (RFP) that convey the needs of the U.S. federal government to offerors, including:
*   The statement of objectives (SOO),
*   The statement of work (SOW),
*   The performance work statement (PWS),
*   Technical requirements documents, and
*   System requirement documents.
(SSP)

requiring activity/agency
A federal agency needing supplies or services. The requiring activity is responsible for obtaining funding or developing the program objective memorandum. The requiring activity is also the organizational unit that submits a written requirement or statement of need for services required by a contract award. The requiring activity is responsible for delivering the services to meet the mission. Finally, the requiring activity provides trained and qualified contracting officers capable of determining whether service contract requirements are being performed in accordance with the contract terms. *(FAR 8.401)*

requiring office
The entity (e.g., a program management office or other organizational entity) responsible for translating user requirements into the requirements documents within the request for proposals (RFP) that communicate those requirements to offerors. *(SSP)*
See also **requirements documents; requiring activity/agency**.

requisition
A request for supplies or services originating from the party actually requiring them. *(SPP)*
See also **purchase request**.

rescission
(1) The unmaking of a contract, or an undoing of it from the beginning. Not merely a termination. It may be effected by mutual agreement of parties, or by one of the parties declaring rescission of contract without consent of the other if a legally sufficient ground exists. *(BLD)*
(2) An action of equitable nature in which a party seeks to be relieved of its obligations under a contract on the grounds of mutual mistake, fraud, impossibility, etc. *(BLD)*
(3) The permanent cancellation of budget authority prior to the time when the authority officially terminates. The rescission process begins when the president proposes a rescission to the Congress for fiscal or policy reasons. Unlike the deferral of budget authority, which occurs unless Congress acts to disapprove the deferral, rescission of budget authority occurs only if both houses of Congress approve the rescission, by simple majority, within 45 days of continuous session. *(DISCS)*

research and development (R&D)
Involves the same type of technical effort as independent research and development, but is sponsored by a grant or required in the performance of a contract. *(FAR 31.205-48)*
Contrast with **independent research and development (IR&D)**.

research and development contract
A contract for basic research (directed toward increasing knowledge); applied research (directed toward improving or expanding new scientific discoveries, technologies, materials, processes, or techniques); or development (directed production of, or improvements in, useful products to meet specific performance requirements through the systematic application of scientific knowledge). *(OPM)*

Rr

research and development program

A program for which the primary purpose is to advance scientific and technical knowledge and apply that knowledge to the extent necessary to achieve agency and national goals. Unlike contracts for supplies and services, most R&D contracts are directed toward objectives for which the work or methods cannot be precisely described in advance. It is difficult to judge the probabilities of success or required effort for technical approaches, some of which offer little or no early assurance of full success. The contracting process shall be used to encourage the best sources from the scientific and industrial community to become involved in the program and must provide an environment in which the work can be pursued with reasonable flexibility and minimum administrative burden. *(FAR 35.002)*
See *research and development contract*.

research, development, test, and evaluation (RDT&E) budget activities

Consists of all efforts funded from an RDT&E appropriation account. There are seven RDT&E budget activities:
- Basic Research,
- Applied Research,
- Advanced Technology Development,
- Advanced Component Development and Prototypes,
- System Development and Demonstration,
- RDT&E Management Support, and
- Operational Systems Development.

(DAAT)

research, development, test, and evaluation (RDT&E) appropriations

In a Department of Defense context, appropriations that fund the efforts performed by contractors and government activities required for the research and development of equipment, material, computer application software, and its test and evaluation, including initial operational test and evaluation and life fire test and evaluation. These appropriations also fund the operation of dedicated research and development installation activities for the conduct of research and development programs. *(DAAT)*

residual inventory (equipment or material)

Items procured for a contract that become excess to the needs of the contract. *(NDIA II)*

residual value

The proceeds, less removal and disposal costs, if any, realized upon disposition of a tangible capital asset. It is usually measured by the net proceeds from the sale or other disposition of the asset, or its fair value if the asset is traded in on another asset. The estimated residual value is a current forecast of the residual value. *(FAR 2.101)*

resistance point

In negotiation, this term refers to the negotiating option or position that represents the point at which a party is disinterested in whether agreement is reached or not—i.e., the point farthest from the target point a negotiator will go, but the point can change. In a contract negotiation, this would be the most a buyer will pay, and the least the seller will accept. Also known as *bottom line*. *(GTY)*
See also *negotiation; target point*.

resolution

A "simple" congressional resolution, designated H. Res (House) or S. Res (Senate), deals with matters entirely within the prerogatives of one house or the other. It requires neither passage by the other chamber nor approval by the president, and it does not have the force of law. Most such resolutions deal with the rules or procedures of one house. They are also used to express the sentiments of a single house, such as condolence to the family of a deceased member, or to comment on foreign policy or executive business. A simple resolution is the vehicle for a "rule" from the House Rules Committee. *(DISCS)*
See also *concurrent resolution; joint resolution* (J Res).

resource plan

In project management terminology, the schedule for the planned expenditure of project resources to accomplish project work scope. *(NDIA II)*

responsibility

With respect to negotiable instruments, means authority to—
- Sign or indorse instruments on behalf of the employer;
- Process instruments received by the employer for bookkeeping purposes, for deposit to an account, or for other disposition;
- Prepare or process instruments for issue in the name of the employer;
- Supply information determining the names or addresses of payees of instruments to be issued in the name of the employer;
- Control the disposition of instruments to be issued in the name of the employer; or
- Act otherwise with respect to instruments in a

responsible capacity. "Responsibility" *does not* include authority that merely allows an employee to have access to instruments or blank or incomplete instrument forms that are being stored or transported or are part of incoming or outgoing mail, or similar access. *(UCC 3-405(a)(3))*

responsibility accounting
See *activity accounting*.

responsibility assignment matrix (RAM)
A graphical chart showing the relationship between the work breakdown structure elements and the project organization elements responsible for ensuring work accomplishment. It identifies the control accounts established for the project. When budget values are included in the chart, it may be referred to as a "dollarized responsibility assignment matrix." *(NDIA II)*

responsibility determination
The process by which a seller is found to be a capable party that has the financial resources, personnel, facilities, integrity, and overall capability to fulfill specific contractual requirements satisfactorily. *(DGBCT)*

responsibility standards
Standards that measure whether the offeror is able to provide the supplies or services. In federal government contracting, to be determined "responsible," a prospective contractor must meet the following responsibility standards—
- Have adequate financial resources to perform the contract, or the ability to obtain them;
- Be able to comply with the required or proposed delivery or performance schedule, taking into consideration all existing commercial and governmental business commitments;
- Have a satisfactory performance record (lack of relevant performance history shall not solely form the basis of the responsibility determination);
- Have a satisfactory record of integrity and business ethics;
- Have the necessary organization, experience, accounting and operational controls, and technical skills, or the ability to obtain them;
- Have the necessary production, construction, and technical equipment and facilities, or the ability to obtain them; and
- Be otherwise qualified and eligible to receive an award under applicable laws and regulations.

(FAR 9.104-1) (See also *FAR* Subpart 42.15.)

See *responsible offeror; responsible prospective contractor; see also satisfactory performance record*.

responsible audit agency
The federal government agency that is responsible for performing all required contract audit services at a business unit. *(FAR 2.101)*

responsible offeror
A capable party that has the financial resources, personnel, facilities, integrity, and overall capability to fulfill specific contractual requirements satisfactorily. Also called a *responsible source* and "responsible contractor." *(CMBOK; NCMA-SB)* (See also *FAR* 9.104-1.) See also *responsible prospective contractor*.

responsible prospective contractor
To enter into a contract with the federal government, a prospective contractor or subcontractor must meet the *Federal Acquisition Regulation's* general responsibility standards to be determined "responsible." *(FAR 9.104-1)* See *responsibility standards*.

responsible source
See *responsible offeror*.

responsive
(1) Describes a bid that meets, without any material deviation, the expressed requirements of a solicitation. *(NCMA-SB)*
(2) When a bidder fully complies with and does not materially deviate from the terms, conditions, and specifications set forth in an invitation for bids (sealed-bid method), it is deemed "responsive." *(P&L I)*
(3) When an offeror materially complies with a solicitation and is capable of being made compliant through discussions, it is deemed "responsive." *(P&L I)*

restitution
(1) In the context of judicial remedies, occurs when the defendant must repay the monetary value he or she received from the aggrieved party for partial contract performance. *(CMBOK)*
(2) The sum to be paid to the nonbreaching party to the position he, she, or it was in before the formation of the contract. *(CMBOK)*
See also *restitution interest*.

restitution interest
In the context of judicial remedies, a promisee's interest in having restored to him or her any benefit that he

Rr

or she has conferred on the other party in a contract. *(RSOC 344(c))*
See *restitution*.

restricted computer software
Computer software developed at private expense and that is a trade secret, is commercial or financial and confidential or privileged, or is copyrighted computer software, including minor modifications of the computer software. *(FAR 27.401)*

restricted rights
(1) A form of limited rights that applies only to computer software. Data protected under restricted rights is referred to as "restricted computer software." *(TIPS)*
(2) The rights of the federal government in restricted computer software, as set forth in a "restricted rights notice." *(FAR 27.401)*
See *restricted computer software; restricted rights notice; contrast with limited rights; unlimited right*.

restricted rights notice
A notice detailing the rights of the parties to the use of "restricted computer software." If a federal government contract identifies and specifies the delivery of "restricted computer software," or if such a requirement is directed by the contracting officer, the contractor is required to affix a "restricted rights notice" to the software in accordance with FAR 52.227-14, Alternate III, (g)(4)(i). The notice obligates the government *not* to use, disclose or reproduce the submitted software except as provided within the notice. *(FAR 27.401; FAR 52.227-14, Alternate III, (g)(4)(i))*

Restrictions on Obtaining and Disclosing Certain Information statute
A federal law (41 U.S.C. Chapter 21) that outlines restrictions on obtaining or disclosing certain information—including contractor bid or proposal information or source selection information—before the award of a federal agency procurement contract to which the information relates. Formerly known as the *Procurement Integrity Act* (PIA). *(41 U.S.C. 2102(a)-(b))*

restrictive requirements
In the case of a pre-award protest, a protestor may claim that the requirements or specifications are unnecessarily restrictive, and thereby prohibit or limit meaningful competition. *(CMBOK)*

retroactive pricing
A pricing decision made after some or all of the work specified under contract has been completed, based on a review of performance and recorded cost data. *(GKPT)*

retrofitting
See *backfitting*.

return on investment (ROI)
A measure of income or profit divided by the investment required to help obtain the income or profit. That is, given the same risks, for any given amount of resources required, the investor wants the maximum income. *(IMA)*

revenue recognition and realization
Generally accepted accounting principles state that revenue should be recognized (realized) when the earning process is virtually complete and an exchange has taken place. There are exceptions to this rule, particularly in the case of percentage-of-completion construction contracts where revenue is recognized over the life of the construction project. The purpose of the revenue realization principle is to provide an accurate representation of the economic substance of revenue-related transactions. *(NCMA-CA)*

reverse auction (RA)
A single buyer of a single item (or lot of items) receives decreasing offers from prospective sellers. The auction ends at a predetermined time, and the item is purchased from the lowest offeror for the lowest offer price. *(ARQ)*
See *auction*.

reverse engineering
A process whereby a product is analyzed to determine the composition of its various design elements for the purpose of producing a like product or performance capability. *(P&L II)*

reverse logistics
The collection of all processes that come into play for goods that move in the reverse direction (i.e., from the buyer to the seller). *(DGBCT)*

reversionary interest
An interest in property (as a possibility of reverter or a power of termination) remaining in the transferor of the property or in his or her successor in interest. *(MW)*

250

DESKTOP GUIDE TO
CONTRACT MANAGEMENT TERMS

Rr

revolving door

The process of federal government employees leaving government service to join private industry. Restrictions on such employment are contained in 18 U.S.C. 207 (for civilian employees) and in 37 U.S.C. 801 (for military employees), as well as in 5 CFR 2637 and 2641. Additional restrictions are contained in the procurement integrity rules. Special statutory provisions governing post-government employment with defense contractors are contained in 10 U.S.C. 2397, *et seq*. *(NS)*

revolving fund

A fund established to finance a cycle of operations to which reimbursements and collections are returned for reuse in a manner that will maintain the principal of the fund (e.g., working capital funds and industrial funds). *(DISCS)*

rights in technical data

The right for the federal government to acquire technical data. If the government has funded or will fund a part of or the entire development of the item, component, or process, then the government is entitled to "unlimited rights" in the technical data. However, if the item is developed by a contractor or subcontractor exclusively at private expense, the government is entitled to "limited rights." Such data must be unpublished and identified as limited rights data. *(DSMC)* (See also *FAR 27.407*.)

See *government purpose license rights; limited rights; restricted rights; unlimited rights*.

risk

(1) A measure of the extent to which an entity is threatened by a potential circumstance or event, and typically a function of:
- The adverse impacts that would arise if the circumstance or event occurs, and
- The likelihood of occurrence.

(FIPS 200)

(2) In federal government contracting, the probability of not attaining the goals for which the party entered into a contract. For the government, the principal risks include:
- The total cost of the acquisition will be higher than expected or unreasonable in relation to the actual costs of performance;
- The contractor will fail to deliver or will not deliver on time;
- The final deliverable will not satisfy the government's actual need, whether or not "acceptable"

under the terms and conditions of the contract; and
- The government's need will change prior to receipt of the deliverable.

(FAI)

(3) In a program management context, a measure of the inability to achieve program objectives within defined cost and schedule constraints. Risk is associated with all aspects of the program; e.g., threat, technology, design processes, or work breakdown structure elements. It has two components:
- The probability of failing to achieve a particular outcome, and
- The consequences of failing to achieve that outcome

(DAAT)

(4) As it pertains to source selection, the potential for unsuccessful contract performance by the offeror. The consideration of risk assesses the degree to which an offeror's proposed approach to achieving the technical factor or subfactor may involve risk of disruption of schedule, increased cost (except in the case of firm-fixed-price contracts) or degradation of performance, the need for increased government oversight, and the likelihood of unsuccessful contract performance. *(SSP)*

(5) In a cybersecurity context, the possibility that a particular threat will adversely impact an information system by exploiting a particular vulnerability. Information system–related security risks are those risks that arise from the loss of confidentiality, integrity, or availability of information or information systems and reflect the potential adverse impacts to organizational operations (including mission, functions, image, or reputation), organizational assets, individuals, other organizations, and the nation. *(CNSSI 4009; FIPS 200)*

risk analysis

A detailed examination of each identified risk, which refines the description of the risk, isolates the cause, and determines the impact of the risk in terms of its probability of occurrence, its consequences, and its relationship to other risk areas or processes. *(DAAT)*

risk assessment

(1) The process of subjectively determining the probability that a specific interplay of performance, schedule, and cost as an objective will or will not be attained along the planned course of action. *(P&L II)*

(2) In a cybersecurity context, the process of identifying risks to organizational operations (including mission, functions, image, and reputation), organizational assets, individuals, other organizations, and the nation, result-

ing from the operation of an information system. A part of risk management, "risk assessment" incorporates threat and vulnerability analyses and considers mitigations provided by security controls planned or in place. *(NIST SP 800-171)*

risk capital
See *venture capital*.

risk-informed decision-making (RIDM)
A process that uses a diverse set of performance measures (some of which are model-based risk metrics) along with other considerations within a deliberative process to inform decision-making. *(NID 8000-108)*

risk management
(1) The process for identification, analysis, and treatment of loss exposure, as well as the administration of techniques to accomplish the goals of a company in minimizing potential financial loss from such exposure. *(F&F)*
(2) The process of planning, analyzing, tracking, and controlling events that could put a project or contract in danger of not being completed on time, within schedule, or within budget. Risk management is a key component in reducing acquisition cycle time and in cutting costs. *(NES-00)*
See also *continuous risk management* (CRM); *risk-informed decision making* (RIDM).

risk owner
The entity, usually a named individual, designated as the lead for overseeing the implementation of the agreed disposition of an identified risk. *(NID 8000-108)*

Robert T. Stafford Disaster Relief and Emergency Assistance Act
A federal law (42 U.S.C. 5121, *et seq.*) that constitutes the statutory authority for most U.S. federal government disaster response activities. In terms of the government's contracting authority, Title VI of this act amended the definition of "national defense" under the Defense Production Act of 1950, as amended (50 U.S.C. App. 2061, *et seq.*), to include emergency preparedness activities and critical infrastructure protection and restoration in response to natural and man-caused disasters. (Also referred to simply as the "Robert T. Stafford Act.")
See also *Defense Production Act of 1950, as amended* (DPA); *disaster or emergency assistance activities*.

Robinson-Patman Act
Section 2(a) of the Clayton Antitrust Act of 1914 (15 U.S.C. 12, *et seq.*), as amended by the Robinson-Patman Act (15 U.S.C. 13), makes it unlawful for any seller engaged in commerce to directly or indirectly discriminate in the price charged to purchasers on the sale of commodities of like grade and quality where the effect may be to injure, destroy, or prevent competition with any person who grants or knowingly receives a discrimination, or the customer of either. *(BLD)*
See *Antitrust Act; Clayton Antitrust Act of 1914*.

rollover of unearned award fee
The process of transferring unearned award fee, which the contractor had an opportunity to earn, from one evaluation period to a subsequent evaluation period, thus allowing the contractor an additional opportunity to earn that previously unearned award fee. *(FAR 16.001)*

rough cut capacity planning (RCCP)
A type of capacity planning that compares requirements to the available capacity at key work centers or critical bottlenecks. It attempts to balance workloads broadly and often takes into account the areas of labor, machinery, storage space, and supplier capacity. *(DGBCT)*

royalties
Any costs or charges in the nature of royalties, license fees, patent or license amortization costs, or the like that are paid for the use of or for rights in patents and patent applications in connection with performing a contract or subcontract. *(GOAT)*
See *royalties and other costs for use of patents*; see also *ownership*.

royalties and other costs for use of patents
The costs of royalties on a patent or amortization of the cost of purchasing a patent or patent rights necessary for the proper performance of a contract and applicable to contract products or processes. *(FAR 31.205-37(a))*

Rule 4 file
A file containing the contracting officer's final decision, the contract, pertinent correspondence, affidavits, and related information that is prepared pursuant to Rule 4 of the "Rules of the Armed Services Board of Contract Appeals" and 48 CFR 6302.4, "Preparation, Content, Organization, Forwarding, and Status of Appeal File." *(GCG)*

Ss

Rule of *Blue and Gold*

A legal precedent established by the Court of Appeals for the Federal Circuit (in *Blue and Gold Fleet, L.P. v. United States*, 492 F.3d 1308 (Fed. Cir. 2007)) that applies to the patent ambiguity exception to contra proferentem in the context of bid protests of federal government contracts. The "Rule of *Blue and Gold*" states that a party who has the opportunity to object to the terms of a U.S. government solicitation containing an error or ambiguity, and fails to do so prior to the close of the bidding process, waives its ability to raise the same objection subsequently in a bid protest action (as described at 28 U.S.C. 1491(b)). Therefore, an offeror must seek clarification *before* it bids or submits its initial proposal if either of the following occurs:

- A U.S. government solicitation contains, or appears to contain, a "patent ambiguity" or "defect"; or
- An offeror has a question or doubt about something contained within the solicitation.

(PAS)

See also *contra proferentem; patent ambiguity; solicitation*.

S

safeguard/safeguarding

The use of measures, controls, or other protection prescribed to protect information systems from a known or expected condition. *(FAR 4.1901; CNSSI 4009)*
See also *information system* (IS).

safety stock

Stock held at a distribution center that is in excess of what the organization expects to sell. The purpose of safety stock is to act as buffer inventory to account for unexpected customer orders, longer than expected manufacturing, or transportation time. *(DGBCT; IMA)*

sale

(1) The exchange of goods or services for an amount of money or its equivalent; the act of selling. *(DGBCT)*
(2) Consists of the passing of title from the seller to the buyer for a price. *(UCC 2-106(1))*

sales

Activities involved in selling goods or services; also, gross receipts. *(DGBCT)*

sales analysis

The breakdown of sales figures by region, product, customer, market, etc. for a given period as a control measure. *(DGBCT)*

sales contract

A business arrangement in which all elements of the transaction are determined and defined between the parties at the time of contract formation, including mutual assent, exchange of consideration, capacity to contract, and legal purpose. *(DGBCT)*

sales cycle time

Measures the time required for a product to sell out completely from the store/shelf (beginning from the day it goes on sale). *(DGBCT)*

salvage

Surplus material or equipment that has a market value and can be sold. *(GKPT)*

sample size

Number of units to be selected for random sampling. *(DGCQI)*

sampling

A method of obtaining statistics from a large body of data without resorting to a complete census of the data. Two broad methods of selecting samples are "probability sampling" (in which sample units are selected according to the law of chance) and "nonprobability sampling" (in which personal choice, expert judgment, or some other nonprobabilistic rationale is used to select sample units). *(HECA)*

Sarbanes-Oxley Act of 2002, The (SOX)

A federal law (*Pub. L.* 107-204) that, among other things, created requirements for enhanced financial disclosures from public companies—including strict requirements pertaining to records retention. Compliance with SOX requires firms to be especially diligent in how they create, record, store, and manage their contracts and related information and records. *(DGBCT)*

"Satisfactory" performance rating

In the case of a past performance evaluation, a "Satisfactory" performance rating signifies that performance meets contractual requirements. The contractual performance of the element or sub-element contains some minor problems for which corrective actions taken by the contractor appear or were satisfactory. *(FAR Table 42-1)*

Ss

See *past performance evaluation*; contrast with *"Exceptional" performance rating; "Marginal" performance rating; "Unsatisfactory" performance rating; "Very Good" performance rating*.

schedule

The project timeline identifying the dates (absolute or relative to a start date) that project tasks will be started and completed, what resources will be required, and upon which milestones will be reached. *(DGBCT)*
See also *delivery schedule; performance schedule*.

Schedule contract

See *Federal Supply Schedule* (FSS) *Program*

schedule performance index (SPI)

A measure of how well a project (or a portion of a project) has actually performed in comparison with the baseline plan. It is an indicator used to determine whether a project will need to increase efficiency to complete on time. It is calculated by dividing the budgeted cost of work performed (BCWP) by the budgeted cost of work scheduled (BCWS). A value greater than "1" is favorable; a value less than "1" is unfavorable. It may be expressed as a value for a specific time period or cumulative to date. The nature of the SPI formula is such that no matter how early or late a project completes, SPI calculations will eventually equal 1.00. *(NDIA II)*

schedule risk

The likelihood that project actions cannot be accomplished within the planned project timeframe. May result from unrealistic schedule estimates or problems with project execution. *(NDIA II)*

schedule risk assessment (SRA)

A formal process used to simulate the execution of a project hundreds or thousands of times to quantify schedule risk and predict the probability of completing events by specific dates. *(NDIA II)*
See *schedule risk*.

schedule variance (SV)

(1) Comparing the earned budget (the value of work accomplished) during a given period of time to the value of work scheduled (planned budget) during the same period of time provides a valuable indication of schedule status in terms of dollars' worth of work accomplished. It represents the quantity (i.e., the value) of the work that is ahead of or behind schedule. In essence, it is an "accomplishment" variance. *(DGBCT)*

(2) The difference between the budgeted cost of work performed (BCWP) and the budgeted cost of work scheduled (BCWS) (i.e., SV = BCWP - BCWS). *(DAAT)*

scope

(1) The work required to deliver the product or outcome of the project. *(CMBOK)*
(2) A general statement defining the parameters or boundaries of expected actions, required performance, or products required. *(DGBCT)*

scoring system

See *rating/scoring system*.

scrap

(1) The loss of labor and material resulting from defects that cannot be economically repaired or used. *(DGCQI)*
(2) Residual material resulting from machine or assembly processes, such as machine shavings, unusable lengths of wire, or faulty parts. *(DOD-MMH)*
(3) Personal property that has no value except its basic metallic, mineral, or organic content. *(FAR 2.101)*

sealed bid

Document enclosed in a sealed envelope and submitted in response to an invitation for bids. Sealed bids received up to the deadline date are generally opened at a stated time and place and evaluated for award of a contract. *(DGBCT)*
See also *bid*.

sealed-bid procedure

A method of federal government contracting that employs competitive bids, public bid opening, and awards. The government issues an invitation for bids (IFB). The IFB is publicized by distributing it to prospective bidders, posting it in public places and on the FedBizOpps website. Sufficient time must be allowed between the time the IFB is publicized and bids are opened publicly to enable prospective bidders to prepare and submit bids. An IFB should describe the government's requirements clearly, accurately, and completely. Unnecessarily restrictive specifications or requirements that might unduly limit the number of bidders are prohibited. The invitation includes all documents (whether attached or incorporated by reference) furnished to prospective bidders for bidding purposes. Agencies must use a fixed-price contract for sealed bidding. After the bids are opened and evaluated, award is made to the responsible bidder whose bid, conforming to the IFB, will be most advantageous

Ss

to the government considering only price and price-related factors included in the IFB. *(FAR 14.101; DGBCT; GOAT; NCMA-SB)*

sealed bidding

(1) A method of contracting that employs competitive bids, public opening of bids, and awards. *(FAR 14.101)*
(2) Procurement by obtaining sealed bids and awarding the contract to the lowest-priced responsible bidder whose bid is responsive. *(DGBCT)*
(3) An acquisition method in which the buyer issues and invitation for bids (IFB). *(CMBOK)*

second source

An acquisition strategy that establishes two or more producers for the same part, system, or service for the purpose of increasing competition or broadening the industrial base. *(P&L II)*

secondary comparison

A means of accomplishing price analysis. Secondary comparisons are used to support primary comparisons. When no primary data are available, a combination of secondary comparisons may result in a determination that a price is fair and reasonable. Types of secondary comparisons include:
- Comparative analysis,
- Historical prices,
- Market data,
- Index numbers,
- Cost estimating relationships,
- Government catalogs, and
- Government estimates.

(NCMA-WS)
See *comparative analysis; cost estimating relationships; historical prices; market data;* compare with *auxiliary techniques; primary comparison*.

secondary obligor

(1) An obligor to the extent that:
- The obligor's obligation is secondary, or
- The obligor has a right of recourse with respect to an obligation secured by collateral against the debtor, another obligor, or property of either.

(UCC 9-102(a)(72))
See *obligor*.
(2) With respect to a negotiable instrument, means:
- An indorser or an accommodation party,
- A drawer having the obligation, or
- Any other party to the instrument that has recourse against another party to the instrument.

(UCC 3-103(a)(17))
See *negotiable instrument*.

Section 8(a) Business Development Program

(1) The 8(a) Program is dedicated to helping small disadvantaged businesses. It provides a wide scope of business development assistance to firms that are "at least 51 percent owned and controlled by U.S. citizens who are economically and socially disadvantaged." (See https://www.sba.gov.)
(2) Section 8(a) of the Small Business Act (15 U.S.C. 637(a)) established a program that authorizes the Small Business Administration (SBA) to enter into all types of contracts with other agencies and award subcontracts for performing those contracts to firms eligible for program participation. *(FAR 19.800)*

Section 800 Panel

A panel tasked with streamlining defense acquisition laws by Section 800 of the Fiscal Year 1991 National Defense Authorization Act (*Pub. L.* 101-189). The panel's official name was the "Advisory Panel on Streamlining and Codifying Acquisition Laws." The panel presented to Congress an 1,800-page study in January 1993 titled "Streamlining Defense Acquisition Laws." *(TIPS)*

Section 809 Panel

An advisory panel on "streamlining and codifying" acquisition regulations established in the 2016 National Defense Authorization Act (*Pub. L.* 114-92). The panel is charged with making recommendations to amend or repeal regulations that the panel considers necessary as a result of their review. (See https://section809panel.org.)

Section 1207 Program

Named after Section 1207 of the DOD Appropriations Act of 1987 (*Pub. L.* 99-661), this program allows the Department of Defense to "set aside" contracts for socially and economically disadvantaged firms. The program also allows the DOD to apply a 10 percent evaluation preference when awarding a contract to a socially and economically disadvantaged business that competes in unrestricted procurements. *(TIPS)*

sector

(1) An area of the economy in which businesses share the same or a related product or service. *(INV)*
(2) Certain commercial activities are common to more than one agency. Many of these commercial activities can be aggregated. For example, an agency may inventory transportation acquisition, operations,

Ss

maintenance, and disposal as independent commercial activities. *(OMB A-76)*

secured party
Means:
- A person in whose favor a security interest is created or provided for under a security agreement, whether or not any obligation to be secured is outstanding;
- A person that holds an agricultural lien;
- A consignor;
- A person to which accounts, chattel paper, payment intangibles, or promissory notes have been sold;
- A trustee, indenture trustee, agent, collateral agent, or other representative in whose favor a security interest or agricultural lien is created or provided for; or
- A person that holds a security interest.

(UCC 9-102(a)(73))

securities account
An account to which a financial asset is or may be credited in accordance with an agreement under which the person maintaining the account undertakes to treat the person for whom the account is maintained as entitled to exercise the rights that comprise the financial asset. *(UCC 8-501(a))*
See *financial asset*.

securities intermediary
Means:
- A clearing corporation, or
- A person, including a bank or broker, that in the ordinary course of its business maintains securities accounts for others and is acting in that capacity.

(UCC 8-102(a)(14))
See *security*; see also *broker; clearing corporation; securities account*.

security
(1) An obligation of an issuer or a share, participation, or other interest in an issuer or in property or an enterprise of an issuer:
- Which is represented by a security certificate in bearer or registered form, or the transfer of which may be registered upon books maintained for that purpose by or on behalf of the issuer;
- Which is one of a class or series or by its terms is divisible into a class or series of shares, participations, interests, or obligations; and

- Which:
  - Is, or is of a type, dealt in or traded on securities exchanges or securities markets; or
  - Is a medium for investment and by its terms expressly provides that it is a security governed by the Uniform Commercial Code.

(UCC 8-102(a)(15))
See also *bearer form; registered form; security certificate*.
(2) A share or similar equity interest issued by a corporation, business trust, joint stock company, or similar entity. *(UCC 8-103(a))*
(3) *Synonymous with "cybersecurity."*
See *cybersecurity*.

security agreement
An agreement that creates or provides for a security interest. *(UCC 9-102(a)(74))*
See also *security interest*.

security assistance (SA)
A group of programs authorized by the Foreign Assistance Act of 1961 (22 U.S.C. 2151), as amended, and the Arms Export Control Act (22 U.S.C. 2751), as amended, or other related statutes by which the United States provides defense articles, military training, and other defense-related services, by grant, loan, cash sale, or lease, in furtherance of national policies and objectives. There are 12 major security assistance programs, of which seven are administered by the Department of Defense and five are administered by the Department of State. The seven programs managed by DOD are included in the DOD-defined security cooperation program. *(DISCS)*
See also *Arms Export Control Act* (AECA); *defense article; defense service; Foreign Assistance Act of 1961* (FAA).

security certificate
A certificate representing a security. *(UCC 8-102(a)(16))*
See *certificate; security*.

security control
In a cybersecurity context, a safeguard or countermeasure prescribed for an information system or an organization designed to protect the confidentiality, integrity, and availability of its information and to meet a set of defined security requirements. *(FIPS 199)*

security entitlement
The rights and property interest of an entitlement holder with respect to a financial asset. *(UCC 8-102(a)(17))*
See *entitlement holder; financial asset*.

Ss

security interest
An interest in personal property that exists by contract as security for payment or performance of an obligation. *(UCC 1-201(35))*

security procedure
In the case of a payment order, a procedure established by agreement of a customer and a receiving bank for the purposes of:
- Verifying that a payment order or communication amending or cancelling a payment order is that of the customer, or
- Detecting error in the transmission or the content of the payment order or communication.

A "security procedure" may require the use of algorithms or other codes, identifying words or numbers, encryption, callback procedures, or similar security devices. Comparison of a signature on a payment order or communication with an authorized specimen signature of the customer is not by itself a security procedure. *(UCC 4A-201)*
See also *payment order.*

segment
One of two or more divisions, product departments, plants, or other subdivisions of an organization reporting directly to a home office, usually identified with responsibility for profit and/or producing a product or service. This term includes U.S. federal government-owned contractor-operated facilities and joint ventures and subsidiaries (domestic and foreign) in which the organization has a majority ownership or less than a majority ownership, but over which it exercises control. *(FAR 2.101)*

Selection of Architects and Engineers statute
A federal law (40 U.S.C. Chapter 11) establishing federal policy concerning the selection of firms and individuals to perform architectural, engineering, and related services for the federal government. Formerly known as the *Brooks Architect-Engineer Act. (40 U.S.C. 1101)*

self-insurance
The assumption or retention of the risk of loss by the contractor, whether voluntarily or involuntarily. "Self-insurance" includes the deductible portion of purchased insurance. *(FAR 2.101)*

self-insurance charge
A cost which represents the projected average loss under a self-insurance plan. *(FAR 31.001)*
See *self-insurance.*

seller
(1) A person who sells or contracts to sell goods or services. *(UCC 2-103(d))*
(2) A contracted party tasked with fulfilling the buyer's requirement for goods and/or services. *(CMS)*
Contrast with *buyer.*

selling
A generic term encompassing all efforts to market a seller's products or services. *(FAR 31.205-38(a))*
See also *selling activity.*

selling activity
Includes the following broad categories:
- Advertising,
- Corporate image enhancement,
- Bid and proposal costs,
- Market planning, and
- Direct selling.

(FAR 31.205-38(b))
See *selling*; see also *bid and proposal* (B&P) *costs; direct selling; market planning.*

Senior Executive Service (SES)
Appropriated fund positions in an agency classified above General Service-15 or in level 4 or 5 of the Executive Schedule, or an equivalent position, which is not required to be filled by an appointment by the president by and with the advice and consent of the Senate. *(DODM 1000.12-M-VI)*

senior procurement executive (SPE)
The individual appointed pursuant to 41 U.S.C. 1702(c) who is responsible for management direction of the acquisition system of the executive agency, including implementation of the unique acquisition policies, regulations, and standards of the executive agency. *(FAR 2.101)*

sensitive property
Property potentially dangerous to the public safety or security if stolen, lost, or misplaced, or that shall be subject to exceptional physical security, protection, control, and accountability. Examples include weapons, ammunition, explosives, controlled substances, radioactive materials, hazardous materials or wastes, or precious metals. *(FAR 45.101)*

separate contract
(1) In the context of contract bundling/consolidation, a contract that has been performed by any business, including small and other than small business concerns.

Ss

(FAR 2.101)
See *"bundling; consolidation;* compare with *separate smaller contract.*
(2) In the context of utility services, means a utility services contract (other than a GSA areawide contract, an "Authorization" under an areawide contract, or an interagency agreement) to cover the acquisition of utility services. *(FAR 41.101)*
See *utility service;* see also *areawide contract; authorization.*

separate smaller contract

In the context of contract bundling/consolidation, a contract that has been performed by one or more small business concerns or that was suitable for award to one or more small business concerns that has been or is being considered for consolidation, along with other separate smaller contracts, into a solicitation for a single contract, a multiple-award contract, or a task or delivery order. *(FAR 2.101)*
See *bundling; consolidation;* compare with *separate smaller contract.*

separable cost

A cost directly identifiable with a particular segment. *(NCMA-CA)*

sequester/sequestration

The cancellation of budgetary resources provided by discretionary appropriations or direct spending law. Under "sequestration," an amount of money equal to the difference between the cap set in the budget resolution and the amount actually appropriated is "sequestered" by the Department of the Treasury and not handed over to the agencies to which it was originally appropriated by Congress. *(CMBOK; 2 U.S.C. 900(c)(2))*

service and warranty costs

Include those costs arising from fulfillment of any contractual obligation of a contractor to provide services such as installation, training, correcting defects in the products, replacing defective parts, and making refunds in the case of inadequate performance. *(FAR 31.205-39)*

service contract

(1) A contract that directly engages the time and effort of a contractor whose primary purpose is to perform an identifiable task rather than to furnish an end item of supply. A service contract may be either a nonpersonal or personal contract. It can also cover services performed by either professional or nonprofessional personnel whether on an individual or organizational basis. *(FAR 37.101)*
(2) Any federal government contract, or subcontract thereunder, the principal purpose of which is to furnish services in the United States through the use of service employees, except as exempted by the Service Contract Labor Standards statute (41 U.S.C. Chapter 67). *(FAR 22.001)*
See also *Service Contract Labor Standards statute.*

Service Contract Labor Standards statute

A federal law (41 U.S.C. Chapter 67) establishing labor standards for such matters as wages and working conditions. It applies to every government contract over a stipulated dollar threshold when its principal purpose is to furnish services to the government. (Formerly known as the "Service Contract Act of 1965.") *(FAR Subpart 22.10)* (See also FAR 22.1003-3 for statutory exemptions.)
See *professional services.*

service-disabled veteran–owned small business (SDVOSB)

A small business concern in which—
* Not less than 51 percent is owned by one or more service-disabled veterans or, in the case of any publicly owned business, not less than 51 percent of the stock of which is owned by one or more service-disabled veterans; and
* The management and daily business operations of which are controlled by one or more service-disabled veterans or, in the case of a service-disabled veteran with permanent and severe disability, the spouse or permanent caregiver of such veteran.
(FAR 2.101)

service employee

Any person engaged in the performance of a service contract other than any person employed in a bona fide executive, administrative, or professional capacity. This term includes all such persons regardless of any contractual relationship that may be alleged to exist between a contractor or subcontractor and such persons. *(FAR 22.001)*
See *service contract;* compare with *exempt employee.*

service level agreement (SLA)

A contract between a service provider and the end user that describes the minimum performance criteria the service provider promises to meet while delivering a

Ss

service. It also typically sets out the remedial action and any penalties that will take effect if performance falls below the promised standard. *(DGBCT)*

service life
The period of usefulness of a tangible capital asset (or group of assets) to its current owner. The period may be expressed in units of time or output. The estimated service life of a tangible capital asset (or group of assets) is a current forecast of its service life and is the period over which depreciation cost is to be assigned. *(FAR 31.001)*
See also *tangible capital asset*.

service mark (SM)
Designates particular manners or modes of service delivery protected as intellectual property. *(DGBCT)*
See also *trademark (™)*.

service recipient
An agency organizational unit, programmatic entity, or chargeable account that receives information processing services from an information processing service organization (IPSO). A service recipient may be either internal or external to the organization responsible for providing information resources services, but normally does not report either to the manager or director of the IPSO or to the same immediate supervisor. *(OMB A-130)*

services
All activities engaged in for other persons for a consideration. Such activities predominately involve the performance of a service as distinguished from selling or leasing property. "Services" includes activities performed by a person for its members or shareholders. In determining what is a service, the intended use, principal objective, or ultimate objective of the contracting parties shall not be controlling. "Services" also includes construction activities and all tangible personal property that will become an ingredient or component part of a construction project. Such tangible personal property retains its character as tangible personal property until it is installed as an ingredient or component part of a construction project. However, sales of tangible personal property that will become an ingredient or component part of a construction project to persons engaged in the construction business are sales of tangible personal property. *(FAR 29.401-4(a))*

servicing agency
The U.S. federal agency that will conduct an assisted acquisition on behalf of the requesting agency. *(FAR 2.101)*
See *assisted acquisition; interagency acquisition; see also requesting agency*.

set-aside
(1) A kind or class of procurement reserved for contenders that fit a certain category (e.g., business size, region, minority status). *(OPM)*
(2) The reserving of an acquisition exclusively for participation by small business concerns. A small business set-aside may be open to all small businesses. A small business set-aside of a single acquisition or a class of acquisitions may be total or partial. *(FAR 19.5(a))*
See *partial set-aside; total set-aside*; compare with *unrestricted procurement*.

settle
To pay in cash, by clearing-house statement, in a charge or credit or by remittance, or otherwise as agreed. A settlement may be either provisional or final. *(UCC 4-104(a)(11))*

settlement agreement
A written agreement in the form of a contract modification settling all or a severable portion of a settlement proposal. *(FAR 49.001)*
See also *settlement proposal*.

settlement date
As it applies to electronic funds transfer, means the date on which an electronic funds transfer payment is credited to the contractor's financial institution. *(FAR 32.902)*
See also *electronic funds transfer* (EFT).

settlement point
In negotiation, the final point(s) of agreement, if this happens. *(GTY)*
See *negotiation*.

settlement proposal
A proposal for effecting settlement of a contract terminated in whole or in part, submitted by a contractor or subcontractor in the form, and supported by the data required by *FAR* Part 49. (A settlement proposal is included within the generic meaning of the term "claim" under false claims acts (i.e., 18 U.S.C. 287 and 31 U.S.C. 3729).) *(FAR 49.001)*

Ss

Severin Doctrine

The federal government has privity of contract with the prime contractor, not with any of the subcontractors under the prime contract. As such, if one of the prime's subcontractors incurs damages through the fault of the government, the subcontractor does not have a direct avenue of recovery against the government. However, under the "*Severin* Doctrine" (*Severin v. United States Court of Claims*, 1943. 99 Ct. Cl. 435), a prime contractor may sue the government for damages incurred by one of its subcontractors through the fault of the government, but only when the prime contractor has reimbursed its subcontractor for the latter's damages or remains liable for such reimbursement in the future. These are the only ways in which the damages of the subcontractor can become, in turn, the damages of the prime contractor, for which recovery may be had against the government. *(S-1943)*

severable contract

A contract divisible into separate parts; a default of one section does not invalidate the whole contract. *(FBL)*

severable expansion

An expansion of currently contracted in-house or inter-service support agreement–provided work that could be provided using the current approach or could, without severe additional administrative burden, be provided by another competitive offeror. Economies of scale are not justification for dismissing new or expanded work as severable; these economies will be tested through competitive offer. *(OMB A-76)*

severance pay

A payment in addition to regular salaries and wages by employers to workers whose employment is being involuntarily terminated. *(FAR 31.205-6(g)(1))*

severe forms of trafficking in persons

Means:
- Sex trafficking in which a commercial sex act is induced by force, fraud, or coercion, or in which the person induced to perform such act has not attained 18 years of age; or
- The recruitment, harboring, transportation, provision, or obtaining of a person for labor or services, through the use of force, fraud, or coercion for the purpose of subjection to involuntary servitude, peonage, debt bondage, or slavery.

(FAR 22.1702)
See also *commercial sex act; sex trafficking*.

sex trafficking

The recruitment, harboring, transportation, provision, or obtaining of a person for the purpose of a commercial sex act. *(FAR 22.1702)*
See *commercial sex act*.

"shall"

Means the imperative. *(FAR 2.101)*

sharing base

In value engineering, means the number of affected end items on contracts of the contracting office accepting the value engineering change proposal. *(FAR 48.001)*
See *value engineering; value engineering change proposal* (VECP).

sharing period

In value engineering, the period beginning with acceptance of the first unit incorporating the value engineering change proposal (VECP) and ending at a calendar date or event determined by the contracting officer for each VECP. *(FAR 48.001)*
See *value engineering; value engineering change proposal* (VECP).

sharp practice

Indirect misrepresentation, unscrupulous shrewdness, or deceit or trickery, just short of actual fraud. Such actions are usually designed for short-term gain, but typically act to the detriment of good long-term supplier relations based on honesty, truth, and respect. *(GKPT)*

Sherman Act

See *Antitrust Act*.

shift premium

The difference between the regular rate of pay to an employee and the higher rate paid for extra-pay-shift work. *(DGBCT)*

shipment

(1) In general, freight transported or to be transported. *(FAR 2.101)*
See *shipper*.
(2) All of the cargo carried under the terms of a single bill of lading. *(46 U.S.C. 40102(21))*

shipper

A person that enters into a contract of transportation with a carrier. *(UCC 7-102(a)(12))*
See also *carrier*.

Ss

shop drawings

Drawings submitted by the construction contractor or a subcontractor at any tier or required under a construction contract, showing in detail either or both of the following:

- The proposed fabrication and assembly of structural elements; and
- The installation (i.e., form, fit, and attachment details) of materials or equipment.

(FAR 2.101)

shop rights

The rights of an employer in the use and/or ownership, without payment of royalties, of an invention or work conceived by an employee in the course of employment, or through the use of the employer's facilities, in which the employee created the invention or work as part of his or her job. Also referred to as "work made for hire" or "work for hire." *(DGBCT)*

should

An expected course of action or policy that is to be followed unless inappropriate for a particular circumstance. *(FAR 2.101)*

should cost

A specialized form of cost analysis designed to estimate what an item or system "should cost" based upon a review of all applicable seller business methods, reflecting reasonably achievable seller economy and efficiency. A should-cost review differs from traditional evaluation methods because it does not assume that a seller's historical costs reflect efficient and economical operation; instead, the review evaluates the economy and efficiency of the seller's existing workforce, methods, materials, facilities, operating systems, and management. This review should include subcontractor procedures when subcontracting is part of the proposal. The result is utilized to develop realistic price objectives for contract negotiation purposes. *(DGBCT; GOAT; P&L I)*
See also *contractor's plant*.

show cause notice

(1) A written delinquency notice informing a contractor of failure to perform within the specified terms of the contract and advising that the government is considering termination for default. It affords the contractor the opportunity to "show cause" why it should not be terminated. *(OPM)*

(2) If termination for default appears appropriate, the contracting officer should, if practicable, notify the contractor in writing of the possibility of the termination. This notice shall call the contractor's attention to the contractual liabilities if the contract is terminated for default and shall request the contractor to show cause why the contract should not be terminated for default. The notice may further state that failure of the contractor to present an explanation may be taken as an admission that no valid explanation exists. *(FAR 49.402-3(e)(1)*
See *default termination*; see also *cure notice*.

shrinkage

An additional quantity of material added to the quantity listed on the bill of materials to provide for spoilage, scrap, waste, and natural attrition. *(DOD-MMH)*
See *attrition*.

sight

Bills of exchange are frequently made payable at "sight" (i.e., on presentment), which then means the bill should be paid without further delay, or within the established timeframe for payment specified by the bill. (BLD)

sign

With present intent to authenticate or adopt a record, to:

- Execute or adopt a tangible symbol, or
- Attach to or logically associate with the record an electronic sound, symbol, or process.

(UCC 7-102(a)(11))
See *signature/signed*.

signature/signed

(1) The discrete, verifiable symbol of an individual that, when affixed to a writing with the knowledge and consent of the individual, indicates a present intention to authenticate the writing. This includes electronic symbols. *(FAR 2.101)*
See also *sign*.

(2) With respect to a record that is not a writing, this term includes the attachment to or logical association with the record of an electronic symbol, sound, or process to or with the record with the present intent to adopt or accept the record. *(UCC 3-602(f))*

significant deficiency

In the context of a contractor business system, refers to a shortcoming in the system that materially affects the ability of officials of the U.S. Department of Defense to rely upon information produced by the system that is

Ss

needed for management purposes. *(DFARS 252.242-7005)*
See *contractor business systems*.

significant military equipment (SME)
Defense articles for which special export controls are warranted because of the capacity of such articles for substantial military utility or capability. These items are identified on the U.S. Munitions List in the *International Traffic in Arms Regulation (ITAR)*. *(DISCS)*
See also *defense article; International Traffic in Arms Regulation* (ITAR); *Munitions List*.

significant weakness
In the context of a contractor proposal received by the U.S. federal government, this term refers to a flaw in the proposal that appreciably increases the risk of unsuccessful contract performance. *(FAR 15.001)*
See *weakness*.

simple interest
Interest computed on the principal of a loan or account. *(MW)*

simplified acquisition
Refers to relatively low-dollar-threshold contracts and transactions using simplified acquisition procedures. Simplified acquisition usually occurs without the elaborate and formal solicitation techniques required by sealed bidding and negotiation. It is often used for very small purchases made using simplified acquisition tools, such as government purchase cards. *(DGBCT)*
See *"simplified acquisition procedures* (SAP)"; see also *"government purchase card* (GPC; P card)"

simplified acquisition procedure(s) (SAP)
(1) Methods for entering into contracts without using elaborate and formal solicitation techniques (i.e., invitations for bids and requests for proposals). They are restricted to purchases under the simplified acquisition threshold. *(GSFC)*
See *"simplified acquisition threshold* (SAT)"
(2) The methods prescribed in *FAR* Part 13 for making purchases of supplies or services. *(FAR 2.101)* (See also *FAR* Part 13.)

simplified acquisition threshold (SAT)
A standard monetary amount (as defined in FAR 2.101) below which simplified acquisition procedures may be used, except for—
• Acquisitions of supplies or services that, as deter-

mined by the head of the agency, are to be used to support a contingency operation or to facilitate defense against or recovery from nuclear, biological, chemical, or radiological attack, where the monetary amount varies based on whether the contract to be awarded and performed, or purchase to be made, is inside or outside the United States; and
• Acquisitions of supplies or services that, as determined by the head of the agency, are to be used to support a humanitarian or peacekeeping operation (10 U.S.C. 2302), where a different monetary amount will be used as the simplified acquisition threshold for any contract to be awarded and performed, or purchase to be made, outside the United States.
(FAR 2.101)

Single Award Schedule (SAS)
Contracts made with one supplier, pursuant to the Federal Supply Schedule Program, to cover delivery to one geographic area. *(NCMA-WS)*
See *Federal Supply Schedule* (FSS) *Program*.

single, governmentwide point of entry
The one point of entry to be designated by the administrator of the Office of Federal Procurement Policy that will allow the private sector to electronically access procurement opportunities governmentwide. *(FAR 2.101)*
See *governmentwide point of entry* (GPE).

single point adjustment (SPA)
A process that sets existing contract cost or schedule variances to zero. It typically accompanies a re-plan of all remaining effort with the goal of completing the project on schedule and on budget. This change is accomplished in the current period (the single point) to avoid making retroactive changes. *(NDIA II)*

single process initiative (SPI)
Eliminates costly multiple processes within contractor facilities. It is the concept of doing things one way where possible; e.g., business processes, quality assurance processes, or manufacturing processes. *(DGBCT)*

single source
One source among others in a competitive marketplace that, for justifiable reason, is found to be most advantageous for the purpose of contract award. *(OPM)*

Ss

single-source negotiation

Negotiation with a single provider, because either the provider is the sole supplier of the product or service, or the relationship with the provider is of strategic importance based on long-term relationships and built on mutual trust. Also called "sole-source negotiation." *(DGBCT)*

single vendor integrity (SVI)

The requirement that all replacement spares and support equipment for a specific system are provided by the same manufacturer that provided the original equipment. *(DISCS)*

site of construction

The general physical location of any building, highway, or other change or improvement to real property that is undergoing construction, rehabilitation, alteration, conversion, extension, demolition, or repair. This term includes any temporary location or facility at which a contractor or other participating party meets a demand or performs a function relating to a U.S. federal government contract or subcontract. *(FAR 22.801)*
See also *site of the work*.

site of the work

In the context of labor standards for contracts involving construction, means the primary site of the work—i.e., the physical place or places where the construction called for in the contract will remain when work on it is completed. This term also includes the secondary site of the work, if any—i.e., any other site where a significant portion of the building or work is constructed, provided that such site is located in the United States and established specifically for the performance of the contract or project. *(FAR 22.401)*
See also *site of construction*.

site visit

An inspection of the site where services are to be performed. Site visits are conducted by offerors or "quoters" to satisfy themselves regarding all general and local conditions that may affect the cost of contract performance, to the extent that the information is reasonably obtainable. *(GOAT)*

Six Sigma

A process improvement strategy that improves output quality by reducing defects. "Six Sigma" is named after a statistical concept where a process produces 3.4 defects per million opportunities. Therefore, it can

also be thought of as a goal, where processes not only encounter fewer defects, but do so consistently (with low variability). *(GLSS)*
See also *Lean; Lean Six Sigma* (LSS).

size standards

Measures established by the SBA to define whether a business entity is "small" and, thus, eligible for federal government programs and preferences reserved for "small business" concerns. SBA establishes small business size standards on an industry-by-industry basis and matched with the North American Industry Classification System (NAICS) codes. The standards are applied by classifying the product or service being acquired in the industry whose definition best describes the principal nature of the product or service being acquired. SBA's size standards are published on the SBA website *(FAR 19.102(a)(1); FAR 19.102(b)(1); 13 CFR 121.101(a))* (See also http://www.sba.gov/content/table-small-business-size-standards.)
See *small business concern*; see also *North American Industry Classification System* (NAICS).

Small Business Act (SBA)

A federal law (15 U.S.C. 631, *et seq.*) providing preferences for small and small disadvantaged businesses in government contracting. *(GCG)*

Small Business Administration (SBA)

The federal government agency whose function is to aid, counsel, provide financial assistance to, and protect the interests of the small business community. *(GSFC)*

small business concern

A concern, including its affiliates, that is independently owned and operated, not dominant in the field of operation in which it is bidding on federal government contracts, and qualified as a "small business" under the criteria and size standards in 13 CFR Part 121. Such a concern is "not dominant in its field of operation" when it does not exercise a controlling or major influence on a national basis in a kind of business activity in which a number of business concerns are primarily engaged. In determining whether dominance exists, consideration must be given to all appropriate factors, including volume of business, number of employees, financial resources, competitive status or position, ownership or control of materials, processes, patents, license agreements, facilities, sales territory, and nature of business activity. *(FAR 2.101)* (See also FAR 19.102 and 15 U.S.C. 632.)

Ss

Small Business Innovation Research (SBIR) Program

A program established under Section 9 of the Small Business Act (15 U.S.C. 631, *et seq.*) that requires federal agencies with research and development budgets in excess of a specified dollar amount to set aside a fixed percentage of their budgets exclusively for small business participation. *(10 U.S.C. 2500(11))*

Small Business Jobs Act of 2010 (SBJA)

A federal law (*Pub. L.* 111-240) to improve federal government assistance to small businesses. The act created the Small Business Lending Fund Program to enhance loan provisions. It provides for parity across federal small business programs by increasing "availability of credit" and alternate size standards, as well as other measures. (See https://govinfo.gov/app/details/PLAW-111publ240.)

small business set-aside

A set-aside reserves an acquisition exclusively for small businesses. A small business set-aside may be open to all small businesses. A small business set-aside may relate to a single acquisition or a class of acquisitions and may be total or partial. For federal government contacts, all acquisitions within a certain dollar range are automatically set-aside for small business. Small business set-asides may be withdrawn by the contracting officer if award would be detrimental to the public interest (e.g., paying more than a fair market price). *(FAR 19.501(a))*

Small Business Subcontracting Program

Any contractor receiving a contract for more than the simplified acquisition threshold must agree in the contract that small business, veteran-owned small business, service-disabled veteran-owned small business, HUBZone small business, small disadvantaged business, and women-owned small business concerns will have the maximum practicable opportunity to participate in contract performance consistent with its efficient performance. Prime contractors must also establish procedures to ensure the timely payment of amounts due pursuant to the terms of their subcontracts with small business, veteran-owned small business, service-disabled veteran-owned small business, HUBZone small business, small disadvantaged business, and women-owned small business concerns. *(FAR 19.702)*

small business subcontractor

A concern that does not exceed the size standard for the North American Industry Classification System (NAICS) code that the prime contractor determines best describes the product or service being acquired by the subcontract. *(FAR 2.101)* (See also FAR 19.102.) See also *size standards*.

small business teaming arrangement

An arrangement where—
- Two or more small business concerns have formed a joint venture, or a small business offeror agrees with one or more other small business concerns to have them act as its subcontractors under a specified federal government contract;
- The small business teaming arrangement between the offeror and its small business subcontractor(s) exists through a written agreement between the parties that is specifically referred to as a "small business teaming arrangement," and the same sets forth the different responsibilities, roles, and percentages (or other allocations) of work as it relates to the acquisition.

In addition—
- Specific to civilian agencies, a "small business teaming arrangement" may include two business concerns in a mentor-protégé relationship when both the mentor and the protégé are "small" or the protégé is "small" and the concerns have received an exception to affiliation pursuant to 13 CFR 121.103(h)(3)(ii) or (iii).
- Specific to the DOD, a "small business teaming arrangement" may include two business concerns in a mentor-protégé relationship in the DOD Pilot Mentor-Protégé Program (see Section 831 of the National Defense Authorization Act for Fiscal Year 1991 (*Pub. L.* 101-510; 10 U.S.C. 2302 note)) when both the mentor and the protégé are "small." There is no exception to joint venture size affiliation for offers received from teaming arrangements under the DOD Pilot Mentor-Protégé Program.
- Regarding the exception to affiliation for offers received from small business teaming arrangement in the case of a solicitation of offers for a bundled contract with a reserve see 13 CFR 121.103(b)(9).

(FAR 2.101)

Small Business Technology Transfer Program (STTR)

A small business program established under Section 9 of the Small Business Act (15 U.S.C. 638) that expands funding opportunities in the federal innovation and development arena. Central to the program is expansion

Ss

of public/private-sector partnership to include the joint venture opportunities for small business and some nonprofit research institutions. *(10 U.S.C. 2500(12))*

small disadvantaged business concern

Consistent with 13 CFR 124.1002, a small business concern under the size standard applicable to the acquisition, that:

- Is at least 51-percent unconditionally and directly owned (as defined at 13 CFR 124.105) by–
  - One or more socially disadvantaged (as defined at 13 CFR 124.103) and economically disadvantaged (as defined at 13 CFR 124.104) individuals who are citizens of the United States; and
  - Each individual claiming economic disadvantage has a net worth not exceeding a specified dollar threshold after taking into account the applicable exclusions set forth at 13 CFR 124.104(c)(2); and
- The management and daily business operations of which are controlled (as defined at 13 CFR 124.106) by individuals who meet the criteria outlined in this definition.

(FAR 2.101)
See *small business concern*.

smart card

See *government purchase card* (GPC; P Card).

smart contract

A computer protocol intended to facilitate, verify, or enforce the negotiation or performance of a contract. *(BBDM)*

socioeconomic programs

Programs designed to benefit particular groups. They represent a multitude of program interests and objectives unrelated to procurement objectives. Some examples of these are preferences for small businesses and for American products, required sources for specified items, and minimum labor pay levels mandated for contractors. *(GPM)*

software

(1) Computer programs that comprise a series of instructions, rules, routines, or statements, regardless of the media in which they are recorded, that allow or cause a computer to perform a specific operation or series of operations. *(FAR 2.101)*
(2) Recorded information comprising source code list-

ings, design details, algorithms, processes, flow charts, formulas, and related material that would enable the computer program to be produced, created, or compiled. This term does not include computer databases or computer software documentation. *(FAR 2.101)*
See also *computer database; computer software documentation*.
(3) A computer program and any supporting information provided in connection with a transaction relating to the program. This term *does not* include a computer program that is included in the definition of "goods." *(UCC 9-102(a)(76))*

software as a service (SaaS)

A software delivery method that provides access to software as a web-based service. *(DGBCT)*

sole-source acquisition

A contract for the purchase of supplies or services that is entered into or proposed to be entered into after soliciting and negotiating with only one source. *(FAR 2.101)*
See also *inappropriate sole-source requirement*.

solicitation

Any request to submit offers or quotations to the Government. Solicitations under sealed bid procedures are called "invitations for bids." Solicitations under negotiated procedures are called "requests for proposals." Solicitations under simplified acquisition procedures may require submission of either a quotation or an offer. *(FAR 2.101)*
See also *invitation for bids* (IFB); *request for proposals* (RFP); *simplified acquisition procedures* (SAP).

solicitation provision

A term or condition used only in solicitations and applying only before contract award. *(FAR 2.101)*

solution

See *capability solution*.

SourceAmerica

See *AbilityOne Program*.

source selection

(1) The process of analyzing submitted offers in accordance with the solicitation evaluation criteria to select the source that has the highest probability of satisfactory contract performance. The value added by this process is in mitigating buyer risk by selecting the offeror

Ss

most likely to satisfactorily perform the contract. This process is part of the "award" life cycle phase. *(CMS)*
See also *award life cycle phase*.

(2) In a federal government context, the process wherein the requirements, facts, recommendations, and government policy relevant to an award decision in a competitive procurement of a system/project are examined and the decision made. *(DSMC)*

(3) Selection of the proposal that represents the best value *(FAR 15.302)*
See also *rating/scoring system*.

source selection advisory council (SSAC)

A group of senior federal government personnel who provide counsel during the source selection process and must prepare the comparative analysis of the source selection evaluation board's evaluation results, when directed by the source selection authority. *(SSP)*
See *source selection*; see also *source selection authority (SSA); source selection evaluation board (SSEB)*.

source selection authority (SSA)

(1) In a federal government procurement, the official designated to make the source selection decision. *(SSP)*

(2) The contracting officer is designated as the source selection authority, unless the agency head appoints another individual for a particular acquisition or group of acquisitions. *(15.303)*
See *source selection decision*.

source selection decision

The source selection authority's (SSA) decision shall be based on a comparative assessment of proposals against all source selection criteria in the solicitation. While the SSA may use reports and analyses prepared by others, the source selection decision shall represent the SSA's independent judgment. The source selection decision shall be documented (i.e., the "source selection decision document" (SSDD)), and the documentation shall include the rationale for any business judgments and tradeoffs made or relied on by the SSA, including benefits associated with additional costs. Although the rationale for the selection decision must be documented, that documentation need not quantify the tradeoffs that led to the decision. *(FAR 15.308)*
See *"source selection decision document (SSDD)"*; see also *"source selection authority (SSA)"*

source selection decision document (SSDD)

The document that reflects the source selection author-

ity's independent, integrated, comparative assessment and decision. *(SSP)*
See *"source selection decision"*; see also *"source selection authority (SSA)"*

source selection evaluation board (SSEB)

(1) Any board, team, council, or other group that evaluates bids or proposals. *(FAR 3.104-1)*

(2) A group of federal government and, if needed, approved nongovernment personnel, representing the various functional and technical disciplines relevant to the acquisition, whose function is to evaluate proposals and report its findings. *(NCMA-SS; SSP)*

(3) Also known as a *source selection evaluation team (SSET)*.

source selection evaluation team (SSET)

A group of military and/or government civilian personnel, representing functional and technical disciplines, that performs the duties of a source selection evaluation board (SSEB) and a source selection advisory council (SSAC). It can also be a subgroup of a SSEB, that is, a group of military and/or government civilian personnel, representing a particular functional or technical discipline that evaluates one area of a contractor's proposal in support of the source selection evaluation board, for example, a "cost SSET." *(DAAT)*
Compare with *source selection evaluation board (SSEB)*.

source selection information

Any of the following information that is prepared for use by a federal agency for the purpose of evaluating a bid or proposal to enter into a federal agency procurement contract, if that information has not been previously made available to the public or disclosed publicly:

- Bid prices submitted in response to an agency solicitation for sealed bids, or lists of those bid prices before bid opening;
- Proposed costs or prices submitted in response to an agency solicitation, or lists of those proposed costs or prices;
- Source selection plans;
- Technical evaluation plans;
- Technical evaluations of proposals;
- Cost or price evaluations of proposals;
- Competitive range determinations that identify proposals that have a reasonable chance of being selected for award of a contract;
- Rankings of bids, proposals, or competitors;
- Reports and evaluations of source selection panels,

Ss

boards, or advisory councils; and

- Other information marked as "source selection information" based on a case-by-case determination by the head of the agency, the head's designee, or the contracting officer that its disclosure would jeopardize the integrity or successful completion of the federal agency procurement to which the information relates.

(41 U.S.C. 2101(7)) (See also FAR 2.101 and FAR 3.104.)

source selection plan (SSP)

A plan that describes how the source selection will be organized, how proposals will be evaluated and analyzed, and how source(s) will be selected. This term refers not only to the plan itself, but also to the document that describes the plan, including the selection criteria, the process, and the organization to be used in evaluating proposals for competitively awarded contracts. The source selection plan is written by the program office and approved by the source selection authority. Typically, the source selection plan consists of two parts:

- The first part describes the organization and responsibilities of the source selection team, and
- The second part identifies the evaluation criteria and detailed procedures for proposal evaluation.

(DAAT; HCS; SSP)
See also *source selection; source selection team* (SST).

source selection team (SST)

A team that is tailored to the unique acquisition and tasked with carrying out a source selection. Composition of the team generally consists of:

- The source selection authority,
- The procuring contracting officer (if different from the source selection authority),
- The source selection advisory council,
- The source selection evaluation board,
- Advisors,
- Cost or price experts,
- Legal counsel,
- Small business specialists, and
- Other subject matter experts.

(SSP)

spare part

An individual part, subassembly, or assembly supplied for the maintenance or repair of systems or equipment. *(DISCS)*

Spearin Doctrine

A legal doctrine derived from a 1918 Supreme Court decision (*United States v. Spearin*, 248 U.S. 132 (1918)) stating that by providing the contractor with specifications to be followed in carrying out the contract work, the U.S. federal government impliedly warrants that, if the contractor complies with those specifications, an adequate result will follow. Also known as *implied warranty of specifications*. *(DGBCT)*
See *implied warranty*.

special competency

A special or unique capability, including qualitative aspects, developed incidental to the primary functions of the Federally Funded Research and Development Centers to meet some special need. *(FAR 2.101)*
See *Federally Funded Research and Development Center* (FFRDC).

special indorsement

(1) In the case of an instrument, an indorsement made by the holder of an instrument, whether payable to an identified person or payable to bearer, that identifies a person to whom it makes the instrument payable. When specially indorsed, an instrument becomes payable to the identified person and may be negotiated only by the indorsement of that person. *(UCC 3-205(a))*
See *indorsement; negotiable instrument*.
(2) In the case of a security, an indorsement that specifies to whom a security is to be transferred or who has power to transfer it. *(UCC 8-304(a))*
See *indorsement; security*.

special item number (SIN)

A group of generically similar (but not identical) supplies or services that are intended to serve the same general purpose or function. *(FAR 8.401)*

special test equipment

Either single or multipurpose integrated test units engineered, designed, fabricated, or modified to accomplish special purpose testing in performing a contract. It consists of items or assemblies of equipment including foundations and similar improvements necessary for installing special test equipment and standard or general-purpose items or components that are interconnected and interdependent so as to become a new functional entity for special testing purposes. Special test equipment does not include material, special tooling, real property, and equipment items used for general testing purposes or property that with rela-

tively minor expense can be made suitable for general purpose use. *(FAR 2.101)*
See also *special tooling; special tooling and special test equipment costs*.

special tooling

Jigs, dies, fixtures, molds, patterns, taps, gauges, and all components of these items including foundations and similar improvements necessary for installing special tooling, and which are of such a specialized nature that without substantial modification or alteration their use is limited to the development or production of particular supplies or parts thereof or to the performance of particular services. "Special tooling" *does not* include material, special test equipment, real property, equipment, machine tools, or similar capital items. *(FAR 2.101)*
See also *special test equipment; special tooling and special test equipment costs*.

special tooling and special test equipment costs

The costs of special tooling and special test equipment used in performing one or more contracts, which are allocated to the specific contract or contracts for which acquired, except when such costs include:

- Items acquired by the contractor before the effective date of the contract (or replacement of such items), whether or not altered or adapted for use in performing the contract; and
- Items which the contract schedule specifically excludes (which shall be included only as depreciation or amortization).

When items are disqualified as "special tooling" or "special test equipment" because with relatively minor expense they can be suitable for general purpose use and have a value as such commensurate with their value as "special tooling" or "special test equipment," this term includes the costs associated with adapting such items for use under the contract and the costs associated with returning them to their prior configuration. *(FAR 31.205-40(b)-(c))*
See "*special test equipment; special tooling*.

specialty metal

Means:
- Steel—
  - With a maximum alloy content exceeding one or more of the following limits: manganese, 1.65 percent; silicon, 0.60 percent; or copper, 0.60 percent; or

- Containing more than 0.25 percent of any of the following elements: aluminum, chromium, cobalt, molybdenum, nickel, niobium (columbium), titanium, tungsten, or vanadium;
- Metal alloys consisting of—
  - Nickel or iron-nickel alloys that contain a total of alloying metals other than nickel and iron in excess of 10 percent; or
  - Cobalt alloys that contain a total of alloying metals other than cobalt and iron in excess of 10 percent;
- Titanium and titanium alloys; or
- Zirconium and zirconium alloys.

(DFARS 252.225-7009(a))

specific enforcement

In the case of a breach of contract, refers to when a court requires the party that breached the contract to complete contract performance. Also called *specific performance*. *(CMBOK)*

specific performance

Synonymous with "specific enforcement." *(CMBOK)*
See *specific enforcement*.

specification

(1) A description of the technical requirements for a material, product, or service that includes the criteria for determining that the requirements have been met. *(NCMA-SB)*

(2) In federal government acquisition, a document prepared to support an acquisition that describes the government's essential technical requirements for purchased items, materials, or services and the criteria for determining whether those requirements are met. *(DODM 4120.24)*

(3) There are generally three types of specifications used in government contracting:

- "Detailed/design specifications": prescribe the design requirements, such as how the item is to be fabricated or what materials must be used. A specification that contains both performance and prescriptive requirements is still considered a detailed specification.
- "Functional specification": A purchase description that describes the deliverable in terms of performance characteristics and intended use, including those characteristics that at minimum are necessary to satisfy the intended use.
- "Performance-based specifications": define an item's functional requirements or capabilities, the

Ss

environment in which the item must operate, the item's interface and interchangeability characteristics, and the criteria for verifying the item's compliance. These specifications do not describe how a requirement is to be achieved, nor do they require the use of specific materials or parts or give detailed design or construction requirements beyond those needed to ensure interchangeability with existing items. *(NES-97)*
See also *guide specification; Spearin Doctrine*.

specification guide
See *guide specification*.

speculative buying
Purchasing material in excess of current and future known requirements with the intention of profiting on price movement. *(GKPT)*

spend analysis
The process of collecting, cleansing, classifying, and analyzing expenditure data with the purpose of reducing procurement costs, improving efficiency, and monitoring compliance. It can also be leveraged in other areas of business such as inventory management, budgeting and planning, and product development. There are three core areas of spend analysis: visibility, analysis, and process. Spend analysis is often viewed as part of a larger domain known as "spend management," which incorporates spend analysis, commodity management, and strategic sourcing. *(DGBCT)*

Spend Under Management (SUM)
In a category management context, this is a top-priority measure of category management performance. It is defined on a three-tier maturity model that tracks maturity on five key attributes that underpin category management: leadership, strategy, data, tools, and metrics. *(GWCM)*

spoilage
A form of waste material resulting from misuse of material or errors in workmanship. *(DOD-MMH)*

sponsor
In the context of a Federally Funded Research and Development Center (FFRDC), the U.S. executive agency which manages, administers, monitors, funds, and is responsible for the overall use of an FFRDC. Multiple agency sponsorship is possible as long as one agency agrees to act as the "primary sponsor." In the event of multiple sponsors, "sponsor" refers to the primary sponsor. *(FAR 35.017(b))*
See *Federally Funded Research and Development Center (FFRDC)*; see also *nonsponsor; primary sponsor; sponsoring agreement*.

sponsoring agreement
In the context of a Federally Funded Research and Development Center (FFRDC), a written agreement of sponsorship established between the federal government and an FFRDC in order to facilitate a long-term relationship between the government and the FFRDC, establish the FFRDC's mission, and ensure a periodic reevaluation of the FFRDC. The sponsoring agreement may take various forms; it may be included in a contract between the government and the FFRDC, or in another legal instrument under which an FFRDC accomplishes effort, or it may be in a separate written agreement. Notwithstanding its form, the sponsoring agreement shall be clearly designated as such by the sponsor. *(FAR 35.017-1(a))*
See *Federally Funded Research and Development Center (FFRDC)*; see also *nonsponsor; primary sponsor; sponsoring agreement*.

spot purchase
A one-time purchase made in the open market. *(DGBCT)*

spread-gain actuarial cost method
Any of the several projected benefit actuarial cost methods under which actuarial gains and losses are included as part of the current and future normal costs of a pension plan. *(FAR 31.001)*

standard
(1) In general, this term refers to a document, established by consensus, that provides rules, guidelines, or characteristics for activities or their results. *(ISO/IEC)*
(2) In an engineering or technical context, this term refers to a document that establishes uniform engineering or technical criteria, methods, processes, and practices. *(DODM 4120.24)*
(3) In federal government procurement, this term means:
- A document that establishes engineering and technical limitations and applications of items, materials, processes, methods, designs, and engineering practices and includes any related criteria deemed essential to achieve the highest practical degree of

Ss

uniformity in materials or products, or interchangeability of parts used in those products; or

- A criterion for determining the effectiveness of the procurement system by measuring the performance of the various elements of the system. *(FAR 10.001; 41 U.S.C. 114)*

See *American National Standards; association standards; company/consortium standards; de facto standards; defense standard; federal standard; General Services Administration (GSA) specifications and standards;," "International Electrotechnical Commission (IEC) Standards; International Organization for Standardization (ISO) Standards; International Telecommunications Union (ITU) Standards; non-government standard (NGS); private-sector standards; test method standard; voluntary/consensus standards.*

standard absorption costing

That type of product costing in which the cost of the finished unit is calculated as the sum of the standard allowances for the factors of production, without reference to the costs actually incurred. *(NCMA-CA)*

standard cost

Any cost computed with the use of pre-established measures. *(FAR 31.001)*

standard direct costing

That type of product costing in which the cost of the finished unit is calculated as the sum of the costs of the standard allowance for the factors of production, excluding fixed factory overhead, which is treated as a period cost, and without reference to the costs actually incurred. *(NCMA-CA)*

standard form (SF)

A specific form prescribed by a federal agency through regulation and approved by the General Services Administration for mandatory governmentwide use. They are each assigned a standard form (SF) number. (See www.gsa.gov.)

standard hours allowed (earned or worked)

The number of standard hours that are chargeable to production for the actual goods produced. *(NCMA-CA)*

Standard Industrial Classification (SIC) code

A code representing a category within the SIC System administered by the Statistical Policy Division of the Office of Management and Budget. The system was established to classify all industries in the U.S. economy.

A two-digit code designates each major industry group, which is coupled with a second two-digit code representing subcategories. SIC codes are published in the *Standard Industrial Classification Manual. (F&F)*
See *size standards*.

standard practice

Specifies procedures on how to conduct certain non-manufacturing functions. Standard practices are developed for functions that, at least some of the time, are obtained through contractors from private-sector firms. *(DODM 4120.24)*

standardization

The process of developing and agreeing on (by consensus or decision) uniform engineering and other criteria for products, processes, practices, and methods for achieving compatibility, interoperability, interchangeability, or commonality. *(DODM 4120.24)*

standardization agreement

The record of an agreement among several or all of the member nations of NATO to adopt like or similar equipment, supplies, and stores; as well as operational, logistics, and administrative procedures. *(DISCS)*

standards of conduct

The ethical conduct of personnel involved in the acquisition of goods and services. Within the federal government, business shall be conducted in a manner above reproach and, except as authorized by law or regulation, with complete impartiality and without preferential treatment. *(STBP)*

start-to-finish (SF)

In project management terminology, a logical relationship that establishes the following rule between two activities: The succeeding task cannot finish until a preceding task starts. (Valid use of a start-to-finish relationship is extremely rare in most project schedules.) *(NDIA II)*
See also *start-to-start* (SS).

start-to-start (SS)

In project management terminology, a logical relationship that establishes the following rule between two activities: The succeeding task cannot start until a preceding task starts. *(NDIA II)*
See also *start-to-finish* (SF).

Ss

state and local government
Includes any state, local, regional, or tribal government, or any instrumentality thereof (including any local educational agency or institution of higher education). *(40 U.S.C. 502(c)(3)(A))*
See also *local government*.

stated capital
The total par value or stated value of no-par issues of outstanding capital stock. Also called legal capital. *(MW)*
See *capital*.

statement of objectives (SOO)
A federal government–prepared document incorporated into the solicitation that states the overall performance objectives of the resulting contract. It is used in solicitations when the government intends to provide the maximum flexibility to each offeror to propose an innovative approach. *(FAR 2.101)*

statement of work (SOW)
That portion of a contract describing the actual work to be done by means of specifications or other minimum requirements, quantities, performance date, and a statement of the requisite quality. The SOW should reflect all work to be performed—communicating the work scope requirements for a program and defining the requirements to the fullest extent practicable. *(DSMC; EVMIG)*
See *design statement of work; functional statement of work; performance statement of work*.

static budget
A budget that is fixed for the entire period covered by the budget, with no changes based on actual activity. *(AT)*

statistical process control (SPC)
The application of statistical methods to monitor variation in a process over time. SPC displays variation in a process to identify special/assignable causes of variation versus common/chance causes of variation. *(SPP)*

status review meetings
Updated information on status, issues, and concerns should be shared between the buyer and seller during periodic face-to-face meetings. The frequency, content, and required attendees for these meetings should be mutually agreed to, and each should have a written agenda. These meetings should augment any written reports required and help serve as a means to continue an open and honest dialogue for issues related to contract performance. *(DGBCT)*
See *pre-performance meeting*.

statute
A law enacted by the legislative branch of government and signed by the president. Identifiable by a *Public Law (Pub. L.)* number. *(FAI)*

statute of limitations
A statute that sets limits to the time in which a lawsuit may be filed in certain causes of action. *(FBL)*

statutory law
The body of law that exists in legislatively enacted statutes, especially as distinguished from common law. *(MW)*
Compare with *civil law; common law*.

Stevenson-Wydler Technology Transfer Act
A federal law (*Pub. L. 96-480*) that allows the head of an agency to loan, lease, or transfer research equipment to educational institutions or certain nonprofit organizations. *(DGBCT; TIPS)*

stipulated damages
A fixed sum or formula that the contract provides as a remedy for partial or full breach of the contract. Also called *liquidated damages*. *(CMBOK)*

stockless purchasing
See *systems contract*.

stock out
Occurs when items normally carried in stock are exhausted. *(GKPT)*

stop-work order
A request for interim stoppage of work, such as when a work stoppage may be required for reasons such as advancements in the state of the art, production or engineering breakthroughs, or realignment of programs. *(FAR 42.1303)*
Contrast with *suspension of work*.

strategic plan
A document used by an organization to align its organization and budget structure with organizational priorities, missions, and objectives. *(AIMD)*

Ss

strategic sourcing

The collaborative and structured process of critically analyzing an organization's spending and using this information to make business decisions. Strategic sourcing involves the establishment or modification of acquisition vehicles to better address procurement needs and/or more effectively leverage spend, market position, market knowledge, and capabilities in contract terms and conditions. This process helps organizations optimize performance, minimize price, evaluate total life cycle management costs, improve vendor access to business opportunities, and otherwise increase the value of each dollar spent. *(GWCM)*

strategic sourcing accountable official (SSAO)

The designated official with the authority to coordinate a federal agency's internal strategic sourcing activities and its participation in governmentwide efforts. *(GWCM)*

Strategic Sourcing Leadership Council (SSLC)

See *Category Management Leadership Council (CMLC)*

strength

In the context of an offeror's proposal received by the federal government, this term refers to an aspect of an offeror's proposal that has merit or exceeds specified performance or capability requirements in a way that will be advantageous to the government during contract performance. *(SSP)*
Compare with *weakness*.

studies, analyses, and evaluations

A subdivision of advisory and assistance services. They are contracted services that provide organized, analytical assessments/evaluations in support of policy development, decision-making, management, or administration. Included are studies in support of research and development activities. Also included are acquisitions of models, methodologies, and related software supporting studies, analyses, or evaluations. *(FAR 2.101)* (See also *FAR* Subpart 37.2.)
See *"advisory and assistance services* (A&AS); see also *engineering and technical services; management and professional support services*.

subassembly

A major subdivision of an assembly consisting of a package of parts, elements, and/or circuits that perform a specific function. *(CNSSI 4009)*
See *assembly*.

subcategory

Governmentwide segmented areas of "level 1" category spend. Also referred to as "level 2." *(GWCM)*
See *category*.

subcontract

(1) A contract or contractual action entered into by a prime contractor or subcontractor for the purpose of obtaining supplies, materials, equipment, or services of any kind under a prime contract. *(FAR 3.502-1)*
(2) Any contract entered into by a subcontractor to furnish supplies or services for performance of a prime contract or a subcontract. This term includes, but is not limited to, purchase orders and changes and modifications to purchase orders. *(FAR 3.901; 3.1001; FAR 22.1702; FAR 22.1801; FAR 44.101)*
(3) Any agreement (other than one involving an employer-employee relationship) entered into by a federal government prime contractor or subcontractor calling for supplies and/or services required for performance of the contract, contract modification, or subcontract. *(FAR 19.701)*
(4) A contract between a buyer and a seller in which a significant part of the supplies or services being obtained is for eventual use in a prime contract. *(DSMC)*
(5) In an equal employment opportunity context, any agreement or arrangement between a contractor and any person (in which the parties do not stand in the relationship of an employer and an employee)–

- For the purchase, sale, or use of personal property or nonpersonal services that, in whole or in part, are necessary to the performance of any one or more contracts; or
- Under which any portion of the contractor's obligation under any one or more contracts is performed, undertaken, or assumed.

(FAR 22.801)
(6) A transfer of commercial items between divisions, subsidiaries, or affiliates of a contractor or subcontractor. *(FAR 12.001; FAR 15.401)*
(7) Any contract in support of a prime contract. *(CMBOK)*
See also *first-tier subcontract*.

subcontract data requirements list (SCDRL)

See *contract data requirements list*

Ss

subcontract management

In the context of the *Contract Management Standard*™, "subcontract management" is in the "post-award" life cycle phase of contract management, within the "perform contract" domain. It is the process of contract management of subcontracts, with the prime contractor being responsible for the performance of its supply chain. The value added by this process is in having a single point-of-contact responsible for:

* Subcontract award,
* Technical and financial performance,
* Monitoring performance, and
* Payment to the subcontractors and suppliers for the work accomplished under subcontract terms.

(CMS)
See *perform contract; post-award life cycle phase*; see also *administer contract; ensure quality; manage changes*.

subcontracting management

Describes the role a prime contractor has in ensuring a subcontractor performs in accordance with its contract with the prime. In a subcontract, the prime contractor delegates some of the required work to another company, the subcontractor. Subcontracting usually occurs where the contracted work, such as the construction of a building, requires a variety of skills. Responsibility for fulfilling the original contract remains with the original contracting party, the prime contractor. *(DGBCT)* (See also *FAR* Part 44.)

subcontracting plan

These plans are required for government acquisitions expected to exceed specific thresholds that have subcontracting possibilities. They must contain goals for both small businesses and small disadvantaged businesses. The goals are stated in terms of percentages of dollars awarded, and are negotiated with the contracting officer or the agency's small and disadvantaged business utilization specialist prior to contract award. The negotiated plan is subsequently incorporated into the contract by reference. Small businesses themselves are exempt from the requirement to submit a subcontracting plan. *(TIPS)* (See FAR 19.703.)
See *individual subcontracting plan; master subcontracting plan; subcontracting preference*.

subcontracting preference

A federal government policy that encourages prime contractors to assist minority companies by requiring that prime contractors develop subcontracting plans.

On all contracts over the simplified acquisition threshold, contractors must agree to allow small and small disadvantaged businesses opportunities to participate in contract performance. *(TIPS)*

subcontractor

(1) A contractor that enters into a contract with a prime contractor or a subcontractor of the prime contractor. *(DSMC)*
(2) Any person, other than the prime contractor, who offers to furnish or furnishes any supplies, materials, equipment, or services of any kind under a prime contract or a subcontract entered into in connection with such prime contract. *(FAR 3.502-1)*
(3) Includes any person who offers to furnish or furnishes general supplies to the prime contractor or a higher-tier subcontractor. *(FAR 3.502-1)*
(4) Any supplier, distributor, vendor, or firm (including a consultant) that furnishes supplies or services to or for a prime contractor or another subcontractor. *(FAR 3.901; FAR 3.1001; FAR 22.1702; FAR 22.1801; FAR 44.101)*
(5) In an equal employment opportunity context, means any person who holds, or has held, a subcontract subject to Executive Order 11246. *(FAR 22.801)*
See also *equal employment opportunity* (EEO); *Executive Order 11246*.

subcontractor employee

Any officer, partner, employee, or agent of a subcontractor. *(FAR 52.203-7(a))*
See *subcontractor*.

subcontractor's rights

A subcontractor has no contractual rights against the government upon the termination of a prime contract. However, a subcontractor may have rights against the prime contractor or intermediate subcontractor with whom it has contracted. Upon termination of a prime contract, the prime contractor and each subcontractor are responsible for the prompt settlement of the settlement proposals of their immediate subcontractors. *(DGBCT)*

subject invention

Any invention of the contractor made in the performance of work under a U.S. federal government contract. *(FAR 27.301)*
See *invention*.

Ss

sublease

A lease of goods—the right to possession and use of which was acquired by the lessor as a lessee under an existing lease. *(UCC 2A-103(w))*
See also *lease; lessee; lessor*.

subline item

A subset of a line item. Subline items may be used to facilitate tracking of performance, deliverables, payment, and contract funds accounting, or for other management purposes. Subline items may be either "deliverable" or "informational." *(FAR 2.101; 4.1004)*
See *line item*; see also *deliverable subline item; informational subline item*.

subsidiary

An entity in which more than 50 percent of the entity is owned directly by a parent corporation or through another subsidiary of a parent corporation. *(FAR 9.108-1)*

substantial bundling

Any bundling that results in a contract task or delivery order with estimated values listed at FAR 7.107-4. *(FAR 7.107-4(a)(1)-(2))*

substantial evidence

Information sufficient to support the reasonable belief that a particular act or omission has occurred. *(FAR 2.101)*

substantial performance

(1) Performance that deviates only in minor respects from contract requirements. *(DGBCT)*
(2) A doctrine that prohibits termination of a contract for default if a contractor's performance deviates only in minor respects from the contract's requirements. *(GCG)*

succession management

In the context of investments, an approach for determining when and how to replace current investments with other investments that provide greater benefits at lower costs. *(AIMD)*

successor

An entity that has replaced a predecessor by acquiring the assets and carrying out the affairs of the predecessor under a new name (often through acquisition or merger). The term "successor" *does not* include new offices/divisions of the same company or a company that only changes its name. The extent of the responsibility of the successor for the liabilities of the predecessor may vary, depending on U.S. state law and specific circumstances. *(FAR 52.204-20(a))*

successor of a beneficiary

A person who succeeds to substantially all of the rights of a beneficiary by operation of law, including a corporation with or into which the beneficiary has been merged or consolidated, an administrator, executor, personal representative, trustee in bankruptcy, debtor in possession, liquidator, and receiver. *(UCC 5-102(a)(15))*
See *beneficiary*.

summary level planning package (SLPP)

An aggregation of far-term work efforts (i.e., scope, schedule, and budget) that are not able to be identified at the control account level, but can be distributed to reporting level work breakdown structure elements. *(NDIA II)*

sunk cost

A cost that has already been incurred and which, therefore, is irrelevant to the decision-making process. *(NCMA-CA)*
See *historical cost*.

superior knowledge

U.S. federal government liability for nondisclosure of information is based on an implied duty to disclose information that is vital for the preparation of estimates or for contract performance. This implied duty is consistent with the general contract law concepts of good faith and fair dealing. *(AGC)*
See *duty of good faith and fair dealing*.

supplemental agreement

(1) A contract modification that is accomplished by the mutual action of the parties. *(FAR 2.101)*
(2) A bilateral written modification to a contract by which the government and the contractor settle price and/or performance adjustments to the basic contract. *(DAAT)*

supplemental appropriation

An act appropriating funds in addition to those provided for in the annual appropriations acts. Supplemental appropriations provide additional budget authority beyond the original estimates for programs or activities (including new programs authorized after the date of the original appropriations act) in cases where

Ss

the need for the funds is too urgent to be postponed until enactment of the next regular appropriations act. *(DAAT; DISCS)*
See also *appropriation; appropriations act*.

supplemental guidance
Statements used to provide additional explanatory information. *(NIST SP 800-171)*

supplementary procurement instrument identifier
The non-unique identifier for a procurement action that is used in conjunction with the government-unique procurement instrument identifier (PIID). For example, an agency may use as its PIID for an amended solicitation, the government-unique identifier for a solicitation number (e.g., "N0002309R0009") in conjunction with a non-unique amendment number (e.g., "0001"). The non-unique amendment number represents the supplementary PIID. *(FAR 4.001)*
See also *procurement instrument identifier* (PIID).

supplier
(1) In general, the individual or concern actually performing services, or manufacturing, producing, and shipping any supplies required by a contract or subcontract. *(AFIT)*
(2) In a federal government context, a distributor, manufacturer, or other entity that provides products to the government. *(DODM 4120.24)*
(3) A commercial entity, as determined by its Dun and Bradstreet (DUNS) number as listed in the System for Award Management (SAM). *(GWCM)*
(4) In project management, a government, commercial organization, or entity from which goods or services are required to complete a program/project. The entity may be internal or external to an organization. Suppliers can include prime contractors, subcontractors, or sub-tier contractors, as well as interorganizational transfers, which are responsible for project execution. Also called a vendor. *(NDIA II)*
(5) In the context of a finance lease, a person from whom a lessor buys or leases goods to be leased under a finance lease. *(UCC 2A-103(x))*
See also *goods; lease; lessor; supply contract*.

supplier goods/services management
Management of any contract, agreement, or purchase order (and any preliminary contractual instrument other than a prime contract) calling for the performance of any work or the making or furnishing of any material

required for the performance of a prime contract; includes managing the purchase of supplies that are consumed in use of become incorporated in other property, thus losing identity. *(CMBOK; DGBCT)*

supplier rating system
A system used to evaluate and rate suppliers' performance, which generally involves quality, service, delivery, and price. Rating formulas vary depending on the nature of the item being purchased, the quality required, and competition within the supplying industry. *(GKPT)*
See *performance risk assessment group*.

supplier relationship management (SRM)
A methodology for managing suppliers aimed at reducing procurement and inventory costs, supporting customization of products and services, assuring quality and timeliness, and improving ongoing processes.

supplies
(1) Includes material, equipment, and stores of all kinds. *(10 U.S.C. 101)*
(2) All property except land or interest in land. It includes (but is not limited to):
- Public works, buildings, and facilities;
- Ships, floating equipment, and vessels of every type, character, and description, together with parts and accessories;
- Aircraft and aircraft parts, accessories, and equipment;
- Machine tools; and
- The alteration or installation of any of the foregoing. *(FAR 2.101)*
(3) *Synonymous with* "item" and "item of supply." *(41 U.S.C. 115)*

supply base rationalization
Determining and maintaining the appropriate number of suppliers by category or item depending on the risk and value of the category or item. Also called "supply base optimization." *(FSCM)*

supply chain
The entire network of entities directly or indirectly interlinked and interdependent in serving the same consumer or customer. It comprises vendors that supply raw material, producers who convert the material into products, warehouses that store, distribution centers that deliver to the retailers, and retailers who bring the product to the ultimate user. *(BD)*

Ss

supply chain function

Management of the flow and storage of materials (raw materials, semi-finished goods, and finished products) from vendor sources through to the ultimate customer. It includes both inbound logistics (materials management and procurement) and outbound logistics (customer service and channels of distribution). *(DGBCT)*

supply chain management (SCM)

The planning and management of supply-side activities to maximize customer value and gain a competitive advantage in the marketplace. It represents an effort by suppliers to develop and implement supply chains that are as efficient and economical as possible. *(INV)*

supply contract

In the context of leasing goods, this term refers to a contract under which a lessor buys or leases goods to be leased. *(UCC 2A-103(y))*
See also *goods; lease; lessee; lessor*.

supply management

(1) A systems management concept employed by some organizations, designed to optimize the factors of material costs, quality, and service. This is accomplished by consolidating the following operating activities: purchasing, transportation, warehousing, quality assurance for incoming materials, inventory management, and internal distribution of materials. These activities are normally combined in a single department, similar to the arrangement under a materials management form of organization. *(GKPT)*
(2) A continuing, evolving management philosophy that seeks to unify the collective productive competencies and resources of the business functions found both within the enterprise and outside the firm's allied business partners along intersecting supply channels into a highly competitive, customer-enriching supply system focused on developing innovative solutions and synchronizing the flow of marketplace products, services, and information to create unique, individualized sources of customer value. *(NES-00)*

supporting obligation

A letter-of-credit right or secondary obligation that supports the payment or performance of an account, chattel paper, a document, a general intangible, an instrument, or investment property. *(UCC 9-102(a)(78))*

surety

(1) An individual or corporation legally liable to the debt, default, or failure of a principal to satisfy a contractual obligation. *(FAR 2.101)*
See *corporate surety; cosurety; individual surety*.
(2) Includes a guarantor or other secondary obligor. *(UCC 1-201(39))*

surplus

(1) Excess funds, including (with respect to a fiscal year) the amount by which receipts exceeds outlays during that year. *(2 U.S.C. 622(7))*
(2) Excess property, including those materials that are in excess of a firm's operational requirements. *(DGBCT)*
See also *surplus property*.

surplus property

(1) Property that is in excess of what an organization needs and that is not required for any foreseeable needs. The property may be used or new, but the same has some usefulness for the purpose for which it was intended or for some other purpose. It includes "scrap," which is material that is damaged, defective, or deteriorated to the extent that it has no value except for its basic material content. *(DGBCT)*
(2) Excess personal property not required by any federal agency as determined by the administrator of the General Services Administration. *(40 U.S.C. 102(10); FAR 2.101)* (See also 41 CFR 102-36.40.)

surveying activity

The cognizant contract administration office or, if there is no such office, another organization designated by the agency to conduct pre-award surveys. *(FAR 9.101)*

suspended

A contractor that is disqualified from federal government contracting and government-approved subcontracting is "suspended." *(FAR 2.101)*
See *suspension*.

suspending official

An agency head or a designee authorized by the agency head to impose suspension. *(FAR 9.403)*

suspension

Action taken by a suspending official to disqualify a contractor temporarily from federal government contracting and government-approved subcontracting. *(FAR 2.101)* (See also FAR 9.407.)
Compare with *debarment*; see also *Consolidated List of Debarred, Suspended, and Ineligible Contractors*.

Ss

suspension of work
(1) An order by the buyer to temporarily halt the work. A "Suspension of Work" clause may provide a maximum time period for such suspension. *(HECA)*

(2) In U.S. federal government contracting, when the contracting officer orders the contractor, in writing, to suspend, delay, or interrupt all or any part of the work of the contract for a period of time that the contracting officer determines appropriate for the convenience of the government. *(FAR 52.242-14(a))*
See **compensable delay**.

(3) Under a construction or architect-engineer contract, an order by the contracting officer for the contractor to suspend work for a reasonable period of time. If the suspension is unreasonable, the contractor may submit a written claim for increases in the cost of performance, excluding profit. *(FAR 42.1302)*
Contrast with **stop-work order**.

sustainable acquisition
Acquiring goods and services in order to create and maintain conditions under which humans and nature can exist in productive harmony and that permits fulfilling the social, economic, and other requirements of present and future generations. Also called **green contracting**. *(FAR 2.101)* (See also FAR 23.103.)

SWOT analysis
A situation analysis in which internal strengths and weaknesses of an organization and external opportunities and threats faced by it are closely examined to chart a strategy. "SWOT" stands for strengths, weaknesses, opportunities, and threats. *(DGBCT)*

synopsis
A brief summary or a condensed version. *(DGBCT)*

synopsis of proposed contract actions
A notice of a U.S. federal agency's proposed contract actions, as required by the Small Business Act (15 U.S.C. 637(e)) and the Office of Federal Procurement Policy statute (41 U.S.C. 1708). *(FAR 5.201(a))*

synopsis of contract awards
A notice of a federal agency's contract awards, as required by FAR 5.301. *(FAR 5.301(a))*

system
(1) The organization of hardware, software, material, facilities, personnel, data, and services needed to perform a designated function with specified results, such as the gathering of specified data, its processing, and delivery to users. *(DSMC)*

(2) A combination of two or more interrelated equipment (sets) arranged in a functional package to perform an operational function or to satisfy a requirement. *(DGBCT)*

(3) *Synonymous with* "information system." *(NIST SP 800-171)*
See **information system** (IS).

system acquisition process
The sequence of acquisition activities starting from an agency or organization's reconciliation of its mission needs or delineation of its requirement needs with its capabilities, priorities, and resources, and extending through the introduction of a system into operational use or the otherwise successful achievement of program objectives. *(DISCS; DSMC)*

system administrator (SA)
The individual responsible for the installation and maintenance of an information system, providing effective system utilization, adequate security parameters, and sound implementation of established information assurance policy and procedures. *(CNSSI 4009)*

system engineering
The application of scientific and engineering efforts to transform an operational need into a description of a system configuration that best satisfies the operational need according to the measures of effectiveness; integrates related technical parameters; assures compatibility of all physical, functional, and technical program interfaces in a manner optimizing the total system definition and design; and integrates the efforts of all engineering disciplines and specialties into the total engineering effort. *(DSMC)*

System for Award Management (SAM)
The primary federal government repository for prospective federal awardee and federal awardee information and the centralized government system for certain contracting, grants, and other assistance-related processes. It includes–

- Data collected from prospective federal awardees required for the conduct of business with the government;
- Prospective contractor-submitted annual representations and certifications (in accordance with *FAR* Subpart 4.12); and
- Identification of those parties excluded from re-

Tt

ceiving federal contracts, certain subcontracts, and certain types of federal financial and nonfinancial assistance and benefits.
SAM provides a common source of vendor sources and vendor data. It consolidates the capabilities of CCR/FedReg, ORCA, and EPLS. *(FAR 2.101; FAR 52.204-7; FAR 52.204-13)*
See also *Data Universal Numbering System* (DUNS) *number*.

system integrity
An attribute of an information system when it performs its intended function in an unimpaired manner, free from deliberate or inadvertent unauthorized manipulation of the system. *(CNSSI 4009)*

system of records on individuals
A group of any records under the control of any federal agency from which information is retrieved by the name of the individual or by some identifying number, symbol, or other identifying particular assigned to the individual. *(FAR 24.101)*

system security
See *information systems security* (INFOSEC).

systems and other concept formulation studies
Analyses and study efforts either related to specific independent research and development efforts or directed toward identifying desirable new systems, equipment or components, or modifications and improvements to existing systems, equipment, or components. *(FAR 31.205-18(a))*
See *independent research and development* (IR&D).

systems contract
A contract that authorizes designated employees of the buying firm, using a predetermined release system, to place orders directly with the supplier for specified materials during a given contract period. One principal objective of systems contracting is to reduce the buyer's inventories to a level as low as is consistent with assured continuity of supply; thus, systems contracting is sometimes referred to as "stockless purchasing." Order releases under systems contracts should usually be made by personnel from the using department. *(DBL)*

tailoring
The process by which individual sections, paragraphs, or sentences of a specification or solicitation are modified to meet the minimum requirements and specific needs of the requestor. *(NCMA-SB)*

takt time
The maximum time per unit allowed to produce a product in order to meet demand. It is derived from the German word *taktzeit*, which translates to "cycle time." *Takt* time sets the pace for industrial manufacturing lines. The formula is: *takt* time = available time ÷ sold units. So, if 42 units are produced in 840 minutes, then it takes 20 minutes to produce one unit (840 minutes ÷ 42 units = 20 minutes per unit). *(DGBCT)*

tampering
Unauthorized modification altering the proper functioning of items or equipment. *(CNSSI 4009)*

tangible benefit
A benefit that can be explicitly quantified—e.g., reducing costs, increasing productivity, decreasing cycle time, or improving service quality. *(AIMD)*
See *benefit*; contrast with *intangible benefit*.

tangible capital asset
An asset that has physical substance, more than minimal value, and is expected to be held by an enterprise for continued use or possession beyond the current accounting period for the services it yields. *(FAR 31.001)*
Compare with *intangible capital asset*.

target cost
(1) A final agreed-upon cost that serves as a basis for computing cost savings in incentive-type contracts. *(DGBCT)*
(2) The estimated cost of a contract as initially negotiated, adjusted for any change in contract requirements. *(GOAT)*

target fee
The fee initially negotiated on the assumption that a contract would be performed for a cost equal to the estimated cost initially negotiated, adjusted for any change in contract requirements. *(DGBCT)*

Tt

target fiscal year
The fiscal year two fiscal years into the future from the current fiscal year; the year for detailed consideration in programming. *(AFIT)*

target point
In negotiation, the point at which a negotiator would like to conclude negotiations—i.e., his or her optimal goal has been reached. Also called "aspiration." *(GTY)* See also **best alternative to a negotiated agreement (BATNA)**; *negotiation*.

tariff
A tax levied by governments on the value, including freight and insurance, of imported products. Different tariffs are applied on different products by different countries. *(DGBCT)*

task order
An order for services placed against an established contract or with U.S. federal government sources. *(FAR 2.101)*

task order contract
A contract for services that does not procure or specify a firm quantity of services (other than a minimum or maximum quantity) and that provides for the issuance of orders for the performance of tasks during the period of the contract. *(FAR 16.501-1)*

tax accounting
Involves the measuring, recording, and reporting of relevant financial information in accordance with tax rules and regulations to interested users (primarily government authorities). *(NCMA-CA)*

tax expenditures
In a U.S. federal government context, this term means those revenue losses attributable to provisions of the federal tax laws which allow a special exclusion, exemption, or deduction from gross income or which provide a special credit, a preferential rate of tax, or a deferral of tax liability. *(2 U.S.C. 622(3))*

tax expenditures budget
In a U.S. federal government context, this term means an enumeration of tax expenditures. *(2 U.S.C. 622(3))* See tax *expenditures*.

tax implications
The tax-cost implications of doing business in for-eign countries can be tremendous; e.g., the foreign country may have a right to assess its own income or value-added tax on the company's global earnings that have a connection to that country. There may be personal tax implications for company employees who are temporarily transferred to the country for contract performance. *(DGBCT)*

Taxpayer Identification Number (TIN)
The number required by the IRS to be used by the of-feror in reporting income tax and other returns. The TIN may be either a Social Security Number or an Employer Identification Number. *(FAR 2.101)*

teaming agreement
An agreement to establish a collaborative relation-ship between or among separate businesses to work together towards a common goal (usually the capture of a specific business opportunity.

teaming arrangement
An arrangement in which—
- Two or more companies form a partnership or joint venture to act as a potential prime contractor, or
- A potential prime contractor agrees with one or more other companies to have them act as its sub-contractors under a specified U.S. federal govern-ment contract or acquisition program.

(FAR 9.601)
See also **small business teaming arrangement**.

TechFAR Handbook
An online handbook that highlights the flexibilities in the *Federal Acquisition Regulation*. The TechFar aids U.S. federal government agencies implement "plays" from the *Digital Services Playbook* that can be ac-complished with acquisition support, with a particular focus on how to use contractors to support an iterative, customer-driven software development process, as is routinely done in the private sector. (See https://playbook.cio.gov/techfar/.)

technical analysis
(1) The contracting officer should request that person-nel having specialized knowledge, skills, experience, or capability in engineering, science, or management per-form a "technical analysis" of the proposed types and quantities of materials, labor, processes, special tooling, equipment, or real property; the reasonableness of scrap and spoilage; and other associated factors set forth in the proposal(s) in order to determine the need

Tt

for and reasonableness of the proposed resources, assuming reasonable economy and efficiency. At a minimum, the technical analysis should examine the types and quantities of material proposed and the need for the types and quantities of labor hours and the labor mix. Any other data that may be pertinent to an assessment of the offeror's ability to accomplish the technical requirements or to the cost or price analysis of the service or product being proposed should also be included in the analysis. The contracting officer should request technical assistance in evaluating pricing related to items that are "similar to" items being purchased, or commercial items that are "of a type" or requiring minor modifications, to ascertain the magnitude of changes required and to assist in pricing the required changes. *(FAR 15.404-1(e)(1)-(3))*
(2) An evaluation—ordinarily conducted by engineering, technical, or specialized personnel—of the technical and managerial qualifications of a contractor to perform a particular contract requirement, and applicability/sufficiency of the technical solution proposed to fulfill the contemplated contract requirements. *(P&L II)*

technical data (TD)
Recorded information (regardless of the form or method of the recording) of a scientific or technical nature (including computer databases and computer software documentation). This term includes recorded information of a scientific or technical nature that is included in computer databases; but *does not* include computer software or financial, administrative, cost or pricing, or management data or other information incidental to contract administration. *(41 U.S.C. 116; FAR 2.101)*

technical data package (TDP)
Normally includes technical design and manufacturing information sufficient to enable the construction or manufacture of a defense item component modification, or to enable the performance of certain maintenance or production processes. It may include blueprints, drawings, plans, or instructions that can be used or adapted for use in the design, production, manufacture, or maintenance of defense items or technology. Examples of technical data packages include research and engineering drawings and associated lists, specifications, standards, process sheets, manuals, technical reports, catalog item identifications, and related information and computer software documentation. *(DISCS)* See *technical data*; see also *"contract data requirements list*.

technical direction
An interpretation of statement of work (SOW) requirements provided by a representative of the contracting officer. Representatives of the contracting officer have no authority to alter the SOW. The SOW can only be altered through use of a contract modification signed by the contracting officer. *(GOAT)*

technical evaluation factors
(1) Factors other than price-related used in evaluating offers for award. Examples include technical excellence, management capability, personnel qualifications, prior experience, past performance, and schedule compliance. *(DGBCT)*
(2) Descriptions of the technical aspects of an offer used to evaluate the merit of the proposed technical approach and/or work to be performed (e.g., technical approach, understanding of the requirement, and compliance with requirement). *(DGBCT)*

technical information
Includes both technical data and computer software. Examples of "technical information" include research and engineering data, engineering drawings, and associated lists, specifications, standards, process sheets, manuals, technical reports, technical orders, catalog-item identifications, data sets, studies and analyses and related information, and computer software executable code and source code. *(DFARS 204.7301)* See *software; technical data*.

technical leveling
Helping an offeror to bring its proposal up to the level of other proposals through successive rounds of discussion, such as by pointing out weaknesses resulting from the offeror's lack of diligence, competence, or inventiveness in preparing the proposal. *(DGBCT)*

technical manual
A publication containing instructions designed to meet the needs of personnel responsible for (or being trained in) the operation, maintenance, service, overhaul, installation, and inspection of specific items of equipment and materiel. *(DISCS)*

technical proposal
An unpriced proposal that sets forth in detail that which a vendor proposes to furnish in response to a solicitation. *(DGBCT)*

Tt

technical risk

In project management, the likelihood that the project, as planned, will be unable to deliver a product to satisfy the technical or operational requirements. *(NDIA II)*

technical specification

Specifications that establish the material and performance requirements of goods and services. *(DGBCT)*

technical transfusion

Disclosing technical information pertaining to a proposal that results in improvement of a competing proposal. *(DGBCT)*

technology transfer

The process by which federal scientific research and development is transformed into commercially viable products and services. *(TIPS)*

tender

(1) An unconditional offer of money or service in satisfaction of a debt or obligation made to save a penalty or forfeiture for nonpayment or nonperformance. *(MW)*
(2) An offer or proposal made for acceptance (e.g., an offer of a bid for a contract). *(MW)*
(3) To present for acceptance (e.g., "tender goods," "tender delivery," "tender payment," "tender performance"); to extend for acceptance or consideration, as in proof of something (e.g., "tender a plea to the court" or "tender an issue"); or to offer for sale (e.g., "tender shares"). *(MW)*

term

(1) A word, expression, or phrase that has a precise meaning in some uses or is peculiar to a science, art, or subject (e.g., legal *terms*, contracting-specific terms.) *(MW)*
See also *undefined term*.
(2) A limited or definite extent of time. (Especially, the time for which something lasts, such as duration or tenure—e.g., *term* of office.) *(MW)*
(3) A portion of an agreement that relates to a particular matter. *(UCC 1-201(40))*
See also *agreement*.
(4) In the *plural* (i.e., "terms") means provisions that determine the nature and scope of an agreement (e.g., "terms" of sale, liberal credit "terms"). *(MW)*
See also *agreement; terms and conditions* (Ts and Cs).
(5) In the *plural* (i.e., "terms"), can also refer to a mutual relationship (e.g., on good "terms"); an agreement or concord (e.g., come to "terms" after negotiations); or

a state of acceptance or understanding (e.g., came to "terms" with his failure). *(MW)*

term contract

Normally covers a 12-month period or may cite another specific time to complete the project or service. *(DGBCT)*

term contracting

A technique by which a source of supply is established for a specific period of time. *(DGBCT)*

term form

A form of cost-plus-fixed-fee contract that describes the scope of work in general terms and obligates the contractor to devote a specified level of effort for a stated time period. If contract performance is considered satisfactory by the government, the fixed-fee is payable at the expiration of the agreed-upon period, upon contractor statement that the level-of-effort specified in the contract has been expended in performing the contract work. Renewal for further periods of performance is a new acquisition that involves new cost and fee arrangements. *(FAR 16.306(d)(2))*
Compare with *completion form*.

terminable interest

An interest that will terminate upon the occurrence of an event or the passing of time. *(MW)*

terminated portion of the contract

The portion of a contract that the contractor is not to perform following a partial termination. For construction contracts that have been completely terminated for convenience, this term refers to the entire contract, notwithstanding the completion of, and payment for, individual items of work before termination. *(FAR 2.101)*
See *partial termination*.

termination

(1) Occurs when either party pursuant to a power created by agreement or law puts an end to the contract otherwise than for its breach. On "termination," all obligations which are still executory on both sides are discharged, but any right based on prior breach or performance survives. *(UCC 2-106(3))*
Compare with *cancellation*.
(2) In federal government contracting, an action taken pursuant to a contract clause in which the contracting officer unilaterally ends all or part of the work; it can be a

Tt

"termination for convenience," in which the ending of work is in the best interest of the government, or a "termination for default," in which the contractor has not performed according to the terms of the contract. *(OPM)*
See *contract termination*; see also *termination for convenience; termination for default* (T4D).
(3) In the context of a lease contract, this occurs when either party pursuant to a power created by agreement or law puts an end to the lease contract otherwise than for default. *(UCC 2A-103(z))*
See lease *contract*.

termination by mutual consent
Commonly used in the commercial contracting environment, termination by mutual consent is a bilateral agreement indicating that the parties no longer wish to be bound by the contract and are terminating both parties' respective rights and obligations. "Termination by Mutual Consent" clauses are sometimes included in the basic contract, though they can also be negotiated and executed during the period of performance. *(DGBCT)*

termination costs
Contract terminations generally give rise to the incurrence of costs or the need for special treatment of costs that would not have arisen had the contract not been terminated, including the following costs peculiar to termination situations:
- Common items costs,
- Costs continuing after termination,
- Initial costs,
- Loss of useful value of special tooling and special machinery and equipment,
- Rental costs under unexpired leases,
- Alteration and reasonable restoration of leased property,
- Settlement expenses, and
- Subcontractor claims.

(FAR 31.205-42)
See *termination*.

termination claim
Any claim or demand by a prime contractor for compensation because of the termination before completion of any contract or subcontract for the convenience of the government. *(AFIT)*
See *claim*.

termination contracting officer (TCO)
The contracting officer assigned responsibility for settling terminations for default or convenience, and

in some cases settling claims and actions involving extraordinary relief. *(OPM)*

termination for cause
See *termination for default* (T4D)

termination for convenience
The exercise of the federal government's right to completely or partially terminate performance of work under a contract when it is in the government's interest. *(FAR 2.101)*
See *anticipatory profit; termination; Torncello Rule*.

termination for default (T4D)
(1) Also called *termination for cause*, a T4D is normally a right of law as well as a right vested as the result of the inclusion of appropriate terms and conditions in the contract. Termination for default can result from one party's failure to perform one or more actions required by the contract. *(DGBCT)*
(2) The exercise of the federal government's right to completely or partially terminate a contract because of the contractor's actual or anticipated failure to perform its contractual obligations. *(FAR 2.101)*
(3)The exercise of the government's contractual right to completely or partially terminate a contract because of the contractor's actual or anticipated failure to perform its contractual obligations. *(FAR 49.401(a))*
See *cure notice; show cause letter; termination*.

termination inventory
Any property purchased, supplied, manufactured, furnished, or otherwise acquired for the performance of a contract subsequently terminated and properly allocable to the terminated portion of the contract. It includes U.S. federal government-furnished property; but *does not* include facilities, material, special test equipment, or special tooling that are subject to a separate contract or to a special contract requirement governing their use or disposition. *(FAR 2.101)*

termination liability
A contingent federal government obligation to pay a utility supplier the unamortized portion of a connection charge and any other applicable nonrefundable service charge as defined in the contract in the event the government terminates the contract before the cost of connection facilities has been recovered by the utility supplier. *(FAR 41.101)*
See also *connection charge; utility service*.

Tt

termination of employment gain or loss
An actuarial gain or loss resulting from the difference between the assumed and actual rates at which pension plan participants separate from employment for reasons other than retirement, disability, or death. *(FAR 31.001)*

termination statement
An amendment of a financing statement which:
- Identifies, by its file number, the initial financing statement to which it relates; and
- Indicates either that it is a termination statement or that the identified financing statement is no longer effective.

(UCC 9-102(a)(80))

terms and conditions (Ts and Cs)
All language in a contract, including time of delivery, packing and shipping, applicable standard classes, and special provisions. The primary function of terms and conditions is to eliminate or reduce the risk of contract ambiguity; often the source of disputes and misunderstandings. *(OPM)*

testing
That element of inspection that determines the properties or elements, including functional operation, of supplies or their components, by the application of established scientific principles and procedures. *(FAR 46.101)*

then-year dollars
See *current year dollars*.

third-party draft
An agency bank draft, similar to a check, that is used to acquire and to pay for supplies and services. *(FAR 13.001)*

third-party services
Services performed by any person or firm other than the buyer and supplier. *(DGBCT)*

threshold
(1) The limiting acceptable value of a measurement or technical parameter, typically a performance requirement. *(AIMD)*
(2) A level of performance measure or a risk metric whose exceedance "triggers" management processes to rectify performance shortfalls. *(NID 8000-108)*

tiered evaluation of offers
Also known as "cascading evaluation of offers," means a procedure used in negotiated acquisitions, when market research is inconclusive for justifying limiting competition to small business concerns, whereby the contracting officer—
- Solicits and receives offers from both small and other than small business concerns,
- Establishes a tiered or cascading order of precedence for evaluating offers that is specified in the solicitation, and
- If no award can be made at the first tier, evaluates offers at the next lower tier, until award can be made.

(DFARS 202.101)

tiering
The incorporation of standards and specifications due to cross-referencing of successively lower levels. Automatic tiering occurs when documents are invoked implicitly by reference in the primary document. *(NCMA-WS)*

time and materials (T&M) contract
A type of contract providing for a fixed hourly rate, including overhead and profit and material at cost plus handling charges. Used when it is impossible to estimate schedule and costs at the time of contract award. *(OPM)*
See also *direct materials; hourly rate; material*.

time value of future cash flows
See *"present value of future cash flows"*

title
In property administration, the legal right to control and dispose of property. *(DGBCT)*

Torncello Rule
In *Torncello v. United States* (681 F.2d 756 (Fed. Cir. 1982)), the U.S. Court of Claims ruled that the "Termination for Convenience" clause could not be used to avoid anticipated profits, unless there had been some change in circumstances between the time of award of the contract and the time of termination. *(AGC)*

tort
(1) A wrongful act other than a breach of contract that injures another and for which relief may be obtained in the form of damages or an injunction. *(MW)*
(2) A violation of a duty, such as to exercise due care,

Tt

imposed by law. *(MW)*

(3) This term also refers to a cause of the action based on such acts described in (1.) and (2.) of this definition. *(MW)*

total allocated budget (TAB)

In project management terminology, refers to the sum of all budgets allocated to the contract. It consists of the performance measurement baseline and management reserve. When an over target baseline is in place, it must reconcile to the contract budget base and any recognized over target budget. *(NDIA II)*

total compensation

In situations where executive compensation must be reported, this term refers to the cash and noncash dollar value earned by an executive during a contractor's preceding fiscal year, which includes the following:

- Salary and bonus;
- Awards of stock, stock options, and stock appreciation rights;
- Earnings for services under non-equity incentive plans (not including group life, health, hospitalization, or medical reimbursement plans that do not discriminate in favor of executives, and are available generally to all salaried employees);
- Change in pension value (i.e., the change in present value of defined benefit and actuarial pension plans);
- Above-market earnings on deferred compensation which is not tax-qualified; and
- Other compensation, if the aggregate value of all such other compensation (e.g., severance, termination payments, value of life insurance paid on behalf of the employee, perquisites, or property) for the executive exceeds $10,000.

(FAR 52.204-10(a))

total contract dollars

The final anticipated dollar value of a contract, including the dollar value of all options. *(FAR 19.701)*

total cost

The total cost, including standard costs properly adjusted for applicable variances, of a contract is the sum of the direct and indirect costs allocable to the contract, incurred or to be incurred, plus any allocable cost of money (pursuant to FAR 32.205-10), less any allocable credits. In ascertaining what constitutes a "cost," any generally accepted method of determining or estimating costs that is equitable and is consistently applied may be used. *(FAR 31.201-1(a))*

total cost basis

A means of pricing equitable adjustments when the costs associated with a claim are not clearly identifiable. Using the total cost approach, an equitable adjustment is calculated as the difference between the contractor's proposed price on the original contract and the actual total cost of performing the contract as changed. This method assumes that all costs expended by the contractor were caused by the change, and the contractor's original estimate was correct and reasonable. *(NCMA-WS; TIPS)*

total float

In project management terminology, the number of work days an activity's finish date can slip before impacting the project's end date. It is calculated by taking the delta between an activity's late finish date and early finish date. Also referred to as "total slack." *(NDIA II)*

total obligational authority (TOA)

The total amount of funds available for programming in a given year, regardless of the year the funds are appropriated, obligated, or expended. Total obligational authority includes new obligational authority, unprogrammed or reprogrammed obligational authority from prior years, reimbursements not used for replacements of inventory in kind, advanced funding for programs to be financed in the future, and unobligated balances transferred from other appropriations. *(DISCS)*

total production cycle time

Total activity time required to produce one unit of product. *(GKPT)*

total quality management (TQM)

The philosophy and principles that continuously improve an organization. It is the application of quantitative methods and human resources to improve the material and services supplied to an organization, the processes within an organization, and the degree to which the needs of the customer are met. *(DGCQI)*

total set-aside

When the entire amount of an acquisition is reserved for small businesses. *(NCMA-WS)*
See *set-aside*.

toxic chemical

A chemical or chemical category listed in 40 CFR 372.65. *(FAR 23.001)*

Tt

trade
The business of buying, selling, or bartering goods or services. *(DGBCT)*

trade acceptance
A time draft or bill of exchange for the amount of purchase, drawn by the seller on the buyer, bearing the buyer's acceptance and the place of payment. *(GKPT)*

Trade Agreements Act (TAA)
A federal law (19 U.S.C. 2501, *et seq.*) that governs trade agreements between the United States and other countries. In particular, the TAA provides the authority for the president to waive the Buy American statute (41 U.S.C. Chapter 83) and other discriminatory provisions for eligible products from countries that have signed an international trade agreement with the United States, or that meet certain other criteria, such as being a least developed country. *(FAR 25.402(a)(1))*

trade balance
The shift between trade surplus (when a country is exporting more than it is importing) and a trade deficit (when the value of the goods being imported are greater than those being exported). *(NES-94)*

trade discount
A discount from the list price offered to all customers of a given type; e.g., a discount offered by a lumber dealer to a building contractor. Contrasts with a discount offered for prompt payment or a quantity discount. *(BLD)*

trade secret
A form of legal protection for any information used in a commercial trade or business that:
- Is not generally known in the trade,
- Is used in secrecy, and
- Affords a competitive advantage.

The Trade Secrets Act (18 U.S.C. 1905) restricts disclosure of trade secrets, and the same provides for civil and criminal penalties for such violations. A company does not need to request "trade secret" status from anyone. Rather, it can declare such a status by adhering to certain practices. *(TIPS)*

Trade Secrets Act
See *trade secret*.

trade terms
Conditions offered, or offered and accepted, as terms for a sale or payment for goods or services. *(GKPT)*

trademark (™)
A distinctive mark of authenticity. Words, symbols, devices, or designs affixed to or placed on an article or its container to identify an article offered for sale. *(DGBCT)* See also *service mark* (℠).

tradeoff
The selection among alternatives with the intent of obtaining the best overall "deal" or "value," as opposed to the best price.

tradeoff process
In a federal government context, a source selection technique that is appropriate when it may be in the best interest of the government to consider award to other than the lowest-priced offeror or other than the highest-technically-rated offeror. *(FAR 15.101-1(a))*

trafficking in persons
The federal government prohibits contractors, contractor employees, subcontractors, and subcontractor employees from:
- Engaging in severe forms of trafficking in persons during the period of performance of the contract,
- Procuring commercial sex acts during the period of performance of the contract, or
- Using forced labor in the performance of the contract.

Contractors and subcontractors must notify employees of the prohibited activities described in *FAR* Subpart 22.17 and the actions that may be taken against them for violations. *(FAR 22.1703(a))*

trainee
In the context of labor standards for contracts involving construction, a person registered and receiving on-the-job training in a construction occupation under a program which has been approved in advance by the Department of Labor, Employment and Training Administration, Office of Apprenticeship Training, Employer, and Labor Services (OATELS) as meeting its standards for on-the-job training programs and which has been so certified by that administration. *(FAR 22.401)*

training and education costs
Costs of training and education that are related to the field in which the employee is working or may reasonably be expected to work. *(FAR 31.205-44)*

transportation
Applying transportation and traffic management con-

Tt

siderations in the acquisition of supplies and acquiring transportation-related services. *(DGBCT)* See *mode of transportation*.

transportation-related services
Procedures for the acquisition of related services such as stevedoring, storage, packing, marking, and ocean freight forwarding. *(DGBCT)*

travel costs
Costs for transportation, lodging, meals, and incidental expenses incurred by employees on official company business. Costs for transportation may be based on mileage rates, actual costs incurred, or on a combination thereof; and costs for lodging, meals, and incidental expenses may be based on a per diem, actual expenses, or a combination thereof. *(FAR 31.205-46(a) (1))* (See also FAR 31.205-46.)

traveling (purchase) requisition
A purchase requisition designed for repetitive use (e.g., inventory items). It contains stock level data, potential suppliers, lead times, and, frequently, prices and predetermined order quantities, as well as other data needed for ordering. The requisition is sent to the purchasing department where a purchase order is prepared directly from it. *(GKPT)*

treaty
A formal agreement entered into between two or more countries. The treaty process includes negotiation, signing, ratification, exchange of ratifications, publishing and proclamation, and treaty execution. Treaties having only two signatory states are called "bilateral," whereas those with more than two parties are "multilateral." *(DISCS)*

tribal government
For federal government purposes, this term means—
* The governing body of any Native American tribe, band, nation, or other organized group or community located in the continental United States (excluding the State of Alaska) that is recognized as eligible for special programs and services provided by the United States, and
* Any Alaska Native regional or village corporation established pursuant to the Alaska Native Claims Settlement Act (31 U.S.C. 1601, *et seq.*).

(40 U.S.C. 502(c)(3)(B))

tribal organization
The recognized governing body of any Native American tribe. *(25 U.S.C. 5304(l))* Compare with *tribal government*.

trier of fact
In a legal sense, refers to the judge in a bench trial or jury in a jury trial that carries the responsibility of determining the issues of fact in a case. *(MW)*

trusted computer system
An information system employing sufficient hardware and software assurance measures to allow simultaneous processing of a range of classified or sensitive information. *(CNSSI 4009)*

Truthful Cost or Pricing Data statute
A federal law (41 U.S.C. Chapter 35) ensuring that the government is provided with sufficient information prior to contract award to ensure that it does not pay excessive prices for its procurements. The statute requires offerors to submit cost or pricing data and to certify that, to the offeror's best knowledge and belief, the data submitted is accurate, complete, and current. Formerly known as the *Truth in Negotiations Act* (TINA). *(41 U.S.C. 3501(a)-(b))*

Truth in Negotiations Act (TINA)
See *Truthful Cost or Pricing Data statute*.

Tucker Act
A federal law (28 U.S.C. 1346(a) and 1491) that waives sovereign immunity from suit for all claims founded upon any contract, express or implied, with the U.S. government. *(NS)*

two-phase design-build selection procedures
A selection method in which a limited number of offerors (normally five or fewer) is selected during "Phase One" of a construction project to submit detailed proposals for "Phase Two." *(FAR 36.102)* (See also *FAR* Subpart 36.3.)

two-step sealed bidding
A combination of competitive procedures designed to obtain the benefits of sealed bidding when adequate specifications are not available. An objective is to permit the development of a sufficiently descriptive and not unduly restrictive statement of the government's requirements, including an adequate technical data

package, so that subsequent acquisitions may be made by conventional sealed bidding. This method is especially useful in acquisitions requiring technical proposals, particularly those for complex items. It is conducted in two steps:

- *Step One*—Consists of the request for, submission, evaluation, and (if necessary) discussion of a technical proposal. The objective is to determine the acceptability of the supplies or services offered. It is the proper step for clarification of questions relating to technical requirements. Conformity to the technical requirements is resolved in this step, but not responsibility.
- *Step Two*—Involves the submission of sealed priced bids by those who submitted acceptable technical proposals in Step One. Bids submitted in Step Two are evaluated and the awards made.

(FAR 14.501) (See also *FAR* Subparts 14.3 and 14.4.)

tying agreement
An agreement or understanding to sell a desired product upon the condition that the customer must buy another of the supplier's products. *(BOE)*

"Unacceptable" past performance evaluation rating
Based on the offeror's performance record, an "unacceptable" past performance evaluation rating means that the federal government has no reasonable expectation that the offeror will be able to successfully perform the required effort. *(SSP)*
Contrast with *"acceptable" past performance evaluation rating*.

unallowable cost
Any cost that, under the provisions of any pertinent law, regulation, or contract, cannot be included in prices, cost-reimbursements, or settlements under a federal government contract to which it is allocable. *(FAR 2.101)*

unauthorized commitment
A nonbinding agreement because the federal government representative who made it lacked authority to do so. Government employees are prohibited from committing or obligating funds in excess of those available. Doing so results in an unauthorized commitment.

In order to convert an unauthorized commitment to a binding agreement, it must be ratified by authorized government representatives. *(DGBCT)*
See *ratification*.

unauthorized disclosure
A type of event involving exposure of information to individuals not authorized to receive it. *(CNSSI 4009)*

unauthorized signature
A signature made without actual, implied, or apparent authority. This term includes a forgery. *(UCC 1-201(41))*
See *signature/signed*.

unbalanced pricing
Exists when, despite an acceptable total evaluated price, the price of one or more contract line items is significantly over or understated as indicated by the application of cost or price analysis techniques. If cost or price analysis techniques indicate that an offer is unbalanced, the contracting officer must—

- Consider the risks to the government associated with the unbalanced pricing in determining the competitive range and in making the source selection decision, and
- Consider whether the award of the contract will result in paying unreasonably high prices for contract performance.

An offer may be rejected if the contracting officer determines that the lack of balance poses an unacceptable risk to the government. *(FAR 15.404-1(g)(1)-(3))*

unclassified
Information that has not been determined, pursuant to Executive Order 12958 or any predecessor order, to require protection against unauthorized disclosure and that is not designated as "classified." *(CNSSI 4009)*
See *controlled unclassified information* (CUI).

uncompensated overtime
The hours worked without additional compensation in excess of an average of 40 hours per week by direct-charge employees who are exempt from the Fair Labor Standards Act (29 U.S.C. 201, *et seq.*). Compensated personal absences such as holidays, vacations, and sick leave must be included in the normal work week for purposes of computing uncompensated overtime hours. *(FAR 37.101)*
See *exempt employees; professional services*.

Uu

unconscionability

An absence of meaningful choice on the part of one of the parties to a contract, together with contract terms that are unreasonably favorable to the other party. Typically, the cases in which unconscionability is found involve gross overall one-sidedness or gross one-sidedness of a term disclaiming a warranty, limiting damages, or granting procedural advantages. The basic test of unconscionability of contract is whether, under circumstances existing at the time of the making of contract and in light of the general commercial background and the commercial needs of a particular trade or case, clauses involved are so one-sided as to oppress or unfairly surprise a party. *(BLD)*

undefined term

In general, a word or phrase given without an accompanying definition to establish its meaning or context. One of the major principles of contract interpretation is that undefined terms in a contract shall be read with their meaning in ordinary usage. Therefore, a party to a contract cannot interpret an undefined term to mean something different than it would normally mean in ordinary usage. *(FAR 1.108(a))*
See *contract interpretation*.

undefinitized contractual action

Those contract actions for which the contract terms, specifications, or price are not agreed upon before performance commences (DFARS 217.7401).
See also *undefinitized item*.

undefinitized item

An item for which a price has not been established in the basic contract or by modification. *(DFARS 204.7101)*
See also *undefinitized contractual action*; contrast with *definitized item*.

undistributed budget

A temporary holding account for budget associated with specific work scope or contract changes that have not been assigned to a control account or summary level planning package. *(NDIA II)*

undue burden

A significant difficulty or expense. *(FAR 39.202)*

unenforceable contract

An otherwise valid contract rendered unenforceable by some statute or law (e.g., a verbal contract that, due to the passage of time, must be in writing to be enforceable). *(DGBCT)*

unequal treatment

In the case of a post-award protest, a protestor may claim that other offerors received some form of special treatment or that all offerors were not treated equally, thereby adversely impacting the protestor's ability to compete effectively. *(CMBOK)*

unexpended balance

The amount of budget authority previously granted to an agency but still unspent and available for future payments. *(DAAT)*

unexpired cost

A cost that may be properly carried forward to future periods as an asset to measure. *(NCMA-CA)*

unfair evaluation criteria

In the case of a pre-award protest, a protestor may assert that one or more of the criteria used to evaluate proposals was unreasonable, unfair, or otherwise inappropriate. *(CMBOK)*

unfair trade practices

The commission of any of the following acts by a contractor:
- A violation of Section 337 of the Tariff Act of 1930 (19 U.S.C. 1337) as determined by the International Trade Commission;
- A violation, as determined by the U.S. Secretary of Commerce, of any agreement of the group known as the "Coordination Committee" for purposes of the Export Administration Act of 1979 (50 U.S.C. App. 2401, *et seq.*) or any similar bilateral or multilateral export control agreement;
- A knowingly false statement regarding a material element of a certification concerning the foreign content of an item of supply, as determined by the secretary of the department or the head of the agency to which such certificate was furnished.

(FAR 9.403)

UNICOR

See *Federal Prison Industries* (FPI)/*UNICOR*

Uniform Commercial Code (UCC)

Uniform law governing commercial transactions, developed by the National Conference of Commissioners on Uniform State Laws and the American Law Institute,

Uu

which has been adopted by all states in the United States except Louisiana, and which is sometimes used to aid in the interpretation and enforcement of government subcontracts. *(GCG)*

uniform contract format

The format (Section A through Section M) that must be used in U.S. federal government solicitations and resulting contracts. The uniform contract format is as follows:

- Part I—The Schedule:
  - Section A—Solicitation/contract form
  - Section B—Supplies or services and prices/costs
  - Section C—Description/specifications/statement of work
  - Section D—Packaging and marking
  - Section E—Inspection and acceptance
  - Section F—Deliveries or performance
  - Section G—Contract administration data
  - Section H—Special contract requirements
- Part II—Contract Clauses:
  - Section I—Contract clauses
- Part III—List of Documents, Exhibits, and Other Attachments
  - Section J—List of attachments
- Part IV—Representations and Instructions
  - Section K—Representations, certifications, and other statements of offerors or respondents
  - Section L—Instructions, conditions, and notices to offerors or respondents
  - Section M—Evaluation factors for award

(FAR 15.204-1(a); FAR Table 15-1)

unilateral contract

A contract formed by the exchange of a promise for an act. In a "unilateral contract," only one party has made a promise and is obligated to perform. An example is a contract that promises a monetary reward to find a missing pet. No one is obligated by such a contract to search for the pet, but if the pet is found, the party who promised the reward is obligated to pay. *(CMBOK; BLD)*
See also *bilateral contract*.

unilateral modification or change

(1) A contract modification that is signed only by the contracting officer, without the concurrence of the contractor. Unilateral modifications are used, for example, to—

- Make administrative changes;
- Issue change orders;
- Make changes authorized by clauses other than a "Changes" clause (e.g., "Property" clause, "Options"

clause, or "Suspension of Work" clause); and
- Issue termination notices.

(FAR 43.103(b))
See *contract modification*; contrast with *bilateral modification*.

(2) In the context of the Cost Accounting Standards, a change in cost accounting practice from one compliant practice to another compliant practice that a contractor with a CAS-covered contract(s) or subcontract(s) elects to make that has not been deemed a desirable change by the cognizant federal agency official and for which the federal government will pay no aggregate increased costs. *(FAR 30.001)*
See *bilateral change*; see also *cognizant federal agency official* (CFAO); *Cost Accounting Standards* (CAS).

unique and innovative concept

When used relative to an unsolicited research proposal, means that in the opinion and to the knowledge of the federal government evaluator, the meritorious proposal—

- Is the product of original thinking submitted confidentially by one source;
- Contains new, novel, or changed concepts, approaches, or methods;
- Was not submitted previously by another; and
- Is not otherwise available within the federal government.

In this context, this term *does not* mean that the source has the sole capability of performing the research. *(FAR 2.101)*

unique entity identifier

A number or other identifier used to identify a specific commercial, nonprofit, or federal government entity. It is among the identification requirements to submit an offer to the government. If the Offeror does not have a unique entity identifier, it should contact the entity designated at www.sam.gov for establishment of the unique entity identifier directly to obtain one. *(FAR 2.101; FAR 52.204-6(c))*
See also *Data Universal Numbering System* (DUNS) *number; generic entity identifier; System for Award Management* (SAM).

unique item identifier (UII)

A globally unique and unambiguous set of data elements marked on items. *(DAAT)*
See *item unique identification and valuation*.

Uu

unit
In value engineering, means the item or task to which the contracting officer and the contractor agree the value engineering change proposal applies. *(FAR 48.001)*
See *value engineering; value engineering change proposal* (VECP)

unit acquisition cost
(1) For government-furnished property, the dollar value assigned by the federal government and identified in the contract. *(FAR 45.101)*
See also *government-furnished property* (GFP); *government property*.
(2) For contractor-acquired property, the cost derived from the contractor's records that reflect consistently-applied generally accepted accounting principles. *(FAR 45.101)*
See also *contractor-acquired property* (CAP); *generally accepted accounting principles* (GAAP).

unit cost
A total cost divided by some related base, such as labor hours, machine-hours, or units of product. *(NCMA-CA)*

unit price agreement
An agreement that provides for the furnishing of an indefinite quantity, within stated limits, of specific property or services at a specified price, during a specified contract period, with deliveries to be scheduled by the timely placement of orders upon the lessor by activities designated either specifically or by class. *(FMR 102-71.20)*

United Nations Convention on Contacts for the International Sale of Goods (CISG)
See *Convention on Contracts for the International Sale of Goods* (CISG).

United States
The 50 States, the District of Columbia, Puerto Rico, the Northern Mariana Islands, American Samoa, Guam, the U.S. Virgin Islands, Johnston Island, Wake Island, the Outer Continental Shelf (as defined in the Outer Continental Shelf Lands Act (43 U.S.C. 1331, *et seq.*), and outlying areas. *(29 CFR 4.112(a))*

unjust enrichment
Where one of the parties to the contract receives benefits in excess of the amount of money involved. *(HECA)*

unlimited rights
The rights of the federal government to use, disclose, reproduce, prepare derivative works, distribute copies to the public, and perform publicly and display publicly, in any manner and for any purpose, and to have or permit others to do so. *(FAR 27.401)*
Contrast with *limited rights; restricted rights*.

unliquidated progress payments
See *liquidation*.

unmanufactured construction material
In the case of a public building or public work, raw material brought to the construction site for incorporation into the building or work that has not been–
• Processed into a specific form and shape, or
• Combined with other raw material to create a material that has different properties than the properties of the individual raw materials.
(FAR 25.601)

unobligated balance
The amount of budget authority previously granted to an agency, but not yet committed, which continues to be available for commitment in the future. *(DAAT)*

unreasonable best value analysis
In the case of a post-award protest, a protestor may indicate that, in a best value procurement, the cost/technical trade-off analysis used to justify an award to other than the highest-rated or lowest-priced proposal was flawed, inaccurate, or otherwise unreasonable in some material way. *(CMBOK)*

unrestricted procurement
Those acquisitions available to all contractors, and not reserved to satisfy social or economic programs of the U.S. federal government. *(TIPS)*
Compare with *set-aside*.

"Unsatisfactory" performance rating
In the case of a past performance evaluation, an "Unsatisfactory" performance rating signifies that performance does not meet most contractual requirements and recovery is not likely in a timely manner. The contractual performance of the element or sub-element contains a serious problem(s) for which the contractor's corrective actions appear or were ineffective. To justify an "Unsatisfactory" rating, multiple significant events in each category that the contractor had trouble overcoming must be identified and how it impacted the

Uu

government must be stated. A singular problem, however, could be of such serious magnitude that it alone constitutes an "Unsatisfactory" rating. *(FAR Table 42-1)*
See *past performance evaluation*; contrast with *"Exceptional" performance rating; "Marginal" performance rating; "Satisfactory" performance rating; "Very Good" performance rating*.

unsettled contract change
Any contract change or contract term for which a definitive modification is required but has not been executed. *(FAR 49.001)*

unsolicited proposal
(1) A written proposal for a new or innovative idea that is submitted to a federal agency on the initiative of the offeror for the purpose of obtaining a contract with the federal government, and that is not in response to a request for proposals, broad agency announcement, Small Business Innovation Research topic, Small Business Technology Transfer research topic, program research and development announcement, or any other government-initiated solicitation or program. *(FAR 2.101)*
See *proposal*.
(2) A research or developmental proposal that is made by a prospective contractor without prior formal or informal solicitation from a purchasing activity. *(AFIT)*

untimely payment
In the case of a subcontract, a payment to a subcontractor that is more than 90 days past due under the terms and conditions of a subcontract for supplies and services for which the U.S. federal government has paid the prime contractor. *(FAR 19.701)*

unusual contract financing
Any financing not deemed "customary contract financing" by a federal agency. Unusual contract financing is financing that is legal and proper under applicable laws, but that the agency has not authorized contracting officers to use without specific reviews or approvals by higher management. *(FAR 32.001)*
Contrast with *customary contract financing*.

U.S. Agency for International Development (USAID)
A division of the U.S. Department of State that provides grants and loans to developing countries for development and foreign policy reasons. *(DGBCT)*

U.S. Army Corps of Engineers (USACE)
The U.S. Army's principal engineering design, construction, research, and development organization. *(DISCS)*

United States Code (U.S.C.)
A consolidation and codification of the general and permanent laws of the United States arranged according to subject matter under 50 title headings. The United States Code sets out the current status of the laws, as amended. The U.S.C. presents the laws in a concise and usable form without requiring recourse to the many volumes of the statutes at large containing the individual amendments. *(DISCS)*

U.S. Court of Claims
See *U.S. Court of Federal Claims* (COFC).

U.S. Court of Appeals for the Federal Circuit
Federal court that, upon dissolution of the U.S. Court of Claims in 1982, assumed the role of the Court of Claims' appellate division. *(DGBCT)*
See *Federal Courts Improvement Act*; compare with *U.S. Court of Federal Claims*.

U.S. Court of Federal Claims (COFC)
Federal court that, upon dissolution of the U.S. Court of Claims in 1982, assumed the role of the Court of Claims' trial division. *(DGBCT)*
See *Federal Courts Improvement Act*; compare with *U.S. Court of Appeals for the Federal Circuit*.

U.S.-made end product
In the context of the federal government's "Buy American" policies, trade agreements, and other laws and regulations governing foreign acquisition, this term refers to an article that is mined, produced, or manufactured in the United States or that is substantially transformed in the United States into a new and different article of commerce with a name, character, or use distinct from that of the article or articles from which it was transformed. *(FAR 25.003)*
See end *product*.

usage of trade
Any practice or method of dealing having such regularity of observance in a place, vocation, or trade as to justify an expectation that it will be observed with respect to the transaction in question. The existence and scope of such a usage must be proved as facts. If it is established that such a usage is embodied in a trade code or similar record, the interpretation of the record

is a question of law. *(UCC 1-303(c))*
See also *course of dealing; course of performance*.

USDA-designated item

A generic grouping of products that are or can be made with biobased materials—

- That is listed by the Department of Agriculture in a procurement guideline (7 CFR Part 3201, Subpart B); and
- For which USDA has provided purchasing recommendations.

(FAR 23.401)

useful life

The prospective period of economic usefulness of a tangible capital asset in an organization's operations. It is evidenced by the actual or estimated retirement and replacement practice of the organization. *(FAR 2.101)*

utility service

A service such as furnishing electricity, natural or manufactured gas, water, sewerage, thermal energy, chilled water, steam, hot water, or high-temperature hot water. *(FAR 41.101)*

V

valid contract

A contract satisfying all of the contract requisites (agreement, consideration, capacity, legal purpose, assent, and form). *(DGBCT)*

valid time-phased requirements

Material that is—

- Needed to fulfill the production plan, including reasonable quantities for scrap shrinkage, yield, etc.; and
- Charged/billed to contracts or other cost objectives in a manner consistent with the need to fulfill the production plan.

(DFARS 252.242-7004(a)(2))

validation

(1) The process of determining whether or not the product delivered at the end of the development process satisfies predefined requirements. *(AIMD)*
See also *verification*.

(2) Acceptance by auditors of reported cost reduction savings and cost reduction reports, based on a selec-

tive review of cost reduction reports and supporting documentation. *(AFIT)*

value adjusted total evaluated price (VATEP)

A tradeoff source selection process where the offeror's total proposed price may be adjusted based on the "value" placed on better performance as identified in the solicitation. *(SSP)*

value-added

The value added to a product or service at each stage of its production and distribution based on its increased value at that stage. *(GKPT)*

value analysis

A systematic and objective evaluation of the function of a product and its related cost; a pricing tool that provides insight into the inherent worth of a product. Value analysis assumes that value is a function of three variables: demand, use, and aesthetics. *(NCMA-WS; OPM)*
See *auxiliary techniques*.

value chain

The sequential set of primary and support activities that an enterprise performs to turn inputs into value-added outputs for its external customers. *(DGBCT)*

value engineering (VE)

(1) An analysis of the functions of a program, project, system, product, item of equipment, building, facility, service, or supply of an executive agency, performed by qualified agency or contractor personnel, directed at improving performance, reliability, quality, safety, and life-cycle costs. *(FAR 2.101; 41 U.S.C. 1711)*

(2) An organized effort to analyze the functions of systems, equipment, facilities, services, and supplies for the purpose of achieving the essential functions at the lowest life cycle cost consistent with required performance, reliability, quality, and safety. *(FAR 52.248-2)*

(3) Value engineering is the formal technique that seeks to eliminate—without impairing essential functions or characteristics—anything that increases acquisition, operation, or support costs. Through it contractors may—

- Voluntarily suggest methods for performing more economically and share in any resulting savings, or
- Be required to establish a program to identify and submit to the federal government methods for performing more economically.

(FAR 48.101(a))

Vv

value engineering change proposal (VECP)

(1) In value engineering, a proposal that requires a change to the instant contract to implement and results in reducing the overall projected cost to the U.S. federal agency without impairing essential functions or characteristics, provided that it does not involve a change in deliverable end item quantities, research and development (R&D) items, or R&D test quantities that are due solely to results of previous testing under the instant contract, or to the contract type only. *(FAR 2.101)*
See *instant contract; value engineering*.
(2) In connection with a federal government architectural and engineering contract, a change proposal developed by employees of the federal government or contractor value engineering personnel under contract to an agency to provide value engineering services for the contract or program. *(FAR 48.001; FAR 52.248-2)*
(3) In connection with a federal government contract for construction, a proposal that requires a change to the instant contract to implement and results in reducing the contract price or estimated cost without impairing essential functions or characteristics—provided that it does not involve a change in deliverable end item quantities only or to the contract type only. *(FAR 52.248-3)*

value engineering proposal

An in-house, agency-developed proposal, or a proposal developed by a contractor under contract to provide value engineering services, to provide value engineering studies for a federal government project/program. *(OMB A-131)*

value proposition

The unique added value an organization offers customers through their operations. *(DGBCT)*

variable budget

See *flexible budget*.

variable cost

A cost that changes with the rate of production of goods or performance of services. *(OPM)*

variable costing

See *direct costing*.

variance

(1) The difference between projected and actual performance, especially relating to costs. *(AFIT)*
(2) The difference between a pre-established measure

and an actual measure. *(FAR 31.001)*
See *standard cost*.

variance analysis

(1) Comparing the total budget with the estimate at completion at the control account level provides a variance expected at the completion of the control account. *(EVMIG)*
(2) The process of examining differences between actual costs and budgeted costs. In management control system terms, a variance can be positive or negative (parallel to the accounting terms of favorable or unfavorable). A "positive variance" indicates the program is under budget or ahead of schedule; a "negative variance" indicates that the contract is over budget or behind schedule. *(NCMA-WS)*

variance at completion (VAC)

The difference between the budget at completion (BAC) and the estimate at completion (EAC) (VAC = BAC – EAC). It may be calculated at any level from the detail level up to the total contract. It represents the amount of expected overrun (i.e., "negative VAC") or underrun (i.e., "positive VAC"). *(NDIA II)*

vendor

An individual, partnership, corporation, or other entity from which items are acquired in the performance of a contract. *(AFIT)*

venture capital

The initial capital (usually paid-in capital) of a new enterprise involving risk but offering potential above-average profits. (Also called "risk capital.") *(MW)*
See *capital*; see also *"paid-in capital*.

"Very Good" performance rating

In the case of a past performance evaluation, a "Very Good" performance rating signifies that performance meets contractual requirements and exceeds some to the U.S. federal government's benefit. The contractual performance of the element or sub-element being evaluated was accomplished with some minor problems for which corrective actions taken by the contractor were effective. To justify a "Very Good" rating, a significant event must be identified and how it was a benefit to the government must be stated. There should have been no significant weaknesses identified. *(FAR Table 42-1)*
See *past performance evaluation*; contrast with *"Exceptional" performance rating; "Marginal" performance rating; "Satisfactory" performance rating; "Unsatisfactory" performance rating*.

vested interest
A present and certain right to the present or future enjoyment of property. *(MW)*

veteran-owned small business (VOSB)
A small business concern not less than 51 percent of which is owned by one or more veterans (as defined at 38 U.S.C. 101(2))–or, in the case of any publicly owned business, not less than 51 percent of the stock of which is owned by one or more veterans–and the management and daily business operations of which are controlled by one or more veterans. A company can only refer to itself as a VOSB for the purposes of federal contracting after being formally approved by the U.S. Department of Veterans Affairs Center for Veterans Enterprise (CVE). *(FAR 2.101)*

Veterans First Contracting Program
Under the Veterans First program, VA contract specialists conduct market research in an effort to seek out veteran-owned small business (VOSB) firms to meet their needs. The Department of Veterans Affairs is the only agency which sets a goal and which tracks participation of VOSBs. (See https://www.va.gov/osdbu/programs/vosb.asp.)

virgin material
(1) Previously unused raw material, including previously unused copper, aluminum, lead, zinc, iron, or other metal or metal ore. *(FAR 2.101)*
(2) Any undeveloped resource that is, or with new technology will become, a source of raw materials. *(FAR 2.101)*

virus
Self-replicating, malicious code that attaches itself to an application program or other executable system component and leaves no obvious signs of its presence. *(CNSSI 4009)*

visual analysis
The visual inspection of an item or its drawings, from which a general estimate of probable value may be made. *(AFIT)*
See *auxiliary techniques*.

void contract
A contract having no legal force or binding effect (e.g., a contract entered into for an illegal purpose). *(DGBCT)*

voidable contract
An otherwise valid contract that may be legally avoided, cancelled, or annulled at the option of one of the parties (e.g., a contract entered into under duress or under false pretenses). *(DGBCT)*

voluntary consensus standards
Standards established by a private-sector body and available for public use. (This term *does not* include private standards of individual firms.) They are characterized by the common and repeated use of rules, conditions, guidelines, or characteristics for products, or related processes and production methods and related management systems. They are developed or adopted by domestic and international voluntary consensus standard-making bodies (e.g., the International Organization for Standardization and ASTM-International). *(FAR 2.101; NES-97; OMB A-119)*
See *standard*.

voucher
See *invoice*.

wage and classification
Guidelines to be used by the contracting office in determining applicable wages for specific classes of employees expected to be employed by the contractor to perform the required services under a proposed service contract. Determinations are made by the Department of Labor in accordance with the Service Contract Labor Standards statute (41 U.S.C. Chapter 67). *(OPM)*

Wage and Hour Division
The unit in the Employment Standards Administration of the Department of Labor to which is assigned functions of the secretary of labor under the Service Contract Labor Standards statute. *(FAR 22.1001)*
See *Service Contract Labor Standards statute*.

wage determination
A determination of the minimum wages or fringe benefits made under 41 U.S.C. 6703 or 6707(c) applicable to the employment in a given locality of one or more classes of service employees. *(FAR 22.1001)*
See *Wage Determinations Online* (WDOL); see also *service employee; wages*.

Ww

Wage Determinations Online (WDOL)

The federal government website for both Wage Rate Requirements (Construction) statute (40 U.S.C. Chapter 31, Subchapter IV) and Service Contract Labor Standards statute (41 U.S.C. Chapter 67) wage determinations (available at http://www.wdol.gov). *(FAR 22.001)*
See *wage determination*; see also *Service Contract Labor Standards statute; Wage Rate Requirements (Construction) statute*.

Wage Rate Requirements (Construction) statute

A federal law (40 U.S.C. Chapter 31, Subchapter IV) that requires all laborers and mechanics employed on U.S. federally funded construction, alteration, or repair contracts to be paid the locally prevailing wage rate (as determined by the Secretary of Labor). Formerly known as the *Davis-Bacon Act. (40 U.S.C. 3142)* (See also FAR 22.403-1.)

wages

Includes–
* The basic hourly rate of pay; and
* Any contribution irrevocably made by a contractor or subcontractor to a trustee or to a third person pursuant to a *bona fide* fringe benefit fund, plan, or program; and the rate of costs to the contractor or subcontractor which may be reasonably anticipated in providing bona fide fringe benefits to laborers and mechanics pursuant to an enforceable commitment to carry out a financially responsible plan or program, which was communicated in writing to the laborers and mechanics affected. The fringe benefits enumerated in the Construction Wage Rate Requirements (Construction) statute (40 U.S.C. Chapter 31, Subchapter IV) include:
* Medical or hospital care, pensions on retirement or death, compensation for injuries or illness resulting from occupational activity, or insurance to provide any of the foregoing;
* Unemployment benefits;
* Life insurance, disability insurance, sickness insurance, or accident insurance;
* Vacation or holiday pay;
* Defraying costs of apprenticeship or other similar programs; or
* Other *bona fide* fringe benefits.

Fringe benefits *do not* include benefits required by other federal, state, or local law. *(FAR 22.401; 40 U.S.C. 3141(2))*

waiver

(1) The voluntary relinquishment by a person of a right that he or she has. *(FBL)*
(2) Acceptance by the buyer of a minor nonconformity that does not degrade the function of the item. *(GSFC)*
(3) A written authorization to accept a configuration item or other designated item, which, during production, or after having been submitted for inspection, is found to depart from specified requirements, but nevertheless is considered suitable "as is" or after rework by an approved method. *(DAAT)*
(4) A decision to not require certain criteria to be met for certain reasons (e.g., national security). *(DAAT)*

Walsh-Healey Public Contracts Act

See *Contracts for Materials, Supplies, Articles, and Equipment Exceeding $15,000 statute*.

warehouse receipt

(1) A receipt issued by a person engaged in the business of storing goods for hire. (UCC 1-201(42))
(2) If goods are stored under a statute requiring a bond against withdrawal or a license for the issuance of receipts in the nature of warehouse receipts, a receipt issued for the goods is deemed to be a "warehouse receipt," even if issued by a person that is the owner of the goods and is not a warehouse. (UCC 7-201(b))

warrant

(1) An official document (Standard Form 1402) designating an individual as a contracting officer. The warrant serves as the contracting officer's certificate of appointment and will state as reference the limits of the contracting officer's authority. *(DAAT; GSFC)*
(2) An official document issued by the secretary of the treasury and countersigned by the comptroller general of the United States by which monies are authorized to be withdrawn from the Treasury. Warrants are issued after appropriations and similar congressional authority has been enacted. *(DAAT)*

warranty

A promise or affirmation given by a seller to a buyer regarding the nature, usefulness, or condition of the supplies or performance of services furnished under the contract. *(FAR 2.101)*
See *express warranty; implied warranty*

waste reduction

Preventing or decreasing the amount of waste being generated through waste prevention, recycling, or purchasing recycled and environmentally preferable products. *(FAR 2.101)*

water consumption intensity
Water consumption per square foot of building space. *(FAR 2.101)*

weakness
In the context of an offeror's proposal received by the U.S. federal government, this term refers to a flaw in the proposal that increases the risk of unsuccessful contract performance. *(FAR 15.001)*
See also *significant weakness*; compare with *strength*.

weighted average cost
An inventory costing method under which an average unit cost is computed periodically by dividing the sum of the cost of beginning inventory plus the cost of acquisitions by the total number of units included in these two categories. *(FAR 31.001)*

weighted guidelines method (WGM)
A cost analysis technique used to ensure consideration of the relative value of appropriate profit factors in establishing profit objectives and conducting negotiations. Used as a basis for documentation and explaining final pricing factors, including the seller's input to total contract performance, assumption of contract risk, performance, and other selected factors. *(OPM)*

whistleblower
See *qui tam action*.

wholesale supply sources
A required source of supply. Certain federal government agencies have been tasked to maintain a stock of common-use items for all government agencies to use (e.g., the Defense Logistics Agency and Department of Veterans Affairs both have stock programs). However, by far the largest program is under the General Services Administration, which offers two methods of accessing its wholesale supplies: distribution centers and customer supply centers. *(NCMA-WS)*
See *mandatory sources*.

wholly owned government corporation
Refers to any of the following government corporations of the federal government:
- The Commodity Credit Corporation (15 U.S.C. 714);
- The Export-Import Bank of the United States (12 U.S.C. 635);
- The Federal Crop Insurance Corporation (7 U.S.C. 1501);
- The Federal Deposit Insurance Corporation (12 U.S.C. 1811);
- The Federal Financing Bank (12 U.S.C. 2281);
- Federal Prison Industries, Inc. (UNICOR) (18 U.S.C. 4121);
- The Financing Corporation (12 U.S.C. 1441);
- The Government National Mortgage Association (12 U.S.C. 1717);
- The National Railroad Passenger Corporation (AMTRAK) (49 U.S.C. 241);
- The Overseas Private Investment Corporation (22 U.S.C. 2191);
- The Pension Benefit Guaranty Corporation (29 U.S.C. 1301);
- The Presidio Trust of San Francisco (16 U.S.C. 460bb);
- The Resolution Funding Corporation (12 U.S.C. 1441(b));
- The Saint Lawrence Seaway Development Corporation (33 U.S.C. 981);
- The Secretary of Housing and Urban Development (when carrying out duties and powers related to the Federal Housing Administration Fund);
- The Tennessee Valley Authority (16 U.S.C. 831);
- The U.S. Postal Service (USPS) (39 U.S.C. 101); and
- The Valles Caldera Trust (16 U.S.C. 698-v4).
(FGCO; 31 U.S.C. 9101(3))
See also *government corporation; mixed-ownership government corporation*.

Wide Area Workflow (WAWF)
See *Invoicing, Receipt, Acceptance, and Property Transfer (iRAPT)*.

will cost
(1) A concept of contract pricing that requires an evaluation of what an offeror estimates it will cost to do the job in a specified future period. *(OPM)*
(2) A projection by an offeror as to what a contract will cost based upon the offeror's best estimate utilizing current methods, historical costs, and forecasts. *(P&L I)*

win theme
Customer-focused messaging; limited, high-level ideas and concepts; and the melding of the buyer's priorities and the seller's differentiators/strengths. It frames the offer as the best overall solution. *(CMBOK)*

Ww

win-win
A philosophy whereby all parties in an acquisition scenario come away gaining some or most of what they wanted (i.e., everyone "wins" something, even though it may not be 100 percent of the goal); the ideal outcome. *(DAAT)*
See also *negotiation objectives*.

women-owned small business (WOSB) concern
A small business that is at least 51-percent owned by one or more women—or, in the case of a publicly owned business, at least 51 percent of the stock of which is owned by one or more women—and whose management and daily business operations are controlled by one or more women. This term also refers to a small business concern eligible under the Women-Owned Small Business Program in accordance with 13 CFR Part 127. *(FAR 2.101)*
See also *Women-Owned Small Business (WOSB) Program*

Women-Owned Small Business (WOSB) Program
Created by the Small Business Act (15 U.S.C. 637(m)), the program ensures women-owned small business (WOSB) concerns and economically disadvantaged WOSB (EDWOSB) concerns have an equal opportunity to participate in federal government contracting and to assist agencies in achieving their women-owned small business participation goals. The program authorizes contracting officers to limit competition, including award on a sole-source basis, to WOSB and EDWOSB concerns eligible under the WOSB Program for government contracts assigned a North American Industry Classification System code in an industry in which the Small Business Administration has determined that WOSB concerns are underrepresented in federal procurement. *(FAR 19.1500(a)-(b); 2.101)* (See also 13 CFR Part 127.)
See *"women-owned small business (WOSB) concern*.

Women-Owned Small Business (WOSB) Program Repository
A secure, web-based application that collects, stores, and disseminates documents to the contracting community and the Small Business Administration, which verify the eligibility of a business concern for a contract to be awarded under the WOSB Program. *(FAR 19.1501)*
See *women-owned small business (WOSB) concern; Women-Owned Small Business (WOSB) Program*.

work authorization
A contractor's internal process for authorizing the commencement of project work. The work authorization system describes the work to be performed in terms of work scope, schedule, and budget. *(NDIA II)*

work breakdown structure (WBS)
(1) A product-oriented structure that depicts the subdivision of effort required to accomplish project objectives. It is an organized method to break down a product into sub-products and, at the lowest level, the tasks to be accomplished. It is used for planning, budgeting, work authorization, performance measurement, tracking, and reporting purposes. *(NDIA II)*
See also *work breakdown structure (WBS) dictionary*.
(2) A direct representation of the work scope defined in the program statement of work. It breaks down that work scope into appropriate elements for cost accounting and work authorization. It is a multi-level hierarchical breakdown that shows how program costs are summarized from the lower elements to the total program level. *(EVMIG)*

work breakdown structure (WBS) dictionary
A listing of work breakdown structure elements with a description of the work scope content for each element—generally what is included, excluded, or other specifics to clearly communicate what is required as well as to segregate the work for work authorization and accounting purposes. *(NDIA II)*
See *work breakdown structure (WBS)*.

work-in-process inventory
The cost of uncompleted goods still on the production line. (NCMA-CA)

work package (WP)
A natural subdivision of control account work scope, schedule, and budget used in planning, controlling, measuring, and reporting project performance. Simply put, a "work package" is a low-level task, a grouping of similar tasks, or a job assignment at whatever level of control is normal for program management within an organization. They are commonly segregated by the elements of cost (i.e., labor, material, other direct costs, or subcontract). An earned value technique is assigned to each work package. Work packages are the point where work is planned, progress is measured, and earned value is calculated. *(EVMIG; NDIA II)*

Zz

working capital

The capital available for use in the course of business activity, including:

- Current assets less current liabilities, or
- All capital of a business except the fixed capital.

(MW)

See *capital*; see also *"fixed capital.*

World Trade Organization Government Procurement Agreement (WTO GPA)

A plurilateral agreement within the framework of the World Trade Organization (WTO) between some WTO members aimed at mutually opening government procurement markets among themselves. The United States is a party to this agreement. *(AGP)*

See also *World Trade Organization Government Procurement Agreement* (WTO GPA) *country; World Trade Organization Government Procurement Agreement* (WTO GPA) *country end product.*

World Trade Organization Government Procurement Agreement (WTO GPA) country

In the context of the U.S. federal government's "Buy American" policies, trade agreements, and other laws and regulations governing foreign acquisition, this term refers to any of the following countries: Armenia, Aruba, Austria, Belgium, Bulgaria, Canada, Croatia, Cyprus, Czech Republic, Denmark, Estonia, Finland, France, Germany, Greece, Hong Kong, Hungary, Iceland, Ireland, Israel, Italy, Japan, Korea (Republic of), Latvia, Liechtenstein, Lithuania, Luxembourg, Malta, Montenegro, Netherlands, New Zealand, Norway, Poland, Portugal, Romania, Singapore, Slovak Republic, Slovenia, Spain, Sweden, Switzerland, Taiwan, or the United Kingdom. *(FAR 25.003)*

See also *World Trade Organization Government Procurement Agreement* (WTO GPA) *country end product.*

World Trade Organization Government Procurement Agreement (WTO GPA) country end product

In the context of the U.S. federal government's "Buy American" policies, trade agreements, and other laws and regulations governing foreign acquisition, this term refers to an article that is wholly the growth, product, or manufacture of a WTO GPA country, or in the case of an article that consists in whole or in part of materials from another country, has been substantially transformed in a WTO GPA country into a new and different article of commerce with a name, character,

or use distinct from that of the article or articles from which it was transformed. This term also refers to a product offered for purchase under a supply contract, but for purposes of calculating the value of the end product includes services (except transportation services) incidental to the article, provided that the value of those incidental services does not exceed that of the article itself. *(FAR 25.003)*

See *World Trade Organization Government Procurement Agreement* (WTO GPA); *World Trade Organization Government Procurement Agreement* (WTO GPA) *country*; see also *end product.*

Z

zero-based budgeting (ZBB)

An elaborate, time-consuming practice of having managers justify all their activities and costs as if they were being undertaken for the first time. ZBB is successfully used in many nonprofit organizations because most costs in many nonprofit organizations are discretionary. ZBB forces managers to define the output of various programs of expenditures and relate inputs to the output. *(IMA)*

zero-based pricing

A form of cost analysis based on reviewing all cost elements and working with internal customers and with suppliers to reduce the total combined cost of purchased materials, equipment, labor, and services. *(GKPT)*

zone of possible agreement (ZOPA)

An area where two or more negotiating parties may find common ground. It is in this area where parties will often compromise and strike a deal. It represents an area of common ground and compromise where a settlement can be reached or an agreement made. Also referred to as *bargaining range. (INV)*

Source Codes

(AAAG)
Agile Alliance, "Agile Glossary" (copyright 2018, Agile Alliance), *available at* www.agilealliance.org/agile101/agile-glossary/.

(AAPM)
Office of the Inspector General, *Acquisition Alerts for Program Managers* (Washington, DC: U.S. Department of Defense, 1987).

(AFIT)
Air Force Institute of Technology, *Compendium of Authenticated Systems and Logistics Terms, Definitions, and Acronyms* (Wright-Patterson AFB, OH: Air Force Institute of Technology, 1981).

(AGC)
John Cibinic Jr. and Ralph C. Nash Jr., *Administration of Government Contracts* (Washington, DC: George Washington University, 1985).

(AGP)
World Trade Organization, "Agreement on Government Procurement" (World Trade Organization, 2018), *available at* www.wto.org/english/tratop_e/gproc_e/gp_gpa_e.htm.

(AI)
John W. Chierichella and Douglas E. Perry, "Negotiating Teaming Agreements," *Acquisition Issues* (Vienna, VA: Holbrook & Kellog Inc. 1991).

(AIMD)
U.S. Government Accountability Office, Accounting and Information Management Division, "Information Technology Investment Management: A Framework for Assessing and Improving Process Maturity" (Washington, DC: U.S. Government Accountability Office, May 2000).

(AMAD)
The American Marketing Association (AMA) Dictionary, *available at* www.ama.org (copyright 2018, American Marketing Association).

(APMP)
Betsy Blakney and Charlie Divine, *APMP Industry Glossary of Terms*, Version 4.0 (APMP, January 2015).

(ARQ)
Bruce G. Linster, PhD, and David R. Mullin, PhD; "Auctions in Defense Acquisition: Theory and Experimental Evidence," *Acquisition Review Quarterly* (Defense Acquisition University, Summer 2002).

(ASPM)
U.S. Department of Defense, *Armed Services Pricing Manual*, "Vol. 1, Contract Pricing" (Washington, DC: U.S. Department of Defense, 1986).

(AT)
Steven Bragg, "Static Budget," AccountingTools.com (October 18, 2017), *available at* www.accountingtools.com/articles/what-is-a-static-budget.html.

(BBDM)
Nick Szabo, "Smart Contracts: Building Blocks for Digital Markets" (1996), *available at* http://www.truevaluemetrics.org/DBpdfs/BlockChain/Nick-Szabo-Smart-Contracts-Building-Blocks-for-Digital-Markets-1996-14591.pdf.

(BD)
BusinessDictionary.com (copyright 2018, WebFinance Inc.), *available at* www.businessdictionary.com.

(BLD)
Henry C. Black, *Black's Law Dictionary*, sixth ed. (St. Paul, MN: West Publishing Co., 1990).

(BOE)
The Boeing Company, *Business Conduct Guidelines* (Seattle, WA: The Boeing Company, 1987).

(CBTR)
Usman W. Chohan, "Cryptocurrencies: A Brief Thematic Review," *Discussion Paper Series: Notes on the 21st Century* (University of New South Wales, Canberra; August 3, 2017).

(CE)
Rodney D. Stewart, *Cost Estimating*, second ed. (New York: John Wiley & Sons Inc., 1991).

(CFR) with specific Title number and Chapter
Code of Federal Regulations.

(CJCSI) with specific instruction number
Chairman of the Joint Chiefs of Staff Instruction.

Source Codes

(CMBOK)
The Contract Management Body of Knowledge (CM-BOK), fifth edition (Ashburn, VA: NCMA, 2017).

(CMPA)
Stanley N. Sherman, *Contract Management: Post Award* (Gaithersburg, MD: Wordcrafters Publications, 1987).

(CMS)
"The Contract Management Standard Publication™ (CMS™)," Version 1.0 (Ashburn, VA: NCMA, 2017), *available at* www.ncmahq.org/apply-best-practices/cmbok-standard.

(CNSSI) with specific instruction number
Committee on National Security Systems Instruction.

(DAAT)
Defense Acquisition University, *Glossary of Defense Acquisition Acronyms and Terms*, 16th ed. (Fort Belvoir, VA: Defense Acquisition University, 2017), *available at* https://www.dau.mil/glossary.

(DAAT-A)
Defense Acquisition University, *Acquisition Encyclopedia, available at* https://www.dau.mil/acquipedia/Pages/acquipedia.aspx.

(DAAT-H)
Defense Acquisition University, Community Hub, *available at* https://www.dau.mil/community-hub#All||title_asc.

(DBL)
Donald W. Dobler, David N. Burt, and Lamar Lee Jr.; *Purchasing and Materials Management*, fifth ed. (New York: McGraw-Hill Publications, 1990).

(DCMA-INST) with specific instruction number
Defense Contract Management Agency (DFCMA) *Instruction.*

(DDMAT)
U.S. Department of Defense (DOD), *DOD Dictionary of Military and Associated Terms* (Joint Publication 1-02) (August 2017), *available at* https://www.jcs.mil/Portals/36/Documents/Doctrine/pubs/dictionary.pdf.

(DFARS) with specific reference to part/subpart/section/subsection/paragraph
Defense Federal Acquisition Regulation Supplement, 48 CFR Chapter 2. *Available at* https://www.acq.osd.mil/dpap/dars/ dfarspgi/current/.

(DGBCT)
Margaret G. Rumbaugh and Dr. John Wilkinson, *Desktop Guide to Basic Contracting Terms*, seventh edition (Ashburn, VA: NCMA, 2012).

(DGCQI)
Boeing Defense and Space Group, *Desktop Guide for Continuous Quality Improvement* (Seattle, WA: Boeing Defense and Space Group, 1990).

(DISCS)
Defense Security Cooperation Agency, Defense Institute of Security Cooperation Studies, *Green Book*, Edition 38.0 (May 2018), *available at* https://www.dsca.mil/publications.

(DLA)
U.S. Defense Logistics Agency, "Understanding the DOD Budget," *Dimensions* (Alexandria, VA: Defense Logistics Agency (April 1991)): 2–3.

(DODD) with specific directive number
Department of Defense Directive.

(DODI) with specific instruction number
Department of Defense Instruction.

(DODM) with specific manual number
Department of Defense Manual.

(DOD-MMH)
Defense Systems Management College, *Department of Defense Manufacturing Management Handbook for Program Managers*, second edition (Fort Belvoir, VA: Defense Systems Management College, 1984).

(DPAP)
Richard Ginman, director, Defense Procurement and Acquisition Policy (DPAP); Office of the Under Secretary of Defense (Acquisition, Technology, and Logistics); U.S. Department of Defense; Memorandum: "Update to the Department of Defense Contracting Officer Representative Tracking Tool" (Washington, DC: DPAP, February 10, 2014).

Source Codes

(DSMC)
Defense Systems Management College, *Subcontract Management Handbook* (Fort Belvoir, VA: Department of Defense, 1988).

(ECON)
Roger N. Waud, *Microeconomics*, third edition (New York: Harper & Row Publishers, 1986).

(EDI)
Margaret E. Emmelhainz, *Electronic Data Interchange: A Total Management Guide* (New York: Van Nostrand Reinhold, 1990).

(EDIW)
Joan M. Ugljesa, "A&D Contract Management Discovers EDI," *EDI World* (Hollywood, FL: EDI World Inc., November 1991): 25; *and* Tom Millhorn and Javier Romeu, "EDI Capabilities Grow to Include Complex Data Transfer," *EDI World* (Hollywood, FL: EDI World Inc., January 1992): 31.

(EO) with specific number
Executive Order

(EVMIG)
U.S. Department of Defense, *Earned Value Management Implementation Guide* (Washington, DC: Department of Defense; April 7, 2005).

(FAI)
Federal Acquisition Institute, *Basic Procurement Course Materials* (Washington, DC: Federal Acquisition Institute, 1991).

(FAR) with specific reference to part/subpart/section/subsection/paragraph
Federal Acquisition Regulation, 48 CFR Chapter 1.

(FASAB Handbook)
Federal Accounting Standards Advisory Board (FASAB), *FASAB Handbook of Federal Accounting Standards and Other Pronouncements*, Version 16 (Washington, DC: June 2017), *available at* www. Fasab.gov/accounting-standards/document-by-chapter/.

(FBL)
Phillip J. Scaletta Jr. and George D. Cameron III, *Foundations of Business Law*, second edition (Homewood, IL: Richard D. Irwin, Inc., 1990).

(FGC)
John Cibinic Jr. and Ralph C. Nash Jr., *Formation of Government Contracts* (Washington, DC: George Washington University, 1982).

(FGCO)
Kevin R. Kosar, "Federal Government Corporations: An Overview" (Washington, DC: Congressional Research Service; June 8, 2011).

(FGP)
C.M. Culver, *Federal Government Procurement—An Uncharted Course Through Turbulent Waters* (McLean, VA: NCMA, 1985).

(FIPS) with standard number
Federal Information Processing Standards, *available at* www.nist.gov/itl/fips.cfm.

(FMR) with specific reference to part/subpart
Federal Management Regulation, 41 CFR Chapter 102.

(F&F)
Friedman & Fuller P.C., *The Government Contractor's Glossary* (Rockville, MD: Friedman & Fuller P.C., 1992).

(FSCM)
J.R. Carter and T.Y. Choi, *Foundation of Supply Chain Management* (Tempe, AZ: Institute of Supply Management, 2008).

(FTH)
U.S. General Services Administration, *U.S. Government Freight Transportation Handbook* (Washington, DC: U.S. General Services Administration, January 2012).

(GACI)
U.S. Department of Defense, Office of the Under Secretary of Defense (Acquisition, Technology, and Logistics); *Department of Defense Guidebook for Acquiring Commercial Items*, Part A: "Commercial Item Determination" (Washington, DC: Department of Defense, February 24, 2017).

(GAO-05-734SP)
U.S. Government Accountability Office (GAO), *A Glossary of Terms Used in the Federal Budget Process* (Washington, DC: GAO, September 2005).

Source Codes

(GCG)
Donald P. Arnavas and William J. Ruberry, *Government Contract Guidebook* (Federal Publications Inc., 1986).

(GKPT)
Donald W. Dobler (ed.), *The Glossary of Key Purchasing Terms* (Tempe, AZ: National Association of Purchasing Management (NAPM), 1996).

(GLSS)
Tracy O'Rourke, Elisabeth Swan, *et al.*; "Lean Glossary"; GoLeanSixSigma.com (copyright 2018, GoLeanSixSigma.com); *available at* https://goleansixsigma.com/category/resources/lean-glossary/

(GOAT)
Federal Acquisition Institute, *Glossary of Acquisition Terms* (Washington, DC: Federal Acquisition Institute, 1998).

(GPBSA)
Office of the Under Secretary of Defense (Acquisition, Technology, and Logistics); *Guidebook for Performance-Based Services Acquisition (PBSA) in the Department of Defense* (Washington, DC: Department of Defense, December 2000).

(GPM)
Stanley N. Sherman, *Government Procurement Management* (Gaithersburg, MD: Wordcrafters Publications, 1991).

(GPMT)
The Glossary of Project Management Terms, Visitask.com (2014), www.visitask.com/GlossaryItems.asp.

(GSFC)
Barry L. McVay, *Getting Started in Federal Contracting* (Westbury, NY: Asher-Gallant Press, 1986).

(GTY)
Roger Fisher and William L. Ury, *Getting to Yes* (United Kingdom: Penguin Group, 1981).

(GWCM)
U.S. Office of Management and Budget, "Government-Wide Category Management Guidance Document—Version 1.0" (Washington, DC: Office of Management and Budget, May 2015).

(HCS)
Judith V. Richardson, *Handbook for Contract Specialists* (Washington, DC: Naval Air Systems Command, 1989).

(HECA)
Cary Cohen, *The Handbook of Effective Contract Administration* (Richmond, VA: Caldwell Consulting Associates, 1985).

(IMA)
Charles T. Horngren and Gary L. Sundem, *Introduction to Management Accounting,* seventh edition (Englewood Cliffs, NJ: Prentice-Hall, 1987).

(INV)
Investopedia Dictionary (copyright 2018, Investopedia LLC), *available at* www.investopedia.com/dictionary.

(ISO/IEC)
International Organization for Standardization (ISO)/International Electrotechnical Commision (IEC), *ISO/IEC Guide 2:2004, Standardization and Related Activities—General Vocabulary* (2016).

(MCS)
Robert N. Anthony, John Dearden, and Richard F. Vancil; *Management Control Systems* (Homewood, IL: Richard D. Irwin Inc., 1972).

(MIL-HDBK) with specific handbook number
Military Handbook (U.S. Department of Defense).

(MSA)
Stuart R. Boyd and Juan A. Montes, *The Management of Security Assistance*, eighth edition (Wright-Patterson Air Force Base, OH: Defense Institute of Security Assistance Management, February 1988).

(MW)
Merriam-Webster Online Dictionary, Merriam-Webster.com (copyright 2018, Merriam-Webster Inc.), available at www.merriam-webster.com.

(NCMA-CA)
Cost Accounting Basics, rev. ed. (Vienna, VA: NCMA, 1990).

(NCMA-SB)
Solicitations, Bids, and Awards (McLean, VA: NCMA, 1984).

Source Codes

(NCMA-SS)
Source Selection (McLean, VA: NCMA, 1984).

(NCMA-WS)
National Contract Management Association, "Workshop Series" (Vienna, VA: NCMA, 1989–1993).

(NDIA)
National Defense Industrial Association (NDIA), *Program Management Systems Committee (PMSC) ANSI/EIA-748-A Standard for Earned Value Management Systems Intent Guide* (Arlington, VA: NDIA, January 2006).

(NDIA II)
National Defense Industrial Association (NDIA), Integrated Program Management Division (IPMD), *Master Definitions List for IPMD Guides* (Revision) (Arlington, VA: NDIA; May 1, 2017).

(NED)
Negotiation Experts, "Negotiation Definitions," Negotiations.com (copyright 2018, Negotiation Experts), *available at* www.negotiations.com/definition/.

(NES-00)
The Contracting Professional as a Business Manager (Vienna, VA: NCMA, 2000).

(NES-02)
William G. Droms and Neal J. Couture, *Financial Analysis: Contract Management Applications* (Vienna, VA: NCMA, 2002).

(NES-87)
Donald P. Arnavas, Gilbert J. Ginsburg, Matthew S. Simchak, and John S. Pachter; *Managing Contract Changes* (Vienna, VA: NCMA, 1987).

(NES-89)
H. Philip Marks and Donald L. Brechtel, *Subcontracts: Government and Industry Issues* (Vienna, VA: NCMA, 1989).

(NES-90)
Daniel M. Jacobs, Janice M. Menker, and Chester P. Shinaman; *Building a Contract: Solicitations, Bids, and Proposals* (Vienna, VA: NCMA, 1990).

(NES-93)
Keith L. Baker, William A. Erie, and Scott J. Parkinson; *Financial Issues for the Contracts Professional* (Vienna, VA: NCMA, 1992).

(NES-94)
National Contract Management Association (NCMA), *Commercial, Environmental, and International Contracting: An Evolving Focus* (Vienna, VA: NCMA, 1994).

(NES-97)
Louis M. Gaudio, Eric L. Gentsch, Phillip H. Harrington, et al.; *Commercial Item Acquisition* (Vienna, VA: NCMA, 1997).

(NES-98)
Delane F. Moeller and Herbert L. McCulloch, *Electronic Contracting* (Vienna, VA: NCMA, 1998).

(NID) with specific directive number
National Aeronautics and Space Administration Interim Directive (NOTE–At the time of this publication, NID 8000-108 was required for use in lieu of NPR 8000.4A, with an expiration date of March 24, 2018.)

(NIST SP) with specific publication number
National Institute of Standards and Technology Special Publication.

(NOM)
The Nature of Markets, "A Masterful Way to Use Business Cycles & Economic Indicators to Make Better Investment Decisions," *Fundamental Analysis Blog* (May 27, 2015), *available at* www.thenatureofmarkets.com/professional-trader-mindset-business-cycles-economic-indicators/.

(NS)
Ralph C. Nash Jr. and Steven L. Schooner, *The Government Contracts Reference Book* (Washington, DC: The George Washington University, 1992).

(OMB A-11)
Office of Management and Budget Circular No. A-11, "Preparation, Submission, and Execution of the Budget" (revised) (Washington, DC: Office of Management and Budget; August 1, 2017).

Source Codes

(OMB A-76)
Office of Management and Budget Circular No. A-76, "Performance of Commercial Activities" (Washington, DC: Office of Management and Budget; May 29, 2003).

(OMB A-108)
Office of Management and Budget Circular No. A-108, "Federal Agency Responsibilities for Review, Reporting, and Publication under the Privacy Act (Reissuance)" (Washington, DC: Office of Management and Budget; December 23, 2016).

(OMB A-109)
Office of Management and Budget Circular No. A-109, "Major Systems Acquisition" (Washington, DC: Office of Management and Budget; November 9, 1979).

(OMB A-119)
Office of Management and Budget Circular No. A-119, "Federal Participation in the Development and Use of Voluntary Consensus Standards and in Conformity Assessment Activities (Revised)" (Washington, DC: Office of Management and Budget; January 22, 2016).

(OMB A-123)
Office of Management and Budget Circular No. A-123, "Management's Responsibility for Internal Control" (Washington, DC: Office of Management and Budget; December 21, 2004).

(OMB A-127)
Office of Management and Budget Circular No. A-127, "Financial Management Systems" (Washington, DC: Office of Management and Budget; July 23, 1993).

(OMB A-130)
Office of Management and Budget Circular No. A-130, "Management of Federal Information Resources" (Washington, DC: U.S. Office of Management and Budget; February 8, 1996).

(OMB A-131)
Office of Management and Budget Circular No. A-131, "Value Engineering (Revised)" (Washington, DC: Office of Management and Budget; December 26, 2013).

(OMB M) with specific memorandum number
Office of Management and Budget Memorandum.

(OPM)
U.S. Office of Personnel Management, *Position Classification Standards for the Contract and Procurement Series, GS-1102* (Washington, DC: Office of Personnel Management, 1981).

(PAS)
Kenneth J. Allen and John B. Wyatt III, "Protests of Ambiguous Solicitations—The Rule of 'Blue and Gold,'" *Contract Management* Magazine (Ashburn, VA: NCMA, September 2017): 52–63.

(PFAL)
U.S. Government Accountability Office, Office of the General Counsel, *Principles of Federal Appropriations Law*, third edition, volume 1 (Washington, DC: Government Accountability Office, January 2004).

(PGI) with specific reference to section/subsection
DFARS Procedures, Guidance, and Information. Available at https://www.acq.osd.mil/dpap/dars/dfarspgi/current/.

(P&L I)
David V. Lamm and William C. Pursch (with assistance from John E. Cannaday, Daniel L. Downs, Richard A. Florek, William J. Hauf, Randal Indvik, Dean R. Matro, Laureli M. Moyle, Michael W. Robinson, Daniel F. Ryan, and Robert Eric Wilson), "A Dictionary of Contracting Terms," *Contract Management* Magazine (Vienna, VA: NCMA, May 1991): 41.

(P&L II)
William C. Pursch and David V. Lamm (with assistance from John E. Cannaday, Daniel L. Downs, Richard A. Florek, William J. Hauf, Randal Indvik, Dean R. Matro, Laureli M. Moyle, Michael W. Robinson, Daniel F. Ryan, and Robert Eric Wilson), "A Dictionary of Contracting Terms Part II," *Contract Management* Magazine (Vienna, VA: NCMA, November 1991): 42.

(PMPM)
Eric Verzuh, *The Portable MBA in Project Management* (Hoboken, NJ: John Wiley & Sons, 2003).

(PW)
Price Waterhouse, *Contracting with the Federal Government*, second edition (New York: John Wiley & Sons, 1988).

Source Codes

(QAC)
U.S. Government Accountability Office, "Quality Assurance Concerns About Four Navy Missile Systems" (Washington, DC: Government Accountability Office, 1987).

(QRFAL)
John E. Jensen, *Quick Reference to Federal Appropriations Law*, second edition (Vienna, VA: Management Concepts, 2006).

(RSOC) with specific reference to section/subsection
Restatement (Second) of Contracts (1981).

(S-1943)
Severin v. United States Court of Claims, 1943. 99 Ct. Cl. 435

(SPP)
Federal Acquisition Institute, *Small Purchase Procurement: An Introduction*, "Desk Guide and Workbook" (Washington, DC: Federal Acquisition Institute, 1986).

(SSP)
Claire M. Grady and Sara A. Higgins; Office of the Under Secretary of Defense (Acquisition, Technology, and Logistics); Defense Procurement and Acquisition Policy/Program Acquisition; *Department of Defense Source Selection Procedures* (Washington DC: Department of Defense, 2016), *available at* www.acq.osd.mil/dpap/policy/policyvault/USA007183-10-DPAP.pdf.

(STBP)
Gregory A. Garrett, *Contract Negotiations: Skills, Tools, and Best Practices* (Chicago: CCH Inc., 2005).

(TAS)
Nadia Hilliard, *The Accountability State: U.S. Federal Inspectors General and the Pursuit of Democratic Integrity*, Studies in Government and Public Policy (University Press of Kansas, 2017).

(TIPS)
Topical Issues in Procurement Series (Vienna, VA: NCMA, 1990-1994).

(TTAB)
Marco Iansiti and Karim R. Lakhani, "The Truth About Blockchain," *Harvard Business Review* (January-February 2017).

(UCC) with specific reference to section/subsection/paragraph
Uniform Commercial Code.

(UNI)
Unisys Defense Systems, *Handbook of Ethical Business Practices* (McLean, VA: Unisys Corporation, 1988).

(U.S.C.) with specific title and chapter/section/paragraph
United States Code (U.S.C.).

(WB)
Webopedia Online Computer and Internet Dictionary, Webopedia.com (copyright 2018, QuinStreet Inc.), *available at* www.webopedia.com.